The Ancient World

HARPER'S HISTORICAL SERIES

Under the Editorship of Guy Stanton Ford

Augustus (Museum of Fine Arts, Boston)

Alexander the Great (Louvre Museum)

Plate 1

The Ancient World

Volume Two

The World Empires: Alexander and

the Romans After 334 B.C.

by

JOSEPH WARD SWAIN

PROFESSOR OF HISTORY UNIVERSITY OF ILLINOIS

HARPER & BROTHERS, NEW YORK

To My Kinsman
JAMES ARNOLD BLAISDELL
Professor of Biblical Literature, Beloit College, 1903–1910
President of Claremont Colleges, 1910–1936
My First and Best Teacher of Ancient History

Contents

Maps

Plates

Preface

IN THE FIRST TWO CENTURIES OF THE CHRISTIAN ERA THE Roman Empire included "the fairest part of the earth and the most civilized portion of mankind." The inhabitants of this empire had achieved a status which the most enlightened leaders of the world today are now valiantly trying to duplicate. During these two hundred years, for the first and only time in the history of the Western World, men might reasonably and confidently look forward to peace in their time. The story of how this happy situation came about is the theme of the present volume.

This is not a History of Rome following the tradition established by the patriotic Livy and telling how the inhabitants of a village on the Tiber went out and conquered the world because of their valor and fortitude. On the contrary, it is the story of how men of diverse sorts and races slowly and painfully created a state that in a moderately satisfactory fashion embodied their ancient longings for unity, peace, and freedom. The Romans had a share in this great enterprise, to be sure, but so did Greeks and Orientals; it was in part the work of soldiers and statesmen, but businessmen, philosophers, poets, and prophets had their share too.

The story begins with Alexander the Great, whose ephemeral empire showed men what could be done and suggested to them blessings that might flow from the political unification of the world. The collapse of this empire was followed by a century of warfare, another century of decay and readjustment, and a third century of horror, but at last the empire of Augustus put an end to those terrible things. This empire endured for two full centuries whereas that of Alexander had begun to disintegrate within two years. Nevertheless the price men paid for peace and security was very high, and their empire was far from perfect. They lost many of those things which formerly had made life most worth living, and eventually the empire itself collapsed in what has been called "the greatest, perhaps, and the most awful scene in the history of mankind." Today, when men again are longing so ardently for peace and freedom, the rise and fall of the Roman Empire has an especial interest, both as an inspiration and as a warning.

Again I must express my thanks to the University of Chicago Press for permission to quote freely from J. M. P. Smith and E. J. Goodspeed, *The Complete Bible: An American Translation.* The two excerpts from Sallust and Pliny, pages 403 and 522, respectively, are reprinted by permission of the publishers from the Loeb Classical Library translations of Sallust and Pliny, Cambridge, Mass.: Harvard University Press. Appreciation is due also to the various museums mentioned for permission to reproduce photographs of their treasures.

JOSEPH WARD SWAIN

March, 1950

Part One: The Hellenistic
World

I Alexander's World Empire

THE NAME OF ALEXANDER STANDS AT THE END OF ONE EPOCH in world history, at the beginning of another." With these words, written in 1833, the German historian Johann Gustav Droysen opened a book that revolutionized the study of Alexander the Great and his successors. Heretofore, scholars had regarded the Macedonian as a mighty conqueror, a spectacular eccentric, and a genius, but they had scarcely considered him a person of such crucial significance in world history. They believed that his story was primarily of romantic interest, that his achievements were largely negative, and that he was followed by a dreary and unimportant period in Greek history that ended only with the coming of the Romans. Scholars today have generally come to accept Droysen's view and share his opinion that few events in ancient history, when judged by their ultimate consequences, were as important as was the invasion of Asia that Alexander launched in the spring of 334 B.C. This invasion may be taken as dividing all ancient history into two halves, one before Alexander the Great and the other after him. The first was the period of oriental despotisms and Greek city-states; the second was the period of world empires.

Though Alexander was one of the world's great generals, his importance rests neither upon his military genius nor upon the wide extent of his conquests. Genghis Khan and Tamerlane each conquered more square miles than he, yet he is far more important in history than either of them—or than both of them and many others

3

of their kind taken together. Alexander's importance lies in the fact that he once held virtually the whole civilized world of his day united under one rule. Many oriental potentates had claimed like achievements before him, but it was Alexander who firmly impressed upon the mind of Greece and Europe that such a thing was possible. Moreover, the oriental empires had included only oriental peoples whose cultures were fundamentally alike, but Alexander united Greeks and Orientals whose ways of life were very different. By bringing these two peoples into more intimate relations than ever before, he forced each to learn from the other, thus unwittingly laying the foundation for a new world civilization to which East and West each contributed a share. This new civilization is called "Hellenistic" to distinguish it from the "Hellenic" civilization of the Greeks before Alexander's day. It rose above race and people, and it was the first truly international civilization in the history of the world.

Alexander's political empire collapsed with his death in 323, but the thirteen years of his public career had been so full of great upheavals that nothing he touched was ever quite the same again. Greeks continued to rule the East because he had effectively smashed all organized opposition. The frontiers that he destroyed could not easily be restored. Commerce between East and West, and even with remote parts of the world, expanded at an increasing tempo. The exchange of ideas between East and West became more rapid. The world was thus united economically and intellectually, just as Alexander's victories had united it politically. In the next century, statesmen, businessmen, and philosophers alike came to the conclusion that their great problems could best be solved by a return to the world unity that Alexander had momentarily achieved.

The task of creating a world federation or a world government was not easy. Alexander's empire was an empire of the sword, and even had he lived longer, this military rule could not have endured. Unity had been bought at the expense of liberty. Alexander's successors therefore had to find a more acceptable form of world federation, and for three hundred years they vainly sought a substitute for the antiquated city-states and despotisms that Alexander had abolished and for the empire that he had failed to establish solidly. At last, the Romans succeeded where the Greeks had failed, and Augustus presided over an empire that reconciled peace and unity with a large degree of local liberty. This Roman Empire endured for more than five hundred years as a living embodiment of the ideal of world unity. Rome then passed that ideal on as a major item in her legacy to medieval and modern times.

When Alexander set out upon his famous expedition, he had neither planned, nor desired, nor foreseen the far-reaching consequences of his campaigns. In fact, he had scarcely caught a glimpse of them before he died thirteen years later. He was merely a romantic young man, bent on adventure and on making a name for himself. But it happened that he came into a world that was ready for just such a career as his. A hundred and fifty years before this time, two successive Persian kings, Darius I and Xerxes I, had tried in vain to drag Greece into their oriental world. Three quarters of a century later, the Athenian Alcibiades, a young fellow of much the same type as Alexander, clever and full of big ideas, had dreamed of mighty conquests, but he got nowhere. Conditions were not yet ripe for the unification of the world. Alexander, on the other hand, easily carried everything before him. Our study of Alexander must therefore be prefaced by a brief review of the rapidly changing world into which he was born.

The Persian Empire

When Alexander came upon the scene, the Persian Empire had long been the world's most impressive political organization. Its enormous spread extended from India in the East to Egypt and the Aegean Sea in the West, from the Black Sea and the Caspian in the North to the Persian Gulf in the South. It included the rich and populous cities of Mesopotamia, Egypt, and Ionia (the Aegean coast of Asia Minor), the fertile valleys of the Nile and Tigris-Euphrates rivers, the pastures of Iran, Palestine, and Asia Minor, and the deserts of Arabia. Its population was made up of a wide variety of races and peoples, including Persians, Babylonians, Syrians, Jews, Arabs, Egyptians, the debris of the old Hittites and other Europeans who had invaded Asia

Minor, and even many Greeks. In culture, these peoples ranged from the primitives of Afghanistan to the highly civilized inhabitants of the great cities. Over it all, a small group of Persian aristocrats ruled supreme.

This Persian Empire was the culmination of two thousand years of Near Eastern imperialism. Ever since the days of Lugal-zaggisi and Sargon (c. 2250) and of Hammurabi (c. 1700), military conquerors had been marching back and forth over these vast territories, establishing empires of greater or less permanence. Sumerians, Babylonians, Egyptians, Hittites, Assyrians, Chaldeans, and Medes, each in turn had their day of glory and each added something to the imperialistic art of governing conquered peoples. Last of all came the Persians. The founder of their greatness was Cyrus (559–29), who in a few years conquered most of the Asiatic territories later held by his successors. His son Cambyses (529–22) added Egypt, and the Persian Empire reached its greatest extent in the days of Darius I (522–486). Darius invaded Europe, thus beginning a long quarrel with the Greeks, but primarily he was the organizer who perfected the administrative machinery for governing the huge domains his predecessors had conquered. This task he performed so well that rather incompetent successors were able to operate his political machine for more than a hundred and fifty years.

In the fourth century, the Persian kings commanded the largest and most feared army in the world. The Persians themselves were good fighters. In the past they had produced generals who were able to muster, maintain, and maneuver huge armies and to win important victories. Lesser Persians had proved themselves excellent soldiers, especially in the cavalry. But Persians formed only a small minority of the population of the Empire, and its other inhabitants did not contribute greatly to its military strength. Many were peace-loving peasants who, from time out of mind, had been ruled by foreign conquerors and who could not have fought well, even had they been inspired to try. The more bellicose peoples of the Empire, on the other hand, were kept powerless by their overlords lest they rebel. It thus came about that the Persian kings were forced to fill their armies with mercenaries. Throughout the fourth century, tens of

thousands of Greeks sought such employment. Many of these mercenaries later remained loyal to their Persian employers, but others
deserted to Alexander when he appeared. The Persians also maintained a navy with which they controlled the eastern end of the
Mediterranean. Unfortunately for them, however, they had to rely
upon Phoenician and Ionian-Greek sailors and admirals, whose loyalty was not always above question.

In spite of its military foundation, the Persian Empire did not rest
upon military force alone. It contained many rich and ancient cities
where trade and industry flourished. From the most ancient times,
trade had advanced hand in hand with empire, and often it was the
traders who led the way, dragging the military conquerors in their
wake. A network of trade routes crossed the Near East in every direction, and whoever kept these routes free from brigands might rule
the land. The Persians were not great traders themselves, but others
might trade safely in all their domains and were encouraged to do so.
The wealthy merchants, largely Arameans or other Semites, were
therefore willing to support the Persian kings, to whom they paid
moderate taxes, knowing full well that they would get back their
money's worth in protection and the elimination of artificial trade
barriers. The ensuing economic prosperity enabled the Persian kings
to raise enormous sums of money. They spent lavishly on their armies
and navies, on their courts and buildings, and on other great enterprises, and still they managed to accumulate huge hoards of gold and
silver. This created the appearance of great wealth and power, but
the subjects who created this wealth had no particular loyalty to the
Persian kings and would have been equally satisfied with any other
ruler who granted them the same advantages.

This lack of imperial patriotism was the greatest weakness of the
Persian Empire. Through the long history of the Near East, its rulers
had made various attempts to inspire loyalty in their heterogeneous
subjects. From early times, oriental kings had used grandiloquent
formulas to describe their own greatness and had developed elaborate court rituals to impress their people. Lugal-zaggisi and Sargon
had spoken of their "dominion of the earth . . . from the rising to
the setting sun," and their successors invented countless variations

on this boastful theme. Others, notably the Assyrian kings, supplemented boasting with terrorism, advertising the cruelty with which they punished their adversaries and making calculated frightfulness a policy of government. Such methods were quite ineffective, however, and whatever patriotism existed was largely religious in nature. Throughout ancient oriental history, kings had made religion an important handmaiden to statesmanship. In Egypt they had declared themselves gods incarnate, but in Asia they merely put themselves forward as agents of the gods. The Persians, too, invoked religion, but they made no effort to stamp out the earlier religions of their subject peoples, and while the empire produced such world religions as Zoroastrianism and Judaism, religion generally was a disruptive rather than a unifying force in their empire.

At the head of the Persian administration stood the king, a descendant of Cyrus and Darius, who was officially called the "Great King" or the "King of Kings." His principal capital was at Persepolis, but there were lesser capitals at Ecbatana and elsewhere. Here the king lived in oriental splendor, surrounded by his harem and eunuchs. His court was so full of factions and intrigue that at times the stability of the empire itself was seriously threatened. Since the kings after Darius I were men of mediocre ability at best, the actual direction of government usually fell to a vizier, who in theory was the king's servant.

For administrative purposes, the Empire was divided into about forty provinces, each of which was ruled by a royal appointee called a "satrap." This provincial system went back to Assyrian times, or perhaps even farther, but it was given its classic form by Darius. Distance made it difficult to hold the satraps in line, however, and in the fourth century the Empire was disturbed by serious revolts. The satraps of central Asia Minor endeavored to set themselves up as independent kings; Cyprus and Phoenicia broke away; and native rulers held Egypt for sixty years. About 360, nearly every Mediterranean harbor from the Black Sea to Egypt was in rebel hands.

At this moment, a new king, Artaxerxes III (358–38), ascended the throne and gave the failing Empire a new lease on life. He put an end to the revolts, reconquered Egypt (343), and for a time made the Persian Empire stronger than ever. Court factions and intrigue continued, however, and in 338 Artaxerxes was poisoned by his vizier, who placed the old king's son on the throne. Two years later, the same vizier poisoned the son and made the incompetent Darius III king in his place. Darius's first (and last) beneficent act was to poison the vizier. This Darius (336–30) was the king against whom Alexander fought.

Greece before Alexander

Though Greece, too, was already an old country when Alexander appeared, her antiquity could not rival that of Egypt or Mesopotamia. About a thousand years before his time, Greece had been the home of the Mycenaean civilization of which dim recollections are preserved in the Homeric poems. Then came decline and a period of darkness, until the thrill of a renaissance spread over the land in the seventh and sixth centuries before Christ. Greek colonists went out to settle along the Hellespont and the shores of the Black Sea, in Cyprus and Cyrene, in southern Italy and Sicily, and even along the Riviera. Trade expanded, and the rising economic prosperity gave some men the leisure and means to cultivate the arts and sciences. After learning what they could from the Orient, Greeks began developing their own ideas in such matters. Early in the fifth century, they emerged victorious from two great wars with the Persians, defeating the forces of Darius I at Marathon in 490 and those of Xerxes I at Salamis and Plataea in 480–79. The resulting enthusiasm brought Greece, and especially Athens, to her highest level. The days when Pericles ruled Athens (461–29) were especially famous, but in a larger way it may be said that Hellenic civilization reached its apogee in the fifth and fourth centuries before Christ.

In the fourth century, there were perhaps eight million Greeks in the world. Half of them inhabited the Greek peninsula, the islands of the Aegean Sea, and Crete, and the other half lived in the cities of Ionia or the colonies. These Greeks, if united, might have slightly outnumbered the true Persians (who alone were a military asset to the Persian Empire), but no political bonds united the widely scattered Greeks. Those living in Greece, the Aegean Islands, and the

Ionian cities were in rather close contact with each other and had many interests in common, but those in the colonies were not much concerned with their kinsmen in the Aegean area. Even the Greeks of Greece had no political unity, and we cannot speak of a "Greek Empire."

The Greek peninsula is divided by its mountains into many valleys, each of which became a tiny independent state; and the Aegean Sea forced an equally parochial character upon the peoples of its islands. From early times, therefore, the typical Greek political organization was the *polis*, or "city-state," which consisted of a single important city with its adjacent fields and villages. Some city-states acquired military and political power, others were weak and poor, but all were fanatically devoted to their autonomy or "liberty." No one city was able to lead or conquer the others, all attempts at federal union foundered, and numerous internecine wars between these city-states were the ruin of Greece.

The disastrous results of this vertical division of Greece between rival city-states were aggravated after the fifth century by a horizontal division between hostile social classes. In each city there were aristocratic and democratic factions whose mutual hostility became more bitter as time passed. During the Peloponnesian War (431–04), Athens had supported and invoked the aid of the democratic factions everywhere, thus encouraging class warfare, and during the fourth century almost every city in Greece suffered at least one violent revolution. Agitators promised the redistribution of property, the cancellation of debts, and the emancipation of slaves. The rich, therefore, lived in constant dread, and their panicky fear made them cruel. They came to prefer rule by foreigners of their own social class to domination by fellow citizens of the opposite faction. Throughout the fourth century, Greece was torn as cruelly by class warfare as by intercity warfare.

The economic and social consequences of these wars were catastrophic. Thousands of farms were destroyed, orchards and vineyards were cut down, cattle were driven away and butchered. Multitudes of peasants were thereby turned adrift in a land not prepared to receive them. Thousands became professional soldiers, fighting

for whatever city or faction might employ them or entering the mercenary armies of such foreign powers as Persia, Egypt, or Carthage.
Others sought new homes in the colonies. Still others flocked to the
cities of Greece, where some of them prospered economically, but
where their influence was more often disastrous. As these displaced
persons could not acquire citizenship in their new homes, they remained alien groups, taking no part in the public life of the cities that
received them and undermining the institutions upon which these
cites rested. The city-state organization became wholly unsuited to
conditions prevailing in the fourth century, and with its decline the
old Greece was doomed.

Panhellenism

Thoughtful persons were much perturbed by these developments
and devised countless programs of reform. The most important of
these programs sought to end the ruinous wars by a political union of
all Greeks. This was called Panhellenism, from the Greek words *pan,*
"all," and *Hellen,* "Greek." The proposal was not new, but it was now
propagandized with renewed vigor. Greeks had long been conscious
of their cultural unity and had been accustomed to contrast themselves favorably with the rest of the human race, whom they haughtily styled "barbarians." This early Panhellenism was based on the
common language, common traditions, and common problems of
the Greek people, and it was promoted by such manifestations of
the Greek genius as the Homeric poems, the Olympic games, and the
Delphic oracle. It was strongest among the aristocratic classes, who
naturally were those most conscious of their cultural unity. The Persian invasions of 490 and 480 brought the Greeks into a temporary
union, called the Hellenic League, but the disruptive forces in
Greece were so powerful that the League could not survive the Persian menace.

The sufferings and disasters of the Peloponnesian War (431–04)
did much to revive the old ideal of a federative Panhellenism. The
Athenian aristocrats had opposed this democratic war from the first,
and in the last years of the long conflict, as Athens was slowly but
relentlessly being pushed to the wall, intellectual leaders of all par-

ties came to regard the struggle as sheer fratricidal slaughter. The fact that Sparta received financial assistance from Persia during these terrible years aroused new anti-Persian feeling in Athens. A little later, in 387, the Persian king took advantage of Greece's distracted condition to reannex the Ionian cities and to impose a humiliating treaty upon the states of Greece. Persia again appeared as the enemy of all Greeks. These events prepared the way for the revived Panhellenism of Isocrates (436–338), an Athenian aristocrat who for forty years filled Greece with propaganda for a Panhellenic union.

Panhellenism had played upon anti-Persian sentiment ever since the invasions of 490 and 480, and Isocrates now devised countless reasons for war against this national enemy. He reminded the Greeks that they had as yet enjoyed no proper revenge for their unmerited sufferings at the hands of Darius and Xerxes, and that their gods had not yet been vindicated against the Persian temple-ravishers of those far-off days. He urged his fellow Greeks to liberate their Ionian brothers from the Persian yoke. (These Ionians had been conquered by Cyrus in the sixth century; they had been independent allies of Athens in the fifth; and they had been reannexed by the Persians after 387.) Isocrates also suggested that the surplus population of Greece might colonize central Asia Minor. He pointed to the wealth of Persia and the opportunities for loot. He urged ambitious men to achieve immortality—or even divinity—by leading the great crusade. It happened that an Athenian soldier of fortune named Xenophon, who had accompanied a band of Greek mercenaries in a raid that almost reached Babylon (401), had written a popular account of his adventures (the *Anabasis*) in which he indicated that Greeks could easily defeat Persians: Isocrates never ceased reminding his fellow countrymen of this important fact. And finally, Isocrates assured the wealthy classes that the war he was urging, and the resulting union of all Greece, would be their strongest safeguard against revolution. It is important to note, however, that Isocrates and the Panhellenists never urged the conquest and annexation of non-Greek peoples. Persians and other Orientals had for centuries been talking of world empires, and had vaguely recognized the essential unity of all mankind, but such ideas were quite foreign to the Greek mind.

Isocrates dreamed of a national union of all Greeks, and if his proposed war against the Persians had once effected such a union, he would willingly have left the "barbarians" to their own devices thereafter. He was a nationalist, not an imperialist, and he never considered substituting a Greek world empire for the Persian one.

Philip of Macedon

Isocrates was an effective propagandist, but Panhellenism lacked a political leader until the appearance of Philip of Macedon. Macedonia was a large region bordering on the northwestern corner of the Aegean Sea and including parts of modern Greece, Yugoslavia, and Bulgaria. Its inhabitants spoke a Greek dialect, but they had taken little part in Greek affairs. The backward Macedonian peasants were considered barbarians by the Greeks, but they were good fighters and they supplied both leaders and rank-and-file to the armies with which Alexander conquered the world.

Philip II of Macedon (382–36) had spent three years of his youth as a hostage at Thebes. While there, he observed the political decline of Greece, noted opportunities for his own aggrandizement, and learned all that the ablest general of the day (Epaminondas of Thebes) could teach about military matters. Soon after returning to Macedonia he became king (359), and quietly set to work strengthening his army and laying his plans for the future. He presently commanded the best-drilled, the best-equipped, and the best-led army in Europe, and he had perfected the arts of diplomacy and bribery. In 346 he was publicly invited by Isocrates to assume leadership of the Panhellenic movement. Philip had little sympathy with the idealistic side of Panhellenism, but he recognized the political advantages to be derived from such leadership, and he gladly accepted the offer.

Meantime, Philip's various aggressions against his neighbors in Thessaly and Thrace had aroused the apprehensions of many Greeks. The Athenian orator and democratic leader, Demosthenes, began denouncing him as early as 351. The aristocratic faction, on the other hand, was led by Aeschines, a pupil of Isocrates, who now became a spokesman for Philip. For several years, the conflict of parties raged at Athens and, to a lesser degree, throughout Greece. Demosthenes accused Aeschines of being in the pay of Philip, and Aeschines replied by charging that Demosthenes was subsidized by Artaxerxes III, king of Persia. As Philip made no secret of his use of bribery, and as Artaxerxes had good cause to be worried over Isocrates' incessant war-mongering, these charges and countercharges may have been only too well founded.

When all was ready, in the spring of 338, Philip marched into Greece. He was met by the armies of the Greek states whom Demosthenes had hastily united in an alliance, but the allies were quickly and decisively defeated at Chaeronea near Thebes. Philip made only moderate demands for the punishment of his opponents, but he ordered all the Greek states to send representatives to Corinth to organize a Panhellenic league. Sparta alone among the important Greek states had not fought at Chaeronea and now failed to send delegates to the congress. Philip arranged the League of Corinth to suit his tastes, and though he allowed it to keep much Panhellenic idealism, he was declared its "leader" (hegemon) and he could dominate it at will. He knew well, however, that most Greeks regarded him as a foreign conqueror, not as a national leader, and he therefore decided to increase his popularity by launching the war against Persia which Isocrates had been urging so eloquently and for so long. If only he could "liberate" and annex the Greek cities of Ionia, he would give ocular proof of his own Hellenism, complete the Panhellenic union, and crown his military career with a spectacular victory over the ancestral enemy of Greece. But he no more dreamed of ruling Persians than did Isocrates. In the summer of 336, he moved a few thousand troops into Asia Minor, but before the war took on serious proportions he was murdered by one of his Macedonian nobles. His son Alexander then ruled in his place.

Alexander's Youth

Alexander was twenty years old when he became king of Macedon, and he ruled for almost thirteen years. His father, Philip of Macedon, had been a man of tremendous energy and iron will, a farseeing and hardworking statesman, the ablest general of his day, and a skillful diplomat. Though somewhat given to debauchery, he did not permit his vices to interfere with his labors. His career was the story of one success after another. Alexander's mother, Olympias, was the daughter of an Epirote chieftain ruling in what is now Albania. A wild and terrible woman, she practiced the orgiastic rites of primitive religions, during which she became an inspired prophetess. Yet she was a person of clear intelligence and great determination. She quarreled with her husband over his frequent infidelities, and he openly suspected her of similar shortcomings. Each met his match in the other, and each was the only person whom the other could not dominate.

Their son Alexander, born late in the summer of 356, inherited much from each of his parents. From his father came not only material things—a well organized kingdom, an excellent army, a corps of well-trained and devoted generals—but also strategic insight, genius as a commander, and remarkable talents as a diplomat, an organizer, and a leader. From his mother came even more: a personal beauty which appealed greatly to the Greeks and a contagious enthusiasm which enabled him to retain the loyalty of generals and soldiers through many trying years. Above all, he inherited from Olympias the romantic nature which drove him ever onward, seeking the end of the earth. From his mother, too, came the nervous instability that sometimes drove him to a savage anger, characterized by rage for destruction, or to an equally extreme repentance, and that, according to some accounts, made drunkenness his major vice. From his mother, too, he inherited a tendency to religious mysticism which enabled him to believe that he had been sent by heaven to perform a great task. He was a dreamer but also a hard worker, generous, frank, and self-confident, and he believed implicitly in his star. Like Napoleon, he was primarily a romantic egomaniac, but he was also a fruitful combination of the mystical enthusiast and idealist with the practical man—a leader fit to create a new world.

Philip provided Alexander with an excellent scholastic education under the philosopher Aristotle, who was his tutor from 343 to 340. The philosopher won his pupil's confidence, introduced him to the intellectual treasures of Greece, indoctrinated him with Greek ideas and ideals, and thus prepared him to be the champion of Hellenism throughout the world. Alexander was also given careful military and

political training: he was regent in Macedonia during his father's
Thracian campaign of 340, and at Chaeronea two years later he
smashed the Theban "Sacred Band" while commanding the left wing
of the Macedonian army. Soon thereafter, Philip married the young
niece of one of his generals, and the bride's father publicly expressed
a hope that this union might lead to a *legitimate* son who would some
day rule the Macedonians. Much offended by these slurs, Olympias
and Alexander stormily withdrew to Epirus. There Olympias remained, though Alexander presently returned to court. A few
months later, Philip was murdered by a Macedonian nobleman. Under the circumstances, it was natural that suspicion should fall upon
Olympias, but Alexander insisted that the murder had been instigated by Darius III, king of Persia. Philip's generals then proclaimed
the young man king of Macedon as Alexander III (336).

Early Campaigns in Greece

Soon after Philip's death, Demosthenes and other Greek politicians had renewed their anti-Macedonian agitation. Alexander therefore hastened down to Greece, suppressed various minor revolts, and
required the League of Corinth to confirm him in his father's position
as *hegemon*. In the following year (335), he marched his armies
north, crossed the Danube, defeated the native tribesmen, and even
received a delegation of Celts from the region now called Romania.
No sooner had he settled this northern frontier than he learned that
the Illyrians to the west had risen in revolt. This rebellion too he
quickly crushed. By this time, Demosthenes was inciting the Greeks
against Alexander yet again, supplementing the power of his oratory
by a lavish distribution of bribes from a fund of three hundred talents provided by the Persian king: he even produced a false witness
who swore to having seen Alexander die in battle. Several Greek
cities thereupon revolted.

Alexander was far from dead, however, and within two weeks he
stood before Thebes, his army reinforced with contingents from the
states through which he had passed. Hoping to awe the city into
submission, he paused to give it time for repentance and negotiation,
but the Thebans elected to fight, and their city was promptly cap-

tured. By Alexander's order it was razed to the ground—excepting the temples and the house once inhabited by Pindar—and several thousand Theban citizens were sold into slavery. Alexander must accept the responsibility for this atrocity—an early instance of his terrible anger for which he is said to have repented afterwards— though the actual work of destruction was done largely by Phocians, ancestral neighbors and enemies of Thebes. Warned by the fate of Thebes, the other Greek cities hastened to submit. Alexander was generous to Athens, partly out of respect for her cultural leadership and partly because he was anxious not to drive the leading naval power of Greece into the waiting arms of Persia: all that he required of her was the exile of one minor anti-Macedonian politician. The Spartans remained outside the League, and Alexander saw fit to ignore their absence. Before the end of 335, he was back in Macedonia, preparing for the invasion of Persia which his father Philip had planned.

Alexander Conquers the East

We have no definite information about Alexander's plans at the moment he first invaded Asia, but it is certain that he then had no inkling of what actually lay before him. His more methodical and cold-blooded father had planned an invasion of Asia Minor with definite and practical ends in view. As a Greek, Philip had wished first of all to win a victory over barbarians and thus inspire the Greek states to forget their defeat at Chaeronea; as the leader of Panhellenism, he had wished to liberate the Greek cities of Ionia from the Persian yoke; and as a king, he had wished to conquer new territories for himself. It is pretty certain, however, that if Philip had once established his control over western Asia Minor to the Halys River, he would have been content to rest upon his laurels. He could have regarded this union of all the Greeks of the eastern Mediterranean area as the crown and completion of his life's work. His declining days could then be spent enjoying what he had accomplished.

The young and ambitious Alexander, on the other hand, could regard such an achievement as only the beginning of a great career. He looked upon the invasion of Asia as a romantic exploit, leading he knew not whither. At first he liked to think of himself as repeating the deeds of his glorious ancestor Achilles, continuing the Trojan War of the Greeks against Asiatics. Further opportunities for glory would doubtless appear after he had won this new Trojan War, but for the moment he could not divine their nature and he was not interested in trying to do so. He merely announced that he would avenge the murder of his father upon Darius.

Alexander had inherited his father's excellent army. To make sure of Macedonia and Greece, it was necessary for him to leave about one fourth of his troops in Europe under the command of one of his father's generals, a man named Antipater. There remained for the invasion of Asia about 30,000 infantry and 5000 cavalry. The old Macedonian army made up more than half of these troops, to whom were added contingents of mercenaries and Greeks provided by the League of Corinth. The bulk of the fighting was entrusted to the Macedonians, however, and the Greeks were taken along partly to give the expedition a Panhellenic complexion and partly perhaps as hostages to guarantee the good behavior of their kinsmen in Greece during Alexander's absence. The Greeks were used largely as garrison troops and in other secondary positions. This army was gradually increased by new detachments, Greek mercenaries as well as Persians and other Orientals; just before his death, Alexander commanded about twice as many troops as when he first entered Asia. At the outset, Alexander's generals were all Macedonians trained by Philip, the most important of them being Parmenio. The army was amply supplied with engineers, surveyors, well-drillers, artillery and siege troops, and a commissary.

Alexander's character is well illustrated by the type of additions which he made to this expeditionary force. He took a staff of scientists to collect information about the countries to be conquered, and poets and historians to tell of his noble exploits. An official record of the expedition, the *Ephemerides* or "Journal," was kept by Eumenes of Cardia, and presumably it was as accurate as official histories usually are; but Alexander also had a publicity agent (Aristotle's nephew, Callisthenes) who told the Greeks what he deemed it good for them to know, and whose reports soon took on fantastic colors.

These additions to the staff were made after the first campaign, when Alexander's plans looked to greater things than he had dreamed of earlier.

Alexander's greatest weaknesses were finance and the navy. He was virtually bankrupt when he set out, his treasury containing only seventy talents (a talent was worth about $1100 in silver value, much more in purchasing value) while he needed two hundred talents a month to pay his soldiers. The army therefore had to live on the country through which it marched, and booty was a matter of prime importance. Not until he had seized the great Persian hoards did Alexander overcome his financial difficulties. His fleet contained only 160 vessels against some 400 in the Persian navy; many of Alexander's vessels were manned by Greeks of doubtful loyalty, and their upkeep cost approximately one hundred talents a month.

Ionia Occupied

Philip had sent 10,000 Macedonians into Asia Minor under the command of Parmenio, but their successes were slight, and at the end of 335 they held only a little territory south of the Hellespont. The expedition proved its value, however, by providing a bridgehead where Alexander's troops might land on the Asiatic shore without facing armed resistance. While Parmenio was organizing the new army, Alexander approached Asia by another route, disembarking near Troy at the spot where tradition reported that Achilles had landed many centuries before. After throwing a spear from his boat to the shore as a token that the land was his by right of conquest, and after offering sacrifices at the ancient sites, Alexander joined the main army and advanced against the Persians.

The Persian army was commanded by a Greek mercenary, Memnon of Rhodes, who had faithfully served successive kings for many years. He wished to withdraw his army slowly, burning the country behind him, while the fleet made a demonstration off Greece to stir up dissatisfaction that would require Alexander's immediate attention. The Persian nobles would listen to no such plan and insisted upon fighting a pitched battle. Apparently they counted on their slight numerical superiority to stop Alexander once and for all. The

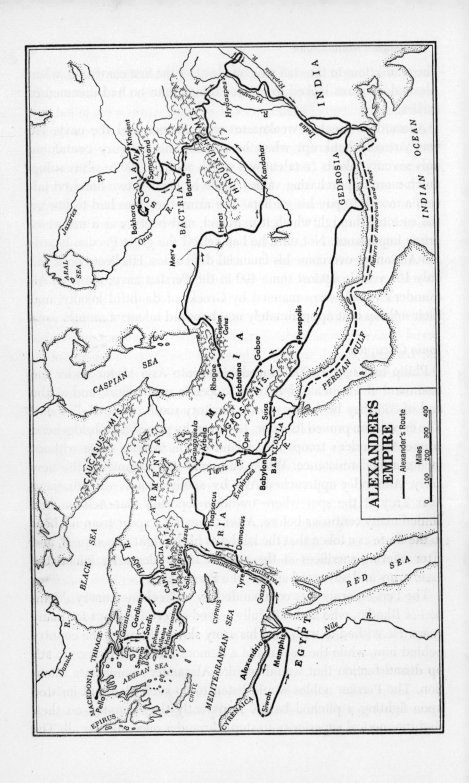

ALEXANDER'S EMPIRE

— Alexander's Route

Miles
0   100   200   300   400

INDIA

INDIAN OCEAN

Hyphasis R.
Hydaspes R.
Hydaspes
Indus R.

Khojent
Samarkand
SOGDIANA
Bokhara
Oxus R.
Jaxartes R.
ARAL SEA

BACTRIA
Bactra
HINDU KUSH MTS.
Merv
Herat
Kandahar

GEDROSIA

Return of Nearchus and Fleet

Caspian Gates
Rhagae
Ecbatana
ZAGROS MTS.
M E D I A
Gabae
Persepolis
PERSIAN GULF

CASPIAN SEA

CAUCASUS MTS.
ARMENIA
Arbela
Gaugamela
Tigris R.
Opis
Babylon
BABYLONIA
Euphrates R.
Susa

Thapsacus
Damascus
SYRIA
Issus
Soli
TAURUS MTS.
CAPPADOCIA
Halys R.

BLACK SEA

Gordium
Sardis
Granicus R.
Ephesus
Miletus
Halicarnassus
CYPRUS

PHOENICIA
Tyre
PALESTINE
Gaza

MEDITERRANEAN SEA

RED SEA

Nile R.

EGYPT
Memphis
Alexandria
Siwah
CYRENAICA

MACEDONIA
THRACE
Pella
EPIRUS
AEGEAN SEA
CRETE

Danube R.

battle was fought late in May, 334, near the Granicus River only a few miles from the Propontis. Here Alexander won a brilliant victory. All but about 2000 of Memnon's Greek mercenaries were killed, and the survivors were sent to work in Macedonian mines as punishment for having fought against Greeks, contrary to the orders of the League of Corinth. The Panhellenic nature of the expedition was further emphasized when Alexander sent the armor of 300 Persian nobles to the Parthenon at Athens with the inscription, "Alexander, son of Philip, and all the Greeks except the Spartans, dedicate these spoils taken from the barbarians of Asia."

Alexander was then free to complete the emancipation of the Greeks in Ionia. When he proclaimed the Ionian cities free, the democratic factions received him joyously. The pro-Persian Greek oligarchs were lacking in enthusiasm, however, for they had prospered under Persian lordship and now they sometimes suffered at the hands of the democrats. Alexander therefore found himself in the anomalous position of depending upon the oligarchies in Greece and the democracies in Asia, of being opposed by the democrats of Greece and by the oligarchs of Asia. Alexander next marched to Sardis, the ancient capital of Lydia, and after an unsavory massacre of the oligarchs at Ephesus, he proceeded to Miletus, where the oligarchs were aided by Persian troops and surrendered only after a siege. Alexander then ordered the rebuilding of Smyrna, which the Persians had destroyed more than a century and a half before. Late in the summer he reached Halicarnassus, at the southwestern tip of Asia Minor, where Memnon resisted stubbornly behind well-prepared defenses. Several weeks of fighting gave Alexander the greater part of the city, but the last citadel was not taken until the following spring. After the capture of the main city, Alexander withdrew most of his troops to winter quarters in central Asia Minor, occupying the ports of Lycia and Pamphylia on the way.

Syria and Egypt

In one summer, Alexander thus accomplished the Panhellenic program urged by Isocrates and prepared by Philip. The ensuing winter (334–3) turned his ambition in new directions. It was obvious that if he were to hold his new conquests, he could not stop now: he must meet and defeat Darius in a pitched battle. Moreover, the Persian fleet still controlled the Aegean, and with it Memnon captured several Aegean islands during the winter. Had the old general not died at this juncture, he might well have made his demonstration against Greece and won the active aid of Athens and Sparta. Alexander's fleet could not hope to defeat the Persian navy, and its cost was too heavy for Alexander's precarious finances: he therefore disbanded it, but only after he had conceived a brilliant plan for eliminating the Persian navy. He would destroy this navy, not at sea but on land, by depriving it of its bases and thus forcing it to surrender. This scheme required that Alexander occupy the whole coast of Asia Minor, Syria, and Egypt, and led him to conquests which he had not anticipated. He therefore advanced eastward through central Asia Minor, crossed the Taurus Mountains, and entered Tarsus. Here he was delayed for several weeks by illness, but after occupying Soli and other cities along the Cilician coast he was finally ready, towards the end of the summer, to advance into Syria.

By this time, Darius III had assembled a huge army with which he hoped to repel the invader. The two forces met at Issus early in October, 333, and here Alexander won his second great victory. The Persians probably outnumbered the Greeks slightly (not in the fantastic proportion of twenty to one given by later writers), though some authorities believe that Alexander had the larger army. In the midst of the battle Darius turned and fled, after which his army retreated. Most of his troops escaped, but Darius's camp, with his mother, wife, and daughters, fell into Alexander's hands. Darius fled to the east, but a considerable body of his troops withdrew to Asia Minor, where they maintained Persian power in Cappadocia and thus seriously threatened Alexander's communications. One of the best Macedonian generals, Antigonus, was detailed to keep the road across Asia Minor open. In this task he was successful, but though he fought three major battles with the Persians, he was unable to drive them from Cappadocia and thus to burst the bottleneck.

Alexander ignored the temptation to pursue Darius across the desert and, persevering in his original plan, he marched south along the Syrian coast. He met his first serious opposition at Tyre, whose capture required a siege of eight months. Alexander's engineers eventually proved their superiority over their Phoenician opponents, the city was captured and destroyed (August, 332), and 30,000 Tyrians were sold into slavery. Meantime, the greater part of the Persian fleet, finding no friendly harbor to enter, had surrendered to Alexander. Some of these very vessels were used by the victor in the last stages of the siege of Tyre. After his victory Alexander continued southward, took Gaza after a siege of several weeks, and late in 332 he entered Egypt without meeting armed resistance. Thus ended his third year of campaigning.

Shortly after the battle of Issus, Darius had begged the return of his family and a treaty of friendship and alliance. Alexander replied with a political manifesto in which he rehearsed at length the crimes of the Persians, claimed to be "Lord of Asia," and ordered Darius to address him as such in the future. Darius sent a second embassy during the siege of Tyre. He now offered a huge ransom (10,000 talents) for his wife and children, promised to surrender all lands west of the Euphrates—that is, the lands Alexander actually held, plus Egypt and the unconquered half of Asia Minor—and agreed to cement an alliance by marrying his daughter to Alexander. Parmenio is reported to have said that if he were Alexander he would accept these terms. "And I suppose," retorted Alexander, "that I would accept them if I were Parmenio." With that, he rejected the whole Persian proposal. Historians have seen in this episode the beginning of a break between the Macedonians of Philip's court—who wished only to add the Greeks of Asia Minor to their kingdom—and Alexander, to whose romantic imagination there were now opening up broad vistas of conquest.

Soon after arriving in Egypt, Alexander had himself crowned king in Memphis, thus becoming the successor of the ancient Pharaohs. That he intended his new position to be permanent is shown by his reforms in Egypt and especially by his founding of a new city at Alexandria to replace Tyre as the commercial metropolis of the eastern Mediterranean. A few weeks later, he made a trip into the western desert to visit the oracle of Ammon at Siwah, which had long

been honored by the Greeks. On the way to the oracle, he received
ambassadors from Cyrene, with whom he made an alliance that
extended his territories westward to the frontier of Carthage, and
soon after his return to Memphis he started east for a final settlement
with Darius. The die was cast. Alexander had decided to take over
the whole Persian Empire.

The Conquest of Persia

In the spring of 331, Alexander passed through Tyre, where he
stopped long enough to regulate many matters concerning Greece,
Asia Minor, and Syria. He then marched east through Damascus,
crossed the Euphrates at Thapsacus, and reached the Tigris somewhat north of the ancient Nineveh. Here he met a great army collected by Darius, and he won his third major victory at Gaugamela
on October 1, 331. This battle marked Darius's supreme effort. At
first it seemed that his greatly superior numbers might bring victory;
but in the end his forces were shattered, and the king fled eastward
to his Median capital at Ecbatana. Alexander again refused pursuit
and turned south to Babylon, where the Persian satrap received him
without fighting. Continuing his march past Susa, Alexander crossed
the mountains to the Persian capital at Persepolis, where he seized
Darius's enormous treasury and burned the royal palace. In our own
day, the charred ruins of this palace have been excavated by American archeologists (see Vol. I, Plate 15).

The burning of Persepolis disposed of the last pretext that Isocrates and the Panhellenists had originally put forward for war against
Persia—namely, vengeance for Xerxes' invasion of Greece in 480.
The Persian Empire was defeated, and the better part of it was in
Alexander's hands. Yet Alexander could not stop. Darius and his
nobles at Ecbatana were assembling new forces to defend Persia
proper from further invasion. In the summer of 330, Alexander therefore marched north from Persepolis. Darius fled toward the Caspian
Sea and Bactria, but after an exciting chase by the Greeks through
Rhagae and the Caspian Gates, his Persian nobles deposed and murdered him. Alexander claimed the entire Persian Empire as his inheritance.

Though Alexander might claim the whole Persian Empire, its eastern half was still held by Persians unprepared to acknowledge the claim. The establishment of his supremacy in these remote regions, and the elimination of minor rivals, forced Alexander into several years of guerrilla warfare which led him through central Persia, Bactria, and Sogdiana (the modern Afghanistan) to Khojent in Ferghana. At last Bessus, the Persian noble who had murdered Darius and assumed the diadem, was captured, mutilated, and executed (328). A few months later the last Sogdianian leader was murdered by his own men and his head sent to Alexander.

An invasion of India followed in 327 and 326. Alexander was lured into this adventure by his pressing need for a spectacular victory after exhausting years of guerrilla fighting, and by his romantic desire to reach the end of the earth. Greek geographers in his day taught that the ocean lay but a short distance beyond the Indus River, that it continued around Asia only a little beyond Ferghana, and that the Caspian Sea was one of its arms. Alexander therefore believed that only a slight advance would bring the whole inhabited East under his power. He entered into an aliance with an Indian prince, Taxiles, whose principality lay east of the Indus in the modern Punjab; but he was compelled to fight this prince's rival, Porus, and defeated him on the Hydaspes River (the modern Jhelum) in his fourth and last great battle (summer, 326). After the victory, however, he made Porus his ally. Alexander then headed east toward where he supposed the ocean to be, but when he reached the Hyphasis (Beas) River, his troops mutinied and he was forced to turn back. After recognizing Porus as the independent king of all this region, Alexander built a fleet and sailed down the Hydaspes and Indus rivers to the Indian Ocean. The year 325 he spent marching the army back through southern Persia to Persepolis while the fleet was brought back by Nearchus through the Indian Ocean and the Persian Gulf. This march, tiring and costly, has been compared to Napoleon's retreat from Moscow in 1812.

Alexander spent the next year (324) reorganizing his vast domain, making a trip to Ecbatana, and dreaming up plans for the future. There is a certain amount of evidence to show that he considered conquering Carthage, which would have carried him westward to the Straits of Gibraltar, and even of adding Italy and Sicily to his empire. While this evidence is not conclusive, it is hard to doubt that Alexander would sooner or later have undertaken such campaigns had his life been spared. At any rate, his contemporaries confidently expected him to follow this course, and ambassadors hastened from the West to seek his favor. His immediate program called for an exploratory circumnavigation of Arabia to open trade between Babylon and Egypt. Just as the argosy was about to sail, however, Alexander fell sick of a fever, and a week later he died (June 13, 323). He was not yet thirty-three years old.

Alexander's Empire

As Alexander's grandiose dreams of conquest were not born until after he had won his first campaigns and seized extensive territories in Asia Minor, he had made no preliminary preparations for governing the various domains that he presently acquired. Governments had to be improvised as he went along, and the resulting structure was a rather ramshackle affair. Only in the last year of his life did Alexander find time for a careful consideration of the larger and more fundamental problems that arose in the administration of so vast and varied an empire, and he died before much could be done to establish a strong government. Though his views developed greatly during the years he spent in Asia, we have only hints from which to guess what was in his mind, and the only progress that we can clearly trace is one toward the aggrandizement of his own personal power and prestige.

Alexander started his public life as king of Macedon and *hegemon* of the League of Corinth. The captured Ionian cities became his allies but they did not enter the League. This program had also been Philip's, and it shows that Alexander, like his father, never took the League seriously except as a means of dominating Greece. At any rate, Alexander dropped his Panhellenic pretensions soon after Granicus. When he reached Caria, he allowed himself to be adopted by the queen of that region, thereby establishing a claim to eventual personal rule there. As he advanced through Asia Minor, he put

Macedonian generals in charge of the various satrapies as temporary administrators. After the victory at Issus, however, he began dreaming of a permanent conquest of the whole Persian Empire and his settlements took on a new character. When he entered Egypt a year later, he had himself crowned Pharaoh in the old Egyptian manner and clearly he intended to keep this position permanently. After the death of Darius, he claimed that the whole Persian Empire was his by right of conquest, and there can be little doubt that, like the Persian kings before him, he thought of himself as the autocrat of the world.

It was not easy for Alexander to maintain himself in so lofty a position, even after the armed forces of Persia had been destroyed. He and his few thousand Greeks had neither the knowledge, nor the skill and training, nor even the numbers necessary for governing the millions of Asia. They were therefore forced to enlist the aid of the Persians whom they had just conquered, and in general they retained the old Persian political institutions and customs, with many of Darius's old officials still in office. Greek generals were rewarded with important satrapies, but there were not enough generals to go around and Persian satraps were sometimes allowed to continue temporarily in the civil administration. Military control of provinces might go to Macedonians, but the local officials almost always continued as before. This policy was, of course, extremely distasteful to those Greeks who failed to get the lucrative posts they expected but which they were not competent to fill, and some of them eventually mutinied in protest. Alexander was acting from necessity rather than choice, however, for until more and better Greeks became available, he simply had to rely upon the old Persian officials. But though he gave satrapies to no less than eighteen Persians, he had replaced all these men except three with Greeks before his death in 323.

Alexander's economic policies were likewise forced upon him by immediate necessity, yet they were destined to have far-reaching effects upon the development of his empire. His dire financial distress came to an end only when Parmenio seized a considerable treasure at Damascus in 333. Later at Babylon, at Susa, and especially at

Persepolis, Alexander captured enormous hoards of gold stored up by the Persian kings. This wealth he spent so lavishly that at the time of his death the greater part of it was already gone. Moreover, Alexander began collecting the customary taxes in the different provinces as soon as he occupied them. The old Persian system of taxation was gradually reformed, however, and the money was collected more honestly and efficiently than before. One man (Harpalus) was made treasurer for the whole empire. Harpalus presently absconded with a huge fortune, but not until he had given the empire financial unity under Greek direction. A uniform coinage on the Attic standard was provided for the whole empire. Alexander also showed great interest in new trade routes and in developing commercial opportunities for his Greek friends. These measures brought a period of economic prosperity and commercial activity that lasted for several decades after Alexander's death.

One of the spectacular policies by which Alexander hoped to perpetuate his domination of the new world empire was the foundation of Greek cities. Isocrates had urged Philip to colonize Asia Minor with Greeks, thus providing homes for the surplus population. Alexander pursued this policy with great success. It is said that he founded, or fundamentally rebuilt, over sixty cities, about twenty of which are now known. Alexandria in Egypt was the most celebrated of these new cities, but most of them were east of the Tigris and they included such famous places as Kandahar, Herat, and Khojent. Some of these cities, especially those in eastern Persia and India, were little more than military colonies inhabited by retired Macedonian soldiers and designed as military posts to prevent uprisings. Others, such as Alexandria in Egypt and Alexandretta in Syria, became commercial metropolises whence Greeks directed the economic life of the region round about.

Greek Supremacy

What then was Alexander's attitude on the fundamental question regarding the respective parts Greeks and Orientals were to play in the new empire? A brilliant British scholar (W. W. Tarn) has recently argued with great force that Alexander rose above all racial prejudice and dreamed of making his empire a melting pot in which Greeks and barbarians would become one people; others insist that Alexander merely intended to Hellenize the East. Alexander's conquests certainly set in motion forces which continued to work in both these directions long after his death, but it is difficult to accept either view in its entirety. Alexander was interested first of all in himself: whatever he did was aimed primarily at exalting his own position. But the pursuit of this egocentric ideal forced him to adopt lines of conduct, hitherto unknown in the ancient world, which eventually led to new ideals and to a new world.

The Greeks were more race-conscious and racially snobbish than the Persians and Romans or many other peoples in antiquity. They customarily drew a sharp line between themselves and the "barbarians" who made up the rest of the human race, and in his early days Alexander had shared these prejudices to the full. Aristotle had taught him that the Greeks were a "master race" while the barbarians, especially those of Asia, were slavish by nature, and he had specifically advised his pupil to act toward the Greeks as a "leader" but toward the barbarians as a "despot." Alexander presently outgrew these early prejudices to some extent, learning from experience that the barbarians were not always as bad as they had been pictured. Perhaps, too, his personal aggrandizement became so great that, in his own mind, Greeks and barbarians alike were so far beneath him that he could no longer see much difference between them. This had been the view of the Persian kings whom he supplanted. But the best explanation of his position seems to be that he always remained a Greek at heart and that he continued to regard Greeks as the most reliable support of his own grandeur, though at times he was forced to use barbarians as well. An examination of Alexander's racial policy supports this view.

A major item in this racial policy may be seen in his famous marriages—first his own marriages, then those of his generals, and lastly those of his soldiers. His first wife was Roxane, daughter of a Sogdianian leader, whom he married in 327. Legend romantically pictured the marriage as a great love match, and Roxane's son (born shortly after his father's death) was chosen by the generals as

Alexander's heir. Three years after this first marriage, Alexander held a great ceremony at Susa during which he took as second wife Barsine, eldest daughter of Darius III. Subsequently, Parysatis, youngest daughter of Artaxerxes III, became a third wife. At Susa Alexander's best friend, Hephaestion, married Barsine's sister, and eighty of his officers accepted lesser Persian ladies. Alexander also offered bonuses to all soldiers who had married oriental women, and some ten thousand Macedonians profited by his generosity.

These marriages are sometimes pictured as part of a deliberate effort by Alexander to promote race fusion and even as proving his recognition of the equality of all races. It is hard to accept this interpretation of the facts. Alexander's second and third marriages were purely political, designed to strengthen his position as heir to the Persian throne. The marriages of his officers apparently were intended to win over members of the Persian nobility who, in Alexander's opinion, should be grateful for the honor of having Greek sons-in-law and brothers-in-laws! The plan failed completely, however, and most of the Greek officers soon abandoned their Persian brides. When Alexander encouraged his soldiers to marry Asiatic women, he most probably was looking forward to the creation of a contingent of half-castes, living near the military posts, upon whom he and his successors could safely rely against both native rebels and foreign enemies. At any rate, a few thousand soldier-marriages could have no deep and lasting effect upon the huge populations of the Orient. It should also be noted that Alexander did not provide Greek wives for Persian men, that he sent no Persians to live in Greece, and that when superannuated soldiers returned to Macedonia, he directed them to leave their oriental wives and half-caste children behind. The race mixture was strictly a one-way matter. Alexander never believed in the equality of Greeks and barbarians, and he certainly had no intention of "contaminating" the blood of Greece by a fusion with Asiatics.

Alexander also retained his old beliefs about the superiority of Greek culture. There is no evidence that he sought to learn anything from the Persians except devices for governing the Empire. When he aped them in the superficialities of court ceremonial and dress, it was because he had learned from them that such ceremonial can enhance the aloofness and grandeur of the sovereign. His curiosity led him to take an interest in new and strange peoples and ideas, just as he took an interest in new plants and animals and the other phenomena of nature, but apparently it never occurred to him that Orientals could have anything important to teach him. As a Greek and a pupil of Aristotle, he could learn nothing from a naked Indian ascetic, even though it might be amusing for a moment to hear such a character tell him that he was no better off than the rest of mankind. Alexander had no more expectation of learning something important from the Persians than the British in India had of adopting Hindu culture or fusing it with their own. On the other hand, he had even less intention of educating the Persians to be Greeks or of "civilizing" them. Then as now, however, long-continued political and cultural domination by an alien minority was impossible, and in the long run Alexander's conquests led to the creation of a new culture to which both East and West contributed a share and in which distinctions of race were of less importance than ever before.

Alexander's Claims to Divinity

One of the most famous of Alexander's acts was the proclamation of his divinity. This aspect of his policy has been much discussed, but even today scholars cannot agree as to whether the idea was Greek or oriental, and some are more inclined than others to concede that Alexander acted with religious sincerity in the matter. The kings of Egypt had claimed divinity from very ancient times, and as they still did so in Alexander's day, he officially became a god when he was crowned at Memphis. On the other hand, there had been very few divine kings in ancient Babylonia and for many centuries no ruler in Asia had put forward claims to divinity. The idea of a divine monarchy was quite out of harmony with the lofty monotheism of the official Persian Zoroastrianism, and there is no evidence that either Darius III and his predecessors or Alexander ever demanded or received divine honors from the Persians.

The idea of a divine king came more naturally to the Greeks than to the Persians. For many centuries, these Greeks had been offering divine honors to the demigods, and Homer portrayed their national heroes as children of the gods, associating with them freely while alive and sometimes living with them after death. Many leading Greek families, including that of Alexander himself, claimed descent from these children of the gods, and we have already seen how seriously Alexander took his alleged descent from Achilles and Heracles: he re-enacted the deeds of the former in the Troad, and he used the latter as an excuse for attacking Tyre. In that city, there was a famous temple dedicated to Melkart, whom the Greeks had long since identified with Heracles. Alexander launched his attack upon Tyre only after the Tyrians had refused to let him enter their city in force to worship his ancestor in this temple.

Moreover, the Greeks were not disturbed by the idea that a man might achieve divinity by noble deeds. Even in the fourth century, various Greek politicians and statesmen had received divine honors while still alive for this very reason—as was the case, for example, with the Spartan general Lysander and the Syracusan tyrant Dionysius. Isocrates had quite definitely held out to Philip of Macedon the hope that he might achieve divinity if he served humanity by uniting all the Greeks. Even Aristotle had thought along somewhat similar lines. In one passage of his *Politics* (iii, 13), he declared that "the best" of mortals was "like a god among men." Aristotle probably did not write this book until Alexander was far advanced in the conquest of Asia, but it seems not improbable that he expressed similar views to his pupil many years before he wrote them down. As it certainly never occurred to Alexander that he might not be "the best," the words of Aristotle may have made a deep impression upon the ambitious and romantic lad of fifteen or sixteen who heard them. From his youth upward, therefore, Alexander was being conditioned to believe in his own divinity, and it is possible to trace the progress of his ideas in this direction through several stages.

When Alexander was crowned king at Memphis, the impressive ceremonies included the offering of divine honors, and a little later he visited the oracle at Siwah, where the priest hailed him as the "son of Ammon." From the priest's point of view, the matter was simple: Alexander had become a god, and a son of Ammon, at the

moment of his coronation, for all the kings of Egypt were gods incarnate. It is more difficult to explain Alexander's reaction, and historians are by no means agreed about this cardinal event in his life.
Was it just one more new experience, or was it a matter for political
propaganda, or was it the great religious experience of his life? Careful scholars hold the latter view, pointing out that he was always
reticent and touchy on the subject of his relations with Ammon.
Plutarch tells us that while in Egypt Alexander was much impressed
by the remark of an Egyptian philosopher that "all men are ruled by
god," but that he replied that "god was indeed the common father of
men, but that he made the best of them peculiarly his own."[1] Aristotle's teaching about "the best" was bearing fruit, and Alexander
clearly believed that he enjoyed some special relationship to the god
—presumably in consequence of his experience at Siwah. There is
no evidence that Alexander ever referred to himself as the "son of
Zeus," yet he allowed others to do so in his presence. As those who
spoke thus were sycophantic flatterers, it is safe to assume that they
would quickly have changed to another tune if this sort of adulation
had not proved conspicuously successful with the young king.

A further stage in Alexander's deification came four years later at
Bactra. He had already adopted Persian dress and other outward
trappings of the Orient, much to the disgust of his Macedonians. He
now ordered that all persons approaching him must prostrate themselves on the ground before him. This ceremony, which the Greeks
called *proskynesis,* had long been customary among the Persians,
who regarded it merely as a mark of deep respect. The Greeks, on
the other hand, regarded it as contemptible slavishness or else as the
rendering of homage to a god. Alexander certainly knew how the
Greeks felt, and presumably he shared their view. The elaborate
ceremony staged at Bactra, at which both Greeks and Persians were
to prostrate themselves before Alexander, was therefore intended to
imply a recognition by the Greeks of his divinity. When the Macedonians refused to comply, Alexander dropped the matter, but he

---

[1] The idea that Zeus was "father of gods and men" was as old as Homer, and in this
statement Alexander, like Homer and Aristotle, uses the word "father" to designate
one having paternal authority, not the loving "Heavenly Father" of the Gospels.

was furiously angry, and presently he executed Aristotle's nephew Callisthenes for his part in the defiance.

Three years later, in 324, Alexander sent an order to Greece demanding that he be granted divine honors there. The order excited a certain amount of opposition, but the Greeks hastened to comply. It was said that Alexander's archenemy, Demosthenes, remarked mockingly that he could see no reason why the Athenians should not recognize the king as the son of Zeus "and of Poseidon, too, if it makes him feel any better." The next year, the Greek states sent ambassadors to Babylon to adore Alexander as a god. Scholars usually explain this demand upon the Greeks by pointing out that it was accompanied by other orders which Alexander had no right to give in his capacity as *hegemon* of the League of Corinth. If he were a god, however, Alexander need not be bound by constitutions. He certainly had the power to enforce his wishes under any circumstances, but it would be well to avoid the show of naked force as long as possible. Religion was therefore invoked to provide a cloak for Alexander's growing absolutism. This, too, was an old oriental custom, but it is equally possible that Alexander was again taking his cue from Aristotle. In the passage cited above, the philosopher goes on to remark that laws cannot be made for these superior persons, each of whom is "like a god among men," for they are themselves the law.

The final question is, what did Alexander himself believe about his divinity? Many writers pass the question off lightly, saying that he was far too sensible to believe any of it—as though he were a rationalistic skeptic with many generations of Christian training behind him. It must be remembered, however, that Alexander was no cold-blooded philosopher like Aristotle. Rather, he was a true son of that Olympias who participated in the frenzied orgies of Dionysus and who, as a Bacchante, felt herself possessed by the god. Alexander was a religious man, most scrupulous in fulfilling all the obligations of religion. Moreover, his unparalleled victories might well seem to require a supernatural explanation, and his romantic imagination, coupled with his deep religious emotions and his Greek training, may then have convinced him of his own divinity. Other men in his state of mind have proclaimed that they had a divine mission to fulfill; it was more natural to Alexander, and more in harmony with Greek ideas, for him to announce that he was a god. He certainly used the divinity for political purposes, but we cannot affirm that he was completely cynical in so doing. By nature he was a believer, and he also believed in his own divinity.

Growing Opposition to Alexander

During his earlier campaigns, Alexander's troops and generals offered little opposition to his schemes. His own enthusiasm inspired them and carried them from one astounding victory to another. Not until he reached the Hyphasis River in 326 did the soldiers refuse to go farther. Opposition arose sooner among the generals. Philip's old officers did not share the young king's romantic temperament and many of them, like Parmenio, would have been glad to make peace after Issus. The breach between Alexander and his father's officers was widened when he began appointing Persians as satraps, and more especially when he gave them commands in the army, and Alexander's growing aloofness alienated them still further.

Dissatisfaction was intensified by the unfortunate affair of Philotas in 330. This young man, the son of Parmenio, had known that a few minor officers were conspiring against Alexander's life, but he had not reported the fact at once. When Alexander later learned of the conspiracy, he suspected Philotas of complicity and ordered him tried and executed; fearing the father's vengeance, Alexander then ordered Parmenio executed without trial, much to the indignation of other Macedonian officers. Two years later came the more tragic affair of Cleitus. This officer had saved Alexander's life at the Granicus and had been his boon companion ever since. One night, during a drunken brawl, the two men fell to quarreling and Cleitus bitterly reproached Alexander, blurting out many of the things of which the Macedonians were secretly complaining. Alexander seized a spear and murdered him on the spot. When the practice of *proskynesis* was ordered shortly after this, Callisthenes refused to go through the prescribed ritual and accompanied his refusal with sarcastic remarks. Soon thereafter a number of pages conspired against Alexander's life, and Callisthenes was hanged as an instigator of the affair. He thus became a martyr in the eyes of many Greeks.

The last and most serious act of insubordination occurred in 324 at Opis in Babylonia. Alexander had decided to send home ten thousand of his soldiers who, because of wounds or age, were no longer fit for active service. These warriors saw in his order a repudiation of old Macedonian soldiers for new Persian friends. A riot followed, during which certain soldiers referred derisively to Alexander's father Ammon. In a fury, Alexander ordered several of the ringleaders arrested and executed. Not until three days later was peace restored, after which nine thousand Macedonians and Persians attended a great banquet, with the former in the higher places. It is far from certain, however, that all was forgiven and forgotten at the love feast of Opis. Had the king not died a few months later, controversies with his troops would undoubtedly have arisen again in more acute form. Alexander's dreams and ambitions were more than his soldiers were willing to support.

Alexander's Prayer at Opis

The affair at Opis was more than just another mutiny. The feast in honor of the reconciliation became an event of high significance. Greek seers and Persian magi opened the ceremonies, and Alexander offered an eloquent prayer for "harmony and fellowship in the empire between Macedonians and Persians." All those present poured a libation and sang a song of victory together. While it is of course possible to take Alexander's supplication for "harmony and fellowship" as a reference to the recent mutiny which had been caused by Greek jealousy, it is equally possible to give the words a broader significance. Perhaps he was thinking of his plans for the future organization of the empire and, for that matter, of the whole civilized world. Some recent writers (notably Tarn) believe that in the exaltation of this happy moment—after the mutiny, the insults to Ammon, the executions, the three days of high tension, and the reconciliation —Alexander managed to express eloquently the ideals that had arisen in his mind during these years of campaigning. If this be the case, we might almost say that the prayer at Opis was Alexander's "Gettysburg Address."

The Greek word here translated "harmony" is *homonoia*, which means, literally, "of the same mind." The Romans translated it by *concordia*, or "union of hearts," which perhaps expresses in English what Alexander had in mind better than the literal translation from the Greek. Isocrates had used the word when preaching Panhellenism, but he envisaged this "union of hearts" as extending only to Greeks; Alexander expanded it to include Persians (Asiatics) and presumably all other inhabitants of the earth as well. The word meant much more than a mere absence of quarrels and war, yet such blessings would inevitably flow from *homonoia*. On the other hand, it did not necessarily imply world conquest. Isocrates, of course, thought of some sort of Greek league under a *hegemon;* Alexander apparently thought of the civilized world under his leadership. If men accepted this leadership freely, as was technically the case with the Ionian Greeks, conquest was unnecessary; if they refused, he conquered them by force of arms. Likewise, one central government was not necessary, for many separate states could unite under his leadership without merging their administrative machinery. Moreover, mere conquest and political union would not be enough, for there must be a union of minds or hearts as well. But how was this change of heart to be accomplished? Probably by religious devotion to the leader, who was also a god. Alexander's imperialism was thus religious as well as military, political, and economic. In the final analysis, it was religion that would lead all men to accept his leadership and cause them to co-operate, regardless of their race or condition, in the new empire he had created. Thus almost four centuries before St. Paul wrote his famous words about there being "neither Greek nor Jew, circumcision or uncircumcision, barbarian, Scythian, bond, nor free," Alexander was thinking in very similar terms. The greatest difference seems to be that Alexander expected to be recognized as leader and god by all.

Alexander's Legacy

Alexander was one of those individuals whom the gods favor, and in nothing was he luckier than in his death. He died at exactly the right moment to assure him an immortal reputation. He had accomplished all that he seemed destined to achieve, and before him lay a stormy period, full of unsolvable difficulties. In his death Alexander therefore resembled Lincoln, who died just as he brought the Civil War to a successful close and before the quarrels with Congress which brought his successor to ruin; Woodrow Wilson, on the other hand, survived the Armistice of 1918 and his triumphant reception in Europe, and buried his reputation for statesmanship in the Treaty of Versailles.

Alexander's unbroken series of military successes had carried him to lands of which no earlier Greek had ever heard. It was of minor import that the West remained unconquered: the conquest of Carthage and Italy would have added little to Alexander's glory. If he had made a western campaign, he would probably have been victorious, but war is always a gamble, and had he met defeat, his reputation would have suffered irretrievably. Regardless of whether Alexander decided to conquer the West or to leave it alone, the day would soon have come when he had no more worlds to conquer and no further opportunities to demonstrate his unquestioned military talents. It would then have been necessary for him to govern the vast empire that he had amassed, and it is doubtful whether he was as well adapted to the routine tasks of administration as he was to the more spectacular feats of military conquest. There is little to suggest that Alexander would have been a conspicuously successful ruler in time of peace. Moreover, had a period of peace allowed a cooling of martial fervor, the Macedonian troops might have raised sufficient opposition to ruin the whole mighty enterprise. Collapse under Alexander would have created infinitely greater disillusionment than did the chaos which later overwhelmed his supposedly less able generals. Alexander's death relieved him from the most hazardous role he could have been called on to play, and it permitted the growth of an extravagant legend which was to be a matter of importance in the subsequent history of the world.

Even while Alexander was alive, Callisthenes had regaled the Greek public with fantastic stories of the hero's superhuman achievements; after Alexander's death, these stories took on still more fanciful forms. In the next century, most writers and thinkers, being Greeks (not Macedonians) or men of mixed Greek and oriental ancestry, had a low opinion of the man who had conquered their fathers. They criticized him bitterly and sometimes pictured him as a vile-tempered drunkard and superbrigand. In still later times, however, beginning in the first century before Christ, writers again went into such raptures over their hero that he lost all semblance of reality. An Alexander legend came into being which was an important factor in the history of the world. Its depiction of the superhuman hero and of the romance and riches of the Orient inspired many an ambitious young man, including such important figures as Pompey and Crassus, Caesar and Antony. Revived at the time of the Crusades, the legend again lured adventurous fortune hunters to the East, and even Napoleon was not insensitive to its attractions.

The legends of romance are not, however, the foundation of Alexander's place in world history. He is important because his armies completed the overthrow of the moribund political systems of Greece and Persia, thus preparing the way for something different. But more especially his importance rests upon the fact that his ephemeral empire caused men to dream of a new and more permanent world empire in which persons of every race might become citizens and in which peace would enable everyone to reap the rewards of his labor. In the course of the present volume, we shall see how men struggled for three full centuries toward the realization of this lofty dream and eventually achieved it under the leadership of a people of whom Alexander may never have heard. Nevertheless, it was during the thirteen years of his active life that the ancient world turned in this new direction. The name of Alexander does indeed stand at the end of one epoch in world history, at the beginning of another.

II The Hellenistic Monarchies

The right to choose the king of Macedon belonged by custom to the leaders of the army, and even before Alexander was decently buried, the generals fell to quarreling among themselves about the succession. Everyone professed a desire to see the Empire and the dynasty continue, but under whom should they continue? Alexander's wife Roxane was expecting a child, and some generals favored delay and the acceptance of this child, if it were a boy; others favored Alexander's feeble-minded and illegitimate half brother, later called Philip III. In either case, a long regency would be necessary, and dissension centered principally about the appointment of a regent. At last a compromise was effected whereby Philip III and the infant Alexander IV were declared joint kings with three leading generals sharing the regency.

The first and most important of the regents was Perdiccas. Being a young man, only a few years older than Alexander himself, he perhaps understood and shared something of his master's ambitions; and just before dying, Alexander had shown his confidence by giving Perdiccas the royal seal. Perdiccas was therefore named guardian of Roxane's expected son and commander of the armies in Asia, which positions he retained until his death two years later. The second regent was a general named Craterus, who was to be Philip's guardian and assist Perdiccas in governing the Asiatic empire. But when Craterus was killed in battle before the settlement could go into effect, Perdiccas was left the supreme ruler of Asia. The third regent was Antipater, an old general of Philip of Macedon who had been ruler of Macedonia and Greece during Alexander's absence and who now continued in that office. As he had never been with the armies in Asia, Antipater failed completely to understand Alexander's dreams, and he remained loyal to Philip's purely Hellenic ideal. Antipater was now over seventy-five years old and he relied much upon his son Cassander. An able general like his father, Cassander, too, wished to retain Philip's system, with the kings of Macedon ruling only the Greeks of Greece and the Aegean area.

Perdiccas assigned a number of Greek satraps to different provinces in Asia. The ablest of these men was Antigonus, a contemporary of Philip, who ever since Issus had been satrap of Phrygia in Asia Minor, keeping open the main highway between Greece and Asia. He retained this province with enlarged borders, but his ambition soared higher, and for many years he aspired to rule the whole Empire himself. Another able general was Ptolemy, who long ago had been impressed by the wealth and defensibility of Egypt and who now got himself appointed satrap of that province. Mention must also be made of Eumenes of Cardia, a civilian who had formerly been Alexander's secretary: he was named satrap of Cappadocia, Pontus, and Paphlagonia, which three provinces in central Asia Minor were as yet largely unconquered. Among the generals were two lesser men who did not cut an important figure at first, though each became prominent later: Lysimachus, satrap of Thrace, presently acquired much of Asia Minor; and a cavalry general named Seleucus became satrap of Babylonia and eventually ruled nearly all the Asiatic provinces.

The Wars of the Diadochi

The twenty years that followed Alexander's death were rendered chaotic by the struggles of these willful men, who came to be called the Diadochi or "Successors." The more ambitious generals believed that they might get the whole Empire for themselves and therefore spoke loudly of preserving Alexander's noble work. Less sanguine rivals sought only a portion of the Empire, since they saw no chance of getting it all, and they solemnly deplored the fact that no mere mortal could perpetuate the noble Macedonian's superhuman achievements. Costly wars were fought with mercenary troops by skillful and unscrupulous contenders, and military action was supplemented by propaganda vigorously defending or attacking Alexander's system and ringing all the changes on loyalty, liberty, and the like, as seemed most expedient at the moment.

The details of this fighting need not delay us. As soon as one general was eliminated, another rose to take his place. Olympias obtained the death of Philip III in 317; a year later Cassander had her assassinated; and in 309 he murdered Roxane and her son, Alexander IV, thus exterminating the old Macedonian dynasty. Thereafter, the generals could no longer pretend that they were trying to save Alexander's empire for his son, and in 306 Antigonus took the title of king for himself. The other generals quickly followed suit. At last, in 301, an important battle was fought at Ipsus in west-central Asia Minor, where Antigonus was defeated and killed by a coalition of his rivals. The victors then divided the Empire amongst themselves. Cassander got Macedonia and Greece; Lysimachus took Thrace and much of Asia Minor; Ptolemy retained Egypt, Cyrenaica, and Palestine; and the rest of Asia went to Seleucus.

Unfortunately, this settlement satisfied no one. Antigonus's brilliant son, Demetrius, escaped from the battlefield at Ipsus and continued to hold Athens, several Aegean Islands, a few cities in Asia Minor, and Cyprus. The death of Cassander (298) opened the way for renewed aggression. Three years later, Demetrius was recognized as king of Macedon, thereby arousing the apprehension of the other kings, who drove him from office: he died a prisoner of Seleucus in 283. Soon thereafter, Lysimachus was deserted by his friends, and in 281 he was defeated by Seleucus at Corupedion. Seleucus then seized the greater part of Asia Minor. A few years later, in 276, the army made Demetrius's son, Antigonus Gonatas, king of Macedon, which position his dynasty retained for more than a century.

Alexander's vast empire thus fell into its natural divisions, with three dynasties of Diadochi ruling Europe, Asia, and Africa respectively, and with a few minor potentates holding various odds and ends. The Antigonid dynasty (sons of Antigonus) ruled Macedonia and dominated Greece; the Seleucids ruled Asia; and the Ptolemaic dynasty ruled Egypt, Cyrene, Palestine and Cyprus. These three Hellenistic dynasties dominated the Near East throughout the third century.

Ptolemaic Egypt

Ptolemy I Soter[1] was the most successful of the Diadochi. Born a lesser Macedonian noble, Ptolemy became satrap of Egypt in 323; he assumed the title "King of Egypt" in 305; and he ruled until 285. He died in 283 at the age of eighty-four. As a young man, he had shown high talent as a soldier, but after the death of Alexander he devoted himself largely to administrative problems. It was he who laid the foundations of Hellenistic Egypt. His son Ptolemy II Philadelphus (285–246) was of a very different type. Fundamentally a man of peace, Philadelphus was interested in literature and art, and he was a voluptuary. Nevertheless, the wealth of Egypt enabled him to maintain large armies and conquer distant places. Under him, Ptolemaic Egypt reached the summit of its power in world affairs and the highest development of its domestic culture. Ptolemy III Euergetes (246–221) resembled his military grandfather in many respects, and in his early years he won important victories; but impoverished Egypt soon lost what he had won. These three were the kings who presided over Ptolemaic Egypt in the days of her glory.

The city of Alexandria served as capital for the Ptolemies and was their most brilliant creation. Built on a peninsula about four miles long and three-quarters of a mile wide, it lay between the Mediterranean and the fresh-water Lake Mareotis. Its principal street, running approximately east and west along the peninsula, was about

---

[1] The practice of numbering kings of the same name was unknown in antiquity and historians usually distinguished them by titles—sometimes titles which they assumed or which were accorded them while they were still alive, sometimes nicknames or titles conferred after death. Thus the first member of this dynasty—all of whom were named Ptolemy—was called Ptolemy Soter, or "Ptolemy the Savior," by the Rhodians because he saved them from Demetrius in 304. The case of the second Ptolemy, Philadelphus, is more complicated: he married his sister Arsinoë, who was therefore called Philadelpha—"Brother-loving"—and the name was transferred to him many years later. Ptolemy III was simply Euergetes, or "Beneficent," Ptolemy IV Philopator, or "Father-loving," and so on through the list to Ptolemy XI Auletes, "Flute-player." The same system was used for the other Hellenistic dynasties.

ninety feet broad—unusual for the ancient world—and was paved, cleaned regularly, and lighted at night. It was lined with shops and bazaars and was the center of the commercial life of the city. Cross streets were laid out at right angles, some of them being almost as splendid as this "Canopic Street." There were magnificent parks and public gardens, and streets and buildings were decorated with many statues and paintings. Aqueducts and underground pipes brought fresh water from the Nile seventeen miles away, and large sewers provided drainage.

Near the center of the city stood the tomb of Alexander, later to be surrounded by the tombs of the Ptolemies. Here, too, were the law courts and the gymnasium, of whose size and architectural beauty the ancient writers speak admiringly. The city also had a hippodrome, a stadium, and a theater, a celebrated museum and library, countless temples to Greek and oriental gods, barracks, an arsenal, and government warehouses and offices. Near the Mediterranean shore stood the palace of the Ptolemies, surrounded by its famous gardens. On an island in the northern harbor, connected with the mainland by a mole nearly a mile long, was the Pharos, or lighthouse, which the ancients numbered among the Seven Wonders of the World. Most of these celebrated buildings were located in the northern and eastern part of the city. South of the western end of "Canopic Street" lay the native quarter with its different architecture, its peculiar sights and sounds and odors, its oriental peoples and its oriental life; it must have presented as great a contrast to the rest of Alexandria as that separating the European and native quarters of a Levantine city today. The only other Greek cities in Egypt were Naucratis in Lower Egypt, near the Canopic branch of the Nile, where Greeks had lived for several centuries, and Ptolemaïs, near Thebes in Upper Egypt.

Ptolemaic State Socialism

Alexandria was a Greek city where the Ptolemies lived in Greek style with their Greek subjects. Elsewhere, the new kings continued most of the political, economic, and religious institutions of the

Pharaohs, though they contrasted strongly with those of ancient Greece. Like the Pharaohs before them, the Ptolemies claimed ownership of all the land in Egypt. This land was tilled, of course, by native Egyptian peasants, but the Ptolemies divided it into estates which they distributed among their Greek followers. The Greek owners and overseers directed the use that was made of the land, indicated the crops to be grown, and sometimes even provided the seed. Under their auspices, new crops, new domestic animals, and new methods of farming were introduced; attention was given to specialized agriculture and gardening; orchards and vineyards became more numerous; and in general the yield of the land was increased. Moreover, as the Ptolemies were constantly being forced to find new land for their retinues of officials and mercenaries, they made every effort to increase the amount of arable land: they drained swamps, and their irrigation projects opened up new districts. The region known as the Fayum, some fifty miles south of Memphis, profited especially by such development.

The Ptolemies also did much to encourage Egyptian industry. In about a dozen industries (including vegetable oils, salt, brewing, papyrus, and textiles), they established state monopolies. Raw materials were bought by government officials at fixed prices, the manufacturing was done in government workshops by workers who were given a share of the profits as well as wages, and the finished products were distributed and sold under state control. Industries not thus monopolized were usually subject to government regulation.

The Ptolemies were the first to cast coins in Egypt, and they established banking as a state monopoly, bankers alone having the right to issue and exchange coins. The local banker was also the fiscal agent of the government in his district, receiving tax money and disbursing the funds spent by the state. Foreign commerce was closely regulated by the state. Much of it was conducted by government officials, partly to dispose of the king's share of the produce of farms and monopolies, and partly to procure raw materials which Egypt could not provide but which were imperatively demanded by industry or by the military forces. Imports included such necessities as metals, lumber, horses, and slaves, as well as Greek luxuries like olive oil and wine, and they were paid for with exports of grain and papyrus, glassware and cosmetics.

The operation of this vast political and economic machine of course required the services of a huge staff of officials. The Pharaohs had developed a bureaucracy which the Ptolemies took over and expanded, thus making Egypt the most thoroughly bureaucratized state of the ancient world. Though the Ptolemies assigned the higher offices to Greeks, the greater part of the work continued to be done by natives trained under the old regime. To this bureaucracy should go much of the credit for the progress and prosperity of Egypt in the third century.

Religious and Racial Policies

The religious policy of the Ptolemies also deserves attention. Like their predecessors the Pharaohs, they presented themselves as gods before their Egyptian subjects. Ptolemy I made no effort to induce his Greek subjects to accept him as a deity, but he actively encouraged the cult of Alexander. Though Ptolemy II assumed divinity before the Greeks, it is difficult to say how seriously he took his godhead. His successors officially called themselves gods. Greek gods were brought to Egypt by immigrants, and their worship was encouraged by the Ptolemies, but the favorites were Dionysus and the other gods worshiped in the mysteries, rather than the great Olympians. However, the Ptolemies betrayed no missionary zeal. They wished to be on good terms with all the gods, and consequently they gave government subsidies to all. They built temples for the Greek gods in the Greek cities, but they also built Egyptian temples for the Egyptian divinities, and even the Jewish God was honored with a great synagogue in Alexandria. The property rights of the Egyptian gods were scrupulously respected, and Egyptian priests were allowed to retain their former liberties. These priests therefore accepted the new regime, and even became its defenders: only Amon and his priests stood aloof, as they had done so often under the Pharaohs of old.

The most significant religious innovation of the period was the worship of Serapis, established by Ptolemy I as a national cult to be shared by Greeks and Egyptians. The new religion contained elements from both Egypt and Greece, deliberately blended together by a committee composed of Greek and native theologians at Ptolemy's order. It was one of the few "synthetic" religions known to history that has been successful. The Egyptian part of the new religion came from the old cults of Osiris, god of the next world, and of Apis, the sacred bull whose mummied remains were piously preserved in a temple near Memphis: the name "Serapis" seems to be a Greek form of Osiris-Apis. The Greek part of Serapis made him resemble Asclepius, the god of healing, or the Dionysus of the mysteries; and Greek sculptors presently endowed him with a human form not unlike that of Poseidon or even of Zeus himself. The first Serapeum—or temple of Serapis—was at Memphis, not far from the Apion; but Ptolemy I erected a magnificent Serapeum in Alexandria which ancient writers considered one of the finest temples in the world. Lesser temples to the new god were built in other Egyptian towns, and the new religion eventually spread to all parts of the ancient world.

The Ptolemies made no attempt to fuse their various subjects into one people but planned to keep Egypt a country where a relatively small number of Greeks ruled over and exploited the Egyptian masses. The Egyptian population was between five and six million at this time, but it is very doubtful whether there were as many as one hundred thousand Greeks in Egypt outside Alexandria. They filled the high government offices, served in the army, held and managed the great estates, conducted large business enterprises, built great engineering works, and looked down upon the natives. Intermarriage with natives was rare and, while there were many half-castes, these unfortunates were never numerous enough to change the racial complexion of the population. Other foreigners were invited to Alexandria, among them the Jews who presently formed an important element in the population. Here they were assigned to one section of the city and granted many privileges; and here, too, anti-Semitism soon raised its head.

The Greek rulers treated the Egyptians as a distinctly inferior group. They subjected them to special taxes and obligations, notably forced labor on roads and canals, from which Greeks and other foreigners were free. Nevertheless, the status of the Egyptian peasants was not changed greatly from what it had been under the old regime, and perhaps their standard of living rose slightly because of the general prosperity. There was a certain amount of grumbling and discontent even in the days of Ptolemy II, and toward the end of the century, when Egypt's foreign wars were unsuccessful and the country was sinking into an economic depression, the natives began to cause serious trouble.

The Seleucid Empire

The second of the great Hellenistic dynasties was that of the Seleucids. Its founder, Seleucus I Nicator ("Conqueror"), had been one of the younger Macedonian generals, only a year or two older than Alexander himself. He seems to have been one of the few Macedonians to understand and share Alexander's ambitions. He alone among the important officers failed to discard the oriental wife whom he married at Susa, and he championed the continuation of imperial unity after Alexander's death. He became satrap of Babylonia in 312; his military exploits carried him to India, where he regained much of what had been lost; and his participation in the battle of Ipsus (301) brought him Syria and all Greek possessions east of the Euphrates. Twenty years later, he defeated Demetrius and Lysimachus, thereby adding most of Asia Minor to his domain; but in 280, when he was about to invade Europe with the intention of rounding out his empire by the acquisition of Macedonia and Greece, he died by an assassin's hand. He was succeeded by his able and energetic son Antiochus I Soter ("Savior"), who continued his father's policies for twenty years (280–261). The next three rulers, Antiochus II Theos ("God," 261–247), Seleucus II Callinicus ("Triumphant," 247–226), and Seleucus III Soter (226–223), were less important personages: their story is not an edifying one, and most of what we know about them concerns their wars and their family feuds and assassinations. After them came Antiochus III (223–187), called "the Great," who pulled the Empire together once more, raised it to its highest glory, and brought it to ruin.

The Seleucids had a far more difficult task than the Ptolemies, and we know much less about them. While the Ptolemies ruled a compact country which was united by geography and economics, by language and religion, and by ancient institutions and traditions, the Seleucids held a huge empire, sprawling over all southwestern Asia and disrupted by these same forces. Geographically, the Seleucid Empire fell into five major subdivisions, each inhabited by peoples of various races and languages and of many stages of culture. The first major division lay east of the Persian Desert and included parts of modern India, eastern Persia, and Afghanistan. Here the Seleucids could not retain their hold. Next came western Persia, inhabited largely by Iranian peoples, most of which was lost during the third century. West of the Zagros Mountains were the Semitic peoples of Mesopotamia and Syria. In central Asia Minor were many peoples whose blood and culture came from that of primitive Armenoid peoples mixed with Hittites, Assyrians, Lydians, Persians, Greeks, and a host of lesser groups. And lastly, along the shores of the Aegean, were the Greek cities of Ionia. Practically the sole bond uniting these various territories and peoples was the fact that they all had been conquered once by the Persians and again by Alexander. The Seleucids usually found themselves forced to follow old Persian practices in governing this vast and heterogeneous empire. The old division into more than thirty satrapies was preserved, and satraps continued to enjoy great independence in their respective territories. The Greek rulers allowed many Persian nobles to retain their old estates, some of which were large and of a feudal nature, with the lord living in a castle and ruling vast areas cultivated by his serfs. Not only in Persia proper but throughout the empire, and especially in eastern Asia Minor, many of these lords remained unreconciled to the new regime. The Seleucids continued the Persian policy of religious toleration, and they carefully refrained from interfering with temple estates. In Asia Minor and elsewhere, these huge temple estates were almost independent countries, ruled over by oriental

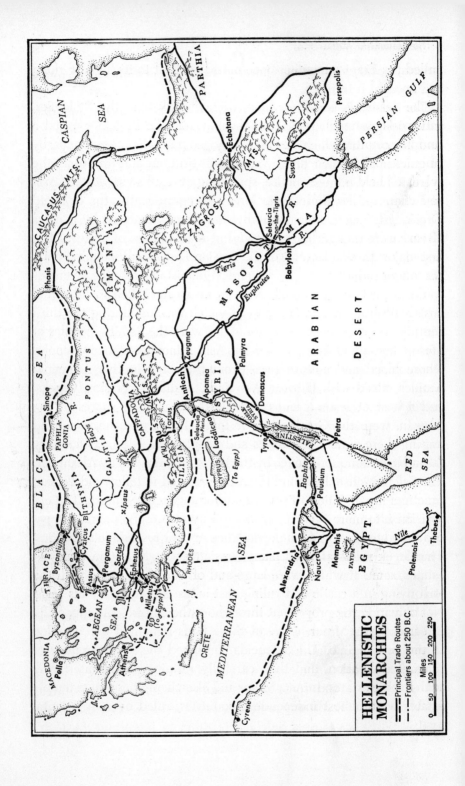

HELLENISTIC MONARCHIES

— Principal Trade Routes
—·— Frontiers about 250 B.C.

Miles
0   50   100 150 200 250

priests, and they sometimes became important centers of anti-Greek agitation.

The Seleucids were more active than the Ptolemies in founding cities designed to help the Greeks dominate their empire. Seleucus I and his son Antiochus I have been called the most prolific founders of cities in all history. Some of the new cities, especially in the East, were military outposts along the frontiers and at strategic points elsewhere. Others were Greek cities with Greek political institutions, Greek law, and a high degree of local autonomy. Thousands of Greeks were thus settled in various parts of the country, and it was hoped that they would be a force capable of dominating and uniting the whole empire.

The capital of the new empire was at Antioch-on-the-Orontes, in northern Syria. Like its rival Alexandria, Antioch was counted among the celebrated cities of antiquity, but little is now known of it. The port of Antioch was called Seleucia-in-Pieria, and farther down the Syrian coast was another new city named Laodicea. Inland, above Antioch, was the fourth great city of this locality, Apamea, a military center where the kings had their enormous arsenals, while the pastures for their cavalry horses and elephants were in the vicinity. The largest of the new cities was Seleucia-on-the-Tigris, recently excavated by American archeologists. Located not far from the ancient Babylon, which it replaced in importance, this Seleucia is said to have had a population of 600,000. At many other places new cities bore these famous dynastic names—those of the first two Seleucids and their wives. And while Antioch was the capital of the empire as a whole, Seleucia-on-the-Tigris was a secondary capital for Mesopotamia and the East, and Sardis held much the same position in Asia Minor.

Information regarding economic conditions is not so abundant as that from Egypt, yet we know that in the third century the Seleucid Empire enjoyed a high level of prosperity. The fertility of Mesopotamia rivaled that of the Nile Valley, and other provinces were very rich. Both Syria and Ionia were famous for their manufactures, notably textiles. Trade was profitable because of the fact that three great trade routes crossed Seleucid territory to India and the East, competing with the Egyptian water route through the Red Sea. These trade routes were an important bond of imperial unity: as long as they were open, the whole empire was prosperous, but when they were interrupted a period of rapid decline ensued.

Conflict of East and West

The political history of Asia under the Seleucids is largely the story of rebellions and the loss of territory. Sometimes the rebels were minor members of the Seleucid family; sometimes they were Greek satraps; and sometimes they were native leaders; but in the long run it was the native populations who tore the empire to pieces. Seleucus I never made good his claim to northern and eastern Asia Minor—Bithynia, Pontus, Cappadocia, Armenia—most of which had not been held by Alexander himself, and as early as 303, the Indian provinces were lost to a native leader. Soon after the death of Seleucus, tribes of Celts invaded Asia Minor from Thrace (277); two years later Antiochus I defeated them in a battle near Sardis, but since he could not drive them out he bought them off with heavy subsidies. The invaders settled in northern Phrygia, where they retained their language and customs into late Roman times. Two large districts were thus lost to non-Greeks.

Other Seleucid territories soon went to Greek rebels or conquerors. During the confusion caused by the Celts, a Greek satrap named Philetaerus set himself up as an independent ruler at Pergamum and founded the Attalid dynasty. It eventually ruled much of northwestern Asia Minor. A little later Antiochus I lost parts of southern Asia Minor to Ptolemy II, and when he died his government could be sure only of the central part of the peninsula, including the great road from Antioch and Cilicia to Ephesus. Ptolemy's armies even seized several Syrian ports, including Seleucia-in-Pieria (245). About 250, a Greek satrap named Diodotus had assumed independence and set himself up as king of Bactria and Sogdiana, now northeastern Persia and Afghanistan.

A little later, in 247, came the establishment of a native Parthian kingdom between Bactria and the Caspian Sea. The leaders of this revolt were the two sons of Arsaces, a Parthian nobleman whose name was perpetuated in the "Arsacid" dynasty. Domestic difficulties prevented Antiochus II and Seleucus II from attempting to suppress this revolt until 228, and then it was too late. The Parthian king had by that time conquered and annexed neighboring Hyrcania; he firmly established himself in northern Persia; and he allied himself to Diodotus II of Bactria. The Parthian kingdom thus founded claimed to be the heir of the Persian Empire of Darius III. Before the end of the third century, it held most of modern Iran, and eventually it was to conquer everything east of the Euphrates, challenge Rome, and defeat her legions.

When Seleucus III was murdered in 223, after a reign of only three years, he was succeeded by his brother, Antiochus III the Great. This young man stood in strong contrast to his immediate predecessors. Acting with energy and intelligence, he regained much of what had been lost and consequently was called by later historians *Restitutor Orbis,* "Restorer of the World." The beginning of his reign was most inauspicious. As soon as he came into power, he was faced with the revolt of two powerful Greek satraps. Molon revolted in Media along with his brother Alexander in Babylonia; and Antiochus's cousin Achaeus led a rebellion in Asia Minor. After spending several years in suppressing these revolts, Antiochus recaptured Seleucia-in-Pieria from Ptolemy IV, but his efforts to seize Palestine led to a costly defeat at Raphia (217). Thereafter, things went better. Antiochus made a great tour of his eastern provinces (209–204), comparable to that made by Alexander. He invaded Parthia, defeated its king, and forced him to pay tribute as a vassal. Advancing into Bactria he fought against Euthydemus, a Greek from Asia Minor who had married Diodotus's daughter and then succeeded his father-in-law as king. When Antiochus found that he could not conquer Euthydemus, he allowed him to retain his royal title and made an alliance with him instead. Antiochus then advanced into India itself, where he forced one of the rajahs to recognize his overlordship and pay tribute in money and elephants. Returning to Seleucia-on-the-Tigris, he assumed the title "Great King" in the ancient Persian style: altering this title slightly, later Greek and Roman historians called him "Antiochus the Great." Antiochus thus regained most of what had been lost since the days of Seleucus I.

In spite of these drains on his resources, Antiochus's army and treasury were able to support further wars, and in 200 he avenged Raphia by inflicting a serious defeat upon the Egyptians at Panium in northern Palestine. After this victory, Antiochus annexed Palestine and forced the young Ptolemy V to marry his daughter Cleopatra. He could then dominate Egypt, and only Greece stood between him and the complete restoration of Alexander's empire. By his interference in Greece, however, Antiochus courted destruction at the hands of Rome.

Macedonia and Greece

The third of the great Hellenistic monarchies was Macedon. This small country had provided the leaders and most of the soldiers for Alexander's campaigns, the leaders and many of the soldiers for the wars of the Diadochi, and large numbers of mercenaries for the later Hellenistic kings. Yet Macedonia had probably changed less during these revolutionary years than any other part of the Hellenistic world. In the days of Philip, Macedonia had been a country of hardy peasants who made excellent fighters, and such it remained a hundred years later. The loss of population through war and emigration had been made up by the natural increase of a fertile people. A few new cities were established early in the third century, and a few men representative of the new Hellenistic world were attracted to the court at Pella; but the country as a whole was scarcely touched by the new spirit. Macedon was a strong military monarchy whose kings played an important part in world politics, but its people remained backward Macedonian peasants.

Antipater and his son Cassander ruled Macedonia for twenty-five years after the death of Alexander. Cassander's death in 298 was followed by two decades of confusion, culminating in the Celtic invasion of 279. The invaders captured and decapitated the Macedonian king, and in the following year they sacked Delphi. After they had wrought great havoc, they were finally driven from Greece and, as we have seen, they invaded Asia Minor in 277. Their expulsion from Greece was due largely to the efforts of Antigonus II, who was rewarded by being chosen king of Macedon in 276.

This Antigonus II Gonatas ("Knock-kneed"), the son of Demetrius and grandson on his mother's side of Antipater, had been a pupil of Zeno, the founder of Stoic philosophy, and he was eager to seem a philosopher king. Poverty supplemented philosophy in moderating his ambition. Though he fought various wars to defend the old frontiers of Macedonia, his policy was not aggressive. In Greece he held only Piraeus (the port of Athens) and the acropolis of Corinth. The latter was useful in dividing Greece and preventing it from uniting against him, and his desire for Piraeus has been explained as a strange expression of his sentimental attachment to Athens and her culture. His love of philosophy led him to invite scholars, literary men, and artists to Pella, but his capital could not rival Athens and he probably did not intend that it should. He ruled for thirty-seven years, until his death in 239, and his Antigonid descendants continued to occupy the throne of Macedon until the Roman conquest in 168.

Meantime, statesmen were again endeavoring to effect a union of the lesser Greek states, such as others had dreamed of before Philip and Alexander. Their successes were now greater than before. Leagues were established which were no longer alliances of mutually jealous cities but unions of the small towns and villages which had suffered from the quarrels of these cities. The most important was the Aetolian League, which by 250 included most of central Greece north of the Gulf of Corinth and to which a few years later Elis in the western Peloponnesus was added. As the League contained no large cities, it had no capital and no leading power, and the temple of Apollo at Thermum was the center where meetings were held. Political power rested in an assembly of all free citizens. The League's few officials devoted themselves to military and financial affairs, and there was an elected council which looked after current business between meetings of the assembly. As time went on, a com-

mittee chosen from this council gradually assumed leadership and became virtually a central government, destroying the early democracy of the League. In strictly local matters each district retained great autonomy.

The great rival of this Aetolian League was the Achaean League. Though originally a union of twelve minor cities in southern Greece, it eventually included the whole Peloponnesus except Sparta, Elis, and Messenia. This League exercised its greatest power in the days when it was led by Aratus of Sicyon (245–213). In the second half of the third century, there were consequently four Greek powers in Europe—Macedon, the Aetolian League, the Achaean League, and Sparta—as well as Athens, which no longer sought to play an important political role. The two leagues were usually hostile to one another, and each consequently sought the friendship of the other's neighbor. Thus Aetolia and Sparta were brought together by their common fear of Macedon and Achaea.

Economic Distress and Attempted Reform

Greece did not share the economic prosperity of Egypt and Syria in the third century. Corinth and a few other cities did well, but the greater part of the country was desperately poor. It was in decline before Alexander, it was weakened by the wars of the Diadochi, and it was drained of energetic young men by the lure of the East. During this third century, there were many attempts to remedy matters by violent social revolutions which destroyed much and remedied nothing. The most celebrated of these revolutions occurred at Sparta under the leadership of Agis and Cleomenes. Sparta had suffered more than most Greek states during the preceding century. Her army, which once had dominated Greece, had shrunk to seven hundred men, and the austere discipline which had once made this army famous had given way before luxurious living. The land had fallen into the hands of a few wealthy persons, and there was much complaint about debt. Sparta cried out for reform.

Agis IV became king of Sparta in 244, at the age of twenty, dreaming that he might bring his country back to her old supremacy by a return to institutions that were supposed to date from the mythical king Lycurgus. The new king's youthful idealism and inexperience were exploited by self-seeking persons, chief among whom was his uncle Agesilaus. His original program called for two major reforms: the cancellation of debts, and a redistribution of the land, with 4500 lots of the best land going to Spartans who would form the army, and with 15,000 lots for the free civil population. Agesilaus persuaded the young king to abolish the debts first and to destroy all evidence for them. Having thus got rid of his own and his friends' debts, he sabotaged the rest of the program. In the period of reaction that followed, Agis and his family were murdered (241) and many of his friends were exiled.

Cleomenes III came to the throne in 237, and after ten years he took up the cause of reform, being led to it, we are told, by Agis' widow and a Stoic philosopher named Sphaerus who had been his tutor. Debts were cancelled again, land was redistributed, and many minor reforms seemed to bring back the old system which had once made Sparta great. Cleomenes' success led discontented people throughout Greece to espouse his cause and presently he became the champion of revolution everywhere. The conservative forces in Greece, led by the Achaeans and aided by Macedon, therefore united against him and he was defeated in battle at Sellasia in 222. After his flight to Egypt (where he was killed three years later), his reforms were abolished by the victorious allies. Nevertheless, his activities gave Sparta the reputation of favoring economic reform, and for many years thereafter reformers everywhere looked to her for encouragement and aid. The Aetolians likewise were supposed to champion the poor, while Macedonia and the Achaean League favored the rich and the economic status quo. Again Greece was split asunder by divisions that were both territorial and social.

Antigonus Gonatas had been succeeded as king of Macedon by his son Demetrius II (239–229), a rather ineffective person. When Demetrius died, he left as heir his nine-year-old son Philip, under the guardianship of his cousin. This regent promptly assumed the crown as Antigonus III Doson, but he adopted Philip as his heir. The new king was an able and energetic man who spent his first years repairing the damage Macedonia had suffered under Demetrius. When Aratus called for aid against Cleomenes of Sparta, Doson organized a Hellenic League of which he became the leader, and after his victory at Sellasia he forced Sparta to join the League. A few months later he died (221) and was succeeded by Philip V.

Much was destined to happen to Macedon and Greece during Philip's long reign (221–179), and he was to suffer great defeats and humiliations. At first, however, everything went well. Philip was called "the darling of Greece," and it seemed that the whole peninsula might soon be united under his leadership. Meantime, important things were happening elsewhere. Antiochus III had become king in Syria (223) and presently started the reconquest of his ancestral domain. The decline of Egypt began with Ptolemy IV (221–203), thus further disturbing the Hellenistic balance of power. And above all, Rome and Carthage went to war in 218. It seemed not unlikely that the victor in this mighty struggle would become a menace to Greece. We are told that at a conference at Naupactus in 217 an Aetolian leader urged the immediate union of all Greeks in view of the "cloud rising in the West." Philip soon began preparing to champion all Greece against these new dangers.

Lesser Greek States

Mention must also be made of a few small but independent Greek states in the Aegean area. The first is Pergamum. The founder of this state was a eunuch named Philetaerus, who had once been a satrap under Seleucus I. He first rose to greatness by stealing 5000 talents (silver value, over $5,000,000) entrusted to his care; he next fought the Galatians; and when he died he was virtually an independent sovereign. His nephew, Eumenes I, succeeded him in 263; and he in turn was followed by his son Attalus I (241), who refused further tribute to the Galatians, assumed the royal title (230), and after various lucky wars ruled the greater part of central Asia Minor for a few years (228–223). Even after losing most of these gains, he still held important territories for the rest of his long reign (241–197). This man's son, Eumenes II (197–160), raised the kingdom to its greatest glory. Pergamum was rich in industry and agriculture and, lying at the terminus of the main road from the East, it was the natural outlet of much of Asia Minor. The Attalids held mercantilist economic ideas and carefully developed the resources of their country. They encouraged literature and art, and though they were only half Greek themselves, they posed as great champions of Hellenism.

The island of Rhodes, at the southwestern tip of Asia Minor, was a commercial center that enjoyed great prosperity in the third century. Rhodes turned against the Cretan pirates who infested the seas and for more than a hundred years the powerful Rhodian navy policed all Aegean waters. The city of Rhodes, situated on a beautiful harbor, was much admired in antiquity and was celebrated for the Colossus, a huge statue of Apollo as sun god that stood near the entrance to the port. When an earthquake shook down the statue and much of the city in 226, funds for relief were sent from all parts of the Greek world—an interesting illustration of the international humanitarianism of the time—and soon Rhodes was again as rich and prosperous as ever. The small sacred island of Delos was another impor-

tant commercial and banking center, though in the third century it
had not yet acquired the importance it attained in early Roman
times.

An Intellectual Revolution

Like the Greek soldiers and politicians, Greek thinkers in the days
after Alexander found themselves face to face with a world such as
they had never known before. At first they expected that this new
world would merely be an expanded Greece, ruled by Greek politicians and dominated by Greek thinkers thinking along traditional
lines. This was not to be the case, however, and these men soon discovered that they, like the contemporary Ptolemies and Seleucids,
must accept fundamentally new ideas and adapt themselves to fundamentally new conditions. Entrance into the new world conquered
by Alexander forced great masses of new information upon their attention, and in this new world a new way of life arose whose practices and ideals differed widely from those of the old Greek city-
states. Before long, the old Greek view of the world was no longer
adequate or even comprehensible to Greeks living in Egypt and Asia
or, for that matter, to those living in Greece itself.

In earlier chapters of this book, we have seen how closely the intellectual life of Greece was associated with the city-states in the
fifth and fourth centuries. Artists, literary men, and philosophers received their inspiration from these cities, they wrestled with their
cities' problems, and they expressed their cities' ideals. They were
very conscious of the fact that they were citizens as well as thinkers.
After Alexander, all this was changed. The cities lost much of their
political freedom, and citizenship lost much of its significance. Governments became autocratic monarchies while private persons
tended to become individuals and citizens of the world. The old
ideals were slowly superseded by new ones appropriate to the new
world governed by foreign dynasties, mercenary armies, and professional bureaucrats.

In the new day, literary men and artists tended to become bureaucrats themselves, showing both the virtues and the vices of such persons. They developed technique to a high finish, they did much solid
and substantial work, but somehow they seemed to lack creative

imagination. Their activities were given direction by the patronage conferred upon them by the Hellenistic monarchs. The Ptolemies wished to make Alexandria the intellectual capital of the world. They founded the great library which is said to have contained a million volumes, and they built the museum for scientific study; they invited distinguished scholars and scientists to conduct researches in these institutions; and they subsidized literary men and artists at their court. The other Hellenistic monarchs pursued similar policies to the best of their abilities, with Pergamum a second great center for artists and scholars. Often, however, the men who received these subsidies were forced to sacrifice their intellectual freedom. They made and said things to which no important person could possibly take exception, and sometimes their speculations were rather far removed from the pressing problems of the political and social world about them.

Athens remained an important intellectual center, a university town sought out by students and professors from far and near. Here, something of the old free spirit still prevailed. As thinkers in Athens were not subsidized by great monarchs, they enjoyed greater freedom of speculation than was common among the scholars of Alexandria. The latter excelled at scientific work and in scholarly studies that had little bearing on contemporary political problems, but Athens remained the home of the philosophers who criticized and formulated the fundamental ideals of the new age.

At first, the Greek thinkers of the Hellenistic world, like their Greek rulers, attempted to maintain an aloof superiority toward Orientals, but just as the Ptolemies and Seleucids were forced to take over institutions created by their Egyptian and Persian predecessors, so Greek scientists and philosophers presently adopted ideas that had long been current in the East. Moreover, nearly all the thinkers who best caught the new spirit and best expressed themselves in this cosmopolitan third century were men who came, not from European Greece, but from the cities along the eastern shores of the Aegean and the Mediterranean. Here Greeks and Orientals had lived side by side for several generations and had begun creating a new civilization centuries before Alexander was born. This blending of Greek

and oriental ideas continued at an ever-increasing tempo until the
Greeks at last were submerged by the Orient. The intellectual history of Hellenistic times is largely the story of the gradual dissipation of the classic Greek heritage and the creation of something new
to replace it.

Hellenistic Art and Literature

The third century saw immense activity among artists. The building
activities of the time required the services of architects, sculptors,
and painters, and such artists were subsidized lavishly by kings and
private individuals. These new patrons of the arts were parvenus and
adventurers, not deeply rooted in the old traditions, but they were
prosperous, they wished to live luxuriously, and they demanded
something new from their artists. They wanted large and imposing
houses, costly furniture, sumptuous decorations, rich food, numerous
slaves, and women embellished with plenty of cosmetics. Size became important, and some works of art—such as the Colossus at
Rhodes—were considered great primarily because they were "colossal." The harmony and simplicity of classic Greek architecture gave
way to elaboration and ostentation, as when simple Ionic capitals
were superseded by the more ornate Corinthian. Sculptors represented their characters in theatrical and unnatural poses, and there
was an air of sophistication about them—that is to say, they were
superficial and insincere. Sometimes artists sought "realism" by portraying ugly things—such as the "Drunken Old Woman"—and in
other cases they seem to have deliberately parodied the great works
of an earlier age. Many times, too, the author obviously was trying to
harrow one's feelings, and the obviousness of his efforts impaired
their effectiveness—as when blood streamed from the wound of the
"Dying Gaul." Compared with the classic, this art often seems cheap
and gaudy (see Plates 2–5).

• Note for Plate 2.   These plates illustrate various types of Hellenistic sculpture. The Tyche, or Good Fortune, of Antioch is a sort of personification of the
city; the swimmer at her feet is the Orontes River flowing past Antioch. This
statue dates from the third century before Christ. The Victory of Samothrace,
likewise dating from the third century, was the work of a Rhodian sculptor.

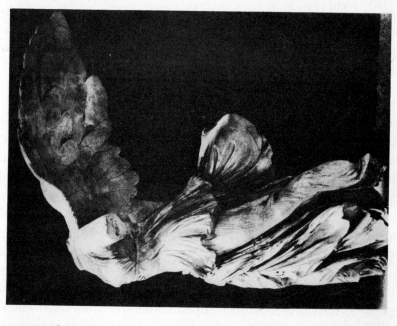

Victory of Samothrace (Louvre Museum)

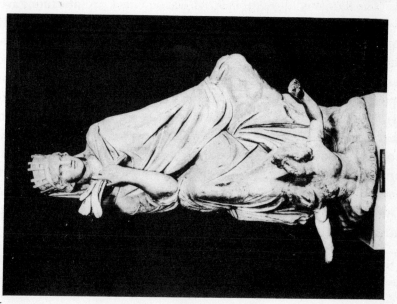

Tyche of Antioch (Vatican Museum)

Plate 2

The Dying Gaul *(Capitoline Museum, Rome)*

Dead Persian *(Terme Museum, Rome)*

Plate 3

Nevertheless, Hellenistic artists accomplished many remarkable things. The most significant work of the period was done in Asia Minor by the schools of Pergamum and Rhodes. Little remains to us from these artists except fragmentary Roman copies of Greek statues, but among them are several of the world's most famous pieces (the Victory of Samothrace and the Gaul and his Wife; and from the second century, the Venus de Milo and Apollo Belvedere). New types of art were also developed in Hellenistic times. The laying out of new cities permitted careful town-planning, an art scarcely known in earlier times. Now parks and open places, beautified by statues, fountains, and gardens, relieved the crowded and unsightly conditions which prevailed in the older cities. The Greeks had formerly paid little attention to landscaping, but they now learned from the Persians, who had long been celebrated for their parks filled with cultivated fruits and flowers. In classic times, statues had sometimes been part of the architecture of temples or other public buildings, but more frequently they were set up as votive offerings around shrines; as new statues were constantly being added, the place must eventually have had a rather cluttered appearance. Hellenistic sculptors continued to make statues for such purposes, but they also made busts and other small works for private houses or gardens, and several of the most celebrated pieces of the time were set up in parks where they must have been very effective.

Literary Activity

Though great attention was given to literary production, Hellenistic literature produced no famous masterpieces. There was a wider reading public than ever before; authorship became a recognized profession; and hundreds of authors composed huge numbers of books. Few works of this period have come down to us entire, but the

---

• Note for Plate 3. The Dying Gaul and the Dead Persian were set up in Pergamum by King Attalus I about 225 B.C. in honor of his victories. The sculptor's obvious sympathy with the defeated peoples recalls the Stoic teaching of the Brotherhood of Man, and it is evidence of the deep longing for peace that came over the Hellenistic world after a century of senseless warfare between Alexander's successors.

extant fragments have not ordinarily caused critics to deplore the loss of the rest. Literature was light stuff, intended to amuse the reader rather than to instruct or convince him.

Athens developed the New Comedy at this time, with Menander (340–291) composing more than a hundred plays. In the plots of these comedies, the social changes brought by the new world can be clearly seen. Reversals of fortune are sudden, both author and audience being quite prepared to believe that nothing is impossible. Old standards of conduct are laughed at, parents are altogether out of date, and youth has the world before it. The bullying father, the intriguing and impertinent slave, the love-sick youth, the amiable courtesan, the soldier back from the wars, all achieve happiness after various amusing adventures. While Menander's comedies thus illustrate the changing times, they seem trivial when compared to those of the fifth-century Aristophanes, for their author had none of his predecessor's zeal for persuading and reforming men. Menander merely wished to amuse his audience, without causing it to think at all. Nevertheless, he was much admired and imitated by later generations. The Latin comedies of Plautus and Terence are often free translations from his; the tradition of comedy which he established reappeared in Molière and Shakespeare (*Comedy of Errors*); and by this circuitous route one of his plays has recently reached Hollywood.

A dramatic type more popular at Alexandria was the mime, a brief skit in which one or several actors "mimicked" characters of everyday life. The mime originated in southern Italy or Sicily, and later was popular in Rome, but it achieved its highest development in

---

• **Note for Plate 4.**   According to an ancient myth Marsyas rashly challenged Apollo to a musical contest; after his victory, Apollo ordered his rival skinned alive as punishment for his presumption. The sculptor who carved this statue, a member of the Pergamene school of the third century, depicted the unfortunate man hung up and about to be flayed. The bronze statue of a Praying Boy comes from the early third century. Students sometimes comment upon the free and dignified manner in which the Greeks approached their gods, contrasting it with the cringing and servile attitudes often assumed by Orientals before their masters, human and divine.

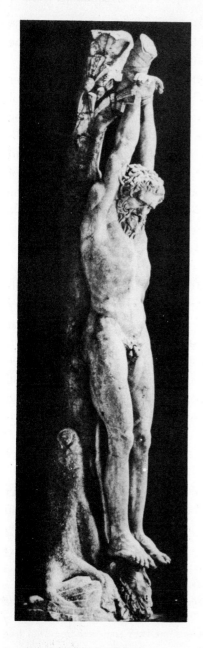

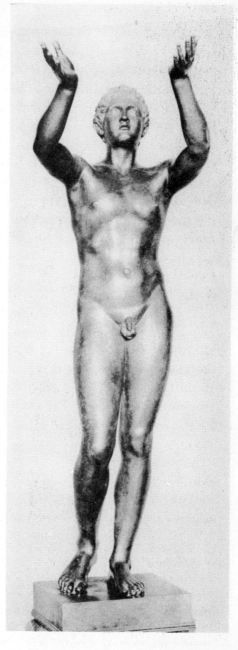

Marsyas About to Be Flayed
(Louvre Museum)

Praying Boy (Berlin Museum)

Plate 4

Drunken Old Woman *(Munich Museum)*

Old Market Woman *(Courtesy of the Metropolitan Museum of Art)*

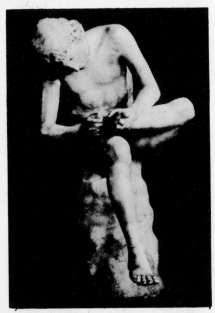

Boy with Thorn *(Uffizi, Florence)*

Parody of Boy with Thorn *(Berlin Museum)*

Plate 5

third-century Alexandria. The authors of mimes sought realism principally by making their dialogue coarse and vulgar, but sometimes they managed to create rather lifelike characters. One writer of mimes was the Sicilian poet Theocritus, who resided in Alexandria under Ptolemy II. His more celebrated poems, however, deal with the lives of Sicilian shepherds. They established a type of pastoral poetry which has persevered to modern times. Perhaps these *Idylls* gave the mild pleasure of nostalgia to rustic Greeks who had migrated to Alexandria and been successful there. At any rate, they inspired Vergil, and they gave us our word "idyllic."

The chief concern of the lesser poets of this Alexandrian period—many of them subsidized by the Ptolemies, and none of them having anything to say—seems to have been to mystify their readers with recondite allusions. Handbooks of obscure mythology were compiled to lighten the labors of these paid poets who hoped to conceal their lack of inspiration behind a façade of elaborate pedantry.

Hellenistic Historians

Third-century historians produced no great masterpieces, yet their influence upon subsequent historical writing was profound. The spectacular career of Alexander, of course, gave them something new to write about, and the popular demand for biographies of the hero was so great that twenty-five such books soon appeared. The best of them was that written by Ptolemy I of Egypt, who had accompanied Alexander and who based his narrative upon the *Ephemerides*, or official record. Ptolemy wrote a sober and accurate account, and the bulk of our reliable information about the wars comes indirectly from him. Most Hellenistic biographies of Alexander approached the hero

---

• Note for Plate 5.   The two statues of old women illustrate another aspect of Hellenistic art, its tendency to depict ugly things in order to be true to life or "realistic." These two terra cottas date from the second century before Christ. The statue of a Boy with a Thorn, dating from the early third century (or perhaps even from the fourth), was very popular in the Hellenistic world and at Rome. Still another aspect of the Greek genius is illustrated in this parody of the famous statue found at Priene.

in a different spirit. Cleitarchus, for instance, paid little attention to fact but invented countless stories to illustrate the Macedonian's marvelous powers. This was the sort of history that the Hellenistic public wanted, and it was widely imitated. The "Alexander romance" took on fearful and wonderful proportions, and for centuries to come such works continued to entertain, amaze, and inspire their readers.

The expedition of Alexander did more than provide historians with a romantic subject to write about: it also broadened the field of their investigations. Historians as well as politicians began to think in world terms, and a few tried to cover the whole world in their histories. Hieronymus of Cardia, a fellow townsman and friend of Eumenes, attempted such a feat for the history of his own generation, while others projected world history back to the very beginning of things. Dicearchus, a pupil of Aristotle who attained distinction in several fields of learning, wrote a *Life of Hellas* which apparently took on a universal character. Our brief fragments show that it began with a description of primitive man (whose first accomplishments were declared to be the domestication of animals and the invention of agriculture), that it spoke briefly of the Ancient Orient, and that it described the cultural as well as the political history of Greece down to Alexander. At first these historians took the attitude—shared by their readers and rulers—that since Alexander and his Greeks had conquered the world, it mattered little what the conquered countries had been before his time. Eventually, however, they realized that these conquered peoples had a history that was both interesting and important. Books appeared which dealt with the histories of India, Babylonia, Phoenicia, Judea, Arabia, Egypt, Ethiopia, Carthage, and Rome. Though written in Greek, these histories were usually the work of native scholars able to use the national records of the country in question. Such at least was the case with Berosus who wrote a history of Babylon, Manetho who wrote about Egypt, and Fabius Pictor who wrote of Rome. But the task of welding these national histories into one great world history lay beyond the powers of third-century scholars, and not until two hundred years later did true world histories appear.

Learned Research

Alexandrian scholars showed even less creative ability in other fields of learning. They studied Homer and the other monuments of classic Greek literature and wrote copiously about them. They established standard texts of the various classics—a task as important as it was difficult at a time when every copy of a book was written by hand and therefore differed somewhat from every other copy—and they made serious efforts to secure the perpetuation of these texts. They commented upon old authors, explaining difficult words and allusions; they wrote dull literary history; and they compiled bibliographies. In fact, their work was surprisingly like much modern "research" in the same fields. Classic Greece was already an alien world that could be understood only by professional scholars, and it is doubtful whether even they comprehended it perfectly. The old Greece had passed away and scholars were preserving a part of the old world that was gone as a heritage to the new world that was coming into being.

Hellenistic Science

Hellenistic scientists were the most brilliant produced by the ancient world. Their achievements were the result in part of the encouragement and subsidies of the Ptolemies, in part of the acquisition by the Greeks of information accumulated through the centuries by oriental priests and scientists, in part of the broadened view of the world that came from Alexander's conquests. Greek knowledge of geography, for example, expanded greatly at this time. We have seen that Alexander's inadequate knowledge of the subject led him to confusion in India, and that he ordered further explorations in the Caspian Sea, the Indian Ocean, and Arabia. These explorations were continued by his successors. The Seleucids sent explorers to India, whence they brought back reliable information regarding the Ganges and the lands beyond which had hitherto been unknown to the Greeks. Others explored the Caspian and still other travelers told vague stories of China itself. Meantime, the Ptolemies were sending expeditions up the Nile, through the Red Sea, and south along the African coast.

Greek geographers also became better acquainted with Carthaginian explorations beyond Gibraltar. Pytheas of Massilia circumnavigated Britain shortly before 300 and wrote a book about his travels. In this book, he reported rumors of an island called Thule (probably Iceland or Norway), located six days' voyage north of England, where day and night each lasted six months. This story seemed quite incredible to most Greeks, but a few scientists accepted it and perhaps even understood the phenomenon. Pytheas also studied the tides of the Atlantic (those in the Mediterranean are so slight as to be almost imperceptible) and correctly attributed them to the influence of the moon. Map-makers located newly discovered lands on maps showing the whole inhabited world. These maps are evidence of the enormous progress made by Greek geographers since the days of Herodotus and even of Aristotle. They are also monuments to the cosmopolitanism of a time when men's minds were reaching out to the whole world.

This new geography was summed up by Eratosthenes, a scholar born of Greek parents in Cyrene about 276. After studying at Athens and Alexandria, he became librarian under Ptolemy III, and finally died at the age of eighty. He was the only man of his day to rival Aristotle in the breadth of his learning. He called himself a philologist, or "lover of learning," and his writings covered such varied subjects as mathematics, astronomy, geography, history, chronology, philology, literary criticism, and philosophy. He even wrote dull poetry. His contemporaries sometimes called him "Beta" to indicate that, although he did well in a variety of fields, he did not rank first in any. Nevertheless, his geographical writings marked an important step in the progress of that science. He believed that the earth is a sphere, and apparently he knew the correct explanation of the long Arctic nights reported by Pytheas. He was the first to mark maps with lines of latitude and longitude, and he invented the zones still used by geographers. When he attempted to mark out the torrid zone, his error was less than one-half of a degree—he put the tropics at 23° 51′ instead of the correct 23° 27′. His study of the tides in the Atlantic and Indian oceans convinced him that these two bodies of water were connected, that the inhabited world was completely surrounded by water, and that India might be reached by sailing around Africa from Spain. His most brilliant achievement, however, was his calculation of the size of the earth from the angles of shadows in wells at different places. He declared the earth's circumference to be 252,000 stades or 24,662 miles; as the true distance is 24,857 miles his error was 195 miles or less than 1 per cent.

Astronomy

While geographers were thus establishing a knowledge of the earth upon solid foundations, other scientists turned their attention to the heavens. In these studies they received great aid from the Babylonians, who had recorded their astronomical observations accurately for several centuries. These observations were continued after Alexander, and one of the greatest of oriental astronomers was Kidenas of Sippar, who early in the third century discovered the precession of the equinoxes (the slow rotation of the earth's axis, causing slight variations in the length of the year) and made a computation of the length of the year which missed the correct figure by only seven minutes and sixteen seconds. Greek astronomers soon absorbed this oriental science and added to it, cataloguing and plotting stars and constructing elaborate theories about the universe.

The most important of the Greek astronomers was Aristarchus of Samos. This man, who flourished in the days of Ptolemy II, is famous for his theory that the sun is the center of the solar system. Aristarchus had made some interesting but very inaccurate computations of the size and distance of the sun and moon, concluding that the sun is about three hundred times as large as the earth. (It really is more than a million times as large.) Perhaps these calculations caused him to doubt whether the larger body revolves around the smaller, but others had prepared the way for his theory. In the fourth century, Heraclides of Pontus had suggested that the planets Mercury and Venus revolve around the sun. Aristarchus completed the theory by declaring that the earth and all the planets follow circular paths around the sun, while the moon revolves around the earth. Though he thus anticipated the views of Copernicus by many centuries, his brilliant suggestion did not convince his successors. Only one Babylonian astronomer, a man named Seleucus, attempted to defend the new doctrine. Unscientific persons declared Aristarchus guilty of impiety, while scientists rejected his theory because they could not harmonize known phenomena with the theory of a circular path for the earth. (Its path really is elliptical.) Aristarchus's great rival was Hipparchus, who lived in the second century and taught that the earth is the center of the universe, and that around it revolve the moon, planets, sun, and stars, their variations being explained by a complicated system of cycles and epicycles. With him the series of great Greek astronomers came to an end.

Mathematics

Such studies as these required solid mathematical foundations. The old Greeks had gone far in their studies of geometry, first under the Pythagoreans and later under distinguished investigators in the fourth century. Then came the most famous of the Greek mathematicians, Euclid, who taught at Alexandria in the days of Ptolemy I. Though he wrote on several branches of mathematics, his fame rests upon his *Elements of Geometry*. This book has remained the standard work on the subject. Later Greek geometricians prepared new editions of Euclid's treatise which differed only slightly from the original. Latin translations presently appeared, and an Arabic translation came in the eighth century after Christ. New Latin translations were made from the Arabic in the Middle Ages, and translations into modern languages were made from the Latin. Even today, school textbooks on plane and solid geometry differ but little from Euclid's work, and nothing essential has been added. "No book in the world except the Bible has had such a reign."

A greater mathematician than Euclid was Archimedes of Syracuse. Born early in the third century, he was murdered by a Roman soldier in 212. Legends tell of his numerous mechanical inventions which included a system of compound pulleys for lifting enormous weights, a burning glass—probably a concave bronze shield—by which he set fire to ships in the harbor, and a water screw to pump out the holds of ships. He also discovered the principle of specific gravity. His primary interest, however, lay in pure mathematics. He showed that

π, the ratio of the diameter to the circumference of a circle, is less than $3\frac{1}{7}$ and greater than $3^{10}\!/_{71}$; he devised a system for expressing huge numbers as powers of 10,000, the largest number for which the Greeks had a name or symbol (*myrios,* whence our "myriad"); and he was proudest of his solution of the problem of the relative volumes of a sphere and a cylinder. His writings also show that he was on the verge of discovering calculus. At about the same time, Apollonius of Perga wrote on conic sections, carrying the subject as far as is possible by the methods of simple geometry and almost discovering analytical geometry. The last of the great Greek mathematicians was the astronomer Hipparchus, whose studies led him to discover trigonometric functions. Strange to say, however, the Greeks knew nothing of algebra, which was developed by Moslems early in the Middle Ages.

Progress in the other sciences was less spectacular. Archimedes' discovery of specific gravity was almost the only addition to the science of physics, though various writers discussed problems relating to light and color, or wrote about magnets. Even less attention was devoted to chemistry. Theophrastus, a disciple of Aristotle, wrote extensively about plants, describing about five hundred species with remarkable accuracy, inventing a method of classifying them, and explaining their distribution by climate and soil. And finally, Hellenistic physicians made many discoveries. By careful observation and the dissection of animals and men, they discovered the nervous system, distinguishing between sensory and motor nerves. They learned the function of the brain and the relation of the arteries and the pulse to the heart. They made extensive use of drugs and diet for healing, and they even performed simple surgical operations. Votes of thanks recorded in inscriptions bear witness to the courage of these Hellenistic physicians in caring for their patients in time of epidemic and to their willingness to work without fee in case of need.

The third century was thus a brilliant period in the history of science, but its great achievements were not followed up. There are many reasons, both social and political, for this failure to go on. The synthesis of Greek and oriental knowledge had been completed, and men had gone as far as was possible with the tools and instruments of measurement then at their disposal. Not until more accurate measurements could be made did a new period of scientific progress begin. These new tools became available in early modern times, and modern scientists then continued from the point where the Hellenistic Greeks had stopped.

Religion and Philosophy

In earlier chapters, we have seen something of the variety of cults and deities in which the religious spirit of ancient Greece found expression.[2] First there were the ancient spirits of field and stream, the Pans and Satyrs, who differed little from the fairies and pixies of later times and whose simple festivals made glad the hearts of the Greek peasantry. Then there were the Olympian gods, made famous by the Homeric poems which had reached approximately their classic form in the ninth and eighth centuries before Christ. These divinities had since fallen into disrepute and they were rarely honored with sincere devotion in the fifth and fourth centuries. A third aspect of Hellenic religion was to be seen in the worship of the patron deities of the various city-states, such as that of Athena at Athens. And finally, there were the ancient vegetation gods, such as Demeter and Dionysus, whose cults, called "mysteries," inspired worshipers by their elaborate rituals and whose theologies taught secret doctrines regarding sin and purification, death and immortality. In the seventh and sixth centuries, these teachings were much expanded by men called "Orphics," or followers of Orpheus. The mysteries appealed especially to city-dwellers of the humbler sort, and they owed much of their success to the fact that they gave color and meaning to otherwise drab and lonely lives. All these forms of religion had been severely criticized in the fifth and fourth centuries, and after Alexander, Greek religion began developing in other directions.

Perhaps the minor deities, such as the Pans and Satyrs, suffered less change than the others for they continued in their old ways until the very end of pagan antiquity. The Olympian gods seemed simply to evaporate, leaving few traces in Hellenistic Greek religion, though

---

[2] For a fuller discussion of the matters summarized in this paragraph, see Vol. I, especially Chap. 10, pp. 322–337.

literary hacks continued to relate their achievements in dull and un-inspired verses. The patrons of the city-states were still honored with worship, and new cults were still set up from time to time, but the heart was no longer in them. When the city-states lost their power and independence, the impotence of their guardian deities became manifest to all. The humble mysteries, on the other hand, prospered greatly in the new age. Having had little or no connection with the old city-states, they did not collapse with them. Their individualistic teachings appealed to the new spirit of Hellenistic times, and their communities of worshipers proved attractive to countless Greeks in the great cities of the new world. The mystery cults provided new religious interests and new friends for persons who had left their old homes and altars to become sojourners in strange new lands. The cult of Dionysus, for example, spread rapidly through the whole Hellenistic world in the third century, and it presently became a matter of concern to statesmen: some feared it as creating a group of persons who might become a menace to the state, while others encouraged it, and similar religions, as bonds uniting Greeks and thus helping assure their supremacy over Orientals. The new world status of the cult was also shown by important developments in the myth of Dionysus: men began to tell how he had traveled as far as India, taking with him civilization as represented by the cultivation of the vine. His career thus came to be modeled on that of Alexander.

The dramatic military exploits of Alexander and his successors also gave theologians and philosophers other new things to consider. The old gods were evidently powerless before the mighty forces impell-ing these conquerors onward. Long before Alexander, the multiplic-ity of the old gods had sometimes been explained by picturing them as different manifestations of one universal deity. Hellenistic think-ers continued this trend toward monotheism, using the words "god" and "gods" and "Zeus" as synonymous names for one supreme power, which sometimes seemed as impersonal and inexorable as the stars in their courses. More commonly, they preferred to think of it as be-ing capricious and capable of helping individual men if it so chose. Some philosophers made a deity of Fortune or Destiny; others ap-proached the monotheism of the later Hebrew prophets. The lofty views of the metaphysicians were too difficult for ordinary people, however, and many who had forsaken the old gods of Greece now rushed into the grossest superstitions in their frantic search for supernatural aid. Sneering at Zeus, they believed devoutly in omens, dreams, incantations, magic, and sorcery.

We have less information about the changes that came over the various oriental religions in the third century. There can be little doubt, however, that they were then going through a rapid evolution, adjusting themselves to the new world by borrowing heavily from each other and, to a less extent, from the Greeks. In the second and first centuries, when information about them becomes more plentiful, we find that they had gone far in this direction. These religions began to spread into the Greek world soon after Alexander, though at first those who worshiped Isis or Cybele or Yahweh in the Greek cities were Orientals who found much the same attractions in these cults that their Greek neighbors found in the mysteries of Dionysus. Presently Greeks too began to worship oriental gods. These deities were powerful throughout the Greco-Roman world from the first century before Christ to the third or fourth after Christ, and only at the end of ancient times were their cults amalgamated, purified, and superseded by Christianity. In the meantime, educated people turned more and more to philosophy as a substitute for religion.

Epicureanism

The philosophical schools of Plato and Aristotle continued to exist throughout Hellenistic times, but their influence declined, and the tendencies of the new age were best expressed in two new philosophies, Epicureanism and Stoicism. Epicurus was born of Athenian parents on the island of Samos in 341. Expelled from that island in 322, he led a difficult and wandering life until he finally settled at Athens in 306. Here friends bought him a house and garden, and here he resided until his death in 270. Epicurus was a man of singular personal charm, able to win and retain the deep affection of all who knew him. His intimate friends and disciples came from every class of society and—what was unusual in those days—included women as well as men. He spent his life discussing philosophy with these friends and writing his numerous books. In Christian times, these writings were destroyed as completely as possible, and we now have only three short essays and a few scraps preserved on inscriptions or papyri. Our knowledge of Epicurus's doctrine therefore comes largely from his enemies or from his greatest follower, the Roman poet Lucretius (99–55 B.C.), whose long poem *De rerum natura* ("On the Nature of Things") set forth the master's teaching. We know, however, that for at least five hundred years Epicurus was held in the highest esteem by followers who reverenced him as a revealer of the truth and a liberator of mankind from superstition.

The heart of Epicurus's philosophy lay in the problem of ethics: how should a wise man conduct his life? Epicurus established the foundations of his ethical system, not with the gods, but in the material world. Following Democritus (a Greek philosopher of the fifth century), he pictured this material world as made up of tiny atoms moving through space in accordance with natural law. While he did not categorically deny the existence of the gods, he declared that they played no part and took no interest in mundane affairs, and he taught that oracles, omens, dreams, and the like were of no significance. After thus clearing his disciples' minds of old superstitions, Epicurus proceeded to point out that what men seek above all else is happiness, and he discussed what best leads to that goal. When it came to recommending specific conduct, Epicurus was not very original: he praised the old virtues as promoting happiness, and he denounced the old vices as leading to distress; but his noble character caused him to rank friendship first among the virtues and to color his whole philosophy with a spirit of humanitarianism.

Epicurus's frequent use of the word pleasure gave unscrupulous opponents an easy point of attack. His teachings were later denounced by both pagans and Christians as a "pig philosophy." Adversaries charged the sect with encouraging gross debauchery. As a matter of fact, most Epicureans were, like their master, austere persons who considered intellectual pleasures the only ones worth having: Socrates drinking the hemlock, they used to say, was happier than a hog wallowing in the mud, and a true philosopher could be happy even on the rack. It would be more accurate to compare Epicureans with the British utilitarians of the nineteenth century who sought "the greatest good of the greatest number," and who held that this good could best be attained by allowing each individual to follow his own enlightened self-interest. A more serious criticism of the Epicurean philosophy—but one, it is interesting to note, that was rarely urged in antiquity—charges that it was fundamentally a philosophy of escape: the Epicurean was no longer a citizen doing his share in common enterprises but a philosopher who was as unconcerned as his gods with the affairs of this world and who, like them, sought only peace and freedom from disturbance with his friends in a secluded garden. In this attitude, as in so many other things, Epicurus was typical of Athens in his day and, for that matter, of the whole Hellenistic world, where there was not much for the citizen to do now that his former duties had been taken over by powerful monarchs, their bureaucrats, and their mercenary soldiers.

Stoicism

The second great Hellenistic philosophy was Stoicism. Its founder, Zeno, the son of a Phoenician merchant, was born on the island of Cyprus in 336. As a young man, he studied at Athens under the great Cynic philosophers (see Vol. I, pp. 489 f.). Shortly after 300, he began lecturing, and he continued in this profession until his death in 264. Following the example of his Cynic teachers, Zeno delivered his lectures as publicly as possible and took his stand in a colonnade or porch beside the agora. As this porch was called the *stoa poikilé*, or "Painted Porch," Zeno and his followers were called "Stoics." Though Zeno received his philosophical education at Athens, he was born and remained a Phoenician. In personal appearance he was clearly a foreigner, his Greek was imperfect, and many of his ideas seem to go back to his early Semitic environment. Modern scholars suggest that his style of speaking, his austere moral earnestness, his close approach to monotheism and universalism, and his interest in the stars, all betray his oriental origin, and he has sometimes been compared to the Hebrew prophets. In spite of these foreign qualities, however, Zeno won the high regard of the Athenians who, shortly before his death, voted him a golden crown and passed a resolution

Epicurus (Courtesy of the Metropolitan Museum of Art)

Zeno (Copenhagen Museum)

Plate 6

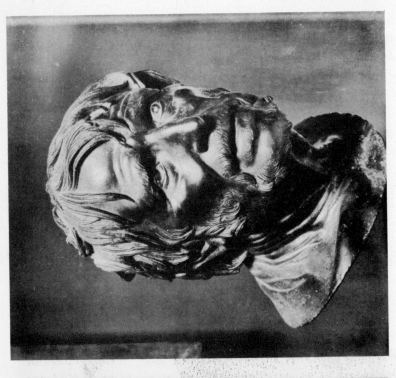

"Tragic Poet" (Naples Museum)

Menander (Museum of Fine Arts, Boston)

Plate 7

in his honor which declared that "he made his life a pattern to all, for he practiced his own teaching."

Leadership among the Stoics next fell to Cleanthes (*c.* 300–232), a native of Assos in the Troad, where Aristotle had once passed a few years. Cleanthes is celebrated especially for his religious poems, several of which have been preserved. His *Hymn to Zeus* is perhaps the finest in the Greek language. He was the theologian of Stoicism. His successor was Chrysippus (280–206) of Soli, a town near Tarsus in Cilicia. These men were the successive leaders of the school in Athens, but Zeno had many other distinguished disciples, among whom may be mentioned Aratus, likewise of Soli, whose long poem *Phaenomena* was translated into Latin by Cicero, imitated by Vergil, and quoted by St. Paul in his famous speech at Athens (Acts 17:28).

Stoicism quickly spread throughout the Greek world and beyond. Even in the third century we hear of Stoics in Babylon and Carthage, and Tarsus became a major center of Stoic teaching, a position which it retained at least until the time of Christ. Stoicism appeared at Rome in the second century before Christ, and there it retained the adherence of intellectual leaders until long after the beginning of the Christian era. It is worth noting that very few of the early Stoic leaders were true Greeks. They came from the oriental towns conquered by Alexander; they were largely or wholly oriental in blood; and often they were more successful than their Greek conquerors in catching the spirit of their new world.

The Stoics, like the Epicureans, concerned themselves primarily with the problems of human conduct, but they laid broader philosophical foundations for their theories. They devoted great attention to the study of logic and to the questions of what a man can know and how he can be sure of anything—speculations for which the Epicureans cared nothing. The Stoics also had a superficial interest in natural science, which provided them with a materialistic view of the world, though they can hardly be called scientists themselves and they attracted few true scientists to their fold. But while the Stoics shared Epicurus's materialism, which taught that the course of nature is inalterably fixed, they showed a more sympathetic attitude than he toward the old religions. Many Stoics, such as Clean-

thes, were deeply religious men, mystically convinced that the
mechanical order of the universe is also a divine order friendly to
man. God, they said, is the "soul" of the universe while the material
world is the "body" of God. But though they continued to talk about
"the gods," their theology was essentially monotheistic. In discussing old myths they used the "allegorical" interpretation. Of course
the myths were not literally true: they were "allegories" or stories
teaching great moral truths—and it is a rare myth from which no
moral lesson can be drawn. The Stoics thus avoided the intransigeance of the Epicureans, and admitted that there was after all an
element of truth in the old myths and gods. Enlightened persons took
these admissions in a very restricted sense, but their unintelligent
contemporaries seized upon them to justify the most degrading
myths and practices, not to mention plain superstition and charla-
tanism. Stoic philosophers must bear a heavy responsibility for the
spread of astrology, which the more forthright Epicureans denounced openly.

Perhaps the Stoics made things too easy for superstitious persons,
but they were only seeking to prove that human beings are fundamentally honest and good, and that the world is a fit place for kindly
people to live in. Since the course of nature is unalterably fixed by
divine law, they said, the wise man will not attempt to change it.
He will instead make his desires conform to nature, accepting the
leadership of what the Stoics called God. Thus one of Cleanthes'
hymns begins, "Lead me, O Zeus, and Thou, O Destiny." If a man
accepts this leadership, he will not be disturbed by any seeming misfortunes that may befall him, for he will know that they are but
parts of a larger plan, and that this plan will eventually work out for
the best.

The changes brought to the world by Alexander and his successors
naturally turned men's minds to social and political theory, and there
was much speculation on these matters. In this the Stoics took a leading part. One of Zeno's earliest writings was entitled *On Kingship*,
and his followers often found occasion to express themselves on social
problems. A considerable body of Utopian literature grew up, usually
under Stoic influence, which described imaginary islands or coun-

tries where everything was arranged according to nature and where everybody was therefore perfectly happy. A certain Euhemerus produced an early work of this sort (about 300), famous especially because in it he propounded the theory that the gods of mythology were men who had been deified by their admirers as a reward for their great services to humanity. A little later, Iambulus, also a Stoic philosopher, wrote an account of the "City of the Sun" (Heliopolis). Even the great Cassander, king of Macedon, is said to have allowed his brother to experiment along these lines by founding the "City of Heaven" (Ouranopolis)—an experiment something like New Harmony and other communistic settlements in America in the early nineteenth century. The inhabitants of this new city were to be called Ouranidae, or "Children of Heaven," and the significance of the project, in its author's imagination, is further shown in that he took the trouble to invent a new language for its citizens to speak—a language that has sometimes been compared to the modern Esperanto. Other writers discussed the ideal king, and how he would differ from a tyrant. Still others wrote on such topics as justice and duty.

Above all, however, the Stoic philosophers played an important part in spreading the new ideal of cosmopolitanism and world citizenship. The old Greek ideal of a free and independent city-state had long since been shattered, and Alexander had given men a momentary glimpse of the world under one ruler. The tragic political history of the next century showed how helpful such world unity might be. The Stoics began speaking of the inhabited world (the *oikumené*) as a unit and they thus implied that it should have only one ruler. They usually expressed a very low opinion of Alexander personally, but they reflected upon his achievements, and better than anyone else they caught the spirit of the new day. It seems most likely, however, that Zeno the Phoenician derived his ideas on world unity largely from the Orient, where great religions such as Zoroastrianism and Judaism had long been preaching the unity of God and of mankind. Several other great Stoics likewise came from oriental cities—such as Tarsus—that had known these empires and religions long before the coming of Alexander. Though these thinkers were much Hellenized, their eastern origin made it easier for them than for the victorious Greeks to understand what was going on in the world, for they could see both sides of the picture. Being conquered peoples themselves, they were perhaps quicker than their conquerors to claim that all men are really equal. At any rate, these Stoic philosophers were for several centuries the leading teachers of world unity, and it was they who popularized the famous phrase, "the Fatherhood of God and the Brotherhood of Man."

Instability of the New Order

The hundred years that followed Alexander constituted one of the great creative centuries in the history of mankind. Alexander's conquests forced his successors to create new political, economic, and intellectual worlds. They could not preserve his world empire, but they never lost sight of his ideal of world unity, and little by little they laid substantial foundations for the world empire that was eventually established by the Romans. The Ptolemies in Egypt built up a bureaucratic system which for a while was remarkably efficient and which later influenced the Roman bureaucracy. The Seleucids, in their efforts to establish free Greek cities within their empire, took the first steps toward reconciling the freedom of a city-state with the international order of a world-empire: the Romans solved the problem much later, approaching it in a very similar way. Even the European Greeks seemed at last to have hit upon a form of League which might eventually unite the whole peninsula. These solid achievements did more to prepare the world for political unity than did Alexander's spectacular but ephemeral victories.

This third century was also one of the most prosperous periods in antiquity. Economic prosperity was due in part to Alexander's expenditure of the huge Persian hoards of the precious metals, and in part to the removal of the restraints that had once hindered trade between Greece and Asia. The opening of new markets and the more intelligent exploitation of the lower classes in the new world also played a part, as did the spirit of enterprise that characterized the new age. International trade developed rapidly and businessmen, like their friends, the politicians, began to think in world terms. They, too, were working for world unity. Meantime, other Greeks devoted their energies to literary, scientific, and artistic creation. They turned their thoughts in new directions, largely under the impact of the new world in which they were living, and they started a new period in the intellectual history of antiquity. A whole new world was brought into being, which thought in terms of world unity and cosmopolitanism.

Nevertheless, then as in our own day, it was easier to dream of world unity and peace than to achieve it. The empires set up by Alexander's successors remained highly unstable. The bureaucracies soon became corrupt, incompetent, and oppressive. Whole populations broke away to form independent states, and other territories were permanently lost to foreign powers. Thinkers lost their originality, and economic prosperity declined. The causes for this decline are not simple. It cannot be said that as a people the Greeks were worn out, or that their physical and mental vigor was declining. But ever since the Peloponnesian War (431–404) economic conditions in Greece itself had been bad, and now they rapidly went from bad to worse. The whole peninsula was caught in the whirlpool of poverty, revolution, and class war, which in turn brought further war and poverty. The Greeks in the East, on the other hand, were at most a few tens of thousands ruling over millions. As they lived in conditions and a climate to which they were not accustomed or adapted, their success demanded constant recruitment in Greece. When the mother country could no longer supply these recruits, the Hellenistic kings had to rely more heavily upon native assistants, and Greek hegemony in the Orient was imperiled. The Greeks simply did not have the numbers or the physical strength to dominate the Hellenistic world. Other factors also contributed to an economic decline during the last quarter of the third century. The stimulus once received from rapid expansion was no longer felt. Trade routes to the East were cut by the Parthians. But, above all, the decline of the Hellenistic Empires was hastened by the incessant wars of the Greek dynasties and by revolts of the native populations.

Wars were inherent in the Hellenistic system, with its unstable balance of power, and they wrought terrific damage throughout the third century. Even greater damage was wrought by native rebellions. The Greeks were not so much of a *Herrenvolk* as they fondly believed—no peoples ever are—and the Orientals soon learned to despise and hate them as they had never hated the Persians. Presently the whole Near East was seething with discontent. Revolts broke out with increasing frequency and were repressed only after incalculable damage had been done. Greeks and Orientals thus tore each other to pieces until Rome intervened and put an end to their suicidal wars.

Part Two: The Roman Republic

III Rome and the West

THE EVENTS OF THE THIRD CENTURY HAD CONVINCED MANY Greek statesmen, businessmen, and philosophers that a return to Alexander's world unity was essential to peace and prosperity, but as is often the case political realities lagged far behind the best thought of the day. Politicians could provide only a precarious balance of power that was repeatedly disturbed by major and minor wars. Though Antiochus III almost re-established Alexander's world empire at the end of the third century, his long wars drove everyone so deeply into bankruptcy that even victory would have availed little. Even if he had completed the task, his world empire would surely have collapsed within a few years. Division and particularism were ingrained in Greek life, and ambitious leaders were so given to quarreling and fighting amongst themselves, that a Greek-ruled world empire was out of the question.

The forces working for world unity were so strong, however, that if the Greeks could not accomplish it someone else was sure to do so. Within a short time the Romans intervened in world affairs and did what the Greeks had proved themselves incapable of doing. They united and pacified the world. Their intervention in the East was accompanied by widespread devastation and suffering, yet it was far less disastrous, even to the Greeks themselves, than a continuation of international anarchy would have been, and in the end it produced a world in which Greeks and Orientals prospered side by side with their Roman conquerors. The Greek historian Polybius, writing shortly after 150 B.C., allowed not quite fifty-three years (219–167) for this Roman conquest of the East, which he erroneously believed to be complete in his day. In reality, the unification of the world required more than another hundred years, and not until the time of Augustus, shortly before the birth of Christ, did the world begin to enjoy that peace and unity for which it had yearned ever since the death of Alexander. The story of how Rome brought about this union of the world forms the major theme in every history of these troubled centuries.

A few recent writers, especially certain German scholars writing between the two World Wars, have depicted Rome's rise to world dominion as proceeding according to a carefully prearranged plan, pursued with ruthless brutality and destructive of all civilization as it proceeded. Such a picture is far from the truth. In the period described by Polybius, and throughout the century that followed, Roman leaders had even less plan for world conquest than Alexander did when he set out upon his invasion of Asia. Alexander at least was embarking upon a joyous adventure from which he vaguely expected great things, but it was with reluctance that the Romans intervened in eastern affairs at all. Repeatedly they withdrew from territories after conquering them, and in later times they especially revered such "isolationist" statesmen as Cato, who had been hostile to all such enterprises. Educated Roman leaders admired Greek culture, for which they even felt a romantic enthusiasm, but they no more desired to subjugate the Greek people than Americans today desire to subjugate Englishmen and Frenchmen.

Moreover, Greek politicians learned to exploit Rome's sympathy long before they learned to fear her power. If one of them found himself in trouble with his neighbors, he was very apt to hasten to Rome with appeals for aid which the Romans were not always able to refuse. The Greeks thus anticipated the policy of the British statesman, George Canning, who early in the nineteenth century boasted that he had "called the New World into existence to redress the balance of the Old." But when Rome had once established herself among the great empires of the world, she was not content merely to redress the Greek balance of power: she eventually insisted upon reorganizing the old world in a way that would stop these ever-recurring calls upon her blood and treasure, and she forced upon it that peace and unity which the Greeks could not gain for themselves.

At this point, therefore, we must turn our attention to the West. Who were these Romans? How were they drawn into an imperialistic career? Where did they learn the secret of empire? The answers to these far-reaching questions can best be discovered by examining Rome's early history and the story of how she established her power throughout Italy and the West.

The Peoples of the West

The lands encompassing the western half of the Mediterranean Sea are more sharply cut off from the East than a hasty glance at the map might suggest. The fertile land in the West is a rather narrow strip, rarely a hundred miles wide, lying between the sea and the surrounding mountains. Though southern Italy and eastern Sicily are easily accessible from Greece by sea, western Mediterranean waters can be entered from the East only through the straits at Messana—barely two miles wide—which cut Sicily from Italy, or through the wider straits which separate Sicily from Africa. Italy can be entered from central Europe only through a few Alpine passes, of which the Brenner is the best. Therefore the peoples of these western lands were not much influencd by Near Eastern civilization in the earliest times, and they were much slower than the Greeks in developing a high civilization of their own. Italy lagged three or four hundred years behind Greece in such matters.

The earliest important inhabitants of this western region were men of Mediterranean race who began to come up out of Africa as the Sahara gradually became desert some ten thousand years before Christ. These men eventually developed a primitive neolithic civilization which implied a knowledge of agriculture and the domestication of animals, but not the use of metals. There is no evidence about their language, but presumably they spoke tongues roughly resembling the Hamitic languages then spoken in Egypt and northern Africa. They form the underlying population of the western Mediterranean area to the present day, and in most of it they were not seriously disturbed by invaders of alien race until after 1000 B.C. Only Italy suffered serious invasions from central Europe during the second millennium—the period from 2000 to 1000 B.C. The northern invaders came in several waves and their invasions were part of a larger folk-movement which carried their kinsmen from central Europe to Asia Minor, Greece, France, and even to Britain and Scandinavia. Those entering Italy spoke languages or dialects akin to Latin and more distantly related to the Hittite, Greek, Celtic, and Germanic tongues. The earliest of them fought only with bronze weapons, but their later successors understood the use of iron. Before the end of the millennium they had established themselves throughout the greater part of the Italian peninsula and had absorbed its earlier inhabitants or reduced them to subserviency.

Carthaginians, Etruscans, Greeks

Higher civilization was first brought to the West by three groups of invaders from the East—the Phoenicians, the Etruscans, and the Greeks—all of whom arrived early in the first millennium before Christ. The earliest were the Phoenicians. In the tenth, ninth, and eighth centuries traders from Tyre established posts in northern Africa from Libya to the Straits of Gibraltar, in southern Spain (especially at Gades), and on the islands of Sicily, Sardinia, Corsica, and Malta. In the seventh century the Carthaginians assumed leadership of all the Phoenician (or, as the Romans said, "Punic") colonies in the West and thus built up a great empire. Thereafter their trading vessels plied the whole Mediterranean, from Phoenicia to Spain, and their navy dominated the western half of that sea. The mercantile civilization of Carthage bore many traces of its Semitic origin; her government was an aristocratic Republic; and in the days of Alexander she was the most powerful state in the West.

The Etruscans were a people from Asia Minor who settled in Italy north of the Tiber River, in the district now known as Etruria or Tuscany. The first comers, who arrived in the ninth and eighth centuries, were merchants in search of iron and other metals, but presently they set themselves up as an aristocracy ruling over Italian

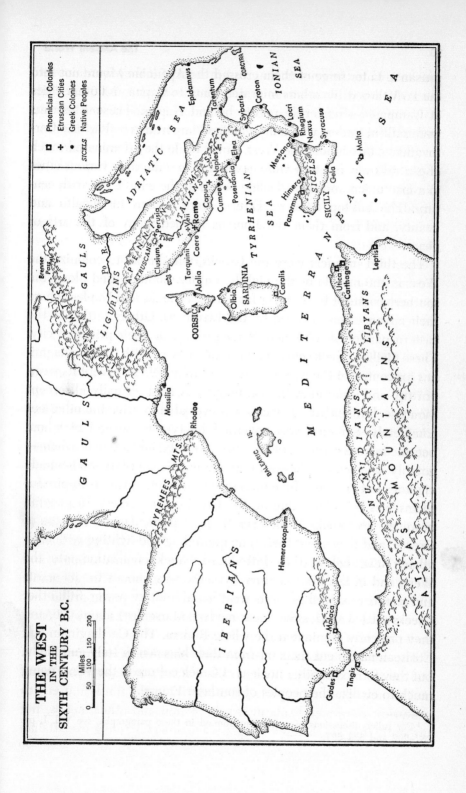

THE WEST
IN THE
SIXTH CENTURY B.C.

Miles
0   50   100   150   200

Phoenician Colonies
Etruscan Cities
Greek Colonies
SICELS Native Peoples

GAULS
LIGURIANS
MTS.
Brenner Pass
Po R.
ADRIATIC SEA
APENNINES
ITALIANS
ETRUSCANS
Clusium
Tiber R.
Veii
Rome
Caere
Tarquinii
Capua
Cumae
Naples
Poseidonia
Elea
Epidamnus
Tarentum
Sybaris
Croton
CORCYRA
IONIAN SEA
Locri
Rhegium
Naxus
Syracuse
Messana
Himera
Panormus
SICILY
SICELS
Gela
Malta
TYRRHENIAN SEA
MEDITERRANEAN SEA
CORSICA
Alalia
SARDINIA
Olbia
Caralis
Utica
Carthage
Leptis
LIBYANS
NUMIDIANS
ATLAS MOUNTAINS
Massilia
Rhodae
PYRENEES MTS.
BALEARIC Is.
Hemeroscopium
IBERIANS
Malaca
Gades
Tingis
GAULS

peasants. Later some of them crossed the Apennine Mountains into the Po Valley while others migrated south to Capua and other cities in Campania—the fertile region behind Naples. These Etruscans were skillful traders who long remained important rivals of the Carthaginians throughout the West. For a while they dominated much of central Italy, but they were never able to unite their various cities in a firm union and their decline began at the end of the sixth century. The hill-top cities of Etruria were famous for wealth and beauty, and from them the Romans learned many of the arts of peace.

The third invaders were the Greeks, who began to colonize the West in the middle of the eighth century. Some settled along the southern coasts of Italy and as far north as Cumae and Naples, where their advance was checked by the Etruscans. Others settled in the eastern part of Sicily, where Syracuse became their principal city. These Sicilian Greeks engaged in frequent wars with the Carthaginians for control of the island: sometimes they held all except its western tip, and sometimes the Carthaginians held virtually all except Syracuse, but neither adversary was ever able to drive the other out completely. Syracuse was governed by tyrants, several of whom became famous for their blood-thirsty cruelty, and a few of whom—notably Dionysius (405–367) and Agathocles (316–289)—made vigorous but unsuccessful efforts to create a united Greek empire for themselves by subjugating all the Greeks of the West. In general, however, the Greeks of the West were as particularistic as those of Greece, and they spent their time quarreling and fighting with each other. Nevertheless, they introduced Greek civilization into the West, and in the third century Syracuse was famous for its artists and scientists as well as for its wealth and military power. Still other Greeks settled at Massilia (near modern Marseilles) about 600, and they presently dominated the whole Riviera. The Carthaginian and Etruscan navies cut them off from their kinsmen in Italy and Sicily, but they formed another nucleus of Greek culture in the West, doing much to civilize the peoples of southern France.[1]

---

[1] For fuller discussions of matters mentioned in these paragraphs, see Vol. I, pp. 287–292 and 522–527.

The Rise of Rome

Rome was the principal city of Latium, a strip of the Italian coastal plain bounded on the north by the Tiber River and Etruria, on the south by Campania. It measured only a little over sixty miles from north to south, and about thirty-five miles at its greatest breadth, yet it contained a dozen sizable towns and many villages. Its early inhabitants, known as Latins, were shepherds and farmers. They had come from central Europe in the second millennium, and in Latium they found a district that apparently had never been occupied by the older Mediterranean peoples of Italy. The hill country behind Latium was inhabited by the Sabines, distant kinsmen of the Latins. At the northern corner of Latium, where Latins, Etruscans, and Sabines came in frequent contact, stood the city of Rome. Each of these three peoples therefore had an important part in the early history of the city.

Rome was built on its famous Seven Hills. Three of these hills—the Palatine, Capitoline, and Aventine—are true hills, surrounded by a small plain, but the other four hills—the Quirinal, Viminal, Esquiline, and Caelian, like the Janiculum and Vatican on the Etruscan side of the river—are merely spurs of the plateau through which the Tiber has cut its bed. Though Roman historians of the first century before Christ assigned the foundation of their city to the year 753 B.C., this date is much too late or too early. Archeologists have found traces of a settlement dating from about 1000 B.C. on the Palatine, and other villages, of somewhat later date, have been found on other nearby hills. Little is known, however, of the history of these villages until shortly before 600, when Etruscan kings began to rule the region. They united the villages into one political community, built walls and fortifications, drained the field at the foot of the Palatine as a market place (the forum), and perhaps even gave Rome the name by which it has ever since been known. As the city was excellently located for commercial purposes, trade prospered under the encouragement of the kings. In the latter part of the sixth century Rome was the largest and richest city in Italy. But though the Etruscan kings did much for Rome, they won such hatred from

the old Latin aristocracy that the last of them (Tarquinius Super-
bus) was expelled and a Republic established. Tradition dated this
expulsion in 509 B.C. Similar rebellions soon drove the Etruscans
from the rest of Latium.

Revolution may have brought "liberty" to a handful of Latin
aristocrats, but it brought bankruptcy to Rome and to Latium. The
Etruscan merchants were driven from the city along with the kings,
and their departure spelled economic ruin for Rome. All Latium suffered in consequence, for it lost the market for its agricultural products. Moreover, the loss of Rome and Latium separated the Etruscans from their kinsmen in Campania and ruined their trade with
that region. They therefore made vigorous but vain attempts to re-
conquer Latium. At the same time Rome and the Latins suffered
repeated attacks by Sabine tribesmen from the hill country. The fifth
century was therefore a tragic but crucial period in the history of
Rome and central Italy.

Toward the end of the century the Romans had so much improved
their status that they were able to carry the war into enemy territory,
and in 396 they captured the Etruscan city of Veii after a long siege.
Scarcely had this victory been won, however, when a new disaster
befell both Etruscans and Romans. Various tribes of Gauls had settled in the Po Valley of northern Italy, whence they made frequent
raids across the Apennines into Etruria. Such a raid reached Rome
itself in 390. The whole city except the Capitoline Hill was captured,
and much of it was destroyed. The Gauls were presently bought off
and withdrew, but during the next fifty years they made other incursions into central Italy, and on each occasion the Romans assumed
leadership in fighting off the invaders.

Rome thus gradually regained the importance she had lost by the
expulsion of her kings, but the new Rome was a military rather than
a commercial city. It owed its importance to the fact that it was a
frontier fortress, the spearhead of Latin and Italian resistance to
Etruscan or Gallic military domination. Its location made access easy
to immigrants from all parts of central Italy, and the city attracted
fighters from all sides. Rome thus developed the military spirit which
later characterized her people.

Rome also began to regain her position as a commercial center at this time. The city was located at the lowest practicable ford of the Tiber, on the main route from Etruria to Campania and southern Italy. This route was crossed by a second road—called the Via Salaria or Salt Road—which followed the Tiber up from the sea to central Italy. The two roads crossed in the forum, or market place, which always remained the center of Rome's public life. Nevertheless, the Romans, unlike their Etruscan, Greek, and Carthaginian neighbors, never distinguished themselves as traders. They policed the forum, organized and regulated the market, protected the traders, and collected fees for their services; but they did very little trading themselves. Rome became a polyglot city, full of Italians, Etruscans, and Greeks, but it was ruled by Latin aristocrats who were landowners, soldiers, and governors rather than businessmen.

These circumstances gave Rome invaluable training for her future role as ruler of the world. The fact that the Roman people were of such diverse origin prevented the rise of that feeling of racial superiority which made the Greeks impossible as world rulers. (The early Latin language had no word for "barbarian": Romans later took over the Greek word, but they applied it only to uncivilized peoples, not to non-Romans in general.) The Romans became the most successful welders-together of races and peoples that the world ever knew before the rise of modern America. As the peoples who migrated to Rome brought with them a wide variety of cultures, Roman civilization became highly eclectic. The Romans took over what they found useful in the cultures of other peoples, but the remarkable tenacity with which they retained their own fundamental social institutions enabled them nonetheless to preserve their own identity. Rome's fundamental institutions therefore deserve our careful attention.

Roman Social Institutions

The basic unit of early Latin society was the *familia*, the household or family. In a legal sense the "family" included not only the father, his wife, and his descendants, but also his retainers and slaves and even his movable and immovable property. At its head stood the father, or *paterfamilias,* who exercised supreme jurisdiction—called the *patria potestas,* "paternal authority"—over all members of the family and who represented it in all its dealings with other families and with the state. His authority over his children extended even to life and death. The high importance of the family tie was impressed upon Romans from earliest childhood, and family loyalty remained one of their major virtues. Families carefully preserved the memory of distinguished forebears and used every possible means to inspire young men to follow in the glorious footsteps of their ancestors. The *mos maiorum* (the "custom of the elders," or family tradition) was taken as a guide to life, and until the end of the Republic in the first century before Christ it had almost the force of law. This patriarchal organization acted as a powerful factor in making Roman society solid and conservative.

From prehistoric times these Roman families had been grouped in larger units, each called a *gens.* In theory, all members of a given *gens* were descended from a common ancestor, and all bore the same name, the *nomen* or *nomen gentilicum.*[2] A writer of the first century before Christ reported that about one thousand such names were known at Rome in his day, but we have no way of determining how many were of ancient origin. The *gens* retained legal authority over many matters, including inheritance and the property of persons dying intestate, and its members held religious ceremonies from which all other persons were excluded.

---

[2] In later times, when the number of individuals in a *gens* was very large, it became customary to add a second name called the *cognomen.* Of course each Roman also had his personal name, or *praenomen.* The full name consisted of the *praenomen,* followed by the *nomen,* and that by the *cognomen.* Both *nomen* and *cognomen* were inherited by the eldest son, but younger sons might take new *cognomina* when setting up families of their own. In case of adoption, which was quite common among the Romans, the adopted person took the *nomen* of his new father but also retained his original *nomen,* supplemented by the syllable *ian,* as an additional *cognomen.* Thus when the son of Lucius Aemilius Paullus was adopted by Publius Cornelius Scipio he became Publius Cornelius Scipio Aemilianus.

There is no uniform practice today as to which name should be selected when only one is wanted: in scholarly works of reference men are listed in the alphabetical order of their *nomina,* but in general writing the *cognomen* is more commonly used. Thus Gaius Julius Caesar and Marcus Tullius Cicero are known by their *cognomina* while Publius Vergilius Maro and Quintus Horatius Flaccus are known by their *nomina.* All that can be done today is to follow accepted usage. When the name has an Anglicized form, this will be used, as Horace instead of Horatius. Thus the Apostle will be called Paul while the Roman statesmen of the same name will be called Paullus.

The name *gens* is of course related philologically to the Greek *genos,* and the two institutions may well have had a common central European origin in the days before the great migrations at the beginning of the second millennium. Subsequent developments gave quite different aspects to the Greek and Latin institutions, and while Greek politicians broke up the *genos* at an early date, the *gens* remained powerful until the decline of the Roman Republic.

Patricians and Plebeians

Throughout Republican times the Roman *gentes* were divided into two groups called respectively "patrician" and "plebeian." The former made up the hereditary aristocracy whose members had effected the Revolution of 509 and who long continued to monopolize the high offices in the new Republic. After the Revolution no new members were admitted to this happy circle, which included only a small homogeneous group of landowners. For a long time the Fabii were much the most important of the patrician *gentes,* but the Claudii, the Cornelii, the Valerii, and a few others played important roles even in these early days. As the names Fabius, Cornelius, and Claudius recur on almost every page of Republican history, it will be well to become familiar with them now.

The plebeians were a more varied group. They included the peasants on the farms of Latium; laborers, artisans, and merchants at Rome; emancipated slaves who had received citizenship; citizens of states absorbed by Rome who continued to live in their ancestral homes as farmers, businessmen, or local aristocrats; and lastly, members of these last groups who had migrated to Rome. Some plebeians were poor, others were rich; some were accustomed to a humble station in life, others had been born aristocrats in their native towns; and some were ambitious and energetic self-made men. The different classes of plebeians had little in common except that they all were ruled by the patricians and none might hope to become patricians themselves.

The patricians owed their power and prestige principally to the ancient institution of clientage. Each patrician family had many plebeian followers, called "clients," who cultivated its fields and rendered it other services, followed its leaders in war, and supported its members in elections. The "patrons," in their turn, looked after and defended the interests of their clients in a patriarchal way. Each client held a small piece of land, called his *heredium,* whose average size was two jugera, or about an acre and a quarter. So small a farm could not support a family under the methods of cultivation then in vogue, but clients were allowed various rights on the common fields. As the patricians had general charge of these fields, the right to use them guaranteed the loyalty of clients to their patrons. Furthermore, the sanctions of religion were invoked, and it was considered a heinous sin for either patron or client to fail in his duty toward the other. This institution of clientage remained fundamental to Rome's whole social and political system, and we shall see that when it went into decline, the old aristocracy and the Republic itself declined as well.

Roman writers of the Ciceronian period believed that the whole population of Rome had once been made up of patrician patrons and their plebeian clients. Such may have been the case in very early times, but in the historical period there were many plebeians who had no patrons. Some were independent landowners, perhaps former clients who had left their farms and patrons because the *heredium* could not support them and had acquired lands elsewhere without benefit of a patron. Others were workers or businessmen in Rome itself, who may perhaps have been clients of the king in the days of the Monarchy but who had no patrons under the Republic. And lastly there were crowds of immigrants from the Italian towns who had acquired Roman citizenship without ever having been attached to Roman patrons. Some of these immigrants were aristocrats from Italian cities who brought their clients to Rome and thus created a large class of clients not attached to the old Roman aristocracy but to Roman plebeians.

The ancient Romans recognized the fact that the plebeians were not a united body, and writers often distinguished the *plebs rustica* from the *plebs urbana.* As a matter of fact, there were at least four distinct sorts of plebeians in Republican Rome. The first group were clients of the patricians, usually working as peasants on farms near their patrons' country estates. Secondly came the independent owners of small farms. Thirdly, there were the urban plebs who had no intimate connection with the aristocracy, but neither did they have close connections or common interests with the rural plebeians. And lastly, there were many well-to-do plebeians who held hereditary estates elsewhere in Italy, or who had made fortunes by trade at Rome, and who took a haughty attitude toward their less fortunate fellow-plebeians. These divisions among plebeians contributed greatly to the continuation of patrician rule at Rome.

Early Roman Religion

The early Romans were an austere and puritanical people in whose lives religion occupied a conspicuous place. The major and minor events of their daily lives were accompanied by religious ceremonies shared by the whole family, with the *paterfamilias* acting as priest; there were great festivals in which the whole community took part; and public meetings or assemblies were always opened with religious rites. Priests were public officials, and the *pontifex maximus,* or chief priest, was one of the most influential men in Rome.

The simplest form of Roman worship consisted in the repetition of complicated formulas, or spells, in an ancient and generally incomprehensible language. The power of the word was believed to be so great that the mispronunciation of a single syllable required the priest to start all over again. On certain occasions there were processions around the fields or villages, which were sometimes solemn and stately while at other times they were characterized by the ribaldry and buffoonery of a carnival. These ceremonies were especially numerous at the great crises of the agricultural year— plowing, first fruits, harvest—for they perpetuated the old vegetation and fertility cults of Mother Earth which had been widespread in the Near East and Europe ever since Neolithic times. On still other occasions there were public or private purifications and sacrifices. The spirits worshiped at such times were supposed to bring fertility, and their worship implied rather elaborate ideas about purity and impurity, sin, the expiation of faults, the soul, immortality, and sacrifice.

Ancient tradition, which now has the support of archeology, declared that the early Italians did not build temples or make statues of their gods. The only deities they worshiped were vague and impersonal forces called *numina*. Some of them served as protectors of the household and farm. Thus the Lares guarded the clearing, the Penates the pantry, and Janus the doorway, while Vesta presided over the family hearth. These were the powers invoked in family worship. Other *numina* dwelt farther afield and were worshiped in the groves or caves, or near the springs and pools, where they were supposed to dwell. Still others personified the great powers of nature and received more universal worship. Roman antiquarians later believed that the oldest of these nature cults was that of the Bona Dea (Good Goddess), a deity so ancient that she had no name, who bestowed fertility upon fields and women: she was an ancient form of Mother Earth. Other ancient cults honored such spirits as Ceres (Grain), Tellus (Earth), Flora (Flowering), and Ops (Harvest). Usually the *numina* were helpful and kindly, especially if they received proper attention from their worshipers, but a few (such as the Furies) were horrible.

When urban life began to affect the rural customs of Latin peasants, religion took on new forms. Many novelties dating from this period can be traced to Etruscan or Greek influence. From the former, Romans first learned to endow their *numina* with human shapes and characteristics, to make statues of them, and to erect temples to them. Under Etruscan influence, too, they developed a pantheon and a mythology. The vague old Nordic sky-god was personified as Jupiter—he and Vesta being the only gods in the Roman pantheon whose Nordic ancestry can be satisfactorily established. While he was worshiped in different Italian towns under various *cognomina,* he became the patron god of Rome as Jupiter Optimus Maximus ("Best and Greatest"). The first and most important temple in the city was erected to him on the Capitoline Hill by Tarquin, the last Etruscan king. It was sacred to Jupiter Capitolinus, but its two wings were dedicated respectively to Juno and Minerva, goddesses of Italian origin brought to Rome by the Etruscans. The Romans also learned from the Etruscans to be very scrupulous about auguries and portents. They had long been in the habit of taking auspices from the flights of birds, while Etruscan diviners prognosticated from the entrails of sheep. Both methods were used at Rome in later times, and the Etruscans introduced a whole elaborate system of divination.

At a somewhat later period the Romans accepted ideas about religion and mythology taught them by Greeks from southern Italy. Gods and *numina* were identified with Greek counterparts: Ceres with Demeter, Liber with Dionysus. Even Jupiter was equated with the Greek Zeus and absorbed the tales of the latter's prowess and perfidy. And while the Romans had no oracles of their own, they often turned to the Greek Sibylline Books which supposedly had been brought from Cumae in Etruscan times. Officials consulted these books in times of public distress to learn what must be done in order to regain the favor of the gods.

More important in Roman religion than mythology and divination (which are of interest chiefly as showing how little imagination the Romans wasted on such things) were their elaborate rules regulating worship and other religious matters. An extensive code of laws known as the *ius sacrum,* drawn up in early times, was observed with great literalness. Various groups, or "colleges," of priests conducted public worship and made sure of the divine benevolence. Thus the Vestal Virgins guarded the sacred fire on the hearth of a temple to Vesta in the forum, while other colleges of priests were responsible for the cults of Jupiter, Mars, and other gods. The two most important of these priestly colleges were the augurs and the pontiffs.

The augurs were responsible for interpreting auspices believed to indicate the will of the gods. Whenever the Romans were about to "inaugurate" an official, hold an election, fight a battle, or perform any other important public act, the magistrate in charge would "scan the heavens," looking for the flights of birds which would indicate whether or not the time was propitious. He would report what he saw to the augur, who stood by with covered head, and the augur's expert knowledge enabled him to declare the auspices favorable or unfavorable. Unless the signs were favorable, nothing more could be done, and stories were told of the sad fates that befell magistrates who disregarded the warnings of the auspices. Long after intelligent people had ceased to believe in such things, an augur could prevent action of which he disapproved by declaring the auspices unpropitious, or a magistrate could delay action by announcing that he was still scanning the heavens.

The pontiffs were even more important. They preserved and interpreted the *ius sacrum*, and they had a large share in the early development of civil and criminal law. They kept records of important events, including omens and portents, and they regulated the calendar. (This last was no easy task, for, up to the time of Caesar, Rome retained a lunar year of twelve lunar months, or 355 days, and from time to time the pontiffs added an extra month to harmonize this year with the solar year.) The pontiffs also declared which days were *fasti* and which *nefasti*. Business was conducted, the law courts were open, elections were held, and so on, only on days that were *fasti*. The pontiffs thus enjoyed great power over all aspects of life at Rome. They were twelve in number, and the college was self-perpetuating, with old members electing new ones to fill vacancies. The *pontifex maximus,* who presided over the college, was elected for life by his colleagues. He enjoyed such prestige at Rome, and even at a late date his powers were so great that realistic politicians like Caesar went to great trouble and expense to get themselves elected to the office. In still later times the emperors always held the office of *pontifex maximus,* whose title and many of whose functions eventually passed to the popes.

Such was Roman religion as it existed in the fourth century. It had far less to do with morals than with morale. The private cults brought members of the household together frequently and in a solemn way, thus strengthening family solidarity, and they accentuated other striking and noble characteristics of the Roman people—their gravity which often bordered on austerity, their self-restraint and perseverance, their courage and fortitude. The public cult, on the

---

• Note for Plate 8. The Roman Wolf, shown on the facing page, was the work of an Etruscan sculptor in the fifth century before Christ. The twins (Romulus and Remus) were added by a Renaissance artist in the fifteenth century.

Plate 8. Roman Wolf

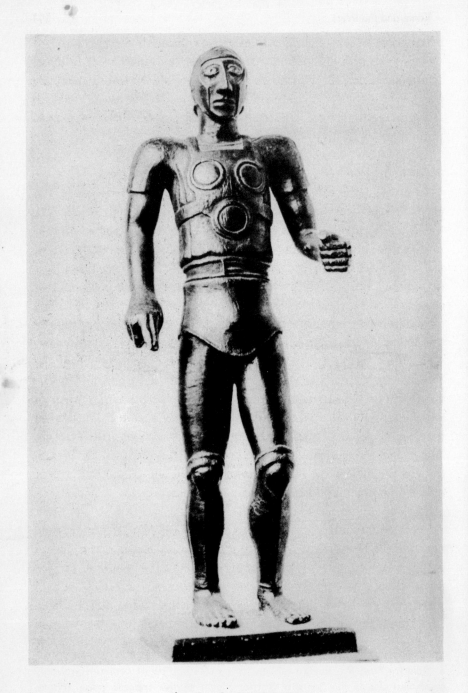

Plate 9.   Samnite Warrior

other hand, evoked emotional enthusiasm through the pageantry of worship and brought all political life under the sanctions of religion. It imposed upon the Roman mind a tremendous awe and reverence for the state in all its manifestations. Roman religion was a powerful factor in creating Roman patriotism, and it played a leading part in promoting social and political conservatism.

Military Organization

After religion, the second great co-operative enterprise of the early Romans was war. At one period the Latins fought much like the Homeric heroes, with chieftains riding about on the battlefield in chariots and challenging opponents to individual combat. Their followers kept up the leaders' morale by shouting and perhaps by a little minor skirmishing on the side, but if the leader were slain or overthrown, his panic-stricken followers were likely to flee. The Etruscan kings brought great improvements to this primitive system. They had learned a new manner of fighting from the Greeks, which they introduced into Rome. Thereafter the backbone of the Roman army consisted of heavy-armed infantry, not unlike the Greek hoplites. They marched into battle to the accompaniment of martial music, drawn up six or eight deep along a solid front. Behind this front, or phalanx, followed various classes of light-armed troops. This military organization prevailed until the invention of the legion, toward the end of the fourth century, and it served as the basis of much of Rome's political and social organization for two or three centuries longer (see Plate 9).

Since each soldier provided his own weapons and armor, men naturally fell into classes according to their economic status, a fact which was recognized when making the levy. The whole army was made up of 193 companies, called *centuriae* or "centuries," which were arranged according to the armor that the soldier could afford. The first eighteen centuries, composed of citizens wealthy enough

---

• Note for Plate 9.   Roman soldiers of the fifth and fourth centuries probably resembled closely the Samnite Warrior shown on the opposite page. (*Photo, Louvre.*)

to provide themselves with horses and complete armor, were called *equites* (horsemen) and served as cavalry. The infantry fell into five classes. The first class contained eighty centuries of men armed with helmets, cuirasses and greaves, shields, spears, and swords; its members formed the phalanx. The second, third, and fourth classes, each twenty centuries strong, had less defensive armor; and the fifth class, with thirty centuries, fought only with slings and stones. There were also four centuries of supernumeraries (armorers, engineers, musicians, and the like) and, last of all, one century of "proletarians" formed a labor battalion. In each class, half of the centuries, called *iuniores*, were composed of men between the ages of seventeen and forty-five, while the other half were made up of men over forty-five, called *seniores*. This organization, known as the "Servian constitution," was popularly attributed to Servius Tullius, an Etruscan king who ruled in the sixth century, though it probably did not reach the exact form described above until the fourth century.

The army was led by the highest magistrates of the state, who nearly always were competent military men. Subordinate command fell to officers called "military tribunes." Since every Roman citizen served in the army for ten seasons, the habits of military order and discipline, as well as many of the less pleasing features of militarism, were graven deep on the character, manners, and thinking of the Roman people. As an educational force, the army was equaled only by the family and by religion at Rome.

Roman Political Institutions

The constitution of the Republic of 509 developed greatly during the next two centuries. Though our scanty information does not enable us to trace its progress in detail, we know that by the year 300 a system was worked out which, with minor changes, remained in force until the first century before Christ. This government made Rome a highly aristocratic republic. In so far as the early Romans thought at all about what modern lawyers call "sovereignty," they thought of it as resting with the senate and the people—the *senatus populusque romanus*, whose initial letters, S.P.Q.R., appear on countless inscriptions as the symbol of the Roman state. The sovereign will of Rome was determined in various assemblies and carried out by popularly-elected officials, whose nature and functions call for brief characterization.

The senate was the most important body at Rome throughout Republican times. It had its origins in the days of the Monarchy when the kings summoned important persons to give advice on public matters. After the Revolution of 509, when consuls replaced the kings as chief magistrates, the senate was perpetuated as a body in which members of the great patrician families debated and determined state policy. At first the senate contained some two hundred members; later this number gradually rose to about three hundred. Senators were appointed for life—by different magistrates at different times, though this official usually had little choice in making his appointments. The law said vaguely that the "best" men should be appointed, which ordinarily was taken to mean those who had already held several high elective offices. As the patricians dominated elections through the votes of their clients, only members of that class had seats in the senate, and all politically-minded families of the class were represented there. The senate therefore was a small and homogeneous body of aristocrats with long political experience who devoted their major attention to affairs of state. The senators were trained in such matters from childhood, and sometimes took their small sons with them to meetings of the senate in order to show them how things were done, knowing that the boys would some day be senators themselves.

Meetings of the senate were usually called by one of the consuls. Republican Rome carefully preserved the fiction that the senate was a purely advisory body, as under the Monarchy; and senators discussed only the questions put to them by the official who called the meeting. However, any senator could probably find some official who would ask his advice on whatever subject he wished to discuss. The order in which senators were asked for their opinions was a matter of prestige, and the man entitled to speak first on every motion—the *princeps senatus,* or "chief of the senate"—was a man of influence and importance. This princeps, the most distinguished man in the senate, was appointed for life.

The senate drew up laws of general purport (*leges*), debated them at length, and voted upon them, and its decrees (*senatus consulta*) settled matters of immediate policy. Except for actual declarations of war or ratification of treaties, the senate directed foreign policy. It appointed many lesser officials, and in general it exercised close supervision over the whole government. Later writers drew idyllic pictures of this old patrician senate, comparing it to an "assembly of kings," and praising the sobriety and patriotism of its members. There can be little doubt that it surpassed Rome's popular assemblies in effectiveness and resolution—and sometimes in wisdom as well.

Popular Assemblies

The people of Rome, or the *populus*, met and expressed their views in various assemblies or *comitia*. All important measures were laid before these assemblies for approval, and here the higher magistrates were elected. Every citizen might attend the meetings of these assemblies in person, but voting was always indirect. Voters were divided into groups; the majority of each group determined its will; and the question at issue was decided by a majority of the groups. Obviously, much depended upon the manner in which voters were assigned to groups, and practical politicians developed great skill at arranging them. An early assembly called the *comitia curiata* was superseded by two others during the greater part of Republican history: the *comitia centuriata* and the *comitia tributa*. Though composed of the same persons, each of these assemblies was organized according to different principles, each dealt with certain questions, and each elected certain officials.

The *comitia centuriata*, as its name indicates, was organized according to the "Servian constitution" of the army, and continued this organization long after the introduction of the legion had rendered the century obsolete for military purposes. At meetings of the *comitia centuriata*, citizens were classified according to their military centuries—that is to say, according to their wealth—with each century having one vote determined by the majority of its members. The organization of this assembly was highly aristocratic. The *equites* made up eighteen of its 193 centuries, and the first class of the heavy infantry made up eighty others. These first two groups therefore had a clear majority in the assembly. In early times these two groups represented the weight of the community; but after the centuries lost their military significance, politicians put the financial requirements for admission to the upper classes so high that only the wealthy few could qualify. Even in the third century the proletarians, made up of artisans and laborers, contained more members than all other centuries combined, yet they cast only one vote in the assembly while the wealthy few cast ninety-eight votes. According to the Roman system, moreover, the centuries voted in sequence, one after another, and voting stopped as soon as one side or the other had a majority, or ninety-seven votes. Only in the unlikely case that the other 192 centuries were exactly tied would the proletarians, who actually made up a majority of the citizens, be called upon to express an opinion at all. Furthermore, the division into *iuniores* and *seniores* gave undue weight to the votes of old men. And finally, as a large percentage of the voters were clients of the patrician families, the elections usually went as the patrician leaders wished. The aristocratic *comitia centuriata* elected the consuls and other high magistrates of the Republic; it had the right to declare war and ratify treaties; it passed laws (*leges*) concurrently with the senate; and it served as a court of appeal for citizens condemned to death.

The other assembly was called the *comitia tributa*. In early times the grouping of its members was territorial: citizens were divided into *tribus*, or "tribes," of which four were "urban" for the inhabitants of Rome, while seventeen were "rural," for the country people. As new territories were added to the Roman domain, their inhabitants were listed in new rural tribes, until by 241 B.C. there were thirty-one rural tribes in a total of thirty-five. No new tribes were created thereafter. Artisans and laborers were usually listed in the four urban tribes, where their votes amounted to little, since the rural vote invariably overwhelmed that of the city. The relative voting strength of moderately well-to-do rural voters was increased by the fact that votes must be cast personally in Rome, and the poorer men entitled to vote in the rural tribes often could not afford a journey to the city for the purpose. Thus the *comitia tributa* came to represent the independent small landholders who were opposed to the aristocratic large landholders on the one hand and to the urban workers on the other. Though this assembly could hardly be called "democratic" in our sense of the term, it certainly was more apt to be anti-patrician than the *comitia centuriata*. Consequently, those opposed to the aristocratic senate were constantly trying to increase its powers. The *comitia tributa* elected the "tribunes of the people" (*tribuni plebis*), and passed resolutions (*scita* or *plebiscita,* whence our word "plebiscite") which after 287 had the same force as laws (*leges*) passed by the senate and the *comitia centuriata*.

Elected Magistrates

These three assemblies—the senate, the *comitia centuriata,* and the *comitia tributa*—determined the will of the Roman people, but officials were necessary to carry out this will and to command armies. Magistrates were therefore chosen upon whom the people conferred *imperium,* or executive authority. *Imperium* was primarily military command, though it extended to civil matters as well. A striking characteristic of the Roman system was that *imperium* was rarely conferred upon one man alone: usually two or more colleagues shared it equally, theoretically in order that neither might become tyrannical. Unfortunately, the two colleagues were not always content with keeping each other from tyranny. Sometimes they even worked at cross purposes, each doing his best to prevent his rival from accomplishing anything at all. In ordinary times, however, each of the colleagues was assigned by the senate to certain specific tasks as his *provincia*—whence our word "province."

The supreme magistrates of the Roman Republic were the two consuls, elected annually by the *comitia centuriata*. A law of 341 forbade re-election until after ten years, but in exceptional cases the senate might permit an able consul (or other official) to continue in a specific command after his year was over. This permission made the official in question a "proconsul," and another consul was elected to perform the regular duties of the office. The consuls were granted very broad powers. They commanded armies in time of war, presided at meetings of the senate and the *comitia centuriata*, and exercised general supervision over the civil administration. As the consuls were the most important men at Rome during their term of office, their names were used for dating all official documents. In time of crisis, when unified command seemed desirable, the consuls appointed a "dictator" who had absolute power when in office but who might not hold office longer than six months. Officials called "praetors," whose principal duty was to preside over law courts, also enjoyed *imperium* and were elected annually by the *comitia centuriata*.

There were various other officials who did not share the *imperium*. The "quaestors" were assistants to the consuls, at first as paymasters in the army, later as general treasury officials. The "aediles" supervised and regulated business in the forum, looked after public property, and served as police court judges. The "censors" took the census, recruited the army, classified citizens by centuries and tribes, and kept official lists of citizens and senators. They also let public contracts and acquired vast powers of appointment, even filling vacancies in the senate. Since the censors investigated the private lives of officials and candidates for office, they presently acquired the evil reputation that censors still enjoy of meddling with private morals. These officials were elected annually by the *comitia centuriata*, all except the censors, who were elected every five years.

The Struggle of the Orders

The first century and a half in the history of the Roman Republic was disturbed by the conflict between patricians and plebeians that later historians called the "struggle of the orders." Our information regarding it is derived largely from Livy, who began writing about thirty years before the birth of Christ and whose views were much influenced by the political controversies of his own day (see p. 459). For his information on these early times Livy relied principally upon writers who had lived fifty or one hundred years before his time, and whose views had been warped by the rather different controversies of their day. These writers in turn depended upon still earlier ones who had compiled their histories from a few written records and much oral tradition and political propaganda. Livy's account of these early struggles is therefore far from satisfactory, yet it enables the critical historian to trace the general course of the disturbances which distracted those unhappy times.

Rome suffered a severe decline after the Revolution of 509. The expulsion of Etruscan kings and merchants left a dearth of economic leadership and led to an economic depression which first affected the urban plebeians, many of whom were thrown out of work and became destitute. Hundreds fell into debt, and a few were sold into slavery by their creditors. Out of these conditions arose the first struggle of the orders, in which the urban plebs demanded economic and political reforms. The ensuing conflict was not so much between patricians and plebeians as between town and country; or rather, it was a struggle of the urban plebeians and their leaders against the patricians and their clients among the rural plebs. The contest was prolonged and bitter, with the rebels frequently resorting to violent measures. Sometimes they rioted, or failed to appear when summoned for military service, or mutinied after induction. Sometimes, as in 468, they refused to take part in elections, leaving the choice of consuls to the patricians and their loyal clients. And on several occasions they organized "secessions," withdrawing from the city in a body and refusing to return until their demands were granted. Revolutionary activity thus became a tradition in Republican Rome.

Political Victories: Tribunes and the Law

The first plebeian victory, perhaps in 494, led to the election of officials called *tribuni plebis*, or "tribunes of the people," whose duty it was to protect plebeians from patricians. In early times two, but later ten, tribunes were elected by the plebeian class from their own number. At first they concerned themselves largely with helping plebeians who felt themselves unjustly treated by patrician magistrates or military officers, but in time they became leaders in demands for further reform. They were declared "sacrosanct," which meant that their persons were inviolable and that anyone injuring them or interfering with them in the performance of their duties was declared an outlaw. Plebeians even took an oath to kill anyone who violated a tribune's sanctity.

As the office of tribune was for a long time the highest to which a plebeian might aspire, ambitious and aggressive men made it one of the most powerful offices in the state. In later times the tribunes obtained the right to attend meetings of the senate, to veto legislation which they considered inimical to the interests of their class, to summon the senate, and to propose laws. Tribunes also won the right to veto the acts of consuls and other magistrates—all except the dictator—and to prosecute officials for malfeasance in office. They were elected annually by the *comitia tributa,* over whose meetings they presided. After 287, as we have seen, plebiscites passed by this body had the same force as laws passed by the senate and centuries.

Another grievance of the plebeians concerned the law. In early Rome, as in all primitive communities, civil and criminal law was unwritten and traditional. In theory, laws were of divine origin, and they were known only to the priests and magistrates, who were trusted to remember them. Naturally these aristocratic officials were especially zealous in remembering laws which favored their caste, and they sometimes permitted or perpetrated injustices against ignorant plebeians. These abuses were only partially remedied by the intervention of tribunes. After many years of agitation the plebeians obtained (about 451) the appointment of a board of ten men (*decemviri*) who replaced the consuls and tribunes for one year and proceeded to codify and publish the laws. These commissioners were all patricians, nearly all were former consuls, and they did their work well; but they did not complete their task in the allotted time and a second board was chosen for the next year. The resulting law code was written on twelve wooden tables which were set up in the forum where all who could read might study it. Unfortunately, only a few fragments of this early code have been preserved, though the "Law of the Twelve Tables" was always thereafter regarded as the fundamental law of the Republic. Out of this code grew the whole enormous structure of Roman law, under which most of Europe still lives.

The first board of *decemviri* was made up of high-minded men, as is shown by the justice of their laws. The second board, on the other hand, was so much concerned with preserving the prerogatives of the patrician class that its laws occasioned tumults and a secession. Order was not restored to the city until the Valerio-Horatian Laws of 449 granted concessions to the plebeians. Even then the populace did not enjoy complete equality before the law, however, for only the aristocratic pontiffs knew the complicated rituals required to open legal action, or the days on which suit might be brought. Almost a century and a half elapsed before the publication of this essential information enabled patronless plebeians to claim their rights in court.

Economic Gains: Agrarian Laws

The distress of the plebeians was economic rather than political, however, though Livy lays less stress on this side of their agitation. Since many of the urban poor were peasants who had migrated to the city in the days of its prosperity, it was only natural that in hard times they should think of returning to their old homes. Unfortunately for them, this was not easily done. They had severed all relations with their former patrons, who now had no obligation or desire to help them, and they soon found that land was not available. The urban plebs then demanded a redistribution of lands. Livy's rather unreliable account mentions twenty occasions in the fifth century when laws ordering such distributions were proposed by tribunes, though not one was actually enacted. The patricians preferred to find lands for the plebs by conquering neighboring peoples. After their victories they usually confiscated a third, or even two-thirds, of the land of the vanquished, which was then redistributed. The patricians retained the lion's share of the spoil for themselves, but many small allotments were assigned to landless plebeians.

In the second half of the fifth century economic distress declined, but the Gallic invasion of 390 brought a new period of suffering. Rural plebeians now suffered as much as their urban cousins, especially those without patrons to help them. At last, in 367, after ten years of agitation, two plebeian leaders, named C. Licinius Stolo and L. Sextius, obtained the enactment of a series of new laws. One law forbade any man to hold more than 300 acres (500 jugera) of public land or to pasture more than 100 head of cattle or 500 head of sheep upon the common fields. A second law eased the condition of debtors by ordering that whatever had been paid in interest should be deducted from the principal of the debt. Subsequent legislation reduced interest to 10 per cent, and later to 5 per cent, and at last a law of 342 forbade interest altogether.[3] A law of 326 made it virtually impossible to enslave a man for debt. By this time, however, the struggle of the orders was drawing to a close, for foreign conquest was relieving economic distress at home.

Plebeians in Office: Patres Conscripti

Plebeian leaders were also eager to be recognized as more nearly the social and political equals of the patricians. Their first victory in this direction came with the Lex Canuleia of 445, by which intermarriage between the orders was sanctioned. Before long, plebeians were also demanding the right to hold high office. The quaestorship was opened to them in 421, and some twenty years later a plebeian became military tribune with consular power. The Licinian-Sextian Law of 367 made it possible for a plebeian to hold the consulship, and the next year Sextius himself was consul. Somewhat later the custom was established of having at least one plebeian consul each year. Toward the middle of the century plebeians held other high offices; after 300 they might become augurs and pontiffs; and in 251 a plebeian became *pontifex maximus*. Since the higher magistrates

---

[3] It must be borne in mind that at this period loans were not investments of capital for machinery or improvements from which rich returns might be expected. They were merely the provision of food to keep the borrower's soul and body together for the time being. Under such circumstances it seemed inhuman to demand interest from the unfortunate borrower. Moreover, the lenders were mostly Greeks or other foreigners unable to protect themselves. It is worth noting that ancient Hebrew law contained a similar prohibition of interest, presumably for the same reason. In later times Roman laws against interest were not well enforced, but the word *fenerator* ("usurer") always carried an evil connotation. In the Middle Ages the Church revived the ancient Hebrew-Roman prohibition of usury and the profession of money-lender was left largely to the Jews—who were allowed to continue in their sinful ways because they would undoubtedly be excluded from Heaven anyhow. Nevertheless, kings and popes frequently turned to these outcasts for loans at interest—and then found moral justifications for not repaying what they had borrowed. The first Christians to authorize interest were the Calvinists, and not until many years later did other Protestants and Catholics follow their example.

ordinarily entered the senate after completing their term of office, the plebeians who held these offices became members of that august assembly; but they were distinguished from its patrician members by being called *patres conscripti,* or "enrolled fathers."

Historians once believed that the *patres conscripti* were ordinary "commoners"—men whose ancestors two or three generations back had been peasants—and regarded their victory as a step toward nineteenth-century democracy. Recent researches (especially those of Münzer[4]) have shown this theory to be untenable. In nearly every case, the plebeians who profited by the new laws and attained high office were descended from the nobility of nearby towns and had rather recently acquired Roman citizenship by choice or conquest. This admission of immigrant nobles into the senate was nothing new. The Etruscan kings had gladly received them into the aristocracy. Thus the Julian family was annexed with Alba Longa in the seventh century and, according to tradition, its members were soon admitted to the senate by the king. The Sabine Appius Claudius migrated to Rome in 504 and was admitted to the senate almost at once. His was the last case of the sort, however, for thereafter the patricians formed a closed circle that would admit no new members.

Few immigrants entered Rome during the difficult years of the early fifth century; but immigration set in anew toward the end of the century, and again after the damage wrought by the Gallic invasions had been repaired. While the newcomers easily obtained citizenship, they had to content themselves with plebeian status, no matter what their position at home had been. Roman historians of a later period tell of various persons (including an ancestor of the Emperor Augustus) who had once been patricians but voluntarily "went over to the plebs": these writers apparently did not understand that such men had been patricians in their native towns but became plebeians at Rome, yet this seems the most plausible explanation of the phrase. The immigrants may have been willing to accept such terms for the sake of Roman citizenship, but they were not satisfied, and before long they were hankering after their old aristocratic standing.

---

[4] For the work of Friedrich Münzer, see note, p. 122.

Many were men of great wealth, numerous clients, and high political capability. They made themselves leaders in the struggle of the orders, aroused the plebeians to protest against their wrongs, and thus gradually built up political clienteles at Rome to match those of the patricians. Eventually they came to be recognized as a "plebeian nobility" beside the "patrician aristocracy."

The victory of these plebeian leaders was hastened by divisions and quarrels among the patricians. The great families might resent the presumption of plebeians who aspired to enter their sacred ranks, but they also vied among themselves for the high offices in the Republic. Canny politicians among the patricians therefore set out to win the favor and votes of the new plebeian nobility and their clients. Some of their concessions were political, others were personal; sometimes they benefited the whole plebeian order, sometimes only its leaders, and occasionally individuals only. The plebeian leaders were granted the right to hold one office after another; and after the Lex Canuleia the great families frequently enlisted the political support of able plebeians who had large clienteles by giving them younger daughters in marriage. Plebeians did not become patricians by holding high office or by marrying the daughters of patricians, but the happy few presently came to form the "plebeian nobility." These new nobles usually maintained close relations with some patrician family which paid them for their political skill and votes with a few high offices. Though plebeian nobles might change their political allegiance for political or other reasons, such desertions were surprisingly rare, and it might almost be said that the plebeian nobles were glorified clients of individual patrician aristocrats.

Many able men entered this plebeian nobility during the fourth and third centuries, but after the defeat of Hannibal (about 200 B.C.) they closed their ranks to form a second hereditary caste. Nevertheless, their early success showed the skill of the patricians at absorbing the peoples whom Rome conquered, gradually giving them positions of importance in the state, and yet keeping final control in their own hands. These successes set the general pattern by which Rome absorbed the Mediterranean world.

The Conquest of Italy

When the Romans set up their Republic in 509, they controlled only the territory immediately surrounding the city and a narrow strip along the Tiber from the city to the sea—a total of not more than three hundred square miles. Within a few years the other peoples of Latium drove out their Etruscan overlords and set up governments of their own. Twelve of these tiny states, fearing Rome and being distinctly hostile to her, united to form the Latin League, which fought a bloody battle with the Romans near Lake Regillus about 496. Etruscan efforts to re-establish their supremacy in Latium forced a union of the two parties, however, and in 493 the Latin League and Rome entered into an alliance that lasted more than a century and a half. Sometimes the cities of the Latin League became restless and revolted, but Rome always forced them back into line. Finally an especially serious rebellion occurred in 341 when the Latins demanded Roman citizenship and a share in the government of the city. They were decisively defeated by the Romans in 338 and, though punished by confiscation of part of their lands, they were received into a liberal alliance by their conquerors. Rome thus firmly established herself as the ruler of Latium and the strongest military power in Italy—a position she had not enjoyed since 509—and she was then ready to start upon her amazing career of conquest.

The first region outside Latium to attract Roman attention was Campania. This beautiful and fertile country was still inhabited by the aboriginal Siculi when the Greeks first arrived and established colonies at Cumae and other points along the coast in the eighth century. Somewhat later Etruscans from the north made the inland city of Capua their chief center. Campania was thus occupied by the two most civilized peoples of Italy; its inhabitants became rich through commerce and industry; and their culture and refinement caused their more barbaric neighbors to accuse them of degeneracy. The wealthy and luxurious city of Capua was singled out especially for the envy and moral disapproval of her rivals.

Bands of Samnites (an Italic people related to the Sabines, who inhabited the hill country behind Campania) began to invade the

ITALY
IN THE
THIRD CENTURY B.C.

Ager Romanus, 500
Ager Romanus, 338
Ager Romanus, 241
Appian Way, 312

Miles

0   50   100   150

ALPS MTS.

CISALPINE GAUL

Po R.

APENNINES

UMBRIA

Ariminum

Ancona

Ager Gallicus

ETRURIA

MOUNTAINS

Tiber

Hadria

CORSICA

ADRIATIC SEA

ILLYRIA

Veii

Rome

LATIUM

SAMNIUM

Capua

Beneventum

EPIRUS

Cumae

Naples

CAMPANIA

Brundisium

Tarentum

SARDINIA

TYRRHENIAN

SEA

MAGNA GRAECIA

Thurii

IONIAN

SEA

Panormus

Messana

Rhegium

SICILY

MEDITERRANEAN

Carthage

Syracuse

MALTA

AFRICA

SEA

lowlands during the fifth century at a time when kindred tribes were vainly attempting to enter Latium. The Samnites took Capua in 424, Cumae in 420, and presently all Campania except Naples was in their hands. The invaders quickly adopted the vices and refinements of their victims and disowned their uncouth kinsmen of the hill country, to whom they now felt vastly superior; but their vigor remained unimpaired, and they were highly prized as mercenaries by Sicilian Greeks and Carthaginians. The Samnites of the hill country were likewise excellent fighters and presently began to covet the wealth of their Capuan cousins. It happened, moreover, that at the time of a threatened Gallic invasion in 354 Rome had made an alliance with the hill Samnites. The Capuan Samnites retaliated by sending aid to the Latins when the League revolted thirteen years later, and during the ensuing war the Romans established themselves in Capua, Cumae, and elsewhere (338). Rome then found it necessary to defend these new possessions against her former allies of the hills, and the great Samnite wars began (326). The story of the various campaigns may be passed over, especially as our knowledge of them comes largely from Livy's highly idealized account. The Roman armies suffered various vicissitudes, but finally they emerged victorious. After the last Samnite war ended in 290, the Samnite territory was added to Rome.

As soon as these wars were over, the Romans turned their attention northward to their old enemies the Etruscans and to the Umbrians, an Italic people living north of Rome and east of Etruria. Both these peoples had been worn down by their long struggle against the Gauls. One city after another was added to the Roman domain until Rome possessed the heart of Italy. By 280 her territories extended from the Tyrrhenian Sea to the Adriatic, from the Gauls of the Po Valley to the Greeks of southern Italy. Italic Italy was Roman territory.

Pyrrhus

Conquest of the Greek cities to the south followed quickly thereafter. The citizens of Tarentum had embarked upon an ambitious policy soon after the death of the Syracusan tyrant Agathocles (289) and the collapse of the empire he had built in southern Italy. The Tarentines hoped to become his heir but they succeeded only in arousing the apprehension and antagonism of their neighbors. When a minor native tribe attacked the Greek city of Thurii in 282, the Thurians preferred to seek the aid of far-away Rome—whose military reputation was just then in the ascendant—rather than that of their nearby Greek kinsmen in Tarentum. Although the Roman senate was disinclined to such distant adventures, the *comitia centuriata* decided to send aid and Thurii was saved. The Tarentines, resenting such interference in Greek affairs, thereupon sank a few Roman vessels that had ventured into their neighborhood in violation of an old treaty. They thus precipitated a war with Rome and hastily summoned to their aid Pyrrhus, king of Epirus. He arrived in Italy in 280 with 20,000 mercenaries and several elephants.

This adventurer was a kinsman of Alexander the Great and son-in-law of Agathocles. After fighting in the battle of Ipsus (301) and ruling Macedon for a few months in 286, he was no longer satisfied with his ancestral but backward kingdom of Epirus. Pyrrhus was a brilliant general, whom Hannibal called a master of strategy, but he lacked stability and did not know how to use his victories. To this day victories which bring the victor no real advantage are known as "Pyrrhic victories." He now hoped that by posing as a defender of Greek liberty against the Romans, and by detaching the Samnites from their recent conquerors, he might found an empire that would include all southern and central Italy.

In his first two campaigns Pyrrhus inflicted severe defeats upon the Romans—and actually marched on Rome itself, but when only forty miles from the city he voluntarily turned back. The expected rising of the Samnites had not occurred, his victories brought him nothing, and his restless spirit craved greater glory. He therefore moved his army into Sicily where he tried to establish a tyranny like that of Agathocles. Checked in this enterprise by native revolts and by the Carthaginians, he returned to Tarentum, and after a defeat by the Romans at Beneventum (275) he took the remnants of his army back to Greece. Here he hoped to find new opportunities for adventure in the chaos that followed the Gallic invasion of Greece in 278. Instead he found death. After Pyrrhus's departure the Romans rapidly conquered the Greek cities, finally taking Tarentum in 272. Little further fighting was necessary, and the entire peninsula of Italy was pacified before 265.

Why Rome Fought

It would be wrong to regard these wars as evidence of a deep Roman plot to conquer Italy or the world. The wars were quite haphazard, as a result of many independent causes. The Romans undoubtedly were bad neighbors, quarrelsome and quick to see intolerable insults in the conduct of others; but the Samnites were equally aggressive, and the Greeks were always fighting. The only ones who developed careful plans for empire building were Greeks such as Agathocles and Pyrrhus. The Romans were not uniformly to blame for their wars; but when they had once embarked upon hostilities their martial virtues and their excellent army eventually won victory. In the end they found all Italy in their hands.

It is worthy of note, moreover, that the Roman "people" were always more bellicose than the responsible statesmen in the Senate. This popular enthusiasm for war is probably to be explained chiefly by the fact that the common soldier saw something tangible to fight for. First of all there was booty to be had from the rich cities of Etruria and Campania, and secondly there was land. Great tracts of land were taken from the defeated peoples and distributed among Romans. Some of the former occupiers of these confiscated fields were killed in the wars, others were sold into slavery: some slaves were brought to Rome, where their standard of living was not one that Roman plebeians would tolerate for themselves; the rest were carried out of the country by Greek and Carthaginian slave traders. Their farms were taken by Romans. It has been estimated that, between 338 and 265, the wars provided new homes for upward of 50,000 Romans, or about one-fifth of the total population. The Roman settlers were established in colonies which were either military posts to defend points of strategic value or else agricultural colonies. Only five military colonies were established during the period in question, each with a garrison of approximately 300 men, but there were fifteen agricultural colonies, each containing between 2500 and 5000 settlers. The agricultural colonies too were planted with an eye to strategy and defense, and they shortly became important centers of Roman political and cultural influence in the peninsula.

The Unification of Italy

The indirect effects of the wars were as important as military conquest in uniting Italy under Roman leadership. The exigencies of campaigning called for military roads. The first to be built was the Appian Way, connecting Rome with Capua, which was begun in 312. During the next two centuries all Italy was covered with a network of splendid highways whose value for the economic and cultural development of the country far surpassed their military importance. During these wars, moreover, the Romans first coined money. In 330 they began casting bronze bars weighing a pound; shortly thereafter they hired Capuans to cast silver and bronze coins for them; and in 269 they began casting small coins in their own mint. When the conquest of Italy was complete, they closed all mints except the one at Rome, and only Roman coins were used throughout the peninsula. The political unification of Italy, which was so quickly followed by widespread Roman colonies, Roman roads, and Roman money, was further strengthened by the resulting growth of trade. Traders were almost always non-Romans, but they knew full well that they owed their prosperity to Roman conquests, and they opposed all efforts by the conquered peoples to regain their independence.

The unity of Italy was further protected by the great respect that all men felt for the Roman army. This fighting machine had been greatly improved during the fourth century. In the early days of the Republic campaigns were fought during the summer months, when work on the farms was light, and the troops went home again each autumn. This system proved impracticable during the ten-year siege of Veii (405–396), and soldiers were enlisted for longer periods. Such troops were paid wages and became the nucleus of a professional army. Somewhat later the state began supplying recruits with weapons and armor, enabling officers to classify men according to their fighting ability rather than their wealth. Then came a fundamental reform in tactics. The great defects of the phalanx had been the difficulties of maneuvering it on uneven ground and of providing reserves immediately in case the enemy broke through the line at an unexpected point. To meet these weaknesses the Romans developed the "manipular legion," which was their great contribution to the art of war and the most formidable fighting machine known to antiquity.

According to the new plan, the heavy infantry was divided into groups called "maniples," which in turn were subdivided into two equal "centuries," each commanded by a centurion. On the battlefield the maniples were staggered checkerboard fashion in three rows, with each maniple separated from the next by a space about equal to its front. The maniples of the first two rows each contained 120 men drawn up in six ranks of twenty men each; those of the third row were made up of *seniores* and, being only half strength, were three ranks deep. The soldiers of the two front maniples were armed with two javelins for throwing and short broad swords; the older men in the rear had long spears primarily for defense. When the charge was ordered, the men of the front maniple ran forward, spread out to form a solid front with their neighbors, threw their javelins at the enemy, and then engaged hand to hand, fighting with their swords. If the line weakened at any point, the second maniple advanced immediately to strengthen it; and the third maniple formed a reserve to be used only in case of extreme necessity. When the army was on the march, it built a fortified camp every night to provide a strong position to which it might retreat in case of surprise or defeat. The legion was composed of twenty full-size and ten half-size maniples, or 3000 men, together with 1200 light-armed troops and 300 cavalry, making the total strength 4500 men. Each consul normally commanded two legions, and the Roman army consisted of four legions of citizens plus a varying number of allies.

Rome's Pattern of Empire

The greatest single factor making for the unity of Italy after the wars, however, was the mildness of the rule that Rome provided.

The peoples of Italy were divided into two groups—"citizens" and "allies"—and each of these in turn was subdivided into two lesser groups. Some of the former group were full Roman citizens; others enjoyed the private rights of Romans, though they could not vote or hold office in Rome. The full citizens were the ancient inhabitants of Rome and the vicinity. About the middle of the third century the territory thus favored, known as the *ager Romanus,* included most of Latium, a little of southern Etruria, part of Campania, and a strip of the Sabine country extending northeastward across central Italy to the Adriatic. Members of the military colonies also enjoyed the rights of full citizenship. All these citizens were closely related to the true Romans by blood, language, and religion; they fought side by side in the Roman legions; they voted in the Roman assemblies; and they formed the backbone of the Roman state. The "citizens without the vote" inhabited the rest of Latium. They could not vote in Rome, but they chose officials for their own cities (*municipia*) and were given great freedom in local matters. They served in the Roman legions beside the full citizens; and they enjoyed all the private rights of Romans.

The allies likewise were of two sorts. The first, called "Latin allies," inhabited the agricultural colonies. Each of these colonies had a government modeled on that of Rome. Its citizens enjoyed the rights of trade and intermarriage with those of Rome and other Latin allies, and they formed special detachments in the Roman army. The others, called "Italian allies," included all those who were not Latins— that is, the Samnites, Greeks, Etruscans, and Umbrians. Each community was bound to Rome by a separate treaty, of which there were about one hundred and fifty, not all alike. In general, however, the Italians enjoyed the right of trade with Rome and usually that of marriage. They supplied separate detachments of troops for the Roman army, with their own officers of the line, but under the command of Roman generals. They elected their own local officials and maintained their ancestral laws and institutions. The Italian cities were not allowed to make treaties with one another, and they entrusted their foreign affairs to the Roman senate. Rome considered any attempt to withdraw from the alliance as ground for war. Very soon, members of the Roman nobility, especially the plebeian nobility, began intermarrying with the nobility of allied Italian states, further strengthening the bonds uniting the two peoples. Much of the wisdom of Rome's policy toward Italy must be attributed to these plebeian nobles.

By this complicated system of government Rome guaranteed her allies a great local autonomy, while assuring her own unquestioned supremacy in Italy. Because of the excellence of the government accorded to the conquered Italians, Rome soon came to be regarded by them as the leader of an Italian League rather than as the subjugator of Italy. In later times these general principles of government were extended to other conquered peoples and formed the basis of Rome's organization of the ancient world. Rome had already discovered that the secret of empire was to assure her subjects almost every liberty except that of starting wars.

Note

Friedrich Münzer

Friedrich Münzer (1868–1944?) spent a large part of his scholarly life preparing biographies of every known Roman of the Republican period for the Pauly-Wissowa *Realencyclopädie der classischen Altertumswissenschaft,* his articles being among the most valuable of all those contained in that enormous work. He was a scholar of a type that became rather common in the twentieth century, a man willing to devote his life to doing small and inconspicuous bits in a large co-operative enterprise, collecting a huge amount of information, and cultivating his tiny field to its very limit. Ordinarily such scholars lacked the large though solid views of the "great" historians, but this was not the case with Münzer. The preparation of these biographies, by requiring him to work out the family connections of hundreds of Romans, forced upon his attention the great importance of a few families throughout the Republican period, their family alliances, and their family feuds. His general views on the subject are set forth in his *Römische Adelsparteien und Adelsfamilien* (1920). The book is badly arranged and difficult to use; a rapid reading is of little help; but the student whose perseverance enables him to go through it carefully will find it the most original and suggestive work on Roman history written in the present century. If only Münzer had learned how to express himself more easily, he would undoubtedly be ranked today among the great German historians of Rome. The fact that he was of Jewish birth (though a convert to Protestantism) made it unwise for German scholars to mention him favorably during the 1930's, and he came to a tragic death in a concentration camp during the war.

IV Rome Becomes a World Power

THE CONQUEST OF ITALY MADE ROME A POWER IN THE Hellenistic world. Her leaders had planned no such distinction for their city, and they assumed their new position reluctantly, but they could not help themselves. The conquered inhabitants of Italy, especially the Greeks, had long since established friendly or hostile relations with various foreign powers, and these relationships Rome now inherited. She was called upon to defend the interests of her allies, and the fulfillment of this duty brought new wars, more annexations and alliances, and wider frontiers to be defended. There is a modicum of truth in the cynical remark that Rome conquered the world in self-defense. The Romans certainly had foreseen no such eventuality when they first went to war with their neighbors, but once embarked upon the stormy seas of conquest, they could find nowhere to stop until they had reached the limits of the civilized world.

Carthage was the first of the great powers of the Hellenistic world with which Rome came in contact. According to an ancient tradition, Carthage entered into a treaty of friendship with Rome soon after the establishment of the Republic (509 B.C.). The terms of the treaty suggest that the Carthaginians were interested principally in stirring up trouble for their Etruscan rivals. No further evidence of friendship between the two powers appeared during the next century and a half, presumably because Rome was too insignificant to attract Carthaginian attention. A second treaty between Rome and

Carthage was concluded in 348. The Carthaginians promised not to establish themselves permanently in Latium and granted Romans trading rights in Sicily and Carthage. The Romans, on the other hand, agreed not to send ships to Libya, Sardinia, or Spain—which certainly was no great sacrifice on their part. A third treaty dated from 306. As Rome had by this time occupied Campania, she was interested in all southern Italy; and though Carthage had just defeated Agathocles, she was still worried about her Sicilian possessions. Each power therefore feared that the other might encroach upon its sphere of interest. By the terms of the new treaty Carthage promised to keep out of Italy while Rome promised not to invade Sicily. A fourth and final treaty, concluded in 279–78, promised mutual aid against the Greek adventurer Pyrrhus, who had recently landed in Italy. Nevertheless, when Rome was besieging Tarentum in 272, after Pyrrhus's departure from Italy, the Carthaginians sent a fleet to aid the Tarentines. The fleet did not enter the fighting, yet the Romans regarded its presence as a violation of the last two treaties.

The First Punic War

The First Punic War broke out eight years later. It is now easy to see the "inevitability" of a great conflict between the two major powers in the West, but at the time it did not seem so inevitable. While the immediate occasion of hostilities was trivial and discreditable to all concerned, it is worth dwelling on briefly as an illustration of how great wars can start. It is perfectly true, however, that if Rome and Carthage had not gone to war on this flimsy pretext they might soon have begun to fight over something else.

Agathocles, the Greek tyrant of Syracuse, had hired a band of Campanian mercenaries who called themselves Mamertines ("sons of Mars"). When his death in 289 left these men without employment, they seized Messana, a Sicilian town situated opposite the toe of Italy. For many years its citizens groaned under their tyranny. During the Pyrrhic wars some ten years later, the citizens of Rhegium, opposite Messana on the Italian mainland, called upon Rome for aid against Pyrrhus. A force of 4000 men was sent to defend them.

These Roman soldiers presently followed the example of the Mamertines by mutinying and establishing a tyranny over Rhegium. Rome was not able to punish their lawless action at once, but eventually she sent an army that besieged the city and killed most of the mutineers. The 300 survivors were taken in chains to Rome, where they were publicly flogged and beheaded in the forum (271).

Three years later Hiero, the new tyrant of Syracuse, decided to exterminate the Mamertines (268). They looked about for aid, some calling on Carthage while others, mindful of their Italian origin, appealed to Rome. The Roman senate, which had agreed in the treaty with Carthage to keep out of Sicily and had recently executed Roman citizens for copying the crimes of the Mamertines, was not at all inclined to intervene. Nevertheless, a reckless and bellicose consul (Appius Claudius Caudex), thinking that a military victory would enhance his political prestige, induced the *comitia centuriata* to send him to aid the Mamertines (264). When Claudius arrived at Messana, he found a Carthaginian general holding the citadel. After tricking this commander into leaving the fortress, Claudius occupied the city. The Carthaginian then went home and was promptly crucified by his indignant fellow citizens. Hiero of Syracuse, alarmed by this Roman interference in Sicilian affairs, allied himself with the Carthaginians to drive out the intruders, but in the first battle his armies were driven back to Syracuse and he sued for peace. The Romans let him off with a moderate indemnity and an alliance. Claudius then attacked the Carthaginians in Sicily, and Carthage hired an army of mercenaries to drive the Romans from the island. The Mamertine brigands were by this time forgotten, and the two great powers found themselves engaged in a war that was rather hard to justify.

The war, thus lightly begun, dragged on for twenty-three years. Rome's armies were superior, but control of the seas enabled Carthage to hire and provision new mercenaries to fight in Sicily. The Romans therefore tried to defeat their enemy at sea. Though they built a fleet—reportedly using a wrecked Carthaginian galley as model—they had no trained sailors and could not use it effectively. One fleet was destroyed by the enemy, another was wrecked by storms. The Romans kept building new and better fleets, however, and gradually they learned to operate them. In 256 a Roman consul (Regulus) landed troops in Africa and almost captured Carthage, but at the last moment a Spartan mercenary defeated the Romans, annihilated their army, and captured Regulus himself. Fourteen years later, in 242, a Roman fleet defeated and destroyed the Carthaginian navy in a battle off the west end of Sicily, and Carthage was forced to sue for peace. Rome demanded that she evacuate all Sicily, agree not to attack Syracuse or her allies, return all prisoners without ransom, and promise to pay an indemnity of 3200 talents (silver value, about $3,500,000; real value several times that amount) during the next ten years (241).

Acceptance of these terms did not bring peace to defeated Carthage. When she could not pay off her mercenaries, they rose in revolt and were joined by native Libyans. Only after three years of civil war, conducted with atrocious cruelty by both sides, did Carthage stamp out the insurrection. Meantime Carthaginian mercenaries in Sardinia had revolted. After suppressing the disturbances at home, the Carthaginians endeavored to pacify that island. The Romans—still somewhat hysterical, no doubt, from the recent war —decided to champion the "liberty" of the rebels. The *comitia* again declared war (238) but Carthage bought peace at the price Rome asked. She ceded Sardinia and Corsica to Rome, thus surrendering command of the Tyrrhenian Sea to the new Roman navy, and she promised another indemnity of 1200 talents. In later times even the pro-Roman historian Polybius admitted that this seizure of Sardinia and Corsica was "contrary to all justice."

Rome After the War

The twenty years that followed the First Punic War, sometimes skipped over lightly by historians, were among the most important in all the history of Rome. Though the Romans had not gone to war with Carthage in order to acquire foreign territory, their annexations dragged them out of Italy physically, politically, economically, and culturally. After the war was over, Roman troops were stationed in Sicily and Roman officials governed the island. They continued the Carthaginian practice of collecting taxes in kind, and sent the grain to Rome. We have no record of the exact amount collected, but even in the third century it must have been considerable. Such vast imports of free grain upset the balance of Italian agriculture. Progressive farmers began cultivating vines and olives instead of wheat, while others, unable to support themselves on their old farms, migrated to the cities. Moreover, the war had developed at Rome a class of businessmen capable of handling the large commercial transactions required to provision the armies in Sicily. These men afterward formed a strong commercial class, and Rome again became a commercial city such as she had not been since Etruscan times. The new commercial classes presently began to weaken the hold of the landed aristocrats upon political power.

Conservative Romans were frightened by the rising power of this new commercial class, and they sought to check it by various political reforms. First they organized the central and east Italian Sabines and Picentes as new tribes, thus bringing the total number of tribes to thirty-five (241). As members of the new tribes might vote in the *comitia tributa,* the voice of the rural voters was increased at the expense of the urban in that body. A few years later an extensive reorganization of the *comitia centuriata* worked in the same direction. The total number of centuries was increased from 193 to 373: the eighteen centuries of equestrians at the top and the five centuries of artisans and proletarians at the bottom of the list were left as before, but the five classes between them were rearranged in such a way that each of the thirty-five tribes had two centuries (one of *iuniores* and one of *seniores*) in each class, thus replacing 170 old centuries with 350 new ones. These changes reduced the political influence of the wealthy equestrians, many of whom were interested in the new commercial enterprises, and they greatly augmented that of the rural voters. Since voting took place only at Rome, those who gained most were the landed aristocrats who could afford to send large numbers of clients to Rome to vote. At about the same time a plebiscite was passed by the *comitia tributa* forbidding senators to engage in trade. This law worked equally well the other way, preventing men active in business from entering the senate.

By such measures as these the old aristocrats retained their firm grip upon the changing government of Rome.

Provincial Administration

The Romans were now faced for the first time with the problem of governing distant provinces inhabited by peoples whose traditions and institutions were quite different from their own. Heretofore they had interfered as little as possible with the local government of the peoples whom they conquered or with whom they made alliances, but this liberal policy was not possible in Sicily. The expulsion of the Carthaginian rulers had left a great part of that island without any government at all. The Romans therefore had to improvise a government as best they could, and Sicily became the first and most significant of their foreign provinces. Here they worked out the principles of provincial administration that they later applied to the whole Mediterranean world.

The first important step in developing Roman provincial administration came in 227 when four praetors were elected instead of two: the third praetor was sent to Sicily, the fourth governed Sardinia and Corsica. The chief duties of these officials were to supervise the collection of taxes and to maintain peace in the islands. The Romans continued to collect the tithe (or 10 per cent tax on crops) which had formerly been paid to Carthage, and they used the old rules and methods for collecting it. They extended a new autonomy to the cities and towns of Sicily, but they left the old social system as they found it. The new Roman government was less arbitrary and oppressive than that of Carthage had been, and the Romans brought peace to the island after centuries of warfare between Greeks and Carthaginians or between the various Greek cities. Under Rome's mild rule the rank and file of the Sicilian people probably were better off than ever before, and the economic prosperity of the whole island rose. Not until a century later were there serious revolts against Roman authority.

The establishment of Roman government in Sardinia and Corsica proved more difficult. The natives were at a low stage of culture and they bitterly opposed Roman dominion. Rome was thus dragged into a series of exasperating wars which she conducted with great cruelty. Thousands of Sardinians were sold into slavery, until the price of slaves dropped so low that they were not worth selling. There was also other booty, and it was here that Roman officials learned to make fortunes for themselves in the provinces. The other unpleasant features of imperialism quickly followed.

First Contacts with Greeks

Romans had already seen something of Greek civilization in southern Italy, and now they saw it to better advantage in Sicily. They were much impressed by what they saw, and from this time forth many Romans were eager to learn what they could from the Greeks. Wealthy families procured Greek slaves who tutored their children, taught them Greek, encouraged them to read Greek literature, and introduced them to the better elements of Greek culture. Some Romans became ardent philhellenists, and there were always a few who tried to pass themselves off as Greeks, but these *Graeculi* ("Greeklings") usually excited the contempt or indignation of their more rugged fellow countrymen.

The first Latin literature arose at this time, but it was largely the work of Greeks or other non-Romans who had been brought to Rome by returning conquerors. The first Latin dramatist was Livius Andronicus, a Greek from Tarentum, who came to Rome in childhood as a slave and whose first play appeared in 240. He wrote both tragedies and comedies, in close imitation of Greek models, and he translated the Odyssey into rude Latin verse. More important than Andronicus was Gnaeus Naevius, an Italian from Campania who fought in the First Punic War and produced his first play in 235. While he was much indebted to the Greeks, he did not ape them slavishly, and he was no "Greekling." He showed greater originality than Andronicus, drawing themes from Roman history as well as from Greek mythology. His epic poem about the Punic War contained the old legend tracing Rome's ancestry back to a Trojan hero, Aeneas, who passed through Carthage on his way to Rome after the fall of Troy. Naevius thus connected Rome to the Greek world, but he indicated clearly that in his opinion Romans would do well not

to adopt a subservient attitude toward the Greeks who had abused
their ancestors so dreadfully. Unfortunately for him, however,
Naevius's plays also contained attacks upon the Scipios and he was
therefore exiled to Utica, where he died about 202. In later times
his writings were admired by many Romans and his ideas were developed by Vergil.

Rome's new position in the world brought political as well as
cultural contacts with the Greeks, though in a rather roundabout
way. Peace had scarcely been established in Sardinia when trouble
arose with a certain Teuta, queen of Illyria. The eastern shore of the
Adriatic Sea, now part of Yugoslavia, had long been held by a barbarous people who had elevated piracy to the dignity of a national
profession. The pirates caused great trouble for the Greek cities of
Italy which were now under Roman rule. When the Greeks asked
Rome for aid against these raiders, the Roman senators at first saw
no reason to shed blood to help any merchants, least of all those
of a conquered people. At the same time they refused to allow the
Greeks to arm themselves in their own defense. Eventually the situation in Illyria became so bad, however, that something had to be
done. Two envoys were sent to Teuta with a formal protest (230).
When she refused to promise better behavior by her corsairs in the
future, the ambassadors started home in high dudgeon. Unfortunately, they were captured by Illyrian pirates on the way, and one
of them was hanged. The Romans charged the queen herself with
ordering this piece of lawlessness and sent an army to punish her
(229). After they had won a victory, they allowed Teuta to retain
the northern part of her territory, but they gave the rest to a certain
Demetrius of Pharos, and they established a Roman outpost at
Dyrrhachium (Durazzo) on the coast of modern Albania. Rome's
efforts to confine the pirates to the Adriatic by dominating the Straits
of Otranto thus forced her to occupy territory on the Greek side of
the Straits.

Within a short time Demetrius secured all Illyria, established a
firm friendship with Philip V of Macedon, and enlarged upon the
piracies of Teuta. The Romans sent a second army against him
(219), and after a second victory they occupied his principal for-

tress and annexed it to the tiny state they had set up at Dyrrhachium ten years before. Demetrius fled to Macedonia, where he continually urged an anti-Roman policy upon the young king, Philip V. Rome was thus drawn into the complicated politics of Greece itself, though several years were to pass before she recognized the true import of her new position. Many Romans disapproved highly of the whole affair and showed their displeasure by exiling Livius Salinator, the consul in command of the second campaign, after charging him with theft of booty.

Popular Unrest at Rome

The war with Carthage, which enabled so many Roman businessmen and aristocrats to become rich and resplendent, had less happy effects upon the Roman peasant. Heretofore plebeians had shared in the profits of wars through land distributions, but as Sicily and Sardinia offered no opportunity for such colonization, the poor got nothing for their struggles in the long war against Carthage. The importation of Sicilian wheat disturbed the agricultural markets and caused further suffering among farmers. The aftermath of the war drove many peasants from their farms to the city, weakening the bonds of clientship and creating large numbers of paupers with no patrons to look after them. The two decades after the war brought a great renewal of popular agitation, and the "struggle of the orders" entered a new phase.

The war was scarcely over before this struggle broke out anew. Two plebeian aediles, brothers named Malleolus, imposed fines on various aristocrats for pasturing cattle on the public lands in violation of the Licinian-Sextian laws of 367. They used the money thus obtained to pave a street on the Aventine Hill (the poor quarter of Rome), to build a temple to Flora there, and to found the Floralian games in honor of that agrarian goddess. The plebeian consul of 238 (Tiberius Gracchus) inflicted further fines on the aristocrats and built a temple to Liberty on the Aventine.

The most important of the new plebeian leaders, Gaius Flaminius, became tribune in 232 (the year when one of the Malleoli was consul), consul in 223, censor in 220, and consul again in 217. As tribune he obtained the passage of a plebiscite distributing lands in the *ager Gallicus* among the plebs. Though this *ager,* a large district in eastern Italy around Ariminum just south of the Po Valley, had been conquered about fifty years before, the new land distributions alarmed the Gauls who had previously occupied the *ager,* and they invaded Roman territory in 225. During his consulship Flaminius won an important victory over them, and during his censorship he built the Old Flaminian Way from Rome to Ariminum as a highway to the *ager.* In 218 he founded colonies at Cremona and Placentia (Piacenza) on the upper Po as new outlets for land-hungry peasants, thus starting Roman expansion in a new direction.

The old aristocrats bitterly opposed these land distributions—perhaps they coveted the lands themselves—and before the plebiscite of 232 was passed they threatened to use troops to stop the tribune. When they discovered a religious flaw in Flaminius's election as consul and ordered him home, he refused to open the senate's letter until after his victory over the Gauls; and when they refused to vote him a triumph after his return to Rome, the populace celebrated one anyhow. During his censorship he built the Circus Flaminius at Rome for popular shows, and during his second consulship he obtained a law designed to relieve debtors by inflating the currency. In later years the aristocracy complained that Flaminius was the man whose measures first began the debauching of the Roman plebs.

Family Factions in Rome

Against this background we may sketch the major outlines of family and party politics at Rome in the period after the First Punic War. During the century preceding the outbreak of that war, three successive members of the Fabian family had dominated Roman politics, holding the powerful position of *princeps senatus* and dealing out consulships and commands among their numerous followers from the minor nobility. When the third Fabius died in 265, his son was already dead and his grandson Verrucosus was only thirteen years old. During the war and the period of confusion that followed, the Fabii lost heavily in political power. They represented the old landed aristocracy of Rome that had conquered Italy and they had little sympathy with the new tendencies of the age. Though Verrucosus held consulships in 233 and 228, and took the lead against Flaminius, his party failed to maintain its former primacy.

The Scipios and the Aemilii were in closer sympathy with the new day. These old patrician families were closely united by marriage, and they had prospered together during the war. One of the Scipios had built the first Roman navy during his consulship in 260, and in the last years of the war other Scipios became prominent. After the war they led Rome's most aggressive faction, and during the late 230's and the 220's they enjoyed almost as complete a monopoly on high office as had the Fabii in earlier days. They stood much closer than the Fabii to the mercantile interests that became so powerful after the war; and whereas the Fabii had little interest in the world outside Italy, the Scipios and Aemilii were already dreaming of making Rome a power in the Hellenistic world. It was they who intervened in Illyria, in 229 and again in 219, thus taking the first steps toward involving Rome in Greek affairs. The rivalry of the Scipios and the Fabii even reached into literature, with the poet Livius Andronicus expressing the views of the Scipionic faction while Naevius stood closer to the Fabii and, as we have seen, was exiled for expressing their views.

The third great faction in Roman politics was that of the Claudii. The founder of this family, Appius Claudius, first came to Rome in 504, five years after the establishment of the Republic, and was at once admitted to the patrician aristocracy. His grandson, of the same name, was leader of the second group of *decemviri* who drew up the Laws of the Twelve Tables in 450 and whose aristocratic views caused him to sponsor many unfair laws. The most distinguished member of the family was Appius Claudius Caecus, censor in 312, who built the Appian Way to Capua and the Appian Aqueduct at Rome, who introduced several popular reforms, and who in his old age rallied Roman resistance against Pyrrhus. The Censor was sometimes accused of aspiring to tyranny, and several of his descendants even more patently entertained such aspirations, until at last the family produced the Emperors Tiberius and Claudius in the first century after Christ. Following the pattern established by

Greek tyrants (see Vol. I, p. 302), the Claudii courted the favor of the mob by spectacular display and public benefactions; and they always posed as great champions of the "people," for whom they really felt an aristocratic contempt. At their best the Claudii were "Tory democrats," and at their worst (which sometimes became very bad indeed) they were utterly unscrupulous rabble-rousers. As they felt themselves superior to everyone else, they were cordially hated by other patricians. They showed little constructive states-manship, but they exploited the sincere idealism of democratic re-formers, or used reckless demagogues for their purposes. Though theirs was almost the only patrician family at Rome that never pro-duced a great general, they often incited the people to war. One member of the Claudian family precipitated the First Punic War in 264; Sardinia and Corsica were seized by consuls attached to the Claudian faction; and on many other occasions in Roman history the Claudii were vociferous warmongers.

Prominent among the plebeian nobility whom the Claudii at-tracted to their faction were the Fulvii, a family from Tusculum, who shared many of the Claudian characteristics and who were the lead-ing plebeian members of the Claudian faction. One Fulvius Flaccus was consul with Claudius Caudex in 264, and his son, the most brilliant member of the family, became consul four times, the first being in 237. The younger Fulvius backed Flaminius in his land program of 232, thus enabling the Claudians to capture the popular gratitude for his benefactions. In revenge, Fabius had Fulvius ex-pelled from the censorship in 230, as usual alleging a religious flaw in his election. Fulvius won a second consulship in 224, during which he prepared the way for Flaminius's consulship the following year. The Scipios and the Fabii then united to defeat the popular leaders and their Claudian exploiters. Each of these factions pro-vided one consul in 222; and in the four following years all eight consuls were members of the imperialistic Scipionic faction.

The Carthaginians in Spain

Carthaginian leaders had meantime set themselves to the difficult and dreary task of reconstruction. Many of the old Punic nobility be-lieved that their best policy was to make Carthage a simple agricultural state. They were willing to forget dreams of empire, and to live at peace with Rome. The business interests and the populace, on the other hand, preferred to continue in their mercantile pursuits and to redeem their losses by building up an empire in Spain. The leader of the latter group was Hamilcar Barca. This brilliant general, member of one of the most conspicuous families in Carthage, had commanded troops in Sicily during the closing years of the First Punic War. He negotiated the treaty of peace and he took a leading part in suppressing the revolt of the mercenaries. He then devoted himself to creating an empire in Spain. Roman writers of a later period saw in his program only preparation for a war of *revanche* against victorious Rome. There can be no doubt that Hamilcar hated the Romans, and he may well have hoped to avenge the defeat in Sicily. Such feeling was not the primary force behind his Spanish policy, however, for his main purpose was to develop new commercial fields to replace the lost markets of Italy and Sicily.

Hamilcar landed at Gades in 237. During the preceding hundred years Carthage had been so occupied with wars in Sicily that her Spanish empire had fallen to pieces. Hamilcar could be sure only of Gades and a few cities along the southern coast of Spain. Within a short time he had founded new trading posts, established Carthaginian power over much of the interior, and acquired the rich silver mines of central Spain. During the nine years of his activity in Spain, Hamilcar conquered the most populous part of the peninsula (the valley of the Baetis, now the Guadalquivir) and made Carthaginian power firm in eastern Spain. He founded a city at the site of modern Alicante, far to the north of the former Punic sphere of influence, and he maintained friendly relations with the natives. His successes were so great that he not only paid the entire cost of conquest from his winnings but also sent great quantities of booty back to Carthage. As his army was composed of mercenaries, his adventures cost Carthage neither blood nor treasure, yet brought her victory and revenue.

Hamilcar was drowned during a battle in 228 and was succeeded by his son-in-law Hasdrubal. The new commander established his capital at an imposing city called New Carthage (now Cartagena) and continued the wars against the Iberians and the Celts. When he was murdered during a personal quarrel (221), command fell to Hamilcar's son Hannibal. Following in his father's footsteps, Hannibal continued the conquest of Spain, making a sudden expedition to the interior and defeating hordes of natives (220). The next year he besieged and captured Saguntum, the last independent town on the Mediterranean coast of Spain. Hannibal's Spanish domains then extended north to the Tagus River on the Atlantic side of the peninsula and to the Ebro on the Mediterranean side.

Roman Protests

At first the Romans paid little attention to the activities of Hamilcar and Hasdrubal in Spain. The Roman senate had not desired the utter destruction of Carthage. It had rendered minor aid to the city during the mercenaries' revolt; it was forced into the Sardinian adventure against its better judgment; and it showed no objection to Carthaginian colonization of Spain. The citizens of Massilia (modern Marseilles) were more deeply concerned, for Punic successes cost them one of their principal colonies. The Massilots therefore complained to their old friends and allies at Rome, who remonstrated with Hamilcar in 231. Hamilcar cleverly retorted that his sole purpose in Spain was to get enough silver to pay Carthage's indemnity from the last war, and asked, Did Rome plan to forgive the debt? Five years later a second Roman embassy negotiated a treaty with Hasdrubal, establishing the Ebro River as the northern limit of Carthaginian expansion and thereby assuring the independence of the remaining Greek colonies.

Nevertheless, the Romans presently entered into an alliance with Saguntum, the only important city south of the Ebro which the Carthaginians had not occupied. Historians still dispute whether or not this act was a breach of the Ebro treaty. Ancient writers apparently were a little troubled in their consciences, for they put forward various absurd excuses—such as Livy's allegation that Saguntum was north of the Ebro. As Hasdrubal did not immediately protest the Roman alliance, the pro-Romans in Saguntum were encouraged to begin intriguing against Carthaginian sympathizers, several of whom they executed soon after Hasdrubal's death. Hannibal was thus stirred to action. After an attack by Saguntines upon one of his subject tribes, he captured the city in 219, though the Romans sent an embassy to warn him not to attack their ally. When the ambassadors could get no satisfaction from Hannibal, they proceeded to Carthage, where they repeated the warning. After the fall of Saguntum, Rome again sent ambassadors to Carthage to present what we today would call an ultimatum, demanding that Hannibal be handed over for punishment. The Carthaginians quite naturally refused to surrender their general, whereupon Rome declared war (218).

Responsibility for this war has been much debated. Patriotic Romans of course protested Rome's innocence and accused Hannibal of deliberately and criminally plotting the whole thing. Postwar defeatists at Carthage, on the other hand, sought to mitigate the punishment of their city by likewise laying the whole blame on him, insisting that Carthage herself had no share in the origin or prosecution of the war. Since spokesmen on both sides were seemingly in accord, ancient writers were virtually unanimous in attributing the war to Hannibal's personal aggression and vindictiveness. Modern scholars are not so sure. They remember that the Romans inaugurated the First Punic War by violating their pledge to keep out of Sicily, that they acquired Sardinia by pure and simple bullying, and that their intrigues at Saguntum—which might be called a second Messana—were the immediate occasion of renewed hostilities. Nevertheless, this aggressiveness was confined to a small faction, and the leaders in this faction seem to have been concerned primarily with immediate personal gains, not with far-reaching plans for conquest. The situation at Rome was complicated by the long war in Sicily, which had aroused a popular feeling against Carthage that was not soon forgotten. The severe terms of the peace treaty of 241, coupled with the Sardinian affair, caused apprehensions in Rome of Punic revenge. The propaganda of Greek intriguers from Massilia added to the confusion, and the death of Hasdrubal, followed by the rise to power of the youthful Hannibal, seemed to offer a suitable occasion for ending the Carthaginian "menace." The truth seems to be that Roman leaders at the time were distracted by varying counsels and uncertain as to their policies. They did not deliberately plan a war but stumbled into one; and Hannibal and the Carthaginians were quite willing to accept the challenge they threw down.

Hannibal and the Second Punic War

The Romans had made no specific preparations for a war against Carthage. They had been occupied with other wars, and perhaps their recent victories over minor enemies had convinced them that Romans did not need elaborate preparations to be victorious. When war was declared, they mobilized only two armies of two legions each, or a little over 40,000 men, more than half of whom were allies. One army was sent to Sicily, preparatory to invading Africa, though plans were changed before it could embark. The second army, commanded by the consul Publius Cornelius Scipio, was ordered to Spain to meet Hannibal, whose military genius the Romans did not suspect. Before Scipio left Italy a serious revolt broke out among the Gauls who had only recently been subjugated by Flaminius, and Scipio's legions were hurriedly sent to repress it. Scipio raised two new legions among the Italian allies, but before he could set sail for Spain Hannibal was well on his way to Italy. Thereafter for several years the Romans were forced to fight on the defensive.

Hannibal, who was soon to prove himself one of the greatest generals in history, was now twenty-nine years old. Drilled from childhood as a soldier, he—like other military geniuses such as Alexander and Napoleon—showed his ability in early manhood. His excellent army had been hardened by fighting against Iberian barbarians, and his campaigns in Spain had given him practical experience in leading troops. The strategy which he later used with such devastating effect against the Romans—a sudden unexpected blow prepared behind clever lures and ambushes—he had already mastered. Studies of Pyrrhus and Alexander had made him familiar with the best Hellenistic warfare. His genius for leadership is proved by the fact that for fifteen years he held his army of mercenaries together on foreign soil without once experiencing a mutiny, an achievement which has ever since excited the admiration of military men.

His ability as a diplomat and statesman equaled his generalship, and his diplomacy embraced the world of his day. Whatever his enemies may have said, it seems clear that he did not desire the utter obliteration of Rome but, like Pyrrhus, hoped to destroy Roman hegemony in Italy, for which he would substitute a new Italian federation under the nominal leadership of Capua but actually dominated by Carthage. Rome would thus have been rendered powerless and Carthage would again have become mistress of the West. From the siege of Saguntum in 219 until his death in 183, Hannibal pursued this aim with a steadfastness and a singleness of purpose that lent plausibility to the story that as a lad of nine he had been led by his father before an altar and there made to swear undying hatred of Rome. It seems more probable, however, that this oft-repeated legend was originally part of the Massilot propaganda used to scare Rome into the "inevitable" war with Carthage. Hannibal was a man of ascetic habits and a fanatic; but Roman charges of perfidy and inhuman cruelty must be discounted as proceeding from the malignancy of an enemy who had suffered too severely at his hands to be fair to his memory.

Hannibal spent the winter of 219–18 organizing his army at New Carthage. In May, 218, he started for Italy, leaving about 20,000 troops in Africa and an army of 12,000 infantry, 3000 cavalry, and 21 elephants under his younger brother Hasdrubal II in Spain. Hannibal's army probably consisted of not much over 40,000 men, including a strong force of Numidian cavalry and a corps of elephants. Since Rome commanded the seas, Hannibal could not count on regular supplies from home, and he had to support his army in Italy as best he could.

Hannibal's Invasion of Italy

The passage of the Pyrenees was resisted by Gauls who caused Hannibal heavy casualties and the loss of valuable time, and he did not reach the Rhone River until August. Here he defeated a Gallic

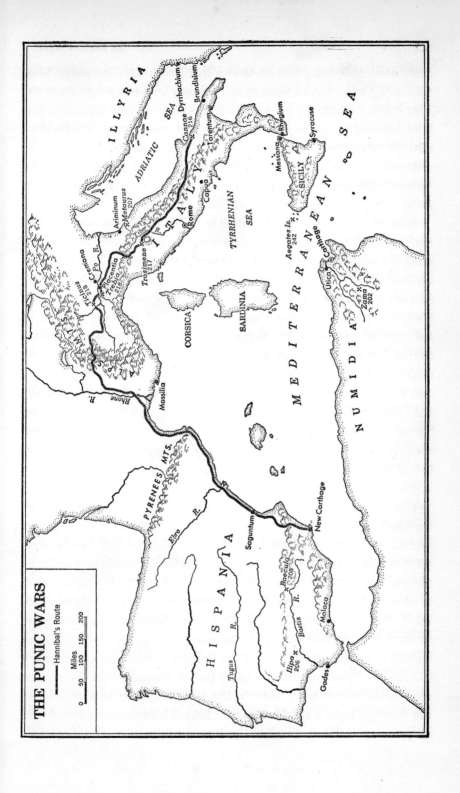

THE PUNIC WARS

Miles
0 50 100 150 200

—— Hannibal's Route

ILLYRIA

ADRIATIC SEA

Dyrrhachium
Brundisium
Cannae 216
Tarentum
Rhegium
Messana
Syracuse
SICILY

ITALY

Ariminum
Metaurus 207
Cremona
Po R.
Placentia
Trebia 218
Trasimene 217
Ticinus 218
ALPS
Rome
Capua

TYRRHENIAN SEA

CORSICA

SARDINIA

Aegates Is. 242
Utica
Carthage
Zama 202

MEDITERRANEAN SEA

NUMIDIA

Rhone R.
Massilia

PYRENEES MTS.

Ebro R.

HISPANIA

Tagus R.

Saguntum

New Carthage

Baecula 208
Baetis R.
Malaca
Ilipa 206
Gades

army and eluded the Roman troops that Scipio had landed at Massilia. In spite of the lateness of the season, he hastened to cross the Alps before winter set in. Again he was resisted by Gauls, and further delays were caused by landslides and early snows. When Hannibal finally entered the Po Valley, late in September, his army was reduced to 20,000 infantry and 6000 cavalry, and nearly all his elephants were gone. Nevertheless, this passage of the Alps has remained one of the famous feats of military history.

After his failure to stop Hannibal in Gaul, Scipio returned to Italy with a small force, but first he made the momentous decision to send the bulk of his army to Spain under the command of his elder brother Gnaeus. Landing at Pisa, Scipio hastened north to resume command of the two legions originally assigned to him. He met Hannibal for the first time and was defeated near the Ticinus, a tributary of the upper Po. Scipio managed to extricate most of his troops, but he was wounded during the fight. Shortly thereafter, the other consul, Sempronius Longus, arrived from Sicily with his army and took command of all Roman forces. Early in December Hannibal destroyed this united army after luring it into a trap on the Trebia River near Placentia. Settling down for the winter, Hannibal made alliances with various Gallic chieftains in northern Italy, enlisted several thousand Gauls in his army, and prepared to march south in the spring.

The Romans at last realized the magnitude of the war upon which they had embarked, and the elections for 217 were held amidst great excitement. A friend of the Scipios named Gnaeus Servilius became the patrician consul, but the popular leader Flaminius was chosen plebeian consul. These two consuls enlisted new armies amounting to eleven legions, or more than 100,000 men. Two legions were already in Spain under Gnaeus Scipio; two were sent to Sicily, one to Sardinia, and two were held in reserve at Rome. The other four legions were sent north against the invaders under the command of Flaminius. Hannibal had crossed the Apennines into Etruria as soon as the passes were open in the spring, and he now ambushed the Romans near Lake Trasimene: here Flaminius was killed and his army annihilated. Too late the Romans remembered unfavorable omens that had warned of impending disaster, and in later years they repeated the old charge, already popularized by Fabius, that Flaminius had neglected the gods.

After Trasimene the Romans lost no time naming Fabius Verrucosus dictator and prepared their city for a siege, but Hannibal was too wise a general to waste troops and time attacking a walled city. He knew that Rome could be besieged successfully only after her allies had deserted her and that her allies could best be seduced by victories over Rome in the field. He therefore freed the Italian and Greek prisoners taken at Trasimene, assuring them that he was fighting against Rome in their behalf, after which he marched his army into southern Italy. Fabius thereupon adopted the strategy which won him the title Cunctator, or "Delayer." He refused to fight the enemy, trusting that time would dampen the ardor of the Gauls and wear down Hannibal's mercenaries; but he kept his own army close on the enemy's heels and thus prevented the Punic leader from dispersing his forces over Italy and besieging fortified cities.

Cannae

Though Fabius's strategy was undoubtedly sound, it cost the Romans and their allies heavily for the Punic army looted farms and villages wherever it went. Roman dissatisfaction with the Fabian strategy was shown at the end of the year when two new consuls were chosen. One was L. Aemilius Paullus, whose military experience led him to favor a continuation of the delaying strategy while his colleague, a vulgar braggart named C. Terentius Varro, shouted for immediate action. The two consuls were constantly quarreling with each other, but at last they decided, in August, 216, to fight a pitched battle against Hannibal at Cannae. Their forces consisted of four over-sized legions, probably more than 50,000 infantry and 6000 cavalry, while the Carthaginians had only 35,000 infantry and 10,000 cavalry. Nevertheless, Hannibal succeeded in completely surrounding the Romans and butchered their army. Roman losses amounted to about 40,000 men, including one consul (Paullus), two quaestors, twenty-nine military tribunes, eighty senators, and several ex-consuls and ex-praetors. Some 10,000 were prisoners in Hannibal's hands, and less than 10,000 managed to escape the stricken field. Hannibal's losses reputedly amounted to about 5700 men—4000 Gauls, 1500 Iberians and Africans, and 200 cavalry. Cannae was the most serious defeat ever sustained by Roman arms, and modern military men have praised it as a "perfect" victory for Hannibal.

On the morrow of Cannae, Hannibal's officers urged him to march on Rome, promising, it was said, that within five days they would dine with him in the Capitol. Hannibal preferred peace and sent his brother Mago back to Carthage to urge negotiations. The Carthaginian senate unwisely replied that it would discuss peace only at Rome. Hannibal then turned his energies to winning over Rome's allies. Capua, the second city in Italy, joined him, and her example was followed by several Campanian and Greek cities, by the majority of the cities of southern Italy, and by some of the Samnites of the hill country. Only central Italy and Etruria remained true to their Roman ally. Early in the following year (215) came the death of Hiero, the aged and pro-Roman tyrant of Syracuse; after months of domestic and foreign intrigue his successors allied themselves with Hannibal. And Philip V of Macedon, seeing an opportunity to drive the Romans from Illyria, entered into an alliance with Hannibal.

The disaster at Cannae did not overwhelm the Roman people. For a few days the city was sunk in mourning, an unchaste priestess and some foreigners were buried alive to placate the gods, and a delegation was sent to consult the oracle at Delphi. But Roman discipline quickly reasserted itself. The senate limited mourning and forbade public discussion of the defeat. It refused to ransom the prisoners or to consider peace. New levies of old men, boys, and even slaves, were raised as a last defense for the city, and loans were floated to finance further fighting. A few weeks later, when word came that another army of two legions had been annihilated by the Gauls in the north, the Roman people again stood firm. Fabius was re-elected consul for 215 and 214, and again for 209, and his son was consul in 213. They continued the policy of refusing a pitched battle, though picking off minor detachments of the enemy here and there. Hannibal was left to wear down his army with fruitless skirmishing and with endless marching and countermarching through southern Italy. His brilliant victories faded into the past and it became evident that, great as his successes had been, they had not been great enough. He had passed the zenith of his career.

The Scipios in Spain

Meantime events had proven the wisdom of Scipio's early decision to persevere in the Spanish campaign in spite of Hannibal's invasion of Italy. Gnaeus Scipio landed his two legions and drove the Carthaginians south of the Ebro before the winter of 218 set in. Publius Scipio was sent to Spain with reinforcements late in the following year (217), and for a while the two brothers made steady progress. In 215 they defeated Hannibal's brother, Hasdrubal, in an important battle on the Ebro, and at last they captured Saguntum in 212. Other events had helped the Romans. The Numidians in north Africa had revolted against Carthage, perhaps with the encouragement of Scipio, and Hasdrubal was called back from Spain to defend possessions nearer home. After the fall of Saguntum he patched up a peace in Numidia and returned to Spain with a large army intended to reinforce Hannibal. In the campaign of 211 both Scipios were killed and the invaders driven back beyond the Ebro. The Romans lost two able generals and the gains of four years, but Hannibal lost his reinforcements.

In spite of their defeats the Romans continued to raise new levies. They had twenty-five legions, or a quarter of a million men, under arms in 212, and they were thus able to carry the war into new fields. When Syracuse made its alliance with Hannibal in 214, the only Roman troops in Sicily were two weak legions composed of the survivors of Cannae. A friend of Fabius named Claudius Marcellus was sent with reinforcements to besiege Syracuse. Though this well-fortified city was defended by many mechanical devices invented by Archimedes, and by aid from Carthage, Marcellus took it in 211 and thus brought all Sicily into Roman hands.

At about this time, too, the Romans felt themselves strong enough to attempt the recapture of Capua. Hannibal failed in an effort to drive the besiegers from their encircling trenches, and a feint which brought him within five miles of Rome did not distract them from the siege. Capua too was taken in 211. Later Roman moralists were fond of saying that Capua was the ruin of the Punic army, and that its luxuries debauched the victors of Cannae. Perhaps this story was edifying to children, but it certainly was not true. Hannibal's troops had never entered Capua, and there is no evidence that they were especially debauched or demoralized at any time. As long as they remained in Italy they continued to fight with their customary skill.

Scipio Africanus and Victory

It was at this juncture that young Publius Scipio, son of the old general of the same name, received his first command. Myths sprang up about this remarkable man even while he was still alive. Men told of his miraculous birth and of his divine inspiration as the son of Jupiter, of his quiet communion with the gods, and of the divine aid he received on the battlefield. Such myths are significant as evidence of the impression that his personality made upon his soldiers. Other anecdotes, of greater historical plausibility, amplify the story: they tell of his personal charm, his romantic enthusiasm, his enlightenment and fondness for conversing with intellectual Greeks and Orientals, his conspicuous success in winning the devotion of his men. He was at once a dreamer and a man of action. Military critics admit his high ability though they rarely consider him comparable to Hannibal as a general. This Scipio was a member of the new generation that grew up during the war and that would no longer tolerate the passive tactics of old Fabius, and he belonged to a family and a political faction that had long been accustomed to look beyond the borders of Italy. He insisted upon aggressive action, he defeated Hannibal and conquered Carthage, and he went down in history as Scipio Africanus.

Scipio had won his spurs in the battle on the Ticinus in 218, where he carried his wounded father from the field. Two years later he was fighting under his father-in-law, Aemilius Paullus, and was one of the few who survived Cannae. In 210, when only twenty-five years old, he was put in command of his father's armies in Spain that Hasdrubal had defeated so disastrously the year before. He at once built up a new army, enlisting many Iberian mercenaries, and within a year he advanced upon New Carthage. His attack was so sudden and unexpected that it met little resistance, and he quickly captured the city. His soldiers later talked of a miracle, with the sea opening to let them pass. As New Carthage was the capital of Spain, its loss was a serious blow to Punic prestige throughout the Iberian peninsula, and the loss of the nearby silver mines was an even more serious blow to their finances. A year later (208) Scipio defeated Hasdrubal at Baecula, though the Carthaginian commander saved most of his army. The final victory in Spain was won at Ilipa (206) over an army led by Hannibal's youngest brother, Mago. When the citizens of Gades deserted to Rome a little later, the Carthaginian empire in Spain was gone.

Meantime, the military situation in Italy had been slowly turning to Rome's advantage. In 209 Fabius recaptured Tarentum, which had revolted to Hannibal a few years before. Hasdrubal led the remnants of his army to Italy after his defeat at Baecula, only to be defeated by the Romans near the Metaurus River south of Ariminum (207). He was killed in the battle, and a few days later the Romans tossed his head into Hannibal's camp. Mago followed his brother to Italy after being defeated at Ilipa, and landed his troops near Genoa. His efforts to rouse the Gauls were unsuccessful, and though he remained in Italy until he died of wounds almost at the end of the war, he was no menace to Rome. By this time Hannibal himself was virtually a prisoner in the toe of Italy. During the ten years since Cannae he had fought no important battle, and though his army was still intact, he must at times have despaired of ever destroying the power of Rome.

Scipio Invades Africa: Zama

Such was the state of affairs when Scipio returned to Rome in 206 and straightway was elected consul for the following year. No sooner was he in office than he began preparing to carry the war into Africa. This aggressive policy was opposed by the Fabians, whose ambitions did not extend beyond freeing Italy of the invader. But Scipio persevered, and in 204 he landed two legions near Utica. He soon entered into an alliance with a Numidian vassal of Carthage named Masinissa—a young man before whom lay a long, adventurous, tumultuous, romantic, and perfidious career. Masinissa had served for several years under Hasdrubal in Spain, but he believed that his interest now lay with Scipio, to whom his cavalry was a welcome addition.

Except for landing his troops safely, Scipio could claim no military success for his first year in Africa. As winter approached, the Carthaginians offered him peace on the basis of mutual evacuation of territory and return to the status quo. While Scipio was pretending to consider terms, he used the negotiations as a blind for sending officers in disguise to spy out the land. In the spring he rejected the proposed terms and resumed fighting. He then proved the effectiveness of his new model army of mercenaries by inflicting a severe defeat upon the enemy. The Roman army was only fifteen miles from Carthage but Scipio, like Hannibal preferring not to attack a fortified town, allowed the Carthaginians to buy an armistice. Severe peace terms were drawn up by Scipio, accepted by Carthage, and sent to Rome for approval. While awaiting a reply, the Carthaginians recalled Hannibal from Italy, and when his troops arrived they broke the armistice by seizing grain ships supplying Scipio's army.

It was with a heavy heart that Hannibal obeyed the order to return home. Reaching Africa in the spring of 202, he created a new army by uniting his own with the remnants of Mago's and enlisting new troops, and toward the end of the summer he moved westward in a vain attempt to prevent Masinissa from joining Scipio. The Roman and Carthaginian armies finally camped near Zama. On the day before the battle the two commanders held a personal interview, but whether they sincerely desired peace, or merely sought an opportunity to appraise each other's minds, no one can say. The next day Hannibal suffered his first defeat. Each army had about 40,000 infantry, but for the first time Hannibal's cavalry was seriously outnumbered, thanks to Masinissa. Moreover, Scipio's troops were seasoned veterans while Hannibal's new levies were of no great value. During the battle Hannibal did all that a good general could do, yet everything seemed to go wrong. His elephants ran amuck; Masinissa drove his cavalry off the field; his raw recruits became panic-stricken and fled; and Masinissa returned from the chase in time to attack the Punic army from the rear, thus completely surrounding it. The army was destroyed, and Hannibal barely escaped with his life (autumn, 202).

Knowing that further resistance was hopeless, Hannibal persuaded his fellow citizens to accept whatever peace terms they could get. A three-months' armistice was purchased, and Scipio's terms were eventually accepted. Carthage surrendered all her empire except the Punic district around the city. Spain and the islands went to Rome; the Libyan territory south of the city became an independent ally of Rome; and Masinissa was made the independent ruler of Numidia. The Carthaginian navy and elephants were surrendered and their replacement forbidden; a hundred hostages were ordered sent to Rome; an indemnity of 10,000 talents[1] was to be paid during fifty years; and Carthage was forbidden to wage war outside of Africa, or even in Africa without Rome's express permission. Neither Hannibal nor Scipio had yet ended his career, but the days of Carthaginian greatness were over.

War with Macedon

Scipio's victory at Zama ended the war with Carthage but it did not bring Rome peace either at home or abroad. In spite of the remarkable steadfastness shown during the disheartening crises of the war, political life at Rome was not suspended and the quarrels of factions

---

[1] This indemnity, like all similar sums in ancient times, cannot be expressed adequately in terms of modern currency. Some writers convert the talent at the rate of $1100, which was approximately its metallic value before the American financial reforms of 1934. Its general purchasing value was at least five times that amount, and it was harder for Carthage to pay this sum than it would be for an equally important modern state to pay many times as much. Nevertheless, it cannot be said that the annual payments of 200 talents were exorbitant. Minor Greek cities sometimes paid as much, Antiochus paid six times as much, and individual Greeks were sometimes fined fifteen or twenty talents. Moreover, the Carthaginians offered in 191 to pay the entire amount at once, but Rome refused to accept it.

continued as bitterly as ever. The Scipionic faction had dominated Rome for several years before 218 and, except for the consulship of Flaminius (during which he was killed at Trasimene), it remained in control until 216. Cannae destroyed the Scipio's prestige, however, and the direction of Roman policy fell to the Fabii, under the dictator and his plebeian associate Claudius Marcellus. Their only serious rivals were the Claudian-Fulvian faction, who elected one consul and all four praetors in 215, and whose leaders, Appius Claudius Pulcher and Quintus Fulvius Flaccus, became consuls together in 212. For two years thereafter the Claudians ruled Rome. Not until 207 was the Scipionic faction able to return to power, but it elected the future Africanus consul for 205. His plans for invading Africa were bitterly opposed by both Fabians and Claudians, who even won recruits among families formerly associated with the Scipios. Before Scipio crossed to Africa, his enemies used obstructionist tactics to prevent him from going, and later they tried to have him recalled or replaced by one of themselves. Even after Zama they continued their attacks upon Scipio, accusing him of plotting to become king. To summarize, the Scipios were in power until 216 and after 207, the Fabians from 215 to 213 and from 210 to 208, and the Claudians in 212 and 211.

The quarrels of factions continued unabated at Rome after the war since conditions encouraged demagoguery and a revival of warmongering. Economic and social life throughout Italy had been profoundly disturbed. Hundreds of thousands of persons had been uprooted from their homes, and political agitators found them an easy field to cultivate. On the other hand, a few persons had found the war extremely profitable, either financially or politically, and were not at all horrified at the thought of further hostilities. The political turbulence of the years immediately after Zama encouraged them to hope for still other wars in which they might win victories that would eclipse Zama. Moreover, conditions in Greece were just then ripe for trouble. The result was that the Romans were soon involved in a new series of wars, and not until twelve more years had passed did they attain the relative repose of peace.

Philip V and the First Macedonian War

When Philip V came to the throne of Macedon in 221, he was the commander of a powerful army; he was the friend and admirer of Aratus, the generous and philhellenic leader of the Achaean League; and he was called "the darling of Greece." The young king apparently hoped to complete the work of Aratus by uniting the various Greek leagues into one Hellenic alliance that would become a sort of Greek super-state (see p. 56). His way was beset with obstacles. His Macedonian advisers favored such panhellenic plans only in so far as they promoted Macedonian supremacy in Greece; the particularism of the Greek states opposed such a union; and the pathetic economic state of Greece, where a few men were very rich while the population as a whole was desperately poor, had by this time made class war endemic throughout the peninsula. The Achaean League, and to a less extent Philip, favored the wealthy classes, while Cleomenes of Sparta had recently championed revolutionists everywhere. After Cleomenes defeat (222) the Aetolians continued to stir up the poor against their Achaean and Macedonian rivals. The first years of Philip's reign were therefore consumed in a war between the Greek leagues (221–217), but once this conflict was temporarily appeased, he welcomed the diversion offered by intervention in Italy.

Philip's mother was the granddaughter of Pyrrhus. The family apparently had not forgotten his old dream of an empire in the West, and in 217 conditions in Italy seemed ripe for its realization. Hannibal's victory at Trasimene suggested to Philip that he might now drive the Romans from Illyria and invade Italy. As soon, therefore, as the war in Greece was over, Philip began preparations for a western campaign. He built a fleet and sailed around Greece to Illyria in 216, but the expedition ended in a fiasco; and a few weeks later Hannibal's victory at Cannae dispelled all hope of a Macedonian empire in Italy. Nevertheless, Philip allied himself with Hannibal in the spring of 215. Civil war immediately broke out in Greece, however, and Hannibal received no aid from his ally.

As Rome's position gradually improved after Cannae, she prepared to defend Illyria against Philip. One legion was sent there in
214, whose commander entered into an alliance with the Aetolians
and their allies, including Sparta and Pergamum (212). The new
allies proposed to confine Philip to Macedonia, and it was agreed
that, while the Romans might loot whatever territories they conquered, the Aetolians were to annex them afterward. Eventually
Philip forced the Aetolians into a separate peace (206), which was
a severe blow to Rome. The Claudians wanted to continue the war
against Philip, but Scipio was anxious to clear up the Illyrian trouble
before invading Africa. He therefore concluded the Peace of Phoe-
nice in 205. Philip allowed the Romans to remain in Illyria, and
they in turn let him retain the corner of that province that he had
occupied.

Philip was encouraged to make peace with Rome by political and
diplomatic developments in the East. Antiochus III of Syria had by
this time completed the pacification of his eastern provinces which
had occupied him for ten years (see p. 53), and he was now turning
his attention to the West. He hoped first of all to settle old scores
with Egypt and later to regain ancestral territories in Asia Minor
and perhaps even in European Thrace. Both Antiochus and Ptolemy
therefore made advances to Philip, each seeking his aid against the
other. Philip negotiated with each, and late in 203 he and Antiochus entered into a secret alliance which neither intended to keep.
Philip merely hoped to make his two rivals fight one another for
their conflict would enable him to seize much of Asia Minor, beginning with the cities held by Egypt. His military and naval successes
in 202 and 201 aroused the apprehensions of Antiochus, brought
open conflict with Pergamum and Rhodes, and convinced the Aetolians that the time for renewed attacks upon Macedon had come.
Philip's Greek enemies then bethought themselves of Rome. When
they decided in 202 to renew the war against Philip, the Aetolians
sent an embassy to Rome, asking for aid; a year later Attalus, king
of Pergamum, and the Rhodians each sent envoys to reinforce their
pleas.

The Second Macedonian War

When the Aetolian ambassadors arrived in Rome, only a few weeks after Zama, senate and people alike were strongly disinclined to further military adventures. The senate reminded the Aetolians forcibly of the perfidy of their separate peace in 206 and sent them

home. A year later the ambassadors of Pergamum and Rhodes were more kindly received. The Roman people certainly were not in a belligerent mood, but the hysteria resulting from the long war against Hannibal had not yet subsided and nervous Romans were quick to see new menaces from abroad. A few listened with fear and trembling when the Greek ambassadors absurdly charged that the alliance of Philip with Antiochus was aimed primarily at Rome. These Romans were only a small fraction of the population, however, and when a declaration of war was proposed to the *comitia centuriata* in March, 200, it was rejected almost unanimously. The Roman people did not want war.

The envoys found better friends in the senate. Many senators were educated men who sincerely and idealistically believed that Rome should defend the liberty of Greece against Philip. More important than they, however, was a senatorial clique composed of men of quite a different kidney, chief of whom was P. Sulpicius Galba. A member of the Claudian faction, Galba had been consul in 211, and for five years had served as proconsul in Illyria, where he fought with more brutality than skill. He was amassing a huge fortune from booty when he was replaced by one of Scipio's friends, and peace was made a little later (206). The postwar attacks upon Scipio gave Galba an opportunity for revenge. He won a second consulship in 200, and again obtained Illyria as his province. It was he who asked the *comitia* to declare war against Philip.

When Galba's request for war was refused, he found other means of achieving his end. A committee of three senators (whose leader, Claudius Nero, also was a member of the Claudian faction) was sent to Greece, ostensibly to investigate the situation and attempt appeasement. Actually they bore a document forbidding Philip to attack any Greek city. From the legal point of view the Romans had not a leg to stand upon, but the commissioners showed the document to various Greek politicians, encouraging them in their anti-Macedonian activities. The Aetolians were already exploiting a petty quarrel to goad Athens into war with Philip, and the Roman committee, arriving early in the summer of 200, further encouraged the Athenians to attack him. Philip's troops invaded Attica and the Romans presented their ultimatum to the Macedonian commander. Philip saw fit to ignore Rome's peremptory demands, continued with his military operations against Greek cities in Asia Minor and Greece, and even ordered the ravaging of Attica. Of course such insolence could not go unpunished. The *comitia* was again assembled in July, 200, and war was declared upon Philip. A small group of bellicose senators thus maneuvered the Roman people into a war which had little justification and which the people did not want.

Within a few weeks Galba landed an army in Illyria. The season was too far advanced for extensive fighting, but in 199 he crossed the mountains and invaded Macedonia. Here he fought several battles, none of which could be called important. Galba induced the Aetolians to declare war on Philip in September, but he got no help from the other Greeks, who remembered his brutality and greed during the first war. As winter approached Galba retired to Illyria whence he was recalled to Rome when his soldiers, who had not wanted the war in the first place, started a serious mutiny.

Flamininus and the Peace

Meantime, Titus Quinctius Flamininus[2] had been elected consul for 198, and early in the spring of that year he took command of the troops in Illyria. Flamininus was now the leader of the Fabian faction, the old dictator (who was his kinsman by marriage) having died in 203. He had shown high military ability when fighting under Marcellus, and his Fabian friends hoped that victory over the Greeks would give him a reputation greater than Scipio's. He shared the Fabian opposition to territorial expansion beyond Italy, but at the same time he was sincerely philhellenic. He spoke Greek fluently, and he had a knowledge and appreciation of Greek culture; he wished the Greeks well and desired to be well thought of by them; he wanted to see Greece "free" but, like most Roman philhellenists, he was very badly informed about the sordid realities of Greek politics. He was, perhaps, a mild foretaste of Woodrow Wilson.

When Flamininus arrived in Illyria to assume command of the troops there, he found that Philip had taken advantage of the mutiny of Galba's soldiers to occupy part of the Roman territory. Attacking Philip's rear, he won an important battle on the Aoüs River (June, 198), massacring 2000 men and driving the rest of the Macedonians back into their own country. At the same time his brother, Lucius Flamininus, persuaded the Achaeans, the Boeotians,

---

[2] This Titus Flamininus must not be confused with Gaius Flaminius, the agrarian reformer, who was consul in 223 and 217, who was killed at Trasimene, and whose son was consul in 187.

and the Spartans to join him, thus dragging nearly all Greece into
the war. Fighting was resumed in the following spring, and Philip
was decisively defeated at Cynoscephalae (June, 197). An armistice was granted and general peace terms drawn up. Philip accepted them at once and the Roman senate ratified them late in the
year.

Flamininus's peace terms declared that all Greeks were to be free,
but they carried the implication that Rome had the right to organize Greece as she saw fit in order to assure this freedom. A committee of ten men was sent to Greece by the senate to arrange the
details of reorganization. By the final treaty Philip was excluded
from Greece, disarmed, and forced to pay an indemnity of 1000
talents to Rome (one-half at once, the rest in ten annual installments); his Greek territories were forfeited to Rome, who would
set up free governments for them; and all Greece was to be free.
The last stages of the negotiations, during which a new map of
Greece was drawn, witnessed heated recriminations, especially from
the Aetolians who coveted extensive territories not awarded to
them.

The treaty at last was completed, and in the summer of 196
Flamininus staged a celebrated scene at the Isthmian games in
Corinth. Just as the races were to start, a trumpeter sounded
for silence and a herald read the peace terms: "The Roman senate
and T. Quinctius [Flamininus], the proconsul, having conquered
King Philip and the Macedonians, leave [the various Greek states]
free, without garrisons, liable to no tribute, and subject to their
own laws." We are told that the excitement following this announce-
ment was so great that no one took any further interest in the athletes. The Greeks were beside themselves with joy, and in their desire to thank Flamininus personally they almost tore the poor man
to pieces.

The task of liberating Greece was not yet complete, however, for
Nabis of Sparta was still preaching social revolution. This able and
energetic man had become King of Sparta in 206 and had resumed
the program of social reform begun by Cleomenes twenty years
before. Debts were canceled, land was redistributed, helots were
enfranchised, the rich were dispossessed. Nabis hoped to rebuild

Spartan power throughout the peninsula by arousing the enthusiasm of the discontented classes everywhere, and he actually occupied a few territories before the Romans arrived in 200. Flamininus opposed such subversive activity. He knew little or nothing of the condition of the poor in Greece; his sympathies were with the educated upper classes; and the Achaeans, Sparta's next-door neighbors and her worst enemies, completed the persuasion of the Roman proconsul. Flamininus went to war with Sparta soon after the celebration at Corinth, charging that Nabis held and refused to liberate Argos. It did not take long to defeat Sparta and free Argos (195), although Nabis's career did not end until he was assassinated by the Aetolians in 192.

The Roman senate had meantime ordered Flamininus home. He had spent the winter of 195–94 establishing pro-Roman and aristocratic governments in various Greek cities, and late in 194 the Romans withdrew. On his return to Rome, Flamininus celebrated a magnificent triumph, exhibiting loot valued at 1200 talents. He had made what he considered a final settlement of Greek affairs, guaranteeing the liberties of all, and he had voluntarily withdrawn when his task was finished. Thereafter Rome insisted that the Greek states accept Flamininus's treaty as the basis of their policies.

Rome and Antiochus III

If the Romans believed that peace had come at last, they were quickly undeceived. The East was still to be pacified. Antiochus III of Syria was still dreaming of reviving Alexander's world empire by victorious wars; and political conditions at Rome would not permit neutrality in any conflict that might arise, even in distant Asia. Though Antiochus had signed a treaty of alliance with Philip V of Macedon in 203, he had neglected to send aid when the Romans attacked his ally a few years later. He had good reason for this inaction, for he had meantime discovered that Philip looked upon the alliance only as a means of obtaining territories in Asia Minor to which Antiochus felt the Seleucids had prior claim. Moreover, his major interest at the moment was Egypt, where chaotic conditions invited intervention.

When Ptolemy IV of Egypt died in 203, a court cabal hushed up the news for several weeks while intriguers murdered his wife and forged a will making themselves regents for the six-year-old Ptolemy V, who was then proclaimed king. As soon as the plot was discovered, the intriguers were lynched. For several years thereafter, incompetent ministers followed one another, and there were frequent native uprisings in various parts of the country. The moment seemed opportune for Antiochus to seize Coele-Syria. (Originally this "Hollow Syria" had been the valley between the Lebanon and Anti-Lebanon mountain ranges in Syria, but by this time the name was loosely applied to a larger area, including southern Syria, northern Palestine, and Damascus.) Antiochus defeated the Egyptian army decisively at Panium, in northern Palestine near the headwaters of the Jordan River (200). He thereby obtained all Palestine and Phoenicia, and Egypt permanently lost territories which she had held for more than a century. Ptolemy V was officially crowned King of Egypt in 197, and four years later he was married to Cleopatra, daughter of Antiochus (193). As Cleopatra remained under her father's tutelage, and dominated her young and weak-willed husband, Antiochus virtually annexed Egypt without going to the trouble and expense of invading it.

Long before he thus completed his Egyptian designs, Antiochus had begun the reoccupation of territories in Asia Minor and Thrace once held by his ancestor, Seleucus I. Soon after the defeat of Philip at Cynoscephalae (197), Antiochus appeared in Asia Minor and began occupying the cities held by Egypt. He established his headquarters at Ephesus, which the Ptolemies had held for half a century and which he apparently took without a fight. Two events then complicated the situation. Attalus of Pergamum died late in 197 and was succeeded by his son Eumenes II. The new king was justifiably afraid of Antiochus, whose schemes included the recapture of Pergamum, once held by Seleucus I. Profiting by his father's successes at Rome in 200, Eumenes decided to seek aid in that quarter, as he continued to do frequently and with greater or less success throughout his long reign of thirty-seven years (197–160). He never let Rome forget the East, even for a moment.

A second complication arose from the arrival of Hannibal at

Ephesus in 195. After his defeat at Zama in 202, the Carthaginian general continued to serve his country, devoting his great energy and skill to reconstruction. His political opponents—defeatists anxious to avoid further trouble by acceding to all Rome's demands —feared lest his successes excite Rome's suspicions and bring reprisals. They therefore sought to placate Rome by complaining of Hannibal's activities, and their reports became so alarming that in 195 a Roman commission was sent to Carthage to investigate the matter. Realizing his personal danger, Hannibal slipped out of the city, escaped to Tyre, and eventually reached Antiochus at Ephesus. He at once began urging the Seleucid king to wage war on Rome, promising that with only a little aid he could soon bring his old enemy to her knees. Antiochus was not particularly interested in Roman adventures, but Hannibal's nagging probably helped turn him against the Republic.

By this time Flamininus had withdrawn his legions from Greece and things were not going at all well in that country. Dissatisfaction was aroused especially by the Aetolians, who had hoped to inherit Philip's supremacy. When they found themselves deprived of that glory, they began complaining loudly of Roman tyranny. Moreover, the Roman settlement had favored the Achaean League and the aristocrats in Greece, which turned popular leaders against Rome. The Aetolians had long since developed great skill at stirring up the masses, and the Roman attack upon Nabis at Sparta was a godsend for their propaganda. At this crucial moment, when Greeks everywhere were anxiously seeking someone to help them throw off the Roman settlement, the Aetolians opened negotiations with Antiochus, inviting him to "free Greece and arbitrate between themselves and the Romans."

Before the Second Macedonian War even the ruling classes at Rome had had only the vaguest notions about Greek and oriental politics. Their fear of the East was largely fear of the unknown. But they understood enough to be careful about maintaining good relations with Antiochus as long as they were hostile to Philip. The three Roman commissioners, who were sent to Greece and who precipitated war with Philip in 200, proceeded to Antioch, where their interviews with the king were most friendly. However, the Romans professed an ancient friendship with Egypt, as Ptolemy II had been the first of Hellenistic monarchs to recognize their growing importance and had made a treaty with them in 273, soon after their defeat of Pyrrhus. After Cynoscephalae the Romans took a firmer stand and expressed displeasure at Antiochus's treatment of their Egyptian friends. But when they sent envoys to protest (196), warning the Seleucid to keep out of Europe and respect the liberties of the Asiatic Greeks, Antiochus retorted that if the Romans would leave him alone he would gladly reciprocate by leaving them alone. He also remarked that he was merely taking back what was rightfully his, suggested that they prove their philhellenism by "freeing" the Greeks in Syracuse, and declared that he was on the friendliest terms with Egypt and even thinking of letting the king of that country marry his daughter Cleopatra. He then proceeded with his original plan of invading Thrace, and from that moment relations between the two powers grew steadily worse.

Party politics at Rome also encouraged a renewal of hostilities, for the Scipionic and Fabian factions were rather evenly balanced and each now regarded war as a means of gaining prestige and votes at the expense of the other. While Scipio's opponents had succeeded in electing Flamininus consul for 198, two members of the Scipionic faction were chosen consuls for the next year, though one consul from each faction was elected for 196. The Scipionic consuls for 197 each tried in vain to obtain Flamininus's command in Macedon. The elections for 196 were held before the victory at Cynoscephalae, but as soon as the rival consuls took office each demanded further hostilities, alleging that Philip had not yet been punished sufficiently, and each hoping to get the command himself. Two tribunes succeeded in having the matter referred to the *comitia,* which voted unanimously for peace, and Flamininus retained his command.

Cynoscephalae brought such prestige to Flamininus and his faction that two Fabian consuls were elected for 195, one of whom, M. Porcius Cato, later became quite famous. These consuls replied to Scipio's attack upon Flamininus by charging that Scipio Africanus had been too gentle with Carthage. They then sent the committee of investigation that caused Hannibal's flight to Antiochus. The great Africanus was forced to seek vindication by standing for a second term. He was elected consul for 194, along with the son of his father's colleague in 218, Sempronius Longus. Scipio resumed the attacks upon Flamininus, severely criticizing his settlement in Greece, predicting war with Antiochus, and demanding the command of the armies still in Greece. The senate refused him the command and ordered Flamininus to bring his army back to Italy at once. Scipio obtained the election of two friends to the consulship for 193, but a year later, after Flamininus had celebrated his victory over Philip magnificently in Rome, Scipio lost a bitterly contested election in which his cousin Scipio Nasica (who was titular head of the family) and his closest friend, C. Laelius, were defeated by Lucius Flamininus (Titus's brother) and a certain Gnaeus Domitius. From that moment Scipio became an out-and-out warmonger. As Antiochus had by this time allied himself with the Aetolians, it was obvious that he would soon overthrow Flamininus's settlement in Greece unless he were checked by Rome. The Fabian party thus came to support a war in defense of its hero's achievements in Greece. Titus Flamininus was sent to Greece by the senate to seek allies in the impending war. Scipio's cousin, Nasica, and his friend, Acilius Glabrio, were elected consuls for 191. Before they took office, however, Antiochus had invaded Thrace and war between Syria and Rome had begun.[3]

---

[3] Perhaps the complicated political situation at Rome during these troubled years will be clarified by the following list of consuls with their political factions. (C) Claudian; (F) Fabian; (S) Scipionic.

202	Ti. Claudius Nero (C)	M. Servilius Pulex (S)	Zama
201	Gn. Cornelius Lentulus (S)	P. Aelius Paetus (S)	Peace
200	P. Sulpicius Galba (C)	C. Aurelius Cotta (S)	2 Maced. War
199	L. Cornelius Lentulus (S)	P. Villius Trappulus (S)	
198	T. Quinctius Flamininus (F)	Sex. Aelius Paetus (S)	
197	C. Cornelius Cathegus (S)	Q. Minucius Rufus (S)	Cynoscephalae
196	L. Furius Purpureo (S)	M. Claudius Marcellus (F)	
195	M. Porcius Cato (F)	L. Valerius Flaccus (F)	Hannibal flees
194	P. C. Scipio Africanus (S)	Ti. Sempronius Longus (S)	R.s leave Greece
193	L. Cornelius Merula (S)	Q. Minucius Thermus (S)	Flam.'s triumph
192	L. Quinctius Flamininus (F)	Gn. Domitius Ahenobarbus (F)	War with Ant.
191	P. C. Scipio Nasica (S)	M. Acilius Glabrio (S)	Thermopylae
190	L. C. Scipio Asiaticus (S)	C. Laelius (S)	
189	Gn. Manlius Vulso (F)	M. Fulvius Nobilior (C)	Magnesia
188	C. Livius Salinator (S)	M. Valerius Messalla (F)	

Victory over Antiochus

The military operations of the war with Antiochus are of minor significance. Most Greek states decided not to choose sides until they saw who would be victorious, but Philip had learned not to fight Rome, and the Aetolians were definitely committed to Antiochus. There were only minor skirmishes at first, but in the following year (191) Antiochus attempted an invasion of Greece. The consul Acilius Glabrio won an important victory over him at Thermopylae and Antiochus fled to Ephesus, leaving his troops to take care of themselves.

Meantime, Lucius Scipio (brother of Africanus) had been elected consul for 190, with Laelius as his colleague. Since Africanus had been consul in 194, he was ineligible for re-election in 190, and Lucius (who was notoriously incompetent) was sent to Greece on the understanding that he would take his famous brother along as legate and allow him to exercise actual command. The two Scipios landed in Illyria in March, 190, and spent the next several months in Greece. Antiochus had by this time put Hannibal, the greatest general of his age, in command of a fleet; but Hannibal was no admiral and in August he was badly defeated by the Rhodians. A few weeks later the rest of Antiochus's fleet was destroyed by the Romans.

Rome then controlled the Aegean and the Scipios crossed to Asia Minor. With the support of Eumenes of Pergamum they advanced upon Antiochus at Ephesus and defeated him in a great battle fought at Magnesia, probably early in January, 189. The next summer was spent in minor operations. The elections for this year, held before the battle at Magnesia, had resulted in another political defeat for the Scipios. One of the new consuls, M. Fulvius Nobilior, a member of the Claudian faction, was sent to pacify the Aetolians; the other, a Fabian named Gnaeus Manlius Vulso, joined the army in Asia and spent the summer of 189 in a campaign against the Galatians by which he extended Roman power over most of Asia Minor west of the Taurus Mountains.

Again there was a peace to be made, and again Roman ignorance of the East proved a great misfortune. Preliminary negotiations were conducted at Rome. The city was filled with smooth-tongued Greek propagandists, mostly from Pergamum and Rhodes, who dragged out discussions while trying to get various concessions for themselves. The final negotiations were held in 188 at Apamea in Syria, where Antiochus accepted his fate. He surrendered all Asia Minor west of the Taurus Mountains and the Halys River to the Romans, but he kept Cilicia, which he had recently taken from Ptolemy; he was assessed an indemnity of 15,000 talents, 3000 to be paid at once and the rest in ten annual installments; and he agreed to send twenty hostages to Rome, among them his second son, later known as Antiochus IV. Rome handed the greater part of Asia Minor over to Pergamum, though her sovereignty over the more distant regions was only nominal. Caria and Lycia, at the southwestern tip of the peninsula, went to Rhodes, and several Greek cities in Ionia and along the Hellespont were declared free. Greece, too, required a new settlement. Aetolia was punished for inciting and aiding Antiochus by loss of territory and an indemnity of 600 talents; Philip was rewarded for his loyalty to Rome by the remission of the unpaid balance of his indemnity of 196. He spent his last years as an embittered though moderately loyal ally of Rome, trying to rebuild his country after the losses caused by his disastrous wars. He died a broken old man in 179.

Antiochus III was assassinated in 187, while robbing a Babylonian temple. After Magnesia, Hannibal fled to Bithynia on the Black Sea; the Romans sent a committee headed by Flamininus to demand his surrender; and as further flight was impossible, the great Carthaginian committed suicide in 183, aged sixty-three years. Flamininus retired to private life. Though Lucius Scipio had done little, he was allowed to call himself Scipio Asiaticus. His brother Scipio Africanus returned home in great glory, but within a short time his political enemies at Rome drove him from power and he spent his last years in virtual exile, grumbling about human ingratitude. He too died in 183, and with him ended the days of the giants who raised Rome to first place among world powers.

Note

Tenney Frank

Tenney Frank (1876–1939) was born of Swedish parents on a Kansas farm. After teaching for a few years at Bryn Mawr, he became Professor of Latin at the Johns Hopkins University, and there he remained until his death twenty years later. Though his early training was as a philologist, and he wrote frequently on subjects connected with Latin literature, his primary interest lay in the history of the Roman Republic. He first attracted attention with a volume entitled *Roman Imperialism* (1914), in which he argued strongly against the then prevailing view that Rome's territorial expansion was caused by the militaristic aggressiveness and mercantilistic economic policies of her governing class. Frank preferred to believe that Rome's early wars were primarily defensive and that the wars in Greece were to be explained largely by Roman philhellenism and by what he called "sentimental politics." In a larger way he always emphasized the idealistic and democratic forces in Roman life. Filled with such ideas, he became an enthusiastic supporter of Woodrow Wilson's policies during and after World War I, and his rather hastily written *History of Rome* (1923) depicts all Roman history from that point of view. Frank's most valuable work is the *Economic Survey of Ancient Rome* (5 vols., 1933–40) to which he devoted the later part of his life. Here are assembled the principal ancient texts dealing with the subject, both in the original Latin or Greek and in translation, while a brief narrative connects and supplements these sources. The first and fifth volumes, dealing respectively with Italy under the Republic and under the Empire, are the work of Professor Frank himself; the intervening volumes, dealing with the various provincial areas from the time of their incorporation into the Roman Empire, were prepared by several American and European scholars.

V The New Imperialism

ROME THUS STUMBLED INTO EMPIRE AND INADVERTENTLY became the most powerful state in the Mediterranean world. No one foresaw or desired such a consummation in 338, when Rome absorbed the Latin League; or in 264, when she first went to war with Carthage; or in 218, when she threw down the gauntlet to Hannibal; or even in 200, when she intervened in Greece, barely ten years before Magnesia completed a century and a half of Roman expansion. Since Roman statesmen had not planned or foreseen world conquest, they were bewildered by their sudden grandeur and uncertain as to future policy. A few followed the line of least resistance, simply adopting the views and ambitions of the Hellenistic kings. They declared that Rome should assume her place as one of the Hellenistic states and perhaps even establish world dominion after the style of Alexander. Thus Scipio Africanus went about boasting that he had conquered the world, and his admirers made him the hero of legends comparable to those of the Alexander romance. An obscure Roman annalist named Aemilius Sura—probably a freedman attached to the powerful and imperialistic Aemilii—put forward even greater claims for Rome shortly after Magnesia. He pictured her as one of the world's great empires, succeeding the Assyrians, the Medes, the Persians, and the Macedonians; and he added an old oriental prophecy to the effect that the fifth empire in this series (Rome) would include the whole world and last forever. A few enthusiasts thus proclaimed Rome's universality and eternity.

Not many Romans shared such vast ambitions, however, for the long wars had left Italy exhausted, and most Romans were more eager to rehabilitate their own country than they were to rule the world. They opposed new adventures, but they were to learn shortly that Rome could not return to her early isolation. She was a Mediterranean power now, whether they liked it or not. The sole question was how she should use her power, and to this question there was no ready-made answer. Only after long experimentation did Rome work out her program for maintaining world peace with treaties of alliance supplemented by force of arms.

The Greeks too were pondering world problems during the twenty years that followed Magnesia. Not being endowed with the gift of prophecy, they failed to realize that the days of their hegemony were numbered, yet they recognized the fact that the new conditions made Greek solidarity more imperative than ever. They therefore strove to assure themselves of continued leadership by the close union and co-operation of all who shared Greek culture, and they developed a federal and cultural imperialism to supplement the military imperialism of Alexander and his successors. At this time too, the Jews, along with other Orientals perhaps, were dreaming of still a different form of imperialism by which the whole world would be united by the worship of one God. These various types of imperialism—military, federal, cultural, and religious—eventually blended into one, and each had its share in advancing Rome's dominion and in establishing the unity of the ancient world.

The Economic Consequences of the Wars

The long war against Hannibal had borne heavily upon the peasants of Italy. The Punic armies, marching up and down the peninsula for many years, had lived off the land. The country was denuded of cattle, crops were carried off or destroyed, vines and trees were uprooted, fields were overgrown and had to be cleared anew, walls were overthrown, buildings were burned. Hannibal boasted that he had destroyed four hundred towns. The civilizing labor of many years was thus lost. The old men, women, and children, who had kept agriculture going during the war, possessed neither the skill nor the physical strength to rebuild the destroyed farms and villages. Even after Hannibal had left Italy, reconstruction could not proceed apace for thousands of men were soon recalled to the colors for the wars in Greece. Moreover, many men never returned to their farms. Some of course were casualties: those lost in the first terrible years had by this time been replaced by a new generation, but losses continued and the wars in Greece took a further toll of lives. Others failed to return for different reasons: some volunteered for service in the armies of occupation in Sardinia and Spain; some were attracted by the opportunities or pleasures they had noted in Rome or other large cities; and others, appalled at the difficulty of rebuilding their devastated farms, simply gave up and took what they could find elsewhere. Rural Italy lacked the man power to rebuild along the old lines.

Reconstruction also required greater financial capital than the peasants possessed. They and their families had been forced into debt during the wars, and now they could not repay what they owed. At a time when they needed ready money to build new houses, buy cattle, and set out orchards and vineyards, they found that they could borrow no more and were even forced to sell what they had in order to pay off old debts. The Roman peasant who had conquered the world then sadly discovered that while doing so he had lost his farm and everything he possessed.

Meantime, other classes of society had been enriched by the wars. Some got their money by profiteering or by selling goods to the army at exorbitant prices; others made fortunes from booty. The old families of the aristocracy usually did very well by themselves, but Rome also acquired a large crop of parvenus. Men with new wealth to invest bought up the farms of ruined peasants at trifling prices. The government, which had borrowed heavily during the wars and now could not pay its obligations, satisfied its creditors by giving them large tracts of the public lands. Sometimes, too, the aristocrats simply appropriated public land and used their political influence to keep what they took. These new landlords rebuilt and improved the farms, which they then rented to tenants—sometimes, no doubt, to the former owners—or, more commonly, entrusted to managers. The agricultural methods used on these estates may be learned from Cato's book *De agri cultura* which was written, probably during the

170's, for the instruction of rich men who knew nothing of farming but wished to check up on their managers. Cato spoke especially of olive orchards and vineyards, which averaged 150 and 60 acres in size respectively. Each farm had a manager and twelve to fifteen workers, most of whom were slaves. Rich men were also eager to secure pastureland, which they filled with cattle and slave herdsmen. Roman agriculture had become capitalistic.

Slavery played an increasingly important part in the agricultural life of Italy after the Second Punic War. Romans had of course long been familiar with this institution, but during the fourth century they had curbed it by legislation: Roman citizens might not be enslaved for debt or other cause, and the emancipation of slaves was encouraged. In the third century, however, slavery revived as prisoners of war provided an abundant supply of captives. Greek slaves were brought from southern Italy, thousands of Sardinians were sold, and after Zama slaves from Africa filled the Roman markets. Greek slaves of the better sort were employed as house servants and tutors for children; they were not treated badly, and emancipation after a few years of servitude became a common incentive to fidelity. But the field hands led wretched lives. They worked under the lash on chain gangs during the day, and at night they were locked in underground prisons. This agricultural slavery was encouraged by the fact that slaves, unlike free men, were not liable to military service, which assured owners of their labor at all times. During the second century, therefore, an ever increasing part of the agricultural labor of Italy was performed by slaves from conquered countries. As these slaves replaced the free peasants who had recently conquered them in arms, many a Roman veteran must have asked himself who had won the recent wars after all.

Italian industry and commerce advanced rapidly at this time, though such progress was not usually the result of the efforts of Romans, who in general were not skillful businessmen. Such matters were left largely to south Italians and Greeks until Campania and the district around Naples became the richest industrial section of Italy. At Rome, trade was conducted largely by foreigners and freedmen. Occasionally, an ambitious Roman aristocrat, unable to resist the lure of the profits to be derived from trade, set up one of his former slaves in business and pocketed a lion's share of the profits, but in general the old-fashioned Romans acquired their wealth in other ways.

The economic and political developments of this period promoted the interests of the social class known as the equestrians. These men were well-to-do citizens of nonsenatorial families whom the censors listed in the first eighteen centuries. During the wars many of them had prospered by provisioning the armies, and afterward they performed other useful services for the state. The old Roman system did not provide a permanent staff of officials, or bureaucracy, to look after the details of government. When special work by civilians was required, the censors let public contracts to private individuals called *publicani*. After the wars these publicans often took contracts to build roads, to erect public buildings, to operate government enterprises such as the silver mines in Spain, and eventually even to collect taxes in the provinces. These undertakings required the contractors to have working capital in amounts such as few Romans possessed or cared to risk in such ventures. Joint-stock companies were therefore organized, whose shareholders usually were equestrians. Not all equestrians engaged in such enterprises, of course, but the publicans were usually the richest and most aggressive members of the equestrian class. As time went on, they sought political power. They performed so many services for the state that it could no longer get along without them, and they used their position to dictate government policies. They lent money to nobles through whom they subsequently put pressure upon high officials, and they even aspired to the high offices once reserved for senatorial aristocrats.

Roman Politics After the Wars

These social upheavals exercised a profound influence upon Rome's political life. Though the various factions of the old aristocracy continued their quarrels with greater vehemence than ever, they gradually learned that the basis of their political power was changing and that they must adopt new methods. Formerly they had dominated elections through their clients; but for more than a century clientage had been declining, and the wars dealt it a body blow. The thousands of peasants who had left their homes no longer felt any obligation to patrons from whom they received no benefits, and they no longer voted as these patrons suggested. Political leaders therefore worked up new clienteles as best they could, promising their followers what they thought expedient or necessary. The highly discontented peasants were willing to listen to anyone who promised them a change of fortune. The Fabian faction, depending largely upon its rural clients, was the first to disintegrate. The Scipios suffered greatly from the attacks of their rivals, though eventually they reorganized their party and regained leadership. The Claudii and Fulvii, on the other hand, were skillful at exploiting the new conditions, and for a few years they prospered accordingly. And at times it seemed that wholly new factions, led by men not members of the aristocracy at all, might shoulder the patricians to one side. The two decades following Magnesia thus became an exciting and crucial period in Roman political history, when men of all parties were trying to adjust their policies to the new world created by the wars.

Cato Attacks the Scipios

Marcus Porcius Cato was conspicuous among Roman politicians of the post-war period. Born in 234 to an independent landowner of the plebeian class, Cato spent his childhood on his father's modest farm. He became an admirer of Fabius, under whom he served in the war against Hannibal, and he began his lifelong quarrel with the Scipios by publicly criticizing their preparations for the African campaign in 205. Meantime, he had attached himself to L. Valerius Flaccus, an aristocrat of the Fabian faction, who was thereafter his political patron: Valerius and Cato served together as consuls in 195 and as censors in 184. After his consulship Cato went to Spain as governor, intensifying his quarrel with the Scipios, who looked upon that province as their private bailiwick. In 192 Cato accompanied his friend Flamininus to Greece, where he conducted propaganda against Antiochus III. A year later he played an important part, perhaps a decisive part, in the battle at Thermopylae, but the glory of that victory went to Scipio's friend Glabrio. These experiences greatly embittered Cato against the Scipios. Moreover, he had seen that all Greece would have gone over to Antiochus, had he won at Thermopylae. In view of Flamininus's recent and idealistic peace settlement with the Greeks, such perfidy seemed outrageous. Cato therefore spent many years hating the Scipios, pouring out his contempt upon Greeks and philhellenic Romans, opposing further imperialistic adventures, and advocating a return to the good old ways. His rugged force of character, his patent honesty, his frugality, his austerity and puritanism, his cantankerousness, his biting wit and oratorical skill, all showed him to be a true Roman of the old school and compensated for the fact that he was a "new man"—that is, one not belonging to the old senatorial aristocracy. His influence was not confined to political life but extended to matters of literature and religion, and his views on economic matters coincided with those of other leaders in his social class.

The war against Antiochus was not yet won when Scipio's enemies resumed their attacks upon him. As early as 190 Cato accused Glabrio, then a candidate for the censorship, of stealing booty at Thermopylae. The scandal was so great that Glabrio was forced to drop his candidacy and abandon his political career; two Fabians (Flamininus and Marcellus) were then elected to the office. After several similar moves against lesser persons of the Scipionic faction, and a few counteraccusations by the Scipios (one against Cato himself), the opposition was ready in 187 to attack the two great leaders. Two tribunes demanded that Lucius Scipio give an account of five hundred talents paid him by Antiochus as part of the indemnity. Knowing that the attack was really aimed at himself, Africanus came to his brother's defense: taking the account books to the senate, he publicly and contemptuously tore them to pieces before they could be examined. This aristocratic hauteur convinced many persons that the books had not been in perfect order, and Africanus himself was attacked: on the day set for his trial he loftily reminded the crowd, in a theatrical manner, that that day was the anniversary of Zama. After three years of uproar, Cato was elected censor for 184 and his friends convicted Lucius Scipio, imposing a heavy fine and prison sentence. Scipio was saved from jail, however, by a tribune who interposed his veto out of regard for the family's services to Rome. Such intervention could not save Africanus's reputation, and he withdrew from Rome to die an embittered old man.

Fulvian Leadership

Cato had been the spearhead of the attack upon the Scipios, yet after his censorship in 184 we hear little about him for several years. Leadership at Rome fell instead to the Claudian-Fulvian faction, which had likewise taken a prominent part in the anti-Scipionic agitation of 185 and 184, when the two brothers Appius and Publius Claudius Pulcher were consuls in turn. This faction was dominated by M. Fulvius Nobilior, who had conquered the Aetolians during his consulship in 189 and who developed great finesse in managing elections. The fall of the Scipios in 184 was followed by three or four years of rapid flux, with members of all the factions holding high offices, until about 180 when Nobilior brought the Claudian-Fulvian party into power. He became censor in 179 and dominated Roman politics until his death four or five years later. Other members of the Fulvian and Claudian families continued in power, as well as two brothers named Scaevola, and a Tiberius Gracchus. The continuity of the faction is shown by the fact that the fathers (or, in the case of Gracchus, the uncle) of these men had been consul and praetors together in the crucial year 215, and that their sons worked together in the equally crucial period beginning in 133 (see the genealogical tables on p. 251 and p. 254).

The Claudian-Fulvian faction won its popularity largely by exploiting the distress of the peasantry. The Scipios had given this problem little attention during the 190's, though Africanus distributed Campanian lands as bonuses to his veterans. During his consulship in 194 he established a few colonies in southern Italy—eight military colonies, intended as a defense against Antiochus, and two agricultural colonies—but they failed to relieve conditions in central Italy. Scipio's enemies then decided to eclipse his efforts by founding colonies in Cisalpine Gaul, thus aiding the Italian peasants who were being dispossessed to make room for the slaves of Scipio's friends. When the colonies at Cremona and Placentia complained of lack of men, six thousand settlers were sent to reinforce them in 190, and Bononia (Bologna) was founded one year later. In each case the leader of the colony was Cato's patron, L. Valerius Flaccus. The new colonial movement was greatly stimulated when Gaius Flaminius, son of the censor of 220, became consul in 187. Like his father, Flaminius was associated with the Fulvii. He continued his father's program of settling the north, and he built the New Flaminian Way (from Rome to Bononia) to facilitate migration thither. Flaminius's colleague was M. Aemilius Lepidus, who had managed to get himself elected as patrician consul though he was a member of the Scipionic faction, hostile to both Flaminius and the Fulvii. He could not allow himself to be outshone in so popular a program and therefore built the Aemilian Way through Cisalpine Gaul from Ariminum through Bononia to Placentia. His efforts were in vain, however, for the Claudian-Fulvian faction had by this time won the allegiance of the discontented peasants, with whose votes they completed the overthrow of the Scipios in 184.

The colonization of Cisalpine Gaul continued rapidly during the next several years. Nine large agricultural colonies were founded there between 184 and 177, providing homes for tens of thousands of settlers. When this expansion aroused the Gauls and Ligurians, the consul Gaius Claudius defeated them in 175, boasting afterward that "by his valor and good fortune he had conquered lands that could be divided among many thousands of settlers." In the following year Q. Fulvius, as censor, opened large districts in the Po Valley to individual settlers. Not only did this program relieve conditions in lower Italy and provide the Fulvii with a large political following: it also Latinized the North. Thereafter the population of the Po Valley resembled that of the old Italy more closely than did the slave-descended inhabitants of the South.

Rome under the Fulvii was less successful in dealing with her Latin and Italian allies. Shortly after Cannae, someone had proposed that the senate admit representatives from these allies to its membership, making Italy a federal republic. By rejecting this proposal the senate committed itself to the policy of dominating the allies. Military exigencies, of course, required a single command in wartime, and Romans got into the habit of ordering their allies about. Unfaithful allies were punished with great severity: Capua was destroyed, its citizens dispersed, and their fields confiscated; and 30,-000 inhabitants of Tarentum were sold into slavery. The allies were sometimes forced to provide troops far in excess of their just share, and Roman generals often discriminated against them when distributing whatever profits the wars had brought. Indemnities and the profits from such sources as the Spanish silver mines went wholly to the treasury at Rome, and Roman soldiers often received larger shares of booty than the allies who fought beside them. The power of officers to punish Roman soldiers was strictly limited by law, but they might punish Latins and Italians as they saw fit.

The Claudians and Fulvians who were so solicitous about the welfare of Roman peasants (who had the right to vote) were especially highhanded toward the allies who had no votes. Q. Fulvius was severely criticized for his violence against the Greeks in southern Italy. G. Claudius gave only half as much booty to allied soldiers as to Romans, in retaliation for which they demonstrated against him during his triumph. Even Tiberius Gracchus, who was the most high-minded and statesmanly of the group, demanded oppressive contributions from the allies for a triumph he celebrated. The new colonies were usually for Roman citizens only, or, if Latins and Italians were admitted, they received smaller allotments than did the Romans. Thousands of Latins had flocked to Rome during the war and the trying postwar years, and had there become Roman citizens; but in 187 and again in 177, during the consulships of Flaminius and G. Claudius, they were ordered to return home because the Latin cities complained that losses in man power made it impossible for them to supply as large contingents of troops as formerly. Such expulsion from Rome violated treaties with the Latins, but the Claudian magistrates insisted upon it, for otherwise they would have had to augment Rome's own military quotas. On the other hand, the Scipios opposed such discrimination, and Cato loudly denounced those who treated the allies as though they were conquered peoples: Claudian-Fulvian highhandedness united even Cato and the Scipios in their protests.

Plebeian Attacks upon the Senate

The Fulvii won a large following among the discontented classes, but even they could not satisfy everyone, and radical agitators outside the faction soon began to use Fulvian methods to obtain honors and offices for themselves. Sometimes these agitators were "new men," and sometimes they were energetic members of the lesser nobility whose ambition was not satisfied with their existing social and political status, but the principal strength of the new faction lay with the equestrians who had prospered during the war and afterward. They were still largely excluded from public office, and even the Fulvii had not cultivated their good will. These new politicians were louder in their appeals to the people than the Fulvii had been, and they vigorously attacked the whole senatorial order. Two plebeian consuls were elected together for the first time in 172, and between 173 and 170 six of the eight consuls and a majority of the praetors elected were "new men."

Typical of the new class of politician was Marcus Popilius Laenas, consul in 173. He was little better than a professional slave-catcher. His name first appears on the records in 180 when he and his brother Gaius were two of the triumvirs who founded Luca. His success as a colonizer led to higher offices, and six years later he was elected consul. In this capacity he provoked an unauthorized war against a friendly Ligurian tribe, in the course of which 3000 Roman soldiers were killed, and he sold his 10,000 captives into slavery. When the senate ordered him to restore these men to liberty, he successfully defied that body, fined the praetor who had criticized him, and repeated his exploit on a smaller scale. The next year two tribunes succeeded in passing a plebiscite against him, but he was saved by his brother Gaius, who followed him as consul. When the senate would not assign Gaius the province he wanted, he refused to transact any public business until threatened with public prosecution, and when he returned from his province at the end of the year he was howled down in the senate. The agitation of these men reached its culmination in 169 when the censors G. Claudius and T. Gracchus were impeached, after complaints by certain equestrians; they es-

caped conviction by only a narrow margin. Had not Rome again
gone to war with Macedon, such disturbances would undoubtedly
have continued with increasing bitterness.

These attacks forced the aristocracy to close its ranks and bury old
feuds. One suspects the hand of Marcus Aemilius Lepidus in much
of this reconciling activity. Grandson of the consul of 232, this remarkable man had entered politics under the aegis of the Scipios.
He held the offices of aedile and praetor in 193 and 191 respectively,
but Nobilior (of the Claudian-Fulvian faction) twice caused him to
be defeated for the consulship, and he did not win that office until
187. Eight years later, in 179, these two political enemies were
elected censors together, and they staged a dramatic reconciliation.
Thereafter Nobilior managed the elections and got his friends
elected to high office, but Lepidus managed the senate, whose membership of course had remained unchanged. Lepidus was chosen
pontifex maximus in 180 and a year later he became *princeps senatus*: holding these two honorable and powerful positions, he dominated the senate until his death in 152. As leader of the senate, he
directed the defense of the aristocracy against the attacks of popular
agitators and healed the divisions by which it was distracted. We
shall presently see that he also had a powerful voice in determining
Rome's foreign policy.

The closing years of the 170's and the early 160's saw a number of
strange but highly important political marriages and adoptions by
members of the Roman aristocracy. As shown by the accompanying
chart, Aemilius Paullus (a distant cousin of Lepidus) allowed his
two eldest sons to be adopted by the childless sons of Fabius Maximus and Scipio Africanus, thus resolving the feud between these
two families. At about the same time Paullus's daughter married
Cato's son—who thus entered the family of his father's old enemy.
The Claudians had no share in these new family alliances; but after
the death of Gaius Claudius, his friend and colleague Tiberius Gracchus married Cornelia, the daughter of Scipio Africanus. Meantime
the Third Macedonian War (171–168) had again upset the Roman
political machine and the new aristocratic coalition was able to gain
control, silencing its plebeian critics.

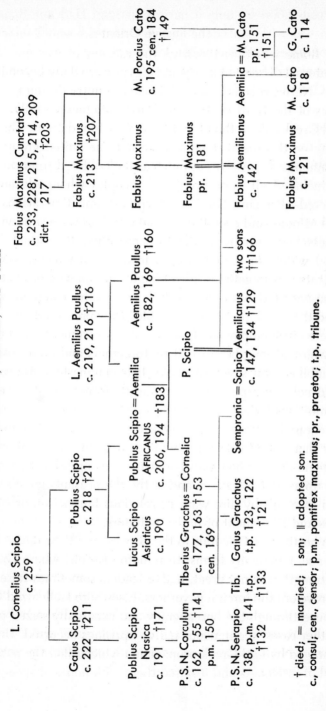

THE SCIPIOS, AEMILII, AND FABII

Fabius Maximus Cunctator
c. 233, 228, 215, 214, 209
dict. 217   †203

Fabius Maximus
c. 213   †207

Fabius Maximus

Fabius Maximus
pr.   ‖181

Fabius Aemilianus
c. 142

Fabius Maximus
c. 121

M. Porcius Cato
c. 195 cen. 184
†149

Aemilia = M. Cato
pr. 151
‖151

G. Cato
c. 114

M. Cato
c. 118

L. Aemilius Paullus
c. 219, 216 †216

Aemilius Paullus
c. 182, 169 †160

two sons
††166

L. Cornelius Scipio
c. 259

Gaius Scipio
c. 222 †211

Publius Scipio
c. 218 †211

Lucius Scipio
Asiaticus
c. 190

Publius Scipio = Aemilia
AFRICANUS
c. 206, 194 †183

P. Scipio

Sempronia = Scipio Aemilianus
c. 147, 134, 129

Publius Scipio
Nasica
c. 191 †171

P.S.N. Corculum
c. 162, 155 †141
p.m. 150

Tiberius Gracchus = Cornelia
c. 177, 163 †153
cen. 169

P.S.N. Serapio
c. 138, p.m. 141 t.p.
†132   †133

Tib.
t.p.

Gaius Gracchus
t.p. 123, 122
†121

† died; = married; | son; ‖ adopted son.
c., consul; cen., censor; p.m., pontifex maximus; pr., praetor; t.p., tribune.

The Restive Orient

While Rome was thus repairing the ravages of war and suffering from internal dissension, Syria and Egypt were daily becoming more restless. Native revolts broke out in each country during the last two decades of the third century, and after Magnesia (189), rebellion rocked Greek rule in the Orient to its very foundations. The peoples who voiced this dissatisfaction were not one united group but differed amongst themselves as much as they differed from the Greeks. They included all those non-Greek peoples whom Alexander had conquered—Persians, Semites, Egyptians, and the various peoples of Asia Minor—and even these racial divisions were subdivided into countless local groups hostile to each other. Individual Orientals differed widely in their attitudes toward the Greeks. The former aristocrats had sometimes been bought, in one way or another, and now co-operated with their Greek rulers; the commercial classes favored the Greek regime under which they prospered; many Orientals were given employment by the new governments; and the peasants, who had long been ruled by foreigners and oppressed by the local nobility, now saw little choice between masters. But sometimes the old nobility aspired to regaining its former prestige; energetic and ambitious Orientals, who had prospered under the new regime and acquired a veneer of Hellenistic culture, thirsted for greater power than the Greeks were willing to grant and, turning against the Greeks under whom they had made such progress, they set themselves up as native leaders; and lastly, the peasants were sometimes driven to revolt by dire want or religious fanaticism, or by the intrigues and incitement of native agitators.

The hostility of Orientals to the Greeks, and their desire for independence, took many forms. In remote districts, where Greek military strength was not great, native leaders sometimes raised armies and drove out the foreign governors. Elsewhere Hellenized Orientals advanced through the bureaucracy and eventually seized power. In still other cases, spontaneous native uprisings occurred. Unrest was encouraged by anti-Greek propaganda which filled the natives with hatred of foreigners and inspired them with hopes of speedy victory under God. Agitators taught men to look back to a glorious past, which they declared superior to anything the Greeks could show, and they foretold a future in which the Orient would again be supreme. The Near East seethed with prophecies of impending doom for the Greeks and a return to the old ways, or, as the prophets usually preferred to say, a return to the rule of God. The constant family feuds and court intrigues which afflicted the Hellenistic empires made it difficult to concentrate upon the suppression of this unrest, and the Greek states were slowly gnawed away by their oriental subjects.

The Seleucid kings began to lose the outlying provinces of their sprawling empire almost as soon as they came into power, and the whole edifice collapsed after Magnesia. The Romans gave most of Asia Minor to Pergamum and Rhodes; Armenia and Atropatene (south of the Caucasus and west of the Caspian Sea) broke away; a native leader made himself king in Elymais (ancient Elam); another set up the nearby kingdom of Characene at the mouth of the Tigris; and the king of Bactria seized much of central Persia. Antiochus's successor retained only Cilicia, a small part of Persia, and most of the Semitic portion of his father's empire. Even these districts were heaving with discontent.

Meantime the Ptolemies had fallen upon evil days and were suffering from the revolts of their subjects. When Antiochus III invaded Palestine in 217, Ptolemy IV armed 20,000 Egyptian natives to fight in the phalanx. These natives acquitted themselves well at the battle of Raphia and contributed to the Egyptian victory; but having defeated the Greeks in the army of Antiochus, they no longer feared and respected the Greeks in Egypt as before. Other factors complicated the situation. An economic decline followed half a century of prosperity; the elaborate system of bureaucratic state socialism began to break down; the loss of Palestine (200) disrupted foreign trade relations and trade routes. Moreover, Greek rule did not extend beyond the First Cataract of the Nile: south of Egypt lay Nubia, whose native rulers often incited Egyptians to revolt. Religion also played its part. The Ptolemies subsidized many Egyptian temples, and the priests repaid such favors with loyalty to the dynasty; but other temples, including those held by the powerful priests of Amon, who had sometimes defied the Pharaohs of old, now became centers of native unrest. When rebels took to rioting they often attacked temples of the former sort while making the latter their headquarters.

A few examples of the anti-Greek propaganda of this period have been preserved. Typical among them is an oracle written in Demotic, the popular language of Ptolemaic Egypt. Though it purports to have been delivered long before Alexander, it actually was composed under Ptolemy IV (221–203). This oracle obscurely sketches the history of Egypt, supposedly as prophecy, from about 360 B.C. down to the time of its actual publication and then runs on into the future, telling of a native ruler to arise in Egypt: "A man of Heracleopolis is he who, after the Aliens [the Persians] and the Ionians [the Greeks], will bear rule. . . . Rejoice over the Ruler which is to be, for he will not forsake the Law." A very similar piece of propaganda is the "Potter's Prophecy," which dates from about the same time. It tells how an inspired potter unrolled the future before one of the ancient Pharaohs, foretelling the coming of the Persians and the Greeks, and at the end prophesying that "the City beside the sea [Alexandria] shall become a place where fishers dry their nets," and that Egypt shall eventually be ruled by a benevolent king coming "from the Sun . . . so that they who are alive and remain shall pray that they who have died may rise again to share the good things." That such prophecies inspired the Egyptian peasants to revolt there can be little doubt.

Native Rebellions

Native uprisings took on a serious character soon after the victory at Raphia (217), especially in Upper Egypt. Here the priests of Amon had always been strong, and foreign aid from Nubia was close at hand. The whole Thebaid threw off the yoke of Alexandria and was governed for twenty years by two successive Nubian kings (206–186). Native rebels were less successful in Lower Egypt, though revolts were frequent. Under Ptolemy V (203–180) the government attempted to appease the rebels by abolishing certain taxes and lightening others, remitting debts owed to the treasury, freeing prisoners, and granting amnesty to rebels. We can read the story on the famous Rosetta Stone (see Vol. I, p. 128, n.) set up in 196, which records the king's concessions, his suppression of a revolt of long standing, his punishment of the "impious" rebels, his gifts to the priests after the revolt had been crushed, and their gratitude. Rebellion soon broke out anew, however, and further attempts were made to establish a native dynasty. The rebels in Upper Egypt were not conquered until 186, and those in the North surrendered two years later. Ptolemy did not long enjoy his triumph, however, for he died in 180, aged twenty-nine years. His queen, Cleopatra I, the daughter of Antiochus III, continued his rule for a few years until she, too, came to an early death in 176. Since her eldest son, Ptolemy VI Philometor, was at that time only seven or eight years old, conduct of the government fell to two regents who brought on the greatest disasters yet suffered by Egypt under the Ptolemies.

These regents, Eulaeus and Lenaeus, were Hellenized Orientals of base origin, who had risen to power under Ptolemy V, and who now governed the kingdom for his son. Eulaeus was an Egyptian eunuch attached to the royal harem; Lenaeus had been a Syrian slave employed as an accountant. Our information regarding their policies is scanty, but it seems clear that they aimed at a nationalistic revolution, giving Orientals positions and power heretofore accorded only to Greeks. Circumstances enabled them to seize power without violence or bloodshed. Eulaeus went so far as to put his own name on copper and silver coins. As the regents' policies made it difficult to collect taxes from either Greeks or Orientals, they, like most revolutionary leaders, quickly went bankrupt. As early as 173 they began debasing the coinage, and when their position grew still more precarious they turned to another device often used by reckless statesmen in like circumstances—agitation for foreign war. The regents promised to regain Palestine and even spoke of annexing the whole Seleucid Empire. Such braggadocio, when addressed to Alexandrian Greeks, was of course a bombastic appeal to the old rivalry with the Seleucids; but to the regents' friends among the natives these words must have sounded like a call to overthrow the Greeks everywhere.

Conditions in Syria were much the same. What remained of Antiochus's empire was inherited in 187 by his son Seleucus IV Philopator ("Father-Loving"). There was little that a king in his position could do except try to repair the havoc of war, and in this Seleucus was moderately successful. His chief minister was an ambitious man named Heliodorus, whose aspirations presently led him to murder his master and attempt to rule as regent for the young heir (176). Unfortunately, we know very little about Heliodorus, except that he was a Hellenized Oriental who had obtained an important post and hoped to govern Syria much as Eulaeus and Lenaeus were just then beginning to govern Egypt. There is evidence to show that even before he murdered Seleucus, Heliodorus was intriguing with discontented Orientals, and we know that Greeks everywhere rejoiced when he was overthrown. Syria barely escaped an oriental government such as afflicted Egypt during the next several years.

The Orientals of Asia Minor had as yet achieved neither the power, nor the leadership, nor perhaps even the class consciousness, necessary to resist the Greeks in similar manner. Perhaps, too, they felt dependent upon the Greeks because of their continuing fear of the Galatians who had invaded Asia in the 270's and who, after establishing themselves in northern Phrygia, had raided their neighbors repeatedly until they were crushed by the Romans in 189. Yet the population of Asia Minor was largely non-Greek and had at times in the third century shown hostility to its overlords. The Persians had colonized in Asia Minor extensively, granting great estates to Persian nobles and lavishly establishing and endowing temples in which Persian priests worshiped Persian gods and were supported by thousands of sacred serfs in the oriental fashion. These Persian settlements were most numerous in Cappadocia and eastern Asia Minor, but they were also found in Phrygia and even farther west, and the Greeks had not destroyed them. Inscriptions show that Persian nobles and priests used Aramaic, the common tongue of the

Near East, and that spiritually they remained Orientals. The Greeks failed completely to win their loyalty.

After Magnesia and the destruction of the Galatians, the natives of Asia Minor became more restless. Pharnaces I, king of Pontus (c. 185–c. 170), tried to set himself up as an oriental leader. His ancestors claimed descent from the highest Persian nobility and had never recognized Seleucid rule, though they had a certain amount of Greek culture and one of them accepted a Greek wife from Seleucus II. Pharnaces now entered into close friendship with Artaxias, an Oriental who had recently freed himself from the Seleucids as king of Armenia. Thus strengthened, Pharnaces seized the Greek city of Sinope on the Black Sea in 183, and threatened neighboring Heraclea until he was defeated by a coalition of his Greek neighbors. In spite of this defeat, native unrest in Asia Minor continued and revolts soon broke out anew. Ten or fifteen years after Magnesia, Greek rule was almost as seriously threatened in Asia Minor as in the rest of the Orient.

Agitation for Greek Solidarity

The wars of the 190's were perhaps more destructive to Greece than the Hannibalic wars had been to Italy. Roman troops in Greece were not especially vindictive—Livy often boasts of their restraint —but they entered nearly every part of the peninsula, where they lived off the country. The worst devastation was usually done by the Greeks who had called in Romans as their allies against other Greeks. Greece had been in a pitiful state before the wars began, and afterward she could not find the long period of repose and recuperation that she so badly needed. Moreover, in restoring autonomy to every tiny Greek state, Flamininus had done much to promote the "Balkanization" of the peninsula. He had not deliberately planned to introduce chaos, but his mistaken conception of Greek "liberty" made anarchy the net result of his treaty. Quarrels and wars between the different states were resumed, and class struggles continued to tear the country to pieces. Responsible statesmen throughout the Greek world were thus brought to realize as never before that some sort of Greek solidarity was imperative if Greeks everywhere were not soon to be overwhelmed by anarchy and self-destruction.

Philip V of Macedon had remained true to his treaty with Rome during the war against Antiochus, for which he was mildly rewarded by the Romans. After the war he persevered, outwardly at least, in this fidelity. He centered his attention upon domestic reconstruction, and when he died in 179 he left Macedon stronger than she had been for many years. Perseus, his son and successor, was an able and ambitious young man who hoped to unite the European Greeks under his leadership, ending Roman influence in Greece and restoring Macedon to her former position as a great world power. He continued his father's domestic policy of cultivating the friendship of the lower classes in Greece—who were inclined to be anti-Roman —and his foreign policy aimed at a close solidarity of the various Hellenistic rulers.

This policy of solidarity was likewise favored by the Hellenistic monarchs of Asia Minor, Syria, and Egypt, though for rather different reasons. To these other Greeks, who had little cause to worry about Rome, Greek solidarity meant primarily a mutual understanding among Greek rulers everywhere in order that each king might have his hands free to deal with his rebellious oriental subjects. The most conspicuous leader in this new movement for Greek solidarity against the Orientals was Eumenes II of Pergamum, but similar views were held by Ptolemy V and Seleucus IV, and especially by Seleucus's younger brother and successor, Antiochus IV. Their common opposition to Orientals led to what might be called Greek

---

• Note for Plate 10. This view shows one wing of the enormous altar to Zeus erected at Pergamum by Eumenes II (197–160). The frieze depicts the Greek gods, representing Greek civilization, defeating the giants who stood for barbarism. This theme undoubtedly was chosen by Eumenes himself, for his whole political career was directed to making Greek civilization supreme over oriental "barbarism" in the Near East. Early in the present century the altar was reconstructed by German archeologists and set up in Berlin; the Russians have since dismantled it and carried it off. (Photo, Berlin Museum.)

Plate 10. Pergamum: Altar to Zeus

Antiochus III of Syria *(Louvre Museum)*

Coins of Antiochus IV of Syria *(British Museum)*

Plate 11

cultural imperialism, which may be contrasted with Rome's military and diplomatic imperialism.

Eumenes II of Pergamum

Eumenes (197–60) was an intelligent and forceful leader who brought Pergamum to the height of her power and glory (see Plate 10 and note). He probably never doubted that the Greeks were going to retain their world supremacy, but his restless non-Greek subjects often caused him trouble. His father, Attalus I, had been a friend and ally of Rome since the days of the First Macedonian War (214–06), and Eumenes continued this friendship after his accession to power. His complaints had been partly responsible for Rome's war against Antiochus III, and he was rewarded for aid granted to Rome during that war with a large part of Asia Minor. His Galatian subjects had been conquered for him by the Romans under Manlius Vulso in 189. It no doubt occurred to him even then that he might be able to use Roman legions for similar purposes again. He therefore desired to remain on friendly terms with his Roman benefactors, but those historians are wrong who depict him as a "lackey" of Rome. (Was Winston Churchill a mere "lackey" of "American imperialism" in 1940 and 1941?) When Eumenes finally had to choose between Romans and Greeks, he chose the Greeks and thereby came to grief. Others perpetuated his policy of using Roman troops to fight Greek battles, and eventually Greek culture was made secure in the Near East by Roman arms. Eumenes misjudged in one point only, for the Romans annexed the Near East to their

---

• Note for Plate 11. The two coins show Antiochus IV Epiphanes of Syria. The first shows him with his own features, the second has him made up with a beard to resemble the traditional statues of Zeus and suggests that Antiochus was the incarnation of the god. The reverse side of the first coin shows Zeus holding a Niké, or statue of Victory, and bears the inscription, "Βασιλέως Ἀντιόχου Θέου ἐπιφανοῦς"—"Of King Antiochus, the god manifest." The second coin shows the same Zeus, who is now represented by Antiochus. The inscription beside the Antiochus-Zeus is the same, but beneath it is added the word "Νικηφόρου"—"Bringer of Victory." It is no longer Zeus in the abstract, or on Mount Olympus, who brings victory, but Zeus incarnate in Antiochus.

own empire before undertaking the permanent defense of Greek culture there.

Eumenes' first step in his program of Greek solidarity was to marry Stratonice, daughter of Ariarathes IV of Cappadocia. This country was inhabited almost wholly by Orientals and contained many Persian estates and temples; Stratonice herself was partly of Persian descent; but Eumenes evidently chose to regard her and her dynasty as Greeks ruling over Asiatics, even though they had a strain of oriental blood in their veins—just as he had. The king of Bithynia, another partly oriental Greek king ruling Orientals, joined the alliance, and these three Greek monarchs defeated the oriental Pharnaces of Pontus. Eumenes also ingratiated himself with the Achaean League, which conferred sundry honors upon him. Meantime Ptolemy V was courting the Greeks, especially the Achaean League, and his brother-in-law Seleucus IV of Syria followed a similar policy. Seleucus sent his daughter to marry Perseus in 177, which called forth enthusiastic demonstrations from the Rhodians and other Greeks. Undoubtedly Ptolemy and Seleucus, even more than Eumenes, thought of this new Greek solidarity primarily as a union against the oriental menace, for Orientals were the only non-Greeks bothering them just then. Moreover, the Romans sent a delegation in 172 to learn the sympathies of these eastern Greeks and found that all were friendly to Rome—all except the Rhodians, who like the Macedonians had no restless Oriental subjects.

Greek Intrigues at Rome

In spite of the efforts of these leaders to create a feeling of Greek solidarity, the lesser states of European Greece continued their customary quarrels with one another and were constantly trying to inveigle aid from Rome against their neighbors. Scarcely a year passed without several delegations arriving in the city to importune the senate or to complain about their rivals. The Romans were at a loss to know what to do. They were still profoundly ignorant of Greek affairs, but they desired peace; they continued to believe that Flamininus had made a perfect settlement of Greek affairs; and traditionally they regarded the Macedonians as inveterate aggressors. The Greeks soon became aware of these foundation-stones of Roman policy and phrased their importunities accordingly. Roman senators, on the other hand, learned that it was not safe to believe anything the Greeks told them—anticipating Vergil's famous warning, *Timeo Danaos et dona ferentes*, "I fear the Greeks, especially when they bring gifts." Often the senate sent commissioners to investigate alleged aggression or treaty-breaking on the spot. The envoys sometimes accepted bribes or were blarneyed into favoring one Greek faction against another; and sometimes they interfered in local politics, obtained the election of favored candidates, or otherwise arrogated unauthorized powers to themselves. But in general the Roman senate was merely annoyed by these frequent importunities, and it became adept at sending complainants home with answers which at first glance seemed friendly enough but which on closer inspection were found to mean exactly nothing at all. Constant repetition, however, led many Romans to believe that there must be some truth behind the ever-recurring charges of aggression; and the Greeks, confused and disappointed, grew hostile and disdainful toward Rome.

Events thus divided Greek statesmen more sharply into anti-Roman and pro-Roman groups, the former being led by Perseus of Macedon and supported by the Greek populace, while the latter was led by Eumenes of Pergamum and supported by the Achaean League and the well-to-do classes in both Greece and Asia. As the quarrel in Greece became more bitter, Eumenes appealed more openly to Rome, and his complaints against Perseus cost him his Greek friends. At last even the Achaean League withdrew the honors it had conferred upon him. In 172 Eumenes went to Rome in person and denounced Perseus in lurid terms before the senate. On his way home he visited Delphi, hoping to restore his declining prestige in Greece by a spectacular appearance at the sanctuary. There he was almost killed by a rock rolled down the hill by unknown assailants. He persuaded the Romans that Perseus was responsible for the outrage, and this incident, coupled with all his other complaints and Rome's traditional mistrust of Macedon, precipitated the Third Macedonian War.

The Third Macedonian War

Perseus had built up a large army and was well supplied with munitions, but he was disappointed in his search for allies. Most Greeks decided, as usual, that they would remain neutral until they saw who was going to win. The Romans, on the other hand, were not prepared for hostilities. At first the populace had opposed war while the senatorial aristocracy regarded it more favorably, partly from philhellenism and partly because they thought a minor war-scare might distract attention from their political opponents whose demagogic agitation was convulsing Rome. After the visit of Eumenes in 172, however, the popular leaders began favoring war and intriguing for commands. Livy says that the senate postponed the war for a year rather than give a command to the demagogue Gaius Popilius Laenas, consul in 172. The delay availed little, however, for Popilius's successors were men of the same stripe, and war was declared in 171. The consuls for 171 and 170 soon proved their incompetence in the field; their demagoguery ruined discipline in the army; and they showed less zeal in fighting Perseus than in looting neutral or friendly Greeks—as the latter complained bitterly in 170.

These events gave the aristocrats their chance, and at the end of 170 they elected Q. Marcius Philippus consul and gave him the command against Perseus. From then on, Roman arms fared better. A year later Aemilius Paullus—who had opposed entering the war—took command and inflicted a shattering defeat upon Perseus at Pydna in June, 168. Though Livy's figures for casualties (20,000 Macedonians and 100 Romans killed) are rather hard to accept, Perseus knew that further resistance was impossible and surrendered a few days later. When war was declared in 171, the second consul, jealous at not receiving the command against Perseus, had started a private war. With inadequate supplies and without permission from the senate, he attempted to reach Macedonia before the first consul by crossing independent Illyria from the Po Valley. The natives resisted his advance and the ensuing Third Illyrian War lasted almost as long as the war against Perseus.

The senate sent twelve commissioners to help Paullus make peace, and again the Romans seemed very generous. Cato had demanded that the Greeks be left to govern themselves, and his advice was followed. After dividing Macedonia into four independent republics and Illyria into three, the Romans exacted an annual indemnity from these peoples that amounted to only one-half the sum formerly paid their kings in taxes. When the Romans seized Perseus's archives, they learned that many Achaeans had intrigued with him during the last stages of the war. They therefore compelled the League to send 1000 hostages to Rome, among them the historian Polybius. An even worse fate was meted out to the Epirotes, who had actively aided Perseus: seventy of their towns were destroyed and 150,000 citizens were sold into slavery.

Pergamum and Rhodes had also aroused suspicion by their conduct. Eumenes too had intrigued with Perseus during the last part of the war after it became evident that the Romans were going to win a more sweeping victory than he anticipated or desired. He thereby lost the confidence of Rome and his Galatian provinces were transferred to a native king. After Eumenes' death, however, the Romans renewed their old friendship with his brother Attalus II (160–138). Rhodes was punished by the loss of Caria and Lycia, provinces in southwestern Asia Minor which she had received in the settlement of 189. These losses caused a serious decline in her revenue, and an even worse blow fell shortly afterwards. Wishing to reward their loyal ally Athens and to punish Rhodes still further, the Romans gave Delos to Athens and made it a free port. The Rhodians complained that their annual revenue from customs fell from 1,000,000 to 150,000 drachmas. The Athenians, on the other hand, gained little or nothing from the gift. The people of Delos suffered most of all, however, for the Athenians presently deported them all to Greece. Delos eventually became an international center for banking and the slave trade, but the merchants who profited thereby were largely Greeks from southern Italy or else Orientals.

A final disaster resulting from this political settlement was that Rhodes could no longer guard the seas from piracy, as had been her practice during the preceding century. Rome was not disposed to assume the task, and the ensuing ravages of pirates and slave hunters were a more serious blow to commerce than was the economic reorganization required by the changed status of Delos. The whole Greek world suffered grievously in consequence of Rome's peace, but again the damage was the result of Rome's ignorance rather than her vindictiveness or her plans for world conquest.

Antiochus Epiphanes

Meantime, events of the utmost importance were taking place in Syria. Antiochus IV Epiphanes, the younger son of Antiochus III and the friend and ally of Eumenes of Pergamum, was about forty years old when his brother Seleucus was murdered in 176. For several years after 189 he had been a hostage at Rome, but when he was replaced by Seleucus's young son Demetrius, Antiochus took up his residence in Athens. His experiences in Rome had convinced him that Syrian armies could never equal those of Rome and that consequently his family must not seek revenge for Magnesia or allow a serious controversy with Rome to arise. They might not like Rome, but they had to live in the same world with her: it therefore behooved them to let bygones be bygones and to seek fields of activity where they would not cross her path. The effects of Antiochus's stay in Greece were equally important. His visit in Athens was pleasant and it culminated in his election to an honorary office which permitted him to cast Athenian coins marked with his name and the Seleucid elephant. He also watched political developments and made contacts with the leading Greeks of his day. Eumenes' program for Greek solidarity met with his hearty approval, and the two men entered into a lifelong friendship which later was sealed by an alliance. The great ambition of each man was the preservation of Greek supremacy in the Near East through the solidarity of Greeks everywhere, and they became the two leading exponents of Greek cultural imperialism.

When news came in 176 that Seleucus IV had been murdered and that Heliodorus was ruling Syria as guardian of the king's young son, Eumenes at once offered to help Antiochus obtain his father's throne. A Pergamese army under Eumenes' brother escorted Antiochus as far as Cilicia, but in order that the new king might seem to come as the free choice of his people, the army marked time at the frontier while he proceeded to his capital. Heliodorus fled and Antiochus took over without meeting armed opposition. We are told, however, that he was opposed at first by some who "favored" Egypt —presumably friends of Heliodorus who wanted a government like that of Eulaeus and Lenaeus—but that after a few months he per-

THE LATER SELEUCIDS

Antiochus III the Great
(223–187)

Seleucus IV Philopator (187–176)		Antiochus IV Epiphanes (176–163)	Cleopatra I †176 = Ptolemy V Epiphanes	

Antiochus †169?	Demetrius I Soter (162–150)	Antiochus V Eupator (163–162)	Laodice = ? Mithradates V of Pontus (150–121)	Ptolemy VI Philometor (180–145)	Ptolemy VII Physcon (145–116)

Demetrius II Nicator (145–139, 129–125)	Antiochus VII Sidetes (139–129)	Mithradates VI the Great of Pontus (121–63)	Cleopatra Thea †121	xxx Cleopatra VII = Antony †30 B.C.

Alexander Balas (150–145) pretended to be an illegitimate son of Antiochus IV; his infant son, Antiochus VI Dionysus, was nominal king from 145–142.

= married, † died, xxx indicates a gap of three generations in the table.

suaded them "by flatteries" and was crowned king of Syria. Apparently he ruled at first as his nephew's guardian, and later the two ruled jointly (in theory at least) until the nephew's death about 169.

As soon as he became king Antiochus turned his attention to advancing Greek solidarity. He was lavish in his generosity to various Greek cities, notably to Athens, while his two chief assistants made conspicuous gifts to the city of Miletus. He also showed his good will toward Rome by erecting a temple to Jupiter Capitolinus at Antioch and by sending agents to Rome in 173 to pay the last installments on the indemnity of 189, which had fallen into arrears. While thus establishing good relations with the other Greeks and with Rome, Antiochus was preparing a great campaign to regain the territories in the East lost by his father and brother after Magnesia

—a program to which Rome could find no possible objection and which would therefore provoke no future conflicts with that power. At the same time he was devising means for strengthening Greek culture in his empire. Before long, however, he was diverted by a war with Egypt which occupied him for two years.

His Invasions of Egypt

The Egyptian war was not of Antiochus's choosing. It was forced upon him by Eulaeus and Lenaeus, though it seems likely that at the last minute the regents' hands were forced by political opponents in Alexandria. Since these two Orientals based their power on their regency for Ptolemy VI Philometor, the obvious line of attack for their opponents was to declare the young king of age. This was done in 170. The regents replied by going to war with Syria and hustling Philometor out of the country to Samothrace—nominally for his safety, more probably to strengthen their own hands by discrediting him as a coward who fled in the face of danger.

Both Eulaeus and Lenaeus were killed in the first battle, where Antiochus completely defeated the Egyptian armies. As soon as Philometor learned of the regents' deaths he returned to Alexandria, opened peace negotiations with his uncle Antiochus, and early in the summer of 169 the two monarchs signed a treaty of peace and alliance at Memphis. Many Alexandrian Greeks showed by their resentment against this alliance that their patriotic hatred of the Seleucids was stronger than their feeling of Greek solidarity. They effected a *coup d'état* by which Philometor's younger brother, commonly called Ptolemy Physcon, was declared king in his place. Antiochus at first aided Philometor against these rebels, but presently he withdrew all his forces from Egypt, keeping only Pelusium, the gateway to Syria. Antiochus had not desired war in the first place, though he undoubtedly was glad to see the end of Eulaeus and Lenaeus, and as a good Greek the last thing he wanted was to wage war against the Alexandrians.

Before long, however, Antiochus discovered that the passions of war, once aroused, do not cool quickly. Soon after his departure from Egypt, the two Ptolemies became reconciled and sent urgent appeals to various Greek states begging for aid against him. Antiochus was infuriated by these unwarranted appeals, which undermined his whole program of Greek solidarity. In the spring of 168 he returned to Egypt, determined to force the Alexandrians to be good Greeks in spite of themselves. He easily occupied large districts in Egypt, had himself crowned king at Memphis, and then slowly advanced upon Alexandria. When only a few miles from the city, he was met by a Roman embassy which ordered him, in the name of the senate, to leave Egypt at once. As Antiochus had long since made up his mind never to fight Rome, there was nothing for him to do but withdraw.

These two invasions of Egypt took place during the Third Macedonian War, which conflict absorbed the attention not only of Rome and Perseus but also of Eumenes and other Greek leaders. Both Eulaeus and Antiochus had undoubtedly taken this war into account when laying their plans. As soon as hostilities between Egypt and Syria opened, both parties sent delegations to Rome seeking her good will, and Antiochus complained of Egyptian aggression. The Roman senate was unwilling to take any action—it did not wish to make new enemies just then—and referred the matter to the Roman general commanding in Greece (Philippus), who suggested to the Rhodians that they mediate. A delegation sent by Rhodes to Egypt for the purpose may have helped bring about Antiochus's first withdrawal. Before Antiochus withdrew, however, Physcon sent a second appeal to Rome, and the senate decided to send an embassy to urge both Antiochus and Physcon to come to terms, threatening that whichever of them refused to do so would no longer be considered a friend of the Roman people. Before the embassy could reach Alexandria, however, Antiochus had withdrawn from Egypt of his own accord, and the ambassadors were left stranded in Greece with nothing to do.

This embassy was led by the notorious Gaius Popilius Laenas whose highhanded activities had caused the senate to refuse him the command in Macedonia upon which he had set his heart when consul in 172. When Antiochus returned to Egypt in the spring of 168, the Romans paid no attention to his activities, for their interest was centered on the campaign against Perseus which was just then reaching its climax. At the time of Pydna, the embassy was still in Greece. Then Popilius decided that a public humiliation of Antiochus would be a fitting substitute for the military laurels he had failed to win in Macedonia. There is no evidence that the senate had renewed its order after Antiochus's second invasion of Egypt began, and Popilius's action was probably more vigorous than the senate had intended; but as it was successful, and as it redounded to the glory of Rome, Romans long continued to boast about it. Centuries later they were still telling with pride how the Roman envoy met the Syrian king and sternly handed him a copy of the *senatus consultum,* ordering him to end the war. When Antiochus replied that he would consult his generals, Popilius traced a circle round him in the sand with a stick and ordered the king to make his reply before stepping outside. Rather than risk antagonizing Rome, Antiochus promised to withdraw from Egypt, whereupon Popilius, throwing all formality aside, embraced him as an old friend—or so the story goes.[1]

His Program of Hellenization

Antiochus was no doubt much chagrined by this experience with Popilius, yet the annexation of Egypt had not been part of his original design, and he did not allow his failure to delay further his program for reorganizing and Hellenizing his empire. During the next few years Antiochus brought to Syria many settlers from Greece, especially from Athens; he founded new cities and gave Greek names and Greek constitutions to old ones; he built gymnasiums and theaters to promote Greek cultural life; he encouraged the worship of Zeus, Dionysus, and other Greek gods; and he introduced Greek

---

[1] The subsequent history of the Popilius family is not without interest since, from generation to generation, it ran true to the form established by Gaius and his slave-catching brother Marcus. Gaius's son, consul in 132, was exiled for his bloodthirsty violence during the white terror that began with the murder of Tiberius Gracchus; this man's son was exiled for *perduellio* (treason) in 105. Two generations later, another member of the family encouraged, but did not take part in, the murder of Caesar (44), and in the next year another Popilius Laenas murdered Cicero. Meantime a daughter of the family had married into a minor branch of the Julius Caesars (only distantly related to the dictator) and her granddaughter became the mother of Mark Antony. This lady's second husband was executed in 63 B.C. for his share in the Catilinarian conspiracy. Through Mark Antony the Popilius Laenases became ancestors of three Roman Emperors: Caligula, Claudius, and Nero.

styles and customs. Perhaps the most important of these measures, in his own eyes, was the refounding of Babylon. He apparently intended to make this city his new capital, thus facing his empire toward the east, forgetting losses in Asia Minor, and avoiding conflict with Rome. But while Antiochus was eager to unify and Hellenize his empire, he was well aware that he could not make his millions of oriental subjects into good Greeks overnight by decree or force. He therefore did what he could to strengthen the Greeks and to encourage Orientals to adopt Greek culture. At the same time he sought the loyalty of the non-Hellenized Orientals by showing sympathy for them and their culture.

The religious aspect of Antiochus's program for unifying the empire is of especial interest and importance. Orientals and Greeks had long been in the habit of identifying their gods with one another. Cyrus had on one occasion equated a Persian god with the Jewish deity Yahweh; Greeks before Alexander had identified Semitic gods with their own gods or demigods; and early Seleucids had encouraged this practice. Antiochus went a step further and gave pre-eminence to a universal and imperial god whose worship might be shared by Greeks and Orientals. The Greeks called this deity the Olympian Zeus while the Aramaic-speaking Orientals called him Baal Shamin ("Lord of the Heavens"), a name long used for such a universal deity. Antiochus had no intention of forcing monotheism upon his subjects, for the existence of other gods was not denied or their worship forbidden; but efforts were made to induce the different peoples of the empire to identify their leading deity with Baal Shamin and worship him as such. The favor shown this deity recalls that shown to Serapis by the early Ptolemies. Presently Antiochus went so far as to declare himself the incarnation of Baal Shamin. Coins cast in 169 show that he took the title "Theos Epiphanes" ("God Manifest") and later coins pictured Zeus or Baal Shamin with Antiochus's own features (see Plate 11). This step was not very revolutionary, however, for ever since Alexander the various Hellenistic monarchs had been proclaiming their divinity.

The second part of Antiochus's program began with the reconquest of Bactria. Antiochus III had recognized Euthydemus as king of that country, made an alliance with him, and assigned to him the task of defending Persia against inroads from the steppes of Turkestan. Euthydemus died about 189 and was succeeded by his son Demetrius. During the next few years Demetrius took three Persian provinces from Seleucus IV, and then set forth upon the great enterprise of his reign, invading India in 183. He occupied the whole Indus Valley, and one of his generals crossed the Punjab desert to the Ganges. The Bactrian kings, Euthydemus and Demetrius, owed much of their success to their skill at handling Orientals, winning the loyalty of the native nobility by taking them into partnership even though they antagonized Greeks settled in the East.

Antiochus decided to put an end to this anti-Greek power, and his first step was to send his cousin Eucratides to Bactria with a considerable force in 168. Before the end of 167 Eucratides had seized all territory west of the Hindu Kush Mountains, and Demetrius was dead. In the spring of 166 Antiochus celebrated his general's victory with an enormous festival at Antioch which is said to have been more magnificent than Aemilius Paullus's celebration of his victory over Perseus. A few months later Antiochus celebrated a "Thanksgiving" at Babylon, where he was hailed as the "Savior of Asia"—that is, as the man who saved Greek hegemony there. In the following year Eucratides invaded India and there defeated Demetrius's general; but on his return to Bactria in 159 he, too, was killed in battle. Menander, Demetrius's son-in-law, was then able to regain his family's former possessions and he governed Bactria and India successfully until his death about 150. His heirs continued to rule over parts of that vast empire even in the first century before Christ, but when they passed away they left scarcely a trace behind them.

The End of Greek Solidarity

After his Thanksgiving at Babylon in 166 Antiochus spent two years pacifying various rebellious provinces, such as Armenia, Elymais, and Judea. In the spring of 163, just as he was ready to advance against the most powerful of the rebels, the Parthians, he died suddenly at Gabae (Isfahan) in Persia. Shortly before his

death he appointed his general Philip regent for his young son
Antiochus V Eupator ("of Good Father"). As Philip was with the
king in Persia, the western provinces actually fell into the hands of
a certain Lysias who had been left to govern them during Antiochus's
campaigns in the East. The fragility of the empire then became
manifest. Nationalistic revolts broke out on every side: Armenia
again became independent under Artaxias; a native dynasty began
ruling Commagene (between Syria and Armenia); Jews and Parthians took the occasion to seize Syrian territory. Moreover, Lysias's
attempts at repression and pacification were cut short in the fall of
162 by the return from Rome of the son of Seleucus IV, who seized
the throne as Demetrius I. He executed Lysias and Antiochus V at
once, but a general named Timarchus managed to hold the eastern
provinces for about two years. The ensuing civil wars were the death
agony of Seleucid Syria.

Popilius Laenas had left Egypt under the joint rule of the two
brothers, Philometor and Physcon. Four years later Physcon drove
his brother out, but was driven out himself by Philometor in 163,
after which the kingdom was divided between the two brothers.
Philometor ruled Egypt and Cyprus thereafter, and Cyrene went to
Physcon. Physcon was still not satisfied and vainly begged the
Romans to give him Cyprus. Disastrous native revolts continued. An
Egyptian named Petosarapis, who had achieved distinction under
Eulaeus, kindled a great rebellion in 166 and soon all Egypt was
ablaze. Almost two years passed before the government destroyed
the last rebel stronghold, and minor revolts and race riots continued for several years longer. The economic damage caused by
these revolts and their suppression was far greater than that caused
by the wars.

The old dream of Greek solidarity, the last hope of Eumenes and
Antiochus, thus vanished into thin air. After the defeat of Perseus
at Pydna (168), the lesser Greek states hastened to hail Rome as the
lord of the world, often showing an unseemly haste to serve their
own interests by denouncing their neighbors. Numerous embassies
were sent to Rome for this purpose, and the Romans came to despise the Greeks who, by fawning and tale-bearing, were constantly

trying to inveigle Romans into supporting their selfish adventures. The Romans were little disposed to intervene further in eastern affairs, but the hope or fear that they might do so remained a potent factor in demoralizing the Greeks.

The Jewish Theocracy and Judas Maccabaeus

The Jews were not an important people in the days of Antiochus Epiphanes, yet for us his relations with them are the most important aspect of his reign. They were the only subject people whose history during these years can be traced in detail, and they therefore offer the best illustration of oriental opposition to Hellenization.

Ever since their return from the Exile in 536, the Palestinian Jews had been a small group living quietly in Judea—the territory immediately around Jerusalem. They were willing to accept rule by the Persians, Alexander, the Ptolemies, or the Seleucids, so long as their successive overlords granted them religious freedom and a measure of local autonomy. During these centuries of alien rule, the Jews gradually organized themselves into a religious state. Their leaders claimed that this state was under the direct rule of God and strove to make the people live according to ancestral customs recorded in the Books of the Law—the Torah, or first five books of the Old Testament. The government of Judea was conducted by the high priests at Jerusalem with the aid of a council of "elders," most of whom were priests, and who were usually enlightened and urbane, familiar with the world, and little inclined to fanaticism. These priests determined matters of general policy and conducted negotiations with the Persians or other higher authorities.

While the priests conducted the government, the real leaders of the people at this time were the scholars who studied and interpreted the Torah and the oral traditions that went with it. They had little knowledge of the world outside Judea. Many of them came from priestly families, others were of humble origin; some attained great power and prestige at Jerusalem, others were obscure teachers in the villages. They won the loyalty of the Jewish peasants whom they instructed in the laws and customs of their fathers. Their theological, legal, ethical, and religious system, which we call Judaism, presently came to differ much from the pre-Exilic religion of Israel. In addition to creating what was virtually a new religion, these scholars were leaders in one of the world's most interesting experiments in theocracy—an attempt to establish a government which in theory was directed by God but which actually was conducted by scholars devoting their lives to the study of what they believed to be his revealed word.

Political conditions in Palestine changed very little when Antiochus III took the province from Ptolemy V in 200. The Ptolemies had continued the Persian policy of liberal treatment for the Jews and had made no effort to Hellenize them. There is no record of unrest during the Egyptian period, yet the Jews willingly opened their gates to Antiochus III after his victory at Panium. He repaid them by continuing the old local autonomy under Jewish law, by providing funds for sacrifices at Jerusalem, and by other special favors. Nevertheless, the high priest (Simon II) caught the spirit of rebellion which was so prevalent in the Seleucid Empire after Antiochus III was defeated at Magnesia, and he built walls around Jerusalem. Though he did not formally denounce Seleucid rule, he may perhaps have looked forward to establishing a completely independent theocracy. His son and successor, Onias III, was highly respected for his piety and, during his early days at least, he showed no open hostility to the Seleucids. He opposed Hellenization of the Jews, however, and he was on friendly terms with Heliodorus before the latter murdered Seleucus IV.

Presently Onias came in conflict with the Jewish family of the Tobiads, who were Hellenized Orientals friendly to whatever government happened to be ruling the Jews. The founder of the family had grown rich by collecting the taxes of Palestine in the days of Ptolemy IV and was therefore closely associated with Alexandria, but his family readily transferred its allegiance to Antioch and led the Hellenizing faction in Palestine. It happened that a Tobiad, who was overseer of the market in Jerusalem and business manager of the Temple, once quarreled with Onias, whereupon the Tobiads denounced the high priest to the king. A bitter struggle arose between the priesthood and the Seleucid dynasty. While the commercial class and the well-to-do landowners, most of whom were somewhat Hellenized, usually sympathized with the Tobiads, the great mass of the Jewish peasantry favored Onias and the priesthood.

Such was the situation in Palestine when Antiochus IV came into power. The new king replaced Onias by his brother Jason, whose Greek name—a substitute for the Hebrew Joshua or Jesus—indicates sympathy with the Hellenizing faction. Three years later Jason was replaced by a member of the Tobiad family named Menelaus, who was even more strongly pro-Greek. Though Jewish writers attributed these appointments to bribery, it seems more probable that they were just a part of Antiochus's general Hellenizing program. At any rate, Hellenization was promoted by Jason and even more vigorously by Menelaus, and the quarrel between the two Jewish factions became extremely bitter, culminating in 170 with the murder of Onias.

Early in his career as high priest, Jason obtained the right to form a separate legal community, called Antioch, for the Greeks and Hellenized Jews living in Jerusalem. This community was given the political status of a Greek city and displayed such symbols of Greek culture as a gymnasium and Greek styles of clothing. The Seleucids had often established separate jurisdictions within an oriental city for Greeks and Hellenized Orientals—something like the "extraterritoriality" enjoyed by Europeans in certain parts of the Orient until quite recently—and a similar Greek community was founded a year later at nearby Ptolemaïs in Phoenicia. For several years the two communities at Jerusalem existed side by side. Menelaus, the Tobiad high priest, was a member of the Greek community even though he ruled the Jewish one.

Antiochus passed through Jerusalem after his first invasion of Egypt and, with the connivance of Menelaus, seized treasures in the Temple worth 1800 talents—such temple plundering being not uncommon after wars. During the second Egyptian campaign a rumor spread abroad that Antiochus was dead. Jason, who by this time had repented of his mild Hellenism and had long been instigating the Jews against Menelaus, at once marched on Jerusalem with about a thousand armed followers. Similar anti-Greek revolts broke out in Syria and at several places along the Phoenician coast. Antiochus punished Jerusalem severely, tearing down Simon's walls and erecting a citadel, not far from the Temple, to be occupied by Greek troops. Around this citadel was built up a new city for the "Antiochenes," whose commander extended his military authority over all Judea, thus reducing the Jewish community to a position of subservience.

These measures aroused great discontent among the Jews, but open revolt might still have been avoided had not Antiochus decided to establish the worship of Baal Shamin in the Temple itself. The steps leading to this decision are not clear. There is no record that Antiochus used violence elsewhere to establish his universal cult. A group of Samaritans—schismatic Jews living just north of Judea, whose legal position as a temple-state was identical with that of the Jews in Jerusalem—had recently requested Antiochus to establish the new worship in their capital city; the cult of Baal Shamin was set up, but no violence was used against Samaritans who failed to participate. It therefore seems probable that Menelaus and his friends sent Antiochus a similar petition, suggesting the identification of Yahweh with Baal Shamin,[2] and that Antiochus anticipated no trouble when he granted their request. At any rate, the new cult was established in the Temple at Jerusalem on the 25th day of Chislev (approximately December) in the year 167, with a statue of Antiochus as Baal Shamin on the altar. Loyal Jews were horrified by a worship which, by a play on words, they called the "abomination of desolation."[3] Opposition led to repressive measures by

---

[2] This identification of Yahweh—the old Jewish God sometimes erroneously called Jehovah—with Baal Shamin was probably not so shocking to Menelaus and to the enlightened upper classes at Jerusalem as it seemed to the common people and to Jews of a later time. More than three centuries before this, the Persian king Cyrus had made a similar identification, and the priests had copied his words into the Scriptures without being scandalized. They are found in the decree of Cyrus permitting the Jews to return to Jerusalem (II Chron. 36:23, Ezra 1:2) which was a sort of Magna Charta for the Jewish state. Here Cyrus declared that "Yahweh, the God of the Heavens," had given him all the kingdoms of the earth. The God of the Heavens, here equated with Yahweh, must have been very similar to Baal Shamin, the Lord of the Heavens, whom Antiochus and Menelaus wished to equate with that same deity.

[3] The Hebrew words translated thus are *Shiquz shomem,* the first of which is a word often used for baals or idols, and the second, "desolation," is merely a pun on

Menelaus and to complaints to Antiochus, until the central government decided that peace could be restored only by stamping out the
old Jewish religion. In the troubled times that followed, copies of
the Scriptures were destroyed and all Jews were ordered to eat pork
that had been sacrificed to the new god. These measures were probably devised by Menelaus himself—nothing of the sort can be found
elsewhere in Antiochus's domain—and they indicate that the struggle was first and foremost between Hellenized and non-Hellenized
Jews, with Greek troops supporting the former and the populace
favoring the latter faction.

The Maccabaean Revolt

At this point a Judean peasant named Judas Maccabaeus roused
loyal Jews to rebellion. He collected an army of resolute men who
were ready to die for their religion, and with them he inflicted one
defeat after another upon the Greeks. As Antiochus was by this time
so deeply engaged in his eastern ventures that he could not spare
enough troops to suppress the revolt in Judea, he withdrew the
orders relative·to the worship of Baal Shamin. In the spring of 164
he offered amnesty to all Jewish rebels who would lay down their
arms, and he promised that those who obeyed might "fearlessly
enjoy their own food and laws, as before." Judas kept his armies together, however, until he entered Jerusalem and purified the Temple
on the third anniversary of its desecration (25 Chislev, 164). Perhaps because of the word "desolation" and the mistranslation of the
word for "shrubbery" by "weeds" in I Maccabees 4:38, modern
writers often picture the Temple as having fallen into ruin. On the
contrary, it had been beautified with statues, shrubbery, and trees
like other oriental shrines in their sacred groves. These alien adorn-
ments Judas destroyed, and the old Jewish worship was resumed.
Jews have ever since commemorated this "rededication" of the
Temple on the Feast of Hanukkah in December.

The Maccabaean revolt was precipitated by religious persecution,

Shamin. Earlier writers usually dated this desecration and the subsequent purification
of the Temple in 168 and 165 respectively. Like all recent writers, I follow the chronology established by Kolbe in 1926 which puts them a year later.

but its fundamental causes reached far beyond the religious sphere. It was basically a revolt against all forms of Hellenization and against the upper classes who had accepted Hellenism: Judas's peasant soldiers showed great vindictiveness toward landlords, for example. Since their program was not only religious but social, cultural, and racial, the mere purification of the Temple was not enough to satisfy the rebels. Judas continued the war and besieged the Greek citadel built by Antiochus at Jerusalem. Meantime, the king had died and been succeeded by his son Antiochus V, with the usurper Lysias actually governing the western provinces. Lysias sent new armies against Judas but, just as he was about to crush the rebels, he was forced to break off the campaign to defend himself against Philip, the lawful regent. Further privileges were therefore granted to the Jews in 162. A formal decree announced that since the Jews were unwilling to be Hellenized and preferred their old ways of living, the king was glad to return the Temple to them and to allow them to follow their ancestral customs. At the same time Menelaus was executed, much to the joy of loyal Jews. This act would seem to indicate that the Greeks considered the Tobiad high priest personally responsible for the unsuccessful efforts at enforced Hellenization. Though the citadel remained in the hands of the Greeks, and the walls which Judas had rebuilt around Jerusalem were thrown down, Judea again became a temple-state under a new high priest.

Most of Judas's followers were now satisfied, but Judas was not. He wanted a wholly independent Jewish state and continued his attacks on the Greeks. Aided by the confusion into which the Seleucid Empire was rapidly falling, the Maccabaean armies raided and pillaged Greek cities along the coast and in Transjordania. They also "smote sinners" (Hellenized Jews and landlords) and inflicted heavy economic damage upon Palestine. In 161 Judas sent a delegation to seek Roman aid and obtained a treaty of alliance by which Rome and Judas each bound themselves not to aid a third party at war with either ally. The Romans also promised to warn Demetrius not to bother the Jews further, but it is most doubtful whether they did so or ever intended to do so.

As Demetrius I was by this time in firm control of Syria, Judas found it increasingly difficult to persuade his followers to persevere in their aggression, and the rebellion came to an end when he was killed in battle in the spring of 160. His brothers were driven into exile, and Judea became so tranquil that when the new high priest died a few months later, the office was left vacant for several years and the government was conducted by Greek officials. Exhaustion of the Jews brought a truce, but before long they resumed their attacks upon the decaying Seleucid Empire and eventually they realized Judas's hopes for complete national independence.

The Book of Daniel

The shock of the Maccabaean uprising caused deep thought among the Jews, who gave brilliant literary expression to their hopes and dreams. Part of the literature of this time is still available. Martyr stories are preserved in various books; Maccabaean hymns have found their way into the Book of Psalms; preachers explained the misfortunes of the time as punishment for the national sin of apostasy; and prophets foretold the imminent fall of Antiochus and the triumph of the faithful.[4]

The most important work of this sort is the Book of Daniel. Though it purports to be the work of a man named Daniel living in the sixth century before Christ, we now know that it was composed during the Maccabaean revolt. One part of the book contains a series of martyr stories calculated to inspire the faithful under persecution —such stories as Daniel in the Lion's Den, and the Fiery Furnace. This portion was written in Aramaic, the popular language of the day, and the stories may well have been old folk tales revived and revised for the occasion. The rest of the book consists of elaborate prophecies, most of them in Hebrew, foretelling the doom of various kings—all of them recognizable as Antiochus Epiphanes. The most detailed of these prophecies closely resembles the "Potter's Proph-

---

[4] Martyr stories in Daniel and II Maccabees; Psalm 30 is definitely marked "For the Hanukkah," and many others are believed to be of Maccabaean origin, notably Psalms 44, 74, 79, 118; the later chapters of Zechariah come from this period, as do shorter passages now found in Isaiah and elsewhere.

ecy" from Egypt mentioned above (p. 180). It occurs in the eleventh
chapter of Daniel which traces, in veiled language, the history of
the Jews from the sixth century to the second, supposedly as prophecy, and ends with a prophecy of the anticipated triumph of the
Maccabaeans. The prophet's knowledge of the sixth century was
poor, but his picture of Maccabaean times is very good. It is easy to
recognize his allusions to Antiochus III (vss. 11–19), Seleucus IV
(20), Antiochus IV (21–40), Ptolemy Philometor (25–27), Heliodorus (20), Eulaeus (26), and Popilius (30), the two invasions of
Egypt (25, 29), and the desecration of the Temple (31). Unfortunately, however, the prophet went on in verses 40–45 to prophesy
a third invasion of Egypt which never took place, and to describe
the overthrow of Antiochus in circumstances far removed from what
actually occurred. Assuming that the author was a fair historian but
a poor prophet, modern scholars can approximate the time at which
he wrote. His story is accurate history up to verse 40, and inaccurate
prophecy thereafter. It seems evident, therefore, that he wrote in
166 or 165, after the beginning of the Maccabaean revolt but before
the purification of the Temple. The book undoubtedly fulfilled its
purpose by inspiring the soldiers of Judas. In later times Christians
accepted the Book of Daniel as the work of one of the major prophets even though the Jews themselves never gave it such recognition.
Hebrew Bibles do not include the Book of Daniel among the Prophets but among the less important Writings at the end.

Jewish Religious Imperialism

Judas Maccabaeus and his followers were extreme nationalists,
but the second century was a time when imperialism and the unification of the world were matters of prime importance to everyone,
and the Jews could not escape the spirit of the times. Greeks were
trying to create a world empire on the basis of a common Greek
culture; Romans were being forced, rather against their will, into the
task of policing the world and were therefore creating a military
world empire instead of the world union based on treaties of alliance
which they would have preferred; and Jews dreamed of a world
empire based on religion. Loyal Jews were willing to die to prevent

the Hellenization of their religion, yet they confidently anticipated a day when all other men would accept their Yahweh as the one true God and worship him at Jerusalem.

The famous prophecy of the Five Monarchies, which Aemilius Sura twenty years earlier had applied to Rome (see page 165), now reappeared with new implications. The second and seventh chapters of Daniel describe the rise and fall of four great empires (those of the Chaldeans—where Sura had said Assyrians—the Medes, the Persians, and the Greeks) and they foretell a Fifth Monarchy. For Daniel this Fifth Monarchy was the anticipated Maccabaean state. Set up by God and composed of the "saints of the Most High," it would eventually fill the whole world and last forever. Analogous ideas are set forth strikingly in a prophecy composed a few years later and now incorporated in the Book of Isaiah. The author of this prophecy tells of five cities of Egypt which "speak the language of Canaan" (*i.e.*, which are inhabited by Jews), mentions a temple of Yahweh in Egypt (probably the one built about 160 by Onias IV, the exiled son of the murdered high priest), holds out hope to the Egyptians that they will soon be freed from their oppressors (presumably the Greeks), and closes with a beautiful passage predicting the eventual reconciliation of all men under God: "In that day there shall be a highway out of Egypt to Assyria [Syria], and the Assyrian shall come into Egypt, and the Egyptian into Assyria; and the Egyptians shall worship with the Assyrians. In that day shall Israel be the third with Egypt and Assyria, a blessing in the midst of the earth, whom the Lord of hosts hath blessed, saying, Blessed be Egypt my people, and Assyria the work of my hands, and Israel mine inheritance" (Isaiah *19*:23–25).

It cannot be said that the Jews invented the idea of religious imperialism, but it was they who at this time gave the concept its finest expression. We shall see that when world unity was at last achieved, religion became one of its foundations. While Antiochus Epiphanes had some inkling of the importance of religion for imperialism, his efforts to exploit a universal cult were unsuccessful. The Roman Emperors likewise failed when they made similar attempts. But when Christianity ultimately appeared as a religion capable of uniting the peoples of the ancient world, its devotees were men influenced in their thinking by this religious imperialism of the Jews. The author of Daniel and the other prophets were prophesying on a scale wider than they knew, and their dreams became a factor of importance in the history of ancient imperialism.

VI The New Rome and Her Allies

T HE THIRD MACEDONIAN WAR (171–68) BROUGHT ROME
no serious problems of reconstruction. There had been no fighting
on Italian soil, Roman casualties were light, and booty more than
paid the cost of the war. In fact, Roman citizens were exempted
from all direct taxes after 167 because the tribute from Macedonia
and Illyria, plus the revenue from Sicily and Spain, was enough to
cover the entire cost of their government. The economic clauses of
the settlement of 168 may have been ill-advised and disastrous to
Greece and the Aegean area, but they encouraged trade between
Italy and the Near East, and the whole Italian peninsula prospered
in consequence. Prosperity provided the upper classes at Rome with
greater leisure and many of them began to enjoy a new and more
highly cultured existence. They familiarized themselves with Greek
literature and philosophy, they encouraged writers and artists at
Rome, and they raised their own cultural achievements to new
levels. Rome entered upon the most brilliant period in her history.
A hundred years later, discouraged and disillusioned Romans such
as Cicero and Sallust retrospectively regarded this period as a
golden age.

The village on the Tiber, whose warriors had gone out and conquered Italy and the world, had by now become a metropolis comparable to the great cities of the Greek world. Rome was the largest
city in the West, with a population of a quarter of a million or perhaps more. Wealthy aristocrats might maintain villas in the hill

country east of the city or around the beautiful Bay of Naples, but Rome remained their chief place of residence. The city was full of their clients and hangers-on, and it was the center of the political life which they made their major concern. The Palatine Hill, over-looking the forum from the south, became an aristocratic residential district, covered with magnificent palaces. None of these palaces is now preserved, even in ruins, but presumably they resembled the gorgeous houses of contemporaneous Pompeii (see Plates 12–13). On the opposite side of the forum lay the slums whose narrow and dirty streets were already lined with huge jerry-built tenements, six or seven stories high, which were a public menace in time of fire or pestilence. Here dwelt thousands of Italian peasants who had been forced from their farms by the competition of slave labor, and here too were the thousands of foreigners who flocked to Rome from every corner of the Mediterranean world, bringing with them their strange manners, customs, costumes, and religions.

Rome was now beautified with many fine public buildings. Three basilicas had been built respectively by Cato in 184, by Lepidus in 179, and by Tiberius Gracchus in 169. These huge edifices were copied from buildings used in the Near East for royal courts—the name comes from the Greek *basilike,* "royal"—and they in turn served as models for the "basilica" type of Christian church (see Plate 28). They consisted of one large rectangular room whose gabled roof was supported by a double row of pillars inside the building. The central section of the room, running the length of the building between the two rows of pillars, was used for the law courts; the aisles outside the colonnades were filled with shops. Many temples were built in Rome at this time; a new stone bridge crossed the Tiber; and streets were paved with cobblestones. Enormous sewers were constructed (one by Cato), and the new Aqua Marcia brought great quantities of excellent water to the city. This famous aqueduct, built by the praetor Marcius Rex between 144 and 140, was sixty-two miles long; for about fifty-five miles the water ran through underground tunnels, but for the last seven miles it was carried through channels supported by high masonry arches. Some of these arches are still standing. More than two centuries later an enthusiastic Roman writer on aqueducts urged his readers to compare this magnificent and useful structure with the idle pyramids of Egypt or with the useless though famous works of the Greeks—an observation with which many Americans might sympathize.

Aristocratic Leadership

Leadership in this new Rome remained firmly in the hands of the old senatorial aristocracy. Shortly before the outbreak of war in 171 this aristocracy had been forced to forget its private feuds in order to present a united front against a group of "new men" who were winning consulships and high commands with the aid of the eques-

---

• Note for Plate 12.   A well-to-do farm in the days of Cato, in the first half of the second century B.C. The house, built around central courts, was made of stuccoed wood or brick, with a tile roof. The owner, or more probably his bailiff, lived in the farthest section, beyond the great court. The large dining room was at the far corner, and sleeping rooms opened on the court. Next to them was the kitchen, whose high roof, over the hearth, had holes to let smoke out. The kitchen was the center of family life, with the Lares and Penates in their traditional niches. Around the second court were the stables and sleeping rooms for slaves. The third wing housed storerooms, workrooms, and wine and olive presses. The fence at the extreme left enclosed a threshing floor. The court adjoining the third wing was filled with large jars for storing wine and olive oil. (Photo, from Ernest Brehaut, *Cato the Censor on Farming* (1933), with the permission of the Columbia University Press.)

The lower picture shows a second century residence at Pompeii, the *Casa della nozze d'argento*. The large room in the center is the atrium. In early Roman times it was perhaps the only room in the house. When houses became more elaborate, the center hearth was moved to a separate kitchen in the rear, but the atrium retained the open roof. In its center was the *impluvium,* a large basin to catch rain water, often beautified with statues and fountains. Back of the atrium a short hall led to a large flower garden court, called the peristyle because it was surrounded by pillars. There was also a vegetable garden outside the kitchen to the right, and to the left was a second large flower garden surrounded by an arcade. The dining room and other formal rooms opened off the atrium, with windows overlooking the gardens; the kitchen and sleeping rooms were off the peristyle court. The whole edifice was about sixty feet wide by one hundred and fifty feet deep.

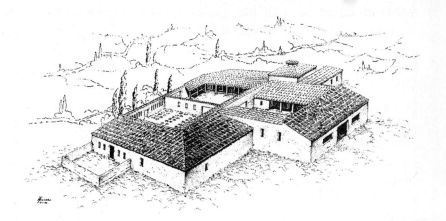

Roman Farmhouse

Pompeii: House of the Silver Wedding, Second Century B.C.

Plate 12

Plate 13.   Pompeii: Mosaic of Alexander at Issus (Naples Museum)

trians. This solidarity of the aristocrats continued after the war, and only twice between 168 and 133 did a "new man" achieve the consulship, each time with the powerful aid of the Scipios. All was not harmony within the charmed circle of the aristocracy, where personal rivalries for offices and honors continued as before, but until the 130's we hear nothing of powerful factions such as those that rent the aristocracy asunder after Magnesia.

Marcus Aemilius Lepidus remained the most highly respected man in Rome until his death in 152. As *princeps senatus* and *pontifex maximus* he exercised great power in the state, and his wide experience in domestic and foreign affairs enabled him to use it wisely. Enlightened and urbane, sharing the broad views characteristic of his family, and little inclined to aggression, he presided well over a peaceful and prosperous Rome. His distant cousin Aemilius Paullus, the victor at Pydna, was honored with the censorship in 164 and died in 160. The prestige of Tiberius Gracchus—now married to Cornelia, the daughter of Scipio Africanus—won him a second consulship in 163, but during that year he quarreled with his Scipionic in-laws and we hear little more about him until his death about 154. Cato remained as active as ever and, though now related by marriage to the Aemilii and other prominent families, he continued his cantankerous outspokenness until silenced by death in 149.

After the passing of these men of the older generation, leadership returned to the Scipios. Scipio Nasica—son of Africanus's cousin and now titular head of the family—succeeded Lepidus both as *princeps senatus* and as *pontifex maximus,* and when he died in 141 the high priesthood passed to his son, who held it until his death in 132. Of

---

• Note for Plate 13. This most famous of ancient mosaics was found at Pompeii in the so-called House of the Faun—a magnificent residence dating from the second century before Christ. The mosaic, made of almost a million tiny pieces of colored stone, was probably based on a Hellenistic Greek painting. It shows a battle between Alexander the Great and Darius, either Issus or Gaugamela. Darius, slightly to the right, and his Persians (with covered heads) are fleeing before the Macedonians who are armed with long spears. Alexander appears bareheaded on horseback in the fragment to the left. (*Photo, National Museum, Naples.*)

far greater stature, however, was Scipio Aemilianus, the son of Aemilius Paullus who had been adopted by the son of Scipio Africanus and married the daughter of Cornelia and Tiberius Gracchus. He was related by blood, marriage, or adoption to all the leading families of his day (see chart on p. 177), and he may be said to represent the old Roman aristocracy at its best. From his first consulship in 147 until his death in 129 Aemilianus remained the most important man in Rome.

After 168 these aristocratic rulers of Rome and Italy followed policies that were satisfactory to a wide variety of persons. Economic prosperity enabled the equestrians to forget their political discontent of pre-war years. Public works at Rome and throughout Italy gave many of them lucrative contracts while foreign trade made fortunes for others. The equestrians as a class therefore approved of the government's policies. The rising generation of Roman aristocrats showed greater sympathy with the Italian allies than the Claudians had shown just before the war. Rich Romans had acquired estates in every part of Italy and felt a new solidarity with their neighbors; some of them married rich wives from the Italian aristocracy; and Roman statesmen such as Aemilianus recognized the importance of Italian good will in the army. When such men were in control at Rome, the Italians found little cause for complaint. Even the lower classes at Rome were fairly well satisfied with their government. As conditions in Italy improved, emigration to northern Italy almost ceased, though peasants continued to drift to Rome and other cities. Here some of them prospered as traders or artisans, frequently with financial aid from their patrons; others dragged out wretched existences in the slums, often as the paid clients of aristocratic politicians. Men of both sorts voted as their patrons ordered. Freedmen too were becoming numerous in the city, where they raised a difficult problem, since they had acquired citizenship along with their freedom. They were often used by their former owners to control elections even though other voters resented being placed on an equality with ex-slaves. By combining statesmanship with shrewd politics, and by exploiting the votes of freedmen and clients, the old Roman families were able to dominate elections and retain their political supremacy.

The Beginnings of Latin Literature

This happy period saw great progress in Rome's intellectual life. Leadership here, as in everything else at Rome, fell to the aristocracy. Ever since the third century aristocrats had been given a Greek education, and Greek influences now touched nearly every phase of Rome's intellectual life. Creative work in literature, philosophy, and the arts was done largely by non-Romans in imitation of Greek models. Philhellenic Romans occasionally went to absurd extremes in aping the Greeks, and scandalized Romans of the old school sometimes tried to check this spread of Greek culture by law. Such laws could not be enforced for long, however, and even their authors could not escape Greek influences. As the poet Horace remarked more than a century later, "Captive Greece took her rude conqueror captive."

Nevertheless, the most influential and the most highly respected leaders of thought at Rome were not the silly "Greeklings" whom Cato ridiculed so unmercifully but stalwart Romans conscious of their own traditions and determined to preserve them. They learned what they could from the Greeks in superficial matters, but in fundamentals they remained thoroughly Roman. Cato was such a man; and though Scipio Aemilianus may have been friendlier to individual Greeks, he was almost as ruggedly Roman as old Cato himself. His closest friends made up that brilliant group of statesmen, writers, and philosophers, sometimes called the "Scipionic circle," who dominated the intellectual life of the day. A hundred years later Cicero was to immortalize these men—Cato, Aemilianus, and the rest—in a series of dialogues and essays portraying them as the epitome of Roman culture.

Ennius, first of the great Latin poets, was a Greek born in southern Italy in 239 and brought to Rome by Cato in 204. He accompanied Fulvius Nobilior on the latter's expedition to Aetolia in 189—to be the Homer of a new Trojan War according to Cato's ironic gibe—

and he was rewarded with Roman citizenship on his return. He translated several tragedies of Sophocles and Euripides into Latin, but his greatest work was an epic poem, entitled *Annales,* in which he traced the history of Rome from ancient Troy down to his own day. Though Ennius was a Greek immigrant, full of Greek ideas, he absorbed much of the old Roman spirit. He praised Fabius as the man who "saved Rome by delaying," and his famous line *"moribus antiquis res stat Romana virisque"*—"The Roman state rests upon an ancient way of life and men"—must have won the approval of Cato himself. In later times Ennius was regarded as the father of Latin epic poetry.

At about the same time, Plautus was writing comedies in Latin. Born in central Italy in 254, Plautus came to Rome shortly before Hannibal's invasion. When he failed in business he took to writing comedies and continued in that profession until his death in 184. Twenty plays by Plautus are still extant. Rome's other great comic poet was Terence. Born in Carthage about 195, he was brought to Rome by a senator from whom he took his Latin name, Terentius, and presently he made the acquaintance of Scipio Aemilianus, who produced one of his plays in honor of Aemilius Paullus. This first play was presented in 166 and was followed in rapid succession by five others before the author's death in 159. In spite of his foreign birth, Terence was highly regarded by later Romans as a master of pure Latin.

Plautus and Terence based their plays principally upon the Greek comedies of Menander, but they added much that was their own and thus partially Romanized them. Their comedies—full of rebellious sons, glamorous courtesans, impudent slaves, tyrannical and unintelligent parents—were profoundly shocking to conservative Romans, who were still devoted to a social system resting in the final analysis upon the *patria potestas.* There was great opposition to the public performance of such subversive plays, and as late as 151 the senate ordered that a theater built by the censors be torn down. Comedies were still performed, with the audience standing up to watch, but such Greek importations did not find a permanent place at Rome. Plautus and Terence had no important successors.

Other writers were developing the truly Roman form of literature known as satire. From early times there had been festivals at which it was permissible for private individuals to criticize prominent men with great freedom. Sometimes this criticism was expressed in the form of dialogues, but more commonly in poetic monologues or diatribes; it usually was pungent and caustic, sometimes it was coarse and scurrilous. Out of this grew the literary satire. The Romans regarded Lucilius, a friend of Aemilianus, as the father of satire. The few remaining fragments of this work show its general character. Sometimes Lucilius lampooned Aemilianus's political opponents, but more commonly he concerned himself with social and literary matters. His bitterest ridicule was aimed at foreign luxury, foreign styles, the bombastic rhetoric taught by Greeks, or the affected Romans who could scarcely utter a sentence without using some Greek word. Lucilius's imitators later included such famous Latin poets as Horace and Juvenal.

Roman Historians

Historians held a high place among writers of Latin prose, and during the second century historical writing became a major form of literature at Rome. Here as elsewhere history grew out of chronicles and annals. From early times the *pontifex maximus* had recorded the names of the consuls and other high officials for each year along with the military events and other striking phenomena such as prodigies and eclipses. At first these pontifical annals were brief and schematic, but gradually they became more copious until they covered Rome's political life in considerable detail. The great families also preserved records of ancestors of whom they were inclined to boast. Unfortunately, however, many of these hero tales had been fabricated long after the event by the imaginative use of the scanty materials available for early times, especially in order to provide distinguished ancestors for families whose prominence dated only from yesterday. It is now difficult or impossible to separate the true from the false in these family traditions.

Scholars and writers in the second century, realizing that popular legend and family brag were feeble foundations for serious history, began to ransack the pontifical archives for materials that would serve as the basis of their works on the history of Rome. While Lepidus was *pontifex maximus* a certain L. Cassius Hemina compiled such a work in four books, called *Annales*. Others followed his example during the next few decades, and at last P. Mucius Scaevola, who served as *pontifex maximus* from 130 to 115, collected and published all the official records in eighty volumes, under the title *Annales maximi*. This publication of course gave a new impetus to historical studies and led to the publication of several large histories of the city. These works were much used by Livy, who wrote a compendious Roman history at the end of the first century before Christ, and since he repeated most of what they said, the earlier works were neglected and lost. Retaining the old annalistic form, these historians recorded events year by year, first mentioning the officials, then the prodigies, then domestic politics, and finally the wars. In later times the pattern of historical writing thus established was used by nearly all Roman historians.

As Rome's intellectual horizon broadened, her historians tried to harmonize her history with that of her neighbors. As early as the fourth century, Romans had claimed descent from the Trojans through Aeneas. Poets developed the idea in the third century, and Q. Fabius Pictor raised it to the rank of sober history. Pictor was a Roman senator who had been sent to Greece in 216 to obtain Aetolian aid against Philip V of Macedon when the latter was preparing his alliance with Hannibal. Perhaps Pictor wrote the history at that time, or perhaps it did not appear until after the defeat of Hannibal—the last extant fragment of the work tells of Roman losses at Trasimene (217). At any rate, Pictor's history was written in Greek and obviously was intended for use as propaganda in Greece. It protests Rome's justice in all her dealings, and it greatly exaggerates her military and naval strength. Pictor's views of Roman history were copied and amplified by many later writers.

Cato's Origines

The most important writer of Latin prose in the second century was Cato. He wrote noteworthy books on agriculture and law, and he published a collection of one hundred and fifty of his speeches. Though Cato ridiculed the efforts of the *Graeculi* to swallow Greek culture whole, and though he sometimes championed traditional ignorance,[1] those modern writers who picture him as the incarnation of bucolic old-fogeyism are far indeed from the truth. He did not oppose culture and the graces of life generally, and his writings show that he was not insensible to literary style, but his standards of judgment were Roman rather than Greek. Even the old legend, preserved by Plutarch, that Cato first learned Greek at the age of eighty is without foundation. He was a propaganda agent in Greece in 192 when he was forty-two, and his writings show that he was familiar with and influenced by many Greek models, including Xenophon and Thucydides.

Cato's most significant writing was his *Origines*, a history of Rome in seven volumes. Only a small part of this work has been preserved, but our few fragments give a good picture of Cato himself and of the dominating ideas of the time in which he wrote. Disapproving of the bald and schematic form of the annals, Cato attempted to make his history a work of literature. The first book told of Rome under the kings while the second and third books dealt with the early history of other Italian communities. This arrangement was characteristic of a time when Romans were showing a new sympathy with the Italians, and it indicated a breadth of view foreign to the earlier annalists and even to Livy a century and a half later. Remarks by ancient writers indicate that Cato's history must have been unusual in other respects as well. In his account of the Second Punic War he mentioned no proper name except that of Hannibal's elephant. He told how the Roman army or the Roman people or the Roman consul acted, but individuals were passed over in silence. The sixth

---

[1] Thus Cato had heard somewhere that all Greek physicians took an oath composed by Hippocrates by which they swore to help Greeks but to kill other patients. He therefore wrote a book of his own on medicine, preserving the traditional Roman remedies. Some of his health hints are given in the *De agri cultura*. His method of curing a sprain, for example, was to split a long reed in a certain manner and apply the parts to the injured spot while chanting "motas vaeta daries dardares astataries dissunapiter." The words presumably had a meaning when the charm was first composed, but in the form given by Cato they mean no more in Latin than they do in English.

and seventh books of the history, dealing with the events of his own day, were much colored by Cato's prejudices, and they included excerpts from a speech he delivered in the last year of his life (149).

Polybius

The great historian of Rome in the second century was not a Roman at all, however, but the Greek Polybius. His father had been a general of the Achaean League and a close friend of its leader, and when the Greeks were defeated in 168, Polybius was one of the thousand hostages sent to Rome. He was then about thirty-seven years old. Aemilius Paullus received the hostage into his own house and made him tutor of his two sons, later known as Fabius Aemilianus and Scipio Aemilianus. Polybius therefore became intimately acquainted with the leading families of Rome and he was an important member of the Scipionic circle. He gradually absorbed the point of view of his Roman friends and persuaded himself that Rome's conquests had been for the best. In his later years he served as propagandist for Rome among his fellow Greeks.

Polybius's *History* told how Rome conquered the world. Only the first five of its forty books remain intact, but extensive excerpts from the others have been preserved. The heart of the history covered the period from 221 to 168 B.C., while an introduction sketched in the background and a conclusion summarized events down to 146. This great work has caused Polybius to be ranked with Herodotus and Thucydides as one of the great Greek historians, a judgment fully justified by his breadth of view, his wealth of accurate detail, and his deep insight. He was particularly interested in the causes of what happened—first, in the general reasons why Rome was able to conquer the civilized world so quickly; secondly, in the special reasons for minor events along the way. But he always kept in mind the practical end of persuading his fellow Greeks to accept Roman rule. Polybius's picture of Greece in the third and second centuries is not a pleasant one, and his account of the Roman character and government is made to support his belief that Rome could set everything to rights. Like every good propagandist, he persuaded himself before he undertook to persuade others; and, like every good historian, he spared no pains to learn the facts and he refused to suppress what he found incompatible with his theory.

The Development of Roman Law

Rome's law was more truly Roman than her literature. Her lawyers expressed the Roman spirit at its best, and their ideas and opinions constitute one of Rome's priceless contributions to the world. The second century was a crucial period in the history of Rome's legal development. Law and religion had always been closely associated at Rome, and in early times both sacred and civil law were preserved and interpreted by the pontiffs. Since these pontiffs all came from the patrician class, law remained a secret of the aristocracy. Attempts were made to secularize and democratize the law, but progress was slow and even the publication of the Law of the Twelve Tables, about 450, did not altogether free the law from patrician control. Roman law, like that of most primitive peoples, was bound up with a rigid procedure not explained in the code, and a citizen who wished to claim his rights had to apply to the priests for essential information regarding rituals and days. Presently one member of the pontifical college was delegated to answer such inquiries. A second step in freeing the law came at the end of the fourth century when Gnaeus Flavius published a collection of the *legis actiones*—that is, of the ritual words that had to be used by a plaintiff to bring a case into court. He subsequently posted in the forum a calendar showing the days on which suits might be brought. Finally, a law was enacted in 300 which admitted plebeians to the college of pontiffs, thereby breaking the legal monopoly of the old aristocracy and closing one chapter in the history of Roman law.

Meantime, Rome's conquests in Italy had begun forcing new developments in the law. When Rome established supremacy over the Latins she gave them the rights of *connubium* and *commercium* (literally, "marriage and trade"), which in practice was equivalent to granting them the full protection of Roman law in civil matters. The Italian allies, on the other hand, retained their own law, and when in Rome they had the status of *peregrini* or "friendly aliens." In later times the free citizens of other allied states enjoyed that same status. The *peregrini* became so numerous that in 242 a special court, under the *praetor peregrinus*, was set up to hear their lawsuits. Thereafter the old court, presided over by the *praetor urbanus*, handled suits between Roman citizens while the *praetor peregrinus* tried cases in which aliens were involved. The urban praetors were closely bound by the old Roman law, called the *ius civile*, or "law of the citizen," but the peregrine praetors, dealing with men not entitled to the privileges of Roman citizenship, were allowed greater freedom in their interpretation of the law.

The *ius civile* had developed in the early days when Rome was primarily an agricultural community and it neglected many relationships arising in advanced commercial life. On the other hand, most of the *peregrini* in Rome were businessmen whose lawsuits dealt with such commercial matters. The peregrine praetors were therefore forced to work out new principles of law to cover the new sorts of cases that arose as Rome's economic and commercial organization became more complex. Moreover, when Roman praetors were sent to govern provinces, such as Sicily and Spain, they followed the peregrine praetors in their free interpretation of the law. It must be added, however, that while praetors sometimes took hints from the law of the peoples they were judging, they rarely incorporated foreign law into their own system. They were Romans, and the law they applied was Roman law stripped of its archaic formalism and developed along the lines of its own fundamental principles. This new law of the peregrine praetors came to be called the *ius gentium*, or "law of the peoples."

The Formulary System

Reforms in legal procedure at Rome presently permitted much of the *ius gentium* to filter into the *ius civile*. In early times suit could be started only by the plaintiff appearing with the defendant before the praetor, going through an elaborate and unalterable ritual, and pronouncing the stereotyped phrases (the *certa verba*) of the *legis actio*—phrases which must contain, among other things, the exact words of the law to which he appealed. The praetor then appointed a *iudex*—a judge or arbitrator, chosen in those days from the senatorial class—who had to be acceptable to both parties. After listening to the complaints and evidence, the *iudex* rendered judgment. The inflexibility of the *legis actio* rendered it burdensome, and the laws which might be invoked under it were inadequate for the new Rome. A new and more elaborate system of civil law and procedure became necessary.

Modernization came through the "formulary system." Writs called *formulae* probably were first used by peregrine praetors to initiate a legal action, but toward the middle of the second century they were authorized for urban praetors as well. Thereafter the ritual of the *legis actio* was dispensed with. The plaintiff merely appeared before the magistrate and stated his case, usually with the aid of a legal adviser. If the praetor approved the suit, he appointed a *iudex* to whom he presented a writ, or *formula,* which had been drawn up in the presence of the litigants, indicating the questions to be decided and the redress to be granted if the facts were found to be as represented. The praetors enjoyed great freedom in preparing *formulae,* and while they could not openly disregard the *ius civile* they could modify or supplement it with equity.

It then became the custom for each praetor, immediately upon entering office, to publish an edict listing the *formulae* that he would grant. This edict was known as the *edictum perpetuum,* or "continuous edict," because it remained in force throughout his year in office. In issuing such edicts the praetors were of course arrogating legislative functions to themselves, for in effect they were listing the wrongs for which they would grant redress and indicating what redress they would grant. Arbitrary action on their part was checked by a law of 67 B.C., which ordered that they adhere to the edict they posted on their first day in office and not invent new formulas later. Each praetor supposedly prepared his own edict, but in most cases he merely copied that of his predecessor, perhaps with a few minor changes. As the praetors were primarily politicians rather than jurists, they must have received careful legal advice in drawing up their edicts for, as modern scholars agree, the law contained in them is law of the highest excellence. In later times these praetorian edicts came to be considered a principal source of Roman law.

Jurisconsults

At this time, too, arose the first great jurisconsults. A certain Tiberius Coruncanius, who became the first plebeian *pontifex maximus* in 253, had introduced the practice of giving public lectures on the law and its interpretation. Following his precedent a group of men learned in the law, called "jurisconsults," began publicly giving out opinions or *responsa*. Sextus Aelius Paetus, consul in 198, was the author of the *Tripertita* in which he gave the texts of the Laws of the Twelve Tables, the interpretations with which the pontiffs had surrounded them, and the *legis actiones* by which complainants might seek redress. This work soon replaced Flavius's publication, and centuries later lawyers still referred to it as "the cradle of the law." Cato wrote on law, as on so many other things, but his legal writings were surpassed by those of his son. The second half of the century was illuminated by the three great jurists who laid the foundation of classical civil law: M. Manilius, consul in 149; M. Junius Brutus; and P. Mucius Scaevola, consul (133) and *pontifex maximus* (130–115), who also published the *Annales maximi*. Publius's son, Quintus Scaevola, likewise consul (95) and *pontifex maximus* (89–82), was perhaps the most eminent Roman jurist of Republican times. In their writings these men discussed and elaborated upon the Laws of the Twelve Tables and the praetorian edicts. Praetors drew up their edicts with the help of such jurisconsults, and the splendid edifice of the Roman law really was their creation.

When praetors and jurists became acquainted with various systems of foreign law, they developed the concept of an ideal law lying behind all actually existing human systems. They believed that this ideal law was common to all men and that in the final analysis it was identical with the *ius naturale*, or "natural law," which philosophers said was inherent in the nature of the universe. The peregrine praetors had this ideal law in mind when formulating the rules of the *ius gentium*, and under the influence of praetors and jurisconsults the civil law itself gradually took on a universal character. The concepts of a *ius gentium* and a *ius naturale* encouraged jurists to create a secular and rational system of law rising above local traditions and national differences. They consciously legislated for all mankind and made Roman law a system fit for the whole world.

New Religions at Rome

The close connection of law and religion at Rome is further illustrated by their parallel development during the second century. For a time Romans showed a tendency to imitate Greek and other foreign religions, but in religion, as in law, fundamental Roman ideas eventually prevailed. The Romans had long been accustomed to admitting the gods of other peoples into the city and even incorporating them into their own pantheon, just as they made these alien peoples themselves allies or even citizens. Sometimes the new deities were identified with old Roman gods but more often they were kept in an appropriate position of inferiority. Their former devotees were allowed to continue worshiping them, but Romans did not do so, and temples might not be erected to them inside the *pomerium*—a sacred line surrounding the heart of the city.

The influx of foreign religious rites and ideas was greatly accelerated during the long war against Hannibal, when men took up new religions and superstitions of every sort in their frantic search for whatever divine aid they could get. Crowds of people worshiped strange gods in the forum and even at the Capitol itself. Once when the authorities tried to remove the new altars they almost precipitated a riot. At last a praetor ordered citizens to surrender all books of ritual and magic, and forbade the use of new forms of worship in public. Such repression was not successful, however, and after the war Rome was still full of foreign fortune-tellers, diviners, and prophets, while old-fashioned Romans were dismayed at the spread of superstition. Cato once expressed amazement that two Etruscan haruspices could meet in the street without winking at each other.

The government itself was not above reproach in this matter of introducing new religions. The Sibylline Books had been consulted frequently during the Second Punic War, and new rites were established as this oracle ordered. On one occasion, in 205, the Books were found to prophesy that Hannibal would be driven from Italy if Cybele, the Great Mother of the Gods, were brought to Rome from her home in Asia Minor. Rome was at that time allied with Attalus of Pergamum, through whom Roman envoys were enabled to obtain a famous black stone representing the deity. It was solemnly received in 204 and placed in a shrine within the *pomerium*, and a great temple to the Magna Mater was erected on the Palatine Hill in 191.

The austere Romans presently found that they could not abide this disorderly goddess. Her worship was conducted by gorgeously-clad eunuch priests and took the form of riotous outdoor processions and wild dances to the beating of drums and cymbals. Her theology of sin and expiation centered around a dying and rising god who conferred immortality upon his worshipers. Neither the theology nor the worship harmonized with ancient Roman ideas as to what a religion should be. Nevertheless, the new cult was defended by important personages. P. Scipio, a cousin of Africanus and father of the Scipio Nasica who became *pontifex maximus*, had been officially delegated to receive the stone at Rome because of his eminent virtues—though Livy slyly complained in his *History* that no one had recorded exactly which virtues these were. Furthermore, the goddess, by performing a miracle, had restored the reputation of a Claudian lady whose chastity had been questioned. The Scipios and Claudians therefore supported the new goddess, and all that her critics could do was to obtain a decree of the senate forbidding Roman citizens to participate in her outlandish worship (187). The cult remained at Rome, and its legalized status later became the means of introducing countless other oriental religions into the city.

Bacchanalia Prohibited by Law

At about this time all Rome became excited over the orgies of the Bacchanalia. Greeks from southern Italy had brought these rites to Rome, where they aroused great popular opposition. The devotees of the new cult were mostly obscure foreigners, or else Romans addicted to strange and exotic practices, and soon they became the subject of many startling stories. They were publicly accused of such crimes as debauchery, false witness, forging wills and seals, and the murder of whole families. There was even talk of a conspiracy against the state. The worshipers of Bacchus probably were guilty of nothing worse than gross superstitions and the noisy worship of a foreign god, but popular feeling rose against them and the ensuing witch-hunts cost several persons their lives. Many were arrested and countless others fled from the city. All this happened just as the anti-Scipionic and anti-Greek agitation was reaching its climax, and in 186 the Fabian consul laid the matter before the senate with a sensational speech. The senate ordered that the Bacchanalian orgies be abolished throughout Italy, with violation of its order being punishable by death.

Though this agitation and the decree of the senate may be explained in part by the political controversies of the day, the ultimate ramifications of the case reached far beyond the immediate political scene. The decree established a general policy to which Rome adhered thereafter. Charges of a conspiracy against the state were hysterical, no doubt, but this was not the whole story. Roman statesmen simply could not think of religion as something distinct from politics. Moreover, the worship of Bacchus was widespread throughout the Hellenistic world, uniting its worshipers in an organized international society whose political potentialities might easily arouse the apprehensions of sober Roman statesmen. The Bacchanalia offered another illustration of the religious internationalism referred to above in connection with the Jews. It is also worth noting that a few years before this time Ptolemy IV of Egypt (221–03) had issued a decree regulating the worship of Dionysus (or Bacchus) along lines very similar to those used at Rome. It is quite understandable that "isolationist" Romans of the Fabian faction would be suspicious of all such religions.

Thanks to the historian Livy and a famous inscription, we know the exact wording of the senate's decree *de Bacchanalibus*. It was concerned only with the political aspects of the new cult. It strictly forbade the formation of an organized group, or church, but it also provided that anyone desiring to worship Bacchus by himself, or with not more than five persons present, might receive special permission from the praetor to do so. The senate thus took the position that it might prohibit a religious organization which it considered politically undesirable and execute a member of the organization for defying such an order. As the historian Mommsen pointed out in a brilliant study, the whole affair of the Bacchanalia may, in a way, be regarded as a dress rehearsal for the prosecution of Christianity several centuries later.

Greek Philosophy

While these exotic superstitions and religions were attracting the attention of the populace at Rome, Greek philosophers were seeking a following among the educated classes there. It cannot be said that the second century was a brilliant period for Greek philosophy. Violent social disturbances and frequent wars did not create an atmosphere conducive to quiet speculation on the nature of man and the universe, and military defeat brought discouragement and doubt. The most typical Greek philosopher of the day was Carneades who, though born at Cyrene in 214, became head of the Academy at Athens. His philosophy was that of an advanced skeptic, and he was especially active in criticizing the teachings of the Stoics. He maintained that certainty about anything—even the existence of God—is impossible and that ideals such as justice, truth, and duty are merely human conventions of relative value. His criticisms and the general disillusionment of the time forced the Stoics to revise their philosophy extensively, abandoning their former broad views on science and metaphysics and confining themselves more closely to the problems of ethics. The new school of Stoicism, sometimes called the "Middle Stoa," was led by Panaetius of Rhodes (c. 180–110) who had studied in the famous schools at Athens and Tarsus. He later became a close friend of Scipio Aemilianus and divided his time between Athens and Rome. As the Epicureans had already gone almost to the extreme limit of skepticism, they could add little to their doctrines at this time.

Such were the Greek philosophers who came to Rome in the second century. At first they met with the same hostile reception as the Greek and oriental religions. Some books of Pythagorean lore were discovered at Rome in 181 and publicly burned by the authorities; eight years later two Epicurean philosophers were expelled from the city; other expulsions followed in 161. Nevertheless, there was a growing interest in Greek thought among educated Romans. Three Greek philosophers, including Carneades, came to Rome on a diplomatic mission in 155, and while in the city lectured to enthusiastic young men of the Scipionic circle. Cato was as hostile as ever, however, and hustled the philosophers out of town as soon as their official business was finished. When Panaetius arrived a few years later, he fared better. While the Romans were horrified by the materialism of the Epicureans and shocked by Carneades' skepticism, they understood Panaetius better and sympathized with him when he talked about duty and virtue. Thereafter educated Romans usually professed some knowledge of Greek philosophy.

It is not easy to evaluate the influence of Greek philosophy on Roman thought in the second century. Presumably the impression made was not deep. Cicero, in a book that was largely fiction, makes one member of the Scipionic circle remark that while he enjoyed philosophical speculations, he reserved them for his leisure moments and did not permit them to influence his activities as a citizen. Whatever influence Greek thought had upon Roman law came through the rhetoric of orators rather than through the ideas of philosophers. Roman poets filled their works with Greek mythology, but no one believed that such stories were either true or essential to religion. A Roman writer of the next century, Varro, stating what was probably common opinion long before his time, distinguished three types of religion: the religion of the state, the religion of poetry, and the religion of nature. The first he considered obligatory upon all citizens; and, as a matter of fact, the Roman state cult, conducted by the *pontifex maximus* and his assistants, was carefully preserved through succeeding centuries and was little influenced by foreign thought. Matters of mythology and theology were a part of the religion of poetry, regarding which an individual might believe as much or as little as he chose. Natural religion stood to the state cult much as *ius naturale* stood to the *ius civile*. Roman thinkers may have been slightly influenced in their views regarding natural law and religion by the Greek philosophers, notably the Stoics, but even in these matters it is wiser not to exaggerate the influence of Greek ideas. The Romans were quick to adopt superficial techniques and styles from others, while in fundamentals such as law and religion they held firmly to their own traditions.

The Third Punic War

For about fifteen years after the battle of Pydna (168) the Romans showed no desire for further wars or for foreign conquest, but then troubles arose in Africa and Spain. After Zama (202) the Carthaginians had scrupulously fulfilled their treaty obligations and were not seriously bothered by their conquerors. Carthaginian merchants even offered, in 191, to pay off the balance of the indemnity at once, but the Romans refused to accept the money before it fell due. Carthage's troubles thereafter came not from Rome but from Masinissa of Numidia.

In the settlement after Zama, Masinissa had received large territories from Carthage, which encouraged him to dream of a Numidian Empire extending from Egypt to the Atlantic. From time to time he snatched new lands from his neighbor. Since the treaty forbade the Carthaginians to go to war, even defensively, without Rome's express permission, there was nothing they could do in such cases but appeal to Rome, who always decided against them. Masinissa's raids continued for forty years until he had occupied a great part of what had been left to Carthage after 202. Though now approaching ninety years of age, Masinissa showed no loss of aggressiveness or vigor—a forty-fourth son was born to him when he was eighty-six years old—and he obviously hoped to round out his empire by the incorporation of Carthage itself.

Toward 155 Carthage's patience was exhausted by the old brigand's depredations, and she took back by force a patch of territory that he had seized. Two years later the Romans sent a commission to investigate, but they did nothing to restrain Masinissa or otherwise improve the situation in Africa. A year or two later the Carthaginians exiled a number of citizens who favored Masinissa, murdered the envoys he sent to demand the recall of these exiles, and went to war (150). In the first battle, the Carthaginian army of 60,-

000 men was defeated and almost annihilated. Carthage had to surrender to Masinissa, whereupon Rome declared war on her (149) for violating the treaty of 201.

Modern writers have devoted great ingenuity and labor to the discovery of economic or imperialistic causes for this Third Punic War, but their efforts have been conspicuously unsuccessful. Such prominent Romans as Scipio Nasica, the *pontifex maximus,* and Scipio Aemilianus could see no need for drastic action against Carthage, and the principal warmonger of the day was the octogenarian Cato, who completed his long career of opposition to aggression and imperialism in this strange way. He had been a member of the commission sent to Carthage in 153, and it was said that thereafter he never closed a speech on any subject without the ominous words, "Carthago delenda est"—"Carthage must be destroyed." The best explanation of the war seems to be, not that the more sober senators were afraid of Carthage (such fears would have been absurd), but rather that they feared Masinissa. If his plan for a great Numidian Empire in Africa were realized, it might someday menace Rome. The Romans went to war, not from fear of Carthage or of her rivalry, but to annex her and thus keep Masinissa or his successors from doing so.

The Romans landed 80,000 men at Utica, the second Punic city in Africa. This city became their ally, and by various promises the Romans persuaded six other Punic cities to join them. They even induced Carthage herself to surrender her arms. It then seemed safe to make extreme demands, and the Romans announced that the city must be destroyed. The enraged and frantic Carthaginians rearmed as best they could and held the Romans at bay until Scipio Aemilianus assumed command in 147. A year later he carried the city by storm. The whole population of Carthage, which by then had been reduced to 50,000, was sold into slavery. The city itself was burned, the fire lasting seventeen days, and the walls—whose massive foundations have been uncovered by modern archeologists—were battered down. The fields were plowed over, sprinkled with salt, and cursed. For many years these ruins were all that remained of the once mighty city. The former Carthaginian territories were incorporated into the Roman province of Africa, under a governor resident at Utica.

Rome's Troubles in Spain

Meantime rebellion had broken out in Spain. Even in the first half of the century there had been complaints of extortion by Roman governors, until the elder Tiberius Gracchus effected various reforms in 181. We hear little more from Spain until 149, when Cato charged a Roman governor with various misdeeds typical of the corrupt provincial governor of the day. Nevertheless, Galba was acquitted in scandalous fashion. Equestrian businessmen and contractors became an even greater curse to Spain than the aristocratic governors. These publicans descended upon the unfortunate country in throngs. They took contracts for all sorts of things, for which the natives were forced to pay exorbitant prices, and they lent money at usurious rates to individuals or communities that had been assessed indemnities. There was little hope for those unfortunates who once fell into the hands of the usurers, and there were some grounds for suspicion that the publicans were not above stirring up trouble in order that cities might be punished and thus forced to contract new loans to pay their fines.

Hostilities in Spain began in 154, apparently with a simple plundering raid into Roman territory by the Lusitani, a tribe inhabiting modern Portugal. The repression of this raid led to a war lasting three years, during which arose a Lusitanian leader named Viriathus. A man of genius, he united much of the Spanish Peninsula under his leadership, and for twelve years he defeated one Roman army after another. At last the Romans hired assassins to murder him (138). His campaigns cannot be traced in detail, however, for Rome's historians skipped hurriedly over wars of which they could not boast. Viriathus's death did not bring peace to Spain, for the struggle was continued by his allies, the Celtiberians. In 137 their army of barely 4000 men forced the surrender of a Roman consul with 20,000 men—probably the most disgraceful surrender in Roman military annals.

After the surrender a treaty was negotiated by the younger Tiberius Gracchus, whom the Spaniards trusted because of their respect for his father, and under the terms of this treaty the lives of the Roman soldiers were spared. As soon as the danger had passed, however, the senate ordered Tiberius's treaty broken, this being the fourth case of major treaty-breaking by the Romans during the war in Spain. New armies were sent out under Aemilianus in 134, and a year later the Celtiberian capital at Numantia was starved into surrender. Aemilianus's force amounted to about 60,000 men while the Celtiberians had barely 4000 at the beginning of the siege. Native losses were heavy and hundreds committed suicide, but Aemilianus was able to parade fifty Spanish captives at Rome in 132 as a warning that a handful of barbarians should not defeat—or trust—a Roman consul again.

These long wars, with their numerous and disgraceful defeats, did much to demoralize the Roman army. Officers and men were primarily adventurers bent upon loot. Army camps were filled with traders buying and selling plunder, and with bootleggers, prostitutes, and other riffraff galore. Even private soldiers were said to own slaves who did their work, and sometimes instead of marching they had themselves carried around in litters by these slaves. No wonder they surrendered to enemies one-fifth as numerous as they. Aemilianus tried to eradicate these shameful conditions in the army, but even he could effect no permanent reform. War and imperialism were already beginning to debauch the Roman people, and unhappy Spain was merely having a foretaste of what the whole Mediterranean world was soon to suffer.

The Decline of the Greek World

After the fleeting dream of Greek solidarity had been shattered at Pydna, Greek history became a dismal story of decline. The politicians ruling European Greece were an unlovely lot, constantly quarreling amongst themselves and vying with one another in servility to Rome. Prusias of Bithynia, Attalus II of Pergamum, the Rhodians, the Ptolemies, and a number of European Greeks took up and perverted Eumenes' idea of seeking Roman aid in their private quarrels. For several years after Pydna they regularly sent embassies to Rome to complain of their neighbors and implore Rome's support. Prusias once had an unhappy inspiration to dress himself as a freedman and kneel before the senators, addressing them as "savior gods." Other Greeks were equally undignified in their importunities, but the most contemptible—and in some ways the most ingenious—of the lot was Ptolemy Physcon.

Physcon had ruled Egypt jointly with his brother Philometor from 168 until 163, when he was expelled and given Cyrene as his share of the inheritance. He also coveted Cyprus, however, and in 161 he obtained permission from the Roman senate to take this island from his brother if he could do so without war. This of course was impossible, and Cyprus remained in Philometor's hands. Six years later Physcon prepared and published a will (preserved on an inscription discovered in Cyrene in 1929) by which he left his kingdom to the Roman people after pointedly mentioning his long-standing friendship and alliance with them: this will presumably was a bribe to purchase Roman aid against Philometor, for when that aid failed to materialize the will was allowed to lapse. Physcon next went to Rome, where he tried to marry Cornelia, the recently-widowed daughter of Scipio Africanus, apparently hoping that her family's influence would assure him the support of Roman legions. When Cornelia rejected his suit, Physcon devised still other intrigues, and he eventually bribed enough senators to obtain a promise of Roman aid in seizing Cyprus. Cato then delivered a strong oration against the plan, and no aid was sent. Moreover, Cornelia and her family were not at all flattered by the Greek king's romantic proposal. A few years later, Scipio Aemilianus (who had married Cornelia's daughter) went on an official mission to the Near East, where he took especial pains to make his fat and flabby would-be step-father-in-law appear ridiculous in public. Physcon had by this time inherited Egypt, which satisfied his ambition; and having learned the uselessness of his endeavors, he importuned the Romans no more.

Roman Governors in Macedonia and Pergamum

While Greek rulers were thus making themselves contemptible, the Greek people were losing confidence in themselves, and slowly but surely they sank into economic and spiritual bankruptcy. Between Polybius (born about 205 B.C.) and Plutarch (born about 45 A.D.), scarcely a writer, artist, or thinker of importance was born in European Greece. The Greeks were not yet so decadent in 150, however, that they would not undertake another war against Rome. The thousand hostages sent to Rome in 167 remained there for sixteen years, but the three hundred survivors were allowed to return home in 151 after Cato had remarked in the senate that the only remaining question was whether their obsequies should be conducted by Roman undertakers or by Greeks. Cato was wrong, however, for the return of the old men revived painful memories and aroused great indignation throughout Greece.

At about this time an adventurer named Andriscus appeared in Macedonia, claiming to be the son of Perseus, the last king of Macedon. Since Rome was then embogged in the Spanish War and about to attack Carthage, many Greeks believed that their hour had struck. Thousands of recruits flocked to the new leader. During the next year Andriscus occupied the four Macedonian republics set up in 167 and even defeated a Roman legion hurriedly sent to defend them. Eventually, however, his army of 20,000 men was destroyed by the Romans. The four republics were resurrected and continued a shadowy existence for several centuries, but Rome stationed a praetor in Macedonia to look after Roman interests there (148).

While anti-Macedonian prejudice had prevented the Achaean League from sending open aid to Andriscus in 149, the League elected an avowed anti-Roman as its general for the next year. A few months later a frontier dispute between Sparta and the League was referred to Rome. As Rome's decision satisfied no one, the League attacked Sparta (147). Pandemonium at once broke loose throughout Greece. The old promises of the popular leaders to abolish debts and redistribute lands were revived; aristocrats and rich men were murdered; Roman envoys at Corinth barely escaped massacre; slaves were emancipated and armed. In response to these disturbances Roman troops hastened to the scene from Macedonia. The consul Mummius arrived with a large army in the spring of 146 and entered Corinth without fighting. After his troops had sacked and destroyed the city, he sold its inhabitants into slavery. This destruction of Corinth was loudly denounced as a needless atrocity. Polybius, who was present, says that he saw Roman soldiers throwing dice on valuable paintings; and later, Greeks revenged themselves upon poor Mummius by telling how, when he saw soldiers carelessly carrying off a priceless masterpiece, he shouted at them that if they injured it he would compel them to paint another just like it! Fighting in the rest of Greece was easily suppressed. The Romans abolished all the Greek Leagues, made separate treaties of alliance with their member cities, and confiscated the lands of Corinth and Thebes. Though Greece was not formally annexed by Rome, it remained under the watchful eye of the praetor in Macedonia.

Our knowledge of the history of Pergamum during the period after Pydna is slight. Eumenes II lost the confidence of his Roman friends by intriguing with Perseus during the last part of the war, but when he died and was succeeded by his brother, Attalus II (160–138), Rome resumed her old friendship. Nevertheless, the days of Pergamum's greatness were over. Her wealth declined, she quarreled and fought with her neighbors, and she was harassed by native unrest. Her last king, Attalus III (138–133), son of Eumenes II, left his kingdom by will to the Roman people. We know neither the time nor the circumstances under which he drew up this will, and we are left to conjecture his motives. It seems plausible to suppose that Attalus shared his father's ideas about Greek and Roman co-operation for the maintenance of Greek culture in the Orient. He had learned from bitter disappointment that the Romans were no longer willing to intervene in the East to protect Greek rulers from their subjects, but it may have occurred to him that if Rome were actually to annex his kingdom she would doubtless preserve the Greek institutions there which the Greeks themselves could no longer defend. At any rate, rebellion broke out as soon as Attalus was dead, and soon all western Asia Minor was ablaze. The chief rebel was Aristonicus who, though reputedly an illegitimate son of Eumenes, recruited his followers among the natives and thus made himself the leader of an oriental popular revolt. He called his followers "Heliopolitans" or "Citizens of the City of the Sun." Stoic philosophers had sometimes written of a Utopia called Heliopolis, but Aristonicus presumably took the name from some oriental solar deity (such as Mithra) with whom his native followers would be more familiar than they were with Stoic philosophy. After much hesitation, the Romans sent troops to occupy their new province (131). Aristonicus defeated the first Roman armies and killed the consul in command, but eventually he was defeated, and in 129 the kingdom of Pergamum was annexed by Rome as the province of Asia.

Syria and Egypt

In Syria Demetrius I had become king (162) about a year after the death of his uncle Antiochus IV Epiphanes. At first he was rather successful in dealing with the various revolts which had broken out in the kingdom: he pacified Judea; he killed the rebel Timarchus, who held the eastern Seleucid territories (160); and he regained most of what his father Seleucus IV had ruled. Before long, however, he fell to quarreling with his neighbors, notably with Ariarathes V of Cappadocia and Attalus II of Pergamum. Bankrupted by these struggles, he withdrew to a castle near Antioch where he spent his days and nights in drunkenness and debauchery, despising his subjects and despised by them. Presently Attalus discovered a young man closely resembling Antiochus Epiphanes, whom he put forward as the old king's son and lawful heir. This fellow was called Alexander Balas. His claims to Syria being recognized by Rome and supported by Ariarathes and Ptolemy Philometor, he landed in 152 at Ptolemaïs on the Phoenician shore. After Demetrius had tried to defend his kingdom and was killed in battle (150), Balas ruled Syria for five years.

Ptolemy Philometor was now almost thirty-five years of age. His Egyptian kingdom had enjoyed peace for ten years and its wealth was such that he could undertake aggressive policies. He, more than any other Greek of his generation, retained something of Antiochus Epiphanes' old dream of Greek solidarity. He therefore married his daughter Cleopatra Thea ("Goddess") to Alexander Balas, whose principal supporter he became. Alexander soon showed his utter incapacity, quarreled with his father-in-law, and was driven out of

Antioch by his subjects. Philometor then transferred his support to young Demetrius II, son of the former king, who was allowed to become Cleopatra's second husband. Philometor visited Antioch in 145, and its citizens begged him to accept their crown and unite the two kingdoms—thus reviving, with roles reversed, the plan of Antiochus during his second invasion of Egypt twenty-three years before —but the scheme came to nothing. A few weeks later, Ptolemy and Alexander fought a great battle. Alexander was defeated and killed, and Ptolemy died of wounds a little later (145). Syria fell into anarchy, and after the death of Philometor Egypt went to his brother Physcon, who ruled as Ptolemy VII Euergetes II. Under his rule Egypt rapidly went from bad to worse.

Two rival kings arose in Syria after the death of Alexander Balas. The guardian of Alexander's infant son (Antiochus VI Dionysus, recognized in Antioch and much of Syria) was a certain Tryphon who proclaimed himself king in 142, thus founding a new dynasty. His rival as king was Demetrius II who held Babylonia and the coastal cities of Phoenicia until he was taken prisoner by the Parthians in 139. His brother, Antiochus VII Sidetes (see chart, p. 191), took over the crown, married Cleopatra Thea as her third husband, killed Tryphon (138), and showed himself to be another strong Seleucid—the last of the line. During the next ten years he reunited most of the territory once held by his father Demetrius I, but he was killed in battle by the Parthians in 129.

Cleopatra Thea then attempted to rule Syria in her own name. This "Goddess" (Thea) was an immensely ambitious woman, utterly unscrupulous, and thirsty for power. She had her second husband, Demetrius II, murdered in 125, four years after the Parthians had released him; she murdered one of her sons; and in 121 she was forced by another son to drink the poison she had prepared for him. The various rivals who thereafter called themselves kings of Syria were in reality nothing more than the leaders of mercenary bands who fought each other and pillaged the unfortunate country.

Parthian Advance

The thirty years that followed the death of Antiochus Epiphanes in 163 were a period of great Parthian advance under Mithradates I.

He had come to the throne in 171, but he did not start upon his career of conquest until almost ten years later. While Demetrius I was ruling Syria, Mithradates conquered Media, occupied much of Bactria, and added most of Persia to his realm. The chaos following Demetrius's death gave him ample opportunity to extend his empire westward. He was received as king in the Seleucid capital at Seleucia-on-the-Tigris in 141, and his authority extended as far south as Uruk. Two years later Demetrius II of Syria launched a great counterattack with the aid of the Greeks throughout the territories occupied by Mithradates, but we have already seen that he was taken prisoner by the Parthians and that all his gains were lost.

Mithradates died in 138 and was succeeded by his son Phraates. A few years later, the strong new king of Syria, Antiochus VII Sidetes, attempted to regain what his father had lost. He received the aid of various pro-Greek factions in Mesopotamia, but he and his mercenaries were a heavy burden to the natives, who soon showed that they preferred Parthian rule. The defeat and death of Antiochus in 129 ended the last effort of the Greeks to dominate Mesopotamia. A few years later, Mithradates II became king of Parthia and during his long reign (122–88) he proved himself a worthy successor to the first Mithradates. He organized the Empire so strongly that it was able to fight the series of great wars with Rome in the middle of the first century before Christ.

The Parthians thus took over the greater part of the old Seleucid Empire. The long-expected kings from the East had at last appeared and had driven out the Greeks. Though the Parthians were only a small aristocracy ruling over a vast territory and though they had no advanced civilization of their own, they were skillful rulers of the peoples whom they conquered. They brought unity and relative peace to the Near East after the chaos that accompanied the decline of the Seleucids. Though Pahlavi, a Persian dialect written in Aramaic characters, was the official language of the Parthian Empire, Aramaic became the common tongue of the whole Near East, and Arameans were employed to look after the details of government. The new unity was a great boon to commerce. The Parthians held the great trade routes between the East and the West and encouraged trade along them. The silk trade with China, which became

an important item before the end of the second century, was facili-
tated by diplomatic relations established by Mithradates II with the
Chinese emperors. Under Parthian rule the cities of Mesopotamia
were granted autonomy, and their economic prosperity is shown by
the fact that modern archeologists have found rich Parthian levels
at practically every Mesopotamian site excavated. The native inhabitants spent little time bewailing the loss of their former Greek
masters. While a part of the Hellenic heritage in the Near East was
preserved by the Parthians, the days of Greek rule were definitely
over. The Parthians and their successors were Orientals, and for
almost two thousand years European influence east of the Euphrates
was negligible.

The Independent Jewish State

Troubled conditions in Syria enabled the Jews eventually to gain
their national independence. After the death of Judas Maccabaeus
in 160, Demetrius I drove the Maccabaeans into exile, but in 157 he
allowed Judas's brother Jonathan to return to the little village of
Michmash, ten miles north of Jerusalem. Here Jonathan continued
the old propaganda against Hellenizing "sinners" and became the
recognized leader of the Jewish nationalists. When Alexander Balas
attacked Demetrius in 152, Jonathan played the two rivals off against
each other. He first persuaded Demetrius to free Judea of all Syrian
troops except the garrison holding the citadel at Jerusalem and to
permit the fortification of the Temple. As soon as he had accomplished this, he induced Balas to outbid Demetrius by making him
high priest and giving him a position at the Seleucid court as one of
the king's "First Friends." A few years later, during the troubles that
followed the deaths of Balas and Philometor, Jonathan besieged the
citadel at Jerusalem, added several towns to Judea, sent troops to
help Demetrius II, and presently deserted to Tryphon, hoping no
doubt for further favors in return. This last piece of treachery was a
mistake, however, for Tryphon had him arrested and executed
(143).

Leadership of the Jewish rebels then passed to Jonathan's brother
Simon. The new leader at once made peace with Demetrius II, and

was rewarded with the title of "high priest and governor of the Jews." The historian of the Maccabaeans records that in the year 142 "the yoke of the heathen was taken away from Israel." Simon obtained the remission of all tribute; taking the coastal cities of Joppa and Gazara, he settled them with Jewish colonists; and in 140 he captured the Greek citadel at Jerusalem. When Antiochus Sidetes attempted in 138 to re-establish Greek power in Judea, his armies were defeated in a minor battle, and for several years the Jews were left in peace. Simon was murdered by his son-in-law in 134, but was succeeded by his son John Hyrcanus. Soon thereafter Antiochus Sidetes again decided to reduce the rebellious province and took Jerusalem after a long siege. Though his advisers urged him to destroy the city utterly, Antiochus preferred more lenient measures. He demolished the fortifications, disarmed the Jews, and demanded an indemnity of five hundred talents together with tribute for Joppa and Gazara. Otherwise he allowed the Jews to return to their old status, with complete religious liberty and with John Hyrcanus high priest and governor. Hyrcanus accompanied Antiochus on his march against the Parthians, but he escaped the enemy, and after Antiochus's death in 129 he became the completely independent monarch of Judea. Never again were the Jews under Greek rule, though their territories were occasionally plundered by Greek mercenary bands.

Hyrcanus raised an army of mercenaries with which he conquered new territories on every side. Coastal cities were added in the west; the city of Samaria, long a rival to Jerusalem, was destroyed and its territory annexed; several cities in Transjordania were captured; Idumea (the Biblical Edom, south of the Dead Sea) was conquered and its inhabitants were forced to accept circumcision. In 122 Hyrcanus sent a delegation to Rome to renew the old friendship dating from Judas's treaty of 161; the ambassadors brought back a new treaty of "friendship and mutual alliance" which had, however, no more practical importance than the earlier one. Hyrcanus died in 104 and was succeeded by his son Judas Aristobulus, who was the first of his family to wear the diadem and to call himself king. He reigned for only one year but he added Galilee—the district north of Samaria—to his possessions and forcibly Judaized its inhabitants, thus following his father in the less lovely aspects of religious imperialism. Alexander Jannaeus then ruled for twenty-six years (103–77) and rounded out the Jewish possessions in Palestine by adding the remaining cities of the coastal plain. Most of the territories once held by David and Solomon were again under Jewish rule, where they remained until the coming of the Romans in 63 B.C.

The Diaspora

Not all the Jewish people lived in this theocratic state in Palestine. At the time of the great catastrophies of the sixth century, when the old Jewish state was destroyed by the Chaldeans (586), many Jews had fled to Egypt and tens of thousands were deported to various parts of Mesopotamia. Fifty years later, the Persian king Cyrus allowed those to return to Palestine who wished (538), but not everyone wished to go back. Many Jews had done so well economically when in exile that they were quite willing to remain there. In fact, the exiles who returned were a select group whose religious ardor made possible the establishment and perpetuation of the theocratic state in Judea. Other exiles had meantime intermarried with the native populations of Babylonia and thus been lost to Jewry. Still others retained their ancestral religion and their national consciousness though remaining in their new homes.

In later years Jews again migrated from Palestine for various reasons. Judea was a poor country, unable to support its population, and the descendants of the returned exiles sought better living conditions elsewhere. Some went to Egypt as mercenary soldiers; others fell into debt and were sold abroad as slaves. Many Jews established themselves in business at Alexandria; others went to Antioch, Ephesus, Tarsus, and the other great cities of the Hellenistic world; and some were expelled from Rome as early as 139. These Jews outside Palestine were said to live in the Diaspora, or "scattering." Even though they kept up their old religion, and maintained relations with the Jews of Palestine, they were led by circumstances into new modes of life.

It was not long before anti-Semitism appeared in the countries where Jewish minorities dwelt. The Jews were inclined to flock together, observing their peculiar customs such as the Sabbath and their dietary laws, and often refusing to marry Gentiles; and sometimes they failed to conceal adequately their consciousness of moral superiority over the rest of mankind. Consequently they were unpopular wherever they went. In the Book of Esther, probably dating from the third century before Christ, there is evidence that the peoples of Babylonia regarded the Jews as different from, and less desirable than, their other neighbors; and the contemporary historian Manetho bears witness to similar views in Egypt. The Gentiles replied to Jewish pretensions of superiority by circulating fantastic stories of their disgraceful or ridiculous practices and history: thus Manetho explained the Exodus under Moses by saying that the Jews had been driven from Egypt because of their filthiness and leprosy. Others accused them of worshiping an ass's head. Greek and Roman writers who mention Jews nearly always betray great ignorance of them and use uncomplimentary language about them. At first anti-Semitism showed itself only in such ways as these, but eventually it assumed more violent forms and, especially at Alexandria, Jews sometimes suffered from mob violence.

The Jews of the Diaspora had taken no part in the Maccabaean revolt and were not much influenced by the religious ideas that sprang up in those exciting days. Babylonian Jews retained the broad interpretation of their religion that is shown in the Jewish writings of the fourth and third centuries, and they continued to learn much from their pagan neighbors. Their Judaism tended to resemble that of the Wisdom literature—such works as the Book of Proverbs, falsely attributed to Solomon—which said very little about Yahweh and the Law. The Wisdom books were concerned primarily with laying down rules for a virtuous and happy life, seeking human rather than divine sanctions for virtue, and speaking always in universal terms. Moreover, conditions in the Diaspora encouraged Jews to neglect the narrower features of the old Judaism and turned their attention to matters not discussed by the Law and the Prophets. Earlier Jewish writers had shown only vague and limited ideas upon the subject of immortality, for example, but in the second and first centuries much was said about eternal life, a general resurrection, and future rewards and punishments. At this time, too, there was a great development of Jewish ideas about angels, and especially about Satan and the "fallen angels" who became powers of evil almost independent of God. New doctrines regarding eschatology, or the end of the world, also became current. The influence of Persian Zoroastrianism is visible in much of this and at just this time the Jews began using Persian religious rites such as baptism. Since the Jews of Babylonia retained close connections with their kinsmen in Palestine, their ideas presently appeared in Palestine itself and eventually were accepted by the most orthodox Jews.

The Jews of Alexandria were more receptive to Greek ideas, and expressed themselves rather differently. Since many of them could not read Hebrew, the Old Testament was translated into Greek for their benefit. The Greek translation of the Torah (the first five books of the Old Testament) dates perhaps from the third century, but the other books came later. This version of the Old Testament is called the Septuagint because legend related that it was made by seventy (in Latin, *septuaginta*) scholars. As the Alexandrian Jews were more willing than those in Palestine to admit new books into the canon (the list of books regarded as inspired Scripture), the Septuagint eventually included several books and parts of books not found in Hebrew Bibles. These additional books are now called the "Apocrypha" and are accepted by some Christian churches while others reject them.[2]

Most of the apocryphal books date from the second century and give interesting information regarding the spread of Greek culture among the Jews. The most important are two historical works, I and II Maccabees, which are our principal source of information regarding the Maccabaean revolt and subsequent events in Jewish history. There are also two pious romances, Tobit and Judith; and several

---

[2] The early Christians read the Old Testament in Greek and therefore accepted the Alexandrian canon without question, just as the Greek Orthodox Church does today; the Vulgate, a Latin translation of the Bible dating from the end of the fourth century after Christ, retained nearly all the new material found in the Septuagint, and it became the standard version of the Scriptures used in the West throughout the Middle Ages and by the Roman Catholic Church down to the present time. The early Protestants went back to the Hebrew canon and rejected the Apocrypha, though these books are sometimes printed in Protestant Bibles in a separate section between the Old and New Testaments. Modern Jews still follow the old Hebrew canon. See Vol. I, chap. VII.

short stories are inserted in the Greek texts of Daniel and Esther. Ecclesiasticus, the first of two books of proverbial wisdom, was written in Palestine by Jesus ben Sirach early in the second century and translated into Greek by his grandson somewhat after 132 B.C. It sets forth the views of a pious and enlightened Jew little touched by non-Jewish culture. The second of these wisdom books, called the Wisdom of Solomon, was written in Egypt early in the first century before Christ. It is full of Greek ideas derived from Heraclitus, Xenophon, Plato, and the Stoics, and it was used by St. Paul and other early Christians.

Sadducees and Pharisees

Religious developments in Palestine took a different course. The old dream of the Maccabaeans had at last been realized and the Jews were an independent people ruled only by God and his priests, but in practice the theocracy was not what enthusiasts had dreamed it would be. As is always the case, practical necessities compelled compromises which idealists deplored. Jews tended to fall into two parties according to their attitude toward the new government. Both parties considered themselves good Jews, followers of Judas Maccabaeus and in no way related to the Hellenizers of the preceding generation; but one party, called the Sadducees, was willing to follow the government in its rather worldly politics while its opponents, the idealistic Pharisees, desired a more devout policy.

The Sadducees professed complete loyalty to the Law though they maintained that this Law consisted only of those precepts that were taught explicitly in the Torah. The Pharisees, on the other hand, insisted upon interpreting the Law in the light of the oral traditions preserved by the Scribes, or scholars learned in the Law. The Pharisees continued to study and interpret the Law, thus founding the line of Rabbis, or Teachers, who eventually produced the great commentaries upon the Law known as the Midrash and the Talmud. They were the men who kept Judaism alive, partly by building up an impressive and satisfying system of religious and ethical precepts well adapted to their people, and partly by keeping Jews separate from Gentiles.

In spite of their attachment to the ancient Law, the Pharisees were the progressive faction among the Jews. They accepted such new doctrines as those concerning angels, the resurrection, and a future life, while the conservative Sadducees rejected them. The Sadducees were drawn largely from the priestly and aristocratic circles in Jerusalem and from the great landowners, whereas the Pharisees won their following among the peasants in the villages. John Hyrcanus and the Pharisees came to an open break whose consequences were so disastrous to him that his successor Alexander patched up a truce. Nevertheless, the Pharisees remained critical. The very name Pharisee meant "separate," and it is often said that they acquired it by separating themselves from the government. The Sadducees, on the other hand, are said to have taken their name from Zadok, a Jewish high priest in the days of Solomon.

A few Palestinian Jews were so dissatisfied with the way things were going under the Maccabaean kings that they were not content with the mild criticisms put forward by the Pharisees. Extremists declared openly that it was impossible to lead a godly life in the existing state. They withdrew to small monastic communities, where they lived apart from the world. There were several such groups of recluses, of which the most celebrated were the Essenes. The houses of this order were scattered up and down Palestine, especially at the edge of the desert and near the Dead Sea. Enthusiasts could withdraw to these refuges to lead pious lives, working part of the day at trades or in the fields, studying the Scriptures, writing pious books, and training children in the true faith. They owned their goods in common, ate and lived together, usually foreswore marriage, and wore a special uniform. In many ways they closely resembled the monks of the Middle Ages or the recluses in the Serapeum and other Egyptian temples of whom we read in contemporary papyri.

Apocalypses and Messianic Hopes

Other Jews expressed their dissatisfaction in other ways. Toward the end of the second century, and throughout the first, there was a marked revival of apocalyptic writing in which prophets foretold a sudden change of things to be brought about by divine intervention. Many Pharisees declared that the Maccabaean princes could not be true kings of Israel since they were not of the Davidic line. The apocalyptists went further and prophesied that a true king of the seed of David would soon arise. They spoke of this coming king as the "Anointed One" or as "Yahweh's Anointed," for David had become king when anointed by Samuel. The Hebrew word for "anointed" is Anglicized as "Messiah," and it was translated into Greek by the word "Christos." A few writers apparently thought of this Messiah as an earthly king, though much better than the present ones; but the shortcomings of the Maccabaean line had disillusioned others regarding a theocracy, and they depicted the Messiah in vaguer and more glamorous terms. But he would surely come, and those who remained faithful to the whole Law would then receive their reward.

VII The Decline of the Roman Aristocracy

THE MIDDLE DECADES OF THE SECOND CENTURY BEFORE Christ had been a brilliant period in the history of the Roman Republic. The destruction of Carthage in the West, and the collapse of the Hellenistic monarchies in the East, left Rome without a serious rival in the Mediterranean world. Her citizens basked in the sunshine of universal flattery and homage. Her upper classes recognized and even appreciated the great achievements of other peoples, notably the Greeks, and they were willing to learn what they could from abroad; but Romans of every class were quite convinced of their own high merit. Nevertheless, the old aristocratic Republic was already doomed, for wars and territorial expansion had profoundly altered the position and political power of every class of society at Rome.

The social class known as equestrians was advancing rapidly. Originally the equestrians had been prosperous peasants, whom the censors listed in the first eighteen centuries of the *comitia centuriata* because they were rich enough to provide themselves with horses when they appeared for military service. In more recent times, the class was made up of business leaders in Rome. Many had been made rich by the wars or by exploiting the provinces; others built the roads, aqueducts, temples, and other public works with which Rome was then embellishing herself; and still others engaged in commerce or lent money to finance commercial enterprises. Business was still done on a small scale at Rome, and the wealth and power of the business leaders were small when compared with what they became a century later, but the equestrians already received careful consideration when they made demands upon the government.

Rising prosperity and power made the equestrians jealous of the political privileges and prestige of the aristocracy into which they could not force their way. Sometimes individual equestrians ingratiated themselves with noble families by making timely loans, by letting senators in on profitable enterprises, or by marrying their well-dowered daughters to the sons of aristocrats in straitened circumstances. Such relationships might prove flattering and profitable to the individuals concerned, but they did not erase the stigma of social inferiority, and as a class the equestrians remained critical of the whole senatorial order. In this opposition they were joined by a host of followers whose business activities led them to share the equestrian point of view in politics and who hoped some day to become equestrians themselves.

A century and a half had passed since the conquest of central and southern Italy, during which time the allies had been left much to their own devices as far as local and domestic matters were concerned. Now the Greek and Italian cities of southern Italy were prospering greatly in their trade with the East because of the treaties Rome made after her victories in the Macedonian wars. Moreover, the more intelligent Roman commanders recognized the importance of the allies to the Roman army, and were careful to treat the Italians fairly. The resulting good feeling is shown by the frequency with which Italian cities formally requested and received permission to replace their old dialects and customs with the Latin language and Roman law. Romans and Italians were slowly amalgamating into one people, each taking much from the other.

Nevertheless, there were always persons at Rome who caused trouble with the allies, especially at times when they were inflated with pride over recent victories. Roman officers sometimes tyrannized over allied soldiers; the allies did not always receive a fair share of the booty and lands they helped to conquer; occasionally petty Roman officials were offensively insolent when traveling through Italian towns and villages. Italians naturally resented these things. Those who migrated to Rome sometimes became wealthy, but they could not become Roman citizens with the right to vote. Italians in general would not have been helped greatly by an extension of the Roman franchise, for they could have voted only if they made the long trip to Rome for the purpose. But to many of them, denial of the ballot at Rome had become a hateful symbol of political inferiority.

Heavy emigration to the Po Valley during the 170's had relieved the suffering of the peasantry, but it effected no permanent cure for the evils brought by lack of land and slave competition. After the middle of the century peasants were still being forced from their ancestral homes by the thousands. Some entered the armies that fought minor wars after the fall of Carthage. Since they were interested primarily in booty, they made inferior soldiers and, as we have seen, they were defeated disgracefully in Spain and elsewhere. Others flocked to the cities, especially to Rome—whose population increased rapidly after the middle of the century[1]—where they supported themselves by day labor and became an urban rabble that contributed much to the debauching of Roman political life.

The rapid growth of slavery brought further troubles to Rome and Italy. One recent scholar (T. Frank) has declared that the importation of oriental slaves was so great as to alter seriously the racial constitution of Italy—that the modern south Italians are descended, not from the Romans of old but from their slaves! This statement is a great exaggeration, yet it contains a modicum of truth. Moreover, the waste and carelessness of slave labor reduced the productivity of Italy, and there was constant danger of slave rebellion. The first recorded insurrection of this sort, in 198, was easily suppressed, but before the end of the century such revolts became more serious matters.

It was always difficult to make the slaves work, and Romans often

---

[1] Unfortunately, we have no reliable population statistics, but Rome's growth may be traced by the growth of her system of aqueducts. Two aqueducts built in 312 and 272 supplied the city with fresh water for more than a hundred years; further building was demanded in the 170's, but nothing was done until 144, when a praetor built the famous Aqua Marcia, whose capacity almost equaled that of the other two combined. In 125 it was necessary to add the Terpula. This supply had to suffice for another hundred years, until Augustus doubled the size of the old aqueducts and added three new ones.

stimulated their industry by promising to emancipate them or their children after a certain period of faithful service. These "freedmen" became Roman citizens. At first they were clients of their former owners, but in many cases the bonds of clientship dissolved quickly. Independent freedmen were numerous at Rome before the end of the second century and were beginning to make their influence felt as voters. These men lacked all feeling for the old traditions which Italian peasants were apt to revere long after they had left their farms. They brought to Rome, instead, the political turbulence that had long characterized Greek and oriental cities, and they swelled the urban mobs that caused such trouble during the last century of the Republic. Even as early as 129 Scipio Aemilianus had to remind the members of such a mob that they were after all only the "stepchildren of Italy." It was perhaps quite natural that these freedmen should be filled with resentment against their former owners, and against all aristocrats and rich men generally.

These social changes all worked to the disadvantage of the old senatorial families that had governed Rome for so long. When slaves replaced the free peasantry, the aristocrats lost the clients who had supported them at the polls. Political leaders therefore sought new ways of attracting the votes of the urban masses, who now made up the majority of the actual voters. Rich men bribed them on a lavish scale, and demagogues promised them sun, moon, and stars—at public expense. The aristocratic tradition was still so strongly entrenched at Rome that the old senatorial families managed to retain most of the high offices until the very end of the Republic. Nevertheless, the coalition of great families under the Scipios, that had dominated the government for so long, was presently superseded by other families of the patrician or plebeian nobility who had won greater favor with the discontented classes. The first to challenge the dominant Scipionic coalition were members of the Claudian faction, then led by Appius Claudius Pulcher who became consul in 143.

The Claudian Faction

The Claudians had long been noted for their perennial hostility to other patrician families as well as for their demagogic proclivities and their propensity for what the historian Livy once denominated "Claudian violence." Their faction had ruled Rome for a few years after Cannae, and in the next year (215) a consul and four praetors had entered into a political alliance that endured through three generations. Claudians had figured prominently in the attacks upon Scipio Africanus in the 180's, and three sons of the Claudian praetor of 215 all rose to consulships, as did the sons of his three colleagues in the praetorship. The Appius Claudius of the third generation, whose star was now rising, was the grandson of the praetor of 215 and throughout his career he co-operated closely with the descendants of his grandfather's colleagues.

Prominent among this Appius Claudius's associates were four members of the Fulvius family. One was Quintus Fulvius Nobilior, son of the censor of 179; the son became censor in his turn in 136, having Claudius as his colleague. The other three Fulvii belonged to the Fulvius Flaccus branch of the family and were therefore closely related to the praetor of 215. Servius Fulvius Flaccus became consul in 135, his cousin Marcus served in 125, and the third Fulvius Flaccus, named Gaius, was consul in 134. The family of Q. Mucius Scaevola, another of the praetors of 215, was now represented by two brothers. The elder was Publius, who became consul in 133 and *pontifex maximus* in 130: his activities as a jurist and a scholar have already been mentioned (pp. 216 and 222). The younger brother was adopted into the Crassus family and was known as Licinius Crassus Mucianus, or simply Crassus. He married Claudius's sister, and was consul in 131. And finally came two brothers, Tiberius and Gaius Gracchus. The elder was Claudius's son-in-law while the younger married the daughter of Crassus. These two young men eventually became prominent in the anti-Scipionic agitation, serving as tribunes in 133 and 123–22 respectively, and giving their names to the more idealistic features of the agitation. These marriages made the Claudian faction resemble a family party.

Appius Claudius was elected consul for 143. Eager to celebrate a triumph, he deliberately attacked an Alpine tribe and eventually won a victory. The attack was made without a formal declaration of war, and when the senate refused him an official triumph, Claudius

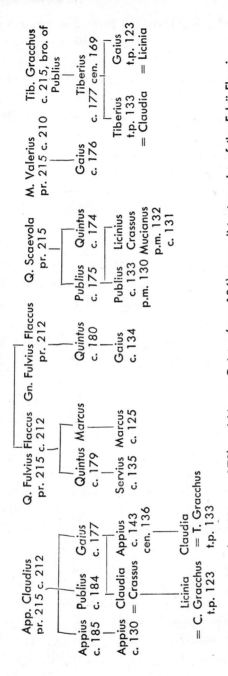

THE CLAUDIAN FACTION

App. Claudius
pr. 215 c. 212

Appius Publius   Gaius
c. 185 c. 184   c. 177

Appius Claudia Appius
c. 130 = Crassus c. 143
                  cen. 136

Licinia   Claudia
= C. Gracchus = T. Gracchus
t.p. 123   t.p. 133

Q. Fulvius Flaccus   Gn. Fulvius Flaccus
pr. 215 c. 212   pr. 212

Quintus Marcus
c. 179

Servius Marcus
c. 135   c. 125

Quintus
c. 180

Gaius
c. 134

Q. Scaevola
pr. 215

Publius Quintus
c. 175   c. 174

Publius Licinius
c. 133   Crassus
p.m. 130 Mucianus
         p.m. 132
         c. 131

M. Valerius   Tib. Gracchus
pr. 215 c. 210   c. 215, bro. of
                 Publius

Gaius   Tiberius
c. 176   c. 177 cen. 169

Tiberius   Gaius
t.p. 133   t.p. 123
= Claudia = Licinia

M. Fulvius Nobilior (c. 189, cen. 179) and his son Quintus (cen. 136) were distant cousins of the Fulvii Flacci.

= married; c., consul; cen., censor; pr., praetor; p.m., pontifex maximus; t.p., tribune.

celebrated one anyhow at his own expense. A year later Scipio
Aemilianus defeated him for the censorship, and the two men spent
the rest of their lives in bitter enmity. The other consul for 143 and
one of the consuls in each of the next three years were likewise hostile to the Scipios though not members of the Claudian faction. In
139 the anti-Scipionic groups joined forces to pass a law requiring
that the popular assemblies vote by ballot rather than by voice as
heretofore. The value of this reform to a man like Claudius is obvious. It emancipated clients from fear of their patrons and enabled
them to vote secretly for popular candidates. A spectacular political
attack upon the Scipios in 138 caused the two consuls (Scipio Nasica
and his close friend Decimus Junius Brutus) to be thrown into prison
because they had allowed a deserter from the army to be flogged.
Even more effective than these measures was the Claudian criticism
of the conduct of the Spanish war that had been dragging on for
upward of fifteen years and in which one general after another suffered disgraceful defeat.

When the Scipionic leaders had thus been discredited in the eyes
of the populace, Claudius and Fulvius Nobilior were elected censors
for 136. Claudius also became *princeps senatus,* and two Fulvii
Flacci were elected consuls for 135 and 134. Meantime, young
Tiberius Gracchus, who was quaestor in Spain in 136, had negotiated a treaty, later repudiated, by which he saved the lives and
liberty of 20,000 Roman soldiers who had surrendered to the Spaniards (see pp. 230 f.). Gracchus was furious at the senate's rejection
of his treaty, but saving the lives of the soldiers gave him such popularity in Rome that he was elected tribune for 133. No sooner was
Gracchus in office than he began agitation for his famous Agrarian
Law.

The Agrarian Law

The Agrarian Law was designed to relieve economic distress by
distributing public lands among the Roman poor. It was, in a way,
a continuation of the program undertaken by the fathers of the
present Claudian leaders when they gave farms in the Po Valley
to peasants willing to settle there, and also of Flaminius's distribu-

tion of the *ager Gallicus* in 232 (see p. 133). Now, however, when new lands were not available for colonization, the Agrarian Law of 133 ordered the distribution of public lands in Italy that had been acquired during the conquest of the peninsula. These lands had been leased by the state to private individuals and had fallen into the hands of rich men, most of whom adhered to the Scipionic faction. Long ago the Licinian-Sextian Laws of 367 had provided that one man might not hold more than 500 jugera (about 300 acres) of this public land, or pasture more than a specified number of cattle on it, but these laws had not been well-enforced. As economic conditions in Italy grew steadily worse during the 130's, it was only natural that someone should suggest relieving the peasants by redistributing these public lands. The matter was brought up by Gaius Laelius, a friend of the Scipios, during his consulship in 140, but it was speedily dropped when opposed by the aristocrats who held the lands in question.

The Claudians revived the idea a few years later. They drew up a law ordering that the state resume possession of all public lands held by individuals in excess of 500 jugera, with an additional allowance of 250 jugera for each of two sons. The holders were to be recompensed for their improvements on the land, and the repossessed fields were to be distributed among the poor in small lots—probably of fifteen jugera (nine acres) each. The law was written largely by Scaevola and Crassus, who were high-minded statesmen and jurists interested in the legal and social aspects of the question, and, as Plutarch remarked, the whole law was very just. Appius Claudius's interest in the measure seems to have stemmed largely from its promise of popularity and votes at the expense of his Scipionic rivals. But the chief proponent of the new law was Tiberius Gracchus. If Claudius imagined that his young and idealistic son-in-law would push the measure merely as part of a vast vote-catching machine, he was shortly to be undeceived.

Tiberius Gracchus

Tiberius Sempronius Gracchus, the tribune of 133, is one of the most famous figures in ancient history. The Gracchi were a distinguished family of the plebeian nobility, and though his mother was Cornelia, daughter of Scipio Africanus, Tiberius made up his mind early in life to emulate his paternal ancestors. His great-grandfather and namesake had once fined a Roman lady for speaking disrespectfully of the plebs, and as consul in 238 he had devoted fines, collected from aristocrats, to building a temple to Liberty on the Aventine.

The Gracchi

Tiberius Sempronius Gracchus (I)
aed. 246, c. 238

Tiberius Gracchus (II) c. 215, 213. †212		Publius Gracchus †217 (?)
Tiberius Gracchus aug. 205, t.p. 187 †174	Publius Gracchus t.p. 189	Tiberius Gracchus (III) (220–154) t.p. 184 c. 177, 163, cen. 169 = Cornelia, d. Scipio Afr.
Sempronia = Scipio Aemilianus	Tiberius Gracchus (IV) (163/2–133) t.p. 133 = Claudia	Gaius Gracchus (154–121) t.p. 123, 122 = Licinia

= married; † died; c., consul; cen., censor; t.p., tribune; aug., augur; aed., aedile.

The Gracchi of this generation had been closely leagued with the Claudii and Fulvii and had sympathized with the agrarian reforms of Flaminius. Tiberius (II), a great-uncle of the tribune, made a reputation in the war against Hannibal, and was consul in the crucial year 215, when the Claudian faction got its start. During the 170's the tribune's father, Tiberius (III) followed a brilliant career in collaboration with Gaius Claudius: they were consuls together in 177 and censors in 169. Though he later married Cornelia, he presently quarreled with Scipio Nasica, titular head of his wife's family, and thereby ruined his political career.

Of the twelve children of Tiberius (III) and Cornelia only three survived childhood: Tiberius (IV) and his younger brother Gaius—the two who have come down in history as "The Gracchi"—and their elder sister Sempronia, who married her mother's kinsman, Scipio Aemilianus. The boys owed much to the careful up-bringing they received from their mother, who became a widow in the year of

Gaius's birth. During the Third Punic War, the young Tiberius had accompanied his brother-in-law Aemilianus to Africa, where he distinguished himself at the age of sixteen. Thereafter, however, he followed consistently in the footsteps of his father and the earlier Gracchi. The success of his first official mission, to Spain, was largely the result of the fact that the Spaniards trusted him out of regard for his father's fairness, and the subsequent repudiation of his treaty by the senate infuriated him the more because it reflected on the good name enjoyed there by the Gracchi. Tiberius was encouraged to co-operate with Claudius in promoting the Agrarian Law partly, no doubt, by his anger against Aemilianus, partly by the fact that his father too had been active in land distributions, but primarily by his idealistic nature.

Tiberius began his agitation for the Agrarian Law as soon as he became tribune in 133. He was an excellent orator and spoke movingly of the pitiful state of those Romans who had conquered the world yet had no foot of land that they could call their own. When the bill was laid before the *comitia tributa,* the aristocrats dared not attack it openly but adopted the more devious method of inducing a tribune named Octavius to veto it. Tiberius first tried to persuade Octavius to withdraw his veto. When this effort failed, Tiberius declared that, since Octavius opposed the will of the people, he no longer represented them and should therefore be removed from office at once. As this proposal was quite foreign to Roman political thought and precedent, Tiberius's associates urged him not to attempt so drastic an innovation. He chose to disregard their advice. The *comitia* was again assembled and voted against Octavius, who accepted their verdict and withdrew from the assembly. A new tribune, friendly to Tiberius, was promptly elected in his place and the Agrarian Law was passed. Shortly thereafter a committee consisting of Tiberius himself, his father-in-law Appius Claudius, and his brother Gaius, was set up to direct the land distributions.

It was about this time that Attalus III of Pergamum died, leaving his kingdom and his treasure to the Roman people (see p. 234). Tiberius at once proposed that the treasure be employed to stock the new farms. We do not know whether or not his proposal became law, or even came to a vote, but the senators saw in it a threat to their control of financial matters. Tiberius then proposed other reforms of an equally radical nature, and crowned them all by announcing that he would be a candidate for re-election. As this step too was contrary to Roman precedent, the fat was in the fire, and Tiberius's enemies accused him of aiming at tyranny. On election day riots broke out. When a group of excited senators demanded of the consul that he take vigorous measures to restore order, Scaevola refused to act, though he assured the senators that he would recognize no election won by violence. At this point Scipio Nasica, the *pontifex maximus,* set himself at the head of a mob that murdered Tiberius together with about three hundred of his followers and threw their bodies into the Tiber.

Party Warfare After Tiberius's Death: Fulvius

The election of magistrates for 132 was held shortly after the death of Tiberius Gracchus and the capture of Numantia by Scipio Aemilianus. It resulted in the choice of two Scipionic consuls, who conducted a reign of terror for several weeks against the friends and associates of Gracchus. Nevertheless, the Agrarian Law remained in force. Tiberius's place on the commission was given to Crassus, and the triumvirs proceeded with their task of surveying and distributing land. Within a short time the anti-Scipionic faction was again in power at Rome. Nasica's boasts about his share in Tiberius's death made him so unpopular in the city that he withdrew to Asia, where he died in 132. His office of *pontifex maximus* went to Crassus, who was subsequently elected consul for 131 in spite of efforts to arouse enthusiasm for his Scipionic opponent by a magnificent triumph for Aemilianus. Rebellion now broke out in Pergamum, and Rome was forced to defend her inheritance. Crassus led an army to Asia, where he was killed in 130. He was succeeded as *pontifex maximus* by his brother Publius Scaevola, the consul of 133. Appius Claudius, too, died in 130.

The land commissioners had by this time precipitated a conflict with the Italian allies. The Claudians of the 130's, like their fathers of the 170's, had little regard for the rights of allies, whose deep resentment they aroused by the Agrarian Law. Rich men among them had leased or otherwise acquired public lands belonging to Rome which they were now called upon to surrender, but the Italian poor got no share in the new allotments. Therefore, while Romans were divided regarding the Agrarian Law, the allies opposed it unanimously. Scipio Aemilianus attacked the law vigorously, arousing great enthusiasm among senators, equestrians, and allies. Then one morning, at the height of the agitation, he was found dead in bed. His death was undoubtedly due to natural causes, but there was a rumor afloat that he had been murdered by the Gracchans—perhaps even by his wife Sempronia. A few years of comparative peace followed, under a succession of Scipionic consuls; the triumvirs ceased distributing land; and Scaevola, the last of Appius Claudius's close associates and now *pontifex maximus,* turned from political activity to legal and historical studies.

Peace did not long endure, however, for the Agrarian Law had aggravated rather than quieted unrest throughout Italy. Ambitious leaders, not acceptable to the aristocratic circle of the Scipios, devised ways of making political careers for themselves by fishing in these troubled waters. Among the new leaders was Marcus Fulvius Flaccus, a member of a family which had furnished Rome with half a dozen consuls. His father, likewise named Marcus Fulvius, had been expelled from the senate by his own brother in 174 for deserting his troops. Brought up under a shadow as the son of the black sheep of his family, the young Fulvius showed great bitterness toward the whole senatorial order. In many ways he resembled Appius Claudius, whose place he took as the chief demagogue in the anti-Scipionic group. He was a reckless and unscrupulous person, interested only in his own political career and in votes, though a very able man after his fashion. Even less that is good can be said of C. Papirius Carbo, who was a "new man," an adventurer, and a rabble-rouser. For a while he worked with the Gracchans; later he deserted to the aristocrats, who elected him consul for 119; and finally he committed suicide when threatened with prosecution for his irregularities as consul. In 130 these two men succeeded Claudius and Crassus on the Agrarian Commission and were active with Gaius

Gracchus in land distributions until the distributions were suspended by Aemilianus in the next year, whereupon they sought more lucrative fields elsewhere for their political activities.

A year or two after the death of Aemilianus the prestige of the Scipionic aristocracy was again shaken by a sensational trial in which a jury of senators acquitted a fellow senator accused of extortion. The revulsion of public opinion made Fulvius consul in 125. At once he proposed that Roman citizenship be extended to all Italians who desired it and that others be granted other privileges. No doubt he expected that this measure would bring him the political support of the new Italian voters and the popularity that he could no longer win by land distributions. The proposal aroused such bitter opposition in all classes of Roman society—especially among the populace, which had no desire to share its privileges with Italians—that Fulvius dropped the matter without ever bringing it to a vote. Blocked on this issue, he decided to seek military laurels instead and spent the next two years in Gaul. His departure from Rome did not close the Italian question, however, for Romans were alarmed by the enthusiasm which Fulvius had aroused among allies resident in Rome, and a tribune expelled all allies from the city. This action, which was arbitrary and illegal, raised the indignation of the allies to such heights that the Latin colony Fregellae revolted. The praetor sent to pacify it took Fregellae by trickery, scattered its inhabitants, and leveled the city to the ground (125).

Metellus

Meantime, a popular leader of quite a different sort was steadily building up the political power which his family was to enjoy for the next two generations. This man was Q. Caecilius Metellus, called "Macedonicus" because as praetor he had pacified Macedonia in 148. A member of the plebeian nobility and son of a consul of 206, he had been elected consul with Claudius for 143, but only after Aemilianus had twice caused his defeat. In consequence, though not a member of the Claudian faction, Metellus cordially hated the Scipios. He unsuccessfully sued a Scipionic general for extortion (138) and successfully defended another man sued by Aemilianus.

He delivered a strong oration against Tiberius Gracchus in 133, and a year later he was elected censor. During the decade of the 120's Metellus carefully kept away from the friends of Gracchus and Fulvius, but two of his followers became censors in 125.

The census of 125 was a matter of major political importance, for the census determined who might vote. In recent decades censors had been rather lax in performing their duties, with the result that, in spite of a growing population, the number of registered voters declined by about 20,000 between 164 and 136. In 131 the number rose slightly, and in 125 it was augmented by 76,000, or almost a quarter of the whole. The most plausible explanation of this sudden increase in the number of authorized voters suggests that the citizens registered by earlier censors had been chiefly clients of the aristocracy, who could be counted upon to vote as directed, whereas Metellus's censors of 125 enrolled as many others as possible in order to gain votes for "popular" candidates. Even Claudius had not gone so far against his own class. The next election returned Metellus's son as consul for 123, but Gaius Gracchus was elected tribune for the same year.

Gaius Gracchus

Strong family feeling urged Gaius Gracchus to avenge Tiberius, and this thirst for revenge drove him to attack the whole senatorial order. "Those worst of men have murdered the best of men, my brother!" he exclaimed in an early oration, and later he prophesied that his measures would utterly destroy the power of the senate. He became a popular reformer who tried to rally as many classes of people as possible to his cause, and in so doing he developed a program that went far beyond anything that either Tiberius or Claudius had ever imagined. Tiberius's followers had by this time obtained the enactment of a law—first proposed in 132 and passed a few years later— permitting the re-election of tribunes as often as the people desired. Gaius took advantage of this law to hold a second tribuneship in 122, and it was alleged that he failed of election to a third term only because of fraudulent counting of the votes. During his two years in office Gaius and his friends presented at least seventeen major laws, most of which were enacted and all of which were highly prejudicial to the interests of the senate.

Two of Gaius's earliest proposals were inspired by memories of 133. The first provided that any official removed from office by a vote of the people should forever thereafter be ineligible to public office. This proposed law was obviously aimed at Octavius, the tribune who had tried to veto the Agrarian Law, and by it Gaius sought to force recognition of the legality of what Tiberius had done. The bill was withdrawn, however, reportedly at the request of Gaius's mother, Cornelia, and this plan for dismissing unpopular officials was never adopted at Rome. A second law sponsored by Gaius decreed banishment for anyone who executed Roman citizens without allowing the *ius provocationis*—the right of appeal to the *comitia*. This law was enacted and, as was intended, it caused the exile of Popilius Laenas, the consul of 132 who had executed several persons during his reign of terror. In later years this law became an important weapon in the arsenal of the Popular Party, and on more than one occasion it was invoked against aristocratic leaders. The Agrarian Law of 133 was re-enacted at the insistence of Gaius, though largely, it is to be feared, out of respect to the name and memory of Tiberius. It is doubtful whether more lands were actually distributed.

Among the more important new laws promoted by Gaius was a *lex frumentaria,* or Grain Law. The price of grain had been rising rapidly, in part because locusts had destroyed much of the African grain crop in 125. The Roman populace could not buy food at prices it could afford. Gaius's law provided that the state should buy grain on the market and sell it in limited amounts to private citizens at a stipulated price. This law has often been denounced as a demagogic measure for buying votes with cheap grain, but the charge is unfounded. The price at which his law ordered the grain sold was higher than the average price had been a few years earlier. His purpose was to provide an "ever-normal granary" and stabilize prices rather than reduce them. It may be taken for granted, however, that Gracchus anticipated popular gratitude for what he did. As the grain distributions required the construction of enormous granaries at

Rome, the law had the further advantage of providing employment. Gracchus further reduced unemployment by building new roads, and by another popular measure he made military service less burdensome.

These social laws were designed to help the poorer classes. Other measures sponsored by Gracchus sought to improve the position of the equestrians against the senate. He first proposed a law by which three hundred (or, according to Livy, six hundred) equestrians would be admitted to the senate, thus doubling (or trebling) the size of that body. This proposal was not carried out, but three other laws helped the equestrians greatly. One regulated the procedure by which publicans were to bid for the right to collect taxes in Asia —the old domain of Attalus, which by this time had been pacified and annexed by Rome. While this system of "farming" the taxes worked rather well at first, abuses eventually became so great that the word "publican" was loathed throughout the Roman world. A second law reformed the courts established for trying senators charged with extortion in the provinces. Jurors for these courts, formerly drawn from the senatorial class, had shown themselves reluctant to convict fellow senators. Gaius substituted equestrian jurors, which of course greatly increased the power of that class: equestrians could now punish the senators who interfered with their activities. The third law reformed the methods of selecting provincial governors. Formerly the senate had selected these governors from the year's praetors—or, in exceptional cases, from the consuls. Supposedly the officials thus selected governed their provinces only during their one year of office, but they often were allowed to remain longer in power as propraetors or proconsuls. Gaius's new law provided that before the consular election each year the senate should announce exactly which provinces were to receive new governors, and that the distribution of provinces should be made by lot among the praetors elected. It thus became possible for antisenatorial praetors to get good provinces.

While there can be no doubt that each of these measures pointed at grave abuses, there is no evidence that the reforms improved, or were intended to improve, the lot of the provincials. In fact, the subject peoples were probably worse off than before, since they were handed over for exploitation to a group of insatiable parvenus who were usually more ruthless than the senators had been. Senators had been corrupt at times, but after all they came from a social class in which traditions of honest government had been maintained for many generations, while the equestrians had no such background to restrain them. Gracchus could hardly have foreseen the ultimate working out of his reforms, yet the fact remains that in his desire to destroy his senatorial enemies he bought equestrian support by giving the publicans a free hand in the provinces.

The Italian Question and Drusus

Gaius's desire to build up an antisenatorial coalition also led him to propose extending Roman citizenship to the allies. Some ancient writers say that under his plan only Latins were to receive Roman citizenship while the Italians were to receive Latin rights; others say that all were to receive full citizenship. From this contradiction it has been plausibly deduced that two laws were proposed, the narrower measure coming first and being followed later by the broader one. In any case, the laws were not favorably received, either at Rome or by the allies, and neither was enacted. Fulvius Flaccus had already discovered that giving citizenship to the allies would be unpopular with the Roman populace, though there was always a chance that such a law might pass the *comitia* if it were associated with grain distributions and other popular measures. On the other hand, it may be doubted whether most Italians really wanted Roman citizenship at this time, and there certainly were other rights and privileges which they wanted more.

Opposition to the proposed law was led by a tribune named M. Livius Drusus, whom Plutarch unjustly accused of being an outrageous demagogue. The Livii were a family of plebeian nobility attached to the Aemilii and the Scipios. They had maintained close connections with the Italians for more than a century (one of them had married the daughter of a prominent Campanian nobleman), and thirty years later Drusus's son came forward as the leading champion of the Italians against Roman oppression. Perhaps Drusus knew better than Gracchus what the Italians really wanted. At any rate, as soon as Gracchus presented his law (or his second law, if there were two), Drusus offered a rival measure granting the Italians more tangible concessions, the chief of which protected Italian soldiers against the tyranny of Roman officers in the army. This law was passed instead of the one proposed by Gracchus.

Perhaps no law on Gaius Gracchus's program has received more varying interpretations from modern scholars than this one on the Italian question. Admirers of the Gracchi picture it as a great democratic measure, an important step in the ancient Roman program of absorbing other peoples and making them good Romans. Much can be said to support this contention. Critics of the Gracchi, on the other hand, maintain that Gaius had little interest in the Italians except as potential voters against the senatorial aristocrats. The franchise would have helped only those Italians who could go to Rome to exercise it. (Many years later the Italians were given the right to vote, but as long as Roman citizens continued to vote at all, they voted only at Rome.) It therefore seems probable that Gracchus was interested only in those Italians who happened to be living in or near Rome and who might therefore support him with their votes.

Gracchus and his friends also furthered the foundation of new colonies. Settlements dating from this period can be identified by their government under duumvirs (two men appointed by the Roman senate) and by their double names, one usually that of a god—as Neptunia Tarentum, Junonia Carthago, or Narbo Martius. Gracchus first proposed two colonies, at the sites of Tarentum and Capua, which had been destroyed during the Second Punic War; Drusus retorted by proposing twelve colonies, which were actually founded in various parts of Italy. More important and more significant than these twelve colonies, however, was Gracchus's elaborate plan for colonization near the site of Carthage. Though his colonies were no doubt intended to relieve overpopulation, they served other ends as well. They were not agricultural colonies, like those founded fifty years before in northern Italy, but cities located at important commercial centers; and their citizens were drawn, not from the poor but from the "best" citizens. They were intended to provide opportunities for the non-senatorial middle class. In Africa, moreover, the allotments of land were large—about 125 acres. Land near Carthage was fertile, and an allotment of this size was more than a proletarian colonist could equip or cultivate. Elsewhere fifteen or twenty acres was the largest allotment granted a peasant and his family. Allotments in Africa were to go only to well-to-do Roman citizens who would form a new Roman aristocracy with native serfs to work their farms.

Death of Gaius Gracchus

After spending six months in Africa in 122, Gaius found that he had been deserted by many of his old associates and followers. He failed of election to a third term, and two Scipionic consuls were chosen for 121. No sooner had Gracchus stepped down from office than his opponents began to attack his laws. Rioting broke out early in 121, and a man was killed. The senate, in something of a panic, ordered the consuls to take care that no harm should come to the Republic. (This incident was the origin of the *senatus consultum ultimum,* or "final decree," which was roughly equivalent to declaring martial law; in later times the "final decree" was used by the aristocrats to suppress popular demonstrations, just as the *ius provocationis* was invoked by the popular leaders against the aristocrats.) The next day the followers of Gracchus entrenched themselves on the Aventine Hill, where the consuls attacked them with mercenary Cretan archers. Gaius Gracchus and Fulvius Flaccus were killed, along with about three thousand of their followers (121). Plutarch reports that on the day before the battle Gaius stood for a long time in the forum, sadly contemplating a statue of his father, and then spent the night quietly at home, while Fulvius passed the night carousing with his friends and was still drunk the next day. Nothing could better summarize the characters of the two men.

After the death of Gaius Gracchus several of his measures were repealed, among them the Grain Law and the law founding a colony at Carthage; other laws were allowed to stand. During the next few

years the Agrarian Law was whittled down by a series of amend-
ments, until in 111 a wholly new law was enacted, part of which has
been preserved in a celebrated inscription. This new law recognized
and confirmed the allotments made since 133 and arranged for the
sale of the remaining lands taken from Carthage and Corinth in
146. It also recognized and perpetuated various ill-defined rights
granted to the Italian allies by a law passed during the consulship
of Livius Drusus (112)—which clause furnishes further proof that
this opponent of Gaius Gracchus was more of a statesman than one
would gather from Plutarch. The settlement of 111 seems to have
been remarkably fair, and it shows that a considerable number of
Roman peasants had acquired homes as a result of the Gracchan
agitation. But the great weakness of the Gracchan agricultural program was also recognized in this new law. The general economic
developments of the time continued to work against the small
farmer, and urban proletarians did not possess the skill required to
work their new farms. The new law therefore permitted them to sell
their allotments—which Tiberius's law had strictly forbidden. Soon
thereafter many peasants sold their land and went back to the city.
In the long run, the Agrarian Law failed to improve economic conditions in Italy.

The importance of the Gracchi does not rest upon their legislation
but rather upon the fact that they were the first to raise their voices
against the power of the aristocratic senate. It was this opposition
that made them heroes. In later times they came to be regarded as
distinguished examples of the high-minded and disinterested popular leader. Such idealization apparently began with Gaius's lauda-
tion of his brother soon after 133. In the next century Cicero praised
the two brothers in his public orations (though in his private writings he was more critical), and Vergil, who better represented the
best at Rome, counted the Gracchi among those who had added
most to the glory of their city. Their mother Cornelia became a
popular heroine, the nobility of whose character was illustrated by
countless stories. Plutarch mentions a statue set up in her honor at
Rome: the pedestal of this statue has been recovered and may now
be seen in a Roman museum, bearing the inscription, "Cornelia,

daughter of Africanus, mother of the Gracchi." The Gracchi were thus more powerful dead than alive, for legend hallowed them as Rome's greatest champions of democracy and humanitarianism.[2]

The Metelli and the Rise of Marius

Metellus Macedonicus was an old man in 121, yet he took part in the final attack upon the Gracchans and he, more than anyone else, may be said to have won on that tragic day, for his family thereafter dominated Roman politics for many a year. During the fifteen year period from 123 to 109, no less than eight members of his family became consuls; four became censors, one was *princeps senatus,* and one succeeded Scaevola as *pontifex maximus.* Though the Metelli had formerly been hostile to the Scipios, they now made their peace with the high aristocracy, or rather, the aristocracy made its peace with them. One of Metellus's daughters was married to Scipio Nasica (son of the man who had led the mob against Tiberius Gracchus); and other Metelli were permitted to marry Fabii and Claudii. Nevertheless, the political power of the Metelli rested with the equestrians. Although these equestrians retained all the rights and privileges that Gaius Gracchus had obtained for them, they turned their backs upon his surviving friends in order to keep their gains. Moreover, they were eager to end the turmoil of the Gracchan period in order to devote their undivided attention to the pursuit of wealth. Typical of these equestrians was M. Aemilius Scaurus. By his own efforts Scaurus had accumulated a huge fortune early in life, though he was often accused of unscrupulousness and dishonesty. He married Metella, the daughter of Macedonicus's nephew, and with the aid of his wife's family he was elected to various lesser offices and eventually became consul (115), censor (109), and *princeps senatus.*

The decade following the death of Gaius Gracchus was marked by a rapid territorial expansion that produced many of the benefits Tiberius Gracchus had expected from his Agrarian Law. Though the Gracchan colonial laws had been repealed, new territories were colonized. Settlement near Carthage had gone too far to be stopped

---

[2] See note on Interpretations of the Gracchi and Barthold Georg Niebuhr, p. 288.

THE METELLI

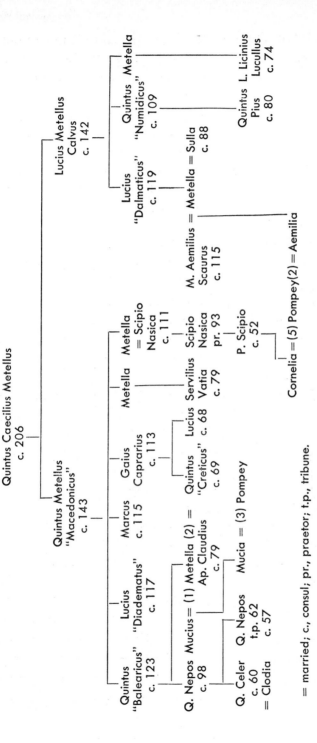

= married; c., consul; pr., praetor; t.p., tribune.

completely and several thousand Romans remained in Africa. Other thousands found new homes in southern Gaul. A fortress had been established at Aquae Sextiae (Aix-en-Provence) in 123, and all southern France (except the small territory of Massilia) was set up as a Roman province called "Gallia Transalpina" in 120. The important colony of Narbo Martius (Narbonne) was founded there in 118, and a great road (the Via Domitia) was built through the province, connecting Italy with Spain. Thousands of settlers established themselves in the new Transalpine province, which was especially beloved by the Romans for its natural beauty and climate. Transalpine Gaul became known as "The Province" and to the present day this part of southern France is ordinarily called "Provence." Other Roman settlers followed the new road to Spain. Meantime, Quintus Metellus, the consul of 123, had conquered the Balearic Islands and founded Palma on Majorca (122), in honor of which he was called "Balearicus." During the next few years conquests were also made along the Dalmatian coast and in Illyria, where Scaurus and his father-in-law, Metellus "Dalmaticus," acquired enormous fortunes and military reputations.

The old aristocracy, which had governed Rome for so long, was beginning to show clear signs of decay. Fifteen years of social struggle had made many aristocrats desire relaxation, or at any rate excitement over less serious matters. Others desired only to parade their wealth. As the equestrian nouveaux riches were only too eager to outdo them in ostentation, the resulting display and debauchery aroused the apprehensions of many good people, including the censors who vainly tried to restrain it in the public interest. Scandal reached its climax when three aristocratic Vestal Virgins were convicted of violating their vows of chastity (113). The judge who condemned them was a notorious demagogue who turned the trial into a political demonstration against the aristocracy. Political corruption and bribery were so prevalent at this time that one visitor to Rome was led to remark as he departed, "A whole city for sale, and soon to fall, if only a purchaser appears." The inner weakness of this gay and corrupt city was ere long to be laid bare in lurid fashion.

War Against Jugurtha

The powerful and picturesque Masinissa had governed Numidia for more than fifty years after the defeat of Hannibal. When the old man died in 148, his kingdom passed to his son, Micipsa, who remained an equally staunch friend of Rome until his death in 118. Micipsa's two sons, Adherbal and Hiempsal, and an adopted nephew Jugurtha, then jointly took over the rule of his kingdom. The most important of the three heirs was Jugurtha, who had inherited many qualities from his royal grandfather and who was soon plotting to obtain the entire kingdom for himself. Hiempsal was murdered, whereupon Adherbal fled to Rome to seek aid in gaining his inheritance. But Jugurtha, who had learned the incredible venality of the Roman aristocrats, sent agents to Rome with full purses to defend his interests. Moreover, the Italian traders in Numidia preferred Adherbal to Jugurtha, and the aggressive equestrians at Rome shared this preference. When the senate refused to intervene in Adherbal's behalf, the equestrians were quick to attribute the decision to Jugurtha's bribes. Scaurus in particular was loudly accused of corruption. Both the dispute between the African rivals and that between the Roman factions continued for several years until Jugurtha captured Adherbal's capital and butchered the king along with several hundred Italians who had aided in his defense (112). Roman intervention was thus made inevitable, but the first Roman armies sent to Africa suffered a disgraceful defeat at the hands of Jugurtha (110). Again the cry of bribery was raised at Rome. It was therefore decided to send the consul himself to Africa in 109. This consul, Q. Metellus (later known as "Numidicus") was a nephew of old Macedonicus. Being a man of unquestioned honesty and a moderately able general besides, Metellus was more successful than his predecessors had been, though his failure to capture Jugurtha caused criticism at Rome to become more vehement than ever.

One of Metellus's officers was a self-made man named Gaius Marius. He had received his early training under Scipio Aemilianus in Spain and had entered politics as a henchman of the Metelli, but when tribune in 119, Marius quarreled with his powerful patrons and it seemed that his political career was over. He went along on the African campaign, however, and soon began sending home reports accusing Metellus of incompetence and of needlessly prolonging the war. This won him widespread favor, especially among the equestrians. On the strength of his promise of immediate victory, he was elected consul for 107 and at once took over the command in Africa.

Marius conducted the war with great vigor, but he could not bring it to a close until a young officer named Sulla—an obscure and impecunious aristocrat, of whom we shall hear more presently—persuaded the king of Mauretania to capture and surrender Jugurtha (106). Jugurtha was taken to Rome, where he died in prison. The western part of Numidia was given to Mauretania, whose king became a "Friend and Ally of the Roman People," and the rest of Jugurtha's kingdom went to his half brother. Rome took no territory for herself (105).

The Cimbri and Teutones

Meantime danger had arisen on another front. Gallic tribes in southern France had been restless for several years, and as early as 125 Massilia had begged aid of Rome. Fulvius Flaccus and other commanders held the raiders at bay until about 113, when the Gauls were reinforced by fresh invaders from the north known as the Cimbri and the Teutones. Roman generals then suffered defeat after defeat until 105, when an entire consular army was annihilated at Arausio (modern Orange) with a loss of 80,000 men. In a panic the Roman people turned to Marius, who had just defeated Jugurtha, and elected him *in absentia* to a second consulship in 104. This reelection was irregular, for no Roman was eligible to a second term as consul until ten years after the first, but war emergency overrode constitutional precedent. When Marius failed to rout the Gauls and their allies at once, he was re-elected consul year after year. Eventually he defeated the Teutones near Aquae Sextiae in 102, and in the following year he destroyed the Cimbri at Vercellae, not far from Turin in the Po Valley.

Marius was primarily a general, but his historical importance is political rather than military. His army, recruited from the urban proletariat, was made up of professional soldiers, rather than citizen levies as heretofore, and his men gave their loyalty to their commander rather than to the Roman state. In return for this personal loyalty, Marius undertook to defend the special interests of his soldiers, even after they had returned to civil life. Thus he gained the political support of his veterans. The change from a citizen militia to a professional army was an inevitable result of improvement in the art of war throughout Hellenistic times: fighting now required more skill than could be expected of an ordinary citizen with a few weeks' training, and the command of armies required more military knowledge than was generally possessed by the aristocrats who had formerly dealt out consulships and commands to prominent members of their cliques. Forces far more formidable than the Gracchi were thus turned against the senate. The new-model army brought forward a new type of political leader who relied primarily upon troops and veterans, just as the old aristocrats had relied upon their clients for votes. Sometimes these new political leaders favored the equestrians, sometimes the aristocracy, and sometimes the populace, but above all they favored themselves. To promote their political ends, they initiated a new period of aggressive warfare, first wars against foreign enemies, then wars amongst themselves, and finally the Republic itself went down in civil war.

Optimates and Populares

The political consequences of Marius's rise to power began to show themselves almost at once. During his first campaign for the consulship he had freely attacked the aristocracy as a class, going far beyond anything that Gaius Gracchus had ever done, and afterward he declared that his election was a victory for "the people." He thus taught ambitious demagogues how to curry favor with the populace by spectacular attacks upon prominent families, and he divided Roman society into two camps: those who attacked the senate and those who defended it. These two groups are often compared to modern political parties, but more commonly they were factions, and their struggles took on more and more the character of class warfare.

Those who defended the senate called themselves the Optimates, literally, the "Best." Their group included the aristocracy as well as many influential men such as the Metelli who had once attacked the Scipios, and others such as the Claudii and Scaevolae who had formerly supported the cause of the Gracchi. They usually were able to control the *comitia centuriata* which elected consuls and praetors. The other group was known as the Populares, or the "Popular Party." Its founder was Marius, though its members idealized the Gracchi and continued to demand reforms of the sort they had proposed. The Populares were usually led by equestrians and a few disgruntled aristocrats, but the bulk of their votes came from the urban masses and especially from Marius's veterans. They usually managed to elect the tribunes. The struggle between these rival factions became extremely bitter. The attacks upon Scipio Africanus and Aemilianus had already given a hint as to what Roman politicians were capable of doing; and scurrilous tribunes now surpassed themselves in demagoguery, character assassination, and violence.

For a short time after the departure of Marius to replace Metellus in Africa (107), the political position of the aristocracy improved at Rome, for Marius was accompanied by large numbers of his followers while his opponents remained in the city. Metellus was allowed to assume the cognomen "Numidicus" and to celebrate a magnificent triumph, thus arousing new enthusiasm for the senatorial cause. A little later the consul for 106, Servilius Caepio, took advantage of this enthusiasm to carry through a new judiciary law to replace the Gracchan law of 122: it provided that thereafter both senators and equestrians, rather than equestrians alone, should sit on the juries that tried senators for extortion. This measure angered the equestrians, widened the breach between them and the senate, and brought new attacks upon the aristocracy. Without a doubt this disaffection helped elect Marius consul five times in succession, contrary to law and precedent. Indeed, senatorial opposition to Marius was largely responsible for these illegalities, for had the senate made him a proconsul, there would have been no excuse for his repeated re-elections.

The first to suffer from these renewed equestrian attacks upon the aristocracy was C. Popilius Laenas—member of a notorious family and son of the consul who had conducted a reign of terror in 132. It was charged that he had surrendered his army in Gaul too readily, and in 106 he was exiled for *perduellio*—a term once limited to treason, or taking up arms against the state, but now applied to anything considered detrimental to the popular interest. A little later Servilius Caepio, who had commanded the army annihilated at Araucio in 105, was attacked by popular leaders and driven into exile, the principal charge against him being that before his defeat he had stolen a great treasure captured at Toulouse. Other important cases followed in rapid succession until the great Scaurus himself was charged with neglecting his duties as augur. Repeal of Caepio's judiciary law in 104 re-established the old Gracchan courts with exclusively equestrian juries. A little later a tribune proposed an agrarian law on the Gracchan model: his bill (which failed to pass) apparently envisaged the division and distribution of the great estates of the rich among the poor, and during the debate he remarked that there were not two thousand men of property in all Rome. Minor revolts occurred at various places in Italy, and in 104 a slave war broke out in Sicily which was not crushed until 100.

Saturninus and Glaucia

Marius lent the weight of his prestige to the popular agitators, with the result that the radical L. Appuleius Saturninus was elected tribune for 103. Saturninus was an aristocrat, formerly associated with the senatorial party, who had progressed by ordinary methods to the office of quaestor in 105. It was his duty to supervise the importation of grain at Ostia, but when rising prices caused complaints he was replaced by Scaurus. He thereupon went over to the Populares, who elected him tribune for 103 and again for 100. At least two of his measures date from 103. The first was a proposed grain law, modeled on that of Gaius Gracchus which had long since been repealed. As grain was then selling at a high price, there unquestionably was need for relief, but Saturninus set the price of government grain at an absurdly low figure—about one eighth of the price asked by Gracchus. When he presented his bill to the *comitia tributa*, another tribune interposed his veto; Saturninus ignored the interruption and his opponents broke up the assembly by violence. Apparently the bill was not enacted. The second measure took the form of an Agrarian Law, though in reality it was a pension scheme for the veterans of Marius's campaign against Jugurtha, granting each soldier an allotment of 100 jugera (60 acres) of land in Africa. When a hostile tribune vetoed the measure, he was stoned off the field, and the law was passed in spite of his protests. At the end of the year Saturninus repaid Marius for his support by helping him obtain another consulship. The next two years, 102 and 101, were filled with charges and countercharges by the leaders of the factions and the turmoil reached a climax in 100.

Since the last Cimbri and Teutones had been defeated before the election of 101, there really was no good reason why Marius should have a sixth consulship. Nevertheless, he decided to run for office once more. Saturninus was again a candidate for the tribuneship while Glaucia, a rabble-rouser of base origin, ran for the praetorship. All three were elected after a campaign marked by violence and even murder. A former slave, put forward by Saturninus as the son of Tiberius Gracchus, was elected tribune.

Saturninus and his friends at once proposed a law establishing new colonies in Gaul. Though the lands were given primarily as bonuses to Marius's veterans, Saturninus and Glaucia obtained allotments for deserving followers among the Roman proletariat. This law differed from those of the Gracchi in more than one important particular. As the lands it distributed lay in the recently conquered areas outside Italy, rich Romans need not fear the confiscation of their estates; but on the other hand, it encouraged demagogues to dream of conquest. The law also included a novel provision that if it were passed by the *comitia tributa* every senator must swear within five days to give it his support. At first the senators demurred, but in the end they all took the oath except Metellus Numidicus, who went into voluntary exile.

Marius was satisfied for the time being with this provision for his veterans and with the exile of his old enemy Metellus, but his friends wanted more. At the end of the year 100 Saturninus sought a third tribuneship while Glaucia stood for the consulship. The equestrians now turned against these men and put up their own candidates. On election day Saturninus instigated a riot in the course of which an equestrian candidate was murdered. The senate quickly passed the "final decree," ordering the consul Marius to arrest his friends. Marius locked them up in the Senate House, but during the night a mob, containing many senators and equestrians, stormed the building, tore the tiles off the roof, and murdered Saturninus along with the other prisoners. No effort was made thereafter to enforce his colonial land law, and a few months later, when Metellus was recalled, Marius withdrew to Asia.

The death of Saturninus in 100 was followed by a brief period of calm, with the senate and the equestrian leaders again united. Unfortunately this *concordia ordinum* ("concord of the orders") did not long endure, for the equestrians were more aggressive than the senators and aspired to take the lead. Conflict broke out in 92 when an equestrian sued a distinguished aristocrat, P. Rutilius Rufus, for extortion in Asia. As the defendant enjoyed a high reputation for probity, it is more than likely that his troubles resulted from the fact that he had interfered with the extortionate practices of rapacious equestrians. The equestrian jury found him guilty and sent him into exile. He returned to Smyrna, where he lived for almost twenty years in peace among his alleged victims though, as we shall see, all Asia Minor was then convulsed with anti-Roman fury.

The Italian War

Meantime a more important storm was rising on the horizon. Relations between Rome and her Latin and Italian allies had reached an acute stage during the 120's, but they became calmer after the death of Gaius Gracchus. When Marius was recruiting his army in 107,

Italians volunteered and fought side by side with Roman soldiers. Concern for his army led Marius to sympathize with these Italian soldiers, just as Scipio Aemilianus had in the days of the Gracchi. On one occasion he rewarded two cohorts for their special bravery by granting them Roman citizenship on the battlefield itself. When senatorial leaders protested that this action was illegal, he replied blandly that amidst the din of battle he could not hear the voice of the laws distinctly. Saturninus's agrarian and colonial laws provided rewards for both Roman and Italian veterans, and all settlers in his colonies were to receive Latin rights. Members of the senatorial faction exploited this concession to alienate the Roman populace from Marius, and their opposition convinced the Italians that they could never obtain justice from the senate. Italian veterans were conspicuous among Saturninus's rioters at Rome in 100. The senate then passed a law in 95 expelling all non-citizens from the city. The author of this law was the consul of the year, Q. Mucius Scaevola, son of the consul for 133 who had helped write Tiberius Gracchus's Agrarian Law. This younger Scaevola was the most famous jurist of Republican Rome, but his legal talents did not keep him from writing a law that was both unjust and unwise. His father's law had caused trouble between Rome and her allies, and the younger Scaevola's law so infuriated the Italians that, for the first time since the conquest of Italy, Rome was faced with a serious revolt. This time the allies demanded Roman citizenship.

At this critical juncture the younger Drusus was elected tribune for 91. This Drusus was the son of the man who, as tribune in 122 and as consul ten years later, had won various rights for the Italian allies. He continued his father's sympathy with the allies, and he was enough of a statesman to recognize the gravity of the situation. Realizing that most Romans were still unwilling to grant serious concessions to the allies, he urged a series of minor reforms in order to build up a party that could be led to the greatest reform of all, full citizenship for the allies. To the plebeians of Rome he offered more colonies, land, and another agrarian law; to the equestrians he held out the promise of admitting three hundred of their number to the senate, thus giving them half the seats in that body; and apparently he planned to hand over the extortion courts—which had been gravely compromised by the recent conviction of Rutilius Rufus—to juries drawn from his reformed senate. He hoped to create a *concordia ordinum* on a larger scale than ever before, with the different factions participating in a national policy. The debates on his measures were accompanied by violence, and though several of the laws were passed, Drusus gradually lost the support of all parties. His laws were declared invalid on the pretext that they had been voted in disregard of unfavorable auspices. The tribune persevered in his program, however, and late in the year he presented a *lex de civitate* extending citizenship to the allies. Before a vote could be taken, Drusus was murdered. He was the last important civilian reformer produced by Rome under the Republic.

The National State of Italia

For the Italians, the assassination of Drusus was the last straw. They severed all connection with Rome and set up a state of their own. Those promoting the revolt were mostly inhabitants of the hill country of central Italy, where Roman civilization had made the least progress. The urban communities, on the other hand, usually remained loyal to Rome. Eight Italian peoples are mentioned as participating in the rebellion. Under the new regime they retained and even increased their local autonomy, but at the same time they created a federal state called Italia. This new national state had consuls and a senate, it coined money, and it established its capital at Corfinium in central Italy about seventy-five miles east of Rome.

Italia raised an army of 100,000 men, most of whom had been trained under Roman generals and whose officers had seen service in Roman armies; but soldiers of the different peoples did not work well together and there really were eight armies instead of one. The Romans found it difficult to raise equal levies to meet this opposition, though they even armed freedmen as second-line troops. The Romans had the advantage of position, however, for they held the seaports and the better agricultural lands, as well as many fortified places within enemy territory. As they controlled the road system, they could shift troops from one front to another more easily than the rebels. The Roman armies were commanded by the consuls for 90, L. Julius Caesar (a distant relative of the future dictator) and P. Rutilius Lupus. The former was already a sick man, the latter was soon killed in battle. Marius, who had commanded only a small detachment at first, was given Lupus's army after his death. The most successful generals, however, were L. Sulla and Pompeius Strabo. The former, once Marius's legate, was now the military hope of the Optimates; the latter became the father of the great Pompey. At the outset the Italians won a series of victories, but before the end of 89 the Romans crushed the rebellion.

Rome did not win the war by force of arms alone. In the end she granted the rebels most of their demands. The Lex Julia (drawn up by Caesar in 90) granted Roman citizenship to all Latin and Italian communities that remained loyal to Rome. A few months later another law extended the privilege to everyone south of the Po who would lay down his arms and register with Roman officials within sixty days. A third law set up Cisalpine Gaul as a Roman province with all inhabitants south of the Po enjoying Roman citizenship while those north of the river received Latin rights.

This sudden creation of about 400,000 new citizens, almost doubling the former number, was a landmark in Roman history. Almost overnight Rome ceased to be a city-state and became a national Italian state. At once it was necessary to define anew the relations of citizens to their local communities and to the national state, specifying what authority the central government should have in local affairs, what position the former allies should hold in Rome, and what voice they should have in the central government. As soon as the Italians had laid down their arms, many Romans began to regret their hasty liberality and sought ways of nullifying their concessions. A new law ordered that all the new citizens be registered in eight tribes, where they would form a minority of less than one quarter in the *comitia*. The indignation of the Italians over this measure was such that a tribune named P. Sulpicius (a Marian who had been a friend of Drusus and whom Cicero later praised as the best orator he ever heard) carried through a second law ordering the censors to distribute the new citizens equally among all thirty-five tribes. This arrangement in turn alarmed the Romans, who saw their government virtually handed over to the Italians. A third measure was therefore enacted by the Optimate Sulla, who became consul in 88. Sulla's law deprived the *comitia tributa* of practically all power and entrusted legislation to the senate and the *comitia centuriata*, which could still be dominated by a few rich men. Under this law, rich Romans shared their power with rich Italians while the political position of the poor in both groups was seriously impaired. None of these three laws was satisfactory, and many a year was to pass before a solution was found for this thorny problem of uniting Romans and Italians in one state.

Continued Disorders at Rome: Sulpicius and Cinna

The Italian problem was not the only one to cause trouble at Rome in 88. The Italian War had been accompanied by much destruction of property, and political pandemonium brought an economic depression. The people were burdened by debt and discontent was becoming prevalent. When a praetor invoked old laws against usury to give relief to debtors, rich creditors stirred up a mob against him, and he was murdered in the forum. Later in the same year the consuls enacted a law reducing debts by one tenth, and subsequently resorted to drastic inflation. As early as 91 Drusus had inflated the currency by one eighth, and in 88 the value of coins was reduced to less than one half of what it had been. The consequent rise in prices inflicted great suffering on the lower classes. Moreover, Rome was still full of refugees from many parts of Italy, who added a turbulent element to the population. And lastly, the victorious Roman armies, which had not yet been demobilized, remained a standing menace to the state. The soldiers were loyal primarily to their leaders rather than to their country, as was luridly proved in 88. When the authorities sent one of the consuls for that year to take over the command of Pompeius Strabo, the soldiers chose to remain under their old general and murdered the consul.

At just this moment it became necessary to send a large army to Greece. Aristocratic and popular leaders vied with each other in raising new troops by promising recruits the loot of the East. Inevitably there was a bitter struggle among politicians for command of the new armies. Command was first given to the Optimate consul Sulla, against the protests of his political opponents. The tribune Sulpicius then incited the mob to drive the consul out of Rome, and a new law transferred the army to Marius. Sulla fled to his troops near Capua, where news of his deposition reached him. His soldiers stoned the messengers to death, and Sulla marched on Rome with his legions, announcing that he would "deliver the city from the tyrants." Marius was unable to put up effective resistance, even though he armed slaves and promised liberty to those who fought for him. After brief skirmishing Sulla entered the city and at once outlawed twelve of his opponents. Sulpicius was murdered, but Marius and his son escaped to Africa. Sulla then held new elections, after which he departed for Greece.

The consuls for 87, elected under Sulla's auspices, were Gnaeus Octavius and Lucius Cornelius Cinna. Octavius adhered to the Optimate faction, but while Cinna's father had been consul in 127, we know nothing about him except his name and year of office. The younger Cinna had at one time opposed Sulla, but he had no political program, and was an opportunist interested solely in office and power. He therefore found it easy to swear that, if elected, he would support Sulla's laws. As soon as Sulla had left for Greece, however, Cinna conveniently forgot his oath, demanded that the Marian exiles be recalled, and ordered that the new Italian citizens be distributed among the thirty-five tribes in accordance with Sulpicius's law. This order precipitated serious rioting, and Cinna fled the city.

After winning the support of a legion left behind by Sulla and recruiting new troops among the Italians, Cinna marched on Rome with four armies. The first he led himself; the second was led by Marius, who had returned from Africa; the third by Q. Sertorius, a moderate and sensible man who later showed high talent as a statesman and soldier; and the fourth by C. Papirius Carbo, son of the consul of 119 who had supported and later deserted Gaius Gracchus. When the Optimates in the senate summoned Pompeius Strabo to defend Rome with an army of veterans from northern Italy, the general unwisely attempted to negotiate with both sides, offering

his support to the one making him the more attractive offer. His
soldiers presently reported that he had been struck by lightning—an
expression which is usually taken to mean that they had murdered
him. Cinna and his friends entered Rome unopposed early in November, 87. A reign of terror lasted for several days, during which
the Optimate consul Octavius was murdered. Sulla's laws were repealed, his property confiscated, and he was outlawed. Many aristocrats then fled to join the general in Greece. Cinna was re-elected
consul for 86, having the seventy-year-old Marius as his colleague.
The old man thus achieved the seventh consulship once promised
him by a soothsayer, but he died two weeks after entering office.

Cinna and Carbo continued to serve as consuls in 85 and 84, apparently without bothering to go through the formality of election.
They had no constructive program and, except for repealing Sulla's
laws, their only accomplishments were the reduction of debts to one
quarter of their former value and a further inflation of the currency.
Their greatest concern was to detach Sulla from his army in Greece.
Late in 86 they sent reinforcements under two generals who were
ordered to take over command of Sulla's troops. Before long, however, one general was murdered by his soldiers, the other died, and
the troops went over to Sulla (85). Cinna at once began raising new
armies, still hoping to fight the now inevitable civil war on Greek
soil. Late in 84, he too was murdered by his soldiers. A few weeks
later Sulla brought his victorious army back to Italy and established
a dictatorship that quickly put an end to all popular demonstrations.

Sulla's Dictatorship

Lucius Cornelius Sulla was born in 138 to a minor branch of the
great patrician family of the Cornelii. One of his ancestors had been
prominent in the Samnite wars, and this man's son, who was consul
in 290 and again in 277, was expelled from the senate by the censors
of 275, allegedly because of his excessive display of wealth. Thereafter the family declined. We know nothing of Sulla's father except
that his early death left his widow and son in humiliating poverty.
Sulla's mother provided him with a good education, however, and in
later years he used to boast of his ability to speak Greek, of his

knowledge of philosophy, and even of his taste in art. As was natural to a boy with such a background, he admired from afar the aristocracy to which he felt that he belonged, and he was deeply distressed by the rise to power of such a nobody as Marius. Sulla received his military training under Marius and took a leading part in the capture of Jugurtha: his hostility to Marius probably came in part from a feeling that his old commander had never given him due credit for this service. At any rate, he allied himself with the senatorial faction by marrying Metella, niece of Marius's old enemy Metellus Numidicus and widow of the notorious Scaurus. In his riper years Sulla was a man of aristocratic joviality, helpful to his friends but heartless to those who opposed him. He was not above pilfering, and he permitted his close associates to perform the most atrocious acts for private gain. His striking appearance, with bright blue eyes and blond hair, made him a favorite with women; he adopted Venus as his patron goddess, calling himself "Epaphroditus" after her Greek counterpart; and it was said that in later life he developed a "drunkard's nose."

Sulla spent more than four years in the East, defeating and making peace with Mithradates (see p. 296) and early in 83 he landed his army at Brundisium, determined to crush the popular leaders at Rome. He then commanded 40,000 men whose loyalty to him was greater than their loyalty to Rome. His opponents were able to muster a force of almost 100,000 men, some of them Italians mindful of Sulla's earlier outrages while others were adventurers concerned principally with loot. Such soldiers were no match for Sulla's veterans, but Sulla was careful not to attack until he had carefully felt out conditions in Italy. He therefore spent the spring and summer of 83 near Brundisium, and during the following winter he occupied southern Italy while his lieutenants were seizing the north. At last Sulla marched on Rome, late in the summer of 82, and after a victory at the Colline Gate he entered the city on November 1. Within a short time he held Italy and all the Roman provinces except Spain, where a "government in exile" under Sertorius resisted his attacks for several years.

Sulla made it his first task to wreak vengeance upon his enemies, whom he more than repaid for their attacks upon his friends during his absence. Several hundred persons were executed the day after he entered Rome, and the systematic extermination of Marians continued for at least eight months. One ancient writer declared that 4700 persons were condemned to death. Another stated, with greater truth, that it was impossible to estimate the number of those who were officially executed or unofficially murdered. Sulla invented the practice of "proscription," publishing (Latin, *proscribere*) lists of persons whom he wished to be rid of, in which he anticipated the modern "purge." A reward was paid for killing the unfortunates whom he listed, their property was confiscated, and their children and grandchildren were barred from political life. According to report, one hundred and five senators were proscribed, but this fate fell even more commonly upon the wealthy equestrians. Many of Sulla's friends enriched themselves by means of proscriptions, and it was alleged that rich men were sometimes proscribed merely because someone else coveted their estates. Those parts of Italy that had resisted Sulla were punished severely. The country of the Samnites and parts of Etruria were laid waste, and in some cases—as at Praeneste and Florence—the entire population was sold into slavery. It was said that the inhabitants of Norba committed mass suicide rather than fall into Sulla's hands.

Constitutional Reforms

When old scores were thus settled, Sulla set about obtaining political and religious sanctions for his new position. On his first day in Rome he notified the senate of his plans—his voice being drowned out occasionally, we are told, by the screams of victims being massacred just outside. On the following day he promised the people that he would soon improve their lot. A little later a law making Sulla dictator was proposed by one of his agents and adopted by the *comitia centuriata*. The dictatorship was an old office at Rome, though one not used since the days of Hannibal. Sulla gave it new significance. Dictators had formerly been special defenders appointed by the consuls when the city was in grave danger from a foreign foe, and they might not hold office longer than six months.

The new law declared Sulla dictator for an indefinite period, and directed him to "make laws and reconstitute the Republic." He therefore resembled the dictators of twentieth-century Europe rather than those of earlier Rome. He received the support of those who profited by the proscriptions, of the senatorial class, and of those who preferred any sort of government to the anarchy of the preceding years; but in the final analysis his power rested upon the army, which he kept mobilized long after the fighting was over. He bought the favor of the proletariat with entertainments and promises; and to strengthen his following in that class he emancipated 10,000 slaves of the proscribed, granting them citizenship and his own name Cornelius. Sulla also sought to surround himself with the aura of sanctity. In the manner of Hellenistic kings he took the title Felix ("Fortunate"), thus putting forward a claim that he enjoyed the special favor of Heaven.

Though Sulla officially championed the senate, he knew that the senatorial aristocracy of his day could no longer fulfill its former role, and he had no desire to see it do so. He preferred to entrust power to a new senate of his own creation. Marius, the wars, and the proscriptions had caused many vacancies in that body, which he now filled with his own appointees; and he doubled the size of the senate, giving it six hundred members, at least three-quarters of whom he had appointed himself. Among these appointees were many soldiers and other "new men" who had supported him. By his orders twenty quaestors were elected annually thereafter, and following their year of office these men entered the senate to replace members who had died during the year. In this way the senate would in the future be elected indirectly by the *comitia centuriata*, which Sulla thought he could control. A politician might embark upon the *cursus honorum* by seeking the quaestorship at the age of thirty, though he could not be praetor until he was thirty-nine or consul until he was forty-two. Although Sulla's changes do not seem great at first glance, they completely reversed the old relationship of the senate to the magistracies. Formerly the senate had been composed of old men who had acquired wisdom by long service as higher magistrates; now the higher magistrates were men who had sat for many years in the senate and thus been thoroughly imbued with its aristocratic spirit.

Sulla's next concern was the reorganization of provincial government. Heretofore, the provinces had been governed by praetors elected by the *comitia centuriata*. In early times these praetors were assigned to specific provinces by the senate, but since the days of Gaius Gracchus assignment had been by lot. Sulla ordered that thereafter the provinces be governed by promagistrates. As there were now ten provinces, he ordered the election each year of eight praetors and two consuls. During their year of office these men were to remain at Rome, but the senate would assign them provinces which they would govern as proconsuls or propraetors during the next year. The law also provided that the governor must leave his province promptly at the end of one year, and it listed various things that he might not do. These provisions were designed less to protect the provincials, however, than to prevent an ambitious proconsul from obtaining a large army and using it to conquer Rome in the Sullan fashion. Consuls and praetors became civilian magistrates who were not permitted to raise armies; and although the promagistrates might command troops, their forces were never large. In case a serious war threatened, armies would be raised by the senate and entrusted to some general as an "extraordinary command." Thereafter, persons planning to follow in Sulla's footsteps usually began by obtaining extraordinary commands from the senate and then turned their troops against their political rivals.

The increased number of praetors led to a reform of the courts at Rome. Sulla established eight permanent courts, or *quaestiones perpetuae,* one for each praetor. As before, civil cases involving Roman citizens were tried by the *praetor urbanus,* while cases involving foreigners were tried by the *praetor peregrinus.* Criminal cases were distributed among the other praetors in the following courts: *de rebus repetundis* (extortion), *de ambitu* (bribery), *de peculatu* (embezzlement), *de maiestate* (treason), *de falsis* (forgery), and *de vi* (assault). A ninth court, *de sicariis et veneficiis,* presided over by an aedile, tried murder and other police cases. Sulla ordered jury panels again drawn from the senate.

In spite of his hatred of the Marians, Sulla did not disturb Cinna's settlement of the Italian question, leaving the newly enfranchised citizens in all thirty-five tribes. They did not seriously affect the *comitia centuriata* however, and upon this body Sulla based his hopes. To prevent a repetition of the Gracchi or Saturninus, Sulla took virtually all power away from the tribunes, and made the office still less attractive by the provision that once a man had been tribune, he could never hold another office.

Other Measures

This reorganization of the Roman government was followed by rewards to his troops for their loyalty. Sulla enacted an Agrarian Law granting them small farms, just as Marius had done for his veterans. This law, like the constitutional reforms, seems at first glance to be merely a continuation of old practices; but here again Sulla introduced a new principle. The land awarded to his veterans was what he had appropriated during the proscriptions. He thus taught his successors to pay for their wars by distributing the estates of political opponents among their troops. During the next fifty years one general after another followed this example, until no one in all Italy felt secure in his property. Some of Sulla's veterans had once been Italian peasants who knew how to work farms successfully; but mostly they had come from the slums of Rome, and years of military life—looting Greece, Asia, and Italy in turn—had not trained them to be good farmers. Within a few years many veterans sold or abandoned their farms and drifted back to the city or else enlisted in the armies of new adventurers.

The distressing economic conditions that had prevailed in Italy for many years began to improve after the establishment of Sulla's dictatorship. The laws by which he attempted to reduce prices probably were not very effective, and he allowed Cinna's debt reduction and financial inflation to stand; but as the booty of Asia removed financial worries for the time being, no further inflation was necessary. The expenditure of vast sums for public building and internal improvements so reduced unemployment that he was able to stop the free distribution of grain. Sulla, like his modern successors, was eager to beautify his capital, for he was conscious of Rome's pre-eminence in the world, and he wished her to seem worthy of her position. New streets were opened, temples were built, the forum was enlarged and paved, whole new sections were added to the city. As the Capitol had accidentally been burned in the days of Cinna, Sulla erected a new one, decorated with marble pillars taken from the temple of the Olympian Zeus at Athens. The lesser cities of Italy profited likewise by his munificence. Sulla patronized art and literature by bringing Greek writers and artists to Rome and encouraging Romans to imitate them. He even championed religion and morality, patronizing the gods and enacting many laws (which he broke himself) designed to prevent debauchery.

This program was completed in less than three years. When Sulla had accomplished most of what he had set out to do, he laid down his dictatorship (July, 79) and retired to private life on an estate near Naples. Here he wrote his memoirs and died the following March, aged sixty years. In an epitaph which he had prepared for himself he boasted that he had never allowed the kindness of a friend or the guilt of an enemy to go unrequited. Another view of Sulla was expressed five hundred years later by St. Augustine, who exclaimed, "Who can even read of such things without shuddering!" In general Sulla's successors shared the latter view of him.

Sulla's dictatorship brought an end to the first phase in the Roman Revolution. He seemed momentarily to have succeeded in checking the political decline of the old Roman aristocracy and the advance of the equestrians. He had handed the government back to the senate, which he reorganized and strengthened. Nevertheless, the system which he established, and the peace and order which he brought back to Rome after so many years of violence, scarcely survived Sulla himself. The bloody and lawless methods which he used to attain his ends, on the other hand, were imitated by successors of every school. Many of Sulla's reforms proved beneficial and were retained, but the foundation upon which he had erected his system —control by his reorganized senatorial aristocracy—was unable to bear its load and quickly crumbled. Of Sulla, as of Caesar, it can be said, "The evil that men do lives after them, the good is oft interred with their bones."

Note

Interpretations of the Gracchi and Barthold Georg Niebuhr

Modern scholars have given the most diverse interpretations of the Gracchi, which interpretations of course reflect the intellectual atmosphere of the interpreters. In the eighteenth century hostile historians belonging to or subsidized by the upper classes depicted the Gracchi as seditious demagogues, eager to give away the property of others. Early in the nineteenth century this view was corrected by the German historian Niebuhr.

Barthold Georg Niebuhr (1776–1831) was born at Copenhagen, the son of a German employed by the Danish government. After completing his studies at Copenhagen and traveling in England and Scotland, young Niebuhr served the Danish government until Freiherr vom Stein gave him a post in the Prussian ministry of finance (1806). Niebuhr was active in the reformation of Prussia which came after Napoleon's victory at Jena, but he quarreled with Hardenberg and resigned in 1810. For a few years he was professor of ancient history in the newly founded University of Berlin; during the Wars of Liberation (1813–14) he published propaganda for Prussia; from 1816 to 1823 he served as Prussian envoy to Rome; and the remaining seven years of his life he passed as professor at Bonn. His most famous book is the *Römische Geschichte*: its first two volumes appeared in 1811–12; the third, carrying the story down to 241 B.C., was published shortly after the author's death; and the rest was put together by pupils from lecture notes.

Niebuhr's greatest service to historiography was his thoroughgoing criticism of the legends of early Rome (see E. Kornemann, "Niebuhr und der Aufbau der altrömischen Geschichte," *Historische Zeitschrift*, CXLV (1931), 277–300), but he was equally proud of his discovery of the Gracchi. Niebuhr was a good German of the Restoration period, an ardent patriot who feared and hated the French Revolution—there is perhaps just one grain of truth in the legend that news of the Paris revolt of July 1830 scared the good man to death—and who hoped rather despairingly for a state guided by patriotic and unselfish aristocrats for the benefit of all. Moreover, he had been much interested in agrarian problems, both in Denmark and during his career under vom Stein, and he wished to see Prussia a land of small peasant proprietors. His opening volumes make early Roman history revolve around the agrarian laws, and in Tiberius Gracchus he found a hero after his own heart, both as a patriotic aristocrat and as a land reformer. He called Tiberius "the noblest among the young men of his time," defended his measures, and declared the prosecution of his followers to be "worthy of the Inquisition." To him Tiberius was a patriotic statesman seeking to strengthen the small farmers who formed the foundation of the nation. "To dwell upon such characters as these," he remarked in a lecture, "is the more delightful as they are seldom met in history; in our day they seem to be quite extinct." See also Fr. Schnabel, *Niebuhr* (1931), and U. Wilcken, *Eine Gedächtnisrede auf Barthold Georg Niebuhr* (1931).

Early in the twentieth century when people everywhere began developing what they liked to call a "social conscience," a new school of historians began to look upon the Gracchi as social reformers of a mildly socialistic hue. Such was the case with Eduard Meyer and more especially with R. von Pöhlmann, whose *Zur Geschichte der Gracchen* appeared in 1907. An interesting and enthusiastic little book (H. J. Haskell, *The New Deal in Old Rome*, 1939) has recently suggested that the Gracchi were simply New Dealers born out of due time, and at the same moment a German scholar (J. Göhler, *Rom und Italien*, 1939, p. 107) saw fit to congratulate Tiberius upon the close resemblance of his Agrarian Law to Hitler's *Erbhofgesetz!* These writers all based their narratives primarily upon Plutarch and Appian, the latter of whom contains a long passage couched almost in the terms of modern social history. The collection of further information from other less obvious sources by scholars such as F. Münzer (whose *Adelsparteien*, pp. 225–81, discusses the Gracchan period in a most enlightening fashion) has shown that the famous agrarian laws really had a rather small part in a large and very complicated movement. The account of the Gracchi in the text above owes much to these recent researches.

VIII The Last Days of the Roman Republic

THE HALF CENTURY THAT SEPARATED THE TRIBUNESHIP of Tiberius Gracchus from the dictatorship of Sulla had been a period of continuous turmoil at Rome. The foundations of the old aristocratic Republic were undermined by social changes that began before the days of Hannibal and swept on with ever-increasing force through the second century. At last the Scipionic aristocracy, no longer able to adapt itself to new conditions, went down just as the Fabians had fallen from power when Rome began expanding beyond Italy. Rich businessmen belonging to the equestrian class now demanded a larger voice in the government. This the frightened Scipios refused to grant, but the Metelli were willing to compromise, and for a while they dominated Roman politics with the aid of their equestrian allies. But the fall of the Scipios so weakened the old political structure that popular leaders like Marius began to appeal directly to the Roman mob. The aristocracy then found a champion in Sulla, who deprived the equestrians of their political gains and restored aristocratic rule in a modified form. His efforts were vain, however, for the equestrians had grown too powerful to be brushed aside, and Sulla's regime collapsed soon after its author's death.

The equestrians and their business allies led Rome into a new period of territorial expansion. In earlier times Rome's expansion had been primarily agricultural, with her peasants seeking new homes in conquered lands. Migration of this sort continued to flow into southern Gaul and Spain, and even into northern Africa, but the important expansion of the first century was that of the business interests into the Near East. A series of wars brought the whole Near East under Roman rule and opened it to exploitation by Roman publicans and capitalists. Ambitious generals learned from Marius that veterans as well as victories might promote their political careers at home; and Sulla showed them how to seize power with armies raised for other purposes. Roman politicians therefore waged countless wars of sheer aggression, culminating in Caesar's famous conquest of Gaul. The final decades of the Roman Republic saw frequent warfare on the frontiers, and these wars furnished a background for the political violence and chaos that prevailed at Rome.

Rome and the East

The Roman senate lost interest in Eastern affairs after the annexation of Macedonia in 148 and the destruction of Corinth two years later. The ruling classes at Rome were deep in domestic strife, or else their attention was engaged in Spain, Africa, and Gaul. Yet while they paid little heed to the moribund Greek dynasties in Syria and Egypt, they could not completely ignore the Greeks of Europe and Asia Minor. Italian merchants had been active at Delos and throughout the Aegean area ever since Pydna (168); and while many, or perhaps most, of these "Italians" were Greeks from southern Italy, they often were financed by Roman equestrians who could force the senate to consider their complaints.

Conditions in Greece and Asia Minor made it even more difficult for the Greeks to forget Rome. Social cleavage was greater than ever in European Greece, where the rich were growing richer while the poor became poorer, and the menace of social revolution was always present. In Asia Minor the conflict between Greeks and natives was growing more intense. Well-to-do Greeks both in Europe and Asia Minor were therefore friendly to the Romans with whom they had commercial dealings, whose policy supposedly favored the *status quo*, and whose armed aid they might obtain in time of danger. Rome's obvious lack of interest after 146 did not discourage these Greeks in the least, and they went right on plotting and intriguing to get Roman help.

The will of Attalus III of Pergamum, by which he left his kingdom to the Roman people in 133, drew Rome into eastern politics once more. As soon as Attalus died, Rome had to send armies to pacify her inheritance. Not until 129 was peace restored and a new province, called Asia, set up in the western quarter of Asia Minor. A few years later Gaius Gracchus obtained the enactment of his law permitting Roman publicans to collect its revenue. These publicans continued the old practice of favoring the Greeks at the expense of the natives, and soon they were cordially hated by the latter for their extortion and cruelty. The publicans and their friends also engaged in business on their own account in Asia, exploiting the natives outrageously, but sometimes passing on a share of their profits to Greeks who knew the country and showed them how far it was possible to go. (The aggressive Roman imperialist, who was bad enough in his own right, usually had a subservient Greek at his elbow, who suggested to him most of the worst things that he did.) The slave trade took on such vast proportions that, when Roman manpower was running low during the war with the Cimbri and the senate asked aid of its eastern allies, King Nicomedes of Bithynia excused himself on the ground that so many of his subjects had been carried off by slave traders that not enough adult males remained to form an army. Occasionally a good governor might attempt to restrain the equestrians, but the fate of Rutilius Rufus (see p. 275) showed the danger of such interference, and the equestrians came to regard Asia as their most valuable province.

Before the end of the second century Rome was forced to establish a second province in Asia Minor. Ever since the destruction of Rhodian sea power in 167, the eastern Mediterranean had been infested with pirates whose principal lairs were in Crete and southern Asia Minor. The passing of the Attalid dynasty in 133 was equally disastrous for the land routes across central Asia Minor, formerly policed by Pergamum but now the prey of brigands. Trade between Syria and the Aegean area, either by land or by sea, became increasingly difficult and both regions declined economically. The Syrian cities presently decided to buy off the pirates and conduct their trade by sea, principally by way of Delos, which re-routing was a further blow to the prosperity of the Roman province of Asia. Moreover, as the pirates and brigands often sanctified their depredations by preaching patriotic hatred of Rome, Italians suffered especially at their hands. At last the senate sent Marcus Antonius (grandfather of the famous Mark Antony) to end the nuisance. He conquered southern Asia Minor and set up the province of Cilicia in 102. It stretched along the whole southern coast of Asia Minor and reached north far enough to protect the highway between Syria and Ephesus. Its boundaries were later pushed even farther north.

Mithradates of Pontus

A new leader then arose in the East in the person of Mithradates VI Eupator, king of Pontus. This kingdom lay in northern Asia Minor, on both sides of the Halys River. Though it was a melting pot of many races, its nobles and priests included many Iranians; and while customs in rural areas were largely oriental, Greek influences had left a deep imprint upon the cities along the Black Sea. The royal family, which had ruled Pontus since the beginning of the fourth century, was sprung from the high nobility of the old Persian Empire (550–330 B.C.), though the kings sometimes married Seleucid wives. Laodice, the mother of Mithradates, was a Seleucid, perhaps a daughter of Antiochus IV Epiphanes of Syria. Her husband, Mithradates V, at first followed a pro-Roman policy, but later he became disaffected and set out to build a great empire of his own in which oriental traditions would predominate. After he was murdered in 120, Laodice (who probably was implicated in the murder) attempted to rule Pontus with the aid of the Greco-Roman faction. Her son Mithradates held different views, however, as he showed when he took the name Eupator—"of Good Father."

Roman writers told many stories to illustrate this new king's great physical and mental endowments, his prowess in sport, his practice of marching all day with the common soldiers and afterward spending most of the night in council, his ability to speak twenty-one languages, and his skill in diplomacy. They also viewed with alarm his indifference to moral considerations—which doubtless was just their way of saying that he was hostile to them, for the modern moralist can discover little ground for choice between his standards and theirs. Probably he was not much more cruel and immoral than any enemy is. Mithradates VI was twelve years old when his father was murdered, and for the next several years he led the life of a fugitive, hiding in out-of-the-way places; but in 111 he returned to his capital at Sinope, threw his mother into prison, murdered his brother, and began to rule in his own name.

Pontus no longer was the powerful state that the elder Mithradates had created. Its army had been allowed to deteriorate, old alliances were dropped, and conquered territories had been surrendered to pro-Roman neighbors. The young king resolved to stop this disintegration by resuming his father's aggressive policy, but, at first, fear of Rome inspired caution. Mithradates therefore directed his early aggressions across the Black Sea to the Crimea, where he was not likely to arouse Roman antagonism. Conditions in the Crimea were not fundamentally different from those prevailing in Pontus itself. A few Greek cities were centers of Hellenistic influence, but the great majority of the people were Sarmatians and Scythians whose cultural affinities connected them with the Iranian East. Mithradates conquered the Greek cities and annexed their territories. He then made alliances with native leaders and before 100 he controlled the whole northern shore of the Black Sea from the Caucasus to the mouth of the Danube. This region became a rich granary and a reservoir of men from which he later drew many of his best soldiers.

Meantime, Mithradates had begun to annex territory in Asia Minor. First he formed an alliance with his neighbor to the west, Nicomedes II of Bithynia, in collaboration with whom he seized and divided Paphlagonia and Galatia. These two kingdoms were "Friends and Allies of the Roman People," but the Roman wars with the Cimbri plus a few well-placed bribes prevented Roman intervention in their behalf (103). The annexation of Cappadocia proved more difficult and caused a break with Nicomedes, who resumed his former friendship with Rome. During the next several years Mithradates and the Romans alternately set up and deposed puppet kings in Cappadocia. Mithradates also annexed Armenia Minor and allied himself by marriage with Tigranes, king of Greater Armenia. Tigranes was a close friend of the Parthians still farther to the east and a valuable ally for Mithradates. He soon invaded Cappadocia and established a king favorable to himself and his new ally. A few years later this puppet king was dethroned (92), at a demand of the Romans delivered by Sulla, who was then governor of the adjoining Roman province of Cilicia.

Mithradates Attacks Rome

Mithradates knew that he must eliminate Rome from Near Eastern politics before he could realize his dream of a vast Anatolian Empire. Moreover, the time for action was drawing nigh. Rome was torn by factional strife which would soon degenerate into civil war; in Asia Minor the activities of the publicans had filled the populace with fear and hatred of Rome, and though the upper classes in the cities were moderately pro-Roman, their good will could be bought. Only a leader was needed, and Mithradates decided to step forward as the champion of Asia against Rome. His first move was against Bithynia whose former king, Nicomedes II, had died in 94. The new king, Nicomedes III, received the blessing of the Roman senate in 91, but a year later Mithradates drove him from his kingdom and set up his half brother in his place. At about the same time Tigranes expelled Sulla's pro-Roman king from Cappadocia.

When the two exiled monarchs complained at Rome, the senate sent a legate to restore them to their thrones. The task was accomplished without much difficulty, but when the legate suggested that the restored kings defray the cost of his expedition, they told him to present his bill to Mithradates. Mithradates refused payment. Nicomedes then attacked him and was quickly defeated (89). The few Roman troops in the vicinity were driven into fortified places or captured—among the latter being the Roman legate whose expense account had precipitated the trouble. It was later reported that he got his money all right—but in the form of molten gold poured down his throat! Nearly the whole of Asia Minor went over to Mithradates, who straightway declared war upon the Romans (88). He inaugurated hostilities by ordering the massacre of 80,000 persons, mostly Italian merchants in Asia. The funds acquired by confiscating their property enabled him to grant remission of all taxes for five years. As the Asiatic Greeks participated in and profited by this bloody day, they were alienated from Rome and recognized Mithradates as the leader of all Asia Minor.

Realizing that he could not drive the Romans permanently from the Near East without the sympathy and support of the European Greeks, and knowing that these Greeks were highly dissatisfied with their present status, Mithradates sent agents to win them over. Soon all Greece was agog from his propaganda. Sometimes this propaganda was characterized by an oriental touch hitherto little known in the West, as is shown by an interesting prophecy supposedly uttered by a dead Roman soldier after the battle of Thermopylae (192). It correctly foretold the tragic course of events during the next hundred years and culminated with the promise that a king from the East would destroy Rome and set all things right once more. Mithradates' advance agents were highly successful, especially among the lower classes in Greece. In the summer of 88 even the Athenians, who had always been pampered by the Romans, were induced to overthrow their pro-Roman oligarchic government, to murder and pillage the rich, and to throw in their lot with Mithradates. A few weeks later, when the king's fleet captured Delos, 20,-000 Romans and Italians were put to death, their property was confiscated, and the island was reduced to a desert. This moment marked the apogee of Mithradates' power. He celebrated his triumph by ordering that thereafter years be reckoned from his victory, by recasting the map of Asia, and by marrying a rich Greek lady from Miletus.

Sulla's Victories

Such were the conditions prevailing in the East when Sulla arrived in Greece with five legions early in 87. The Greeks and their Asiatic allies resisted Sulla's advance so furiously that he was unable to enter Athens until March of the following year. He then notified the Athenians that out of regard for their illustrious ancestors he would spare their lives, but he pillaged their city in shocking fashion. The Asiatic army, sent to Greece by Mithradates, was finally de-

NEAR EAST
IN THE DAYS OF
MITHRADATES

Miles
0   50   100   150

CRIMEA

BLACK   SEA

Danube R.

THRACE

Byzantium

Heraclea

BITHYNIA

Sinope

Halys R.

GALATIA

PONTUS

Zela
✗ 67, 47

Nicopolis
66 ✗

Pergamum

A   S   I   A

CAPPADOCIA

ARMENIA
MINOR

Smyrna
Sardis

Ephesus

Miletus

Athens

AEGEAN SEA

DELOS

Tyana

PISIDIA

CILICIA

Tarsus

PARTHIA

Euphrates R.

LYCIA

Antioch

RHODES

SYRIA

CRETE

CYPRUS

COELE-SYRIA

Damascus

MEDITERRANEAN   SEA

PALESTINE

Jerusalem

CYRENAICA

Alexandria

E   G   Y   P   T

Nile R.

feated in two great battles near Thebes. Mithradates withdrew his surviving forces from Europe, and Sulla proceeded to pacify Greece with great brutality.

These Roman victories gave the Greeks of Asia Minor much food for thought, and they began to regret their hasty alliance with Mithradates. Revolts broke out in various Greek cities, which forced Mithradates to follow in the footsteps of Aristonicus and set himself up as champion of Asia against Greeks as well as Romans. He canceled debts, redistributed land, freed slaves, and proclaimed a social revolution—all of which he called granting freedom to Asia. This new freedom for Asiatics was enforced by a reign of terror in the course of which several hundred Greeks lost their lives. In the spring of 85 the Romans occupied Bithynia and Pergamum, and a few weeks later Mithradates accepted the peace terms Sulla offered. He surrendered all his earlier conquests in Asia Minor, paid Rome an indemnity of 3000 talents, and became a "Friend and Ally of the Roman people." Though Sulla re-established the "free" governments overthrown by Mithradates in European Greece, the fate of that country in his day was pathetic. First, various Greek demagogues had dispossessed the rich. Then Mithradates' generals and Sulla had supported their armies at the country's expense. Next, Sulla looted the country systematically. And finally, the new rulers set up by Sulla took their revenge on the people; Romans following in Sulla's train bought huge estates at ridiculous prices; and pirates and brigands made away with much of the remaining movable property. Whole cities were destroyed, never to be rebuilt, and the next several years were among the saddest in the whole history of Greece.

In Asia the Romans were even more rapacious for, in spite of Mithradates' looting, the land was still rich enough to excite the conquerors' greed. The Greek cities of Asia were assessed an indemnity of 20,000 talents—nearly seven times the amount imposed upon Mithradates himself—and soldiers were billeted on private citizens who were compelled to pay them wages as well as feed and clothe them. Cities unable to pay their indemnities borrowed the money from Roman financiers at ruinous interest. When it came to looting Asia, the agents of these moneylenders were serious rivals of the publicans who had returned on the heels of Sulla's army. The Romans were more detested than ever, and Asiatics of every sort stood ready to support Mithradates again when opportunity permitted him to challenge Rome once more.

The Second and Third Mithradatic Wars

The so-called Second Mithradatic War was a brief affair of no great consequence. When Sulla returned from the East to conquer Italy, he left part of his army in Asia under a lieutenant named Murena. Late in 83 this man invaded Cappadocia on the pretext that Mithradates was rearming. As soon as Mithradates had defeated Murena, he complained to Sulla about this breach of the peace. The Roman general had no desire to take on another enemy at the moment and ordered Murena to desist. During the next several years the Romans were too busy with domestic affairs to pay much attention to the East, and Mithradates was allowed to build up such power that in 74 he was prepared once more to challenge Rome.

Nicomedes III of Bithynia was one of those Greek kings who ruled over many non-Greeks and, like Eumenes II of Pergamum a century before, he looked to Rome for military aid against the rising tide of the Orient. When he died in 74 he bequeathed his kingdom to Rome, just as Attalus III had left Pergamum to her in 133, presumably for a similar reason: he wanted to make sure that the Romans would actually defend Greek Bithynia against her orientalizing neighbor Mithradates. As soon as Nicomedes was dead, however, Mithradates occupied a large part of the kingdom and thereby precipitated the Third Mithradatic War with Rome (74–63). The Roman armies in Asia were commanded by L. Licinius Lucullus, a member of the aristocracy to whom Sulla had dedicated his memoirs and whom he had named guardian of his young son. Being an able general, Lucullus soon drove Mithradates from Bithynia, and before 70 he had occupied and reorganized all Asia Minor west of the Halys River. The king fled into the domains of his son-in-law, Tigranes of Armenia. Lucullus invaded Armenia with inadequate forces in 69, and though he won a few surprising victories, he could not occupy the mountainous country into which Tigranes withdrew. Mithradates saw his chance, returned to Pontus, and in 67 he again ruled over most of his earlier kingdom. Lucullus's troops were mutinous, Lucullus himself was being attacked bitterly by rivals at Rome (see p. 311), and he was relieved of his command late in that year. Though his successor delivered the final blow, it was Lucullus who destroyed the power of Mithradates.

The new Roman commander was Gnaeus Pompey, often called "Pompey the Great." When Lucullus's command was transferred to him, Pompey was already in Cilicia, engaged in a war against pirates. He at once took up his new task with such energy that in 66 he shattered Mithradates' army. The king fled to the Crimea, where he raised new armies and was said to be planning an invasion of Macedonia or perhaps even of Italy from the north. But his own subjects revolted against his heavy impositions, and Mithradates committed suicide in 63.

Meantime, Tigranes had made peace with Pompey, who thereupon turned south into Syria to regulate its affairs. The Seleucids had long since ceased to rule this unhappy land in anything but name, and the country was torn between numerous native chieftains whom the Romans called "brigands." Pompey occupied the whole eastern shore of the Mediterranean, taking Jerusalem in 63. He then reorganized the Near East. Western Pontus was added to the province of Bithynia set up by Lucullus, and the rest was divided between the neighboring kings of Armenia and Galatia, who were allowed to continue ruling as "client-kings" under Roman supervision. The Crimean territories went to Mithradates' son. The province of Cilicia was extended northward to include much of central Asia Minor, with its important trade routes. Syria was annexed as a Roman province, and Palestine was left under a native ruler friendly to Rome. Roman territory thus reached eastward to the Euphrates and the Syrian desert, beyond which the Parthians ruled supreme. They were soon to inherit Mithradates' position as champions of oriental culture and as Rome's great rival in the East.

Egypt and Cyrene

A word must also be said about the state of Egypt early in the first century. The long reign of Ptolemy VII Physcon came to an end in

116 and was followed by many years of fighting between his sons. His grandson was a protégé of Sulla, and when he was lynched by his subjects on the nineteenth day of his reign, in the year 80, the legitimate line of Ptolemies died out. An illegitimate son of Ptolemy VIII by one of his concubines was then set up as king with the aid of Mithradates, at whose court the young man had been educated. This Ptolemy XI (80–51) received the epithet Auletes, "Flute Player," and was often pictured as an utterly contemptible person. His brother became the independent king of Cyprus, which was thus separated from the Egyptian Empire.

Behind these dynastic quarrels were forces that were even more effectively tearing Egypt to pieces. Native unrest had continued throughout the second century, and frequent revolts played havoc with the economic life of the country. These uprisings were often led by the priests of Amon, who were especially powerful in the southern part of the country until Ptolemy VIII destroyed the ancient city of Thebes in 85. Auletes adopted a more sympathetic attitude toward the natives and was thus enabled to restore the semblance of domestic peace and to start on the long road to economic recovery. His oriental sympathies may also account in part for the low opinion of Auletes expressed by writers belonging to the Greek faction in Alexandria: it was not that Auletes did nothing, as they alleged, but that he did things of which they did not approve. At any rate, Egypt was really prosperous during the reign of Auletes' daughter and successor, the famous Cleopatra (51–30). Until the reforms begun by Auletes were able to bear fruit, however, the debility of Egypt invited attack from abroad. Pompey apparently had no plans for annexing the country, but we shall see that several of his contemporaries plotted armed intervention.

Under Ptolemy Physcon, Cyrenaica had been reunited with Egypt, but after his death it passed to his illegitimate son, Apion. When Apion died in 96 he left his kingdom by will to the Roman Republic. As Rome at first made no effort to take over her inheritance, government fell to leaders in the Greek cities. At the time of the outbreak of the Third Mithradatic War in 74, however, when the senate was accepting its legacy from Nicomedes of Bithynia, a Roman governor was sent to Cyrenaica.

New Leaders at Rome

Meantime, Sulla's reforms were being tested out at Rome and were quickly found wanting. As soon as the dictator was dead, opposition arose among the old aristocrats who dreamed of resuming their former position in the state, untrammeled by his reform of their order. The first leader of this opposition was L. Aemilius Lepidus. He had once attached himself to Sulla, who allowed him to plunder Sicily unmercifully, yet when he became consul in 78 he turned conservative reformer. He demanded a second consulship for himself, pardon for the sons of those whom Sulla had proscribed, the return of confiscated lands to their former owners, and, to color this aristocratic program with a democratic hue, he added a request for the restoration of the power of the tribunes. Unable to gain his ends by political means, he vainly invoked military force and died soon after his defeat (77). His agitation, though futile, uncovered widespread discontent. Many Marians raised their heads, and large districts of Italy, including most of Etruria, went over to the rebels.

Two other episodes during the next few years showed the weakness of the Sullan regime. Several opposition leaders had escaped to Spain where, under the leadership of Sertorius, they maintained an independent government in exile. They ingratiated themselves with the native Iberians and defied Sulla. Though strong armies were sent against them, they remained undefeated until Sertorius was murdered in 72. Secondly, all Italy was thrown into a panic in 73 by the revolt of Spartacus, a Thracian slave in training to be a gladiator. With about seventy companions, Spartacus escaped from his prison near Capua and was quickly joined by thousands of runaway slaves and poverty-stricken peasants. These recruits he whipped into a formidable army of 40,000 men, arming them with weapons snatched from Roman legionaries sent against them. At first Spartacus tried to lead his men north through Italy to central Europe, the original home of most of his followers; when that move failed, he turned south and attempted to reach Sicily, and finally he tried once more to escape to the north. He was defeated and killed in 71, and 6000 of his followers were crucified along the highways of Italy.

Perhaps the greatest weakness in the Sullan system was the fact that Sulla left no strong successor. The purges of the preceding decade, first by the Marians and later by Sulla, had eliminated most potential leaders among their contemporaries. Sulla's close associates were usually scoundrels attracted by loot and they proved quite incapable of continuing his regime. They remained in office for a few years and gathered in more loot, but power soon passed to young men of a new generation. Some of the new leaders sprang from old families of the aristocracy and others were of recent equestrian origin; some had followed Sulla, profiting financially from the proscriptions, but others had opposed him while he was alive—though he had usually seen fit to ignore their juvenile opposition. Most of them had been under thirty at the time of the dictator's death; they began to fill high offices about 70; and they remained in power until the death of Caesar a quarter of a century later. All in all, they were a group of remarkable men, and we know them better than we know the leaders of any other period in the history of the ancient world.

Pompey

One of these young men was the Gnaeus Pompey whose campaign against Mithradates has already been mentioned. His father was Pompeius Strabo, the Optimate consul of 89 who probably was murdered by his own soldiers in 87. The younger Pompey, born in 106, was among the first to join Sulla in 83. He brought with him three legions (probably faithful soldiers of his father) and, though only twenty-three years old, he was gratefully hailed by Sulla as Imperator. After he had played an important part in the defeat of the Marians in Italy, Pompey was sent to Africa to destroy the rebels there. This task he accomplished in so thoroughgoing a fashion that Sulla permitted him to assume the title Magnus ("the Great"). He became one of Sulla's closest associates, and many regarded him as a probable successor. In 77, however, jealous rivals saw to it that he was sent to Spain against Sertorius. Here Pompey met his match, and not until the chief rebel's assassination in 72 did he crush the enemy. When Pompey returned to Rome in 71, seven years after Sulla's death, he felt himself ready to embark upon a great political career.

In spite of his early associations, Pompey did not propose to perpetuate the Sullan system. In the first place, this system could not provide him with adequate opportunities for an immediate career. When he returned from Africa calling himself "Magnus," he was not yet old enough to be a candidate for the minor office of quaestor or to become a senator, and when he returned from Spain he had not yet taken the first step in the *cursus honorum*. Only after a wait of seven years could he have sought the consulship, and even that high office could scarcely provide permanent satisfaction to a man of his vast ambition. In the second place, Pompey's close associates, being members of the equestrian order, had no patience with the antiquated aristocrats who insisted that only members of their own class might enjoy distinguished political careers. These associates, upon whom Pompey principally relied, turned him more strongly against the Sullan system. But it must be admitted that Pompey had no broad political program of his own. His talents were those of a general rather than those of a statesman. When commanding troops he was energetic, resolute, and resourceful, but when faced with political problems he was hesitant and awkward. Pompey could command soldiers but he could not lead men.

Crassus

A second of the young men who now rose to power, Marcus Licinius Crassus, was about nine years older than Pompey and belonged to an ancient family of the lesser nobility. His father, a general in the Italian War, had committed suicide in 87 to avoid being captured by Cinna. Young Crassus fled to Spain, where he remained in hiding until Sulla's return from the East. Hastening back to Italy, Crassus ingratiated himself with the dictator, fought successfully under him at the Colline Gate, and subsequently acquired enormous wealth from the proscriptions.

Crassus advanced through the *cursus honorum* until he became praetor in 73, and in 72 he was sent with six legions against Spartacus. His mission was not an easy one, and he was frequently outgeneraled by the slave; but after suffering several humiliating defeats he destroyed the main body of Spartacus's troops. The last survivors of the slave revolt attempted to escape from Italy but were destroyed by Pompey, who came upon them as he was returning from Spain. Pompey thereupon claimed credit for saving Rome. This claim intensified the jealousy that had separated Crassus and Pompey ever since the early days of their rivalry for Sulla's favor. Moreover, military defeat at the hands of a slave brought a stigma that Crassus could never forget and that darkened his mind for many years to come.

By this time the wealthiest man in Rome, Crassus held large amounts of real estate—often seized or bought for a song during the proscriptions, or acquired in various disreputable ways—and owned huge gangs of slaves. Though his contemporaries believed him dominated by the vice of avarice, the charge was rather unjust. Crassus spent his money freely when there was something he wanted, and what he wanted above all else was power. To gain this power he employed many expedients. At times he played the millionaire demagogue, posing as a champion of the people and helping the poor in spectacular ways. Once he honored Hercules with an enormous banquet to which he invited everyone in Rome; food was heaped high on thousands of tables in the streets; everyone could have all he wanted; and still great quantities spoiled because no one could eat or drink any more. He also gave each citizen of Rome a three-months' supply of grain. Such philanthropy was not forgotten by the Roman populace. At the same time Crassus lent money to senators and later blackmailed them into giving him their political support. At times his agents terrorized Rome with gangs of slaves and gladiators. He had learned from Sulla the political value of an army, but he realized that his own talents lay in other directions. He preferred to intrigue behind the scenes while the more hazardous tasks were performed by hired agents. But like Pompey, he had no carefully thought-out political program. He was a big businessman eager to dominate the state, partly in order to use its power in promoting his various business enterprises, partly to check his rival Pompey, but mostly for the pleasure of considering himself a great man.

Caesar

A third member of the new generation was Gaius Julius Caesar. Caesar was born in 100 of a patrician family that traced its ancestry back to the mythical Iulus, the son of Aeneas and the grandson of Venus herself. In spite of this distinguished lineage, however, the

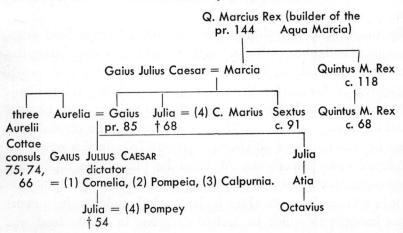

THE FAMILY OF JULIUS CAESAR

= married; † died; c., consul; pr., praetor. It is not certain whether Aurelia was the sister or the cousin of the three brothers named Aurelius Cotta. Lucius Julius Caesar, consul in 90, and his son Lucius, consul in 64, belonged to another branch of the family.

Julii did not play a prominent part in Roman politics until the first century before Christ. Three of the family, in addition to the dictator, then won consulships and others held lesser offices, while marriages gave the Caesars intimate contacts with several other political families. Caesar's father died during his praetorship in 85. Caesar's mother Aurelia, on the other hand, belonged to a family that had provided Rome with consuls in every generation since the First Punic War, and her three cousins (or perhaps brothers) named Aurelius Cotta each became consul in the years after Sulla. Moreover, Aurelia was a niece of the Rutilius Rufus whose honesty in denouncing extortion led to his downfall in 92. Caesar's grandfather had married Marcia, daughter of Marcius Rex, the praetor of 144:

this family falsely claimed descent from Ancus Marcius, a legendary king of Rome. Though all these families adhered to the aristocratic faction in Roman politics, Caesar's aunt Julia became the fourth wife of Marius, the leader of the Populares.

When Caesar was only sixteen years old, he was named a priest of Jupiter and married Cornelia, the daughter of Cinna; their daughter Julia was born one year later. Caesar was ordered by Sulla to divorce Cornelia and, when he refused, his property and that of his wife were confiscated. He was deprived of his priesthood, and he would have been proscribed had not his mother's kinsman Cotta intervened in his behalf. Caesar then left Rome to take part in the Second Mithradatic War, from which he did not return until after Sulla's death. He was not implicated in Lepidus's abortive revolt of 77, but a year later he brought charges of extortion against two of Sulla's associates. On a second visit to Asia, Caesar spent his time studying oratory and philosophy: though the young Epicurean could hardly be called a great philosopher, he was a well-educated man and second only to Cicero among the orators of his day.

Back in Rome by 73, Caesar was first noted for his debts and his romantic escapades. Soon, however, he became active in politics as a member of the college of pontiffs and as quaestor for 68. Just at this time his aunt Julia died, and at her funeral he delivered a powerful oration praising her family and himself. When his wife Cornelia died a few weeks later, he again contrived to turn the funeral into a political rally. Up to this point Caesar, like the Cottas and the Rexes, had been working with the old aristocrats to moderate the Sullan regime, but after Cornelia's death he changed sides and took as his second wife Pompeia, a granddaughter of Sulla. The year 67 he passed in Spain as proquaestor, and when he returned to Rome he changed sides once more and threw in his lot with Crassus.

Cicero

The fourth of the new leaders who dominated Rome after Sulla was Marcus Tullius Cicero. An equestrian born at Arpinum in 106, Cicero received an excellent literary education in both Latin and Greek, and he became Rome's most powerful orator. He took a genuine interest in literature, philosophy, and other matters of purely intellectual import, but he always considered that his profession was politics. Cicero's political activities have been much discussed, often praised, and as often censured. Scholars who merely repeat Cicero's own opinion of himself are apt to hail him as the greatest of the Romans. Others sometimes picture him as little better than a comedy character. There can be no doubt that he was a careful trimmer, irresolute, and willing to defend the disgraceful actions of his social betters. He was a wind-bag and a boaster, and at the same time given to fawning before the great. A scholar in politics, he shared to the full the pathetic and ludicrous qualities often attributed to such misplaced persons. Yet for all his many weaknesses, Cicero remains a man to admire, a man of intelligence and courage living in a rough and difficult time. In such homely virtues as honesty and patriotism he far surpassed most of his distinguished colleagues. His influence upon his own day was great, and few Romans have exercised a more powerful influence upon posterity.

As a young man Cicero studied law under the great Scaevola and served for a short time in the army. Here he made the acquaintance of Pompey and developed an enduring admiration for the great man. Pompey did not always reciprocate these sentiments, though he was always ready to make use of Cicero's talents. The two men differed profoundly in their attitude toward Sulla. Early in his career as a lawyer, Cicero defended a victim of the proscriptions and won his case; afterward he found it expedient to travel in Greece and Asia in the guise of a student. Upon his return to Italy after Sulla's death, Cicero married a rich, domineering woman and acquired fame and fortune at the bar. His clients were mostly rich equestrians, and throughout his political career Cicero staunchly supported that class. Starting up the *cursus honorum,* he became quaestor in 75, entered the senate a year later, and spent three years as proquaestor in Sicily.

Cicero's big chance came in the year 70, when he brought charges of extortion against Verres, a Sullan who had served in Sicily as propraetor from 73 to 71. His handling of the case was so masterly that Verres went into exile without attempting a defense, and Cicero kept the memory of the affair alive by publishing his speeches. Cicero quickly learned, however, that though his oratory had enhanced his reputation with the populace, it had offended Verres' aristocratic friends who dominated Roman politics. The next year he redeemed himself in their eyes by defending another aristocrat, a certain Fonteius, governor of Transalpine Gaul, who was likewise accused of extortion by his subjects, the Allobroges. Modern historians suspect that Fonteius was no less guilty than Verres, except that his poor province afforded fewer opportunities than Sicily, yet Cicero obtained an acquittal and thus put himself in the irreproachable position of having prosecuted the guilty and defended the innocent, regardless of their social status. The publicity resulting from these two cases assured Cicero's rapid advance in the *cursus honorum*.

Cato

At this time the political stage was crowded with secondary characters about whom we are much better informed than is usual in ancient history, chiefly because of the light thrown on them by over nine hundred of Cicero's letters that have been preserved. Among these lesser lights was Cato, sometimes called Cato Minor, greatgrandson of the old censor and nephew of the tribune Livius Drusus (†91). Constantly parading his family and his honesty, Cato was easily held up to ridicule by his opponents. He was not a great statesman, or even a very skillful politician, yet he became leader of the most reactionary aristocrats in the senate. To Crassus and Caesar he was either a nuisance or a joke; he sometimes caused Cicero to wring his hands in despair; but to later generations Cato became a hero because of his heroic opposition to Caesar.

The Rivalry of Pompey and Crassus

Pompey and Crassus planned to use their respective victories over Sertorius and Spartacus as steppingstones to brilliant political careers. As each had learned politics in the Sullan school, each advanced to Rome at the head of his army under the pretext of awaiting a triumph. But as neither general could seize the city without first defeating the other, and as neither was reckless enough to assume the odium of renewing civil war or skillful enough to make his rival seem the aggressor, the two men patched up a temporary truce, with each supporting the other for the consulship of the year 70. The senate passed a resolution permitting Pompey to stand as a candidate before reaching the legal age or going through the *cursus honorum;* and the two armies, encamped just outside the city, guaranteed that their respective generals would be elected.

During their year in office Pompey and Crassus re-established the tribunes in their old powers, reformed the jury panels to give the majority of places to the equestrians, and brought about the election of censors who expelled sixty-four of Sulla's more infamous henchmen from the senate. These three laws seemed to revive the spirit of Gaius Gracchus: the judiciary law was of course a great boon to the equestrians, while the other two laws were direct attacks upon the power of Sulla's reformed senate. At the same time anti-senatorial feeling was being further inflamed by Cicero's attacks upon Verres.

The events of the year 70 may therefore be taken as marking the beginning of the end of the Sullan system, but their full import did not appear at once. Two Sullan consuls were elected each year for the next three years; Cicero made haste to defend the aristocratic Fonteius in 69; so keen an observer as Caesar decided that it might be a good idea to marry Sulla's granddaughter; and perhaps the most significant fact of all was that neither Pompey nor Crassus received the proconsulship that normally followed a term as consul. We know nothing of how this came about. It is possible, of course, that the consuls did not wish to leave Rome, or that the provinces assigned to them were too insignificant to be attractive. But in view of their open use of military force at the time of their election, and their subsequent anti-senatorial legislation, it seems most likely that the Sullan senate refused to allow them any excuse for raising new armies. Moreover, Pompey and Crassus detested and feared each other as bitterly as the old senators feared and detested them both. Each would have done his best to prevent the other from getting troops.

Pompey was only thirty-six years old when he laid down his consulship. He had then completed the public career open to him and he spent the next two years living at Rome as a private citizen. He had not forsaken politics, however, and was eagerly awaiting new opportunities. The Mediterranean Sea was at that time infested with pirates—some of them instigated by Mithradates, no doubt, but others merely following an ancient and honored profession. When Roman business interests demanded that such depredations be stopped, a tribune named Gabinius proposed a law giving Pompey an "extraordinary command" against the pirates (67). This proposal terrified both Crassus and the conservative senators, for they feared that Pompey might march on Rome with his new army after defeating the pirates, but the bill was passed after riotous demonstrations by equestrians and the populace. Pompey then threw himself into his new command with such vigor that the pirates were swept from the seas within three months.

The campaign against the pirates was not yet concluded when another tribune, C. Manilius, sought popular acclaim by proposing that the command against Mithradates be transferred to Pompey. Lucullus had just allowed the king to escape from Armenia and regain his old kingdom; his soldiers were discouraged and mutinous; and he had antagonized the equestrians in Asia by attempting to curb their rapacity. The Manilian Law therefore won widespread approval. Cicero delivered an oration in favor of the proposal, praising the equestrians and Pompey; Caesar added his support; and the measure was passed in spite of the opposition of both Crassus and the old aristocracy. Pompey then remained absent from Rome for five years, during which period his political enemies in their nightmares saw him returning to Rome at the head of his army as a new Sulla.

The Alliance of Crassus and Caesar

Crassus had returned to money-making after his consulship, but he did not forget his political ambitions or his hatred of Pompey. When his rival obtained the command against Mithradates, Crassus at once sought to balance it with new powers for himself. He perhaps felt justified in fearing that his own name might stand first on new proscription lists when Pompey returned, and apparently he decided that the best way to defend himself against such a fate was to become a Sullan dictator himself before Pompey's arrival. At any rate, he and Caesar entered into an alliance which looked in this direction and which soon threw all Rome into turmoil.

Conditions in Rome at this time encouraged machinations such as theirs. A considerable number of persons who had profited by the Sullan disturbances were now in financial straits once more. Many of Sulla's veterans had been unwilling or unable to cultivate the farms he had given them and, having sold the farms and spent the money, they were now paupers in Rome waiting for someone to buy their support with new largess. Dissolute nobles, having run through fortunes acquired from proscriptions, were looking for new sources of easy money and were not above a little lawlessness in getting it. Bright young men had learned how to manipulate the Roman mob and were eager to practice their new profession. Crassus and Caesar set themselves at the head of these diverse groups and formed a new "Popular Party." Obviously, however, the two leaders had no deep personal attachment to democracy: they merely planned to exploit the populace for their personal aggrandizement.

Crassus's first step in his new program was to get elected censor for 65. He at once prepared to enroll as citizens the Gauls living north of the Po River, whom Caesar had already encouraged to demand more than the Latin rights they then enjoyed. The two friends apparently hoped to obtain the votes of Gauls living in Rome and to recruit armies among those across the Po. The scheme miscarried, and in 64 the senate ordered all Gauls in Rome to leave the city lest another attempt be made to enfranchise them. Crassus was then forced to resign the censorship before he got around to the purge of the senate that he had contemplated.

Meantime Caesar had been elected aedile for 65. He set up in the forum the trophies of Marius that Sulla had torn down, and he won the hearts of the populace by the lavishness of his shows. On one occasion he exhibited combats between no less than 320 pairs of gladiators. He was restrained from using more only by an order from the senate, which feared lest he use an army of gladiators to capture the city. To meet his enormous expenses he borrowed millions from Crassus, thereby cementing their alliance.

The Conspiracy of 65

The most important intrigue in which Caesar and Crassus were implicated grew out of the so-called First Conspiracy of Catiline. Lucius Sergius Catilina belonged to a family of the minor nobility and had been notorious for his excesses during Sulla's proscriptions. In 68 and 67 he served as propraetor in Africa and was sued for extortion on his return. Late in 66 two henchmen of Crassus, the consuls-elect for 65, were convicted of bribery and disqualified. Catiline wished to stand for the consulship at the new election thus made necessary, but unfortunately he was still awaiting trial. He therefore entered into a conspiracy with the two disqualified consuls to seize power after murdering the new consuls on New Year's Day, 65. The authorities suspected that something was brewing and provided adequate guards on the appointed day. The plot degenerated into a minor riot, and though a second futile attempt at assassination was made on February 5, the whole matter was so carefully hushed up that we now know very little about it.

It was later alleged that both Crassus and Caesar, who were censor and aedile that year, had been implicated in the plot, Crassus hoping to be made dictator with Caesar his next in command. The charge seems most improbable, for Caesar's uncle, Aurelius Cotta, was one of the consuls marked for death. Moreover, a dictatorship without an army could have done Crassus no good. It seems more likely that after the plot had failed, Crassus exploited it to his own advantage. His influence over senators who owed him money was enough to prevent an investigation, and he even obtained the appointment of one of the conspirators, Gnaeus Piso, as propraetor in Spain. The resulting confusion offered Crassus his chance.

It happened that Ptolemy XI Auletes had recently been expelled from Egypt by his subjects, which provided a plausible excuse for Roman intervention there. It was charged, furthermore, that the ousted king's predecessor had bequeathed Egypt to the Roman people—which was most unlikely as Rome had done nothing to take over her supposed inheritance, either at the time of the king's death or subsequently. A tribune friendly to Crassus presented a bill authorizing Caesar to occupy Egypt. Such an occupation would require a large army, of course, and the army could be used equally well to check Pompey. Piso would hold Spain; Cisalpine Gaul, friendly to Crassus and Caesar because of the franchise bill, would provide soldiers for the necessary armies; and Crassus would direct everything from Rome. All these dangerous implications of the bill were quickly recognized. Senators, equestrians, and the friends of Pompey united in attacking it, Cicero delivered an oration against it, and the measure was defeated in the *comitia*.

Far from being discouraged by their failures in 65, Crassus and Caesar, now out of office, turned their attention to the election of 64. Catiline, who by this time had stood trial and been acquitted in scandalous fashion, was one candidate for the consulship. The second was another notorious senator, Gaius Antonius, an uncle of Mark Antony. Their principal rival for the office was Cicero, who ever since the trial of Verres had been busily making a career for himself. While serving as praetor in 66, Cicero had the good fortune to preside at the politically important trial of a popular tribune; a letter he wrote at the time shows that he was much less interested in the evidence than in the effect which conviction or acquittal would have on his own political fortunes. A little later, Cicero thought of defending Catiline in return for political support, but Catiline preferred other defenders. As election day approached, Crassus spent money freely for his candidates while Cicero concentrated his attack upon Catiline. Cicero won first place at the polls, with Antonius a poor second and Catiline a close third.[1]

Cicero's *Annus Mirabilis*

Cicero never tired of talking about his marvelous achievements as consul in 63, which he called the *annus mirabilis* or "wonderful year." His opponents kept him on the griddle every minute, and his sur-

---

[1] The whole political situation at Rome just before the election, and Cicero's campaign methods, are vividly set forth in a little essay by Cicero's brother Quintus, sometimes called *De petitione consulatus* ("On Seeking the Consulship"), which is published with Cicero's letters.

vival of their repeated attacks is a tribute to his political agility. Their first attack took the form of an Agrarian Law which, seeming to follow the Gracchan tradition, provided that ten commissioners should distribute to the poor all the remaining public lands in Italy as well as land in the provinces, specifically including Egypt. Other land was to be bought at public cost and distributed. Though no names were mentioned, the law virtually deprived Pompey of his booty from the East (it would be used to buy land from aristocrats at high prices); it assured Caesar an army (to enforce the annexation of Egypt); and it provided the means for Crassus to build a great political machine at Rome through land distributions. Moreover, anyone who criticized the law would, of course, be accused of grinding down the faces of the poor. Nevertheless, Cicero, as he boasted later, surpassed his opponents in demagoguery and misrepresentation, and the bill was withdrawn.

Cicero's next step was to buy off his colleague Antonius. This he accomplished by handing over to him the rich province of Macedonia to which Cicero had been appointed proconsul for 62. (After plundering Macedonia unmercifully for three years, Antonius was eventually tried for extortion; though ably defended by Cicero, he was found guilty and went into exile in 58.) A few weeks later Caesar retaliated by attacking the principle of the *senatus consultum ultimum*. A certain Rabirius was charged with the murder of Saturninus thirty-seven years before. As he had committed the murder after the "final decree" had been issued, his conviction would imply that the decree carried little or no weight. Cicero defended Rabirius, who undoubtedly would have been acquitted had not Caesar called the whole thing off before it was too late to conceal his defeat. A law was next brought forward to pardon the sons of those proscribed by Sulla. Much as Cicero hated the Sullan system, he had to secure the rejection of this law to prevent Crassus and Caesar from gaining credit with the populace for their attack upon the dictator's memory. On other occasions minor riots had to be pacified. Thus Cicero thwarted all Caesar's schemes except two: Caesar managed to get himself chosen *pontifex maximus*, at an enormous cost in bribes, and a little later he was elected praetor for 62.

The election of consuls for 62 took place in September, 63. Catiline was once more a candidate, backed by Crassus and Caesar, while Cicero backed two other men. Both sides spent money freely. Though Cicero's candidates were elected, Cato at once sued one of them for bribery—not out of love for Catiline or Crassus, but because Cato was a Stoic who professionally favored justice though the heavens fell and an aristocrat in whose eyes the successful candidate was not aristocratic enough. Cicero had to defend his man. As there could be no doubt of the defendant's guilt, Cicero studiously ignored the evidence, abused his opponents, and got the jury to laughing at his jokes. Cicero won an acquittal, and Cato went away muttering that the consul seemed to be quite a witty fellow.

The Catilinarian Conspiracy

Mithradates had by this time been defeated and Pompey was expected home at any moment. Realizing that it would be futile and dangerous to oppose a returning hero, Crassus and Caesar abandoned their earlier policies and prepared to seek peace with Pompey. Catiline was not gifted with equal caution, however, and prepared to seize the government of Rome by force. He assumed the role of a popular leader, successor to the Gracchi, Saturninus, and Cinna. A few persons may have believed in his sincerity, but most of his followers were decadent aristocrats hoping to escape their creditors, adventurers hungrily looking forward to new proscriptions, veterans of Sulla who had failed as farmers, and members of the Roman rabble already thoroughly debauched by Crassus and Caesar. Though Catiline was undoubtedly a man able to inspire enthusiasm and loyalty among his followers, his plot to seize Rome with this motley crew was foredoomed to failure.

Cicero seems to have learned something of Catiline's plans at an early date from the mistress of one of the conspirators, but he had no proof to lay before the senate. His speeches were therefore limited to vague and unconvincing charges. At last, however, on October 21, he was able to present evidence that troops were being recruited in Etruria and he prophesied a general massacre for the 28th. The senate promptly passed the "final decree" and ordered an army under Antonius to suppress the insurgents. Catiline was checked, but only for a moment. On November 6 he made ready to join his troops after arranging for the murder of Cicero. The consul was warned, the attempted murder was foiled, and Catiline stayed in Rome. Two days later Cicero delivered an impassioned oration against him before the senate (his "First Catilinarian") exposing the attempt at murder, reviving his old charges, adding new ones of a more definite character, and urging Catiline to leave the city. Catiline left that very night, and the next day Cicero triumphantly delivered his "Second Catilinarian" before the people, hailing the flight as a confession of guilt. The senate voted Catiline a public enemy.

Nevertheless, Catiline's friends in Rome continued to plan a general uprising for December 16. At this critical moment delegates arrived from the Allobroges (see p. 309), seeking redress for their ancient grievances. The delegates were lured by Catiline's friends into joining the conspiracy—perhaps not a difficult feat, for the Allobroges knew Cicero only as the slick lawyer who had saved the scoundrelly Fonteius from punishment. In the nick of time better-informed friends convinced the Allobroges that no help could be expected from Catiline and even induced them to give positive evidence enabling Cicero to arrest Catiline's ringleaders in Rome. Cicero told the people what had happened in his "Third Catilinarian," and the senate debated the fate of the arrested leaders on December 5. A death sentence was favored until Caesar made a powerful speech in defense of his former associates, urging that they be incarcerated in different Italian towns, and that after the immediate danger had passed they be given a calm trial. Caesar's proposal seemed likely to prevail until Cato's reply and Cicero's "Fourth Catilinarian" persuaded the senate to decree death. Five conspirators were executed at Cicero's order that very night.

Catiline's conspiracy thus collapsed, and early in the following year Roman troops destroyed his army, which had dwindled by desertions from more than 10,000 to about 3000 men. On the day of the battle Antonius feigned illness rather than fight against his old friend, but Catiline fought bravely and died with his followers.

Partisans continued to hail him as a champion of the people, and four years later, when Antonius was convicted of extortion in spite of Cicero's defense, they decorated Catiline's tomb with flowers.

Aftermath of the Conspiracy

Cicero was quite sure that he had saved Rome, but popular hostility to him arose even before Catiline's death. Metellus Nepos, a cousin of Pompey's wife, had come back to Rome from the East early in 63 to prepare the way for the general's triumphant return. He was elected tribune for 62, and soon after taking office (December 10, 63) he proposed a law calling Pompey home to restore order in the Republic and to put an end to Cicero's "tyranny." He accompanied his proposal with stinging attacks upon the consul. On the last day of the year Cicero took the usual oath that he had faithfully fulfilled the duties of his office. He had planned to detail his achievements in a long oration, but Nepos silenced him as soon as he had pronounced the formula of the oath. Three days later, when Cato (who was also tribune) vetoed the bill recalling Pompey, Nepos filled the forum with gladiators who rioted until the senate in a panic voted the "final decree." Nepos fled to Pompey, vowing vengeance. The bill lapsed, and Pompey thereby lost his chance to return lawfully at the head of his army.

During the next few months all Rome was filled with sly whispers and jokes at Cicero's expense. His scholarly education was held against him. His claim in his early speeches to have "discovered" so much for which he offered no proof caused his enemies to throw the word *comperisse* ("discovered") in his teeth. Crassus once brought the house down by remarking in the senate, with dead-pan humor, that he owed his life, his wife, his home, and his country to Cicero. Most important of all, it was charged that the consul's execution of the five conspirators had been illegal in that they had not been given an opportunity to appeal to the *comitia* under the *ius provocationis*.

Cicero spent much time replying to these attacks. When a minor Greek poet named Archias was sued for something in 62, Cicero undertook his defense. Virtually ignoring the case in hand, he delivered a famous discourse upon the advantages of a literary education. Actually he was defending himself against the damning charge of being a high-brow. He wrote and published histories of his consulship in Greek and Latin, in prose and in verse. The Latin poem began with an oft-quoted line *"O fortunatam natam me consule Romam"* ("Rome, fortunately born, having me as consul") which still excited Roman mirth two centuries later. He begged the distinguished Greek historian Posidonius to write an account of the "wonderful year"; but the wily Greek, who was a friend of Pompey, replied gravely that his pen was unequal to so mighty a theme—words which Cicero mistook for sincere praise. At this same time (June, 60) we find Cicero editing and publishing ten orations originally delivered in 63. Among them were the four "Catilinarians" which are still sometimes read in high schools. These speeches do not give us what Cicero said at the time of the conspiracy so much as what he wished that he had said when he came to think it over three years later. In fact, the opening paragraphs of the "First Oration," as they now stand, cite several persons less guilty than Catiline whom earlier consuls had executed without trial. They seem to be Cicero's *ex post facto* defense of himself for executing the five conspirators a month after the original oration was delivered!

The First Triumvirate

Pompey finally landed his army at Brundisium in December, 62, and to the amazement of many he at once disbanded all but a small bodyguard. The menace of civil war vanished, and even Crassus, who had fled with his family to Asia Minor, now felt safe in returning to Rome. The reasons for Pompey's unexpected conduct are not clear. It may be that the fears of his enemies had been exaggerated, and that he had never planned to capture Rome. Perhaps he doubted that his troops would follow him, since he had no good excuse for attacking the city; or he may have believed that the authorities, cowed by the knowledge that he could quickly muster his veterans whenever he wished, would recognize his supremacy without resistance. It has even been suggested that Pompey had already entered into some sort of deal with Caesar, possibly through the mediation of Metellus Nepos. At any rate, he dismissed his soldiers, proceeded to Rome as a private citizen, and passed the next several months receiving congratulations and offers of co-operation from friends and acquaintances. Cicero was particularly active, though not very successful, in trying to install himself as the general's political advisor. Toward the end of September, 61, Pompey celebrated a triumph lasting two days, which was the most magnificent Rome had ever seen.

Yet Pompey was not satisfied. The senate's ratification of his *acta* —that is, his settlement of the Near East—was held up when Lucullus and Cato persuaded the senate to scrutinize each item separately before confirming the *acta*. (Lucullus, it will be recalled, had been Pompey's predecessor in the East.) Moreover, Pompey needed lands to distribute among his veterans as bonuses, but when a friendly tribune proposed a law providing them, the opposition was so strong that the bill had to be withdrawn. It was annoying to have Cicero constantly boasting that he had saved Rome from Catiline while Pompey was merely defeating Orientals. Cicero was just as annoyed at Pompey's unwillingness to take energetic measures for the perpetuation of the *concordia ordinum* that he had built up against Catiline. Thoroughly disillusioned and fearful lest he lose the adulation he craved, Pompey began seeking new friends.

Meantime, Caesar had gone off to Spain in 61 to serve as propraetor, but he had already planted the seeds of his clandestine alliance with Crassus and Pompey which came to full fruition in 60 and is now called the "First Triumvirate." It cannot have been easy to bring the two former enemies together, but Caesar accomplished the feat by offering each of the rivals exactly what he most desired. Pompey was to have his *acta* ratified and get lands for his veterans; Crassus and his friends among the publicans were to have a reduction of payments due to the state on certain unprofitable contracts; and after his consulship Caesar was to have a province to govern with an army. This secret alliance was presently fortified by Pompey's marriage to Caesar's only daughter, Julia.[2] Julia had inherited

---

[2] Caesar's matrimonial career is an important guide to his political progress. His first wife was Cornelia, daughter of Cinna; the second, married in 67 before he first went to Spain, was Pompeia, granddaughter of Sulla. Shortly after Pompey's return, Caesar divorced Pompeia, under circumstances to be described later, but the scandal

Cicero (Capitoline Museum, Rome)

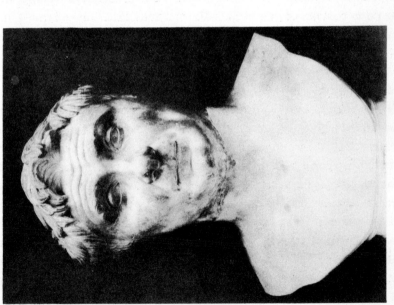

Pompey (Copenhagen Museum)

Plate 14

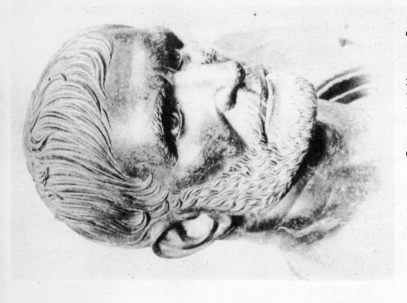

Conservatori Museum, Rome

Museum of Fine Arts, Boston

Plate 15.　Two Unknown Romans of the Late Republican Period

her father's intelligence and she was so successful in preventing a break between the triumvirs that her death, late in 54, was a catastrophe for the Republic. Caesar also invited Cicero to become a minor partner in the triumvirate, to which he would contribute his respectability and his oratory. Cicero wisely declined the honor. As soon as the triumvirate was firmly established, Caesar announced his candidacy for the consulship, to which he was elected late in 60.

"The Consulship of Julius and Caesar"

Caesar's colleague as consul in 59, M. Calpurnius Bibulus, was an extremist in the senatorial faction and the son-in-law of Cato. He was of no help to his friends, however, for he passed his consulship as a voluntary prisoner in his own house after a gang of Pompey's veterans had handled him roughly. His sole acts were to issue opprobrious manifestoes against Caesar from time to time. Wags therefore spoke of "the consulship of Julius and Caesar," rather than the official "of Bibulus and Caesar." Caesar made it his first task to supply Pompey with the land secretly promised him for his veterans. Pompey's soldiers terrorized the voters and two Agrarian Laws were passed in spite of opposition by Cato and Cicero. Pompey's *acta* were ratified, and the amounts owed the state by Crassus's publicans were reduced by one-third. One of Caesar's laws, which won the approval even of Cicero, was designed to curb extortion in the provinces; and another provided that abbreviated accounts of all debates in the senate should be posted in the forum in a daily bulletin called the *Acta Diurna*. (Was this Caesar's reply to Cicero's recent publication of his speeches of 63 in highly revised form?)

Caesar's greatest concern was to obtain a province, primarily that

---

with which her name was connected merely served as a pretext. The divorce really was part of his breach with the senatorial aristocracy and a step toward the alliance with Pompey. On the other hand, Pompey had divorced his third wife, Mucia, shortly before his return from the East, with Caesar indicated as corespondent. Mucia's cousin, the tribune Metellus Nepos, thereupon transferred his allegiance to Caesar, for whom he performed yeoman service; and Pompey married Caesar's daughter Julia. Caesar took as his third wife Calpurnia, the daughter of Calpurnius Piso, a debauched aristocrat attached to the antisenatorial faction and a close friend of the Clodius whose intrigue with Pompeia had given Caesar an excuse to divorce her. Caesar found his new father-in-law useful for various odd jobs—including a consulship—and Cicero once delivered an oration against him as a roundabout way of attacking Caesar.

he might have troops to command. The senate had allotted rather insignificant proconsulships to the consuls for 59, but Caesar forced through a new law giving himself an "extraordinary command" in Cisalpine Gaul, to which Transalpine Gaul was presently added. The attraction of these provinces lay in their restlessness. The Allobroges, having exhausted all legal methods of securing redress from Fonteius and other extortioners, rose in revolt in 61 and were precariously pacified only after several months of fighting. They might revolt again at any moment. Moreover, the Helvetii, a tribe living in the north of Switzerland, were planning to invade Gaul. The governor of Gaul would therefore need a large army. The law gave Caesar command of the two provinces for five years and allotted him three legions. In the spring of 58 the Helvetii began their migration, and the ensuing wars carried Caesar on his famous campaigns beyond the Rhine and into Britain. At the end of nine years he had pacified and annexed the whole territory lying between the Pyrenees, the Rhine, and the ocean; he was in command of ten devoted legions; and he had inspired the Roman populace with high enthusiasm for a governor whose exploits eclipsed those of Pompey himself.

Clodius, "the Gangster in Roman Politics"

It was shortly after Caesar's departure for Gaul that the notorious Clodius rose to prominence at Rome. Publius Clodius Pulcher was the son and grandson of Claudian consuls, and in him the ancient Claudian traditions of demagoguery and violence reached their fullest expression. He has aptly been called "the gangster in Roman politics." As a rabble-rouser Clodius was unsurpassed, but his power rested primarily upon his gangs of armed slaves and hoodlums who rioted and fought with clubs and stones, or even with swords. Clodius began his public career by fomenting mutiny in the army of his brother-in-law, Lucullus, during the Third Mithradatic War, but Cicero testified to his loyalty during Catiline's conspiracy of 63. Late in the year 62 Clodius was caught violating religious mysteries in the course of an intrigue with Caesar's second wife Pompeia. Caesar refused to testify against him—though he divorced Pompeia with the famous remark, "Caesar's wife must be above suspicion." Cato sued Clodius for sacrilege, however, and Cicero gave incriminating testimony. Only by the extensive bribery of jurors did Clodius secure an acquittal. The next several years he devoted to revenging himself upon Cicero and Cato. At first Caesar held him in check, but when his two enemies attacked the Agrarian Law, Caesar gave Clodius a free hand.

As Clodius wished to be tribune, an office to which patricians were ineligible, Caesar permitted him to be adopted by a laborer several years younger than himself and thus to change his official status. The plebeian Clodius was elected tribune for 58, and within a short time he brought his attacks upon Cicero to a climax. He secured the passage of a law which "deprived of fire and water"—that is to say, outlawed—anyone who executed Roman citizens without trial. Though he cleverly presented the law as a popular measure designed to prevent the senate from invoking the "final decree" against opponents, it really was designed only as a means of destroying Cicero, who had executed the five Catilinarian conspirators without allowing them to appeal to the *comitia*. Passage of this law forced Cicero to spend several wretched months in exile. During his absence, Clodius's gangsters tore down his house on the Palatine, and the ground was dedicated for a temple to the goddess Liberty. Clodius next had his vengeance upon Cato, sending him off to Cyprus, which had just been annexed by Rome. Cato hesitated to accept the commission until Clodius remarked, with characteristic humor, that it was Cato's duty to go as he was the only man in Rome honest enough to be entrusted with so important a mission. When Cato returned to Rome after an absence of three years, Clodius added further to the gaiety of the city by charging him with embezzlement.

Clodius had by this time entered into an unholy alliance with Crassus, who found the gangsters useful in terrorizing Rome. Pompey was seriously concerned for his own position and set up a rival gangster named Milo, a son-in-law of Sulla. During the next several years violence and terrorization by gangsters were the order of the day at Rome. The streets were often stained with blood, and no prominent politician dared appear in public unless accompanied by an armed retinue. Meantime, speculators had cornered the grain market at Rome and were enriching themselves by forcing up the price. Pompey ingratiated himself with the public by sponsoring government distributions of grain. By managing the distributions

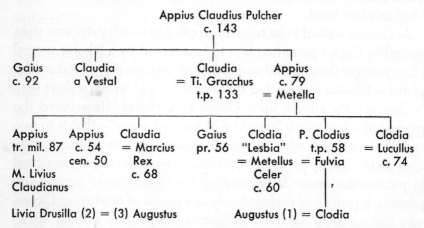

THE CLAUDII IN THE FIRST CENTURY B.C.

Appius Claudius Pulcher
c. 143

| Gaius c. 92 | Claudia a Vestal | | Claudia = Ti. Gracchus t.p. 133 | Appius c. 79 = Metella |

| Appius tr. mil. 87 M. Livius Claudianus | Appius c. 54 cen. 50 | Claudia = Marcius Rex c. 68 | Gaius pr. 56 | Clodia "Lesbia" = Metellus Celer c. 60 | P. Clodius t.p. 58 = Fulvia | Clodia = Lucullus c. 74 |

Livia Drusilla (2) = (3) Augustus   Augustus (1) = Clodia

= married; c., consul; cen., censor; pr., praetor; t.p., tribune; tr. mil., military tribune. The numbers in parentheses indicate the sequence of marriages: the marriage of Livia and Augustus was her second and his third marriage.

Pompey was able to build up a powerful political machine, and by attributing the high prices to Crassus and Clodius, he made his enemies appear as villains while he posed as savior of the people.

While at the height of his difficulties with Clodius, Pompey bethought himself of Cicero, then languishing in exile, and decided that he could use the good man's oratorical ability to advantage. Cicero was therefore recalled in September, 57, but only after several bloody battles between Clodius and Milo. As soon as he reached Rome, Cicero set himself to redeeming his own position rather than Pompey's. His legal training enabled him to discover a flaw in the dedication of his property to Liberty. He got his land back, and his oratory persuaded the senate to build him a better house at public expense. It was he who induced the senate to make Pompey grain distributor, and presently he even found the courage to propose a reconsideration of Caesar's Agrarian Law. At about the same time a senator named Domitius Ahenobarbus, a brother-in-law of Cato, announced his candidacy for the consulship of 55 and promised that if elected he would terminate Caesar's command in Gaul. It seemed that the triumvirate was about to founder.

The Triumvirs at Luca

Such was the state of affairs at Rome in the spring of 56 when Caesar summoned his two colleagues to Luca, a small town near the border between Cisalpine Gaul and Italy. Here the triumvirs renewed their old alliance and allotted each other provinces, though their spirit did not bode well for the future: each had to make concessions, but each sought to arrange them in such a way as to create bad feeling between his two fellow triumvirs. Crassus, coveting a rich province and an army, had set his heart on Syria. It was a relatively new province, not yet thoroughly looted by the Romans; it was full of Pompey's friends, whom he could replace with his own henchmen, thus greatly impairing the prestige of his rival; and above all, war with the Parthians seemed imminent and would provide the excuse for an army that might equal Caesar's. Pompey, on the other hand, had been interested in Spain ever since the days of Sertorius and was eager to command an army there. But at the same time he wanted to remain in charge of the grain distributions at Rome. Caesar decided that his best policy would be to let his colleagues have what they wanted while he contented himself with a renewal of his command in Gaul for another five years. Pompey and Crassus would soon fall to quarreling, and when they entered their respective provinces each would be far from Rome while Caesar's army would be on the frontiers of Italy. Cicero was given short shrift, and in his private correspondence he was soon bewailing the fact that he had been such an "utter ass" as to attack Caesar. But when he was called upon to deliver a public oration blessing the work of the triumvirs, he did so in his best style. The poor man's spirit being utterly broken, he retired from public life to devote himself to literature and philosophy.

Pompey and Crassus, of course, had to be consuls again before they could become proconsuls. As it was now too late to announce their candidacy for the regular elections of 56, they used legal obstruction and gangster violence to prevent any election at all being held that year. Then, early in 55, the two triumvirs were elected consuls for the remainder of the year, being aided by soldiers sent by Caesar for the purpose. During this year Caesar's legions massacred nearly half a million Germans, crossed the Rhine, and invaded Britain. The senate then voted to give thanks to the gods for twenty days. Cato, opposing the measure, showed his courage by suggesting that Caesar be handed over for punishment to the survivors of the Germanic tribes he had recently massacred. This unorthodox suggestion regarding the proper treatment of war criminals caused Cato to be severely beaten by Caesar's plug-uglies, but the old aristocrat showed his courage by resuming his attacks as soon as he was able to attend meetings of the senate again. The principal achievement of the two triumvirs at Rome during their second consulships was the enactment—after protracted rioting and bloodshed, and a public fist fight between the consul Crassus and a senator—of a law whereby provinces were distributed exactly as prearranged at Luca.

Crassus was so eager to start work in Syria that he left Rome and his consulship in mid-November. Upon arriving in his province he found that the Parthian situation was fully as bad as he had hoped and at once he began preparing for war. After a minor skirmish in the fall of 54 he launched his major campaign early in 53. He was easily led into a trap and defeated. Though he managed to retreat into the city of Carrhae, he was murdered by Parthians a few days later (June, 53). The loss of about 30,000 Roman soldiers, the humiliation of defeat, and the encouragement of Rome's foreign enemies on every front, were the more important consequences of Crassus's final adventure.

The Death Agonies of the Republic

The years after Luca witnessed the death agonies of the Roman Republic. Pompey remained sole consul at Rome when Crassus departed for the East, late in 55. His popularity was augmented by the dedication of an enormous theater built with money from his Eastern campaigns, and by shows in which five hundred lions and four hundred tigers were killed fighting with condemned criminals while twenty elephants engaged in mortal combat. Though he raised three new legions for service in Spain, Pompey insisted upon remaining at Rome to direct the grain distributions. A legate was sent to govern his province, which was a serious violation of the law as well as of the agreement reached at Luca. A worse blow befell the triumvirate a few months later with the death of Julia in September, 54. Caesar attempted to repair the breach by suggesting that Pompey marry his great-niece Octavia who, though only twelve years old, would divorce her present husband for the purpose. Caesar would return the favor by divorcing Calpurnia and marrying Pompey's daughter. Pompey rejected these flattering proposals and married a charming lady with an enormous dowry, the widow of Crassus's son.

Political conditions in Rome went steadily from bad to worse. It was openly said that Pompey was planning to set himself up as dictator, and color was lent to the charge by the fact that he used violence to delay any election of consuls for 53 until the year was more than half gone. A tribune who was Pompey's cousin publicly proposed the dictatorship, but the proposal was checked by Cato. Clodius then announced his candidacy for the praetorship of 52. At the same time Milo, who had severed his connections with Pompey, was being backed by the conservative aristocracy for the consulship. Factional violence became so great that no election could be held. One day, early in January, 52, when the two candidates and their retinues happened to meet outside Rome, Clodius lost his life in a pitched battle. His wife Fulvia and his followers carried his body to Rome, placed it in the Senate House, burned the building down as a fitting funeral pyre for their hero, and proceeded to celebrate a terrifying wake amidst the smoking embers. Milo was charged with murder and, despite Cicero's lame defense that the murder of Clodius was a public service, Pompey had his ungrateful agent exiled to Massilia. As no consuls had been elected for 52, the senate made Pompey sole consul—which was virtually a dictatorship—though in August he accepted his new father-in-law, Metellus Scipio, as colleague.

Meantime, Caesar was finding the year 52 the most difficult of the

Gallic War. As soon as the Gauls learned of the Parthian victory over Crassus and of the pandemonium at Rome after the death of Clodius, a leader named Vercingetorix rose in revolt and won an important battle at Gergovia. His success did not last long, however, and he surrendered to Caesar at Alesia three months later. Gaul was then thoroughly pacified. The following year Caesar published his *Commentaries* as a propaganda document, giving his version of all that he had done for Rome since his consulship. During the brief period of Caesar's danger in 52 his enemies at Rome attacked him openly; during 51 they were rather quiet; but the two consuls elected for 50 were openly hostile to him. That year, censors were elected who purged the senate of his more ardent supporters, usually on charges of immorality, and before long the senate began to discuss winding up his affairs.

Caesar Crosses the Rubicon

Careful observers of political life at Rome were declaring as early as 51 that a break between Pompey and Caesar was inevitable. The two champions were already maneuvering against each other, each trying to put the other in as bad a light as possible and force him to take illegal action. Controversy centered primarily about ending Caesar's command in Gaul. Unfortunately, the records now available do not tell us definitely when this command was supposed to end. Dates suggested by modern writers vary from March 1, 50, to December 31, 49. The date was of great importance, however, for the following reasons.

Cato and others had long been threatening to sue Caesar for various illegalities as soon as he laid down his command, but proceedings could not be started at once because a Roman official could not be sued while in office. Caesar sought to protect himself by being elected to a second consulship before laying down his command. The new consulship and a subsequent proconsulship would make him invulnerable for several years to come. On the other hand, Caesar was equally eager to ruin Pompey's career with lawsuits. Pompey's command in Spain was supposed to end simultaneously with Caesar's in Gaul, for they had been granted at the same time, after Luca. However, as Pompey had held the consulship in 55 and 52, he could not legally hold it again until ten years had passed. (His third consulship, in 52, had been illegal though possibly excusable because of the crisis.) As Caesar's first consulship had been in 59, he clearly was eligible to run in 49 for the consulship of 48. If he were elected, he would be in a position to start legal proceedings against Pompey. Pompey therefore induced the senate to prolong his pro-consulship until five years after the end of his third consulship, or until December 31, 47. He further forestalled Caesar with a law (which he justified as a means of discouraging bribery) providing that no consul could become a proconsul until five years after his consulship. This provision would leave Caesar out of office in 47 while Pompey was still proconsul. Pompey won this round. Nothing daunted, Caesar insisted upon becoming a candidate *in absentia* for the consulship in the election to be held late in the summer of 49, and there was little doubt that, unless his enemies forced him from his command before the elections, he would be elected consul.

During the summer of 50 the question of appointing a successor to Caesar as governor of Gaul was raised several times in the senate, but on every occasion it was vetoed by the tribune Curio, a former associate of Clodius. Pompey then persuaded the senate to order two of Caesar's legions to the East to meet an alleged Parthian men-ace. Caesar, sure that he could retain their loyalty, let them go. Pom-pey held them at Capua, while Caesar made good his loss by re-cruiting new forces in Gaul. Caesar clearly won this round. Curio then proposed that both generals lay down their commands simul-taneously: on December 1, the senate voted 370 to 22 in favor of his proposal, but it was vetoed by a tribune hostile to Caesar. The next day the consuls invited Pompey to assume command of the two legions now at Capua in order to defend Rome against Caesar, a commission which Pompey joyfully accepted. Caesar had by this time established headquarters with one legion at Ravenna, at the southern tip of Cisalpine Gaul. This arrangement was quite within his rights as commander of the province, but it indicated that the use of force had occurred to him. As soon as Caesar heard of Pom-pey's new command, he summoned two legions from Gaul and sent three others to Narbonne to guard the Spanish frontier against Pompey's legions stationed there. Caesar then announced that he would accept Curio's proposal and lay down his command if Pompey would do the same. Pompey refused, and it was with difficulty that Curio had Caesar's message read to the senate on January 1, 49. During the next few days Rome was in turmoil, with Pompey trying to find some way of ousting Caesar at once, while Caesarian tribunes vetoed every proposal he made. Cicero arrived in Rome on January 4 and, as he wrote later, concluded that "our friends [the Pompeians] desired war, while Caesar did not desire it but did not fear it."

At last, on January 7, Pompey warned Caesar's tribunes not to appear in the senate again, thus abrogating one of the fundamental liberties of the Roman people. The tribunes promptly rushed off to Caesar's camp. The senate, thoroughly alarmed, relieved Caesar of his command, appointed Ahenobarbus his successor, passed the "final decree," and began levying troops. As soon as Caesar learned what had happened, he marched on Rome, allegedly to defend the tribunes, to guard the sanctity of the Roman constitution, and to save Rome from slavery. His enemies, as might be expected, accused him of attacking the Republic. The truth is that one faction had no more claim to represent the Republic than did the other. On the morning of January 11, 49, Caesar crossed the Rubicon—the frontier between Cisalpine Gaul and Italy—uttering the famous words, "The die is cast!"

IX The Civil Wars

THE CIVIL WAR BETWEEN CAESAR AND POMPEY WAS AT
first little more than a continuation of the gang warfare with which
Clodius and Milo had distracted Rome for so long. Soldiers fought
for their leaders rather than for their country or for a cause, and
both they and the general public remained remarkably unimpressed
by the idealistic pronunciamentos of either side. The conflict was
not a struggle between the aristocracy and the people but a quarrel between factions, all of which were led by members of the upper
classes. Only as a last resort, after the failure of the weapons more
commonly employed in Rome's factional warfare—intrigue, law
suits, *vituperatio*, rioting, and matrimony—did the great antagonists
draw the sword. Moreover, the factions at Rome in the late fifties
were three rather than two: the Pompeians, the Caesarians, and the
Sullan aristocracy who dominated the senate and were led by Cato.
Even after crossing the Rubicon Caesar retained, or acquired, the
support of several old patrician families (including the Aemilii, the
Servilii, and some of the Claudii), but most senators threw in their
lot with Pompey. Cato and his friends, with their customary fatuous-
ness, believed that they could safely allow Pompey to eliminate
Caesar. Afterward they would themselves eliminate Pompey and
his forces!

At the beginning of the war Pompey had about ten legions—six
legions in Spain, two of doubtful loyalty at Capua, and several scattered and inexperienced cohorts. He hurriedly recruited more troops
in Italy, some of whom were veterans while others had never seen
service. Many of these recruits deserted at the first opportunity.

Other legions were raised later in the provinces, and Pompey's fleet enabled him to command the seas. Caesar, on the other hand, had the same number of legions, made up entirely of seasoned legionaries devoted to their leader heart and soul. Their skill, like his military genius, had been perfected by years of fighting in Gaul.

Caesar's Victories

Though Caesar was accompanied by only one legion when he crossed the Rubicon, and reinforcements from Gaul could not be expected in less than a month, he hastened south into Italy, seizing the strategic points as he advanced. At his approach Pompey, the senate, the consuls, and most of the high officials at Rome fled pell-mell to Capua and thence to Brundisium. Caesar followed them down the length of Italy, repeatedly offering to negotiate and carefully abstaining from plundering or fighting. Ahenobarbus finally made a stand at Corfinium with the two legions from Capua, but his men soon compelled him to surrender. After letting the general go, Caesar enlisted the soldiers in his own army: they had been taken from him by Pompey barely a year before. Pompey crossed the Adriatic to Greece early in March, taking with him whatever troops he had managed to scrape together. Caesar then returned to Rome, where he found only one praetor and a few senators. He first confiscated the treasury and then put these few men in charge of the local government. All Italy was thus won in an almost blood-less campaign of sixty days.

Caesar could not follow Pompey to Greece until he had secured his rear by destroying the Pompeian army in Spain. A Spanish campaign of forty days ended with the battle of Ilerda (49), after which Caesar enlisted volunteers and allowed the other defeated Pompeians to return home. The rest of Spain surrendered without fighting. On his way back to Rome Caesar captured and annexed the ancient Greek city of Massilia, in spite of defense offered by Ahenobarbus with part of Pompey's fleet. Meantime, the former tribune Curio had been sent to seize Africa. He failed in the attempt, losing his life in the process, and for several years Africa remained a rallying point for Pompeians. When Caesar reached Rome, late in the

Plate 16. Julius Caesar *(Naples Museum)*

Octavia *(Louvre Museum)*

Livia *(Copenhagen Museum)*

Cleopatra *(British Museum)*

Plate 17

summer of 49, he was made dictator for a few days to enable him to straighten out a number of matters and to hold elections. He and a trusted friend were chosen consuls for 48.

Pompey had by this time assembled all the Roman troops he could find in the East and to them he added levies of Orientals. In January, 48, Caesar crossed the Adriatic to Dyrrhacium, where he and Pompey entrenched themselves and glared at one another for several weeks. At last Pompey hit upon a weak spot in Caesar's lines and, breaking through, forced Caesar to retreat. A month later Caesar had his revenge at Pharsalus in Thessaly. Though outnumbered two to one, he destroyed Pompey's army, killing about 6000 men and taking 24,000 prisoners, half of whom he at once enlisted in his own army. Barely 10,000 Pompeians escaped. Caesar's losses were about 1200. Pompey fled to Egypt, where the regents treacherously cut off his head and preserved it in brine as a gift for Caesar (September, 48).

Caesar presently arrived in Egypt with about 3000 soldiers. He came to capture Pompey, not to conquer the country, but once there, he decided to end the old dynastic quarrel—and incidentally realize his own old dream—by making Egypt subservient to Rome. After the death of Ptolemy XI Auletes in 51, the throne of Egypt had descended to Ptolemy XII and his sister-wife, Cleopatra VII. The royal pair soon fell into the hands of rival factions, Cleopatra was driven out, and a regency set up. Caesar executed the regents for having dared lay hands on a Roman citizen (Pompey) and restored Cleopatra to her throne. When the hostile faction besieged him in the royal palace, Caesar was in great peril until friends in Palestine and Syria arrived with hastily collected reinforcements. Ptolemy was killed in the fighting, and Cleopatra became one of Caesar's many mistresses, later attributing to him a son whom she named Caesarion. At last Caesar ordered her married to her younger brother (Ptolemy XIII) and departed, leaving three legions to protect her— or to punish her in case she proved ungrateful. He sailed to Antioch and advanced through Asia Minor until he met and defeated Pharnaces, son of Mithradates, at Zela in Pontus (August, 47). It was this victory which he announced with the famous words, *Veni, Vidi, Vici*

("I came, I saw, I conquered"). Master of the East, Caesar returned to Rome late in 47.

While Caesar was thus occupied in the East, various Pompeian leaders who had escaped from Pharsalus were assembling troops in Africa. In fact, the not-implausible suggestion has been made that Caesar deliberately encouraged them to make a final, futile stand by circulating lurid stories of his own decline as proved by his entanglement with Cleopatra. At any rate, his enemies collected a strong and well-drilled army, under able leaders, and made an alliance with Juba, king of Numidia. Crossing to Africa, Caesar annihilated their forces at Thapsus (April, 46). Whatever Pompeians were not present at the battle fled to Spain—all except Cato, who committed suicide at Utica after sententiously announcing that he did not care to survive Liberty. Numidia was annexed and Caesar returned to Rome, where he celebrated a magnificent four-day triumph for his victories over four enemies—over the Gauls, the Egyptians, Pharnaces, and Juba, but, it is important to note, not over Pompey or Cato or any other Roman. His wars were not quite finished, however, for the fugitives from Africa built up a new army in Spain under Sextus Pompey, son of the triumvir. Caesar met this army at Munda (March, 45). Though Sextus escaped to fight later against Caesar's successors, his army was destroyed. No armed force that could resist Caesar remained anywhere in the Roman world.

Caesar quickly learned, however, that it was not enough merely to defeat his enemies on the field of battle. Sometimes his own followers caused him much trouble. It was of course inevitable that many adventurers—including a number of bankrupt aristocrats—should attach themselves to him in the hope of profiting by proscriptions and other war measures. When these men learned that Caesar's program did not include an immediate redistribution of wealth for their benefit, they began to regret their trust in him and decided to revive the methods of Clodius and Catiline. The first of the new revolutionists was Caelius Rufus, praetor in 48, who had once been an intimate of Clodius as well as a friend and correspondent of Cicero. When his first efforts to gain a popular following failed, Rufus allied himself with Milo (who had returned from his exile in

Massilia) and the two men resumed the anarchistic activities that had prevailed in the fifties. Both were soon killed by Caesar's troops. A little later, similar disturbances were instigated by Dolabella, an affable but rakish and bankrupt young aristocrat who had married Cicero's daughter and who proved a heavy cross to his father-in-law. Elected tribune for 47, Dolabella sought popular support by proposing to reduce debts and rents. When his colleagues protested, he instigated a series of riots; about eight hundred people were killed, yet Caesar eventually pardoned the young man. Sometimes dissatisfied soldiers urged Caesar to end the war. One legion mutinied after the Ilerda campaign of 49, and after Pharsalus several legions were sent back to Italy, where they riotously demanded their discharges and the rewards promised by Caesar. Not until his return in 46 were they completely pacified.

Caesar's Dictatorship

Many grave political problems demanded immediate attention at Rome. As the senate and the old political machinery could not function in these chaotic times, Caesar, like Sulla, had himself made dictator. The first dictatorship, in the summer of 49, lasted only a few days and was important chiefly as an indication of what was to follow. After Pharsalus he was named dictator a second time, with Mark Antony as his "master of horse" (first assistant). Antony was sent to govern Italy, but he fell into Caesar's disfavor because of his inability to stop the gangsters and mutineers. He was therefore replaced by M. Aemilius Lepidus, scion of a famous family, before whom lay a distinguished career. After Thapsus ten annual dictatorships were voted to Caesar at one time, with his third term beginning in April, 46, and his fourth a year later. Early in 44 he was made "perpetual dictator." In each case Lepidus was his master of horse. Caesar held his second consulship in 48; two of his friends served in 47; he accepted a third consulship in 46, with Lepidus as his colleague; and he was sole consul for most of 45. In 44 he served a fifth consulship with Antony—who by this time had been forgiven —and he made arrangements for Dolabella to succeed him when he left Rome. Caesar's power and prestige were by this time so great that he easily managed the elections of lesser officials, and he began promising offices to his friends two or three years in advance. As time went on, and Caesar's power was magnified, the senate obsequiously offered him still other honors. Sometimes these were traditional offices, but more frequently they were new ones created especially for him. Some of these offices he accepted, others he declined. Actually, his government was never anything less than a dictatorship, and though he liked to have the semblance of legality on his side, he showed that, if necessary, he could do without it.

When his power had been made secure by the destruction of the armed forces of his enemies, and more or less legalized by dictatorships and consulships, Caesar had to decide what to do with this power. He had gone far since the days of his youth when he had been a foppish aristocrat turned rabble-rouser, notorious for his debts and adulteries; but it is not certain that his ultimate aims had changed greatly. It was said of him that once, while on his way to Spain, he declared that he would rather be first in the village through which he was then passing than second in Rome; and on another occasion he remarked that Sulla showed he did not understand the rudiments of politics when he resigned the power he had gained. A desire to be first dominated Caesar's whole career. While he had a realistic knowledge of the world and of how to direct its forces to his own advantage, there is no evidence that he had a real program of social or political reform or even that he had thought deeply upon such matters. But as he drove the Pompeians from one region after another it became necessary for him to govern these regions. He threw himself into the task with his customary vigor, and a considerable amount of reform was accomplished within a few months. The nature of these reforms was dictated, first by the immediate exigencies of war, and secondly by Caesar's desire to strengthen and perpetuate his personal supremacy. His statesmanship was not much concerned with other issues. His reforms sometimes resembled measures taken or urged by the Gracchi and Drusus, Marius and Sulla, Pompey and Crassus, and even by Cicero. In a sense it might be said that Caesar summed up the reform movement of the preceding hundred years, preserving much of what was practicable and rejecting the rest. Yet it is equally true that the reformers whose ideas Caesar exploited would have disavowed him as their legitimate successor. His purpose was less to make Rome strong or Romans happy than to make himself secure in his supremacy.

Caesar's Reforms

As Caesar's power rested, in the final analysis, upon military force, it was of the utmost importance that he should retain the good will of his legionaries. He faced the same problems regarding bonuses that had haunted Marius, Sulla, and Pompey, and he made the customary land distributions, but he always profited from his predecessors' mistakes. While the property of a few eminent Pompeians was confiscated and distributed, the greater part of the land Caesar gave his veterans was bought with funds raised by the sale of booty. Moreover, Caesar was careful to scatter his veterans up and down Italy, with only a few in one locality. He could then easily summon them to the colors again in case of need, and at the same time he could prevent their assembling against his will. This arrangement also made it possible for the veterans located in each community to learn something about farming from their neighbors. Other veterans received land in the provinces, where it was more easily available and where a trained army reserve was needed to guard against native uprisings and Roman aristocrats. Veterans not adapted to agricultural life were sometimes sent to new cities where they engaged in commerce or industry. Many such cities were founded in Spain and other western provinces, and there were a few in Greece and the East. These new cities also received civilian settlers from Rome and other parts of Italy, and natives flocked to them from the surrounding countryside.

Caesar's military requirements made necessary a new provincial policy, or rather, a great extension of policies dating back at least to Marius. Caesar had recruited many soldiers in the provinces, first in Cisalpine Gaul, later in Transalpine Gaul, and still later in other provinces. These provincial legionaries were rewarded with Roman citizenship. Other provincials who had aided Caesar in nonmilitary ways received the same reward. Sometimes whole communities were granted Roman citizenship, the most conspicuous case being Transpadane Gaul, where Caesar recruited many of his best troops and to which he extended Roman citizenship in 49. Though Caesar seized much booty during the wars, he did not loot the provinces extensively afterward, showing himself much less rapacious than the Pompeians. The provincials therefore preferred him to Pompey and the senators. Nevertheless, Caesar's provincial policies were determined by enlightened expediency rather than by sympathy with the provincials or a desire to incorporate them more fully into the Empire.

It was also necessary for Caesar to rid himself of the political opposition at Rome that centered in the senate. From early youth Caesar had shown his contempt for that body, which he now treated in the most highhanded manner. A considerable number of senators had been killed in the wars, and others were in exile. Caesar filled their places with men subservient to himself, and increased the total membership to 900, more than two-thirds of whom were his own appointees. Among the new senators were many from social classes hitherto far removed from such honors. Some were Roman businessmen, some were influential Romans from the provinces, a few were non-Roman provincials. Even in 49 Caesar put two Allobroges into the senate, greatly to the dismay of the aristocrats. He paid little attention to this senate of his own creation and frequently issued decrees in its name which it had not passed or even seen. Cicero complained to a friend that he received letters from people all over the world thanking him for voting in the senate for laws in their behalf when, as a matter of fact, he had never heard of the laws or the persons so favored. It must be added that the senate would undoubtedly have passed any law that Caesar asked for, and that he merely saved time by ignoring it and issuing lists of senators who were falsely said to have voted for his laws.

Less respectable opposition, or possible opposition, was also eliminated. Severe laws against violence stopped the rioting of gangsters who had for so long made orderly government impossible in Rome. Caesar again abolished all but the most ancient *collegia* or trade guilds, which had been used by Clodius and others as propaganda centers: Clodius had even organized his gangsters as a *collegium*. Thereafter it remained the constant policy of the Roman government to forbid all associations which might possibly take on a political character. Caesar reduced the number of persons receiving free food from 320,000 to 150,000, and worked out a system to minimize the political importance of whatever relief was given. His colonies overseas also assisted this program of pacification by draining away from the city many of those most likely to respond to the appeals of demagogic agitators.

Caesar's legislation was largely inspired by the needs of the moment—including the need to make things run smoothly and the need for popular applause—but there were a few more general reforms. The most famous of the latter is the Julian calendar, which he introduced in 46. Heretofore, the Romans had used a complicated year of twelve lunar months, of 29 or 30 days each, with an extra month thrown in as the *pontifex maximus* determined. The addition of the extra month was often advanced or delayed for political reasons. Caesar introduced the year of 365¼ days, which was used throughout the civilized world until slightly reformed by Pope Gregory XIII in 1582. The Julian calendar was used in Anglo-Saxon countries until 1752, and in Russia and eastern Europe until the early 1920's. Sumptuary laws were usually expected of major Roman statesmen, and Caesar added his share, though neither he nor anyone else obeyed them. He sought to raise the standards of family life (he of all persons!) and, though an Epicurean atheist in private, he made a public display of piety and sought to rehabilitate the old Roman religion. He also launched a great building program, somewhat similar to Sulla's and Pompey's: he enlarged and paved the forum, erected the magnificent Julian basilica beside it, and built a temple to his ancestress Venus Genetrix. Even these great constructions were only a small part of what he promised Rome.

The Ides of March

Caesar was never vindictive toward his enemies. To be sure, he seized and sold the estates of Pompey and his senatorial friends, but in general he was anxious to placate his enemies. His widely advertised clemency stood in sharp contrast to the threats of reprisals frequently uttered by exiled Pompeians. After Pharsalus, for example, Cicero wished to make peace, which so incensed Cato that thereafter Cicero feared the Pompeians more than he feared Caesar. He returned to Italy, where his son-in-law Dolabella protected him from Antony until Caesar forgave him. Marcus Brutus was another of Caesar's forgiven enemies. This proud young aristocrat, who was Cato's son-in-law, had ample personal reasons for detesting both Pompey and Caesar. The former had executed his father for his share in Lepidus's revolt of 76, the latter had seduced his mother. Nevertheless, Brutus swallowed his pride and joined Pompey's army. After Pharsalus Caesar forgave him, made him governor of Cisalpine Gaul in 46, and arranged his election to the praetorship for 44. He was much attached to the young man, for whom he apparently was planning a brilliant career. At Brutus's request Caesar also forgave Gaius Cassius, a competent officer who had saved something of Crassus's army at Carrhae and had later won minor victories over the Parthians. Cassius, too, became praetor in 44. Countless lesser opponents enjoyed Caesar's clemency. Even Sulla and Pompey profited from it to the extent of having their overthrown statues set up once more. In fact, Cato was almost the only opponent whom Caesar would not forgive, even in his grave. When Cicero published an encomium on the dead leader, Caesar replied with a vituperative tract entitled *Anti-Cato*.

Caesar knew very well, however, that many persons still remembered his usurpations and the deaths of Pompey and Cato. It seemed to him that these unfortunate episodes could best be erased from the popular memory by military victories on a colossal scale over non-Romans. He therefore prepared a great campaign against the Parthians, who had not yet been punished adequately for defeating Crassus and enslaving his soldiers. Caesar was ready to start east in March, 44, but before he could leave the city he was assassinated by a group of conspirators. Several pardoned Pompeians were in the group, including Brutus and Cassius, as well as men such as Decimus Brutus and Trebonius who had been with Caesar ever since the Gallic wars. These men had become alarmed at Caesar's growing power, as was traditional with the Roman aristocracy whenever one of its members rose above the rest. They also ran true to form when they accused Caesar of planning to abolish the Republic and establish himself as king. Though it is hard to believe that so shrewd a politician would have harbored such plans, his opponents found the charge a convenient one. Their rallying cry was "Liberty" and, as everyone knows, they murdered Caesar on the Ides of March— March 15, 44 b.c.

The Caesar Myth

From that day to this Caesar has been much praised and much blamed. Both friends and enemies created myths about him such as surround all the famous men in history. In fact, the myth-making began long before his death. Caesar contributed to it himself when he wrote and published his famous *Commentaries,* and his friends accelerated it during the Civil wars. The "Liberators" who murdered him concocted a very different myth to justify their bloody deed. And finally, Caesar was scarcely dead when various associates sought to gain popular favor by shouting his praises and then claiming that they, and they alone, were his true heirs and successors. They also found that it was easier to carry through their own schemes if they falsely attributed them to the great Caesar. As all this began only a few days after Caesar's death, it is virtually impossible now to separate the truth from the myth. Some historians regard Caesar simply as a tyrant; others consider him the greatest man that ever lived. In the middle of the nineteenth century the German historian Theodor Mommsen[1] pictured him as a sort of superman—a great democratic leader with an elaborate and admirable program of social and political reform, prepared at the outset of his career and carried through with the unerring instinct of genius. Mommsen's high reputation, aided by contemporary aspirations along these lines, imposed his views upon the learned world for many a year. More recently, however, other historians have, with greater truth, pictured Caesar as a lucky opportunist who was primarily a destroyer.

---

[1] See note on Theodor Mommsen, p. 368.

Regarding Caesar's military talents there can be no doubt. Though we know his campaigns in Gaul only through his own account, they show that he was one of the world's great generals. He had a genius for inspiring the devotion of his soldiers and the populace. He had a flair for the dramatic, and he was as reckless with his own life as he was with his soldiers'. He was an orator, a well-educated man, a true aristocrat. In his complex personal character, in his combination of sensuality, good nature, literary culture, military skill, and aristocratic superiority, Caesar resembled Sulla rather than any other of the reformers. He was wise enough, however, not to compromise his rule at the outset by permitting proscriptions and other acts of violence such as had aroused hatred for Sulla. Caesar showed little reverence for the past and its institutions, yet there is nothing to show that he possessed the ability to create new social and political institutions better than those which he destroyed so freely.

It is easy, though not very profitable, to speculate upon what Caesar might have done if he had not been murdered. His admirers are persuaded that he would have done great things to help the human race. It must be pointed out, however, that at the time of his assassination he had made little progress toward solving the great problems facing the Roman state. There is even less reason to accept the dire prognostications of other eminent historians that Caesar would have made Rome into an oriental despotism resembling that of the fourth century. This view is as absurd as it would be to declare that he was going to make Rome into a twentieth-century totalitarian state or introduce the New Deal. We simply do not know what Caesar would have done—and neither did he. Moreover, it is always well to remember that modern Caesar-worshipers base their rhapsodies upon what they think he was going to do rather than upon what he actually did.

The Liberators and Mark Antony

The assassination of Julius Caesar was more foolish than political assassinations usually are, both in the larger aspects of the plot and in the details of its execution. The murder did not restore liberty of any sort: it merely renewed civil war. The assassins did little more than clear the way for Antony and his associates, who destroyed them and their social class with a ruthlessness of which Caesar would have been incapable. The conspirators were equally blind in arranging the details of the assassination. Apparently they assumed that once Caesar was out of the way, Liberty and their idealized Republic would automatically descend from the skies. They had made no plans about what to do after plunging their daggers into his body. Heroes like themselves could not be bothered with such details as the election of a new consul or the naming of a new dictator to carry on the government of Rome during the crisis, or with securing the treasury or the military forces, or even with defense against Caesar's friends at Rome. Immediately after the murder, Brutus favored the senate with an oration on Liberty to which no one paid any attention. When the crowd outside began shouting for vengeance upon the assassins, a bodyguard of gladiators provided by Decimus Brutus escorted the trembling "Liberators" to the sanctuary of the Capitol. During the afternoon of the 15th, Marcus Brutus and Cassius ventured down into the forum to harangue the mob on the blessings of Liberty, but the howls and menaces of those whom they had just set free caused them to flee for their lives.

Caesar's death left the consul Antony the most powerful man in Rome. Antony belonged to a family of the plebeian nobility that had been prominent in Roman politics for three generations. His grandfather, a famous orator and statesman, added Cilicia to the Roman Empire; his father won the name "Creticus" by fighting Cretan pirates; and his uncle, Gaius Antonius, served as Cicero's colleague in the consulship of 63. On his mother's side, Antony was the great-grandson of Marcus Fulvius, who was killed with Gaius Gracchus in 121, and he was related to the Popilius Laenases and others of the less reputable nobility. After the death of Antony's father in 74, his mother Julia married Lentulus Sura (consul in 71), who was executed by Cicero as a Catilinarian conspirator. Born in 82, young Mark Antony doubtless was much influenced by these stirring events of 63. Plutarch even suggests that his hatred of Cicero dated from that time. Antony became an intimate friend of Curio

(the tribune friendly to Caesar in 50) and Curio brought him to
Clodius, with whom he became closely associated. Antony first saw
military service in Syria, and in 54 he joined Caesar in Gaul. With
Caesar's aid he was elected Curio's successor as tribune for 49, and

THE FAMILY OF MARK ANTONY

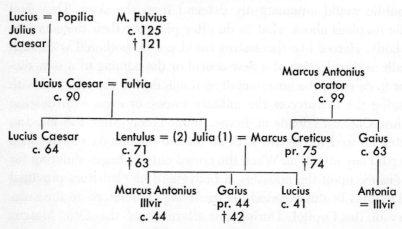

Antony = (1) Fadia, (2) Antonia, (3) Fulvia, (4) Octavia, (5) Cleopatra.

= married; † died; c., consul; pr., praetor; Illvir., triumvir. Antony's second
wife was his cousin Antonia; his third, a more distant cousin, was the widow of
Clodius and Curio; his fourth was the sister of Octavian and by her he became
the ancestor of three Roman Emperors: Caligula, Claudius, and Nero. The Lucius
Caesars from whom Anthony was descended were only distantly related to the
dictator.

---

played an important role in the days just before Caesar crossed the
Rubicon. He commanded Caesar's left wing at Pharsalus and later
was sent to govern Italy. After Curio's death, Antony married his
widow Fulvia, who was also the widow of Clodius. This Fulvia, a
wild and strong-willed woman, extremely ambitious and utterly un-
principled, was already his kinswoman and a worthy daughter of
the ancient Fulvian family. She it was who instigated the mob that
burned down the Senate House when Clodius was murdered. Her
violence continued after she became Antony's wife, and she probably was responsible for much of the evil he did during the next few
years.

Antony Takes Control

On the fatal Ides of March, Antony had no foreknowledge of what was going to happen, but being endowed with a greater sense of reality and more resolution than the Liberators, he quickly maneuvered himself into a strong position. When some of the conspirators suggested killing Antony, Brutus insisted that bloodshed be kept to a minimum. One of the Liberators therefore held Antony in conversation while Caesar was being murdered, and afterward allowed him to escape and barricade himself for a time in his own house. That very night Antony visited Caesar's wife, Calpurnia, and obtained from her the dictator's war chest and papers. Meantime, Aemilius Lepidus, Caesar's master of horse, had occupied the city with a legion, and the Liberators discovered themselves to be virtually his prisoners in the Capitol. Antony had no desire, however, to avenge Caesar by the slaughter of his opponents. He merely wished to make a career for himself, and he was quite willing to forgive the assassins, or even to co-operate with them if they would co-operate with him. He therefore invited them to a meeting of the senate on March 17, and to prove his good intentions he sent them his young son as a hostage.

Cicero opened the meeting of the senate with a few general remarks in praise of Liberty, after which Antony brought up the more pressing question of confirming Caesar's acts. He pointed out that, if Caesar had been a tyrant, his acts should be declared invalid and his corpse thrown into the Tiber. At the same time he reminded the senators that most of them owed their positions to Caesar and that many had been promised further rewards. Were they prepared to sacrifice themselves? Moreover, Lepidus's troops, who had been promised bonuses, might show resentment if the promise were invalidated. Under the circumstances debate seemed superfluous, and the senate sheepishly ratified all Caesar's acts—both those which he had officially proclaimed and those which he had intended to proclaim! As Antony had Caesar's papers, he alone had proof of Caesar's intentions, and during the next few weeks he used these papers in a most highhanded fashion, destroying some and forging others. The senate also granted amnesty to the assassins, ordered that Caesar's will be read, and decreed a public funeral. When the will was opened it was found that Caesar had left his gardens across the Tiber to the Roman people, and 300 sesterces (about $12) in cash to each Roman citizen; his great-nephew Octavius was named as his adopted son and given three-fourths of his estate; and the rest of his property was divided among various heirs, some of whom had joined the conspiracy. The funeral was held on March 20 in the forum. Mark Antony lashed the crowd to a frenzy with a demagogic oration—the historic foundation of Shakespeare's "Friends, Romans, countrymen"—and Caesar's body was burned as hundreds of persons threw gifts on the blazing pyre. That night the mob tried to set fire to the houses of Brutus and Cassius, and one unfortunate man, mistaken for a praetor who had spoken favorably of the assassins, was torn limb from limb in the street.

After this exciting week came a lull, with Antony and the Liberators pretending to work together for the greater good of Rome. Though Caesar had appointed most of the members of the senate, his appointees were timeservers who had failed to lift a finger in his defense when he was being murdered before their eyes. Their chief concern was the advancement of their careers, and they cared little which party advanced them. The enlightened public likewise had no preference between the factions. In one of his letters Cicero quotes a friend as remarking on April 7 that if Caesar, with all his genius, could not find a way out, surely no one could. Decimus Brutus, the most realistic and resolute of the Liberators, had spoken despairingly of flight from Rome as early as March 17, and early in April he withdrew to Cisalpine Gaul—the province that Caesar had assigned to him for 44—where he began recruiting an army at his own expense. Marcus Brutus and Cassius fled the city, and Cicero was reduced to wringing his hands.

Before long Antony too was raising an army, enlisting many of Caesar's veterans. He arranged to have the provinces of Macedonia and Syria assigned to himself and Dolabella for 43, while Brutus and Cassius were ordered to Crete and Cyrene respectively—two second-rate provinces where they could do no harm. Antony next

rigged a plebiscite ordering him to exchange Macedonia for Cisalpine Gaul and Gallia Comata (the northern part of Gaul, recently
conquered by Caesar) but permitting him to keep the six legions
Caesar had left in Macedonia. Decimus Brutus was thus maneuvered into a position where he must either surrender his province
and his troops or else openly defy the sovereign will of the Roman
people. Antony seemed to be winning all along the line.

The task of governing Rome had fallen to Antony as consul. He
undertook to restore order by executing a few people who made
riotous demonstrations in memory of Caesar and by tearing down a
pillar set up in Caesar's honor in the forum. He also carried a law
abolishing forever the office of dictator. Large numbers of appointments were announced and, if we are to believe Cicero, offices were
often sold at enormous prices by Antony's wife Fulvia. Veterans had
been promised land, and Antony gave it to them. A law reorganizing
the municipalities of Italy, for which Caesar may have jotted down
a few disconnected ideas, was hurriedly thrown together and enacted: this was the famous Lex Julia Municipalis, part of which is
preserved on a bronze tablet found in southern Italy. Roman citizenship was extended to Sicily, and Antony issued a law prepared by
Caesar granting special privileges to the Jews. At length, on June 2,
44, Antony obtained a law appointing a commission to examine
Caesar's papers and issue all other laws found therein. This commission consisted of himself and Dolabella, and for years to come he
continued to issue laws which purported to come from Caesar's
papers. In fact, the forging of memoranda attributed to Caesar became a recognized form of legislation, and Augustus issued such a
law forty years after Caesar's death.

Octavian

Early in the summer of 44 the political situation at Rome was greatly
altered by the arrival in the city of Caesar's legal heir. This young
man, first known as Octavius, then as Octavian, and finally as Augustus, was the grandson of Caesar's sister Julia. His father's family
was obscure, though the father himself (G. Octavius) had reached
the praetorship at the time of his death (58). Born on September

23, 63, the young Octavius was only eighteen years old on the Ides of March, and less than a year had passed since he first attracted Caesar's serious attention. He had accompanied the army to Spain during the Munda campaign of 45, though sickness kept him from active service, and it was later arranged that he should win his spurs on the projected Parthian campaign. Meantime, he was at Apollonia, in Epirus, nominally studying oratory but actually awaiting orders to join a legion that was being drilled nearby.

Caesar had adopted the boy in a will dated September, 45, though Octavius was not notified of his good fortune. As Caesar did not foresee his impending death, he cannot be charged with deliberately turning Rome over to an inexperienced youth eighteen years of age. In fact, it seems most improbable that Caesar intended this will to be more than a stopgap. After his anticipated victories in Parthia, he would have more leisure to make a permanent settlement of his affairs and to arrange about a successor. Meantime, the boy's name would serve very well in the will, for no one could regard him as a second Caesar. It has even been suggested, not implausibly, that the man whom Caesar was most seriously considering as his political heir was none other than Brutus himself!

Octavius did not learn of his uncle's death and his own adoption until almost the end of March. He then crossed to Italy at once, with only a few friends, to claim his inheritance and, as he loudly announced, to execute vengeance upon his "father's" murderers. His only asset at this moment was his name.[2] When he reached Naples Octavian entered into friendly relations with Cicero, but refused to see Brutus, the murderer. Cicero regarded him as a convenient rival to set up against Antony, did what he could to promote his fortunes, gave him advice, and tried to fill him with Ciceronian ideas as to a proper government for Rome. It is more important, however, to note that during his stay in Naples Octavian had many long conferences with Balbus, who had been Caesar's principal secretary and business agent.

---

[2] By the adoption Octavius became Gaius Julius Caesar Octavianus, but he always called himself Caesar. Ancient writers followed him in this practice, thereby often filling their narratives with confusion. Modern historians call him Octavius for the period before 44, Octavian for the years from 44 to 27, and Augustus thereafter.

Early in May Octavian proceeded to Rome where he took up his residence in Caesar's house. The populace received him enthusiastically but, as is easily understood, Antony refused to take him seriously. Offended at this cool reception, Octavian publicly demanded of Antony why the assassins had not been punished or Caesar's legacies paid. He then devoted himself, with a skill and astuteness that would have done credit to a seasoned politician, to the task of winning public favor at Antony's expense. His amazing success can best be explained by assuming that he had discovered experienced though obscure friends, presumably associates of Balbus in Caesar's household, who filled him with good advice which he was wise enough to follow. Antony replied with counterattacks until his friends warned him that his troops might desert unless he became reconciled with Caesar's heir. The two men therefore established a formal friendship, though neither was sincere and each began preparations for a great struggle with his rival.

Meantime, other prominent persons were leaving Rome. Lepidus had taken his army to Spain, Dolabella (now second consul) had gone to Asia where he presently murdered one of the Liberators (Trebonius) and later committed suicide. Brutus and Cassius left Italy early in August, saying that they would gladly accept exile if they could thereby bring peace to Rome. They went to Macedonia and Syria respectively, where they began raising armies. Cicero, utterly discouraged, decided to withdraw to Greece until the next year when new consuls might improve conditions. At the last minute, however, he changed his mind and returned to Rome, arriving there on August 31. The old man had found courage at last and resolved to do his utmost to overthrow Antony.

Attacks upon Antony

Antony had called a meeting of the senate for September 1. Cicero ostentatiously failed to attend, but on the next day he appeared and, in Antony's absence, delivered a scathing attack upon the consul. This speech (now known as the "First Philippic," because of its resemblance in form and manner to the terrific attacks which Demosthenes had made upon Philip of Macedon three hundred years before) was followed by others until the fourteenth and last was delivered in April, 43. The most relentless (and also the most scurrilous) of the Philippics was the second, which was never delivered as an oration, but circulated in manuscript during the winter. Contemporaries rated these Philippics as Cicero's finest literary productions, and he paid for them with his life.

Decimus Brutus's military preparations were advancing so rapidly during the autumn of 44 that Antony could no longer ignore them and he began preparations to drive Decimus from his province by force of arms. At the same time, Octavian too was raising two legions —quite illegally, of course—and toward the end of November he crowned his achievements by seducing two of Antony's legions, exploiting Caesar's name and offering higher pay. Nevertheless, Antony marched north with his remaining troops and shortly before the end of the year he besieged Decimus at Mutina. A few days later the consuls for 43 were sworn in. Both men were Caesarians hostile to Antony and willing to co-operate with Cicero and Octavian. The senate declared war on Antony in February, 43, largely at Cicero's instigation, and the two consuls marched against him, taking Octavian and his legions along. Antony was defeated in two battles fought near Mutina in April, but both consuls were killed and Decimus Brutus managed to escape.

The next few weeks were a period of great confusion. Antony withdrew westward, crossing the Alps into Transalpine Gaul, where he again faced a coalition of his enemies. Lepidus, now hostile to Antony, advanced against him from Spain; Plancus, the Caesarian governor of Gallia Comata, came down from the north with another army; and Decimus Brutus, who had also crossed the Alps, joined Plancus. It seemed that Antony was doomed. Suddenly, however, his soldiers began fraternizing with those of Lepidus, and both armies refused to fight. At the demand of their troops, Antony and Lepidus renewed their old friendship, and both were declared public enemies by the senate. Plancus withdrew to the north, though presently he too joined Antony. Decimus Brutus, deserted by most of his soldiers, attempted to escape to Marcus Brutus in Macedonia. He was captured and killed by a Celtic chieftain in Switzerland.

Octavian took no part in the pursuit of Antony after Mutina. Instead, he returned with his legions to Rome, where the faction of the Liberators was gaining in strength, with Antony almost eliminated and with Brutus and Cassius holding the East. This faction presently showed its optimism by making an admiral out of Sextus Pompey—who had recovered from his defeat at Munda and was active as a pirate—and giving him much of Sicily. Impressed by the strength of the Liberators, the senators saw no need to favor Octavian further. Even Cicero dropped his protégé with the unwise remark, "The young man is to be complimented, honored, and got rid of." When the senate showed reluctance to give him everything he wanted, Octavian marched his army into Rome and succeeded in getting himself elected consul to fill out the year of the two consuls killed in battle. The new consul was still one month under twenty years of age.

Immediately upon assuming office, Octavian paid out of public funds the 300 sesterces bequeathed by Caesar to each Roman citizen and put a law through the *comitia* banishing whatever Liberators still remained in Italy. After this energetic answer to Cicero's jest, Octavian made peace with Antony. Everyone knew that the public and the armies were tired of war, and that the soldiers were in a position to force a reconciliation upon their commanders. Octavian therefore met Antony and Lepidus near Bononia in October, 43, and there the three men formed the alliance since known as the Second Triumvirate.

The Second Triumvirate

First of all, the new triumvirs agreed that their arrangements should be published and that they should be legally recognized for a term of five years as "Triumvirs for Reorganizing the State." They carefully avoided the word "dictator," though their position was not very different from that of Sulla during his dictatorship, and the words about reorganizing the state were taken from his title. The triumvirs next distributed provinces among themselves. Antony took Cisalpine Gaul and Gallia Comata, valuable for recruiting troops; Lepidus kept Transalpine Gaul and Spain; and Octavian got Africa, Sicily, Sardinia, and Corsica. As the islands were actually in the hands of

Sextus Pompey (the Liberators' admiral) and Africa was in the hands of another enemy, it is clear that Octavian was definitely the third man among the triumvirs. The amazing thing is that he was there at all. The three allies then proceeded to confiscate large amounts of land for their veterans and to prepare proscription lists, partly to rid themselves of their enemies and more especially to acquire funds for their empty treasuries. It is said that 300 senators and 2000 equestrians were proscribed. Among them were Antony's uncle (Lucius Caesar, the consul of 64) and Lepidus's brother (the consul of 50), though both managed to escape.

The most eminent of the triumvirs' victims was Cicero, whose death Antony demanded. At first Cicero thought of flight, but on second thought he calmly awaited his fate. His actual murderer was a man whom he had once defended on a charge of parricide— Popilius Laenas, the last member of that notorious family whom we shall have occasion to meet. His head and hands were cut off and sent to Antony, who had them nailed to the rostrum in the forum, where the orator had spoken so often. Fulvia publicly spat upon the head and pierced its tongue with hairpins.

Two other aspects of the triumvirate deserve our attention. The soldiers demanded that the new alliance be sealed by the bonds of matrimony, as in the days of Pompey and Caesar. At their insistence, Octavian was married to Clodia, daughter of the gangster Clodius by his wife Fulvia, and therefore the stepdaughter of Antony. The triumvirs also wrapped themselves more closely in Caesar's mantle by requiring an oath from all senators and magistrates that they would maintain Caesar's acts, and they accorded him divine honors. Caesar thus became the *Divus Iulius* ("the deified Julius") and Octavian saw fit to call himself *Divi filius* ("son of the god").

While the triumvirs were establishing themselves firmly in the West, Brutus and Cassius were raising armies for the Liberators in Greece and Asia. Their methods were harsh in the extreme and brought ruin to large districts which had already been plundered ruthlessly by a long succession of Romans from Pompey to Dolabella. In the summer of 42 they had a force of nineteen legions, plus cavalry and archers. This army included large numbers of aristocrats and a few idealists enamored of Liberty (among them the poet Horace), but the rank and file were mercenaries who had to be paid in advance and who were given the right to loot Greek cities. Early in the year 42 Antony and Octavian crossed to Greece with twenty-eight legions, leaving Lepidus with three legions to govern Italy and with twelve other legions in Gaul and Spain. Several of the legions under Antony were detached for various services in Greece, and late in the summer the main force of nineteen legions met the approximately equal force of the Liberators at Philippi in eastern Macedonia. After extensive maneuvering two battles were fought. In the first battle (October 23) Marcus Brutus got a little the better of Octavian but Antony defeated Cassius, who committed suicide. About three weeks later Brutus fought the combined armies of his enemies, was defeated, and killed himself. Most of his army joined the triumvirs, who were now opposed only by Sextus Pompey.

Octavian in the West

On the morrow of Philippi the victors entered into an agreement defining their relations anew. Antony's prestige as a general was now at its peak, for it was he and not Octavian who had defeated the Liberators. In fact, Octavian was so sick during most of the campaign that he could not have helped greatly even had he been a trained military man. Nevertheless, the two victors united to despoil Lepidus, who had few troops and little wealth left, and whom they accused of intriguing with Sextus Pompey. They first rectified the assignment of provinces agreed upon in 43. Cisalpine Gaul was made a part of Italy, as Caesar had planned. Antony took Transalpine Gaul from Lepidus, adding it to Gallia Comata, which he retained. Octavian took Spain, with the understanding that Africa should go to Lepidus if he proved his innocence and could conquer the province. While many soldiers insisted upon being discharged, eleven legions of veterans from Philippi remained. Of these Antony got eight, Octavian three, and Octavian was to receive two other legions from Antony's army in Gaul. It was further agreed that Antony would pay the veterans a cash bonus while Octavian found them lands. Octavian therefore returned to Italy to distribute land while Antony went to Asia Minor, partly to extort funds for the soldiers and partly to regulate the chaotic conditions prevailing in that part of the world after the elimination of the Liberators.

Octavian's task was not an easy one, and his health was failing again. He found no evidence against Lepidus, whom he sent off to Africa, but Antony's lieutenant in Gaul refused to surrender the two promised legions. It was quite impossible to find lands enough for all the veterans, and on one occasion Octavian was almost murdered by a mob. Eventually he distributed enough land to convince the veterans that he, rather than Antony, was the soldier's friend—a task made easier for him by Antony's failure to pay the promised cash bonuses. Meanwhile, Sextus Pompey was daily becoming more troublesome. He still held Sicily and Sardinia, and his pirates were causing famine at Rome by interrupting the transport of grain. Lastly, Antony's wife Fulvia and his brother Lucius were in Italy, doing all they could to destroy Octavian.

It is not surprising, therefore, that civil war broke out again in the fall of 41. Octavian managed to drive Lucius into Perugia, where starvation forced him to surrender (February, 40). All veterans and townspeople were pardoned, but a considerable number of officials were executed, and the town itself was burned to the ground. Lucius was spared, and eventually became governor of Spain, while Fulvia fled to her husband and died shortly afterward—much to the relief of everyone, if we may believe the ancient authors. Octavian pacified another revolt in Campania and spent the summer of 40 in Gaul, collecting the two legions promised by Antony and forcibly taking over nine others and Gaul itself in addition. Meantime, Antony was on his way back to Italy after opening negotiations with Sextus Pompey for an alliance against their common enemy Octavian. Learning of this treachery, Octavian managed to steal a march on his rival. He had divorced Clodia during the war against Lucius and Fulvia; now he hurriedly married Scribonia, a woman several years his senior, whose niece was the wife of Sextus Pompey.

Octavian's troops forbade Antony to land at Brundisium, and for a moment it seemed that still another civil war would break out. The legionaries made it clear, however, that they would not fight, and thus compelled their leaders to patch up their differences. A third and final distribution of provinces followed. Octavian this time got Illyria and all the provinces of western Europe, Antony took the East, and Lepidus was allowed to retain Africa. These arrangements merely meant that the triumvirs would be made proconsuls in their respective provinces by the senate, and it should be noted that the triumvirs did not yet have the effrontery to give Italy away. Italy was still governed, in theory at least, by consuls elected in the old manner. In practice, the triumvirs named the consuls, selecting candidates long in advance.

The reconciliation at Brundisium was sealed by Antony's marriage (November, 40) to Octavia, the elder sister of Octavian. Ancient writers agree that Octavia was a woman of remarkable beauty and refinement who, though forced into a difficult position, played her part with great skill and tact, preventing war between her husband and her brother for several years. This policy of appeasement was hailed joyously by the legions and by the peoples of Italy. (Vergil's Fourth Eclogue, predicting an early return of the Golden Age, was published in connection with Octavia's marriage.) A few months later, public opinion forced the two allies to make peace with Sextus Pompey. Meeting at Misenum near Naples, they agreed that Sextus was to be governor of Sicily and Sardinia, which he actually held, and of Achaea (Greece). In return for this recognition he was to cease his piracies and supply grain to Rome.

These dreams of peace were premature. Within a year Sextus had renewed his depredations, and Octavian was preparing for war against him. Octavian's first efforts were unsuccessful, and his fleet was destroyed. Antony remained neutral, apparently hoping that the two contestants would destroy each other, but at last his own need of troops forced him to beg aid of Octavian. The two triumvirs then met at Tarentum in the spring of 37, and again only Octavia's skill prevented civil war. A settlement was reached, and the triumvirate, which theoretically had expired on January 1 of that year, was renewed for another five years.

Octavian attacked Sextus again in the summer of 36, and won a battle in September of that year. Sextus fled to the East, planning to join Antony or the Parthians, but was captured and executed in Asia Minor. During the campaign against Sextus, Lepidus had landed twelve legions in Sicily and made ready to demand a larger share of the world. When his troops deserted to Octavian, he had to make peace. Octavian took full advantage of the situation to expel Lepidus from the triumvirate and take over his province. Although Lepidus was allowed to retain the office of *pontifex maximus*, given him by Antony soon after Caesar's death, he took no further part in politics until his death in 12 B.C. At the age of twenty-seven Octavian found himself supreme in the West.

Octavian now entered upon his third and final matrimonial venture. The marriage to Scribonia had not survived the troubles with Sextus Pompey. Toward the end of 39, on the complaint that he was "thoroughly disgusted by her outrageous temper," Octavian divorced her on the very day that she gave birth to his only child, Julia. A little later (January, 38) he married Livia Drusilla under circumstances so scandalous that one night in Rome a statue of Virtue fell on its face and had to be purified in the sea at considerable trouble and expense—or at least, so it was said. Though Livia was not yet nineteen years old, she already had a three-year-old son (the future emperor Tiberius) and she presented her first husband with a second son, Drusus, three months after her marriage to Octavian. This unconventional marriage was, however, a fitting symbol of Octavian's desire for political appeasement, for the bride was closely connected with her new husband's chief enemies. Her father was descended from Appius Claudius, the consul of 143, and had been adopted by Livius Drusus, the tribune of 91. Proscribed by the triumvirs in 43, he had committed suicide after fighting under Brutus at Philippi. Livia's first husband, Tiberius Claudius Nero, had also fought against Octavian, but after the peace of Misenum he divorced her in order that she might marry the victor. In spite of its strange beginning, the marriage was most successful. Livia was a woman of great beauty, strong character, and high intelligence, who helped her husband greatly throughout his long life, always urging him in the direction of clemency and appeasement.

Antony and the East

After Philippi, Antony turned to the East. He apparently shared the popular view of his day that these lands of inexhaustible wealth existed primarily to be looted by Romans, and here he hoped to raise the money to pay off his soldiers. As a financial speculation his expedition was a dismal failure, and it raised political and military problems that occupied him for the rest of his life. Antony's achievements in the East were bitterly criticized by Octavian, whose charges have been repeated by uncritical historians down to our own day. It is not wise, however, to accept Octavian's propaganda at face value. Antony's settlement of the Near East entitles him to a high place among Rome's great empire builders, and Octavian secretly recognized its merit, in spite of his denunciations, since he retained it after he had eliminated Antony.

The Romans now held most of the eastern coast of the Mediterranean. Palestine and central Asia Minor were ruled by native princes friendly to Rome, called "client-kings," and only Egypt was nominally independent. Pompey and Crassus had looted the eastern provinces and client-kings at will for fifteen years after the conquest of 63. Pompey demanded their aid when civil war broke out, and Caesar punished those who gave it by demanding more of them. The Liberators were unquestionably the most brutal of all in their exactions. When Antony arrived in 41 he found the East picked bare. Since the money he so urgently needed was not available in Asia, he turned his attention to Egypt, a wealthy country as yet unlooted by the Romans. First he summoned its queen, Cleopatra, to a conference at Tarsus, and a few weeks later he visited the country in person. Before anything could be accomplished, however, his attention was distracted by a Parthian invasion of Syria.

The Parthians had held Mesopotamia for almost a hundred years, and everywhere they were recognized as the greatest military power in the East. Discontented Orientals in Syria and Palestine looked to them as possible saviors who would bring back freedom to the East. The Jews, whose kinsmen in Babylon prospered under Parthian rule, were especially inclined to be pro-Parthian. Nevertheless, the Parthians had up till now made no serious effort to push west to the Mediterranean. They gave Mithradates no help, and they made peace with Sulla and Pompey. The attack of Crassus was sheer aggression on his part, and the Parthians did not follow up their victory at Carrhae. Though there were plundering raids into Roman territory during the next few years, the small numbers of those engaged indicate that no permanent conquests were planned. Pompey sought Parthian aid before Pharsalus, as did the Liberators before Philippi, but in neither case was the Parthian king, Orodes, willing to intervene in Western affairs.

The Liberators had communicated with Orodes through a man named Labienus—the son of Caesar's aid in Gaul and the only important Caesarian to desert his cause for Pompey's. Labienus entered the service of Orodes after Philippi and persuaded him to attack Syria. The invasion began in the spring of 40, led by Labienus himself and by the king's son, Pacorus. Within a few weeks the invaders had occupied all Syria. Here the brutalities of Cassius and Antony had aroused deep hatred among the natives, who welcomed the Parthians. A few Roman troops, once commanded by the Liberators, went over to Labienus. After occupying Syria, Pacorus advanced to Palestine, where he captured the high priest Hyrcanus and re-established an independent Jewish state under Hyrcanus's nephew and rival, Antigonus. Labienus proceeded westward, occupying Cilicia and southern Asia Minor almost to the Aegean, and meeting little resistance. The client-kings of central Asia Minor joined him, and at the end of the year 40 the greater part of the Roman East was in Parthian hands.

Brief reconnoitering in Tyre convinced Antony of the hopelessness of resistance in Syria. He therefore withdrew to Ephesus, where he organized new armies, and then hurried to Italy to procure more troops. Early in 39 he sent an able officer to command the Roman troops in Asia Minor, and during the next few months Labienus was driven back to Syria, defeated, and eventually killed. Pacorus had returned to Parthia, but in the spring of 38 he again attacked Syria, where he too was defeated and killed. A Roman general entered Jerusalem after a protracted siege in the summer of 37, and Roman territory was freed from the Parthians after more than three years.

During most of 38 and 37 Antony was at Athens preparing a great campaign against the Parthians which should avenge Crassus, prevent further incursions, and perhaps carry the Roman eagles over the whole empire once ruled by Alexander. He had Caesar's plans for such a campaign, but the events of 40–38 had shown that military preparations alone were not enough. A political settlement of the Near East must be made before the legions could safely be led into Parthia. As Antony had taken the precaution of having all his acts ratified in advance by the Roman senate, a settlement of the East was accomplished in 37. He distributed kingdoms among various client-kings of his own choosing. Heretofore, client-kings had been the hereditary rulers of the countries in question. Now they were native commanders selected by Antony because of their loyalty to him and their ability to govern. In general, his choices were fortunate, and they kept the Near East for Rome.

Meantime, King Orodes of Parthia had selected one of his sons, Phraates, to be his heir, and this young man, after murdering his father, had taken over the kingdom. In the spring of 36 Antony marched against Phraates, following Caesar's plan of taking the upper route through Armenia and Media to invade Parthia from the north. When Antony reached Media, near the Caspian Sea, he was badly defeated—partly because of the treachery of his ally, the client-king of Armenia—and forced to make a disastrous retreat. Antony won the devotion of his men by his courage and perseverance during the retreat, but after regaining Syria he broke down completely. For many weeks he spent his days and nights in a drunken stupor. By 34 he had recovered sufficiently to punish the traitorous king of Armenia, though he could not bring himself to invade Parthia again. In part his demoralization was caused by the calamitous defeat he had suffered, and in part it was caused by Cleopatra.

Antony and Cleopatra

Cleopatra, the second daughter of Ptolemy XI Auletes and his sister-wife, was born in 68. She had two sisters, one older and one younger than herself, and two brothers, both named Ptolemy, who were born about 61 and 59 respectively. The elder sister was murdered by her father, the younger by Cleopatra herself; her two brothers became her husbands in turn, the first being killed in battle, the second poisoned by his sister-wife. As Cleopatra's parents were brother and sister, she had only one grandfather and one grandmother, from each of whom she inherited much. Her grandfather was Ptolemy VIII Soter; her grandmother, a demimondaine who had reached the top in her profession by becoming the king's concubine, must have been a woman of great force of character since she managed to retain that position for several years and bore her royal lover at least three children. From her grandfather came Cleopatra's dreams of empire, from her grandmother came her personal character. Though not exceptionally beautiful, Cleopatra possessed an unforgettable personality, great intelligence and charm, and unfaltering determination. When only twenty years old she became Caesar's mistress for reasons of state, and three years later, shortly before the dictator's death, she journeyed to Rome in a vain effort to entice further favors from him. In later years she could without compunction use her sex or her poison bottle as circumstances suggested. Octavian's propagandists depicted her as the most magnificent harlot in history. Sentimentalists like Plutarch pictured her and Antony as great lovers who deemed the world well lost for love. Nevertheless, the bare truth seems to be that, whatever Antony's feelings toward her may have been after the Parthian disaster broke his spirit, Cleopatra never regarded him as anything more than a tool of her soaring ambition. This ambition led her to dream of reestablishing and ruling the ancient empire of the Ptolemies or even that of Alexander himself.

Antony first made Cleopatra's acquaintance in 54, when he was a young cavalry officer helping restore her father to his throne and she a girl of fourteen. No doubt he saw her frequently when she was at Rome ten years later and he was consul. Sentimental historians date the great love affair from her resplendent visit to him at Tarsus in 41, when he was at the height of his fame as victor over the Liberators at Philippi. She may at this time have begun to include his aid in her plans for the future: he followed her to Egypt after a few weeks, and she bore him twins significantly named Alexander Helios ("Sun") and Cleopatra Selene ("Moon"), but it seems likely that at this juncture Antony was more deeply interested in money for the veterans of Philippi than he was in romance. Moreover, Antony married Octavia shortly after his departure from Egypt in the spring of 40, and he found no trouble at all in keeping away from the Egyptian siren for more than three years.

Late in the summer of 37, when Antony was making his settlement of the Near East preparatory to the Parthian campaign, he summoned Cleopatra to Antioch and again consulted her wishes. He gave her the whole coast of Palestine and Phoenicia except Tyre and Sidon, all southern Syria including Damascus, Transjordania east of the Jordan River and the Dead Sea, the island of Cyprus, and parts of Cilicia. Aside from Cyrene, and a few cities in the Aegean area, Cleopatra now held everything that the Ptolemies had ever held except Judea and Galilee. She begged hard for these districts too, but Antony had already given them to Herod (the man mentioned in the Gospels as ruling at Jerusalem when Jesus was born) and he would not withdraw his gift. A mighty feud thus arose between Cleopatra and Herod, who were well-matched antagonists. Herod saw through her completely, and she recognized in him the chief obstacle to her ambitions. She used every manner of intrigue to ruin him, to which he replied in kind, even complaining to Antony that she had tried to seduce him and suggesting that it might be a good idea to have her poisoned.

If Antony was already in love with Cleopatra in 37, he did not allow his heart to interfere with his judgment. In general he treated her as a client-queen. His gifts to her did not differ essentially from those he made to other client-kings, and he expected in return the same substantial military aid from her that he expected from them. There was, however, one important difference. He recognized the twins, "Sun" and "Moon," as his own, and probably it was at this time that he married Cleopatra—though evidence as to the exact date of the ceremony is scanty and conflicting. Since he was still married to Octavia, this eastern marriage had no legal standing in

Rome, where Cleopatra was regarded as Antony's mistress. Nevertheless, the marriage was recognized as valid throughout the East, and apparently it was her idea rather than his. During the Parthian campaign Cleopatra was at Alexandria, where she gave birth to a son whom she named Ptolemy Philadelphus after the greatest of her Ptolemaic ancestors. But when Antony returned from Parthia a broken man, Cleopatra began to dominate him completely and his policies no longer aimed at strengthening or augmenting the Roman Empire, or at securing his position in that Empire, but rather at expanding her domains until they equaled or surpassed those of Alexander.

Antony celebrated his victory over the king of Armenia by a magnificent triumph at Alexandria in 34, much to the indignation of patriotic Romans who thought that generals might celebrate their triumphs only at Rome. Moreover, Antony made the situation much worse by proclaiming the so-called "Donations of Alexandria" amidst all the splendors of oriental pageantry. Antony sat on a high throne, more like a Hellenistic king than a Roman general, and beside him sat Cleopatra, robed as Isis. On lesser thrones sat her children: Caesarion, the twins, and Philadelphus. Antony then announced that Cleopatra had been Caesar's lawful wife and that her child Caesarion was the dictator's legitimate son. (This declaration was aimed at Octavian, who claimed to be Caesar's heir and was now declared a usurper.) Antony pronounced Cleopatra Queen of Kings and Caesarion King of Kings, joint rulers of Egypt and Cyprus. To each of his own children by Cleopatra he donated kingdoms. To Alexander Helios he gave Armenia, Media, and Parthia; to Ptolemy Philadelphus, Syria, Cilicia, and the overlordship of all the client-kings of Asia Minor; and to Cleopatra Selene, Cyrene and Libya. Cleopatra and her children thus received the whole of the Asiatic and African possessions of Alexander the Great, except the Roman province of Asia. However, much of the territory thus given away still remained to be conquered. Antony reserved for himself the Western World, which his son (by Fulvia) would inherit. In other words, Antony and Cleopatra and their various children would jointly rule the whole world from India to the Atlantic, from the

English Channel and the Danube to the Sahara and the Indian
Ocean. It was a grandiose dream, worthy of their combined ambitions, but before it could be realized the Parthians must be conquered, and Octavian must be driven from Italy. These two things
lay beyond the power of the royal lovers.

Octavian Destroys Antony

The story of how this house of cards collapsed can be told quickly.
Though Antony and Octavian had been maneuvering against each
other ever since they entered into their last agreement at Tarentum
in the spring of 37, they had carefully preserved the outward forms
of friendship. Antony's marriage to Cleopatra was, of course, a major
change in policy, as well as an insult to Octavian, but just then Octavian was too deeply engaged with Sextus Pompey to begin a fresh
quarrel with Antony. The Donations of Alexandria could not be
ignored, however, and the year 33 was marked by acrimonious correspondence and mutual recriminations between the two triumvirs.
At the end of the year the triumvirate expired, and no attempt was
made to renew it. It had long since been arranged that two of Antony's friends were to be consuls in 32, and Antony and Octavian
would serve together in 31. On their first day in office Antony's two
friends launched a great attack upon Octavian, and a few days later
he replied with a bitter attack upon Antony in the senate, promising
to give proofs of the latter's misdeeds at the next session. Without
waiting to hear Octavian's proofs, Antony's friends—including the
two consuls and almost 400 out of 1200 senators—fled to Ephesus,
where Antony and Cleopatra were already assembling troops. Some
of these senators were undoubtedly sincere partisans of Antony.
Others, it is to be feared, merely expected him to win, for they deserted back to Octavian with equal alacrity as soon as Antony's star
began to decline.

Military preparations and vigorous propaganda campaigns filled
the rest of the year 32. Antony accused Octavian of cowardice at
Philippi as well as of cruelty and greed; Antony was reproached so
effectively for his drunkenness that he wrote a pamphlet in self-
defense. Each was charged by the other with all manner of debauch-

ery and perversion, as was customary in classical vituperation. Antony divorced Octavia, whose brother very successfully dramatized her expulsion with her children from her depraved husband's house. Octavian's most effective charge was that Antony had been bewitched by Cleopatra and intended to hand his fellow citizens over to this oriental queen, who would move the capital of the world from Rome to Alexandria. When two deserters informed Octavian that Antony had deposited a will with the Vestal Virgins, Octavian seized the document and read it aloud before the senate and in the forum. The will, bearing out the Donations, declared that Caesarion was Caesar's legitimate son, made large gifts of Roman territory to Antony's children by Cleopatra, and requested that his body be buried beside hers in Alexandria. Octavian thus seemed to prove his charges and convinced countless Romans that Antony had become the slave of Cleopatra, who was about to attack them with all the forces of Asia. As Asiatics had recently defeated Roman armies under Crassus and even under Antony himself, all Rome was terrified. After persuading the cities of Italy and the West to swear allegiance to him, Octavian formally declared war upon Cleopatra. He was wise enough, even then, to avoid openly attacking Antony, a Roman. The latter had no choice, however, but to come to the aid of his wife Cleopatra—and thus prove himself a traitor to Rome.

Antony's navy, including Cleopatra's contribution, consisted of about 500 ships of the line, probably the most powerful fleet the world had yet seen. The army which he planned to use against Octavian consisted of nineteen legions, plus auxiliary troops, or perhaps 75,000 infantry and 12,000 cavalry all told. Octavian's propaganda later pictured this army as made up largely of cowardly Greeks and Orientals. Such was not the case. The legionaries were almost all Italians who had served in the East for several years; and though Antony's press gangs were active in Greece, the kidnapped Greeks were used only in subservient capacities such as rowers and carriers. Antony's greatest difficulty was with his own high officers, most of whom hated Cleopatra. Knowing the popular effect of Octavian's charges against her, they were constantly urging Antony to send her back to Egypt. When he finally succumbed to their pressure, Cleopatra refused to leave, for she knew Antony and feared that in her absence Octavia might once more reconcile her husband and brother, thereby ruining Cleopatra's prospects. During the summer of 32 Antony moved his army into Greece, but he made no effort to land in Italy. He dared not land with Cleopatra, and she would not let him land without her. They prepared, therefore, to defeat Octavian in Greece. Antony's troops occupied most of southern Greece, though not Thessaly or Macedonia, and the general disposition of his forces suggests that his first concern was to prevent Octavian from attacking Egypt. He had been forced into defensive strategy.

Actium and After

Octavian crossed the Adriatic early in 31, accompanied by about 400 ships, 80,000 infantry, and 12,000 cavalry. The campaign centered around Actium. Here a rather large lake was connected with the sea by a narrow channel. Octavian built his camp on the northern tongue of land separating the lake from the sea, while Antony had his camp on the southern tongue, and his ships held the lake and channel. Octavian's navy won the first victory, destroying some of Antony's ships and establishing a naval base several miles to the south of the channel. This move severed Antony's communications, forcing him to carry all his provisions overland by a long and difficult route. Antony's generals now urged him to withdraw to central Greece, where his proved strategical skill would undoubtedly defeat Octavian. Cleopatra vetoed their plan, which would have required the sacrifice of her fleet, leaving Egypt open to attack by Octavian. When Antony supported her veto, several of his high officers deserted. Antony then moved forces around the lake and managed to establish a line across the neck north of Octavian's camp, thus cutting his opponent off from all land communication. If Octavian's fleet could be destroyed or driven away, starvation would force surrender. As desertions by officers hostile to Cleopatra were by this time becoming alarmingly frequent, Antony decided to risk a naval battle. His fleet sailed out of the channel on September 2, 31, in an attempt to outflank Octavian's line on the right in order to drive his fleet south. The maneuver failed, and Antony's fleet was lost.

Historians once wrote of the terrific fighting in this battle, taking their cue from ancient writers skilled in composing imaginative battle scenes. The most recent and authoritative student of the campaign (Tarn) comes to the conclusion that "it was scarcely a battle at all." According to this view, Octavian won because Antony's troops refused to go on fighting for a cause which seemed to them that of the Egyptian queen. We have seen the fraternization of troops change the course of events repeatedly during the civil wars, and the Battle of Actium seems to have been the supreme example of such mass desertions. Tarn believes that only ten or fifteen ships out of Antony's armada fought at all. Cleopatra's own fleet remained loyal to her, and with it she escaped to Egypt. Antony got away with a few vessels and followed her. The rest of his fleet turned back to shore without ever coming to grips with the enemy, and surrendered to Octavian a few days later.

The disaster at Actium unnerved Antony more than the Parthian campaign. Though he still had seven legions in the East, he made no effort to organize further resistance, but lived alone in a little house on the shore at Alexandria. Cleopatra bore her reverses more calmly, and began making new plans. She and Antony apparently had feared that something might go wrong at Actium, for they had put their entire war chest aboard her flagship before the battle, and it was consequently saved. As Octavian needed funds desperately to pay for the war, he went to Egypt to get Cleopatra's treasure in the summer of 30. On the way he was joined by Antony's legions and client-kings, and entered Alexandria without meeting opposition.

Antony committed suicide and, after vain negotiations with Octavian, Cleopatra followed his example. Perhaps the famous story of the asp (or cobra) is true. In any event, Octavian seized both the treasure and Egypt, the only Mediterranean state left that was not already a part of the Roman Empire. Caesarion was too dangerous a rival for Caesar's heir, and Octavian had him put to death along with Antony's son by Fulvia. Antony's three children by Cleopatra were taken to Rome, where the twins were led in Octavian's triumph. The girl was later married to Juba, the client-king of Mauretania. The fate of the boys is unknown. It may be added that Antony's two daughters by Octavia each played an important part in Roman history. The younger was married to Livia's younger son, Drusus, and became the ancestress of three emperors—Caligula, Claudius, and Nero—while the elder sister was destined to be Nero's other grandmother. All this, however, lay in the far distant future. In 30 B.C. men knew only that Octavian was master of the world, and they hoped that at long last the wars were over.

Note

Theodor Mommsen

Theodor Mommsen (1817–1903) is by common consent the most important historian ever to concern himself with ancient Rome. The son of a Schleswig pastor, Mommsen studied law at Kiel, and his interest quickly centered in Roman law. These studies led him to other aspects of Roman history, though he never forsook his first love. After three years of travel and study in Italy—which remained a second fatherland to him—Mommsen became professor of Roman law successively at Leipzig, Zürich, and Breslau. In 1858 he went to Berlin as professor of Roman history. Here he remained for the rest of his life, the most famous professor in this famous university at the time when German universities were at the peak of their glory.

Mommsen was no scholarly recluse. From his student days he had taken an active part in the nationalistic and liberal movement that culminated in the Revolution of 1848. He edited a radical newspaper at Kiel in 1848, and he was accused of helping foment the May riots in 1849. Brought to trial in 1850, he was sentenced to nine months' imprisonment. At a second hearing, however, he was acquitted—on the ground that, being a university professor, he could not be expected to foresee the consequences of his acts! Nevertheless, he was dismissed from his professorship and spent two unhappy years at Zürich.

Mommsen had not thought of writing formal history until the fall of 1848, when he was asked by a Leipzig publisher (later his father-in-law) to write a history of Rome. The three large volumes of the *Römische Geschichte*, covering the period from the beginning to the battle of Thapsus (46), appeared between 1854 and 1856. At once the work attracted wide attention by its learning and its brilliant literary style, and because the ideas it expressed were in harmony with the spirit of the times. Mommsen was a disillusioned forty-eighter, tired of romantic dreams; and though as a school-boy he had written an essay (later privately printed by his family) declaring that great men were at best a necessary evil, he now decided that Germany needed a strong ruler to achieve what the idealistic revolutionists had failed to accomplish. These views appear throughout the history, and especially in the last part (written at Zürich) where he deals with the period from the Gracchi to Caesar. Most of the blame is laid upon the Roman nobility, who are pictured as strikingly like the German nobles of the 1840's. Tiberius Gracchus comes out a fine example of the liberal reformer of 1848, "a tolerably able, thoroughly well-meaning, conservative patriot, who simply did not know what he was doing." Gaius Gracchus was no wishy-washy idealist but a practical statesman aiming at "autocracy of the Napoleonic type" (*i.e.,* like Louis Napoleon). Cicero was "a statesman without insight, opinion, or purpose . . . never more than a short-sighted egotist"; he was "a journalist in the worst sense of that term" and a lawyer "who could find reasons, or at least words, for everything." Cato was "one of the most Quixotic and one of the most melancholy phenomena in this age so abounding in political caricatures." Caesar, according to Mommsen, was "the entire and perfect man," a man who cannot be pictured to the life. "As an artist can paint everything save only consummate beauty, so the historian, when once in a thousand years he encounters the perfect, can only be silent before it." A critic has observed that Mommsen maintained this reverent silence through eight closely printed pages of panegyric.

This adulation of Caesar may have helped prepare the way for Bismarck and Germany's age of blood and iron. If so, we must recall Mommsen's own remark about Tiberius Gracchus and say that the historian himself simply did not know what he was doing. All his life he remained an old-fashioned liberal forty-eighter, and for many years he took an active part in politics, first as a member of the Prussian Landtag and later in the Reichstag. His criticisms of the Iron Chancellor were so vehement that Bismarck once thought of suing him for libel. In his last years Mommsen was despondent and critical of the course taken by the new kaiser, William II.

The general public still associates the name of Mommsen primarily with the *History of Rome,* but in his later years Mommsen himself spoke slightingly of this work and preferred to base his reputation upon his *Römisches Staatsrecht* (3 vols., 1871–5), a constitutional history of Rome, and more especially upon the *Corpus Inscriptionum Latinarum.* He had begun dreaming of such a collection of inscriptions in his student days, and he never allowed it to slip far from his thoughts. This enormous collection of 200,000 inscriptions from all parts of the Roman world was published by the Berlin Academy and though Mommsen received the aid of many collaborators, it remained his work. No other publication has added so much to our knowledge of Roman history, and the work is not yet finished.

Mommsen was also active in promoting several similar co-operative enterprises. He was a man of tremendous physical and mental energy, and a bibliography of his writings lists 1513 titles. This list includes many brief notes, as well as translations and reprintings. Scarcely a year passed between 1850 and 1903, however, in which Mommsen did not publish a book or major article. The years between 1870 and 1914 knew few German students of ancient Rome who were not his pupils, and his influence reached scholars in every part of the Western World. It can truthfully be said that no one will ever again write on Roman history without being indebted for something to Theodor Mommsen. The biography which Mommsen deserved was never written, and it is now too late, for most of his private papers were destroyed during the bombing of Berlin. For a brief account of his life and a sympathetic criticism, see L. D. Hartmann, *Theodor Mommsen* (1908), which contains several of his political writings in 1848.

X The Roman Revolution

T

HE POLITICAL AND MILITARY EVENTS DESCRIBED IN THE last three chapters give only a superficial view of the great revolution that was changing the face of the ancient world in the first century before Christ. The greater and more fundamental revolution was economic and social, intellectual and religious, rather than political, and out of it came a whole new world. Yet this new world, which we call the Roman Empire, was not the creation of the eminent Romans whose wars and battles, marriages and divorces, intrigues and murders, we have duly chronicled above. The Divine Julius and his like spent their time strutting about in the ruins of their world, making what they considered distinguished political careers for themselves, but actually they were only destroying what other men had created. Caesar and his friends and rivals happened to rise to the top in the chaos that accompanied the world-shaking collapse of the Roman Republic and the Hellenistic Empires. They exploited these conditions as best they could, but they did not create them, and sooner or later they all were destroyed by forces which they could neither control or comprehend.

Three hundred years had now passed since Alexander the Great had hewn out an empire that included most of the civilized western world of his day. The Hellenistic monarchs had ruled this Greek and oriental world until their wars, failing man-power in Greece, and rebellions by their oriental subjects brought them to ruin. Their passing created a vacuum into which Rome was irresistibly drawn since she was the only military power in the Mediterranean world with the strength to enforce peace. In the second century before

Christ the Romans had been most reluctant to assume this burden, but they could not resist forever, and eventually they learned that, willy-nilly, they must rule the world. The conquests of the first century before Christ were accomplished with great cruelty, and brought out the worst side of the Roman character, but while spectacular adventurers were looting the East, countless less eminent persons—Romans, Italians, Greeks, and Orientals—were doing their bit in other ways to make Rome the center and capital of the Mediterranean world.

Rome thus took over the heritage of the Hellenistic world. The East got Roman rulers in place of Greek, and Rome ceased being a city-state on the Tiber to become the capital of a world empire. This great and fundamental revolution had the most sweeping effects upon the government, the economic and social life, and the intellectual life of everyone, both in the East and in the West. It brought disturbances which unleashed the Civil wars and wrought terrible damage everywhere, but out of them came the Roman Empire of Augustus and his successors. While the coming of this Empire marked a new era in both East and West, the changes in Rome and Italy were greater and more far-reaching than those in the East, and to them we must first turn our attention.

The Economic Revolution in Italy

The Italian peasant had fallen upon evil days in the second century, and the wars made matters still worse in the first. The small farmer was pushed aside by the slave, and everywhere there was an increase of large estates, much to the dismay of critics who declared them the ruin of Italy. After the Gracchi, nearly every prominent politician in Rome expressed a desire to break up these great estates and get the peasants back on the land. It is to be feared, however, that the politicians were seeking votes rather than improved agriculture, for their other activities actually hastened the decline of the peasantry. From Sulla to Octavian every successful general dispossessed thousands of peasants in order to distribute their land among his veterans. In many cases the veterans who got the land knew little or nothing about farming, and they certainly had no desire to break their backs laboring in the fields: they yearned instead for the pleasures and excitement of the cities. As soon as opportunity offered, they sold their farms and rushed off to Rome. The farms were added to neighboring estates while their former owners sank back into the urban rabble. The declining price of grain, because of heavy importations from abroad, drove other peasants from their farms, and slave competition ruined countless others.

The social and political effects of these changes were deplorable in the extreme, yet the new agriculture was profitable economically to the big landowners, and in the long run it enriched rural Italy with more diversified farming. Part of the poorer land acquired by rich men was withdrawn from cultivation and converted into pasture, with a few slaves tending large herds of cattle. The more fertile land was given over to vineyards, olive orchards, and truck gardens, often worked by slaves under the direction of a bailiff. When Varro published his book, *De re rustica,* in 36 B.C., he declared that all Italy was a garden whose equal could be found nowhere on earth. Perhaps he was exaggerating for patriotic reasons, yet he made it abundantly clear that there were still many small farmers in Italy and that the Italian garden was not cultivated entirely by slaves or veterans ignorant of the science and art of agriculture. As soon as settled conditions returned, and farms were no longer seized by desperate politicians to pay off their troops, the fertile Italian soil made agriculture prosperous once more.

This specialization in agriculture rested upon, and encouraged, a great expansion of overseas trade. In the second century Sicily and Sardinia had been the great granaries of Rome; in the first century Africa became equally important; and after 30 B.C. great quantities of grain were brought to Italy from Egypt. On the other hand, Italian luxuries, such as wine and olive oil, were sent abroad. The first markets were in the West, but after the wars had disrupted agriculture in the East, Italians found markets for their fancier produce there. There was also a constant demand for oriental luxuries at Rome, and after Pompey had cleared the seas of pirates in 67, trade grew rapidly.

Other forces further encouraged the rapid expansion of Italian commerce during the fifty years after Sulla. The enfranchisement of all Italians promoted the growth of trade, for the South Italians and Italian Greeks, who thereby received the rights and privileges of Roman citizens and the protection of Roman arms, were especially skilled in such matters, able to exploit their new position throughout the Empire. The provisioning of armies provided magnificent opportunities for profiteers. Traders accompanied and followed the armies, cheaply buying booty from soldiers and valuables of every sort from the desperate inhabitants of conquered cities. Officers and soldiers acquired tastes for the luxuries of the distant places they had seen and conquered, and in later years those who had money to spend created a market for such things in Italy. Thus the ruins of Pompeii, where Sulla settled a colony of his veterans, show strong Asiatic influence in the architecture and decorations of this period. In earlier and later times the artistic influences here were quite different, which suggests that many of the new householders were veterans of the Asiatic campaign.

As the Italians did not pay for the imports thus received with exports, trade at first was merely a form of booty-snatching. As time went on, however, intelligent traders came to realize that in the long run the normal methods of trade were the more profitable. A large and powerful class of men appeared, among them both Easterners and Westerners, whose commerce covered the Mediterranean and whose loyalty went to the Romans who policed this entire area.

Perhaps the Romans who profited most from the economic changes in the first century were the businessmen and bankers who organized the companies of publicans to collect taxes in the provinces. Ever since the reforms of Gaius Gracchus the right to collect these taxes had been awarded to the highest bidder, but as the collection required liquid capital and a knowledge of the province, there was little competitive bidding and the contracts were let at low figures. Before long these companies branched out into other forms of banking activity, lending money to cities and sharing in various business enterprises. In the rough and tumble period here under discussion, these companies and their agents did many discreditable things, and the publicans were detested throughout the

East. But at Rome they enjoyed great influence because of their connections with men like Crassus or, as we shall see, even with Cato and Brutus. Nevertheless, they, like the traders mentioned above, were more than mere robbers. They made Rome the banking capital of the world, and they united the Roman Empire by financial bonds that were as important as the commercial bonds forged by the traders or, in the long run, the military conquests of the generals.

Less need be said of Italian industry at this time. In general it was organized on a narrow basis, catering only to local markets. Manufacturers of military equipment were perhaps the principal exception to this rule, though Capua was already known as a center for iron and bronze work and various Etruscan cities were beginning to make names for themselves by their pottery and other manufactured goods. The foundations of a larger industrial system were already laid, however, and as soon as peace returned Italy began exporting goods to the West in large quantities.

The Social Revolution and the Republic

These economic developments produced revolutionary effects upon the various social classes at Rome and it was they that caused the collapse of the aristocratic Republic. In the old days Rome had been governed by the senatorial aristocracy, which was an hereditary caste of great landowners. Each family had its clients, made up of peasants in the vicinity of its estates, and each had intricate matrimonial and political connections with other aristocratic families. The senators as a class found little trouble in managing elections and dominating the Republic. In the first century, however, many of these families became bankrupt; they were forsaken by their clients; and they were hated by social classes that had become wealthy and powerful as a result of the newer economic developments. Their decline brought an end to the old Republic.

The decline of the aristocracy was first of all financial. The aristocrats had always considered government their especial prerogative, but by this time a political career had become an expensive luxury by which an honest man could quickly bankrupt himself. Rich parvenus were rapidly raising the standard of living in aristocratic

Rome, and the old families found it difficult to live up to the new standards set by the nabobs who had just returned from looting the East. Even the wealthier of the old families, such as the Claudii, were often short of ready cash, and the poorer nobility had to draw heavily on their accumulated capital. Moreover, several factors were just then co-operating to raise the price of land. The conservative old owners did not always have the intelligence or skill required to apply the new agricultural methods, and other men could make more money than they out of their land. The possession of large landed estates brought social distinction, and many a wealthy profiteer was willing to lose money on estates bought at exorbitant prices which would establish him in society. Needy aristocrats were tempted to sell their estates at what seemed high prices and were then forced to eat up their capital. Fear of proscriptions encouraged others to sell while it was still possible to get something in return. As social prejudice prevented aristocrats from engaging openly in trade or other legitimate business, those who disposed of their land had to invest their funds in such enterprises as the joint-stock companies of publicans, and during the Civil wars these funds were often confiscated along with the lands still held by the old nobles. Deprived of its land, the old Roman aristocracy went bankrupt.

Financial bankruptcy was presently supplemented by decimation. Hundreds of aristocrats lost their lives as well as their property by the proscriptions of the Second Triumvirate, and countless others were killed at Philippi or committed suicide afterward. Other members of the aristocracy survived, of course, especially those who happened to be too old or too young to meet death in battle or by proscription, but their families died out ingloriously during the next hundred years. The pages of Tacitus contain many notices of the ignoble expedients used in the first century after Christ by members of once great families to secure a livelihood. With the passing of the old nobility, the old Roman Republic lost its heart and soul.

At the same time the peasants who forsook their farms, and the veterans who would not or could not operate or retain their allotments, were flocking to the cities and especially to Rome. Here some found employment, and a few prospered, but many lived wretchedly

and precariously from the public grain distributions. Other ambitious and energetic young men sought new homes outside Italy,
and often the admirable features of old Italian life were better preserved in southern Gaul, Spain, and Africa than in Italy herself.
Nevertheless, the population of Italy, and especially that of Rome,
was growing steadily during this whole period, and conditions in the
city's slums grew worse rather than better. Young men who saw no
future for themselves except in the breadlines, in competition with
these human wrecks, often joined the armies of ambitious generals.
Caesar was able to transmute such recruits into an efficient army,
though the similar armies of his successors often refused to fight for
the generals who fed them.

Those who won most politically by the social revolution were rich
businessmen of the equestrian class. The equestrians were no longer
limited to the members of the first eighteen centuries in the *comitia*,
for all were now admitted to that class who had 400,000 sesterces,
or slightly less than $20,000 in modern cash value. Some had many
millions. Being ambitious, energetic, and able, these equestrians resented their social inferiority to the senators whom they secretly or
openly despised, and they formed the main support of those political
leaders, from Pompey to Octavian, who were overthrowing the Republic.

The Old Aristocrats in the New Day

These social changes were far more potent in destroying the Republic than was the violence of the Civil wars. In fact, the violence
of the years that preceded and followed Caesar's crossing of the
Rubicon was evidence that the old political order at Rome had already broken down. The senatorial class no longer enjoyed the
power and respect necessary to govern the Republic, but until this
aristocracy was utterly destroyed by the Second Triumvirate its
members were strong enough to prevent others from peacefully taking over the government. Until the very end of the Republic, a
distinguished political career was virtually impossible for a "new
man." Cicero was the first such man to obtain the consulship since

96, and only two others achieved it before the death of Caesar.

The political struggle at Rome therefore developed into a conflict between the stiffly old-fashioned families (eventually led by Cato) who would admit no new blood into their ranks, and the newer and more compliant families (such as that of Pompey) or old but formerly undistinguished families (such as Caesar's) which were willing to co-operate with outsiders for the sake of power. But even those who made concessions to the equestrians in return for aid never intended to let their base allies usurp leadership. When they had achieved power, they were therefore faced with very grave problems regarding their old aristocratic relatives and associates and their low but no longer humble allies. Successful leaders were of course courted by many people. Pompey allowed himself to be accepted by the old families, and finally he fitted his program to theirs, not having the intelligence to see that he was inviting disaster by listening to such advisors rather than to the allies who had raised him to power. Caesar managed to reverse the process. He "forgave" his aristocratic enemies, he admitted them to his friendship, but he did not take their advice, and he was murdered by them for his insolence. The triumvirs solved the problem by liquidating the aristocracy.

The pathetic career of Cicero shows how difficult it was for an able man not belonging to a senatorial family to achieve a political career under the late Republic. His lack of political connections and of an hereditary clientele goes far to explain his ineffectiveness, his irresolution, and the abject attitude toward his social betters for which he has been ridiculed by Mommsen and so many others. Cicero knew perfectly well that his consulship was a gift from the aristocrats at a moment when they were badly frightened by Caesar and Catiline, and that all chance of future preferment, or even of future political activity, would vanish at his first sign of independence. Plutarch preserves an interesting piece of gossip to the effect that Cicero was forced by his wife Terentia to testify against Clodius at the famous and portentous trial because she suspected him of planning to divorce her and marry Clodia—the notorious dema-

gogue's equally notorious sister (see p. 393). Terentia is said to have
used this method to break up the match. The story is not incredible,
for the Claudii had repeatedly shown themselves more ready than
most noble families to accept the services of able men wherever they
could find them. Had Cicero managed to ally himself with the aristocracy, his subsequent career and the history of Rome might have
been very different. Yet even Cicero, with the huge wealth and
clientele of the Claudians at his disposal, could not have saved the
old regime.

Cicero made strenuous efforts to create a following for himself
without relying upon old-style clients. The little tract entitled "On
Seeking the Consulship," allegedly written by his brother Quintus in
64 when Cicero was a candidate for that office, describes many of
the tricks in vogue among politicians. It was well to know everybody, he wrote, and to say things to please every one and offend
no one. The politician must curry the favor of as many groups as
possible, acquiring a reputation for liberality by promising everything to everybody. He must attach himself to the great, or at least
seem to have done so. He must persuade or hire large numbers of
persons to follow him about in the forum, thus giving the impression of having a large clientele. He must carefully calculate before-
hand the effect of his speeches and judicial decisions upon leading
men and the general public. And finally, he must constantly resort
to *vituperatio*—abusing his opponents and circulating scandalous
but credible stories about them. Though Cicero obviously took this
brotherly advice to heart, he failed utterly to build up a following.
He did these things self-consciously and badly; his rivals did them
naturally and well. After all, Cicero's chief asset was his oratory, and
that was not enough. Oratory had little lasting effect upon the educated upper classes, and one sometimes wonders whether the Roman
rabble could really follow the involved phraseology of a Ciceronian
oration. (Of course, Cicero may have spoken more simply when
addressing the populace and put the speech into high-flown oratory
only when he published it later.) At any rate, others addressed the
mob more persuasively than he. Cicero was in many ways the most
modern—or perhaps the most nineteenth-century—politician in

Rome. In spite of conspicuous lapses, he was an idealistic man of high ability. But if statesmanship begins with the art of getting elected to office, Cicero was an inferior statesman.

Political Demagoguery

The more successful politicians won popular favor by conferring conspicuous benefits upon the people, either individually or as a body. Crassus owed much of his following to his largess, but such prodigality as his was quite beyond the means of any except multimillionaires and booty-rich generals like Pompey and Caesar. Most politicians preferred to court the populace with benefits for which the bill could be sent to the public treasury. Therefore the aedileship was much sought after, since its holder could prove his love for mankind with magnificent gladiatorial combats—especially after 65, when Caesar set new standards of lavishness in exhibitions of this sort.

The free distributions of grain provided politicians with even greater opportunities. Grain distributions had been started by Gaius Gracchus, revived by Saturninus, and abolished by Sulla. The new system, whereby tens of thousands of persons received their entire food supply at public expense, was inaugurated at the time of the Catilinarian conspiracy by Cato. It was greatly expanded by Clodius, and it was manipulated for several years by Pompey. Though reduced by Caesar and again abolished by the triumvirs, grain distributions were soon revived by Octavian. History thus shows, among other things, that factional affiliation had nothing to do with the matter. The device was fundamentally an aristocratic one, however, for in former times clients had expected material aid from their patrons. The aristocrats now tried to shift the cost to the state while retaining the personal gratitude of the public. Unfortunately for them, more skillful politicians soon overbid them and robbed them of gratitude as well as clients. At times the grain distributions were doubtless necessary to prevent starvation, but though they often consumed half the income of the state and though they were abolished more than once, it proved impossible to keep them abolished, because some politician was always trying to prove his love of humanity and attract votes by reviving them. Until the very end of the ancient world, the imperial government kept the Roman populace quiet by donations of bread and shows—*panem et circenses*. In fact, these two gifts seem to have been about all that the populace desired, for neither Caelius Rufus nor Brutus was able to rouse the mob to action, though the latter promised Liberty and the former offered to cancel debts and divide the wealth of the rich among the poor.

Pompey discovered still other methods for building a clientele. He had been a wealthy man even before Sulla's proscriptions enabled him to rise in the world. On his enormous estates in many parts of Italy he had thousands of old-style clients, and his various activities at Rome—notably the grain distributions—enabled him to create a huge following in the city. His great contribution to the science of practical politics, however, was his exploitation of patronage in the provinces. First in Spain, later in Asia Minor and Syria, he gave lucrative positions to hundreds of his henchmen. Caesar complained that he found all Spain full of Pompey's clients. Pompey invested much of his new wealth in these provinces, especially by lending money to Asiatic cities or client-kings at usurious interest to enable them to pay indemnities to Rome. His personal business agents—called "procurators"—infested the provinces, where they enjoyed great power and odious reputations. Pompey also ingratiated himself with the old nobility by allowing his aristocratic friends to share personally in the profits of empire. Perhaps these favors were a major reason why many of them preferred Pompey to Caesar.

More important still among the new clients were veterans. Marius had inflicted this scourge upon the Roman people when the necessities of war compelled him to recruit a mercenary army. Sulla expanded the system, and Pompey used veterans on an extensive scale for political purposes. Caesar soon surpassed him, however, making his veterans into a veritable clientele, treating them as a loyal patron should, and expecting them to reciprocate with the political support due from clients. We have already seen how Octavian's early career was made possible by the fact that he managed to inherit the loyalty of these veteran-clients. He never forgot the lesson, and to the end of his days he remained a model patron to Caesar's veterans and his own.

Caesar Offers Careers to Talent

These various developments were the true cause of the collapse of the Roman Republic. Nevertheless, those who profited by the revolution were neither the veterans and reliefers who later were kept quiet with bread and circuses, nor the generals who attained high offices only to be pushed aside by others, nor the political nonentities whom Caesar or his rivals appointed to the senate, where they forgot their benefactors as quickly as they were themselves forgotten. Those who really won the revolution were the thousands of hitherto disregarded lesser persons who now for the first time found real opportunities for advancement. Prominent in this group were the Italians, leading men in the small towns once allied to Rome. They had become Roman citizens in the eighties, and thereafter they could vote if they were present at Rome, though they might not yet aspire to office there. Caesar befriended these Italians, appointing many of them to important posts, and Octavian continued this policy on a larger scale. Even before Actium he could truthfully boast that he represented "all Italy," for he and Caesar had made the Italians feel that at last they were really Roman citizens. The other group to profit greatly by the Roman Revolution were the equestrians. They included Romans and Italians, and even a few rich men from the provinces. Their progress had been rapid ever since the second century. Sulla tried in vain to check them; they had favored Pompey; but Caesar gave them the recognition they demanded, and Octavian drew important advisors from their numbers. In the long run Caesar and Octavian won because they, like Napoleon, had convinced their followers that they provided a career open to talent.

Two men may be mentioned as typical of those who prospered politically by the revolutions of the first century before Christ. Titus Pomponius Atticus was a Roman equestrian born in 109. After receiving an excellent education and inheriting a fortune, he withdrew to Greece during the last phases of the Marian struggle and in the days of Sulla he bought large estates in Epirus at depreciated prices.

Twenty years later he returned to Rome, took the cognomen Atticus, and devoted himself to various banking and business enterprises ranging from book publishing to the training of gladiators. His genius for friendship enabled him to associate freely with all the important men at Rome and while he had no desire to hold public office, he became a political power of importance behind the scenes. He had been a schoolmate of Cicero, with whom he maintained an intimate friendship throughout his life: we still have more than four hundred letters addressed to him by the orator. Atticus's friends also included everyone else of importance in Rome. As a young man he had impressed Sulla favorably, and in later years he was the friend and confidant of Pompey, Caesar, Brutus, and Octavian-Augustus. His sister married Cicero's brother Quintus, and his daughter Pomponia married Agrippa, Octavian's right-hand man. His granddaughter Vipsania became the first wife of the future Emperor Tiberius. Nevertheless, Atticus was not destined to be the ancestor of an imperial line. Pomponia was divorced by Agrippa, that he might marry Augustus's daughter Julia; several years later, after Agrippa's death, Augustus ordered Tiberius to divorce Vipsania for the same reason; and Vipsania's son Drusus, who remained Tiberius's heir, died in 23 A.D., allegedly poisoned by a rival.[1]

Lucius Cornelius Balbus was a man of quite a different type who likewise prospered during the revolutionary years. Born to a wealthy family belonging to the native aristocracy of Gades, Spain, and brought to Rome by Pompey, Balbus acquired Roman citizenship and accumulated an enormous fortune. He was Caesar's agent as early as 60, helping him organize the First Triumvirate. In later years his multifarious services as Caesar's confidential secretary and

---

[1] Drusus's daughter Julia was murdered in 43 A.D. at the order of Messalina, the infamous wife of the Emperor Claudius, and for forty years her friend Pomponia Graecina wore mourning for her. This Pomponia was undoubtedly a relative, though not descended from Pomponius Atticus, who left no male heirs to perpetuate his name. Tacitus tells us (*Ann.*, xiii, 32) that in 57 Pomponia "was accused of some foreign superstition," which scholars often interpret as meaning Christianity. This supposition is strengthened by the discovery, in a Roman catacomb dating from the early third century, of an inscription commemorating a Pomponius Graecinus who was a Christian and presumably a relative of this lady. It would be pleasant to think that the family of our Atticus was among the first upper-class families at Rome to embrace Christianity, but it is best not to be too sure.

business agent were invaluable, and his power immense. On one occasion Cicero remarked that he had noticed that whatever Balbus said or did was later ratified by Caesar. Balbus was equally valuable to Octavian, who rewarded him with the consulship in 40. Thereafter

The Family of Atticus

T. Pomponius Atticus	AUGUSTUS	Pomponia = Q. Cicero

Pomponia = (1) Agrippa (2) = (2) Julia

Vipsania = (1) TIBERIUS (2) = (3) Julia (2) = (2) Agrippa

Drusus = Livilla (sister of CLAUDIUS)

Emperor's names are in small caps. The Julia mentioned twice is one and the same person.

we hear less of Balbus, though he remained in Octavian's entourage, and our last glimpse shows him with Agrippa beside Atticus's death-bed in 32.

Agrippa, too, was an equestrian like Atticus, and we shall presently see that he and the Etruscan Maecenas should be counted with Octavian himself among the direct founders of the Roman Empire. These two companions of Augustus will appear frequently in the next chapter.

The Revolution in the Provinces

The half century separating Sulla's dictatorship from the battle of Actium was also marked by great changes in the provinces of the Roman Empire. In Sulla's day there were ten provinces, to which four others were added during the next twenty years.[2] Then Caesar added Africa Nova (Numidia) in 46, and the triumvirs set up two more provinces at uncertain dates. Illyricum, along the eastern shore of the Adriatic, was ruled by the governor of Cisalpine Gaul until

---

[2] The first ten provinces, with the dates of the establishment of each, were as follows: Sicily, 227; Sardinia-Corsica, 227; Hither Spain, 197; Further Spain, 197; Macedonia, 148; Africa, 146; Asia, 129; Narbonensis, 121; Cilicia, 102; and Cisalpine Gaul, 89, which became part of Italy in 42. The next four additions were Cyrenaica, 74; Bithynia, 74–64; Crete, 67; and Syria, 63. Cyprus was annexed as part of Cilicia in 58.

the incorporation of that province into Italy in 42 made a special government necessary; and at about the same time Greece, formerly under the general supervision of the governor of Macedonia, became the province of Achaea. Client-kings ruled Thrace, central and eastern Asia Minor, Palestine, and Mauretania under the triumvirs; and a few recently conquered territories, notably Gallia Comata, were still under military rule awaiting a permanent settlement. When Octavian annexed Egypt (30), he gave it a special status in the Empire. In later years he rounded out the Empire in several directions, especially in the Danube Valley, but before his death the days of the great annexations were over.

When the various provinces were first set up, one after another, each was given an elaborate charter, or *lex provinciae*, under which it was governed thereafter. While these charters differed widely according to conditions in each province, a few general principles underlay them all. Details might be changed from time to time at Rome, especially regarding such matters as the appointment and tenure of Roman officials, but the *lex provinciae* itself was a treaty not easily altered. In the first century before Christ a Roman promagistrate (proconsul or propraetor) was sent out to govern each province, while a proquaestor received and forwarded to Rome the tribute collected by the publicans. The governor had Roman troops to defend the province from foreign aggression and to maintain domestic peace but, except in case of war, he spent most of his time in the administration of justice. All cases concerning Roman citizens came to him to be settled according to the *lex provinciae* or, if that proved inadequate, according to the governor's own edicts or the general principles of Roman law. The tribute coming in from the various provinces usually was enough to defray the entire cost of the government at Rome, and Roman citizens were relieved of all direct taxes after 167. It is only fair to add, however, that under ordinary circumstances the sums taken by Rome as tribute were probably no larger than would have been required by "free" local governments had Rome not annexed the province, taken over its defense, and put a stop to local wars.

The Roman provinces were simply administrative units, uniting

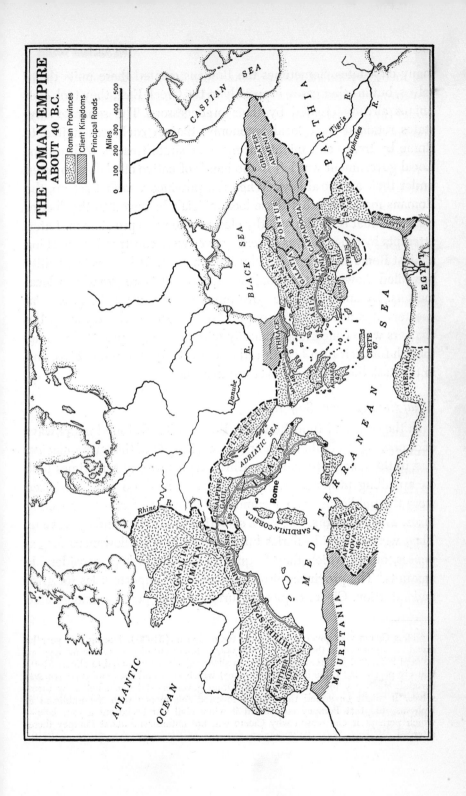

THE ROMAN EMPIRE
ABOUT 40 B.C.

Roman Provinces
Client Kingdoms
Principal Roads

Miles
0 100 200 300 400 500

many city-states. Sometimes the Romans created these units themselves, but in other cases, especially in the Greek East, they took over
unions already created by their predecessors. The separate city-
states retained their local autonomy, though each was united to
Rome by treaty and might not make separate treaties with others.
Local government was left in the hands of native officials who acted
under their ancestral laws. When the province was first set up, the
Romans made sure that these local officials belonged to the "better
classes"—that is, to the wealthy classes who were pro-Roman. Later,
attempts by other natives to seize power were construed as rebellion
against Rome and suppressed by Roman arms. As long as tranquility
prevailed, however, the Romans did not interfere greatly in local
matters. By and large, the government provided by the provincial
charters was not unjust or oppressive. The men who drew up the
charters were concerned primarily with assuring a peaceful regime,
though for their own benefit rather than that of the provincials, and
in this task they generally were successful.

What the Provinces Suffered

In the course of time, however, Roman officials found many ways
of oppressing and robbing their subjects in spite of the *lex provinciae,*
and in the first century before Christ their rapacity sometimes took
on appalling proportions. As we have seen, those most criticized
were the publicans, who accumulated enormous fortunes collecting
taxes. The governors, too, were sometimes dishonest and oppressive.
They were not paid salaries but received liberal allowances for expenses, out of which they frequently saved and kept considerable
amounts.[3] The provinces also provided many opportunities for graft
and extortion. Cicero depicts in lurid—though perhaps exaggerated

---

[3] Thus Cicero was governor of Cilicia for one year (51–50). During this year he
saved and returned to the treasury 1,000,000 sesterces out of his expense money; but
he kept 2,200,000 sesterces for himself. In silver value this amounted to almost $100,-
000 (in purchasing value it was much more) which, over and above all expenses, was
certainly good pay for one year's work. Other governors did much better by themselves. It might be added that Cicero invested this money with the publicans at
Ephesus, and that Pompey confiscated it when civil war broke out a year later—
which perhaps is one reason why Cicero was not enthusiastic about Pompey thereafter.

—colors the crimes of Verres in Sicily, and another illustration of this side of Roman imperialism came under his observation while he was governor of Cilicia.

One day a certain Scaptius appeared before Cicero and demanded military aid in collecting a large debt owed by the citizens of Salamis in Cyprus. Investigation revealed that Scaptius was charging the Salaminians interest at the rate of 48 per cent a year on the pretext that loans to cities were illegal and hence not collectible at law. It was also shown that powerful friends at Rome had subsequently persuaded the senate to legalize this particular loan, and that when, in the previous year, Roman cavalry had been sent to collect the interest, the local senate took refuge in its meeting-house where five senators died of starvation before the others finally agreed to pay at the extortionate rate. And finally, it came out that the real lender of the money was none other than the noble Brutus himself. Amazed at these disclosures, Cicero refused to authorize the use of troops again. Instead he induced the citizens of Salamis to offer interest on the loan at the legal rate of 12 per cent, which Scaptius haughtily refused. Our knowledge of the affair stops at this point, but it is not improbable that Cicero's successor helped Scaptius get his money. When Cicero returned to Rome, he was duly punished for his audacity in opposing the interests of his betters. Brutus's uncle, Cato, during whose rule in Cyprus (58–55) the loan had been made, persuaded the senate merely to return thanks to the gods for Cicero's accomplishments in Cilicia rather than to order the triumph upon which Cicero had set his heart. The right to starve provincial senators who disliked paying 48 per cent interest to Roman aristocrats seems to have been a fundamental aspect of that Liberty upon which Brutus and Cato descanted so eloquently.

The provinces suffered grievously during the Civil wars. Campaigns were fought in most of them, and Roman generals did their best to defray expenses by looting before and after each battle. Greece was especially unfortunate, for she was forced to bear the burden of three major campaigns—Pharsalus, Philippi, and Actium —and the armies that ranged over her countryside were those particularly given to looting—those of Pompey, Brutus, and Antony.

When Caesar's troops captured Pompey's camp at Pharsalus, they
were amazed to find countless works of art and other treasures seized
in the Greek cities. Even when fighting for their very lives, Pompey's
aristocrats found it impossible to make their itching fingers behave.
Antony's troops on the eve of Actium lacked this aristocratic refinement of taste, but if Plutarch's account is to be trusted, they made
up for it with excessive brutality. Greece was left in a pitiful condition, and though it enjoyed a slight revival in the first two centuries
of the Christian era, it never again became a factor of real importance in the economic life of the Mediterranean basin. Other provinces were less unfortunate, but all suffered severely, and many years
passed before their former prosperity returned.

Caesar's opposition to the hated Pompeians made him more popular than the other Roman generals in the provinces. He augmented
this popularity by promising many things to the provincials, but we
can discern no large plan of his for reorganizing the Empire. As a
matter of fact, Caesar probably had not thought deeply upon the
matter. At first the triumvirs merely passed provinces around among
themselves in the traditional way, but presently another spirit began
to appear. After Octavian obtained Gaul by the settlement at
Brundisium in 40, he sent his friend Agrippa to reorganize and govern it. Agrippa was a brilliant administrator who helped the province
greatly. Other such men were given governorships in later years,
and in the long run they made the provinces the principal gainers
from the imperial system of Augustus.

What the Provinces Gained

It would be easy to multiply illustrations of the dark side of Roman
imperialism in the first century before Christ, but we must not forget
that there was also a brighter side and that the way was already
being prepared for better times. Not all provincial governors were
men like Verres, or even minor imitators of Pompey and Brutus.
Many did their work honestly and well, but they are unknown to
history because no one sued them for extortion when they got home.
While Cicero was not a great provincial administrator, he did what
he could to check the extravagances of Romans in his province, and

his efforts apparently won him the gratitude of the Cilicians. Undoubtedly there were many others like him. Moreover, the charges brought against governors were frequently just a part of that general *vituperatio* which every Roman politician had to give and take. Even those governors who committed grave crimes were not wholly bad. Cicero was very severe upon a certain Gabinius, a governor of Syria who accepted enormous bribes, yet the Jewish historian Josephus considered Gabinius a good governor—and Josephus was not given to praising those who oppressed their peoples. If only we had a complete list of the provincial governors and their works, we undoubtedly would find a high average of ability and integrity during these last years of the Republic.

At any rate, it is certain that during the fifty years here in question many things were done in the provinces which were later to prove blessings. In the first place, the Romans brought peace and protection from domestic and foreign enemies. We have frequently had occasion to refer to the disastrous intercity wars in Greece before the coming of the Romans, and conditions in Gaul were much the same before Caesar's conquest. By stopping such wars and threats of war, the Romans conferred an enormous benefit upon the provinces. This benefit may have been obscured for a time by wars among the Romans themselves, but when the Civil wars were over, it appeared that foundations had been laid for the beneficent *pax Romana* inaugurated by Augustus. Moreover, the Romans brought stable government, thus ending the fear of social revolution that had obsessed the Greek cities for so long and driven them to such extremes of repression and explosion. When the governing classes knew that Roman arms would keep them in power, they no longer feared possible rivals, and their relief from fear in turn brought the populace relief from tyranny. It is true that the local governments supported by Rome were highly aristocratic. They rested, as Cicero remarked, upon the "better classes." But these better classes were a commercial rather than an agricultural aristocracy, whose interests favored peace, the perpetuation of Roman rule, and the closer union of the various parts of the Empire for commercial reasons.

The Romans also developed and improved the road system of the

Empire. There had, of course, been roads long before the Romans came. The Persians had built their famous Royal Roads, the Hellenistic monarchs had improved them, and even Gaul had fair roads before Caesar, as is proved by the speed with which he marched his legions about. Roman engineers greatly improved the surfaces of these roads and built new ones; Roman armies made them safe from robbers; and Roman governors centered their attention upon the districts traversed by them. In fact, the Roman province has been well described as a road and its defenses. Cisalpine Gaul was the Aemilian Way from Ariminum to Milan; Transalpine Gaul was the Domitian Way from Italy to Spain; Macedonia was the Egnatian Way from the Adriatic to the Aegean; and Cilicia was the road from the Aegean to Syria. Cicero spent his year in Cilicia traveling back and forth along this road from Laodicea to Tarsus. While these roads were primarily routes for the Roman legions, their economic value to the provinces was greater than the tribute exacted by Rome, and they were as important as the legions in holding the Empire together.

The Romans had not at this time developed an imperial patriotism among their non-Roman subjects, nor had they tried to do so. Nevertheless, many of the measures taken during these fifty years tended in that direction and later became the foundation of such patriotism. The Latinizing of Italy was virtually complete, and Latin culture was rapidly spreading through the western Mediterranean area. Italian colonists in Gaul, Spain, and Africa, as well as the Italian business men who followed or even preceded the legions, and the governors and their trains, all carried with them the Latin language, Roman customs, and Roman law. Presently the superior merits of this Roman culture were obvious even to the natives, and they adopted it willingly.

On the other hand, the Romans were quite willing to see Greek culture prevail throughout the East. In the Asiatic provinces they supported Greek culture against its oriental rivals, thus continuing the policy urged by Eumenes II of Pergamum more than a century before. In countries whose culture was far different from that of Greece or Rome, the Romans found it convenient to establish client-kings—natives with a veneer of Western culture—who governed in Rome's interest. When these countries became more civilized, they were annexed and given Roman provincial governors. Meantime, Greek or Latin culture was strengthened and encouraged in these districts by the foundation of new cities and all the other devices formerly used for the same purpose by Seleucids and Attalids.

The great Roman generals—Pompey, Caesar, Antony—were very free in conferring Roman citizenship upon provincials who aided them conspicuously. This citizenship carried with it economic and financial privileges, legal rights, and social distinction, all of which were hereditary, and it was much sought after. ("With a great sum obtained I this citizenship," declared an army officer mentioned in the New Testament. "But I am a Roman born," boasted Paul of Tarsus in reply.) These proud possessors of Roman citizenship came to form a new cosmopolitan aristocracy devoted to Rome. The Mediterranean world was thus being made ripe for unity, economically, socially, and politically. Even the Civil wars did not nullify the unifying achievements of these fifty years, and on these foundations was built the glorious Augustan Age.

Intellectual Criticism of the Old Order

Much has been written in ancient and modern times about the moral decay of Rome in the first century. It is well to remember, however, that complaints along these lines had been a standard feature of Roman political propaganda, at least since the days of Cato the Censor, so the lurid tales of political agitators need not always be taken as giving completely objective pictures of Roman society in their day. It cannot be denied that men's views on many matters were changing rapidly, partly because of changed social conditions, partly in consequence of a hundred years of Greek education. Whether these changes are taken as denoting progress or decay depends, of course, upon the point of view of the critic, but in any case the change was accompanied by vigorous criticism of the old social order.

The poet Ennius had declared, long before these changes began, that the Roman state rested upon an ancient way of life and men.

In his day men's conduct and ideas still were determined to a remarkable degree by the *mos maiorum* (ancestral custom), as set
forth in the strongly organized patriarchal family and religion. A
century later this was no longer the case. Enlightenment and intellectual criticism had undermined these foundations of the social
order. Persons who continued to exercise rigorously the old *patria
potestas* were now regarded as brutes, and those who trembled before Jove's lightning were considered superstitious old fools—as indeed they were in each case. Educated men and women had come
to regard blind devotion to tradition as odious or ridiculous, and
public regard for the ancient religious cults declined to such a
degree that Varro once expressed a fear lest the old gods perish
because of the neglect of their worshipers. This spirit of freedom
and emancipation reached its climax in the years immediately following Pompey's return from the East in 62. Money then circulated
freely, the whole world seemed safe, and life was gay and easy for
the upper classes at Rome.

The New Woman

One phase of this new freedom found expression in the changed
position of women. Though Roman women had always received
more liberal treatment than their sisters in Greece, their emancipation now went to such lengths that the apprehensions of old-
fashioned Romans were deeply stirred. The decline of the patriarchal family, in which marriages were a family affair arranged by
the parents, led to an increasing number of divorces, often on
frivolous pretexts. Even Cato could not resist the spirit of the times,
and when another man declared that he wished to marry Cato's
wife, and she confessed a desire to marry him, Cato would not refuse
a divorce. He even attended his wife's second wedding. When the
new husband presently died, leaving his entire fortune to his wife,
Cato at once remarried her—thus prompting Caesar's sneer that the
austere Stoic had done very well by himself in renting out his wife
to the old millionaire. Cato's half sister Servilia, the mother of
Brutus, was a new woman of another type. Beautiful, intelligent,
highly educated, and ambitious, she became Caesar's mistress. He

gave her, among other things, a pearl of fabulous price, and many years later he permitted her to buy the estates of condemned Pompeians at trivial prices. Even as an old lady Servilia played politics successfully behind the scenes. Still other new women began to play a more open part in Rome's political life. Hortensia, daughter of a famous orator, became a skilled and respected pleader in court, and at the opposite extreme Fulvia, wife in turn to Clodius, Curio, and Mark Antony, showed her skill at rousing the mob in the forum. And Livia Drusilla, Octavian's third wife, became one of the most influential persons of her day (see Plate 17).

Clodia, sister of the notorious tribune Clodius, is often cited as an illustration of the decadent aristocratic lady of the time. What we know of her is derived almost wholly from two enemies, Cicero and the poet Catullus, each of whom defamed her remorselessly. She seems to have been a brilliant and talented young woman who, during these gay years, made herself the magnet holding together a group of wits whose lighter diversions were interspersed with serious discussions of literature, philosophy, and politics. She was the mistress of Catullus—one of Rome's best lyric poets. He glorified her in his poems as "Lesbia" while in her favor, and he damned her with equal genius when she cast him off for another. It was she who made Catullus a great poet. We have also seen that Cicero was suspected of wishing to marry her, which may account in part for his later venom against her.

Clodia's young friends sometimes turned their wit to stripping away the sham from such prominent political figures as Cicero. They came to admire the realistic political methods of her brother Clodius, who cynically invoked democratic idealism when it seemed expedient and at other times terrorized Rome with hoodlums and armed slaves. The bright young men of Clodia's acquaintance soon shed whatever principles or convictions they may once have held, and they made the *mos maiorum* a subject for mirth. They wished only to acquire position and wealth as quickly as possible and to scintillate while doing so. Yet Clodia's friends were able and attractive young men, and several of them went far.

Another of Clodia's lovers was Caelius Rufus, whom she later

accused of trying to poison her. Rufus was a young aristocrat who
had studied oratory under Cicero just as his teacher was preparing
to run for the consulship, and thus had ample opportunity to observe
the great man in his shirt sleeves. Later he wrote a series of brilliant
letters to Cicero during the latter's proconsulship in Cilicia, keeping
him posted on political and other events in Rome; and we have
already seen how he joined Caesar in 49, became praetor in 48, and
was killed when he attempted to supplant the dictator by stirring
up the lower classes against him. Other young men who frequented
Clodia's circle included Curio, Dolabella, and Mark Antony. Their
number also included Sallust, who became one of Rome's great historians.

It must not be assumed, however, that all the ladies of the Roman
aristocracy resembled Fulvia or Clodia. The more conventional of
them usually escaped the attention of historians, but Appian, in his
account of the proscriptions, recounts many of their heroic deeds.
One Roman matron of the highest type was immortalized by her
husband in a beautiful inscription, a fine monument of Latin literature, that is now known to scholars as the *laudatio Turiae.* Here her
husband records how she courageously defended the estate while
he was serving in Pompey's army and how she saved his life at the
risk of her own during the proscriptions. She obtained his pardon at
the cost of all her jewels and of insults and even blows from Lepidus.
When she bore him no children, she offered to let her husband divorce her, but he indignantly refused. For forty-one years they lived
together happily while she managed the household and cared for his
mother as for her own. Modest, gracious, unostentatious, and
friendly, religious without being superstitious, she had performed
every wifely duty well.

Greek Philosophy: Lucretius and Cicero

Other young Romans were meantime absorbing from Greek
philosophy ideas that were quite incompatible with the old Roman
scheme of things. Old Cato had foreseen the dangers of a Greek
education and had denounced them; but during the century following his death Greek ideas spread rapidly at Rome. After Sulla many

young Romans studied philosophy at Athens or in other Greek cities, and Rome was full of Greek teachers and philosophers. Greek philosophy led to speculation about political and social matters along lines that were foreign to the Roman spirit, and it raised grave doubts about the religion which had played so great a part in justifying the Roman *mos maiorum*. Cato and Brutus called themselves Stoics; Sulla, Caesar, Cassius, and Atticus confessed to being Epicureans; and Cicero preferred his own blend of Platonism and Stoicism. While these philosophical sects differed in many ways, they all agreed in explaining away the old religion.

The most impressive of these attacks upon the old religion is to be found in Lucretius's great poem *De rerum natura* ("On the Nature of Things"). T. Lucretius Carus was born about 99 and died in 55. We know little about his personal life except that he belonged to an aristocratic family and that he left his poem unfinished. Though he was much admired and imitated by Vergil and others of the next generation, he seems to have lived as a recluse, little known in his own day. The *De rerum natura* is an exposition, in six books, of the Epicurean philosophy. The mechanical aspects of atoms and the void do not lend themselves readily to poetic treatment, yet amidst the discussions of such matters Lucretius delights the reader with many passages of rare poetic beauty dealing with nature and man. Through the whole poem runs a high moral earnestness rarely surpassed in literature. Lucretius was filled with humanitarian zeal and he was persuaded that a knowledge of the truth—that is, of Epicurus's philosophy—would free men from the sufferings which he attributed to the old religions. Early in the poem, after a moving account of the sacrifice of Iphigenia, Lucretius exclaims, "How great the evils which religion can accomplish!" He then explains belief in such figments of the imagination as gods and human immortality as the product of fear. "Fear first brought the gods into the world!" One of the most interesting parts of the poem is a long passage in which he traces the history of life on earth and the progress of humanity from crude savagery to civilization, implying that if men have already accomplished so much, they could do even more if freed from this fear. Such an attack upon religion for moral reasons throws a brilliant light upon conditions at Rome in the poet's day, when the official religion actually constituted a bulwark of class tyranny. At the same time the lofty spirit of humanitarianism which inspired Lucretius shows conclusively that he was at heart a deeply religious man. One of his keenest modern critics has written a chapter entitled "l'anti-Lucrèce chez Lucrèce"—"Lucretius Against Himself." He was in truth an inspired religious prophet, and like all great prophets he bitterly denounced the conventional religion of his contemporaries because it did not come up to his own high standards.

Lucretius was a Roman aristocrat, a member of the class that felt itself born to rule, yet he said little of politics. It is perfectly clear that he had only horror for the whole militaristic and imperialistic system of the post-Sullan period; and though disgust with the world of his day drove him to philosophy, he continued in the belief always shared by the best Romans that good laws and good magistrates can do much to improve the state of suffering humanity. The charge of defeatism and world-flight has often been leveled against Epicurus and his disciples. Perhaps some of them deserve it, but not Lucretius. It is not by defeatism and world-flight that a man becomes one of the world's great philosophical poets, fit to be mentioned with Dante and Goethe and Milton.

Cicero too was deeply influenced by Greek philosophy, though in a different way, and he was equally anxious to use its teachings to improve Roman society. In his later years he speculated and wrote much on philosophical, ethical, and religious subjects, especially after the death of his beloved daughter Tullia in 45. These writings often take the form of dialogues, in the Platonic style, and while Greek ideas are discussed, and sometimes accepted, the words are put into the mouths of famous Romans of earlier days (especially the circle of Scipio Aemilianus) and are given a thoroughly Roman sense. As we would expect, however, the most important of his writings are those devoted to political theory—the *De re publica* and the *De legibus.*

The *Republic,* begun in 54 but not finished until three years later, weighs the merits and weaknesses of various forms of government; and the *Laws,* at which Cicero was working in 46 though it was not published until after his death, describes imaginary political and religious institutions supposedly fit for all "free" men. Cicero pictured his ideal state as a restoration of the old Roman Republic, but in reality it was something quite new. He believed that this state would unite the merits of monarchy, aristocracy, and democracy. Each class of society would have its place and its share in the government, thus realizing that same "concord of the orders" which Cicero had preached in 63. Cicero's state, unlike Plato's, would be a world state rather than a city-state, for he had learned—partly from the Stoics, perhaps, but more especially from the events of his own day—that the civilized world was one world and that consequently there should be "one law, eternal and immortal, for all races and times." Cicero's most original contribution to the actually existing Roman government was the idea that there should be a leader to direct the state with the aid of the "best men." The second book of the *Republic* contains a history of early Rome—wholly legendary, of course—showing that all the kings except the last were leaders of this sort. A long section then discusses the qualities such a leader should have. Some writers have suggested that in composing this passage Cicero was drawing an idealized portrait of Pompey; more likely he was thinking of himself.

Historians and Scholars

An interesting and instructive way to trace the intellectual development of the first century is to study the works of the Greek and Roman historians then writing about earlier times. A people can be judged by the history in which it believes, and especially is this the case with Romans of the revolutionary period. Their historians were not scholarly recluses but public men, so closely associated with the events of the day that their changing views, if properly studied, form an excellent index to the thinking of their contemporaries. Moreover, history was the most important type of literature flourishing at Rome in the last days of the Republic. The only significant poets were Lucretius and Catullus; oratory was rapidly degenerating into mere panegyric and invective; and other types of literature scarcely existed. History itself showed a sad decline from earlier standards, yet the Roman historians well expressed the thought of their day and became potent forces influencing the minds and actions of their fellow men.

Of course Rome, like every other city, had always had historians, and in early times these men had created a mythical history of Roman origins. Part of this historical romance was vaguely true, but more of it was not, and it is to be feared that, in the minds of most Romans, the mythical part seemed more important than that which was true. The myth, for example, told how Romulus, the founder of the city and its first king, was the son of the war god Mars and of a Vestal Virgin, named Rhea Silvia, who was descended at several generations from Venus. Romulus allegedly gave his new city its laws and customs, directing it along the warlike path it was destined to follow. The second king, Numa, completed the laws and organized the Roman religion, with the aid of the nymph Egeria whom he secretly visited at night in a grove near the city. The last three of Rome's seven kings were Etruscans (this bit of the legend was vaguely true), and the last of them was driven out by Lucius Brutus, who "established liberty and the consulship." Legend then went on to recount the great deeds of countless heroes of the Republic during its early days.

All Roman schoolboys were carefully indoctrinated with this legendary history of Rome, and its influence in determining their later character and conduct cannot be passed over lightly. Marcus Brutus, the "Liberator," may be cited as an extreme case of the influence of legendary history. He mistakenly believed himself descended from the Lucius Brutus who drove out the last king and founded the Republic, and he joined the conspirators in the fond belief that he would be emulating his glorious ancestor in murdering Caesar. If legend thus powerfully influenced the actions of a man of Brutus's intelligence and education, what must it have done for lesser Romans?

Besides this legendary history there was a more accurate version preserved in the archives of the *pontifex maximus* and, as we have seen, in the politically calm days at the middle of the second century scholars began rewriting Roman history from these ancient records.

Historical criticism thus undermined the old legends to a considerable extent and encouraged the general social criticism that began at the end of the century. But at the same time new schools of historians arose who concocted a "new history" and put it to political use. The scholarly history that had begun to appear in the second century was largely still-born, being quickly superseded by this new propagandist history.

History as Political Propaganda

Much of the new history was biographical, or autobiographical, and frankly panegyric. Even in the second century there had been laudatory biographical sketches of such heroes as Scipio Africanus and Cato, and after the Gracchi this form of writing took on new importance. Gaius Gracchus published an oratorical biography of his brother Tiberius, emphasizing his humanitarian zeal and recounting the portents which showed that he was under divine favor; Sulla wrote his autobiography in semifabulous form, stressing the divine aid he received on many occasions; and Pompey hired literary men to write his life, incorporating therein large sections from the Alexander romance. In reality the writers who composed these biographies were creating a literary portrait of the ideal leader, and their writings later had an influence in determining the history of Rome. We shall see that in the period of reconstruction that came after Actium, Augustus was presented to the public as a sort of composite incarnation of all these idealized portraits. The historians of the Republic must therefore be counted among the founders of the Roman Empire.

The best of the autobiographers was Julius Caesar, whose Commentaries are the only works of the sort that have come down to us complete. Caesar was intelligent enough to omit the absurdities that defaced most of the works just mentioned—being an Epicurean, he did not believe in portents and divine intervention—and he gave a simple, straightforward, and thoroughly credible account of his campaigns. There is no way to verify the accuracy of his narrative of the Gallic wars, though we know that his contemporaries sometimes criticized it severely. His account of the Civil wars, on the other hand, may be compared with other accounts, which bring out its merits and its defects. In it we must admire the skill with which Caesar exaggerated his own good points, passed over his failures, and yet created the impression of complete candor. He made it appear that he did everything possible to avoid a break with Pompey, that he did not shed very much Roman blood, and that after hostilities opened he was always in perfect control of the situation. Caesar was one of the world's master propagandists, yet there is something about these books which raises them above the level of mere propaganda.

While panegyrists were thus embellishing and idealizing the lives of popular leaders, other writers were composing more general histories of Rome. At least six persons wrote accounts of the Gracchan troubles within a few years of Gaius's death, and several wrote about Sullan times. These authors frequently began with summaries of Roman history from the time of Romulus, and in some cases the introductions were longer than the narratives of contemporary events. The authors professed to be writing impartial history, of course, yet their works were as highly propagandist as were the panegyrical biographies. They wrote history to defend one faction or the other in the mighty struggle of their own day, finding precedents in the past for everything that happened. They thus projected the Gracchan agitation and the Marian disturbances back to the very dawn of Roman history. Most of these writers favored Sulla, but the best of them, C. Licinius Macer,[4] defended the popular side. In order to convict his opponents of error and develop the achievements of the popular party, Macer diligently studied whatever ancient records he could find. This scholarship caused Livy, who lived fifty years later, to quote him more frequently than any other Latin writer, and he became the main source for the "struggle of the orders" on which Livy focuses the early history of the Republic.

---

[4] Macer had held high offices before Sulla and was tribune in 73; the aristocrats accused and convicted him of extortion in 66, and he died shortly thereafter. Cicero presided at his trial, and wrote to Atticus that his chief interest lay in the effect of his decisions upon his approaching candidacy for the consulship. Various legends presently grew up about Macer's sudden death upon his unjust conviction. Cicero, *ad Att.* i, 4; Plutarch, *Cicero*, 9; Valerius Maximus, ix, 12, 7.

Livy's account of the fourth century before Christ therefore reflects Rome's class struggles at the beginning of the first.

Mention must also be made of Asinius Pollio, who wrote a history of Rome from the founding of the First Triumvirate to the battle of Philippi. After serving with Caesar in Gaul, Pollio crossed the Rubicon with him—from Pollio we learn the celebrated story of how Caesar said, "The die is cast!"—and later he supported Antony. Pollio was consul in 40, but he retired to private life when Antony and Octavian quarreled. Writing in a calmer period, after the wars were over, Pollio produced a rather dispassionate history much used by later writers. His history, like all those mentioned here, is now lost, but we know much of what it contained from quotations and summaries by two second-century writers, Plutarch and Appian.

Sallust

Among the historians of the late Republic was one whose genius raised him far above the others. C. Sallustius Crispus was born in the Sabine country in 86, and as a young man he went to Rome seeking a career. He apparently was a member of Clodia's circle, and his intrigue with the wife of Pompey's gangster Milo caused her husband to give him a public horsewhipping which the poet Horace was still laughing about thirty years later. After serving as quaestor in 54, Sallust became tribune in 52. He then distinguished himself by his demagoguery and shared with Fulvia leadership of the mob that burned down the Senate House after Clodius's death. In 50 he was expelled from the senate by a Pompeian censor because of his disordered private life—plus his Caesarian sympathies. Caesar soon returned his henchman to the senate, entrusted him with two minor military commands, and in 46 appointed him governor of Africa Nova. Sallust made himself a millionaire before his patron's death, but he fell into disfavor with the Second Triumvirate. He retired to his villa on the outskirts of Rome in the magnificent *horti Sallustiani*, "Sallustian gardens," (later the residence of Emperors) and devoted the remaining years of his life to literature. He died in 34.

Sallust published a scurrilous *Invective* against Cicero in 54— perhaps at the order of Caesar's father-in-law, Calpurnius Piso, whom Cicero had attacked a short time before. Early in the Civil wars he wrote and published two enthusiastic *Letters* to Caesar, flattering his hero extravagantly and suggesting various reforms. After his retirement from politics Sallust turned to historical writing. His first two productions were brief monographs, entitled respectively *De Catilinae coniuratione* and *Bellum Jugurthinum,* which have survived entire. Then came the *Historiae,* covering the years 78–67 in five books. Although it was widely used by later writers in antiquity, only fragments of this work now remain.

The end of Sallust's life thus stands out in sharp contrast to its beginning, but we can trace the steps by which the debauched and demagogic spoilsman became a moralist and a philosophical historian. The *Catiline* was as much a defense of Caesar and an attack upon Cicero as was the *Invective*. It has even been suggested that he wrote the book in the hope of ingratiating himself with the triumvirs, just as his *Letters* had brought him important appointments from Caesar. During the years since he wrote the crude *Invective,* Sallust had learned to make his propaganda more subtle and effective by posing as an impartial historian. He did not attack Cicero directly, but systematically belittled his part in the Catilinarian affair, sneered at him, used irony against him, and patronized him. He quoted the orations of several persons, but none from Cicero, the most noted orator of the day. By a refinement of wit and malice he even had Catiline deliver a speech to the conspirators with the opening words of Cicero's most famous oration, *Quo usque tandem!* Careful scholars believe that Sallust drew most of his facts from Cicero's posthumously published history of the conspiracy, entitled *De consiliis suis,* merely retelling them in another style in order to defame Cicero. Sallust also attacked the whole aristocracy, picturing Catiline as a typical member of that class, and returning time and again to their general moral decay—of which he had seen so many illustrations in his own youth. Evidently the subject grew upon him as he wrote, and presently he found himself attempting a serious inquiry into the causes of the Roman Revolution. The *Jugurtha* continued these investigations, showing an earlier stage of aristocratic decay, and the *Histories* carried them still further, opening with a terrifying ac-

count of Sulla's dictatorship and praising such popular heroes as
Sertorius and Macer.

A pessimistic strain ran through Sallust's books as he sadly deplored the decline of civilization. At first he thought that this decline
had begun with the destruction of Carthage in 146, but in the *Histories* he traced it still further back, making all Roman history a
story of decadence except for a few periods. In the early years of
the Republic and the time of the Punic wars, for example, fear of
foreign enemies had kept Rome pure. This degeneration he attributed to personal avarice, luxury, and political corruption. Sallust's vivid depiction of these vices[5] gave his writings a highly
moralistic turn which made him a favorite with the philosophers and
even with the Christians.

World Histories: Pompeius Trogus

While these historians were writing in the spirit of the factional
quarrels at Rome, others were composing histories from quite a different point of view. The writers already mentioned concerned
themselves with Roman history; others preferred to study the past
of the various peoples of the Roman world and to write world history. Various attempts at such synthesis had been made after Alexander's armies had momentarily given political unity to the world,

---

[5] An example of Sallust's skill in depicting vices may be seen in his character sketch
of the noble conspiratress Sempronia. "Now among these women was Sempronia, who
had often committed crimes of masculine daring. In birth and beauty, in her husband
also and children, she was abundantly favored by fortune; well-read in the literature
of Greece and Rome, able to play the lyre and dance more skillfully than an honest
woman need, and having many other accomplishments which minister to voluptuous-
ness. But there was nothing which she held so cheap as modesty and chastity; you
could not easily say whether she was less sparing of her money or her honor; her desires were so ardent that she sought men more often than she was sought by them.
Even before the time of the conspiracy she had often broken her word, repudiated her
debts, been privy to murder; poverty and extravagance combined had driven her
headlong. Nevertheless, she was a woman of no mean endowments; she could write
verses, bandy jests, and use language which was modest, or tender, or wanton. In
fine, she possessed a high degree of wit and charm" (*Cat.*, 25, Loeb tr.).

These unforgettable lines may best be taken as an example of standardized Roman
vituperatio. They may or may not contain an element of truth; but the same charges,
sometimes in identical words, are brought by other writers against Clodia, Fulvia, and
many others. Sallust probably selected Sempronia as the victim upon whom to show
his skill because she was the mother of Decimus Brutus, Caesar's friend who later became one of his assassins.

and they were renewed after Roman arms had repeated Alexander's achievement. While patriotism kept Roman writers from realizing that other peoples had an important past, several first-century Greeks or Greek-speaking Orientals wrote world histories.

Thus a certain Alexander, nicknamed Polyhistor, who was brought to Rome from Miletus as a slave in the days of Sulla, wrote separate histories in Greek of some fifteen eastern countries. It was from him that later Greeks and Romans learned most of what they knew about oriental history. At about the same time Diodorus, a Sicilian Greek who lived at Rome from about 60 to 30, compiled an immense work which included within a single narrative the history of mankind from its beginning to Caesar. About half of his book is still extant. The most important of these eastern universal historians was Nicolas of Damascus, born in 64. As a young man Nicolas was employed as tutor for the twin children of Antony and Cleopatra. After Actium he ingratiated himself with Herod of Judea, whom he served as minister for many years, and in his old age he attached himself to Augustus at Rome. His great work was a history of the world in 144 books, of which considerable fragments survive. It covered everything from the Creation, through the oriental empires, the Greeks and Alexander, the Hellenistic monarchies and Rome, down to Herod and his own day. His was the most ambitious attempt made in antiquity to write universal history, and his book reflected the point of view of the East and the client-kings, of Antony and Cleopatra and the "Donations of Alexandria," rather than that of Rome and the West.

These universal historians collected huge masses of material which they had neither the time nor the skill to criticize, digest, or put in readable form. History and mythology were inextricably commingled in their works, and details were hopelessly wrong. The shears and paste-pot were their principal tools in research. From the standpoint of the modern scholar, they committed almost every sin of which a historian is capable. About all that can be said in their favor is that they often showed a wider, profounder, and truer comprehension of what was going on in the world about them than did their more polished Roman contemporaries. In the long run, these men prevailed. Their conception of the course of world history was in closer harmony with the facts, and it could more easily be reconciled with the Biblical history of the Christians. Eventually Christian writers adopted it and passed it on to the Middle Ages and the early modern world.

Pompeius Trogus was the only important Latin universal historian, and he was not a Roman. His grandfather, a native of Transalpine Gaul, received Roman citizenship from Pompey; his father helped Caesar in Gaul; but of the historian himself we know nothing. He probably did not finish his history until a dozen years after Actium, yet he belongs to the period of Caesar and the Second Triumvirate. His ambitions and his point of view were then settled, and the sources upon which he relied for facts and ideas date from this period. In his *Philippic History* Trogus wrote the history of the world from the beginning to his own day in forty-four books. The first six books were devoted to the oriental monarchies and early Greece; Philip of Macedon appeared in Book VII; and the remainder of the work, as its title suggests, was concerned with Philip's Hellenistic successors and the coming of the Romans. As the different cities and nations appeared upon the stage, the history of each is traced to legendary origins, and thus something is said about nearly every Mediterranean people.

Trogus was distinctly anti-Roman, speaking bitterly of Rome's aggressiveness and keeping her in the background as much as possible. Only in Book XLIII did he give a cursory sketch of Roman origins, in which he emphasized her early lawlessness, and this he followed immediately with an equally full account of the origins of Massilia, stressing her civilizing influence! He devoted two whole books to the Parthians, two more to a eulogy of Rome's archenemy Mithradates, and he was very kind to Hannibal. This anti-Roman bias may have been occasioned by Trogus's Gallic ancestry, or by unfortunate experiences at Rome, but in large part it was a legacy of the Greeks and Greek-speaking Orientals from whom he learned his history. He set forth the historical views of Rome's eastern critics. However, he admired neither the Persians nor the Macedonians. He was primarily an anti-imperialist, and his sympathies went to

~~those who fought against the great empires~~—to the Greeks at Marathon, later to Mithradates and to the Parthians. Trogus was rarely mentioned by his pagan successors—perhaps because of his defective Roman patriotism—but in the third century there were many persons, even in the Latin West, who were rather glad to see Rome's orthodox history exploded. Trogus's history was then revived and abbreviated by a man named Justin, whose abridgment received the respectful attention of both pagans and Christians.

Two other deeply-learned men of this period deserve notice because of the breadth of their views and their importance for later writers and thinkers. One was the antiquarian M. Terentius Varro. Born in the Sabine country in 116, Varro was educated at Rome and Athens. He held the offices of tribune and praetor, served as a member of the commission that put in force Caesar's Agrarian Law of 59, and in 49 he commanded two Pompeian legions in Spain that surrendered to Caesar. After forgiving the commander, Caesar employed him to collect books for a great library that he planned. Thereafter, until his death in 27, Varro devoted himself entirely to his studies. He was an immensely learned man, whose seventy-five books in over six hundred volumes (rolls of papyrus) covered an enormous field—philosophy, philology, law, mathematics, history, agriculture. His *Antiquitates*, published in 47 and dedicated to Caesar, contained a great amount of recondite information about ancient rites, ceremonies, religious and political practices, and the like, and it is to his studies of Roman chronology that we owe the traditional date 753 for the founding of Rome.

Another influential thinker of this period was the Greek philosopher Posidonius. He was born at Apamea in Syria about 130 and spent his youth as a student in Athens. He later lived in several Greek cities, was awarded citizenship at Rhodes, traveled as far as Spain, and died at Rome in 51. His intellectual interests were as wide as his travels. Though best known today as a philosopher and as the renovator of Stoicism, Posidonius also wrote on natural science and geography, and he composed an important history, continuing that of Polybius and chronicling world events from 146 to Sulla's dictatorship. This book is now lost, but modern scholars suspect that it had a great influence upon subsequent writers in antiquity. Posidonius was also much interested in astrology, and it was he who formulated the general principles of that art which are still repeated today by its practitioners.

The first century before Christ was thus a period of great intellectual activity in the Roman world. Men of many sorts were wrestling with the problems raised in their rapidly changing age, and their answers were of more than academic importance. They intensified the confusion of the times, and they influenced all subsequent history. For example, it is possible to point out many close similarities between the ideal state depicted in Cicero's *De re publica* about 51 B.C. and the actual state established by Augustus a quarter of a century later. Most of the other Roman writers mentioned above likewise contributed something to the Augustan system. Nor did the influence of these writers stop with Augustus. They were rather under a cloud during the great days of the Roman Empire, it is true, for conditions then were very different from those prevailing in the last days of the Republic. In the fourth century, however, the Republican writers again rose to prominence, for society was once more going through rapid changes and the ideas and writings of the earlier revolutionary period again seemed both interesting and important. When writing his great work on *The City of God*, early in the fifth century, St. Augustine relied heavily upon these various first-century writers for his knowledge of ancient Rome and his appreciation of her grandeur. From Varro St. Augustine derived his knowledge of the old Roman religion; from Trogus even more than from Livy he learned the course of profane history; and from Cicero he took fundamental ideas regarding the nature of government. Sallust's story of Rome's moral decline he swallowed whole, drawing largely upon the *Histories* for his illustrations of the decay of the pagan city. It is a far cry from Clodia's gay garden parties to the moralizings of the greatest of the Church Fathers, yet we can clearly trace the line connecting them.

Part Three: The Roman Empire

XI Augustus's World Empire

OCTAVIAN'S VICTORY AT ACTIUM, FOLLOWED BY THE deaths of Antony and Cleopatra, brought an end to the Roman Republic and to the Hellenistic Age. The Roman and Hellenistic worlds were united, and Alexander's dream of world unity at last was realized by Octavian. The new master of the world began where Alexander had stopped, and again it fell to a young man to rule the civilized world. It is an interesting coincidence that when Cleopatra died in 30 B.C., Octavian was just thirty-two years old, within a month of Alexander's age at the time of his death in June, 323. During the intervening three hundred years, however, much had happened to lighten the task of world government. The idea of world unity was no longer merely the dream of a conquering genius, but was shared by men of every sort and condition. The world had learned its need for unity from businessmen and from philosophers, as well as from Hellenistic kings and from Roman generals, and above all it had learned the lesson from its own tragic sufferings under the Hellenistic system of rival monarchies. At last men were prepared economically, idealistically, and politically for the world empire that Rome had created by military force. Octavian succeeded where Alexander's successsors failed—and where Alexander himself would doubtless have failed too—because his empire had foundations more substantial than the brilliant victories upon which the Macedonian conqueror had based his hopes. The Roman built upon foundations laid by others, it is true, yet his success bears wit-

ness to a genius equal to that of the more dazzling military hero who
preceded him.

Octavian and His Associates

Octavian had now been in public life for almost fifteen years, and
he had acquired the qualities and experience required of a ruler and
pacifier of mankind. He was a person of high intelligence, great
tact, and infinite patience, able to distinguish what was possible
from what was not. He knew how to retain the loyalty of his friends,
and he possessed an amazing skill at sensing public opinion. He had
received a careful education in his youth, and in later years he bestowed honors and important posts upon his teachers, but he was
burdened with no doctrinaire theories about government. Had he
been so encumbered he would never have survived the chaotic decade following Caesar's death. Though many of his teachers and
much of his education had been Greek, he did not absorb the cosmopolitan spirit then shown by so many Greeks, but remained as
thoroughly Roman as old Cato himself. He had learned much from
such widely different Romans as Caesar and Antony, Pompey and
Cicero, and even from the younger Cato, and he was a model of
Roman dignity and sobriety. He therefore was well fitted to champion Roman institutions, the Roman way of life, and the Roman *mos
maiorum.*

Historians have sometimes accused Octavian of being a "hypocrite of genius." In support of this charge, they point to his deathbed
remark that he hoped he had played his part well, a statement which
might, of course, be twisted into a confession of conscious hypocrisy.
Nevertheless, the profounder students of Octavian's career believe
in his fundamental sincerity. While he was immensely ambitious
and insisted upon holding first place in his new world, he was willing
to conceal his power behind the ancient forms of liberty. This con-
cealment was not proof of hypocrisy so much as evidence of a statesmanly realization that, if he were going to rescue the world from
civil war, he must retain old forms while adding new powers to the
central government. He therefore made peace with the old aristocracy, "restored" the Republic, and announced a return to the good

old days. At the same time he avoided frightening those who had profited by the revolution, and he convinced everyone of the beneficence of his rule. Meantime, he and his assistants were quietly building up a new political machine which gradually took over the government. Few people in his day realized how far the old Rome had been left behind, and even Octavian failed to recognize the extent of his changes.

Ancient writers were so bedazzled by Octavian's glamor, and so intent on perpetuating his name, that they paid little attention to his associates. It is therefore difficult to write the biographies of these helpers, though they were men of high ability and importance. First among his assistants was Octavian's boyhood friend, Marcus Vipsanius Agrippa. He was beyond question the ablest general and administrator of his generation. Agrippa commanded the armies which waged the most difficult campaigns, he organized new provinces, and he pacified unruly peoples from Spain to Syria. He set up new administrative machinery, constructed roads and other public works in many parts of the Empire, and beautified Rome and the provinces with temples and monuments. When we reflect upon these multifarious activities, we cannot fail to suspect that Agrippa's share in founding the Roman Empire was about as great as Caesar's or Octavian's. Though an equestrian by birth, he was recognized as Octavian's heir for several years before his death in 12 B.C., and his descendants eventually ruled the Empire. Octavian's other lifelong friend and associate was Gaius Maecenas, an Etruscan noble whose gifts for diplomacy were first revealed during the negotiations at Brundisium in 40 B.C. Like Octavian, Maecenas was quick to sense public opinion, and we shall see that his encouragement of artists and literary men brought the intellectual leaders of Rome over to Octavian's side.

Restoration of the Republic

Soon after returning from Egypt in the spring of 29 B.C., Octavian took up the task of making his leadership of the new world secure. First he celebrated a three-day triumph for his various victories. The spoils of Egypt enabled him to pay off his soldiers and to provide more than 100,000 veterans with homes in Italy or the provinces. In every case the land thus distributed was bought rather than confiscated, as had been the usual procedure. Vast sums were devoted to public works in Italy, and Octavian presented each Roman citizen with 400 sesterces (about $16). These spectacular events, plus the end of the wars, made Octavian the most popular man in the world.

Political reform next claimed Octavian's attention. For many years he had been formulating his plans, and the first steps toward the establishment of a new political order had been taken long before Actium. Octavian had often promised that the Republic would be restored as soon as possible, and now that his last enemies were destroyed, there was no good reason why his promise should not be fulfilled. Important people were showing dissatisfaction with his delays, and there was a growing enthusiasm for the old Republic. Octavian therefore went before the senate on January 13, 27 B.C., and formally returned the government to the Roman senate and people. This act did not mean that the government automatically became what it had been before Caesar crossed the Rubicon. No intelligent person expected or desired that to happen. It simply meant that the senate would again have a share in formulating public policy. As Octavian and the senate had already agreed on the powers each would hold, appropriate legislation was enacted at once. Four years later, in 23 B.C., the *comitia* passed a fundamental law defining Octavian's position in greater detail. Further constitutional changes were introduced during succeeding years, but before Octavian's death in 14 A.D. he and his associates had worked out the general lines along which the Roman world was governed for almost three hundred years.

When Octavian laid down his extraordinary commands in 27 B.C., the senate conferred upon him the title "Augustus." As this honor came at just the time when the wars ended and Octavian's civil career began, historians emphasize the change by calling him Augustus thereafter—though he always called himself Caesar. His life as Augustus was not characterized by dramatic events. He took part in only one more military campaign, against the Cantabrians in Spain (26–24). Thereafter he devoted himself conscientiously to the routine work of administration. His health was always bad, and on several occasions his life was despaired of, yet he outlived nearly all his early associates. In his old age there were few persons in active political life who could remember a time when he had not been head of the state.

Shortly before his death, Augustus prepared a statement of his achievements which was later inscribed on his mausoleum in Rome and displayed in various provincial cities. This statement he entitled simply *Res Gestae* ("Things Accomplished"). Though the original inscription at Rome has been lost, parts of several copies—either in Latin or in Greek translation—have been found, and almost the whole text is now available. Here Augustus listed his military victories and triumphs, the offices he held and others he refused to accept as being inconsistent with old Roman institutions, and the laws by which he tried to restore the old Roman manner of life. He detailed his gifts of money and food to the people, his buildings and public works, and the shows and gladiatorial combats he provided. He enumerated his territorial additions to the Empire, and the colonies he founded, and finally he specified the honors bestowed upon him by the senate after he had ended the Civil wars. These were the things for which Augustus wished to be remembered. Soon after completing this statement he died, on August 19, 14 A.D., aged seventy-five years. A few weeks later the senate proclaimed him *Divus Augustus* and ordered that he receive divine honors.

The New Republic

In the *Res Gestae* Augustus declared, "I transferred the Republic from my own control to that of the senate and Roman people. . . . Thereafter I stood ahead of others in authority though I held no more power than my colleagues in various magistracies." The word here translated "authority" (*auctoritas*) refers to the influence enjoyed because of prestige and popularity while "power" (*potestas*) is the term indicating what a magistrate might legally do. This phrase sums up what Augustus wanted the general public to believe about his position in the Republic after 27. He wished his position to be that of a leader, freely accepted by the people because of his superior merit and achievement—a leader such as Cicero had written about in his *Republic* and *Laws.* His first formal step toward such leadership was the oath of fidelity which he administered to the peoples of Italy and the West just before the Actium campaign. Similar oaths were taken later by the inhabitants of other parts of the Empire. The title "Augustus" pointed in the same direction, for it implied that he was something more than an ordinary man—yet not a god—and that therefore he deserved such leadership. Many years later, in 2 B.C., the senate conferred upon him the title *pater patriae* ("Father of the Fatherland") which perhaps meant more to ancient Romans, with their traditions regarding the *patria potestas,* than the same words signify to us today. The most satisfactory title found to express the new leadership, however, was *Princeps* ("First") which indicated that its bearer was the First Citizen of Rome. Augustus's successors retained these titles until Diocletian's reforms three hundred years later, and the Roman government during these three centuries is sometimes called the "Principate."

Whatever the theory may have been, Augustus did not rely solely upon his prestige. He made his position secure by very slight modifications of powers long held by consuls and tribunes. Augustus had been consul in 43 and in 33; he held the office every year from 31 to 23; and he served twice thereafter, making a total of thirteen terms. In 27 he arranged with the senate that consular *imperium* (command) should be given him in all the important provinces where troops were stationed, which automatically made him commander of their armed forces. This assignment of provincial commands followed old Republican precedent, except that Augustus held a large number of important provinces while no possible rival might hold more than one. Thereafter provinces were classified as "imperial" and "senatorial," with all the former under Augustus's direct control while the latter were assigned to various senatorial governors. When Augustus laid down the consulship in 23, he was granted proconsular *imperium* in all parts of the Empire for ten years, and this grant of power was formally renewed by the senate for five or ten years at the end of each period (see map, p. 437).

Augustus's second fundamental powers were those of the tribune.

Since adoption by Caesar had elevated him to the patrician class, he was not formally eligible to the tribuneship. Nevertheless, in 36 the senate had granted him the *tribunicia potestas* ("power of tribune") formerly held by Caesar, and either in 30 or in 23 it extended this power for life. After 23, Augustus advertised the *tribunicia potestas* as his most important power, mentioning it first in inscriptions and decrees requiring the use of official titles. It made his person sacrosanct; it gave him the power to veto legislation or the acts of other magistrates and to propose laws; and above all, it made him appear the champion of the people in succession to the great tribunes of Republican times. Since he was granted these offices for life or for many years, he was not under any necessity of being re-elected every year. Though there were other consuls and tribunes, he was recognized as superior to them all, holding what was called *imperium maior* after 23. His position was thus freed from the weaknesses which had made continuous policy impossible under the old Republic. In later years Augustus accepted further offices, notably that of *pontifex maximus*, which he took over in 12 B.C. after the death of the triumvir Lepidus. On the other hand, he refused the office of dictator when it was offered him in 22, and he scrupulously avoided obvious innovations, such as a life consulship. The proconsular *imperium* and the *tribunicia potestas* gave him all the political power he needed or desired.

The Position of Senate and Magistrates

Since Augustus had proclaimed himself the champion of Liberty and the Republic, he was always circumspect and deferential toward the senate, yet conditions were such that he was not likely to have serious trouble with that body. When he returned to Rome from Actium he found a senate with over a thousand members, many of them unworthy persons who had entered under the triumvirate. Before "restoring" the Republic, he eliminated about two hundred of these men, and further purges were held from time to time until only six hundred senators remained. Vacancies caused by deaths were filled, as under the Sullan constitution, by the quaestors elected each year. Since Augustus controlled the election of these quaestors, he indirectly controlled admission to the senate. Before long there were few, if any, senators who did not owe their position to him. Moreover, Augustus enjoyed great powers of patronage, and senators who wished to profit by them must stand in his good graces. Leading senators were therefore loud in their loyalty, and the others hastened to fall into line. In fact, Augustus's difficulties with the senate came, not from its opposition, but from its obsequiousness, from the fulsomeness of its flattery, and from the honors it voted him which he deemed it unwise to accept.

Augustus, on his side, was careful to favor the old aristocratic families when making appointments, thus lessening the likelihood of effective opposition among them. But while he included young men of the great families among those whom he recommended for the quaestorship—and thus eventually for the senate—he also recommended able young men not drawn from that class. As "new men" thus became numerous in the senate, they founded a new aristocracy whose quarrels with the old families were soon to become a matter of high political importance.

Augustus avoided the appearance of setting aside Republican institutions and magistracies. The *comitia centuriata* and the *comitia tributa* met and transacted business more freely and peacefully than during the last years of the old Republic. Augustus submitted projected laws to the tribes, and the assemblies elected magistrates in the traditional way. Augustus's prestige was so high, however, that the assemblies always followed his wishes. The laws he proposed were always passed, and the candidates he recommended for office were always elected. In fact, it was not worth while to run for office unless the candidate enjoyed his recommendation, and elections became cut-and-dried affairs. Soon after his death his successor transferred to the senate the right of electing magistrates, yet no one complained of a lost liberty. The functions of the various magistrates were sometimes modified, but only to a slight degree. Since Augustus was a sort of supertribune, there was not much for the other tribunes to do, and for the same reason the consulship became rather an empty honor. During the Civil wars it had been rare for a consul to fill out an entire year in office. Augustus perpetuated this system, and it became the regular practice to elect supplementary consuls (*consules suffecti*) who presided during part of the year after the regular consuls had resigned. In this way Augustus flattered the vanity of more persons and at the same time increased the supply of ex-consuls available for tasks which, according to Republican tradition, could be assigned only to men who had held the highest magistracy.

Reorganization of the Army

Augustus's extensive military reforms centered about the establishment of a standing army. After Actium, he had sixty legions under arms, of whom he discharged rather more than half as soon as possible. Only twenty-five legions remained in 14 A.D., and for more than a century thereafter the number never rose above thirty. There were an equal number of auxiliary troops, or a total standing army of about 300,000 men. This army was made up of professional soldiers who enlisted for long periods—twenty years for the legionaries, twenty-five for the auxiliaries—and who were paid fixed wages and given fixed bonuses when discharged. The high command was entrusted to *legati* appointed by Augustus, and loyal to him rather than to the senate or to Rome in the abstract. About half the legions were stationed along the Rhine-Danube frontier, and most of the remainder were in Syria, Spain, and Africa. There were virtually no troops in the senatorial provinces, and in Italy there were only the nine cohorts (of 1000 men each) of the praetorian guard—elite troops serving as Augustus's bodyguard. At first only three cohorts were stationed at Rome, but later all nine lived in a large camp just outside the city. Augustus also maintained a permanent navy, whose principal bases were at Misenum near Naples and at Ravenna on the Adriatic.

This vast military establishment had far-reaching political and social consequences. The legionaries were Roman citizens, almost always of Italian birth, but they were stationed in frontier provinces where they usually found wives and where they often settled after their discharge. They became a powerful factor in Romanizing the provinces. Officers served shorter periods than the enlisted men, and

they moved from one province to another, thus acquiring an imperial
rather than a purely Roman or Italian point of view. The auxiliaries,
on the other hand, were provincials who received Roman citizenship
when discharged. Though the higher officers of the auxiliaries were
Romans, or at least Italians, the lesser commands fell to provincials.
Any man of ability might have a distinguished career in the army.
After serving his term he would return to his own people a person
of consequence, highly Romanized and thoroughly devoted to the
imperial system. The army thus became a factor of prime importance in the creation of imperial patriotism and of loyalty to Augustus.

Bureaucracy and Finance

While seeming to restore the old Republic, Augustus and his associates were really laying the foundations for a government by
bureaucrats, though in their day bureaucracy did not take on alarming proportions. The Roman government under the old Republic
had had almost no permanent personnel. Routine business was handled by the few elected officials and their personal assistants and
slaves, or else by slaves belonging to the state. Tasks beyond the
abilities of these men were assigned to the publicans, who eventually
came to form a sort of civil service. The collection of taxes in the
provinces was entrusted to publicans, as were the direction of the
mint, the care of roads, and countless other public duties. The grain
distributions required the services of many permanent employees,
and for this purpose Pompey had set up a staff whose organization
apparently followed lines worked out by Crassus and other wealthy
men in their private businesses, where positions of trust were given
to personal agents. Caesar entrusted important tasks to his slaves,
freedmen, and clients: the mint and the collection of taxes, for
example, were handed over to his personal slaves. Octavian inherited Caesar's slaves and generally managed to retain the services of
his freedmen and other civilian employees. Starting with this corps
of assistants, he and Agrippa slowly built up a bureaucracy of professional administrators, using personal slaves and freedmen for
many tasks but also drawing many assistants from the equestrian

order. These officials were paid good salaries, but they held office only at his pleasure, and he insisted that they perform their duties competently. Inevitably, the interests of efficiency required that more and more work be transferred from the corrupt and incompetent senatorial aristocrats to the various functionaries trained under Augustus.

The maintenance of this bureaucracy and of the large standing armies was of course highly expensive. Since former Republican officials had not been paid salaries, and booty had usually made wars self-supporting or even profitable, the old Republic had not needed an elaborate tax system. In fact, Roman citizens had paid no direct taxes since 167 B.C., and the indirect taxes (principally import duties and a tax on the manumission of slaves) had not been high. The provinces, on the other hand, had been taxed heavily and dishonestly. Their tribute had provided not only the costs of provincial government and the government of Italy and Rome, but also numerous public works at Rome and even the feeding of a large part of the Roman populace.

As income from booty virtually ceased after the conquest of Egypt, new sources of revenue had to be found. Augustus collected the old taxes more honestly, returning to the treasury at Rome a larger portion of what was actually paid. He also imposed various new taxes, such as an inheritance tax and a sales tax, upon Roman citizens and provincials alike. When these combined revenues proved inadequate for the rising costs of government, he made up the deficit out of his private funds. He was by far the richest man in the world, for he had inherited huge properties from Caesar and acquired enormous holdings during the proscriptions and the Civil wars. He received many gifts and bequests from wealthy men, and the vast revenues of Egypt he retained as his own. His payments to the treasury ran into the hundreds of millions, until his private possessions became virtually public property whose revenue went to the state.

There were several separate treasuries at Rome. The old treasury, under the direction of the senate and called the *aerarium Saturni* because the money was kept in the temple of Saturn, received the taxes collected in Italy and the senatorial provinces, and it supported the governments of those districts. The *fiscus* received taxes from the imperial provinces, and supported their government and the army. The *patrimonium* was Augustus's private wealth. A fourth treasury, known as the *aerarium militare*, was founded in 6 A.D.; into it certain new taxes were paid and from it soldiers drew their pensions. As the *aerarium Saturni* was always the most hard-pressed, Augustus gradually took over more and more functions which it could not afford, and the senate lost power correspondingly.

Social Legislation

Augustus's efforts to preserve as much as possible of the old Republican scheme of things were not limited to constitutional matters. He was careful to retain the old system of social classes and eager to revive the old Roman virtues. As in former times, members of the senatorial order were permitted to wear a broad purple (*purpureus,* actually crimson) stripe on their togas and were given the high magistracies. Equestrians, who wore a narrow stripe, might hold less important offices and commands. It was always possible for the emperor to raise a man to a higher class. Augustus realized, moreover, that outward forms were not enough, and that the Roman people needed to regain something of their former character if they were to regain their former greatness. He fostered a revival of the old religion by restoring temples, reforming priestly colleges, and reviving old ceremonies. Unfortunately, his success in this undertaking was no greater than one would expect from the preaching of an enlightened skeptic who thought a little more religion might be a good thing for the lower classes.

Augustus sought to strengthen the power of the family, which had once played so important a part in Roman life and which had recently changed so much. He also wished to strengthen the old Italian population against the flood of immigrants (largely slaves and freedmen from the Orient) which was threatening to submerge it. He therefore sponsored various laws to raise standards in marriage and to encourage childbearing. Privileges and exemptions were given to the heads of large families, divorce was made more difficult, and adultery was severely punished. These social laws were the least successful part of his program. Augustus's own private life was open to serious reproach, and the debaucheries of his daughter Julia scandalized all Rome until at last even her father learned of them and sent her into exile (1 B.C.). In Julia's defense it is only fair to repeat that on the very day she was born her father had divorced her mother Scribonia for political reasons, and that, regardless of Julia's wishes, she had been married to each of his heirs in turn. Such cynical use of marriage for political purposes was perhaps not the best way to convince Julia and the world at large of the sanctity of the marriage bond.

The Julio-Claudian Line

One of Augustus's most difficult problems concerned the succession. Being an ambitious man, he wished to found a dynasty, and he had excellent reason to fear that civil war would be resumed at his death if an heir were not ready to take over at once. The precarious state of Augustus's health lent urgency to the problem, and the fact that he had no sons made it difficult. His choice fell first upon his nephew Marcellus, whom he adopted and married to Julia in 25 B.C. This young man, who was much admired by those who knew him, died within two years. Augustus next turned to Agrippa, who was married to Julia in 21. The new heir was the second man in Rome, with the *tribunicia potestas* and a proconsular *imperium* inferior only to that of Augustus himself. Five children were born to Agrippa and Julia before he died in 12 B.C. Augustus hoped that one of his two grandsons might be his successor. Again his hopes were frustrated, for death claimed both boys in their early twenties, this being perhaps the most painful tragedy in their grandfather's long career. Nothing now remained for Augustus to do but adopt his stepson Tiberius, which he did in 4 A.D. Tiberius peacefully succeeded Augustus ten years later.

The problem of a successor arose once more when Tiberius's only son Drusus died in 23 A.D. There was by this time little serious opposition to the Empire as such, but the memory of Augustus was so strong that it seemed desirable to choose an heir from his family.

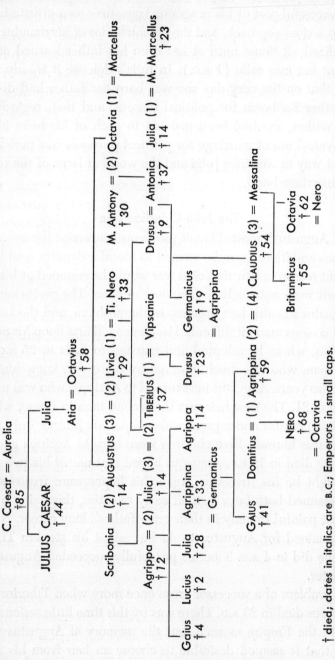

† died; dates in italics are B.C.; Emperors in small caps.
= married; numbers in parentheses indicate sequence of marriages. Thus Augustus (3) = (2) Livia indicates that Livia was Augustus's third wife, he her second husband.

This "Julio-Claudian" family fell into two groups—the "Julians," who were descended from Augustus himself through his daughter Julia and Agrippa; and the "Claudians" who, like Tiberius, were descended from Augustus's third wife Livia and her first husband, Tiberius Claudius Nero. The intrigues and cabals of these two factions distracted the court at Rome, and their struggles make up a good part of the lurid but one-sided tale told by the historian Tacitus in his *Annals*.

It long was the custom to accept Tacitus's dismal but unforgettable chronicle as the essential history of the first century. Writers commonly pictured Augustus's four successors (Tiberius, Gaius, Claudius, and Nero) as respectively a hypocrite, a madman, a fool, and a monster. Today historians paint more flattering pictures of the Julio-Claudian emperors who ruled the world for half a century after the death of Augustus.

Tiberius

Tiberius was born in 42 B.C., the son of Tiberius Claudius Nero and his wife Livia. He belonged to the distinguished Claudian family through both parents. Three years after Tiberius's birth, Livia divorced her first husband to marry Octavian. Tiberius therefore grew up at court, where he creditably performed the various tasks with which he was entrusted. For ten years he shared the government with his adoptive father and was well prepared to assume power when Augustus died in 14 A.D. He was less careful than Augustus in preserving Republican forms, but under him Italy and the provinces prospered. Had it not been for the court cabals, Tiberius would undoubtedly have been recognized as a worthy successor to Augustus.

Tiberius's aristocratic origin led him to favor the old families, even in the ten years before Augustus died, and for a short time it seemed that he might complete their reconciliation to the new regime. Instead, his favors only antagonized the newer families who supported the Julian faction, and who found a champion in Germanicus. This popular war-hero was a nephew of Tiberius, but he had been brought into the Julian faction by his marriage with Agrippina—

a granddaughter of Augustus. After Germanicus's death in 19 A.D., a second and more deadly rival to Tiberius arose in the person of Sejanus, a man of equestrian origin who was connected with the new families. His unquestioned talents raised him high in Tiberius's favor, until he became prefect of the praetorian guard. Sejanus presently began plotting to succeed his benefactor. According to rumor, Sejanus first poisoned Drusus, the son of Tiberius by his first wife and grandson of Agrippa, and then did his best to marry the young man's widow. As she was a sister of Germanicus, Sejanus was aiming by this move to become the guardian of Tiberius's grandchildren and rule in their name. For several years he successfully deceived the old man, whom he had persuaded to retire to the island of Capri near Naples, thereby acquiring a free hand for himself in Rome. Eventually, Sejanus was found out and executed (31 A.D.). This treachery of his most trusted friend was a blow from which Tiberius never recovered. He became suspicious of everyone, and he so hated the senate and Rome that he never again returned to the city. At last he died in retirement in March, 37, aged seventy-seven years. Tiberius was bitterly reviled by his senatorial enemies as a tyrant, but he was a competent administrator who saw the needs of the Empire clearly and found ways to meet many of them.

Gaius, or Caligula

The next emperor is often called Caligula though his name was Gaius—or, in full, Gaius Caesar Augustus Germanicus. He was born in 12 A.D., the son of Germanicus and Agrippina. When a child he was affectionately nicknamed Caligula ("Little Boots") by his father's soldiers because of his fondness for strutting around in military boots. He was raised by Livia and, after her death in 29, by his grandmother Antonia, the daughter of Mark Antony and Octavia. The boy had detested his great-grandmother Livia, but he was fond of Antonia, who apparently filled his mind with respect for Mark Antony and his political ideas. Antonia was responsible for the fall of Sejanus, and it was she who arranged that Gaius should live thereafter with Tiberius at Capri as his heir apparent.

The young man was not quite twenty-five years old when he came

to power, and he was received enthusiastically. Senators were relieved of the fear under which they had lived during Tiberius's embittered last days, and Gaius inherited the idealized reputation of
his father Germanicus. Nevertheless, the senate and army contained
a strong faction of old aristocrats who supported Tiberius and his
system. Though this opposition had no recognized leader capable of
playing a part analogous to that played by Germanicus in the early
years of Tiberius's reign, Gaius and his friends considered it a menace. To offset its influence, the new emperor sought to capitalize his
descent from Augustus and thus to share his great-grandfather's popularity. He greatly expanded the worship of the *Divus Augustus* and
even claimed divinity for himself—this being one way to advertise
his Augustan descent. Gaius also squandered vast sums in shows,
buildings, and unsuccessful frontier wars. When the old senatorial
families still opposed him, he went out of his way to insult the senate,
on one occasion naming his horse a member of that body. Several
plots were formed against him, and at last he was murdered in January, 41, after a reign of slightly less than four years.

Immediately after the death of Gaius, the conspirators called a
meeting of the senate to proclaim a restoration of the Republic. It
was plain to be seen, however, that no one really wanted the old-
style Republic and that each of these self-styled "Republicans" secretly hoped to become emperor himself. Two days were filled with
the quarrels of rival candidates. Meantime, the praetorian guard was
taking more effective steps to perpetuate the political system to
which it owed its existence. Soon after the assassination of Gaius, a
squad of praetorians captured his uncle Claudius and carried him
off to their camp. Here Claudius won over the guard by promising
each soldier an enormous gift (15,000 or 20,000 sesterces, $600 or
$800). At their bidding, the senate obediently proclaimed Claudius
emperor, and the last attempt to restore the Republic failed igno-
miniously after forty-eight hours.

Claudius

Claudius had been born in 10 B.C., a younger brother of the great
Germanicus and a grandson of Livia. He was a sickly child, slower

than others in his intellectual development. His backwardness made him the butt of family jokes and caused Augustus to keep him out of sight as much as possible. Though in time he outgrew his weaknesses, it was only after his reputation as a fool had been so thoroughly established at court that no one took him seriously. As a young man Claudius had shown scholarly tastes which were encouraged by his tutor, the historian Livy. This tutor, who had remained a Republican and a Pompeian at heart, made a deep impression upon his pupil. Many years later Claudius quoted him in speeches to the senate and professed to be continuing old Roman traditions as set forth by Rome's greatest historian. Under Livy's encouragement young Claudius undertook to write a history of Rome since the death of Caesar, but when he expressed views differing widely from Augustan orthodoxy, he was forced to abandon the project. His subsequent studies were confined to the safer fields of Etruscan and Carthaginian antiquities, though he ventured to write a defense of Cicero. As works of scholarship these books probably did not stand in the first rank—we know them only by title—but because of them Claudius's critics held him up to ridicule as a pedant. The training that Claudius underwent in his historical studies bore fruit later in his patience with routine details of government, his humane view of Rome's mission in the world, and his use of evolutionary concepts of government in an effort to solve contemporary problems.

When Claudius came to power he found himself handicapped by the fact that his veins contained none of the precious Julian blood of which Gaius had been so proud. He therefore strove to surpass his predecessor in vociferous loyalty to the memory of Augustus, and in official documents he declared that Gaius had been a lunatic. In general, however, Claudius was a conscientious and hard-working man, responsible for an immense amount of good, but he could never live down the popular conception created by his enemies, who ridiculed his alleged stupidity and pedantry and his matrimonial misfortunes. His third wife Messalina was a thoroughly debauched woman who cared for nothing but pleasure. She sold honors and offices, ruthlessly destroyed her enemies, and it was said that she even went through a marriage ceremony with a man who hoped to murder Claudius and succeed him as emperor. She was finally put out of the way by Claudius's agents in 48. Claudius then married his niece, the younger Agrippina (daughter of Germanicus and the elder Agrippina) who by an earlier marriage was the mother of Nero. Claudius apparently hoped that this union would effect a reconciliation between the Julian and Claudian families. He had his new wife declared Augusta and put her portrait beside his own on coins. He married her son Nero to his daughter Octavia, and even set aside his own son Britannicus in favor of his stepson Nero. When Claudius died in 54, at the age of sixty-three, he was promptly declared a god by the senate. Agrippina's enemies later declared that she had poisoned Claudius with a dish of mushrooms.

Nero

Nero's father, Gnaeus Domitius Ahenobarbus, was a degenerate member of a distinguished Republican family. Though Domitius is supposed to have remarked that no son of his and Agrippina's could possibly fail to be a monster, the boy received a careful education. His tutor was the eminent Stoic philosopher Seneca, who later became his prime minister. When Claudius died, Nero was not yet seventeen years old. At once he was proclaimed emperor by the praetorians and accepted by the senate. During the next five years Agrippina and Seneca waged a desperate struggle for the control of Nero. Seneca won by lauding the boy's artistic genius, by encouraging his taste for athletics and shows, and—so it was said—by procuring him mistresses. Nero came to hate his mother so cordially that in 59 he had her murdered. Seneca then governed the Empire with the aid of Burrus, prefect of the praetorian guard. When Burrus died in 62 his post went to a young man named Tigellinus, whose skill at debauching the emperor so far surpassed Seneca's that the philosopher withdrew in despair to private life. Seneca had been virtual ruler of the Roman Empire for several years, and he ruled so well that the period of his power has since been called the "golden quinquennium."

Nero was popular as long as Seneca ruled, but he lost public favor after Tigellinus took control. Under this malign influence Nero divorced his wife Octavia, who was an estimable woman, and married his mistress Poppaea. Octavia was exiled and later executed. A disastrous fire at Rome in 64 gave Nero's enemies further opportunity for criticism, some of them alleging that he had started the fire, or at least that he had "fiddled while Rome burned." A plot was formed against Nero in 65, which was discovered only at the eleventh hour. Seneca himself was implicated, and with several others he was forced to commit suicide. At about this time, too, Nero murdered Poppaea in a fit of temper. As he was both unhappy and afraid at Rome, he made a spectacular visit to Greece in 66. Here he competed for various literary, artistic, and athletic prizes and each time he was awarded first place—even, according to reports, in competitions which he had not entered. In return for this empty flattery, he showered substantial favors upon the Greeks, exempting the province from all tribute.

Affairs at Rome had taken a turn for the worse during Nero's absence, and his ministers insisted that he come home. Shortly after his return, several legions on the Rhine frontier revolted, and the senate declared Nero a public enemy. He attempted flight, but finding it impossible to escape, he committed suicide—whimpering, it is said, "What an artist dies in me!" (June 8, 68). He was only thirty years old. Though bitterly maligned by later Romans, and branded antichrist by Christians, Nero was in some ways pathetic rather than terrible and, like Gaius, he had little influence upon the development of the imperial system. With Nero, the family of Augustus and the Julio-Claudian line came to an inglorious end.

Early in the year 68 certain senatorial aristocrats had begun plotting against Nero. The conspirators planned to establish their authority with legions brought from the Rhine frontier. Their first champion, a man named Vindex, aroused the legions in Gaul but was easily defeated and killed by loyal troops. It was news of this revolt that caused Nero's flight and suicide. The senate and praetorians at once proclaimed as his successor an old man named Sulpicius Galba, the last member of a noble family prominent in Roman politics for three centuries. The historian Tacitus sums up Galba's character as "free of vices rather than distinguished by virtues," and declares that "all men would have considered him equal to empire, had he never been an emperor." Galba ruled for only a few months. His obvious incompetence soon tempted a certain Otho—heretofore known only as a discarded husband of Poppaea—to march on Rome early in 69 with legions from the Rhine. Galba was murdered, and Otho took his place. Otho fared no better than the claimant whom he displaced, and within four months he committed suicide after being defeated by legions under the command of a general named Vitellius. Before the year was out, the armies of still another commander, Vespasian, defeated and killed Vitellius. The year 69 is therefore called the "year of the four emperors." The last of the four, Vespasian, was a strong man who ruled well for ten years, founded a new dynasty, and opened a new chapter in Rome's imperial history.

Rome and Italy in the First Century

The Roman Empire reached its natural limits in the days of Augustus. On the west and north it was bounded by the ocean, the Rhine, the Danube, and the Black Sea, and on the east and south by deserts. Within these frontiers there dwelt perhaps sixty-five or seventy million persons.[1] They could reasonably claim to constitute the civilized world, for the Romans were ignorant of the civilizations then

---

[1] We have the figures for three censuses taken by Augustus but they included Roman citizens only: in 29 B.C. there were 4,063,000 citizens; in 9 B.C., 4,233,000; and in 14 A.D., 4,937,000. A census taken by Claudius in 48 showed 5,984,072 citizens. It is very difficult to calculate the total population of the Empire, and all published estimates contain much guesswork. The most systematic study was made long ago by J. Beloch (*Die Bevölkerung der griechisch-römischen Welt*, 1886), who placed the total figure under Augustus at about 54,000,000, distributed as follows by millions: Italy, 6; Gaul, 5; Spain, 6; North Africa, 6; Sicily and the islands, 1; Danube provinces, 2; Greece and the Balkans, 3; Asia Minor, 13; Syria and Palestine, 6.5; Egypt, 5.5. Nearly all subsequent investigators have regarded Beloch's figures as too low, especially those for Italy, Gaul, Spain, Syria, and Egypt. They would add 2,000,000 or 2,500,000 for each of these areas, and 2,000,000 to 3,000,000 elsewhere. Others would put the total considerably above the maximum of 70,000,000 suggested in the text. The population of the Empire rose to almost 100,000,000 toward the middle of the second century, the increase being especially notable in Syria, Egypt, North Africa, Spain, and Gaul.

flourishing in China and India. Agrippa collected a large amount of statistical information about the Empire, taking censuses in various provinces and estimating their resources, primarily for the purposes of taxation. On the basis of these investigations he prepared a great map, with an elaborate commentary. Augustus ordered the map displayed publicly in order to impress people with the extent of Roman rule. Though both map and commentary have disappeared, the latter was used by such writers as the geographer Strabo (who wrote about 6 B.C.) and Pliny the Elder (23–79 A.D.). From their works, and from historians and recent findings of archeology, it is possible to attempt a survey of the Roman world in the first century.

The New City

The troubled decade preceding the Civil wars had shown that the old Republican system could not even govern the city of Rome in a satisfactory manner. The activities of Clodius showed what could happen. Caesar and the triumvirs pacified the city with their troops, but it remained for Augustus to establish permanent order. He therefore stationed three "urban cohorts" of one thousand men each—not to be confused with the praetorian guard—in the city as a police force under the command of the *praefectus urbi*. This prefect, who received his appointment from the emperor, was a senator of consular rank who eventually took over most of the municipal government. The first fire department (the *vigiles*) was organized under the command of a prefect of equestrian rank.

Meantime, other bureaus had been established to look after other necessary aspects of the government of the city. A famine in 23 B.C. forced Augustus to resume grain distributions, and in 2 B.C. he made arrangements whereby 200,000 persons received free food thereafter. Even for persons who were not paupers the food supply was a matter of serious concern until 6 A.D., when an office was set up under a *praefectus annonae* to make sure that grain arrived regularly and in quantities sufficient for all. This prefect also bought food for the army, and eventually the operations of his office covered most of the Empire. Agrippa had built new aqueducts and sewers and had set aside two hundred of his own slaves to keep them in repair. These men he bequeathed to Augustus, who made them the nucleus of a new bureau.

As it was desirable to find something to occupy the attention of the lesser men whose political power had passed to the emperor's agents, Augustus divided the city into fourteen wards and subdivided these into 265 precincts, in each of which citizens elected petty officials to perform minor functions. Actually, these officials had nothing to do except conduct a few religious ceremonies. The government of the city was held tightly in the emperor's hands, but Rome was better governed, and a safer and healthier place in which to live, than it had ever been before.

Augustus wished Rome to be a beautiful city, worthy of her position as queen of the world. He therefore spent millions in embellishing his capital. On the Palatine Hill he built an imposing palace to serve as his residence and to house his offices. He erected temples and basilicas in the forum, and when the old forum was no longer large enough, he opened a new one near by, dominated by the temple to Mars the Avenger which he had vowed at Philippi when he avenged Caesar's death. The emperor built or rebuilt eighty-two temples in the city as well as several libraries, theaters, and baths. He also prepared a magnificent mausoleum for himself and his family. Roman nobles were asked to rebuild or repair public buildings which their ancestors had erected, and if they were financially unable to do so, the emperor gave them the money.

In all these public works Agrippa was the emperor's most energetic assistant. As aedile in 33 B.C., he had distinguished himself by donating more than one hundred beautifully decorated fountains to the city and by setting up three hundred bronze or marble statues. Agrippa later constructed baths, a portico, a bridge across the Tiber, and especially the temple which was rebuilt after a century and a half as the Pantheon. The emperor's other great counselor, Maecenas, tore down many old buildings in the heart of the city to make way for a system of public parks which was to be much expanded by other emperors of the first century. Perhaps the most celebrated monument of the times was the "Altar of the Augustan Peace," erected by the senate to glorify Augustus and the *pax Romana* (see Plate 18). Its magnificent sculptures commemorated the idealism of the Augustan age. In his last days Augustus uttered the celebrated boast that he had found Rome brick and left it marble. Though he was speaking figuratively, referring to the Roman constitution which he had put on a firm foundation, his boast was as true architecturally as it was politically.

The New Italy

Though the government of Italy outside the capital was not much changed by Augustus, the whole peninsula profited by the establishment of the Empire. The reforms of the revolutionary period had raised all Italian communities to the rank of Roman municipalities, with a high degree of autonomy in local matters. Italians continued under Augustus to elect their own city officials, and notices written on the walls of Pompeii indicate that down to the destruction of the city in 79, elections there aroused greater popular interest than had been shown in Rome for many years.

Augustus greatly improved the roads of Italy, and gave aqueducts or amphitheaters to many cities. Under his rule private citizens likewise invested enormous amounts in building all over Italy. Among the great commercial cities were Puteoli, near Naples, which was

---

• Note for Plate 18. The upper picture reproduces one panel of the frieze of the Ara Pacis Augustae, or "Altar of the Augustan Peace," set up in Rome by Augustus in 13 B.C. The central figure in the panel is Tellus, or Mother Earth, with children playing on her lap, grain and flowers in the background, fruits, a cow, and a sheep beside her. She represents the fertility and prosperity of the whole world, as encouraged by the Augustan Peace. The two figures beside Tellus—Air, to the left, with a swan, and Water riding on a sea monster— complete the idea of Augustus's universal dominion. The frieze had several other panels, all developing the theme of the Augustan Peace, and it is often said to represent the highest achievement of Roman Imperial art.

The second picture shows a religious ceremony known as the Suovetaurilia, or sacrifice of a pig, a sheep, and a bull. The tall officiant at the right is burning incense on the altar, preparatory to sacrificing the victims held by assistants. The carving dates from the middle of the first century after Christ, and it has been suggested that the celebrant is an emperor, probably Tiberius or Gaius.

Panel of the Ara Pacis *(Uffizi, Florence)*

Suovetaurilia *(Louvre Museum)*

Plate 18

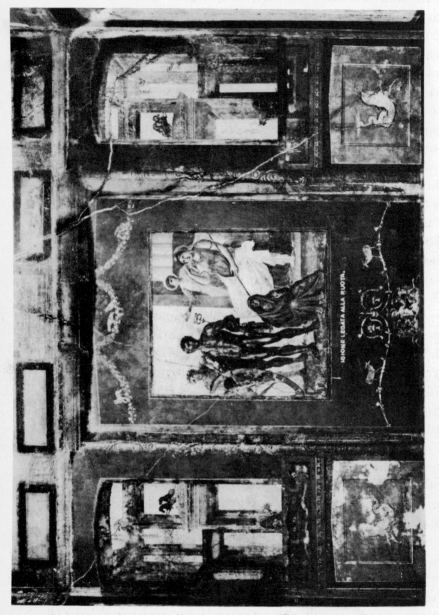

Plate 19. Pompeii: Wall Paintings in the House of the Vetii, First Century A.D.

a port for eastern trade, and Aquileia (at the head of the Adriatic) whence traders crossed the Alps to Germany. Large-scale manufacturing was of course unknown, but there were important industrial cities such as Capua, noted for its iron and bronze work, and Arretium, whose red glazed pottery was exported to all parts of the Roman world. The ruins of Pompeii contain many buildings dating from this period, whose size and elaborate construction show how wealthy the city then was (see Plate 19). Italian agriculture too was prosperous, with its wine and oil among the major articles of export. Liberty and peace had brought prosperity to all Italy. Rome and Italy were of course the economic center of the empire, and they profited tremendously therefrom, but it could no longer be said that they lived largely on loot from the provinces.

This economic prosperity fostered a fundamental social revolution in Rome and Italy. New classes of rich men arose who pushed aside the old aristocracy and gave a new tone to society. Many of the newcomers were men of humble origin whose type is well depicted in the *Satyricon,* a picaresque romance written by Petronius in the days of Nero. This book now circulates in free translation because of its pornography. Nevertheless, it furnishes readers who can overlook such blemishes with an illuminating social history of the time. Petronius recounts the rollicking adventures of a pair of scoundrels wandering through southern Italy. The climax is reached with a banquet at the rich Trimalchio's villa. Trimalchio was a freedman who became a millionaire by exporting wine from Italy, and then set himself up as a country gentleman. No longer under the necessity of demeaning himself with trade, he lent money to other freedmen—mostly Greeks and Orientals—who made his profits for him. Everything Trimalchio touched turned to gold, and his estates in Italy and Africa were so numerous that he could not keep track of them all. At the banquet attended by the two rascals, Trimalchio entertains his haphazard guests by relating his achievements and airing his views on life. For him, he says, a man is worth what he has, and it makes little difference how he got it. His amusing views on literature and art were equally characteristic of the nouveaux riches who prospered in the first century of the Empire.

Trimalchio's gaudy vulgarity and ignorance make up only half the story, however: the other half concerns his creator, Petronius. Petronius was a member of the old aristocracy who had once been an able provincial governor. Later he served as Nero's *arbiter elegantiae* —a foretaste of our own Emily Post. He was amused at Trimalchio, but not indignant; and though his satire was keen, he was quite resigned to the world he pictured. In fact, his aristocratic resignation went still further, for when he incurred the jealousy of the powerful Tigellinus, Nero ordered him to commit suicide. We are told by Tacitus that Petronius obeyed in a graceful manner. While Petronius was making this gentlemanly exit from the world, men of Trimalchio's sort were progressing to new and greater triumphs. The career of Trimalchio and that of his creator thus epitomize much of the social history of Rome and Italy under the early Empire.

The Western Provinces

The Romans had established themselves in Spain one hundred and seventy-five years before Actium, but their progress there was so slow that they held no more than two-thirds of the peninsula when Augustus began to rule. The southern province, Baetica, which consisted largely of the valley of the Baetis (Guadalquivir) River, was inhabited by peaceful farmers who caused little trouble. The other Spanish province, Tarraconensis, once a narrow strip along the Mediterranean coast, had gradually extended westward into central Spain. This province was a quagmire which engulfed one Roman army after another. Augustus was at Tarraco from 26 to 24 directing campaigns against the natives, after which he celebrated a triumph. Not until 19, however, did Agrippa crush the last resistance. A third province, Lusitania, was then carved out of western Spain and modern Portugal.

Many Romans had settled in Spain under the Republic, and colonies of veterans were sent out by Caesar and the triumvirs. Settlement continued actively under the Empire. Augustus built a great road, following earlier routes, from Narbonne south along the coast to Terraco and New Carthage. A branch of this road descended the

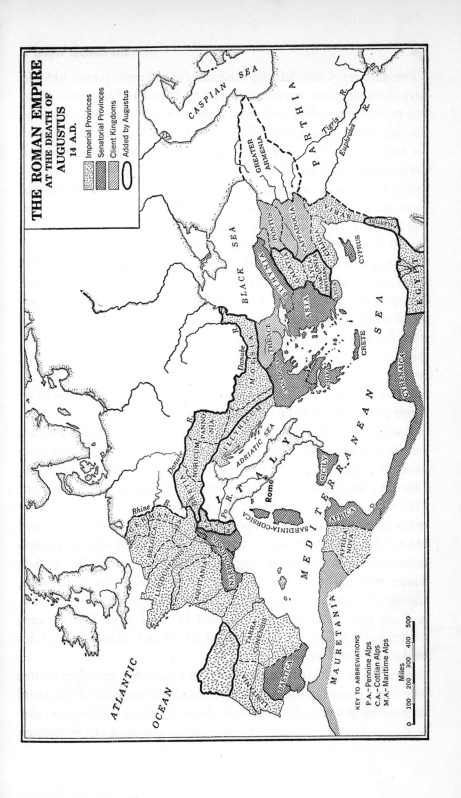

THE ROMAN EMPIRE
AT THE DEATH OF
AUGUSTUS
14 A.D.

Imperial Provinces
Senatorial Provinces
Client Kingdoms
Added by Augustus

CASPIAN SEA

PARTHIA

GREATER ARMENIA

Tigris R.

Euphrates R.

BLACK SEA

PONTUS

BITHYNIA

CAPPADOCIA

GALATIA

SYRIA

LYCAONIA

CILICIA

PISIDIA

PHRYGIA

PAMPHYLIA

LYCIA

CYPRUS

PALESTINE

EGYPT

CYRENAICA

CRETE

THRACE

MACEDONIA

MOESIA

ACHAEA

PANNONIA

ILLYRICUM

NORICUM

RAETIA

VINDELICIA

Danube R.

Danube R.

Rhine R.

GERMANIA

BELGICA

LUGDUNENSIS

AQUITANIA

NARBONENSIS

ADRIATIC SEA

I T A L Y

Po R.

Rome

SARDINIA-CORSICA

SICILY

MEDITERRANEAN SEA

AFRICA

AFRICA NOVA

MAURETANIA

TARRACONENSIS

LUSITANIA

BAETICA

ATLANTIC OCEAN

KEY TO ABBREVIATIONS
P.A.—Pennine Alps
C.A.—Cottian Alps
M.A.—Maritime Alps

Miles
0   100   200   300   400   500

Baetis through Corduba and Hispalis (near Seville) to Gades. In
later years all Spain was covered with a network of fine roads. There
was prosperous trade along these highways and by sea to Italy. The
Spanish mines, producing silver, copper, tin, iron, and lead, were
the richest in the Roman world, and Spanish olives and dried fish
were much esteemed. Urbanization made rapid progress and cities
were given Latin rights or other privileged status. In the days of
Nero, there were 175 cities in Baetica, 50 of them autonomous; the
149 cities of Tarraconensis included 45 that were thus privileged;
and 10 of the 46 cities in Lusitania enjoyed similar status. Romanization progressed so rapidly that, according to Strabo, along the
Baetis the natives were "not far from being Romans." They had
"completely changed over to the Roman mode of life, not even remembering their own language any more." Probably Strabo was
referring especially to Spaniards living in the cities, for he pictured
the rest of Spain as much more backward. Yet even if the north and
center were not deeply Romanized, Spain was so peaceful that before the time of Nero the three legions originally stationed there by
Augustus could safely be reduced to one.

Rome's second great province in the West was Africa Proconsularis, the ancient territory of Carthage. The Romans had made no
effort to colonize this district after their destruction of Carthage in
146, but colonists began to settle there in the days of Gaius Gracchus
(122 B.C.). Nearly twenty years later Marius found homes for many
of his veterans in the African province, and more immigrants arrived
in the days of Caesar and the triumvirs. The estates of Roman capitalists took on enormous proportions in the post-Sullan period.
There was much shuffling of ownership during the Civil wars,
though the general system remained unchanged until it was said,
perhaps with some exaggeration, that in the days of Nero six men
owned half of Africa. Nero executed all six and added their estates
to the *patrimonium.*

Africa was primarily an agricultural country, a principal source
of Rome's grain supply. Native workers tilled the fields of a handful
of wealthy Romans. Nevertheless, parts of Africa had been urban-
ized. The Carthaginians started this development, and the Romans

granted autonomy to the cities such as Utica that helped them in the Third Punic War. Italian businessmen soon became prominent in the cities, and Italian settlers were organized in municipalities. It was said that Caesar, shortly before his death, decided to rebuild Carthage, but nothing was done until Augustus sent out colonists in 28 B.C. The new city became the most important in Africa, and in the second century it was the third largest city in the world. Augustus also established municipal institutions as best he could elsewhere in the province, though in many cases his "municipalities" were merely the villas of rich Romans or trading posts near army camps. The Roman cities whose splendid ruins may still be seen in Africa date in general from the second and third centuries.

The protection of the province required constant attention, with natives frequently raiding it from the desert. Frontiers were therefore pushed back, partly to obtain more land and partly for the better defense of what was already held. Caesar had annexed the territory west of Africa Proconsularis as Africa Nova. When Augustus found it too difficult to govern this vast open territory, he returned it to a client king, Juba II, who was descended from Masinissa and Jugurtha. Later Claudius reannexed the whole of modern Algeria and Morocco as the province of Mauretania in 42, but many years elapsed before this region was effectively held. Roman culture in both the old and the new Africa was confined largely to the Roman settlers for, unlike the Spaniards of Baetica, the African natives adopted few Roman institutions. They continued to speak their Punic and Libyan dialects, and when the Roman ruling class had been eliminated in the last days of the Empire, the natives gladly received the Mohammedan conquerors from the East whose Arabic language and culture were kindred to their own.

The Gauls

Gallia Narbonensis had been made a Roman province in 120 B.C. though Massilia and much of the Riviera remained independent until annexed by Caesar in 49. The eastern frontier of this Gallic province lay somewhat west of the line now separating France from Italy, and its northern frontier ran southwest from Geneva, Switzer-

land, to the Pyrenees behind Narbonne and Toulouse. The rest of
Gaul, to the Rhine and the ocean, was called Gallia Comata or the
Three Gauls, and it was the part conquered by Caesar in his cele-
brated campaigns between 58 and 50 B.C.

The government of the new territory was organized by Agrippa,
who divided it into three districts—later advanced to the status of
provinces—which corresponded only roughly to the three parts of
all Gaul immortalized by Caesar in the opening sentence of his
Commentaries. Southwestern Gaul, from the Pyrenees to the Loire,
became Aquitania; the region from the Loire to the Seine was known
as Lugdunensis; and Belgica lay northeast of the Seine. All three
districts were governed from Lugdunum (Lyons). Agrippa accepted
the sixty-four tribal groups of old Gaul as the basis of his regime,
granting to each a large measure of self-government, usually under
the native aristocracy. Representatives of the different tribes were
allowed to assemble at Lyons in a *concilium* to discuss matters of
common interest to the three provinces.

Agrippa and Augustus connected the Three Gauls with Italy by
an elaborate set of roads. The old Via Domitia was rebuilt from
Turin over the Mont Genèvre Pass and down the Durance to Arles,
thence to Narbonne and Spain. This road remained Rome's principal
highway to the West, though the Via Aurelia, following the coast
from Rome to Narbonne, was also completed at this time. The main
route to Lyons lay farther north, passing through Aosta, another
Augustan foundation, and across the Little St. Bernard Pass. Under
Claudius a fourth route was built, crossing the Great St. Bernard
north from Aosta through Switzerland to the Rhine valley and Belgium. Agrippa also planned an elaborate system of roads in the
Three Gauls, but not much was done toward building them until the
days of Claudius (see map on p. 503).

Archeology has shown that the pre-Roman Gauls were a more
civilized people than Caesar's narrative would indicate. Though the
country was largely agricultural, there were some commercial and
industrial cities even before the coming of the Romans. The upper
classes were receptive to Greek culture emanating from Massilia or
perhaps from Greece itself by way of Celtic peoples on the upper

Danube. Though tribes such as the Allobroges gave Rome trouble in the years between Domitius and Caesar, there was so little unrest thereafter in Narbonnese Gaul—or Provence—that it was made a senatorial province in 22 B.C. Its capital was the old Roman colony Narbo, though Arles on the Rhone presently rivaled the older city in commercial importance. Augustus's liberality toward the province is witnessed by many fine remains: the amphitheater at Arles, the amphitheater and Maison Carrée at Nîmes (the latter a temple in honor of the emperor's two grandsons, dedicated in 1 A.D.), the arch and theater at Orange, and Agrippa's Pont-du-Gard, whose three tiers of arches carried an aqueduct across a valley near Nîmes (Plate 20). Though Massilia remained a Greek city, visited by young Romans eager to complete their education in Greek, Roman culture advanced rapidly in Provence, and we have the word of Pliny the Elder that on the whole this province was more Italian than Gallic.

The Three Gauls were less quick to accept Romanization, but they caused their Roman governors little trouble. In the second century before Christ there had been a great Gallic empire, centering in Auvergne (central France), which later fell to pieces. The ensuing confusion and the quarrels of rival local leaders paved the way for Caesar's intervention and success. The mutual hostility of the Gallic tribes aided the cause of Rome in later times, and their common fear of the Germans reconciled them to the presence of Roman legions. The aristocrats of Gaul were soon learning Latin and accepting other Roman institutions. It seems probable, however, that the lower classes continued to speak their Celtic dialects until the fourth century when missionaries from Rome Christianized them.

The Emperor Claudius had been born in Lyons and was always fond of his native city. He extended the rights of Roman citizenship rather freely in Gaul, and obtained the admission of Gallic nobles to the senate. When this measure aroused opposition, he defended it in a celebrated speech—now preserved on a bronze tablet in Lyons— in which he expressed advanced and enlightened views about making the Roman Empire a common fatherland for all its inhabitants. So successful were the Roman governors in winning the confidence of the Gauls that in 68 only a few Gallic nobles supported Vindex and Galba. Unfortunately, Vitellius's legions sacked Gaul as though it were a newly conquered province and, when they were withdrawn in 69 to fight in Italy, a Gaul named Civilis raised the standard of revolt. A Gallic Empire was proclaimed and an assembly was held at Rheims (May, 70). Here the Gallic leaders decided to remain loyal to Rome and the revolt collapsed before Roman legions arrived to stamp out its last vestiges. Even this abortive Gallic Empire bore evidence of Rome's influence, however, for it was to have been organized on a Roman model. This proved to be the last national resistance which Rome met in Gaul.

The Northern Frontier

The northern frontier of the Empire caused Augustus trouble throughout his life, and it was not firmly established until more than a century after his death. Caesar had made the Rhine a western boundary for the Germanic tribes, but the southern limits of Germany were ill defined. Illyria—roughly, modern Yugoslavia—was very loosely held by the Romans, and in 35 and 34 B.C. Augustus was forced to wage serious wars in its defense. The decade of the twenties saw further fighting there. Roman armies were sent north from Illyria, and from Italy across the Brenner Pass, into modern Austria and Bavaria, where they occupied everything north to the Danube (15 B.C.). Augustus thus added even more extensive European territories to the Empire than those added by Caesar. Claudius set up these new territories as the provinces of Pannonia, Noricum, and Raetia.

As it was desirable that troops stationed in these Danubian provinces should have safe and easy communication with those guarding the Gallic frontier, efforts were made between 12 and 9 B.C. to advance the Rhine frontier eastward to the Elbe. Tiberius and his brother Drusus were in command, and the latter gave his son the name Germanicus in honor of his victories. The campaigns as a whole were not successful, however, and presently they were discontinued. Several years later a Roman army of three legions, sent to punish a raid into Gaul, was trapped and exterminated by the

Aqueduct Near Nîmes, France

Maison Carrée, Nîmes, France

Plate 20.   Roman Provinces Under the Empire, First Century

Baalbek (reconstruction)

Doura: Men Sacrificing (Courtesy, Oriental Institute)

Plate 21

Germans in the Teutoburger Forest, between the Ems and Weser Rivers (9 A.D.). Though Germanicus partially avenged this defeat in 14, Tiberius decided thenceforth to seek no new territories. The frontier therefore remained where Augustus had left it—along the Rhine to Lake Constance in Switzerland, and thence north to the Danube. Gaius waged an unimportant war against the Germans and planned to invade Britain, but he failed to achieve the renown which was all he sought in either case. Claudius invaded and annexed Britain in 43. He also built the Via Claudia Augusta from Aquileia

---

• Note for Plate 21.   The famous temple here somewhat schematically reconstructed was located at Baalbek, a village some fifty miles northwest of Damascus in the old Coele-Syria—the region lying between the Lebanon and Anti-Lebanon mountains. Its enormous ruins still attract visitors. Here the Seleucids had founded—or refounded—a city which they called Heliopolis (Greek for "City of the Sun") because the site had long been a center for the worship of an oriental sun god. Under Augustus or Tiberius the city became a Roman colony and, like many Syrian cities, it was a center for the mingling of Graeco-Roman and oriental cultures. The largest of the three temples was begun in the days of Nero or perhaps a little earlier, the second dates from the time of Antoninus Pius, and the small "Round Temple" in the lower left was built in the third century, perhaps under the Emperor Philip the Arab. Though built in the Greek-Hellenistic style, the temples were dedicated to Syrian Baals—the larger to the sun god, whom the Romans identified with Jupiter, the others to lesser deities. The magnificent entrance and arcades are likewise Greek, but in the two later temples a certain number of oriental features appear, especially in the minor decorations. The floor of the largest temple is about fifty yards by one hundred, the whole temple area is about two hundred yards by three hundred: only a few modern cathedrals are larger. The lavishness of these temples, and of others built at Palmyra and elsewhere in the Near East at this time, is evidence of the economic prosperity brought to this part of the world by the Roman Empire. The drawing is reproduced from Theodor Weigand, *Baalbek*, Vol. I (1921).

The three men sacrificing in the lower picture are from a wall painting found at Doura on the middle Euphrates in modern Iraq. The painting dates from the first century after Christ and has attracted great attention as it is our earliest example of the new oriental style that presently spread to the West and developed into Byzantine. See J. H. Breasted, *Oriental Forerunners of Byzantine Painting* (1923).

across the Brenner Pass to Augsburg. Not until the very end of the
century did the Romans seriously resume aggressive measures, and
in the second century a frontier was finally established which gave
them the security Augustus had sought.

The Eastern Provinces

Conditions were very different in the eastern provinces of the Empire, and Roman policy there differed correspondingly. In general,
the western provinces were places of sparse population and low
culture before the Romans arrived, and there tens of thousands of
Roman or Italian emigrants found new homes. The Romans deliberately tried to Latinize the West, and in our own day the prevalence
of the various Romance languages there and the dominance of the
Roman Catholic Church still bear witness to the extent of their
enduring success. The eastern provinces, on the other hand, were
densely populated and highly civilized long before the Romans
came. The few Roman colonists sent to the East by Caesar or Augustus (most of them Greek or oriental freedmen) were soon merged
with the general population and left no traces behind them. The
numerous cities of the eastern provinces remained centers of Greek
culture throughout the period of Roman dominion. As the better
Romans of every period felt a high respect for Greek culture, they
never attempted to stamp it out. Indeed, they made it their task to
protect Greek culture against that of the Orient. Greeks and Orientals eventually learned much from Rome, but Rome never tried to
Latinize the East.

In general, Augustus and the Romans favored the Greek cities
against the oriental countryside, the Greeks against the Asiatics, and
the rich Asiatics (who usually were more or less Hellenized) against
the lower classes. These policies paid rich dividends. Trade and industry flourished in the East, the upper classes became reconciled to
Roman rule, and Greek civilization prospered. In fact, Hellenism
made more rapid progress in the Near East in the centuries of Roman
rule than it had under the Greek successors of Alexander the Great.
In consequence of these policies, however, the Orientals turned

against Rome, and it was in the provinces where they were most numerous that Rome met with stiffest resistance.

Greece and Asia Minor

Greece had suffered grievously from Sulla, Caesar, the Liberators, and Antony, and writers such as Strabo draw a pathetic picture of her condition in the days of Augustus. Perhaps they exaggerated to some extent, comparing her present status with what they believed she had been in the days of her glory, but there can be little doubt of her wretchedness. Many Greek cities were almost depopulated, fields were uncultivated, and the people were reduced to abject poverty. However, the worst was over, and in the first century after Christ Greece enjoyed the blessings of peace for the first time in her history. Though conditions began to improve, progress was slow, for Greece was poor in natural resources. Caesar and Augustus sent colonists and built new cities in the peninsula. Caesar planned a new Corinth but, as in the case of Carthage, it was Augustus who actually rebuilt the city. Recent excavations have shown that this new Corinth was well-built and prosperous and that it was a thoroughly Greek city. Augustus also founded Nicopolis ("City of Victory") near Actium, and he rebuilt Patrae on the southern shore of the Gulf of Corinth. Colonists were sent to various places in Macedonia, notably Philippi and Pella, the former capital, which Strabo says was nothing but ruins a few years before. Exhaustion assured peace, and Achaea and Macedonia could safely be made senatorial provinces with their governors residing respectively at Corinth and Thessalonica (today Salonika). Both provinces continued to live under their old laws—Macedonia according to the *lex provinciae* of 148, and the Greek cities (of which there were over forty) under treaties inspired by the principles underlying Flamininus's treaty of 196 which was virtually a *lex provinciae* for Greece. These Greek cities were members of various leagues, called *koina*, which were permitted by Rome to transact a certain amount of public business. There was a *koinon* for all Macedonia whose assembly met at Beroea, not far from Thessalonica. Soon after the establishment of the Empire, one of Augustus's generals pushed the frontiers north from Macedonia to the Danube, and Claudius organized the new territory as the province of Moesia. Thrace—the territory between Macedonia and the Black Sea, north of the Aegean and the Straits—was governed by a client-king. Augustus left this king undisturbed but Claudius annexed his territory, thus bringing everything south of the Danube into the Empire.

Western Asia Minor had likewise been plundered flagrantly during the last years of the Republic by publicans and proconsuls, and especially by Sulla and the Liberators. The recovery of these provinces was more rapid than that of Greece. They enjoyed natural advantages lacking to Greece; their population was larger and more vigorous; and they were the chief outlet for the whole of Asia Minor. Cities such as Pergamum, Ephesus, Sardis, Smyrna, and Miletus were highly prosperous even in the first century of the Empire, and their prosperity increased steadily thereafter. The governments of Bithynia and Asia were left much as before, and a third province—called Lycia and Pamphylia—was set up in the southern part of the peninsula. The cities of Asia were largely autonomous, and in each case the province was really a league of cities, a *koinon*, with a representative assembly. The man at the head of the league— called the "Asiarch" in Asia, and by a corresponding title in each of the other provinces—was a personage of high importance. When the client-king of Galatia died in 25 B.C. his territories were added to the Empire, and after Cappadocia was annexed in 17 A.D. all central Asia Minor was Roman territory. In Hellenistic times these central districts had been rather backward culturally, but urbanization was now encouraged, and they were Hellenized by the Romans.

Egypt and Syria

Augustus's most important territorial acquisition was Egypt. This country retained a special status within the Empire, partly because of its wealth and partly because of conditions prevailing there before the annexation. Egypt had long been governed by an elaborate bureaucracy which was taken over by the Romans. An equestrian prefect was put in charge of the province, and Romans held the highest offices in the bureaucracy. The administration was made more efficient, but otherwise the government went on much as before. In fact, imperial officials at Rome probably learned much about administration from these Egyptian bureaucrats. Roman efficiency and engineering skill led to an improvement of irrigation, and thus to increased crops, which enabled Rome to obtain an increasing share of the grain used to feed the Roman populace from Egypt.

Roman administrators ruthlessly suppressed the native revolts which had been the ruin of Egypt. The energy with which they pacified an uprising soon after the death of Cleopatra showed the Egyptians that a new master had arrived, and the Romans had little trouble with natives for a century and a half thereafter. The rabble in Alexandria presented a more difficult problem. Always an unruly people, these Greeks now resented the diminished prestige of their city, for the Romans were less inclined than the Ptolemies to grant them special privileges. They had learned not to show their hostility to the Romans too openly, however, and they expressed their discontent primarily in anti-Semitism. The Jews had been especially favored by Caesar, and the early emperors continued these favors. Discontented Alexandrian patriots retaliated with bloody pogroms. Riots broke out under Gaius, and it was said that 50,000 Jews perished in such a demonstration under Nero. A set of recently discovered papyri, called the "Acts of the Pagan Martyrs," recounts in moving language the tribulations of Alexandrians who suffered at the hands of Rome. A few of these "martyrdoms" came as early as Claudius, the "martyrs" having expressed their Egyptian patriotism chiefly at the cost of Israel.

When Pompey annexed Syria in 63 B.C., Greek power had disintegrated, even in this fragment of the former Seleucid Empire. The Roman proconsuls at first exercised their authority only in the vicinity of Antioch and in the various Greek cities, wherever they might be. The rest of Syria was divided up among a large number of petty client-kings called ethnarchs or tetrarchs. Twenty-three such rulers were still in power in the days of Augustus, but Syria was gradually consolidated and the petty kings eliminated. Thus ended the anarchy that had for so long distracted the country, and in spite of the heavy impositions of Pompey, Crassus, and Cassius, the Romans actually brought prosperity to Syria. Her cities again became famous as centers of industry, and Syrian merchants traveled as far afield as Gaul and Spain. Their extensive trade with India and the East through Palmyra, and with Arabia through Petra, has led a recent writer to compare the Syrian merchants of the first century with the Venetians and Genoese who served as middlemen between East and West in early modern times.

Antioch was the second city in the East, famed for its beauty and luxury, and Syria as a whole was one of the richest provinces of the Empire, having a population perhaps twice that which it supports today. The Seleucids had established Greek colonies at many places, and in the cities the Romans continued this work in Hellenization. In the army camps, men spoke Latin; in the cities, the upper classes spoke Greek; but workers in the cities and inhabitants of the villages alike continued to speak Aramaic.

Judea

The best-known of the client-kings was Herod of Judea, often called Herod the Great. We have relatively full information regarding him, thanks to the Jewish historian Josephus (37–c. 100 A.D., see p. 518), whose works deal primarily with the political history of the Jews. Incidentally these histories also throw much light upon the nature of client-kingship in general and upon the struggle of Eastern and Western culture in the Levant. After Rome's settlement of the East in 63, Herod's father ruled the Jews for almost a quarter of a century, receiving his power from Pompey and skillfully retaining it under Crassus, Caesar, and Cassius, until he was poisoned in 43. Herod inherited his father's character and position, and for several years he was Cleopatra's chief rival for the favor of Antony. After Actium he ingratiated himself with Augustus, and thereafter he remained in power until his death in 4 B.C.

Under Herod the Jewish state attained its greatest territorial extent, including all modern Palestine and much of Transjordania. Herod devoted great thought and care to building up the economic resources of this kingdom. He stamped out brigandage, brought

large districts under cultivation by new irrigation projects, introduced new crops, encouraged industry in the cities, and founded
Caesarea. This city, with its excellent harbor, became the port connecting Judea with the outer world. The resulting prosperity enabled
Herod to spend lavishly without crushing his subjects with taxes.
The city of Jerusalem was improved and embellished, especially by
the magnificent Temple which he built. The beauty of this "Third
Temple" is praised even in the Gospels. Herod did not confine his
benefactions to Judea or the Jews. He made numerous gifts to the
cities of Syria, Asia, and Greece, erecting theaters, stadiums, and
temples to pagan gods. He was even responsible for reviving the
Olympic games. Such expenditures roused the indignation of pious
Jews, yet they undoubtedly were made for political purposes to
combat the anti-Semitism so prevalent among the Gentiles. As the
Jews were popularly criticized for making money among the Greeks
and sending it to Jerusalem, Herod saw fit to return part of this
"tribute" to the Greek cities in a spectacular manner. Herod also
used his influence with Augustus to preserve the privileges granted
to Jews everywhere by Caesar and others.

All this, however, shows only one side of Herod's activity. Herod
was an Oriental, only two generations removed from the desert, yet
he had acquired the outward signs of Hellenism. He owed his position to Augustus's belief that he could make Judea a fit part of the
Roman Empire. His buildings were partly to prove to the world that
he was as civilized as anyone; and though his court was permeated
with harem intrigue in true oriental style, he subsidized Greek
scholars and philosophers to show his interest in intellectual matters.
Patronage of learning was part of the Hellenizing program expected
of every client-king.

In spite of his great benefactions, Herod was hated by his Jewish
subjects. He tried to seem a good Jew, retaining such institutions as
the sanhedrin (the Jewish "senate") and avoiding direct offense to
Jewish religious prejudices. Still, in the eyes of his people Herod
remained a usurper and an oppressor sent by the Gentiles. His Hellenizing activities aroused the old fires of religious fanaticism and
kept the people from forgetting the independence they had once

enjoyed under the Maccabaeans. As Herod grew old, his position became more difficult, and in his very last year he repressed revolts with bloody fury, vague echoes of which perhaps survive in the Biblical story of a "Massacre of the Innocents."

After Herod's death more serious revolts broke out, and three legions of Roman troops were required to restore order. Several thousand persons were killed during the fighting, and the Roman commander afterward crucified about two thousand rebels. Meantime Augustus had divided Herod's kingdom among three of his sons. Archelaus received Judea, Samaria, and Idumea, with the title of ethnarch. Antipas received Galilee (to the north) and Perea (east of the Dead Sea) as tetrarch; and Philip became tetrarch of the rest of Transjordania. Archelaus soon showed his incompetence and was removed after a rebellion in 6 A.D. Philip ruled until his death in 34, and Antipas, the ablest of the three, stayed in power until banished to Gaul by Gaius in 39. He was the "Herod Antipas" mentioned in the Gospels in connection with John the Baptist and once characterized by Jesus as "that fox."

After the fall of Archelaus, Judea and Samaria were governed by a Roman procurator resident at Caesarea, while matters of purely local concern were left to native officials at Jerusalem and Sebaste (Samaria). The fifth of these procurators was the famous Pontius Pilate, who ordered Jesus crucified. He held office from 26 to 36 A.D. Though he built a great aqueduct to provide Jerusalem with fresh water and made other needed improvements, Pontius Pilate was in constant trouble with the Jews. As last he was recalled by Tiberius when he had trouble suppressing a riot. A few years later, Gaius conceived the unfortunate idea of setting up his own statue in the Temple. News of this resolve was received by the Jews with consternation, and civil war would certainly have broken out had not Gaius been murdered before his orders were carried out. Claudius decided that only a client-king could restore order in the seething province. He therefore placed the friendly Herod Agrippa—a grandson of Herod—over the whole of the former kingdom. This man was soon accused of conspiring with the other client-kings of the East against Rome, and after his sudden death in 44—two versions of which may be found in Josephus and the Acts of the Apostles—Claudius returned to the system of procurators. For the next twenty-two years a series of these officials tried in vain to maintain order in Palestine.

The Jewish War

The Jews were the one people in the world whom the Romans could not govern, and in their rebellions, political, nationalistic, cultural, economic, and religious factors were inextricably commingled. Josephus—who wrote for Roman readers and put as good a face as possible on everything—would have us believe that the rebels were simply cutthroats and brigands. Perhaps some of them were, but the great majority were actuated by other motives. Peasants hated the rich landowners and resented the Hellenism of the rich. Josephus names several rebels who wished to be kings, some perhaps in the ordinary secular sense of the word, others obviously conceiving of themselves as the Messiah long foretold by the Jewish prophets. Josephus also uses such words as "magicians" and "impostors" for these men. During these troubled years at least a dozen men claimed the messiahship, or their followers claimed it for them. A certain Judas of Galilee, whose father had been executed by Herod, took part in the revolt of 4 B.C. and was active again in 6 A.D. His sons were crucified for rebellion in 46, and his grandson was a revolutionary leader in the sixties. This Judas organized a group of fanatics, known as the Zealots, who continued the old Maccabaean tradition of fighting or using assassination and terrorism to establish the kingdom of God. Hundreds flocked to their standards, and the Zealots kept all Palestine in confusion. Great revolts which the Romans could not suppress broke out at Caesarea and Jerusalem and in Galilee in 66. A year later Rome sent 50,000 soldiers from Syria under Vespasian—the future emperor—and the rebels were gradually wiped out. Before the Romans could attack the capital itself, however, Nero had committed suicide, and Vespasian had begun plotting to seize power for himself. After a delay of several months, he started west in 69, leaving his son Titus in charge of the operations against the Jews.

When Vespasian became emperor, at the very end of the year, he

needed a spectacular victory to consolidate his position. Titus was
therefore ordered to take Jerusalem by storm. The city had already
been under siege for several months, starvation was imminent, and
extremists among the Zealots were in control. When Titus delivered
the final attack, these Jews fought with the fury of religious fanatics,
but they could not stand against the disciplined legions. The Zealots
fought their last desperate fight in the Temple itself, where thousands of them were butchered. Jerusalem was razed to the ground
and thereafter no Jew might come within one hundred miles of the
site. Titus's triumph at Rome was a magnificent event, featuring the
famous seven-branched candlestick and the table of the showbread
which he had taken from the Temple (see Plate 23). Some 2500
Jewish prisoners were compelled to fight wild beasts in the arena.
Rome thus celebrated the destruction of the last enemy within the
Empire. Jews outside Palestine had shown little sympathy with the
rebels and were allowed to retain their many privileges.

XII Imperial Idealism and Early Christianity

AUGUSTUS BROUGHT AN END TO THE CIVIL WARS AND GAVE Rome a firm and enduring government. He made his city the capital of the civilized world, and to that world he promised peace and prosperity. Blessings such as these, coming after a hundred years of chaos and bloodshed, seemed the greatest gifts that men could possibly desire. Their author won the loyalty of all who could remember the horrors of the old regime or appreciate the benefits of the new. Enthusiasm magnified Augustus's achievements to heroic proportions and proclaimed that with such a leader nothing was impossible. This exalted optimism was given literary expression by the writers of the day, chief among whom stood Vergil, the poet of Imperial Rome.

Vergil

Publius Vergilius Maro was born on October 15, 70 B.C., at Andes, a village not far from Mantua in Cisalpine Gaul. Though he may have been partly of Celtic blood, most of his ancestors presumably were Romans or Italians who had settled in this new province in the second century. Since Andes lay north of the Po River, its people did not gain full Roman citizenship until 49 B.C., and they were ruled by provincial governors until after Philippi. Nevertheless, Vergil was as thoroughly Roman as Augustus himself. His father, a moderately well-to-do farmer, gave his son the best education available, first at Mantua, then at neighboring Cremona and Milan, and finally at

Rome, whither the boy was sent in 53. Vergil apparently took no part in the political and military events of the next several years, during which he spent his time studying poetry and philosophy. Though influenced by such Alexandrians as Theocritus and Aratus, he learned to write Latin verse from Lucretius, who also inspired him with the Epicurean philosophy. When his father's farm was confiscated by Octavian for a veteran after Philippi, the great Roman patron, Maecenas, introduced him to Octavian and procured for him a new farm near Naples. The friendships thus begun endured for life. Vergil accompanied Maecenas to Brundisium when the treaty with Antony was being negotiated in 40, but thereafter he took no part in public affairs. He devoted his life to poetry, living principally at Naples. Here his tomb is still shown at a beautiful spot overlooking the bay.

Vergil's first important work was a set of ten short poems known as the *Eclogues,* published in 37. Some of these poems deal in Theocritan style with country life and the loves of shepherds, one describes the origin of the world in the manner of Aratus, two express gratitude to Octavian, and the Fourth, written in 40, prophesies the impending return of the Golden Age (see p. 355). During the next several years Vergil was occupied with a longer work, the *Georgics,* which he read to Octavian in 29. Though nominally a handbook on agriculture describing the proper care of fields, trees, cattle, and bees, this poem contains some of Vergil's most polished and beautiful verse. It really is a hymn to Italy and her people—to her forests, fields, and vineyards, and to the men who cultivated these fields and built her cities—to Italy the rich mother of fruits and men. If we wish to trace the development of Italian nationalism, this great poem cannot be ignored.

The Aeneid

Vergil then turned to the great work of his mature years, the *Aeneid.* In this long epic he retold the story of how the Trojan hero Aeneas escaped when his city was captured by Agamemnon and the Greeks, and how he migrated to Italy, where his descendant Romulus eventually founded Rome. The legend was an old one, and Vergil merely took what he found; but the story had assumed many forms, and the version of it that we know is his creation. Ten years of labor brought the poem to its present form, but Vergil was still unsatisfied and he was planning to devote three years more to polishing his masterpiece when he died in 19 B.C. In spite of Vergil's dying request that the imperfect poem be destroyed, the *Aeneid* was published at Augustus's order.

Vergil was the most scholarly of poets, widely read in Greek and Latin literature. Though he learned much from Homer and other predecessors, he is at his worst when he most closely approaches these models. Vergil's poetry lacks Homer's vividness; his gods and heroes are less human; his battle scenes soon become tiresome, for he was a civilized man who could not understand the sheer joy of slaughter. His many direct translations from the Greek are rather stilted. But Vergil's imitations of Homer are less significant than his deviations from that model. The task he had set himself differed widely from Homer's. He wished to tell the story of Rome, which to him was the greatest story that could be told. Homer's *Iliad* dealt with one episode in the Trojan War—a war caused by the elopement of someone's wife with another man and ending with the destruction of that city; the *Odyssey* told how its hero Odysseus reached home after being driven o'er land and sea for ten long years; but that was all, and none of these events led to any very important consequences. Vergil's Aeneas, on the other hand, carried civilization to a new home and set in motion forces which eventually enabled Rome to impose peace and law upon the civilized world. While Agamemnon and his friends delighted in fighting and in the destruction of cities, Aeneas and his followers preferred to build cities. They fought well, but they did not fight joyfully, and their delight was in the arts of peace. Twice Vergil found occasion to sketch the history of Rome: once in telling how Aeneas descended into the lower world and there saw Rome's future heroes, and again in describing Aeneas's shield on which were depicted great events that were to come. Both passages were suggested by Homer, but Vergil handled each in his own way. Achilles' shield was decorated with scenes from everyday life, and in the lower world Odysseus saw his old friends (as did Aeneas) but he caught no glimpse of a future beyond his own homecoming. In Vergil's analogous accounts Aeneas saw the whole future glory of Rome. Homer's greatness lies in his portrayal of the hearts of men, Vergil's in a cosmic sweep that covered the whole earth and its history.

Critics have sometimes considered the *Aeneid* an allegory designed to flatter Augustus. They see the "pious" Aeneas playing the role of Augustus—the great statesman and leader, the protector of civilization, who shares Aeneas's filial care for his father (Caesar). Augustus himself had already drawn this comparison on coins. The faithful Achates such critics identify as Agrippa, and Dido as Cleopatra. Aeneas, of course, leaves her as Augustus or any true Roman would, whereas everybody knew that the worthless Antony succumbed to the wiles of his oriental queen. Such interpretations give a very superficial picture of Vergil's mind and purposes—though he may have seen parallels between recent events and the story he was telling.

Following a period of unprecedented destruction and slaughter, Vergil made it his task to glorify the labor which the founding of Rome had cost and the virtues which had made her greatness possible. He was one of the world's great pacifists, quick to see the sordid underside of military glory. He sympathized most with those who suffered most—including Dido. A tinge of melancholy runs through the poem, and everywhere we find the feeling that life is fundamentally a tragedy. *Sunt lachrymae rerum.* Nevertheless Vergil had come to the conclusion that, if Rome were to fulfill her great mission in the world, these terrible things had to be. Troy had to be destroyed; the most just of men had to die miserably; Dido had to kill herself; and long and bloody wars had to be fought in Latium. Many of his companions deserted Aeneas along the way, but he remained firm, always obeying the gods. "I do not seek Italy of my own will," he said to Dido as he forsook her; and when he met her in the lower world, he sighed at her "unjust fate" as she silently turned from him with her eyes fixed on the ground. The austere Aeneas possessed a full measure of the old Roman virtues of stead-fastness and courage, perseverance and devotion to duty, and in the end he reached the goal that destiny had set before him. It was Vergil's hope that the Roman people, filled with such virtues as these and inspired by such heroes, might ever continue in their high mission of teaching men the arts of peace and repressing those who would disturb that peace. Surely an empire built at such cost, by such people, and for such purposes, must last forever. The gods themselves could not will otherwise.

The Lesser Augustans

Vergil, like his hero Aeneas, was essentially a solitary man, standing aloof from and transcending his contemporaries. He brooded upon the events of his day, but he caught its noblest enthusiasms, and he expressed Rome's imperial idealism in an immortal epic. Other writers lived on a less exalted and solitary plane, yet their works too glorify the Augustan Age, making it the most brilliant in the history of Latin literature. Some of these writers stood closer to Augustus than did Vergil, and perhaps they could sense the everyday views and the common sentiments of cultured people at Rome better than Vergil could in his retreat at Naples.

Horace and Ovid

Quintus Horatius Flaccus was born in 65 B.C. in southern Italy, the son of a freedman. After a few years in Rome, he went to study philosophy at Athens in 45. Here he joined the armies of Brutus in 43 and fought at Philippi in 42. Though forgiven by Octavian, he lived miserably at Rome until Vergil introduced him to Maecenas in 39. Five years later Maecenas presented Horace with a farm in the Sabine country not far from Rome—the spot has been identified and the foundations of his house may still be seen—where he lived hap-pily until his death in 8 B.C. When Augustus invited the poet to be his private secretary, Horace refused the post, but he became a sort of poet laureate, occasionally writing verses on order when great

events were to be celebrated. His *Epodes* had been written in the
period of discouragement after Philippi, and their spirit betrays
their origin. During the decade of the thirties Horace wrote two
books of *Satires*, vividly depicting everyday life in Rome, especially
its less pleasing aspects. These were followed by the short lyrics
called the *Odes*. In his later years Horace wrote the *Ars poetica* and
other poetic *Epistles* dealing with philosophy and the principles of
literary criticism. His reputation rests primarily upon the *Odes*, three
books of which were published in 23; a fourth book followed ten
years later.

Horace was as enthusiastic as Vergil over the achievements of
Augustus. He was perhaps more lavish in his praise of the emperor,
but he could not be so sure of the future. This skepticism was shared
by many people, perhaps by Augustus himself, and it is reflected in
the philosophy expressed by Horace in the *Odes*. Get what pleasure
you can day by day, and remember that love, wine, and philosophy
are less dangerous than politics: *carpe diem!* This refrain is repeated
again and again in verses that have since charmed countless readers.
Nevertheless, Horace was fundamentally a moralist. The disillusioned Republican, skeptical of all political reform, decided that
society could be saved only by a return to such old Roman virtues as
those likewise praised by Vergil—simplicity in living, perseverance,
steadfastness, wisdom, courage, and reverence. Such views are set
forth especially in the six "Roman Odes" at the beginning of the
third book, but they permeate Horace's whole work, giving a high
moral seriousness to his light and graceful lyrics.

The third of the great Augustan poets was Publius Ovidius Naso.
Born in central Italy in 43 B.C., Ovid belonged to the new generation
which had not actually experienced the Civil wars and proscriptions.
He was trained as a lawyer, and for a while he held various minor
offices; but his interests lay in the social life of the capital, where he
associated with the gay young members of the best families who
were taking to dissipation now that politics no longer offered them
careers. Ovid then wrote his witty but licentious *Ars amatoria*, or
"The Art of Love." Ten years later, in 7 A.D., Augustus banished him
to Tomi on the Black Sea, nominally because of the immorality of

this poem, actually because of a scandal involving persons high at court in which Ovid had a part. In spite of repeated and pathetic efforts to obtain pardon, he died at Tomi in 17.

Ovid is best known for his *Metamorphoses*, retelling old fables in light and vivacious verse. It was largely from this work that the poets and painters of modern Europe learned their Greek mythology. During his last years at Rome, Ovid composed a more serious work, the *Fasti*, the first half of which has been preserved. Here he described and explained Rome's countless religious ceremonies, arranging them according to their places in the calendar. He roundly praised Augustus and the Roman Empire, and perhaps he dreamed of becoming a national poet, in succession to Vergil. Such a distinction was far beyond his talents. Lighthearted and entertaining, he might accumulate antiquarian lore, but he could not be convincingly serious except when lamenting his exile.

Livy and the Greek Historians

The historian Titus Livius was the sole writer of important Latin prose in the Augustan Age. Livy was born in 59 B.C., at Padua in Cisalpine Gaul, and he died in 17 A.D. Of his life we know little except that he went to Rome, became acquainted with Maecenas and Augustus, was tutor to the Claudius who became emperor, and wrote an enormous history of Rome. He never ceased deploring the fall of the Republic, which caused Augustus teasingly to call him "Pompeianus"; but the emperor recognized his merit and encouraged him in his work. Livy wrote 142 books, which would run to about eight thousand printed pages, in which he covered the history of Rome from Aeneas to the death of Drusus in 9 B.C. We still have the thirty-five books which deal with the periods from the beginning of Roman history to 293, and from 218 to 167. There are also extant brief summaries (the *Periochae*) indicating the contents of each of the lost books. Livy did his work so thoroughly and so well that his history was at once accepted as the standard work, and no Roman ever attempted to supersede it. Earlier histories presently disappeared, and later writers merely epitomized Livy.

When Livy set to work, soon after Actium, he was as discouraged as Horace. He tells us that he took refuge in the past in order to escape from the horrors of his own day. In the end, however, he produced a noble prose epic, comparable to the *Aeneid* as a glorification of Rome. As a prose epic it is unsurpassed, although as a history it is open to many criticisms. It is the story of how the heroic citizens of a small town on the Tiber went out and conquered the world. It tells little or nothing about those whom the Romans conquered, and it suggests no reasons for Rome's successes save Roman virtue. Even old Cato gave his history a broader base by telling something of the Italian cities. Livy makes Roman history resemble an inverted pyramid. Nevertheless, he tells an inspiring story, and he shows what the better Romans liked to believe about their past.

A few Greek writers deserve mention, even in a brief survey of the intellectual development of the Augustan Age. Dionysius of Halicarnassus arrived in Rome as a young man about 30 B.C. Here he presently absorbed the views of the aristocrats whose sons he tutored. He set himself up as a literary critic and promoted the so-called "Attic revival" by insisting that writers having nothing to say should say it in pure Attic Greek. He is best known for a history of Rome covering the period from Romulus to the First Punic War, the first half of which has been preserved. It is a superficial and bombastic work, full of endless speeches, all written by Dionysius himself and therefore all just alike. This history was designed primarily to flatter the old aristocrats. Yet Dionysius had a real interest in antiquities, he read widely, and once in a while his sources of information were better than Livy's. He lacks Livy's force and solidity, however, and his writings may well have strengthened the Roman belief that Greeks of that day were a lightheaded lot—or, as Livy put it, *laevissimi.*

A much more important person was the geographer Strabo, who was born in Pontus, probably of Greek parents. His *Geography,* finished in 6 B.C., is a description of the Roman Empire, province by province, beginning with Spain and following the Mediterranean around to north Africa. Strabo was a highly intelligent man who

collected valuable information and appreciated to the full the blessings brought by the Roman Empire. He also continued Polybius's
history down to his own day.

The reigns of Tiberius, Gaius, and Claudius saw little literary activity of a memorable sort. The generation had passed which knew
the great days of Augustus, and the enthusiasm of those days had
grown cold. Men who might have produced significant literature
were out of harmony with the spirit of the times and spent their
leisure either in frivolities or in composing privately circulated books
of scandal. There were many minor poets, but serious writers limited
themselves to anthologies, epitomes, and works of antiquarian erudition. People who wrote for publication said nothing, and those who
had something to say dared not publish their opinions. Only in the
time of Nero do we detect the dawn of the new period sometimes
called the Silver Age of Latin literature.

Emperor Worship

Not everyone expressed his enthusiasm for the new regime along the
lines chosen by Vergil and the other literary men of the Augustan
Age. Some people found it more natural to ascribe divinity to their
new ruler. It had long been the custom to offer such honors to
Hellenistic kings, a practice which in some cases went back to im-
memorial antiquity. Hellenistic rulers often assumed or were accorded titles to indicate their superhuman nature. *Soter*, or "Savior";
Euergetes, "Beneficent"; *Theos Epiphanes*, "God Manifest"; or simply *Theos*, "God." Roman officials had received similar homage and
titles from Greeks and Orientals in Republican times. Flamininus,
for example, was hailed by the Greeks in 197 as "Titus the Savior,"
buildings were dedicated to him and to Apollo, and he was worshiped along with Roma. During the next century and a half other
Roman generals and proconsuls received similar honors in Greece
and Asia Minor. Pompey was hailed as a god and savior after his
victory over Mithradates, but Cicero declined the honor of a temple
in Asia. Inscriptions in various Greek cities hail Caesar as *Soter*,
Euergetes, or *Theos*. These honors were generally inspired by a

lively expectation of favors to come, and sometimes they may have been extorted by the Roman official in order that he might have something to crow about at home. But occasionally, as in the case of Flamininus, they were doubtless evidence of sincere gratitude and enthusiasm expressed in traditional ways.

All this took place only in the East, however, for Republican Romans did not offer divine honors to any human being. Romulus and other mythical characters were supposed to have become gods. Elaborate mythologies grew up about such heroes as Scipio Africanus and the Gracchi, telling of their supernatural births and superhuman powers. Generals such as Sertorius and Sulla inspired their troops by claiming a special intimacy with the gods. But living men were never deified at Rome as they were in the Hellenistic East. In his last years Cicero speculated, in his *Republic,* upon the possibility that heroes might receive a special status in the next world—a status somewhat similar to that of saints in the Christian heaven—though he knew no way of telling which heroes had been so honored, and he did not suggest that they be worshiped. Enemies accused Caesar of planning to proclaim his divinity and demand divine honors at Rome, but such accusations had little foundation. Servile senators may have sought to flatter him, or his enemies may have suggested it to make him unpopular, but Caesar himself evinced no desire to achieve such glory. He liked to do things in style, and he may have been impressed by the outward trappings of divine royalty in the East, but certainly there was no reason why he should have envied the grandeur of the most eminent divine monarchs of his day—his mistress Cleopatra and her father, Ptolemy the Flute Player.

During the excitement following Caesar's death, his partisans began calling him *Divus Iulius*—the Deified Julius. At about this time a comet appeared in the sky which, they claimed, was his soul being received into heaven. The triumvirs secured his deification by a decree of the senate on January 1, 42. Thereafter, Caesar was officially the *Divus Iulius,* with a temple and priesthood in his service. This adulation doubtless was inspired by ideas similar to those expressed by Cicero rather than by imitation of contemporaneous Hellenistic practice.

Divus Augustus

The *Divus Iulius* took on great political importance in the struggle between Antony and Octavian, for each of the protagonists sought popular favor by calling attention to his devotion to the new god. Antony was a priest in Caesar's cult, and Octavian called himself *divi filius,* "son of the god." On the other hand, each saw fit to charge his rival with harboring divine ambitions for himself. Octavian accused Antony of masquerading as Dionysus or Osiris, and Antony retorted that Octavian had pretended to be Apollo. The fact that this sort of charge was bandied about shows how much the Roman public still disapproved of divine rulers. It was inevitable that Antony, being associated with the divine Cleopatra, should be hailed as a god by the Orientals, and he may have encouraged such attentions; but it is quite impossible to say what he would have done in Rome, had he won at Actium. Octavian was careful not to claim divine honors for himself, both because he recognized the feelings of the Roman people and was loudly denouncing Antony for such un-Roman conduct, and because it was obviously to his advantage that his adoptive father should be the only man recognized as a god. He did, however, permit other unusual honors for himself, and the very name "Augustus" implied that he was something more than an ordinary mortal. Soon after his death, someone swore that he had seen the soul of the emperor rise to heaven, like Caesar's comet. The senate accepted this statement as proof that he had been received among the gods, and ordered a cult of the *Divus Augustus.*

Nevertheless, Augustus was not really a god in the popular estimation, even though he was more than an ordinary mortal. He was a hero or demigod about whom gathered a popular mythology full of miraculous stories showing prowess equal to that of the lesser figures of the pantheon. Many of these stories have been preserved by Suetonius, writing about a hundred years later. He tells us, for example, that Augustus really was the son, not of his reputed father Octavius, but of the god Apollo, who visited his mother Atia in the form of a snake and left a mark upon her which she bore through life. Many marvelous events during his infancy were duly recorded to prove his divine origin and foreshadow his future greatness. His power over the forces of nature was shown by miracles, as when it was said that a barren tree burst suddenly into bloom at his approach. Ample warnings are said to have enabled him to prepare at leisure for death, which came exactly on the day foretold. All this reminds us of the Alexander legend and of the myths regarding various oriental gods and saviors. It pictures Augustus as a supernatural being, fit to be "Master of the World" and "Savior"—a sort of pagan Messiah who saved the world by bringing it peace and prosperity. Vergil had envisioned such a Messiah when he wrote his Fourth Eclogue, and in the First Eclogue he hailed Octavian as a "god." Others dreamed similar dreams during the terrible years of the Civil wars, and legend presently lent Augustus all the characteristics of this expected "Savior." Inscriptions show how often Augustus was hailed as "Savior," and the legends show what sort of being this Savior was expected to be.

Significance of Emperor Worship

During the half century after Augustus's death the cult of the *Divus Augustus* was, among other things, a matter of dynastic import. Successive emperors sought to capture something of Augustus's popularity by professing to follow his policies and by paying conspicuous regard to his memory and his cult. The Julians exploited the cult to emphasize the fact that they, and not the rival Claudians, were the true heirs of the *Divus Augustus*. Tiberius was not deified after his death, but Gaius was unwilling to wait for death before receiving divine honors.

Gaius's claims to divinity have been the cause of much discussion. Claudius declared publicly that his nephew had been insane, and modern writers sometimes view Gaius's religious policy as conclusive proof that the uncle was right. It is quite probable that many of the stories told of Gaius's extravagances were the invention of Claudian detractors. There can be no doubt, however, that he demanded divine honors while still alive. Some writers, recalling his descent from Antony, regard such ideas as an inheritance from his great-grandfather Dionysus-Osiris. More probably they were his way of reminding the public that he was descended from the *Divus Augustus*. The Republican philosopher Cicero had suggested that heroes might obtain divinity by services to the people; a second step was taken when the senate recognized that such deification had actually taken place in the cases of Caesar and Augustus. Further reflection might suggest that these heroes performed their services only by divine power and that they must consequently have been more than mere mortals all the time. Finally, it did not seem unreasonable to suppose that this spark of divinity might be passed on to descendants whose deity was proved by the services of their ancestors and who might be recognized as divine before death. Gaius's deity thus flowed from that of Augustus.

Claudius could not continue along these lines, since he was not descended from Augustus. He obtained the deification of his grand-mother Livia, however, and after his death the senate recognized him as the *Divus Claudius,* much to the amusement of his Julian enemies. Seneca, who was devoted to the Julians, published a clever and scurrilous satire on the *Apocolocyntosis,* or "Pumpkinification," of Claudius. His successor Nero, being a Julian, claimed divine honors for himself while still alive. The Julian emperors rested their claims to power partly upon a divinity inherited from the *Divus Augustus,* and the divinity of the emperor fulfilled the same function in the first century that the divine right of kings did in early modern times. In the final analysis, emperor worship was merely a spectacular way of teaching that government should rest in the hands of lawfully constituted authorities rather than fall to any usurper who could raise an army.

Had the divinity of the emperor rested upon nothing more than the propaganda of rival factions, however, it would not have been of such great importance. Divine honors were offered to the emperors, and their deity was proclaimed by countless persons all over the Empire who had no direct interest in the dynastic quarrel. Inscriptions hailing Augustus as *Soter, Euergetes,* or *Theos,* are far more numerous than those pertaining to any of his predecessors, and there can be no doubt that these expressions of enthusiasm were often spontaneous and sincere. The East had many reasons to be grateful to Augustus. As time went on, these demonstrations were better organized, and the cult of Roma and Augustus was established in each province, with the ruler of the *koinon* serving as high priest. This cult also appeared in the West in the days of Augustus. An altar to Roma and Augustus was dedicated at Lyons in 12 B.C., and the other western provinces presently followed suit. The wide variety of forms taken by the cult is conclusive evidence that it came about, not on orders from Rome, but as the spontaneous expression of popular feeling in the provinces. In fact, the central government sometimes checked the demonstrations of the people.

Tiberius and Claudius would not tolerate temples to themselves, and they insisted that divine honors be offered only to Augustus, who thus came to represent the Empire as a whole. Emperor worship was, therefore, a popular demonstration by which people of all sorts showed their enthusiasm for, and loyalty to, the new regime. Their sentiments differed little from those of modern chauvinists. They may have addressed the emperors as gods, but they knew perfectly well that these emperors were not like other gods. There are hundreds of votive inscriptions whose authors thank various deities for miraculously saving them from sickness or danger. Not one has yet been found whose author thanks an emperor for such a service. Emperor worship was the ancient form of what some people nowadays call the "religion of patriotism" or the "idolatry of the national state."

Philosophical Speculation

Emperor worship stimulated and expressed the sentiment of imperial patriotism, but it gave no answer to the religious and philosophical problems of the day, and it provided no guide to life. Likewise, the old cults, which had formerly seemed to bring divine favor, could no longer arouse the enthusiasm of the educated classes. The old Roman gods had lost their efficacy, and Augustus's efforts to revive the old Roman religion ended in failure. The cults of heroes such as Hercules and Aesculapius, who had once been benefactors of humanity, were somewhat more successful, but everywhere people wistfully sought a new religion. The first century of the Christian era was a time of much philosophical and theological speculation, and it was primarily to the Greeks and Orientals that the Romans looked for light. Hundreds, and perhaps even thousands, of "philosophers" wandered about the Empire preaching their doctrines to those who would listen. Some eked out a wretched existence begging from the poor. Some won fat livings by smoothly exploiting the foolishness of wealthy women. Others undoubtedly were sincere and candid thinkers, and a few preached with the self-sacrificing ardor and zeal of missionaries.

Romans were not ordinarily of a speculative temperament, and at a time when the whole world was changing fundamentally even the Greeks found little leisure or desire to formulate elaborate abstract theories. Men concerned themselves primarily with day-to-day problems of a practical sort, endeavoring to arrive at solutions accurate enough for practical purposes, and asking what lines of conduct a wise man should follow in such a world. Their view of the world was determined to a surprising extent by theories founded on oriental astrology, and their ethics derived principally from Greek Epicureanism and Stoicism.

Astrology

Astrologers, then as now, presented their science to the public as dating from hoary antiquity. As a matter of fact, it was then relatively new. Its fundamental postulates resulted from a fusion of Semitic solar and astral mythology with scientific astronomy. In the eighth century before Christ, astronomy had advanced to the point of establishing the signs of the zodiac and predicting eclipses, but not until a century or two later do we find the first hints of belief in an intimate connection between the planets and the lives of individual men. The great advances of scientific astronomy in the third and second centuries led to further developments in astrological theory, and early in the first century before Christ its main outlines were established. Countless persons, Orientals and Greeks, took part in the elaboration of these theories, prominent among them being Posidonius, Cicero's Stoic friend from Apamea in Syria. The really great theoreticians of astrology lived in the opening centuries of the Christian era. Astrologers had been expelled from Rome as early as

139 B.C., but not until a century later did these "Chaldeans" and "mathematicians" appear in the West in considerable numbers. In the first century after Christ they were mentioned frequently, and thereafter astrological ideas underlay much of the thinking that went on in the Roman world.

This vogue of astrology must not be dismissed as merely another chapter in the long story of human superstition and error. It was partly that, of course, yet that was not all. Individual astrologers may have been clever charlatans who took as much money as they could get for predicting ambiguous futures to superstitious people. Nevertheless, their doctrine deserves attention. In the final analysis, astrological theory rested upon the premise that everything happens regularly and in an ascertainable manner—a premise which also underlies all modern science. This conception of the uniformity of nature was one of the great intellectual achievements of the ancient world, made long before this time, but its popularity in first-century Rome was not wholly unconnected with the political events of the day. The turbulence of the preceding century, which disturbed or magnified or destroyed the lives of so many people regardless of their moral faults and virtues, had prepared men for the fatalistic doctrine that a man's fortune does not depend upon himself but upon remote and inexorable forces which he can never hope to control. Poetry and mythology suggested that this Fate, as certain and as unswerving as the stars in their courses, was somehow related to the heavenly bodies. Practicing astrologers persuaded willing listeners that an individual's horoscope—the position of the various planets in the signs of the zodiac at the moment of his birth—could be made to reveal his whole subsequent career. Astrology therefore appeared plausible to persons in every class of society.

Augustus, Tiberius, and Nero believed firmly in astrology— though they expelled certain astrologers from Rome for making predictions that embarrassed them. Horace advised strongly against counting "Babylonian numbers," but Vergil wrote of the *sidera conscia fati*—"stars conscious of Fate"—and St. Paul occasionally used the technical terminology of astrology in his Epistles. In the second decade of the Christian era a certain Manilius wrote a long poem, the *Astronomicon,* in which he described the universe in astrological terms. Manilius was a high-minded rationalist, singularly free from vulgar superstition, and a man of true poetic feeling whose admirers have exaggeratedly declared him the peer of Lucretius. The difficulty of his poem has kept it from being popular, but it shows how deep was the impression made by astrology upon the best minds of the Roman world.

Ethical Teaching

In a world dominated by Fate and governed by successful soldiers the individual man was apt to feel lost. When the enthusiastic Augustan Age declined into the more humdrum period of the Julio-Claudians, many people found that life did not offer them as much as they thought it should. Those who wished only for material prosperity did very well. Petronius's Trimalchio, for example, and countless others of high and low estate were quite satisfied with the world and worried little about philosophical and ethical problems. There were more serious persons, however, who asked themselves whether the undoubted blessings of the new regime were enough, and who wondered how an individual ought to conduct himself in this strange world. When old Cato heard that Greek philosophers were teaching ethics at Rome, he snorted that regarding such matters men only needed to know the laws—and obey them! This attitude had long since passed away, and during the first century ethical problems were the matter of deep thought and discussion.

Philosophers of every sort preached virtue to their disciples, usually urging what they called a life in conformity with nature. A man should not struggle against Fate, they said, but should accept whatever comes, and a philosopher should do so gladly. To him the only things worth while should be virtue and his own soul, both of which are independent of Fate and all other externals. These preachers denounced the spectacular vices of the rich and such weaknesses as avarice, ambition, and fear of death. They compared philosophers to athletes or soldiers who must constantly be in training, and they laid out extensive programs by which men might strengthen themselves morally. Taking over the Greek word for athletic training, *askesis,* they taught an "ascetical" doctrine that developed into the "asceticism" of later times. If a man underwent such training, he would be rewarded with peace and freedom. The bludgeonings of Fate would mean nothing to him, for he would remain the captain of his soul. When nineteenth-century science brought back a fatalism somewhat resembling that taught by the ancient astrologers, the English poet W. E. Henley expressed similar ethical ideas in his well-known poem, *Invictus.*

We must not think of the Stoic philosopher merely as a man whose head was bloody but unbowed, who kept a stiff upper lip while his world was crashing about him. Such descriptions may fit the Stoic sage, but the Stoics themselves admitted that few persons could achieve such perfect "apathy." Other people too had their ethical problems, and to them Stoicism offered a high moral guide. The Stoics were cosmopolitan and humanitarian, preaching against slavery and the gladiatorial shows, emphasizing such virtues as justice, mercy, and charity. They idealized the younger Cato and Brutus rather than Caesar, and they spoke of God in language that was deeply religious. They were the most nearly modern of ancient philosophers.

The most eminent of the first-century Stoics was Lucius Annaeus Seneca (4 B.C.–66 A.D.). For several years he was Nero's prime minister, governing so well that some people wished to see him emperor. Seneca also wrote Stoic tracts and works of edification. A century and a half after his death, the Christian apologist, Tertullian, claimed that Seneca was often a Christian—*Seneca saepe noster.* Others, unwilling to believe that a pagan could hold such noble sentiments, forged a series of letters to show that St. Paul had expounded the teachings of Christianity to the philosopher-statesman. During the Middle Ages Seneca was one of the most popular of the pagans, while thinkers and poets of modern times owe to him many of their most famous thoughts.

The Mystery Religions

While philosophy might satisfy members of the intellectual class, ordinary mortals craved a more emotional worship and more positive assurances of future felicity than philosophy could give. Such long-ings were often satisfied by the Greek and oriental mystery religions. They were very ancient religions, going back to the fertility cults which had appeared throughout the Near East in Neolithic times. Their long history had left its mark upon them, of course, and they differed widely among themselves, those in Greece having followed lines of development rather different from those taken by their oriental rivals. These cults received new attention in Hellenistic times, and under the Roman Empire they enjoyed their greatest prosperity. There was at this time a general "syncretism," or min-gling of cults, each borrowing from the others and inventing new ceremonies and beliefs, and all religions thus came to resemble each other more and more.

These cults were called "mystery religions" because they centered around certain "mysteries"—ceremonies or sacraments—in which only those who had been "initiated" might participate. A man was initiated only after careful training, during which the significance of the mysteries was explained to him—hence our use of the word "mystery" to indicate something not understood by the uninitiated. In addition to its elaborate and colorful ritual, each mystery religion had a revealed theology describing the nature and purposes of the gods and explaining the origin and subsequent history of the world and man. Each laid great emphasis upon sin and the necessity for purification, each preached various forms of asceticism, and each promised a glorious immortality to its devotees. Finally, each re-ligion had its recognized initiates and a professional clergy inter-ested in missionary activity.

Greek mysteries had been brought to Italy by the earliest Greek settlers in the eighth and seventh centuries before Christ, and their reputation soon spread throughout southern Italy. Much mystical thinking was associated with the name of Pythagoras, a Greek who lived at Croton in the sixth century. Views similar to his appeared at Rome in the second century, and a hundred years later Nigidius Figulus—a friend of Cicero—revived Pythagorean ideas about the transmigration of souls while teaching a morality of abstinence and asceticism. Even Seneca was attracted by this teaching in his youth.

These Neo-Pythagoreans spread the doctrine through Italy and as far as Asia Minor, Egypt, and Palestine. Meantime, other religious leaders were developing the mysteries of Dionysus. The efforts of the senate, early in the second century before Christ, to suppress this cult had proved unsuccessful, and in the first century after Christ Bacchus was worshiped in all parts of the Empire by persons of Greek or Italian descent. The Orphic theology associated with this cult underlay Vergil's account of Aeneas's visit to the lower world, and houses or chapels have been discovered at Pompeii and Rome whose wall paintings illustrate Orphic and Pythagorean teachings. The mysteries of Demeter at Eleusis also attracted the attention of many Romans. Both Cicero and Augustus were initiated there, and under Claudius these mysteries were established in Italy for the benefit of pious Romans.

Oriental Religions

The Greek mysteries were presently supplemented by various cults of oriental origin. The first oriental religion to appear in Rome was the worship of the Phrygian Cybele, the Great Mother of the Gods, which was introduced by the Scipios in 204 B.C. A temple to the Great Mother was built on the Palatine Hill in 191, and the position of her priests in Rome was assured by law. Nevertheless, Cybele remained unpopular until the end of the Republic because she was worshiped in a boisterous and flamboyant manner highly repugnant to Romans of the old school. Augustus, however, was favorably inclined toward the goddess, whom he associated with Troy and the supposed Trojan ancestry of the Julian family: when her temple was destroyed by fire in 3 A.D., he rebuilt it in magnificent style. Several passages in the *Aeneid* mention Cybele with deep respect. Claudius showed her even greater favor, reducing restrictions upon her public worship, introducing her festivals into the official Roman religion, and giving her priests an official standing. Thereafter Rome, rather than Pessinus in Phrygia, was the world capital of the cult of Cybele. Undoubtedly Claudius was actuated by political motives, hoping to control a religious force which he could not resist.

The worship of Isis was established by Egyptian merchants at

Puteoli before 105 B.C. and at about the same time in Pompeii. A few years later the worship appeared in Rome. At first Isis attracted little attention from native Romans, but four times between 58 and 48 B.C. the senate thought it necessary to order the destruction of her temples in the city. Such tactics proved powerless against the new religion, and in 43 the triumvirs reversed the old policy by ordering the erection of a temple to the goddess at public expense—though the order was not obeyed. The wars against Cleopatra brought Isis into disrepute at Rome, and a few years later Vergil spoke contemptuously of the dog-faced gods of Egypt. Priests of Isis were again in trouble under Tiberius, but Gaius gave them official recognition and built a great temple to Isis in Rome.

A third important oriental god was Mithra, a Persian deity whose worship was introduced from Asia Minor by Pompey's soldiers on their return from his war against Mithradates (see Plate 25). Eventually this religion became the most important of the three, but during the first century it attracted less attention. While such exotic religions were tolerated, and even received legal recognition, they did not attract many true Romans. They remained primarily the religion of oriental immigrants, merchants, slaves, or freedmen, and their progress may be taken as an index to the advance of these social classes. Even in the next century Romans like Juvenal continued to express contempt for such outlandish worship.

Basically these various religions were fertility cults, centering around the return of life in the spring. Great ceremonies were held at this season in honor of a god who had died and risen again, or rather, of a mythical man beloved by a goddess, who had been killed and then rose as a god. In the cult of Cybele, as regulated by Claudius, this annual festival lasted from the 15th to the 27th of March. On the first day, worshipers celebrated the birth of Attis. Next came the observance of his *Epiphania*, or "Manifestation," when Cybele found him floating in a basket on a Phrygian river. Worshipers passed the succeeding days in fasting and abstinence until the celebration of the death of Attis on the 22nd. His funeral two days later was characterized by frenzied grief, sacrifices, and offerings of blood —wherefore the day was called *Sanguis*, "Blood." At dawn on the

following day, March 25—then considered the first day of spring—
the priest announced the resurrection of Attis, and the day was given
over to rejoicings called *Hilaria*. The last act of the sacred drama
came on the 27th when a procession conducted the statue of Cybele
through the streets and washed it in a brook. Similar festivals were
celebrated by the devotees of Isis and of various other oriental
deities.

While these spring ceremonies were the most spectacular and the
most important, they were by no means the only ones. The temples
probably had services of some sort every day. While the Easter
festival in the spring assured men of immortality, other lesser rites
reminded them of their sins and purified them. Most of these religions, for example, celebrated a strange rite called the *taurobolium*.
In this ceremony, a bull was sacrificed, and the penitent allowed the
warm blood to trickle over his body in the belief that his sins would
be washed away by the blood of the bull.

The Jewish religion differed greatly from these oriental mysteries
—in fact, it was not a "mystery" at all—yet it too played a notable
part in the religious life of the Empire. Jews had reached Rome in
the second century and had been expelled from the city as early as
139 B.C. They soon reappeared and became numerous in the days of
Caesar, and in the first century after Christ every important town
had its synagogue. Judaism then attracted the attention of sober
Gentiles who desired a new and better religion. Some became prose-
lytes, but a larger number, finding the strict observance of the
Mosaic Law too difficult, merely accepted Jewish monotheism, attended services in the synagogue occasionally, listened to the reading of the prophets, and shared the Messianic hope. Jews spoke of
such persons as "God-fearing" Gentiles. Though it is possible to
detect reminiscences of Isaiah in Vergil's Fourth Eclogue, efforts to
count him among the "God-fearing" have proved unsuccessful.
There can be no doubt, however, that important personages at Rome
were interested in Judaism, and it was said that even Nero and his
mistress Poppaea were among this number. Others tried to identify
the Hebrew God (whose name was probably pronounced Yahweh,
not Jehovah), with various pagan gods. The Asiatic Sabazios, for ex-

ample, was associated with the "Lord of Hosts" (*Yahweh Sabaoth* in Hebrew). Still others showed at least a slight knowledge of Judaism by invoking the name of Yahweh in magic formulae or when cursing and swearing.

Gnosticism

Along with these new religions came a philosophy that reached nearly every class of society. It was called "Gnosticism," from the Greek word *gnosis*, "knowledge." This new knowledge, which apparently arose in Egypt, was a vague and fluctuating hodgepodge of doctrines derived from Greek and oriental mysteries, from astrology, from Pythagoras and the Orphics, from Plato and the Stoics, even from Judaism, and eventually from Christianity itself. It had its sacred books, such as the revelations of Hermes Trismegistus— the Thrice Great Hermes—which were composed in Egypt in the first century after Christ. Gnostics declared that their gnosis was not mere human knowledge but the revealed wisdom of God, and that it provided infallible answers to the deepest questions that disturbed men.

The Gnostics distinguished sharply between spirit and matter, beween God and the world. They urged the cultivation of the former and the neglect of the latter, identifying sin with matter and purity with spirit. They praised poverty, celibacy, and contempt of the world, and they taught a mode of life by which men might free themselves from the temptations of the "flesh" and of "matter" to become "psychic" or "spiritual." Such ascetic renunciation of the world was not enough, however, and men could achieve perfection only by divine aid. After declaring that all men are by nature material and sinful, the Gnostics promised them a *Soter*, or "Savior," who would free them from their sins. To those who persevered in spiritual ways, and achieved "salvation," these ancient Gnostics promised the greatest boon of all—a blessed immortality.

Jesus of Nazareth

Nowhere was religious effervescence more active than in Palestine. The victory of the Jews over the Seleucids in the second century before Christ had led to the establishment of a theocratic state under the Maccabaeans. Thereafter, pious Jews, inspired by the prophets and Daniel, looked forward to a time when all men would worship Yahweh and thus form a theocratic world empire. The stormy events between 63 B.C. and 70 A.D. caused great confusion in Palestine, where religion and politics were inextricably commingled. The aristocratic Sadducees were willing to accept Roman rule if they could retain their own social and religious prestige. The Pharisees were willing to obey the Romans for the time being if they were not obliged to violate the Mosaic Law in so doing. The Essenes, believing that a man could not live according to the Law in such secular society, withdrew to monastic retreats, and the Zealots prepared to drive out the Romans by force of arms. The controversies of these parties raised the people to a high pitch of political and religious excitement. Apocalypses and other prophetic literature foretold the imminent intervention of God to set things right once more, ethically, politically, or religiously. Countless persons expected that the long-awaited Messiah would soon appear, and several enthusiasts believed themselves to be this Messiah or else were hailed as such by their followers. Among those so hailed was Jesus of Nazareth.

While it is not possible to give the exact chronology of Jesus' life, we may safely reject the computations (made in 525 by a Roman monk) from which our Christian era is reckoned. Jesus was not born in the year 1. Two of our four Gospels tell us that he was born under Herod the Great, who died in the spring of 4 B.C. All four Gospels agree that he was crucified under Pontius Pilate, who was procurator of Judea from 26 to 36 A.D. One Gospel declares that Jesus was "about" thirty years old when he began to preach, after having been baptized by John the Baptist, who in turn had begun to preach in the fifteenth year of Tiberius. The Evangelist probably counted this fifteenth year from October 1, 27 to September 30, 28, and thought that Jesus began preaching at some time after the latter date. There is no clear indication of the exact length of Jesus' ministry, but it probably lasted about a year and a half.[1] By putting these scraps of

---

[1] According to the Gospel of Luke (4:16–32), Jesus, early in his ministry, attended the synagogue at Nazareth, "as his custom was," where he read and commented upon

information together, we may conclude that Jesus probably was born about five years before the turn of the century. It may be taken as fairly certain that he was crucified on April 7, 30 A.D. There is, of course, no evidence regarding the exact day of his birth, and not until several centuries had passed did Christians agree to observe Christmas on December 25.

The Gospels indicate that the beginning of Jesus' preaching was connected with that of John the Baptist. Concerning this remarkable man we find information in the Gospels and in the writings of the Jewish historian Josephus, published in 93 A.D. John was an ascetic living in the desert beyond the Jordan. He prophesied the immediate coming of the Messiah, and he urged his followers to repent and be baptized for the remission of their sins. His success was such that Herod Antipas, who then ruled Galilee and Transjordania, ordered him to be executed lest the excitement lead to political revolt. Jesus was among those whom John baptized. Jesus presently left John, though continuing to speak highly of him, but others remained loyal disciples to the Baptist and eventually carried John's teaching as far as Alexandria and Ephesus.

His Preaching and Crucifixion

Our knowledge of the life of Jesus comes entirely from the four Gospels. Liberal scholars in the nineteenth century were in the habit of selecting appropriate passages from these Gospels to depict Jesus as an amiable teacher of ethics whose views were best set forth in the Sermon on the Mount. These writers declared that by such teaching Jesus antagonized the priests, who had him put to death, and that legend presently cast a halo of miracle about him as it did about Augustus and so many others. Scholars today draw a more complicated picture.[2] Many now prefer to regard Jesus as a visionary whose mind was full of the Scriptures and the apocalyptic

---

a passage in the prophet Isaiah. A recently discovered ancient lectionary, listing the passages of Scripture to be read in the synagogues Sabbath by Sabbath over a three-year cycle, indicates that this passage should have been read on the Sabbath Day, December 18, 28. Assuming that this lectionary was then in use at Nazareth, Professor Olmstead has computed (*Jesus*, p. 281) that the ministry of Jesus lasted exactly 475 days.

[2] See note on The Quest of the Historical Jesus, p. 488.

ideas of his day and who shared the views then commonly held by
Jews about God, the world, angels, devils, the resurrection, and the
Messiah. His first preaching resembled that of John the Baptist and
may be summed up in the words, "The Kingdom of the Messiah
is at hand." The nature of this Kingdom Jesus illustrated effectively
and with supreme artistry by parables and pointed stories. He also
uttered the ethical teachings just mentioned, though in such matters
he differed less than was once supposed from the best contemporary rabbis. Jesus' importance as a teacher is shown, as someone
has remarked, not by the Pharisaic doctrines he accepted but by
those he left out.

The Gospels tell us repeatedly how Jesus' teaching was reinforced
by marvelous works, notably works of healing. These "miracles"
were once brushed aside as pure mythology, but today we cannot
be quite so sure. Many of the stories undoubtedly lack historical
foundation, but perhaps not all of them. The reported cures were
usually worked upon demoniacs or other persons whom we today
would call psychoneurotic. Modern psychiatrists know that neurotics
may react in a manner similar to that described by the Gospels
—though of course such reaction is not now considered "miraculous." One or two such cures, plus a few coincidences, would have
been enough in those days to convince everyone that the healer
possessed supernatural powers and to set in circulation other badly
authenticated stories of his prowess. Though these cures and stories
helped spread the reputation of Jesus far and wide, the most important effect of the cures was upon Jesus himself. As he shared the
popular view of such illnesses and cures, he gradually was convinced
by what he saw that he possessed supernatural powers and that God
had chosen him for a central part in the impending establishment
of the Messianic Kingdom. He was thus led to reflect long and
deeply upon his relation to God, the Kingdom, and the divine plan
governing the universe.

Jesus had passed his early life at Nazareth in Galilee, which was
the most restless part of Palestine. Here Judas of Galilee had organized his Zealots at about the time Jesus was born. Here two

thousand of the Zealots were crucified when Jesus was a boy (6 A.D.). Here the last great revolt was to break out in 66. Nevertheless, Jesus did not share the political views of his rebellious neighbors. In fact, the nonresistant pacifism which is so prominent in his teaching seems to have been aimed primarily at the Zealots, one of whom (Simon) presently became one of the Twelve Apostles. Jesus believed that the Messianic Kingdom would come only by act of God and that its coming could best be hastened by personal reforms of a religious and ethical sort.

Herod Antipas, learning of the popular excitement that centered around Jesus, came to fear him as he had formerly feared John the Baptist, and planned to do away with him. Jesus was warned and withdrew to the cities of Phoenicia, then to Caesarea Philippi, and finally to Jerusalem. The first three Gospels picture the visit to Jerusalem as lasting only a week. The Fourth Gospel, perhaps with greater accuracy, describes a longer visit, followed by retirement beyond the Jordan and a return one week before the crucifixion. When entering Jerusalem on this last occasion, both Jesus and his followers were in a state of high excitement, as appears in the stories of the Triumphant Entry. They seemed certain that it was only a matter of days, or perhaps of hours, until the Messiah would be revealed.

The Sadducees were terror-stricken when they learned of this commotion, fearful lest the Romans mistake it for political rebellion and send troops to pacify the city. They therefore anticipated trouble by seizing Jesus themselves. Arresting him late at night, they hurried him off to Pilate early the next morning before the populace learned what had happened. Since it was the time of the Passover, when disturbances might be expected, Pilate had come up from Caesarea to Jerusalem to be on hand in case of trouble. He condemned Jesus to death as a revolutionary leader aspiring to kingship (which was his misunderstanding of the claim that Jesus was the Messiah) and ordered him crucified under the sardonic placard, "This is the King of the Jews." During the hearing before Pilate Jesus refused to deny that he was the Messiah, and to the very end he confidently expected that God would suddenly reveal him as such. Only with his dying breath did he cry out, "My God, my God, why hast thou forsaken me?"

The Early Church

During the confusion attendant upon the arrest and crucifixion of Jesus, many of his friends and disciples had fled back to Galilee, but before long some of them were excitedly saying that they had seen him alive. Theologians may dispute about the psychological processes by which the disciples reached this conviction, but the fact that they were so convinced remains one of the major events in world history. Within a short time they were confidently proclaiming in Jerusalem that Jesus was risen from the dead, that he had ascended into Heaven, and that he would shortly return in glory to establish the Messianic Kingdom. Their preaching was so successful that several thousand persons in Jerusalem soon shared their expectation of an immediate Second Coming.

These persons formed what may be called the first Christian Church. They believed that Jesus was the Messiah who had wickedly been put to death by the Jews, that he had risen from the dead, and that he would soon return to establish his Kingdom. Anyone who accepted these propositions might become a member of the church. These Christians continued to consider themselves good Jews. They frequented the Temple, they observed the Mosaic Law, and they carefully studied the Scriptures, especially those passages which dealt with the Messiah. Their excitement showed itself in such phenomena as "prophesying" and "speaking with tongues," a fairly common accompaniment to great religious excitement. Since all earthly possessions would soon be of no value, the Christians pooled their goods, lived a communistic life, and distributed food freely to the poor. The community was presided over in these earliest days by the twelve Galilean disciples who had been closely associated with Jesus from the first. (The traitor Judas, who had betrayed Jesus to the priests, was replaced in order to keep the old number.) When these men found that they had no time for the management of the community, they chose seven assistants, called "deacons," who attended to the common meals and charities while the Twelve devoted themselves to preaching.

The execution of Jesus had failed to bring peace in Jerusalem, and when new commotions arose, the Jewish authorities again intervened. One of the Seven—a man named Stephen—was stoned to death, whereupon many Christians fled the city. The Galilean disciples had been fishermen and other humble persons of narrowly Jewish background, but the converts in Jerusalem were a more cosmopolitan group including many "Greeks"—*i.e.*, Jews who had lived abroad and spoke Greek. Stephen and others of the Seven belonged to this class. Among those leaving Jerusalem were many "Greeks" who were inspired with missionary zeal and began making converts of their own to the new faith. Christian communities thus arose in various parts of Palestine, in the coastal cities such as Joppa and Caesarea, and even as far away as Damascus and Antioch. It was in the latter city that the disciples were first called Christians.

Jerusalem remained the Christian center, where the Twelve continued to preach and to preside over the church organization. Nothing is known of the history of the church at Jerusalem during the next ten years. This would indicate that the first wave of enthusiasm died down to some extent and that the disciples were more passively awaiting the Second Coming. When the Emperor Gaius ordered his statue set up in the Temple in the year 40, the Jews were thrown into a frenzy of excitement. Some of them apparently believed that this threatened action would be followed by the immediate appearance of the Messiah. Though the statue was not set up, thanks to the timely assassination of Gaius, several persons appeared within a short time who claimed to be the Messiah. A certain Theudas— whom Josephus calls an "impostor," meaning that the man claimed to be the Messiah—attracted many followers before he was captured and beheaded by the Romans. The sons of Judas of Galilee were crucified at about the same time, and still other "robbers" were killed or driven away.

It seems very probable, though there is little direct evidence, that the Christians shared the prevailing excitement and momentarily expected the return of Jesus. Perhaps these expectations are reflected in apocalyptic passages in the Gospels predicting just such events as those taking place in 40 as heralding the Second Coming (Mark 13). At any rate, when Herod Agrippa assumed the government of Palestine in 41 and began the restoration of order, he first took steps against the Christians, presumably because he considered their Messianic agitation dangerous to the peace of his kingdom. One of the Twelve (James the son of Zebedee) was beheaded—this being a punishment for political rather than for religious offenses—and Peter was arrested but escaped and fled the city. The action taken against these men was connected with the disturbances that followed Gaius's ill-advised order and indicates that the early Christians were thought to have had a part in them.

Perhaps it was the failure of the Messiah to appear at this critical moment, when he was so confidently expected, that caused the Christians to reconsider their hopes and to decide that they should not expect the Second Coming until the whole world had been converted to Christianity. At any rate, Christian leaders now became more active than before in propagandizing their faith. A meeting of church leaders was held in Jerusalem at which it was decided that Gentile converts need not observe the whole of the Mosaic Law, as the first Christians had insisted. Shortly thereafter several of the Twelve Apostles set out on great missionary journeys. Peter went to Antioch, and early tradition plausibly reports that he later reached Rome, where he eventually was crucified. John eventually appeared in western Asia Minor, and others of the Twelve evangelized other peoples.

The community at Jerusalem retained its primacy in the church, however, and leadership here fell to James "the Just," a brother of Jesus who had not been prominent before the crucifixion and who was not one of the Twelve. James was killed by a mob in 62, after which the Christians chose a new leader named Symeon, a cousin of Jesus, who ruled for many years and died at an advanced age in the reign of Trajan. The choice of these two men is highly significant, for it shows a desire on the part of the community to keep leadership in the family of David, the first king of the Jews. At this time Christians were already proving the descent of Jesus from

David by the two different genealogies now found at the beginning of Matthew and Luke; and Symeon was related to Jesus through his father Clopas, a brother of Joseph, through whom the Gospels trace the Davidic descent. Shortly before Titus besieged Jerusalem, the Christians in the city fled to Pella beyond the Jordan. After the disasters of 70 most Christians were of Gentile origin, and the group once at Jerusalem no longer enjoyed its old prestige and leadership.

Paul of Tarsus

Shortly after the death of Stephen, the Christians won a great recruit in the person of Paul of Tarsus. A Jew of the Diaspora, born to a family of importance and inheriting Roman citizenship, well-educated and familiar with the world, Paul differed noticeably from the earlier disciples. At first he persecuted the Christians but, as the celebrated story tells us, while on the road to Damascus to arrest disciples there he underwent a psychological experience which converted him to Christianity and changed the whole course of his life. After being baptized at Damascus he withdrew to Arabia, and not until three years later did he visit the disciples at Jerusalem for the first time. He then passed several years in Tarsus and Antioch, preaching to Jews and Gentiles—that is, to those "God-fearing" Gentiles who already had an interest in Judaism and who frequented the synagogues. When the second burst of missionary enthusiasm arose during the early forties, Paul became very active. He and Peter were the men largely responsible for liberalizing the terms on which Gentiles might become Christians, and soon after the council at Jerusalem he set out on his famous missionary journeys to Asia Minor, Macedonia, and Greece. He lived in Corinth for a year and a half, for about two years in Ephesus, and he paid briefer visits to several other cities in the Aegean area.

It was Paul's custom to revisit his churches occasionally and to keep in touch with them through friends and correspondence. He also carefully trained a group of assistants to expand the work which he started. This activity continued for about ten years, interrupted only by brief visits to Jerusalem and Antioch. Presently Paul began seeking larger fields. He planned to visit Rome, and even spoke of going to Spain. Before starting west, however, he once more visited Jerusalem and while there was arrested during a riot instigated by the Jews. For two years he was held at Caesarea awaiting trial, until he exercised his right as a Roman citizen to appeal his case to Rome, whither he was sent under guard. Again Paul awaited trial for two years but was meantime granted considerable freedom to preach in Rome. At this point, about the year 62, the narrative of the Acts of the Apostles abruptly ends. According to plausible tradition, Paul was presently freed by the Romans, visited various places, possibly including Spain, and eventually was again arrested and executed at Rome in the year 67.

Paul's Imperial Religion

Paul's importance does not rest solely in the many churches he founded. He always insisted that he had not learned of Christianity from the other disciples but directly from God, and his Christianity certainly differed widely from that of the Jerusalem group, with whom he quarreled on more than one occasion. In his youth Paul had been educated as a Pharisee, and had therefore been taught great reverence for the Mosaic Law. Yet as a Christian he preached freedom from this Law. When the Jerusalem group wished to retain the Law, even for Gentile converts, Paul insisted that it was no longer necessary. The ardor with which he defended his position shows how fundamental he considered this matter. Paul's repugnance to the Law may have come in part from a personal experience of its inadequacy, but its fundamental causes lay much deeper.

As a Pharisee, Paul had doubtless shared the belief of the prophets that Judaism would some day be the religion of all mankind, and as a Roman citizen—a distinction of which he was very proud—he appreciated the universalism of the Roman Empire. In his early days Paul had perhaps hoped to make Judaism the religion of the Empire, and this fervent hope may explain the violence of his attacks upon the Christians who were undermining Pharisaic Judaism. But life in the Diaspora had shown him how difficult it would be to persuade Gentiles to assume the yoke of the Law. Then came his conversion to the Christian faith. He threw the Law overboard, and in Christianity he found a religion which retained the good points of Judaism, but which might more easily become the religion of the whole world. He wished Christianity to be a Judaism made over for Gentiles, and only abandoning the Law could make it a universal religion, fit for the whole Roman world. This imperial ambition inherited from Judaism seems to be the key not only to Paul's attacks upon the Law, but also to his statesmanship in founding a series of closely affiliated communities across the whole Empire from Syria to Rome—or perhaps even to Spain. They were cells from which a religious world empire was to grow. Many centuries elapsed before Paul's dream was fulfilled, and the Roman Empire became a Christian state. Nevertheless, the fact remains that Paul was, in his way, one of Rome's great empire-builders, and that he caught the spirit of the first century as well as did Augustus or Vergil, with whom he deserves to be compared.[3]

Paul's ideas included more than the religious unification of mankind. He was also a theologian, starting with Pharisaism but adding other ideas of many sorts, and turning all these ideas in a new direction. He had little knowledge of Greek literature and philosophy, belittling them with the comment, "The wisdom of this world is fool-

---

[3] Much more might be said of Paul's imperialism and his sympthay with Rome's imperial system. In the early days of Nero he made the famous remark, "The powers that be are ordained of God." The Jews of the Diaspora usually favored the imperial system which encouraged business and protected them somewhat from anti-Semitic violence. Paul also had good reason to favor the Romans as a citizen of Tarsus ("I am a Jew of Tarsus in Cilicia," he proudly declared, "a citizen of no mean city."). This city had been sacked in 43 by Cassius the Liberator, but it was restored by Antony, and it received numerous favors from Augustus. Paul's family, being Roman citizens, undoubtedly shared these favors, indirectly at least, and their associates were the ones most favored. Moreover, Tarsus had long been the center of a celebrated school of Stoic philosophy, which under Augustus was led by a certain Athenodorus. This man had been Octavian's tutor in Epirus just before Caesar's death. He followed his pupil to Rome in 44, helped him greatly during the next few years, and had a share in developing the principles underlying the Empire. He had been a pupil of Posidonius; Cicero spoke highly of him and received his aid when preparing the tract *De officiis;* and Strabo was his personal friend, telling us most of what we know about him. Athenodorus presently returned to Tarsus to teach philosophy, and when the city fell into confusion about 10 B.C., Augustus ordered him to give it a new constitution. Athenodorus then had a large share in governing the city until his death in 7 A.D. As a young man Paul undoubtedly heard much about his distinguished fellow-citizen. Modern scholars have attributed certain similarities between Paul's views and Seneca's to their common knowledge of Athenodorus, and it is not at all improbable that Paul's political and imperialistic views derived in part from the ideas of this Greek theorist of Roman imperialism.

ishness with God." He was more deeply indebted to the mystery religions. Like them, Paul spoke of the flesh and the spirit, sin and punishment, forgiveness, salvation, death and immortality, and to him Jesus seems to have been primarily a dying and rising god. Paul discussed the problems with which the mysteries were concerned and he expressed himself in their language, but he always added something and omitted much. He was in many ways representative of first-century thought—not so much the thought of the intellectual elite as that of the common man newly rallied to the Empire.

Finally, Paul possessed one of the most striking and interesting personalities of the ancient world. Deeply convinced that he had been set apart, even from his mother's womb, to preach the Gospel, Paul voluntarily gave up a life of ease to become a wandering preacher. Frail in body and afflicted with a serious infirmity, he deliberately faced labors such as might have daunted a stronger man. His intensely active mind poured forth the volcanic eloquence of his Epistles, upon which foundations others reared the mighty edifice of Christian theology. He was the great organizer of the early church. Though differing from Jesus in temperament as much as a man well could, he amply deserved his fame as the second founder of Christianity.

The First Churches

Meantime, other missionaries had been founding churches elsewhere. Some invaded Asia Minor, where they aroused Paul's wrath by interfering with his converts and teaching them to obey the Jewish Law. Christians soon appeared in Rome, and as early as 41 Claudius expelled some of them from the city on charges of disturbing the peace. A Christian community was founded at Alexandria at a rather early date, perhaps in the sixties, by missionaries from Rome. Strange to say, however, this church did not become important until more than a century later. Christianity was thus established in the great centers of the Roman Empire before the death of Nero, when there were also a few churches outside the Empire in the East.

When Paul and other missionaries came to a new community, they usually went first to the synagogue. Taking advantage of the common liberty of speaking, they undertook to prove to the assembled congregation from the Scriptures that Jesus was the Messiah. Such preaching frequently led to disputes, which resulted in the Christians being excluded from the synagogue. Thereafter they held their meetings in private houses or other rooms. In Ephesus, for example, Paul taught in a room that was used at other hours as a school. The Christians held regular religious ceremonies of their own, closely resembling those in the synagogues, with reading and explanation of passages from the Law and the Prophets, singing Psalms, and prayer. They held these ceremonies even in places where they continued to attend the synagogues and in Jerusalem where they worshiped regularly in the Temple. They soon added distinctive rites of their own.

The first of the new ceremonies was baptism "in the name of Jesus," by which converts became members of the Christian community. The second ceremony was a solemn eating of bread and drinking of wine in memory of the last supper of the disciples with Jesus on the eve of the crucifixion. This latter ceremony—simply called "breaking bread" in the Acts of the Apostles, but later called the Eucharist—was regularly observed on the first day of the week. The principal services in the synagogues were, of course, on the Sabbath (Saturday), but after the Christians left the Jewish communities they discontinued the Saturday services and centered their worship around the Sunday celebration of the Eucharist. In addition to these ceremonies, the Christians would also eat an ordinary meal together from time to time, those who could afford it bringing their own food and something extra for the poor. Such a meal was called an *Agape,* or "Love Feast," and was perhaps a relic of the communism of the earliest days (see Plate 27).

The First Christians

Most of the early Christians were persons of humble origin, coming from the lower levels of the artisan-merchant class of the large cities. Many were, or had been, slaves. As Paul remarked, there were "not many wise after the flesh, not many mighty, not many well-born"; they were rather the "foolish," the "weak," the "lowly," the "nobodies." The early church was a great democratic and cosmopolitan society in which there could not be "Greek and Jew, barbarian,

Scythian, slave and free." In it all men were equal. The early Christians were serious, sober, hard-working persons who found in their religion and its promises a release from the humdrum life to which they were reduced. Christianity, like the mystery religions, brought hope and color to the lives of people whose position in the world seemed rather hopeless. Unlike the mysteries, it gave ordinary people opportunities for companionship and activity. It organized them into a close society, and it made them a separate people. It won their undying loyalty, which even the persecution of the emperors could not break. After three centuries of struggle, these Christian communities realized Paul's old dream by absorbing the Empire itself. Thus the rise of Christianity became the most important event in the history of the Roman Empire.

Note

The Quest of the Historical Jesus

The problem of the life of Jesus is at once the most important and the most baffling of all those that face the student of ancient history. Until the eighteenth century it was left largely to the theologians. Then English and French deists began to criticize the Gospel narratives. Their criticisms were philosophical rather than historical, centering especially around the miracles, but they convinced thoughtful persons that a simple rewriting of the Gospels cannot make sober history. In the historically-minded nineteenth century, Biblical scholars gradually took up the methods of criticism that historians use when examining the sources for other historical events. They began talking about the "Jesus of history," whom they contrasted favorably with the "Christ of theology," eulogizing the former but often abandoning the latter to the attacks of rationalist critics. Sometimes they indulged in such attacks themselves. Only after much wrangling did scholars come to regard the rise of Christianity as a social phenomenon worth studying dispassionately for its own sake. These various studies were pursued by scores of eminent scholars, only three of whom may be mentioned here.

David Friedrich Strauss

David Friedrich Strauss (1808–1874) was born at Ludwigsburg in Württemberg, the son of a rather well-to-do merchant. After taking a theological degree at Tübingen, serving for a few months as assistant to a country pastor and teaching in a secondary school, Strauss went to Berlin to study theology under Schleiermacher and philosophy under Hegel. Though Hegel died a few weeks after Strauss's arrival, the young man drank deeply of the Hegelian philosophy, which he later taught at Tübingen. Here he published his famous *Leben Jesu kritisch bearbeitet* in 1835, when only twenty-seven years of age. The book created such scandal that no German university would employ its author, and though he presently received a call from the Swiss university at Zürich, popular protests forced its withdrawal before he met his first class. Fortunately, his father had left him an income large enough to keep off poverty, and thereafter Strauss lived as an independent author and lecturer, though until almost the end of his life his books enjoyed no popular success.

Like many German intellectuals of his day, Strauss became deeply interested in the political agitation of 1848. He published a satire on Frederick William IV of Prussia under the title "Julian the Apostate, or the Romantic on the Throne of the Caesars," and he unsuccessfully stood as a candidate for election to the Frankfort Assembly. A few weeks later he was elected to the Württemberg parliament, but his ineptitude as a politician soon brought about his forced resignation. Life was further saddened for him by his marriage to an opera singer who was not well suited to life with a man of his scholarly and retiring character: after five years of marriage they separated. Strauss's sensitive nature suffered much under the abuse heaped upon him throughout life by his opponents. He died in 1874 after a long and painful illness which he bore with the same fortitude that he showed under his many other misfortunes and disappointments.

The *Leben Jesu* is a work of 1480 pages, full of untranslated quotations in Latin, Greek, and Hebrew, and addressed to scholars only. Nevertheless, it created a sensation in Germany and throughout Europe. It ran through four German editions in five years, it was translated into French by the positivist philosopher E. Littré (1840), and into English by the novelist "George Eliot" (1846). The book's distinguishing feature is its mythological interpretation of the Gospels. This method had already been used by the rationalists to explain away miracles and other difficulties, especially those of the Old Testament. Strauss applied it to the Gospels with a ruthless thoroughness that showed his genius. In fact, Strauss was more severe upon the old rationalists than upon orthodox interpreters, holding them up to ridicule because of the half-hearted manner in which they applied their criticism and their mythological interpretations to the Gospels. With great acuteness and learning, he examined one Gospel story after another in the most minute detail, and in every case he rejected it as the creation of early Christian mythmakers carried away by their love of the miraculous or, more frequently, by their desire to have all Old Testa-

ment prophecies fulfilled in the person of Jesus. Strauss never questioned
the fact that there had once been a man named Jesus, who was baptized
by John the Baptist, preached in Galilee and Jerusalem, gathered about
him a group of disciples, and eventually was crucified; but after his criticism was finished, not much more than this remained of the traditional life
of Jesus. At no place in the book did the author sketch a life of Jesus as
he believed it had actually happened: he merely discussed the episodes
which he had decided to reject.

In spite of its purely negative character, and though its criticism is
much more radical than that used by scholars today, Strauss's *Leben Jesu*
is perhaps the most important single book ever written on the subject. Its
ridicule put an end to the old-fashioned rationalists who arbitrarily explained away episodes of which they happened to disapprove but retained
others, no better authenticated, which met their private approval. Strauss
was a theologian, not a historian, but his criticisms forced scholars to re-
examine the evidence for the life of Jesus. They then began to judge this
evidence by the criteria that are used in judging the historical evidence
regarding Alexander the Great or Napoleon. In so doing, they transferred
the topic from the province of theology to that of history.

After several years during which Strauss wrote upon other matters in
order to avoid the controversy aroused by his great work, he returned to
his old field with a book entitled, *Das Leben Jesu für das deutsche Volk
bearbeitet* (1864). This was an entirely new book, not a re-editing of the
other. Here the life of Jesus is presented in biographical fashion. Much
that was rejected in the earlier book is now admitted, and the story is not
very different from that found in other "liberal" lives of Jesus appearing
at about that time. Finally Strauss summed up his views on religion and
philosophy in a book entitled *Der alte und der neue Glaube* ("The Old
Faith and the New") (1872). Hegelian idealism here gives way to scientific materialism and Darwinism. At last Strauss had written a book with
wide popular appeal, and edition succeeded edition throughout the remainder of the nineteenth century. Nevertheless, philosophers could not
take it seriously, and romantic enthusiasts found it dull, smug, and unin-
spired. The youthful Nietzsche published a review of it in which he administered a fearful lashing to the hapless old man: his diatribe is still
worth glancing over as an example of what a man of genius can do if he
lets himself go. The historian von Treitschke was equally severe upon the
author of the *Leben Jesu* in his great history of Germany in the nineteenth
century. More sympathetic and truer accounts of Strauss may be found
in the biographies by his friend, the historian of Greek philosophy,
Eduard Zeller (1874) and by Theobold Ziegler (1908). The *Gesammelte*

Schriften (12 vols., 1876–78) contains the second *Leben Jesu* but not the first.

Ernest Renan

Perhaps the *Vie de Jésus* of Ernest Renan (1823–1892) best sets forth the "liberal" interpretation of Jesus that was widely popular in the second half of the nineteenth century. Renan was born in Brittany and studied for the Roman Catholic priesthood at a theological seminary in Paris. His studies of the Old Testament, and of German commentaries upon it, raised doubts in his mind regarding the orthodox interpretation of the Scriptures. He therefore withdrew from the seminary without completing his course or being ordained (1845). He presently established a warm friendship with a young man (Marcellin Berthelot, later a distinguished chemist) who filled him with enthusiasm for natural science and for the materialistic philosophy then associated with it. Before long, Renan was a renowned Semitic scholar. The French government sent him on an archeological expedition to Phoenicia, and on his return he became Professor of Hebrew at the Collège de France (1861). Two years later the *Vie de Jésus* appeared. Its brushing aside of miracles and its calm assumption of the simple humanity of Jesus aroused great scandal: within a year the attacks, criticisms, diatribes, and refutations it provoked numbered almost a hundred, not including countless articles in newspapers and magazines. Nevertheless, the book enjoyed a tremendous success: sixty thousand copies were sold within five months, and as many more within three years. A popular edition eventually raised sales well above a million and a quarter copies. Translations quickly appeared in ten languages. The book is a classic, still easily available in inexpensive editions (Everyman's Library, Modern Library).

The storm of abuse that greeted the *Vie de Jésus* so frightened the Emperor Napoleon III that he dismissed Renan from his professorship. The Emperor's numerous critics at once hailed Renan as a martyr to freedom of thought. In a panic, Napoleon offered to restore Renan to his old position, but Renan haughtily declined. After the fall of Napoleon, and the establishment of the Third French Republic in 1870, Renan resumed his professorship and continued his studies of early Christianity with six further volumes of a *Histoire des origines du Christianisme,* carrying the story down to the end of the second century. He also published a five-volume *Histoire du peuple d'Israel* (1887–94), a charming autobiography entitled *Souvenirs d'enfance et de jeunesse* (1883) in which he describes the evolution of his theological views, and lesser works on scholarly, literary, and popular themes. During the last twenty years of his life Renan was one of the most highly esteemed men in France and his death brought forth tributes from persons of every sort.

The author of so long a book as the present one may be permitted a part of one note for a family legend—even though this legend may possibly be what Strauss would have called a "philosophical myth," *i.e.*, a story which is not historically true but which none the less embodies a general truth. I have been told that, soon after the English translation of Renan's book appeared in this country, my grandfather—a Congregational minister in a New England city—procured a copy. His father, then an elderly man, picked up the volume, glanced over the first few pages, and was so horrified that in that book he read no more. My grandfather persevered to the end, commented that "M. Renan forgets that Christianity rests not upon the Sermon on the Mount but upon Calvary," and consoled himself with the reflection that "America is still too profoundly Christian a nation to be disturbed by one more infidel book." Several years later my father read the book and was converted by it. When I first read the *Vie de Jésus*, in my student days, I admired its beautiful French prose but I could not understand the commotion it caused.

Albert Schweitzer

Albert Schweitzer (1875–   ) has been hailed as one of the geniuses and saints of our day. When still a young man he made an international reputation for himself with a theological work entitled *The Quest of the Historical Jesus* (1906); he is a great organist whose book on J. S. Bach is considered the best in its field; and he has passed most of his mature years as a medical missionary in Africa. Schweitzer spent his childhood at Günsbach in Alsace, where his father was the village pastor, and he took a degree in philosophy at Strasbourg. After continuing his theological and philosophical studies at Berlin, and studying music at Paris, he began to teach in the theological faculty at Strasbourg and to preach in the cathedral. It was during these years that he wrote his famous books on Jesus and Bach. Even as a young man Schweitzer had been skeptical regarding the then-current views of "progress," and was inclined to see the dark underside of things. These reflections led him to the conclusion that duty required him to devote his life to improving the lot of men less fortunate than himself. He decided that he might continue his scholarship and music until the age of thirty, but that thereafter he must lead a more active life. He therefore took a doctor's degree in medicine and in 1913 he left his happy surroundings at Strasbourg to found a hospital at Lambaréné in French Equatorial Africa. Here he has since remained, except for vacations in Europe which he fills with concert tours to raise funds for the hospital.

Nevertheless, Schweitzer has found time to continue his studies and his writing as well as his music. Being an Alsatian, bilingual, and with deep and sympathetic appreciation of the good points of both Germany and France, he was much upset by the outbreak of war in 1914. This catastrophe fortified the doubts he already felt about the future of European civilization and caused him to reflect at length upon such matters in his African refuge. He expressed himself in a comprehensive work, the first two volumes of which are called, in the English translation, *The Decay and Restoration of Civilization* (1922) and *Civilization and Ethics* (1923). A few years later Schweitzer continued his New Testament studies with an important work, planned while he was still at Strasbourg, *The Mysticism of Paul the Apostle* (1930). In spite of these books, however, his most brilliant and most important work is the one on Jesus, entitled *Von Reimarius zu Wrede* in the first edition (1906) (after two German critics who mark the beginning and the end of his story), and renamed *Geschichte der Leben-Jesu Forschung* in the much enlarged second edition (1913). The English translation bears the title, *The Quest of the Historical Jesus* (1910).

Though the greater part of this book is made up of accounts and criticisms of earlier students of the life of Jesus, Schweitzer finds a place in it for his own views as well. These views he had sketched in a brochure published as early as 1901, but he now gave them their classic expression. According to Schweitzer's theory, Jesus confidently felt himself to be the Messiah foretold by the prophets, and the whole course of his public ministry was dominated by this conviction: he was certain that God would soon establish a new and better Kingdom upon earth, and that he had been selected to play a major part in the great drama. In putting forth these views, Schweitzer broke definitely with the "liberal" writers, who were quite unwilling to attribute such "nonsensical" ideas to Jesus. This apocalyptic interpretation of Jesus was not original with Schweitzer, but it is he who gave it its most forceful expression and who persuaded scholars of its correctness. More recent writers differ with him on minor points, but in general they regard his interpretation as our best guide to the career of Jesus. *The Quest of the Historical Jesus* is the most important contribution to our knowledge and understanding of his life that has appeared in the present century.

Hostile critics sometimes aver that Strauss was a mere pedant while Renan was a dilettante skeptic, and they accuse each of lacking all religious feeling. Such a charge cannot possibly be leveled against Schweitzer. The most superficial reader of his books must recognize in him a man of deep religious feeling. His theology is Unitarian and his sympathies are with such left-wing Protestants as the Moravian Brethren in Germany and the Quakers in this country. On the last page of his great book Schweitzer sums up his studies in a few striking sentences. Jesus was mistaken about many things, Schweitzer admits, and for us today his Messianic dreams are only a matter of ancient history, but the heart of Jesus' message still remains what it has always been: "Follow me." How Schweitzer interpreted these words we may observe in his whole subsequent career. See George Seaver, *Albert Schweitzer: the Man and his Mind* (1947), Hermann Hagedorn, *Prophet in the Wilderness: the Story of Albert Schweitzer* (1947), and especially, Albert Schweitzer, *Out of my Life and Thought* (1933).

XIII A Century of Peace

When Nero committed suicide in June, 68, Titus Flavius Vespasianus was commanding the legions in Palestine. A year later, on July 1, 69, troops stationed in Egypt proclaimed Vespasian emperor, and his own legions followed suit after a few days. Friends in the West watched over his interests there, and in his behalf an army from the Danubian provinces marched on Rome. Vitellius, the third man who had vainly tried to rule Rome in that chaotic year, was murdered on December 20, and on the 21st the senate recognized Vespasian as emperor, passing a *lex de imperio* to define his position. No one offered the new emperor serious opposition, and when he finally reached Rome, late in 70, the world was once more at peace.

For more than two years, men everywhere had been dreading a return of the horrors that accompanied the fall of the Republic and were prepared to accept any ruler who could avert such calamities. They welcomed Vespasian with open arms. They quickly made him into a superhuman hero, telling stories of how he had miraculously cured a paralytic in Egypt simply by touching him while his spittle had restored sight to a blind man. Writing a full generation later, the historian Tacitus assumed that of course the Jewish prophets were referring to Vespasian when they foretold a king (Messiah) who would arise in Palestine and rule mankind. It was therefore easy for Vespasian to present himself as a new Augustus bringing peace and order to a distracted world.

The new emperor belonged to an undistinguished family and to a class of society whose members would never have enjoyed political

495

careers under the Republic. He was born (9 A.D.) in a central Italian
village, but after various peregrinations his father eventually settled
as a moneylender in Switzerland. Vespasian advanced through different stages of the imperial bureaucracy without the aid of intrigues
at court, but in the days of Nero he fell into temporary disfavor by
inadvertently dropping asleep as the emperor sang. His appointment
to the Palestinian command in 67 was both a recognition of his military ability and evidence that he was not considered politically
ambitious. Two years later, however, he rose to supreme power. His
success brought an end to the Julio-Claudian system under which
the highest offices were reserved for members of the old Republican
aristocracy, which had been virtually wiped out by Nero and the
wars of 68 and 69. Thereafter the world was governed by officials
who, like Vespasian himself, were drawn largely from the upper
middle classes of Italy. The Julio-Claudian dynasty had ruled during
a century of transition, and the advent of the Flavian dynasty (Vespasian and his two sons) marked another step in the progress of the
imperial system.

The Flavian Emperors

The revolts of 68 and 69 had convinced most Romans that only a
strong central government could prevent successful commanders
from renewing civil war at their pleasure. The new *lex de imperio*
therefore granted Vespasian powers never held by the Julio-Claudians. The new emperor had himself elected consul every year; he
revived the censorship, with its great powers of appointment; and
he made a member of his family prefect of the praetorian guard.
Above all, Vespasian saw to it that his offices should be inherited by
his son, saying, "Either my son will succeed me or no one will."
When Vespasian died in 79, his son Titus took over, and Titus's early
death in 81 brought a younger son, Domitian, to power. With the
murder of Domitian in 96, the Flavian dynasty came to an end.

Under Vespasian and his sons the provinces of the Roman Empire
entered upon their golden age. Vespasian had visited almost every
province in the Empire, from Britain and Africa to Syria and Egypt,
and he knew something of their problems. Spain was the most for-

tunate of the provinces under the new regime. About four hundred communities received municipal autonomy, and many new cities were founded. The charter of Malaga, which is typical of this time, granted local self-government, Latin rights to all citizens, and full Roman citizenship to all officeholders. Gaul, the Danubian provinces, and Africa also prospered under Vespasian, and their Romanization advanced rapidly. Fewer changes were made in the East, but everywhere an efficient and honest government put an end to the looting which had disgraced the Republic and which even Tiberius had not wholly eradicated. An excellent example of the new type of administrator who flourished under the Flavians may be seen in Julius Agricola, who for many years was governor of Britain and whose life was charmingly written by his son-in-law, the historian Tacitus.

Vespasian's troubles were primarily financial. The treasury was empty when he came into power, large sections of Rome and Italy were devastated and needed immediate relief, many imperial estates had been occupied by private persons, and the collection of taxes was unusually difficult. It was said that Vespasian estimated that forty billion sesterces ($1,600,000,000) were needed to put the Empire back on its feet. The government was therefore forced to extreme measures in raising money, though even hostile critics admitted that the money thus raised was afterward spent wisely. Vespasian's efforts to increase the imperial revenues were resented at the time, but in the long run they resulted in a juster distribution of taxes. Heretofore, Rome's revenue system had been a complicated and uneven patchwork, with certain provinces taxed very lightly or—as in the case of Greece under Nero—entirely exempted from tribute, while others were ground down by exorbitant demands. Vespasian increased taxes everywhere as much as possible and for a while the whole world suffered to the limit of its capacity, but after the initial stringency was over, a new system of taxation was devised that was both adequate and fair to all the provinces. Even Vespasian, however, did not dare levy direct taxes upon Roman citizens, and Italy was largely spared.

Vespasian died in June, 79, and was succeeded by his son, Titus.

The new emperor had been carefully trained for his post. He had been his father's chief assistant, serving as consul and censor with him, and even sharing with him the *imperium* and the *tribunicia potestas*. He was popular at Rome and he continued his father's policies with great success, until he died suddenly at the age of forty-two (September, 81). In spite of his merits and popularity, Titus's reign is remembered chiefly for a series of disasters for which he was in no way to blame: a fire at Rome destroyed the Capitol and much of the city; a plague carried off thousands of victims; and the famous eruption of Mount Vesuvius (August 24, 79) buried Pompeii and Herculaneum.

Titus was succeeded by his brother Domitian, who was twelve years his junior. Domitian was less able than Vespasian and he had received less careful training than Titus. He was thoroughly familiar with public affairs, however, and during the first years of his rule he successfully maintained the family policies and popularity. Like his two predecessors, he claimed to follow in the footsteps of Augustus, Tiberius, and Claudius. He provided honest administration, he was a great builder, and he bought the favor of the populace with games and bread. Nevertheless, efficiency and administrative centralization required heavy taxation and gave rise to charges of tyranny, or, as his biographer Suetonius put it, "Lack of money made Domitian rapacious, and fear made him cruel." An active opposition arose in the senate, and in 88 a military revolt was attempted by the commanders of four legions in Germany. As most of the troops refused to participate, the revolt was easily crushed and its ringleaders were executed or exiled. During the next few years discontent was kept alive by popular demagogues calling themselves "philosophers," until 93 when Domitian expelled a considerable number of them from Italy. Jews and Christians also suffered persecution at that time. Severe punishments did not end the plots against Domitian's life, however, and he was murdered in September, 96.

The Good Emperors

Among the conspirators who planned the assassination of Domitian was a senator named Marcus Cocceius Nerva. Born in an Umbrian town about fifty miles north of Rome, in 30 A.D., he belonged to a family that had first become prominent under Octavian. Though a friend of Nero, Nerva had continued his career under the Flavian emperors, and after the death of Domitian he was proclaimed emperor by the senate. He prevented civil war, but when Domitian's friends in the praetorian guard and army demanded the punishment of the assassins, Nerva allowed his accomplices to be executed. Throughout the remainder of his reign the army remained surly. The aging emperor's most important act was the adoption of Trajan as his heir, and he died after a reign of barely sixteen months (January, 98).

Trajan (Marcus Ulpius Traianus) was a native of Italica, a town near Seville in Spain, where he was born in 52. Though descended from Italians who had emigrated in the second century before Christ, it is not improbable that he had Spanish blood too in his veins. Since Trajan's three successors likewise belonged to Italian families long resident in the provinces, his accession marked a further expansion of the governing class comparable to that effected when the Italian Vespasian succeeded the Roman Julio-Claudians. Trajan was with the army at Cologne when Nerva died, but he had no important rival and was accepted at once by the senate as Nerva's heir. Not until several months later did he reach Rome. Trajan was primarily a military man, the last of the great conquerors who added new provinces to the Empire. He also proved himself an able administrator. He won the cordial support of the senate and the intellectual classes, and he persuaded people everywhere that a new day of liberty had dawned. After ruling serenely for more than nineteen years, he died in August, 117.

Publius Aelius Hadrianus was born at Rome in 76. His family on both sides had lived for several generations in Spain, his father's ancestors at Trajan's birthplace, Italica, and his mother's people at Gades. Left an orphan when ten years old, Hadrian was educated by his father's cousin, the Emperor Trajan. He married the emperor's niece and was adopted by Trajan—who had no sons—a few days before the old man died. Being of a peaceful disposition, and having no desire for conquest, Hadrian concluded the Parthian war in which Trajan had been engaged, surrendered two eastern provinces recently taken from the Parthians, and devoted the twenty-one years of his reign to domestic administration. More than half of his reign Hadrian spent in travels which took him from one end of the Roman world to the other and to practically every province in the Empire. He was strongly philhellenic, and fond of living at Athens, where he spent about seven years all told; but more than any of his predecessors Hadrian tried to view all the provinces of his vast empire with impartial sympathy.

A glance at Hadrian's great building program reveals many of his fundamental ambitions and gives evidence of the wealth and prosperity of the Empire in his day. At Rome he rebuilt the Pantheon which had been constructed by Agrippa in 27 B.C. but was struck by lightning in 111 (Plate 23). His magnificent villa, a few miles from Rome, was lavishly decorated with scenes from all parts of the Empire as a sort of museum and monument to imperial unity. Hadrian also erected a huge tomb for himself at Rome near the Tiber: it is now the Castel Sant' Angelo. Hadrian's philhellenism made him especially generous to Athens, where he erected many buildings and completed an enormous temple to the Olympian Zeus. Started by the tyrant Peisistratus shortly after 550 B.C. and continued almost four centuries later by that ardent philhellenist, Antiochus IV Epiphanes of Syria, the temple was at last completed as a shrine for the whole Greek world. The Pantheon, dedicated to all the gods, and this temple to the Olympian Zeus are fitting symbols of Hadrian's desire to see Greeks and Romans unite on equal terms in his world empire. Countless other cities, both Greek and Latin, were beautified at Hadrian's expense, scholars and artists were encouraged, and great efforts were made to revive the ancient glories of Greece and Rome.

In his later years Hadrian centered his hopes for the succession in Marcus Annius Verus, who later became the Emperor Marcus Aurelius. As the fifteen-year-old boy obviously could not succeed him at once, Hadrian in 136 adopted the man to whose daughter Marcus was betrothed. The new heir took the name Lucius Aelius Caesar, thus establishing the practice of using the name Caesar for the heir

Vespasian *(Naples Museum)*

Trajan *(Munich Museum)*

Hadrian *(Vatican Museum)*

Marcus Aurelius *(Louvre Museum)*

Plate 22

Pantheon

Reliefs from Arch of Titus

Plate 23

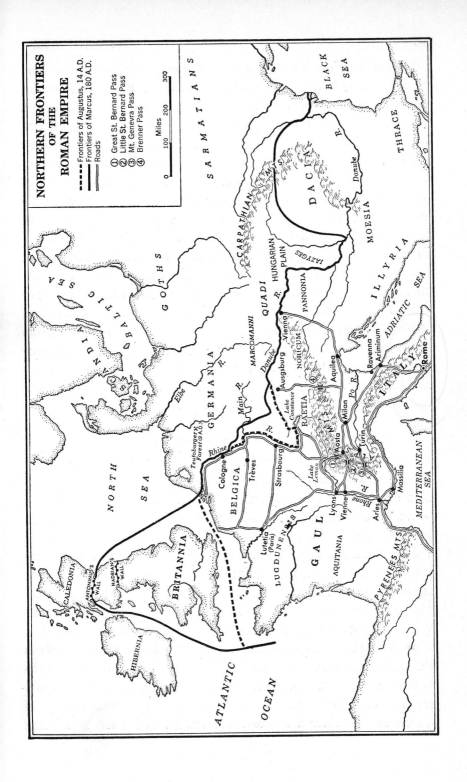

NORTHERN FRONTIERS
OF THE
ROMAN EMPIRE

············ Frontiers of Augustus, 14 A.D.
———— Frontiers of Marcus, 180 A.D.
═══ Roads

① Great St. Bernard Pass
② Little St. Bernard Pass
③ Mt. Genevra Pass
④ Brenner Pass

Miles
0   100   200   300

BLACK SEA

THRACE

SARMATIANS

CARPATHIAN MTS.

DACIA

R. Danube

MOESIA

IAZYGES

HUNGARIAN PLAIN

PANNONIA

QUADI

R.

Vienna

ILLYRIA

ADRIATIC SEA

MARCOMANNI

Danube R.

NORICUM

Ariminum

Ravenna

GOTHS

GERMANIA

R.

Augsburg

Aquilea

Po R.

Ravenna

ITALY

Rome

BALTIC SEA

Elbe

Main R.

Lake Constance

RAETIA

ALPS

Milan

Turin

Aosta

CANDIA

Teutoburger Forest 9 A.D.

Rhine

Cologne

Treves

Strasbourg

BELGICA

Lake Leman

Massilia

MEDITERRANEAN SEA

NORTH SEA

Lutetia (Paris)

LUGDUNENSIS

GAUL

Lyons

Vienne

Rhone R.

Arles

AQUITANIA

PYRENEES MTS.

BRITANNIA

ANTONINUS'S WALL

HADRIAN'S WALL

CALEDONIA

HIBERNIA

ATLANTIC OCEAN

beyond the Rhine, his successors abandoned such ambitions. The
weakness of the Rhine frontier was shown during the civil wars of
68 and 69, and Vespasian decided to strengthen it by occupying a
large corner of southwestern Germany. This shortened line facili-
tated the quick movement of troops from the Danubian to the Rhine
provinces. Domitian repeated the maneuver on a broader scale, and
Antoninus completed the task by cutting off another corner from
Germany and strongly fortifying the whole northern frontier. The
limes erected under Antoninus remained the boundary of the Empire thereafter. Claudius had invaded Britain, but neither he nor his
successors conquered Scotland. Hadrian therefore built a strong wall
across the island a little south of the present Scottish frontier to prevent raids into Roman Britain, and a few years later Antoninus built
a second wall about seventy-five miles farther north, from the Firth
of Forth to the mouth of the Clyde.

Trajan's first conquest was Dacia, the territory lying north of the
lower Danube which is now the part of Romania that is called Tran-
sylvania. The Dacians, a Thracian people much influenced by the
Scythians and other northern barbarians, had been defeated by a
Roman army in 73 B.C., and again in 29 B.C. A century later, in 84
A.D., they were powerful enough to invade the Roman province of
Moesia, where they destroyed an army sent by Domitian to punish
them—the first serious defeat suffered by Roman arms since the disaster of Varus in the Teutoburger Forest (9 A.D.). Trajan invaded
Dacia in 101 and six years later he annexed the country. The new
province contained important mines of gold and silver, and its king
had accumulated a vast hoard of these precious metals. Trajan relieved his financial embarrassments by confiscating this treasury.
Perhaps a desire for the mines and metals was the principal reason
why he attacked Dacia. The province was presently colonized by
settlers from all parts of the Empire and given a Latin culture. It
was the only eastern province to be Romanized, and the work was so
well done that, in spite of many subsequent invasions and the ab-
sorption of countless invaders, the Romanian people still speak a
language of Latin origin.

Between the Danubian provinces and Dacia lay the Hungarian

Plain, inhabited by a people akin to the Sarmatians of southern Russia, and north of the bend of the Danube were various Germanic tribes. These barbarians were not a serious menace until the middle of the second century when the Goths, who formerly dwelt along the Baltic coast, began moving southward, driving others before them. Roman garrisons were swept aside as the barbarians crossed the Alps into Italy and when they besieged Aquileia at the head of the Adriatic in 167, they became the first enemies to set foot on Italian soil since the defeat of the Cimbri in 100 B.C. Marcus Aurelius hastened to the defense of the frontier and spent the remainder of his life fighting barbarians. Though the Roman legions soon proved their superiority by driving out the invaders, Marcus Aurelius decided that peace could be preserved only if the Hungarian Plain and modern Slovakia were annexed by Rome and a new frontier established along the Carpathian Mountains. While preparing to invade this territory, the emperor died, early in 180. His successor discontinued the campaign, and the frontiers remained where they had been before. Had Marcus lived long enough to establish the Carpathian frontier, the subsequent history of the Roman Empire and of Europe would undoubtedly have been very different.

The Parthian Wars

The line separating Roman territory from the Parthians was the only other ill-defined frontier. Augustus and the Julio-Claudians had gradually transformed various eastern client-kingdoms into Roman provinces, and Vespasian made an extensive reorganization of the East after the capture of Jerusalem in 70. Thereafter, Armenia was the only seat of serious trouble within the Empire. The great importance of Armenia lay in its control of the only practicable military road from Syria to Parthia. The Parthians therefore inspired native unrest to keep the road from Roman hands. Armenia was pacified under Nero, when the Romans forced the king to surrender his crown and receive it back as the gift of Rome. Domitian, too, had trouble here and contemplated an invasion of the country, but he died before executing his plan. Trajan therefore inherited a bad situation, and after the Dacian campaigns were finished he began pre-

paring for war in the East. He easily occupied Armenia in 114, and
after annexing it as a Roman province he prepared a great campaign
to eliminate the Parthian menace that had disturbed the Near East
for so long.

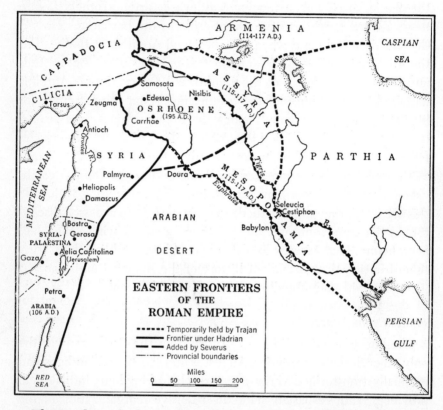

EASTERN FRONTIERS
OF THE
ROMAN EMPIRE
- - - - - Temporarily held by Trajan
————— Frontier under Hadrian
━ ━ ━ Added by Severus
—·—·—· Provincial boundaries

The Parthians had won their greatest military victories in the days
of Crassus and Antony, when the armies of Orodes II (57–37 B.C.)
defeated and annihilated Roman legions. In 19 B.C. Augustus concluded a peace that proved to be highly advantageous to the economic life of both empires, for it reopened the great caravan routes
across Parthia which connected the Western World with India and
China. The Romans were not satisfied, however, and constantly
sought new routes to the Far East which would not cross Parthian
territory. The Red Sea offered the best alternative route, and Augustus annexed a part of Arabia at the head of that sea. In 106 Trajan

continued this policy by adding to the Empire the Nabataean kingdom whose capital was at Petra, south and east of the Dead Sea.

Though the Parthians made no attempts to obtain territory along the Mediterranean after 37 B.C., they continued to resist Roman advances. They sent aid to Armenia in the days of Nero and again when Roman armies invaded that country in 114. Trajan used this as an excuse for advancing against them. From Armenia, he invaded northern Mesopotamia, which he annexed as two provinces. A second campaign carried him south to Ctesiphon and left most of the Semitic part of the Parthian Empire in his hands. Trajan soon found, however, that he could not hold this territory, and shortly before his death he began to withdraw. Hadrian followed the same prudent policy, evacuating the two new provinces in Mesopotamia and restoring Armenia to its former position as a client-kingdom.

Forty years of peace followed until, in the early days of Marcus Aurelius, new troubles in Armenia led to another Parthian war. This war opened with two major victories for the Parthians (163), but the co-emperor Verus and his general (Avidius Cassius, a native Syrian of whom we shall hear again) occupied Armenia and repeated Trajan's march to Ctesiphon. A few frontier cities and a large tract of desert were annexed by Rome, after which peace reigned for another thirty years. War was resumed in the last decade of the century, and there was further inconclusive fighting early in the third century. By this time, however, the days of the Parthian Empire were numbered. It collapsed from internal weakness in the 220's, and was succeeded by the Sassanian or Third Persian Empire.

The Empire in the Second Century

"If a man were called to fix the period in the history of the world during which the condition of the human race was most happy and prosperous, he would, without hesitation, name that which elapsed from the death of Domitian to the accession of Commodus." Such is the judgment Edward Gibbon expressed in 1776 in an opening chapter of his *History of the Decline and Fall of the Roman Empire*. Slightly more than a hundred years later, in 1885, another great historian of Rome, Theodor Mommsen, wrote, "To many regions in

both East and West imperial Rome brought a level of good government which, though modest in itself, has not been equaled before
or since. If an angel of the Lord were to judge whether the domain
ruled by the emperors was governed with greater intelligence and
humanity then or now, whether the refinements of civilization and
national prosperity in general have advanced or fallen back, it is
very doubtful whether the decision would favor the present." And
in 1926 the distinguished Russian-American historian of antiquity,
M. Rostovtzeff, published a brilliant picture of the economic felicity
of the second century.[1] Each of these scholars echoes in his own way
the enthusiasm of second-century writers, who were quite certain
that they had been chosen by fate to enjoy the world's culminating
period of liberty, civilization, and human happiness.

A Benevolent Despotism

Nearly everyone in the second century believed that the emperors
of that time resembled the ideal king of the Stoic philosophers—the
"best" man devoting his whole thought and energy to helping the
people. Each emperor chose his successor. Theoretically, this system
insured that the man chosen would be the best available, and in
practice it provided well-trained and conscientious administrators
who inherited power without serious risk of civil war. The emperors
insisted that they were merely the "first citizens" of Rome, while in
reality they were exalted bureaucrats who directed the civil service
and the army. Though they doubtless had the best intentions in the
world, these bureaucratic emperors could not help becoming more
and more authoritarian, until at last they were benevolent despots.
The civil administration was conducted by their appointees. Taxes
were levied as the emperors saw fit. Legislation fell entirely to them,
and the force behind their rule lay in their armies. Even in the days
of Hadrian the Roman Empire was definitely committed to the principles of centralized absolutism.

The senate still retained high prestige, its members had the sole
right to certain high and lucrative positions, and the emperors pre-

---

[1] See notes on Edward Gibbon, p. 531, Theodor Mommsen, p. 368, and M. Rostovtzeff, p. 533.

ferred to avoid controversy with it. But the senate no longer was
what it once had been, either in power or in personnel. Its members
acquired their seats by first being elected quaestors. Any young man
of the senatorial order could stand for election, and after Tiberius
had transferred elections to the senate, the senators themselves
chose their future colleagues from these candidates. The senators
thus chosen were largely an hereditary caste, to which the emperors
arbitrarily added new members from time to time. Among the Italian aristocrats who continued to make up the majority of the senate,
many took their duties rather lightly and were inclined to let more
energetic members do the work. As the emperor's nominees usually
were men of the latter sort, they became more influential than their
numbers would suggest.

Even in the days of Caesar there had been a few senators from
the provinces, and under Trajan they became numerous. About one
thousand senators from the reigns of Hadrian, Antoninus, and Marcus are known to us by name. They were probably the more active
members of that body, and they do not show a fair proportion of
the Italian aristocrats who regarded membership in the senate primarily as a social distinction. The origins of about half these known
senators can be determined: almost three-fifths were Italians, but
over two-fifths were provincials. At first Gaul and Spain provided
the greater part of the provincial senators, but even under Trajan
and Hadrian there were many Africans, Greeks, and Orientals in the
senate. Under Marcus Aurelius the Gauls and Spaniards almost disappeared, and about a quarter of the senators of known origin were
Greeks or Orientals. The emperors thus made the senate represent
the whole Empire and especially its more significant parts.

Nevertheless, the power and prestige of the senate declined as
those of the imperial bureaucracy rose. This bureaucracy, dating
from the days of Augustus, had been systematically organized by
Claudius. It was directed by various secretaries who looked after
different branches of the administration. Thus the secretary *ab epis-
tulis* conducted the emperor's correspondence with provincial governors and other officials all over the Empire. The secretary *a ration-
ibus* had charge of the finances, the *a libellis* dealt with petitions

presented to the emperor, and the *a cognitionibus* looked after judicial cases appealed to the emperor. The secretary *a studiis* was at once archivist, finder of precedents, and author of the emperor's speeches.

Augustus and Tiberius had used equestrians as well as personal slaves and freedmen as their assistants. Claudius used freedmen whose insolence sometimes seemed intolerable to the old aristocrats. Otho and Vitellius, during their brief reigns in 69, gave indications that they intended to return to the appointment of equestrians, and their example was followed by the Flavians. The Good Emperors virtually eliminated freedmen, and the bureaucracy became the sphere of political activity of the equestrian order. Hadrian gave these officials ranks roughly corresponding to those in the army, with salaries and titles fixed for each grade. At the head of the whole bureaucracy stood two praetorian prefects who were chosen by the emperor from the equestrian order, who were responsible directly to him and who were, next to him, the most important men in the Empire. These prefects virtually directed the government. The preponderance of power thus had passed from the aristocratic senatorial order to the upper middle-class equestrians, or rather, to the emperor supported and aided by his equestrian bureaucrats.

Prosperity of Rome and the Provinces

Rome remained the capital of the Empire, the largest and most important city in the world. The Flavians and the Good Emperors were active builders and their buildings were far superior, both in construction and in appearance, to anything yet seen in the West. Rome became a beautiful city. It was also one of the most cosmopolitan cities in history, with inhabitants drawn from every corner of the Empire and a population estimated at a million and a half for the period of Antoninus. Ships from all the Mediterranean lands came to its harbor at Ostia—rebuilt by Claudius and expanded again in the second century—bringing the products of the whole world. Nevertheless, we can already detect in this Rome of the second century the first faint signs of impending collapse. Here were 200,000 persons supported in idleness by the grain distributions, and the government dared not reduce the number. The upper classes were beginning to flee the city which had once attracted them, leaving it to foreigners and reliefers. Even the emperors—notably Hadrian—preferred to live elsewhere.

Italy and the provinces showed equal signs of prosperity. Throughout the Empire, from Syria to Spain and Africa, were countless cities which, as recent archeological exploration has shown, were well-built and prosperous places. Some were old cities, restored and beautified; others were new cities built by the Romans. As further evidence of the prosperity of the time we might cite the number of rich men who, like modern American millionaires, left monuments to themselves in the form of public buildings or foundations to promote the general welfare. Not until quite recent times have public benefactions appeared so frequently. And finally, the general prosperity of the century is shown by a great increase in population. It has been estimated that the population of the Empire rose from seventy to one hundred millions—an increase of about 50 per cent —during the century and a half between Augustus and Antoninus. Only since 1800 has this phenomenon been surpassed.

The cities of the Empire could still boast of their ancient liberties. Each was governed by its *curia,* a body of native officials who in local matters could do about as they pleased—unless, of course they pleased to make war on their neighbors, engage in piracy or brigandage, or otherwise disturb the Roman peace. The provincials were expected to bear the cost of the army and of the imperial administration, but taxation was not exorbitant, and intelligent people knew that they got their money's worth in peace and security. The cities could levy further taxes and spend money about as they saw fit. If they fell deeply into debt, as they often did, a Roman official was sent to straighten matters out. Moreover, Roman citizenship was extended rather freely, especially to politicians and to the more substantial citizens. These Roman citizens dominated the political life of the city, giving it an aristocratic and pro-Roman character. Rome thus managed to preserve local liberty within a world organization. Local laws were retained, but Roman law was put beside them and was often accepted voluntarily because of its superiority. Local citizenship remained, with the added privilege of Roman citizenship. Civic loyalty remained, supplemented by a new imperial enthusiasm and loyalty. Old religions were unmolested—unless they sanctioned barbarous practices such as human sacrifice—but emperor worship and the imperial cult stimulated imperial patriotism, and participation in the new cult was expected of all as a token of loyalty to the imperial system.

The Lower Classes

Different forms of landholding prevailed in different parts of the Empire, but the growth of large estates was favored by the forces of economics and by Roman sympathy with the well-to-do classes. The owners of these great estates usually lived in the cities and left the management of their rural properties to stewards. No doubt peasants sometimes resented the conduct of individual landlords or their agents, but there is no evidence of widespread discontent in the second century. In fact, the general prosperity, coupled with the elimination of arbitrary local government, did much to raise the economic status of the peasants, who are to be counted among those profiting most from the imperial system. "It is in the agricultural towns of Africa," wrote Mommsen, "in the homes of the vine-dressers on the Moselle, in the flourishing townships of the Lycian mountains, and on the margin of the Syrian desert that the work of the imperial period is to be sought and found." In such places as these, men went on living in their villages as before, though with a higher standard of living. They might retain their old languages, religions, and social institutions as freely as they pleased. The peasants of the West eventually absorbed much Roman culture, but in Syria and Egypt they failed utterly to adopt the European way of life.

Conditions among the lower classes of the cities were quite different. In the older cities there was, of course, an hereditary native population accustomed to local conditions and fitting into the local scheme of things; but changing populations were rapidly breaking this old system down, and in the newer cities there was no such traditional foundation. Traders, freedmen, and slaves filled every city with a population of varied origin that neither knew nor cared about the cultural traditions of their new homes. A few might become wealthy and ostentatious, but those who failed to grow rich led drab lives in the slums of the great cities. Participation in political life was denied them and their daily toil did not make life seem worth living. Entertainment was found only in the gladiatorial combats and wild-beast hunts whose brutalizing influence was often denounced by moralists. It was among this disinherited urban proletariat, however, that ideas from all parts of the Empire were blended together, that preachers of new superstitions and religions found their following, and that a new civilization characteristic of the new Empire was gradually taking shape.

The best escape open to urban workers from their humdrum life was provided by the *collegia*. Ever since ancient times there had been associations of persons in a given trade or craft. During the last years of the Republic such associations had been exploited politically by men like Clodius, and the Julio-Claudian emperors forbade all private associations that might become centers of such agitation. It was soon found desirable, however, to relax the law enough to permit burial associations. All sorts of people then organized themselves, ostensibly for burial, and in the calmer days of the second century, when the government no longer feared its subjects, new *collegia* could be founded in which burial played a very minor part. These associations were primarily social organizations. Each group contained only a few members, and it had no connection with other groups in the same trade or the same town. Members elected their own officials, sometimes they owned their meeting halls or other property, and incidentally they buried their dead. They also held banquets together, marched in parades, and made other public appearances. Groups were of all sorts, varying in character with their members. Within each group there usually was a good deal of democracy. Nearly anyone—even a slave—could be elected to an office, which increased his self-respect and gave him a feeling of importance. The welfare of the society was something which concerned all its members. Lodges of this sort did much to make life tolerable for the city proletariat until, in the third century, the government's attempts to regulate them robbed them of most of their attractions.

/ *Critics of the Imperial System*

Though most men in the second century believed that their age marked the high point in human history, and were grateful to the emperors who made such things possible, there were always a few who criticized the imperial system. A certain number of "philosophers," usually calling themselves "Cynics," continued to deliver public diatribes against the emperors, chiefly to emphasize the vanity of earthly glory. The emperors usually paid little attention to such attacks—Vespasian once remarked, apropos of such critics, that he would not kick a cur for barking at him—but the public was sometimes scandalized.

Of greater significance were the revolts of minor nationalities, usually peoples or tribes living in out-of-the-way corners of the Empire, little touched by Graeco-Roman civilization. Several such minor revolts are mentioned as occurring during the second century, but their repression caused the authorities little trouble. The most important such uprising, toward the end of the century, was that of Avidius Cassius. Though a native Syrian, Avidius had commanded armies under Marcus Aurelius and Verus, aiding in the defeat of the Parthians in 166. He had also governed several eastern provinces. In 176 he proclaimed himself emperor and was recognized in Cilicia, Syria, and Egypt. He even had partisans at Rome, where it was rumored that Marcus Aurelius's wife was one of them. Though Avidius was murdered after a rule of one hundred days, his attempt served warning that new undercurrents were moving in the East.

The Jews were always a case by themselves and the source of frequent trouble. Though all Jews had been expelled from Palestine in 70 A.D., when Jerusalem was demolished by Titus, many had since then returned to their old homes while others made up a large element in the population of neighboring provinces. In their new homes they were restless, and sometimes they were subjected to anti-Semitic violence by the populace. They kept in constant touch with their Babylonian kinsmen, with whom they shared the national hope of again establishing a Jewish state. Their first revolt occurred during Trajan's Parthian campaign of 115. Beginning in Cyrene, it spread to Egypt and Cyprus and later to Palestine itself. In Cyprus the victorious Jews perpetrated many atrocities upon the Gentiles, and in Egypt the Gentiles retaliated with equal fury against the Jews. The Jews of Babylon also revolted and were repressed, but not until after Trajan's death were those within the Empire pacified.

The site of Jerusalem remained a waste until 130, when Hadrian ordered the building there of a new city to be called Aelia Capitolina. (Aelius was Hadrian's family name.) This new city was to have a temple to Jupiter Capitolinus on the spot where Solomon's Temple had once stood. Once more the Jews revolted, this time under the leadership of a certain Bar Kochba who claimed to be the Messiah, and of Akiba, the most eminent student of Jewish law in his day. The rebels seized Palestine, but their success was short-lived, for of course the Roman legions were ultimately victorious. More than half a million Jews were slaughtered, in addition to the uncounted thousands who died during the war. Again all Jews were excluded from the province, whose name was changed from Judaea to Syria Palaestina.

Literature in the Second Century

The general prosperity of the second century provided what might have been the material foundation for an active intellectual life, but there was little in the general atmosphere to stimulate men's minds. Important cities had public libraries, theaters, auditoriums for lectures, and even professors of literature who were supported at public expense. Private individuals built and endowed similar cultural centers in other cities. There was a large class of men who earned their living by traveling from town to town delivering lectures or reading their literary compositions. Nevertheless, intellectual interests were limited to a rather narrow circle. It is perhaps true that at this time a larger portion of the population than ever before was able to read and write, yet, judged by modern standards, this portion was still pitifully small, and a study of the intellectual history of the period shows that persons interested in literature, science, and philosophy were rapidly dropping into sterility.

Latin Writers of the Silver Age

Literary men living under the Flavians and Trajan created the Latin literature of the Silver Age. The most distinguished of these writers was the historian Tacitus. Born early in the reign of Nero, Publius Cornelius Tacitus followed a conventional political career until he attained the consulship under Nerva, but his fame rests upon his writings. He published a *Dialogue on Orators,* a life of his father-in-law *Agricola,* the *Germania*—a somewhat idealized account of the peoples and customs of Germany—and two great historical works, the *Annals* and the *Histories.* Between them these histories covered the period of the Julio-Claudians and Flavians. Though the ancients regarded him less highly than Sallust and Livy, modern scholars usually consider Tacitus the greatest of the Latin historians. Rejoicing in the freedom which prevailed under Trajan, "when it is possible to think what you please and say what you think," Tacitus looked back with horror upon the preceding hundred years of Roman history. While claiming to write *sine ira et studio*—without passion and prejudice—he composed a terrific and unforgettable indictment of the imperial regime of the first century. Though he developed only the darker side of the picture, and passed over much in silence, his literary powers were such that his views have only recently been questioned. His story, centering in Rome, dealt largely with the emperors and the Roman nobility while the people and provinces received scant attention.

A second writer of the period was Gaius Suetonius Tranquillus, who wrote the celebrated *Lives of the Twelve Caesars.* Though Suetonius lacked the keen insight and literary ability of Tacitus, he collected a great amount of information, good, bad, and indifferent, and his book has remained popular because of the scandalous gossip it contains. He also wrote other lives, especially of Roman literary men, most of which are now lost. Contemporary with these two writers, and a friend of both, was C. Plinius Secundus, usually called Pliny the Younger to distinguish him from his uncle of the same name. The uncle, a learned man in the days of Vespasian who wrote a *Natural History* recording much of the science and superstition of the time, was killed during the destruction of Pompeii in 79. Pliny the Younger, born at Como in 61, was a successful lawyer and a friend of Trajan. He is known especially for his letters, which depict the life of an aristocrat in the second century. This life must have been a pleasant one, refined and easy, but without much for a man to do, and if we compare these letters with those of Cicero we are not surprised that Pliny's social class gradually lost its power and importance. Pliny was stationed in Bithynia from 111 to 113. During this time he conducted an extensive correspondence with Trajan which gives us an excellent picture of Roman provincial administration in the second century.

The only poet of the period worth mentioning is the satirist Juvenal. He was born about 55 at Aquinum, a small town in Latium, practiced law for several years, and eventually was exiled (probably by Domitian). Juvenal spent the latter years of his life writing the *Satires* which, except for those of Horace, are the most celebrated in the Latin language. These harsh and bitter poems show us a very different world from that of Pliny. Juvenal liked to think that he came from old Latin stock (he really was the son of a freedman) and he did not approve of the new cosmopolitan Rome, filled with inferior peoples from all over the earth—with the Syrian Orontes emptying into the Tiber, as he once expressed it—where old Roman customs and manners were ignored or forgotten by a crowd of pushing and intriguing foreigners. These various writers of the Silver Age did their best work in the days of Trajan. Thereafter, until the fourth century, the stream of Latin literature ran very low.

Greek Writers

Greek letters had reached their lowest ebb during the first century of the Christian era. The desolation to which Greece and much of the Greek world had been reduced during the last years of the Roman Republic did not provide an environment able to produce thinkers, artists, or scholars. Even when material conditions improved under the Empire, a generation or two elapsed before the great tradition could be resumed. The writings of the minor Greek authors of the first century are lost, and the little we know of them indicates that they were of slight value. A few Jews, writing in Greek, were more important. One of these, Philo of Alexandria, a theologian and critic of the Scriptures, flourished about 40 A.D., and his works were later used by Christians though ignored by Jews and Greeks. Except for the various New Testament writers, who will be discussed elsewhere, the only other important writer in Greek in the first century was the Jewish historian Josephus.

Josephus, the son of a high priest, was born at Jerusalem in 37 A.D. He visited Rome, where he ingratiated himself with Nero's mistress, Poppaea, and shortly before the Jewish rebellion of 66 he was made governor of Galilee. His intrigues were partly to blame for that outbreak, but he deserted to Vespasian, under ludicrous and disgraceful circumstances, and was present when Titus captured Jerusalem in 70. Vespasian then hired Josephus to write an Aramaic history of the Jewish War to dissuade other Orientals from taking up arms against Rome. The burden of this dramatic history, of which we have only a Greek translation, is that the Jews fought as valiantly as men could fight, but their struggles against the Roman legions were hopeless. After completing this assignment, Josephus spent several years at Rome composing his great *Jewish Antiquities*. Published in twenty books in 93, this work covered Jewish history from the Creation to 66 A.D. The first half is largely a rewriting of the Old Testament narrative, but much of the second half, beginning with the return of the Jews from the Captivity in 536 B.C., is based on Greek sources. For the most recent period Josephus seems to have drawn a little upon the Roman archives. Josephus defended the Jews before the Romans but, like Polybius before him, he believed that the Roman Empire was a good thing and tried to bring his fellow Jews around to this view. All his efforts were in vain, however, and pious Jews have never forgotten his treason. His writings were preserved by the Christians, partly because of a brief and problematic reference to Jesus and partly because his story of the events leading up to the destruction of Jerusalem could easily be made to show God's judgment on the Jews for their rejection of Jesus.

The economic revival that came with the Empire eventually brought a literary renaissance in the Greek world and the second century produced two well-known Greek writers. Plutarch, born at Chaeronea near Thebes in the days of Claudius, was the first important literary man born in European Greece since Polybius two and a half centuries before. After studying at Athens and visiting Egypt, Plutarch spent several years as a lecturer in Italy under the Flavians. In middle life he returned to Chaeronea, where he became a priest of Apollo; he died early in the reign of Hadrian. His writing dates largely from the second half of his career, though several of his essays had doubtless already served as lectures. About sixty of these essays make up the *Moralia*, dealing with a wide range of what we would call social topics. Plutarch's reputation rests principally upon his *Parallel Lives of the Greeks and Romans*. This is a set of fifty biographies, arranged in pairs, of Greeks and Romans who followed similar careers—Alexander paired with Caesar, Demosthenes with Cicero, and so on. The biographies were based upon a vast amount of study, and Plutarch liked to parade his antiquarian erudition. He was much interested in religious matters, and he declared that his purpose in writing was primarily ethical, to enable people to improve their morals by the study of great models. It is interesting to note that the models he chose were all politicians or generals and that, in spite of his Greek birth, he showed little prejudice in favor of his fellow countrymen. The *Lives* stand high among the most interesting books in ancient literature. It was from them (in North's famous translation) that Shakespeare drew the material for his plays dealing with ancient times; and many leaders of the French Revolution had in their youth read Plutarch as ardently as they read Rousseau.

Lucian, who lived a generation later, did his best work in the days of Marcus Aurelius. Born at Samosata on the Euphrates, he spoke only Syriac in boyhood, and his Syrian mentality shines through his works. After living in Antioch for several years, he traveled as far as Gaul and eventually settled in Athens. Here he composed the numerous brief essays or dialogues in which he poked fun at traditional beliefs and superstitions, ridiculing the Olympian gods and Homeric heroes. Lucian dismissed Homer himself as a "liar" and Socrates as a tiresome old fool; he attacked the rhetoricians and

moralists of his own day; and he satirized society generally. His light
humor and keen wit make his satires resemble Juvenal's no more
than a rapier resembles a meat axe, but it is well to remember that
Lucian was an outsider, a Syrian, with no hereditary emotional attachment to the things he ridiculed. Critics often compare Lucian
to Voltaire, and the comparison is good. Each was an iconoclast as
well as a wit, and each stood at the end of an epoch, scoffing at ideas
which had once been the foundation of society, but which had long
since lost their potency. Both Lucian and Voltaire were doing their
bit to prepare for a new world which they did not foresee and of
which they certainly would not have approved. The fact that Lucian
won wide applause for such satire shows how rapidly society was
changing in the days of Marcus Aurelius.

The Darkened Face of Learning

We also possess the works of lesser writers from the second century, who are well characterized in Gibbon's famous epigram, "A
cloud of critics, of compilers, of commentators, darkened the face
of learning." Among the lecturers, or "rhetors," the most eminent
was Dio Chrysostom (literally "Mouth of Gold"), while a certain
Aelius Aristides published, among other speeches, an encomium *To
Rome* which expressed the enthusiasm of the educated classes for
the imperial system. This century also produced a number of historians. They compare badly, both in intelligence and in literary
ability, with the great historians of earlier times—or with Tacitus or
even Suetonius for that matter—but they have preserved valuable
information. Arrian, who held a consulship in 146, published a life
of Alexander the Great which remains our best source of information regarding the Macedonian general. At about the same time,
Appian, a Roman bureaucrat from Alexandria, wrote a long history
of Rome in Greek. Pausanias compiled an *Itinerary of Greece,* an
antiquarian guidebook with valuable information about the Greece
of his own day.

Writers on scientific subjects were likewise compilers rather than
thinkers, yet some of their writings were destined to be highly influential. Galen, a native of Pergamum who lived in Rome under

Marcus Aurelius, was the most celebrated of ancient physicians after Hippocrates. His numerous writings, summing up what was known in his day, were the foundation of most medical science until the sixteenth century. Galen's contemporary, Claudius Ptolemaeus of Alexandria, summarized the geographical and astronomical knowledge of antiquity, setting forth the "Ptolemaic" system of astronomy which prevailed until the sixteenth century. In those days the term "scientist" would also have included astrologers. Ptolemy himself dabbled in this "science," but the most eminent astrologer of the century was Vettius Valens, who probably flourished under Hadrian. Vettius's system of astrology was substantially that used by practitioners of the art today.

The second century continued the earnest moral speculation of the first, and nearly every writer of the time was primarily a moralist. Tacitus and Plutarch preached morality through their histories. Satirists like Juvenal and Lucian were much concerned with moral problems. Even scientists like the elder Pliny could not resist the temptation to moralize about nature. The popular and fashionable moralists and sophists are known to us principally through Lucian's caricatures, though it is evident from other sources that some of those whom he ridiculed were highly regarded by other intelligent contemporaries.

It was at this period, too, that Roman Stoicism achieved its most brilliant expression. The first of the great Roman Stoics was Seneca, Nero's minister, and the succession was continued by the slave Epictetus and by the Emperor Marcus Aurelius. While Epictetus himself wrote nothing, a collection of his sayings was preserved by his pupil Arrian, the historian of Alexander mentioned above. Marcus Aurelius's *Meditations* were written by the emperor in Greek during his last campaign against the barbarians. These philosophers and moralists reflect the finest qualities of their age—its cosmopolitanism, its humanitarianism, its essential kindliness, its growing repugnance to slavery and to the brutal public shows. They also show the weaknesses of the age and the beginnings of despair. The Stoics spoke and wrote eloquently about virtue and duty, providence and law, freedom and submission to fate, they preached the Fatherhood of God and the Brotherhood of Man, and yet they were always oppressed by a feeling of uneasiness and perhaps even of fear. They realized that fundamental things were changing, and they did not know what would be the outcome. Juvenal grumbled querulously about the passing of old ways. Lucian laughed at ideas that were already doomed. And the Emperor Marcus Aurelius set his teeth and insisted that, in spite of everything, he still was the Master of his Fate, the Captain of his Soul.

Christianity in the Second Century

When Pliny was governor of Bithynia in 112, his attention was called to the Christians in his province, and he wrote a long letter telling Trajan what he had learned about them. Trajan replied briefly, setting forth the government's attitude toward the new religion. Pliny's letter is our first description of a Christian community from the pen of a pagan and part of it deserves quotation at length:

"They [Christians and ex-Christians whom Pliny had haled into court] affirmed that their guilt, or error, consisted solely in their habit of meeting on a certain day before it was light, when they responsively sang a hymn to Christ as to a god and took an oath never to commit any fraud, theft, or adultery, nor to falsify their word, nor to deny a deposit when it was called for. After this it was their custom to separate and later reassemble for food, but food of an ordinary and innocent sort; but they had ceased even from this after my edict in which, acting on your orders, I forbade such assemblies. I thought it desirable to extract the truth by torture from two female slaves, called 'deaconesses,' but I found nothing worse than depraved and excessive superstition. . . . Many persons of every age and rank, and of both sexes, are and will be endangered, for this contagious superstition has spread not only to the cities but also to the villages and even to the country; yet it seems possible to check and correct it" (Pliny, *Epist.* x, 96).

The "certain day" of course was Sunday, and it seems probable that at the first assembly, before dawn, the Christians celebrated the Eucharist, or Communion service. Pliny's information was not very complete, for this service was secret, and even under torture the deaconesses did not tell all that happened. It is possible to see in the prohibitions mentioned by Pliny a reflection of the Ten Commandments, with the nondenial of a deposit being all that a Roman lawyer could make out of the command, "Thou shalt not covet." The second assembly—which was readily discontinued whereas the first was not—was the ordinary meal called the *Agape*. The insistence upon the innocent character of the food at this meal suggests that people were already charging the Christians with eating human flesh—perhaps because of a misunderstanding or willful misrepresentation of reports about the Eucharist. Pliny's remarks about the number, social position, and residence of the Christians show the growing strength of the new religion. While the urbane and enlightened Roman magistrate considered it merely a *superstitio prava immodica,* the truth is that at this very moment Christianity was rapidly changing from the religion of a small group of enthusiasts, united principally by their common expectation of the speedy return of Jesus as Messiah, into that of a well-organized society. It extended into practically every province of the Roman Empire, with a literature of its own and a way of life that set its members apart from the rest of the world.

The New Testament

The earliest Christian writings which we possess are the Epistles which Paul wrote to various churches during the fifties and sixties of the first century. They were written for quite specific purposes— to settle quarrels that had arisen, to correct abuses, or to denounce other preachers who were introducing new doctrines or trying to "steal" the churches from Paul. They were not primarily treatises on theology—as students often assume—though Paul would sometimes express his views on a few theological questions after disposing of the main matter in hand, just as he would throw in a few ethical precepts and words of encouragement. Toward the end of the first century someone published a collection of ten or more of these Epistles. We have no evidence as to the identity of the editor, or as to how he got copies of the letters included in his collection. Presumably he was a friend and admirer of Paul, perhaps his secretary. At any rate, he took certain liberties with the letters, rearranging them slightly: our two Epistles to the Corinthians, for example, are obviously made up of a least six separate letters. At a later date the collection was augmented by the inclusion of three other epistles (I and II Timothy and Titus) which probably were not Paul's work. Thereafter the thirteen Epistles were read publicly in the churches from time to time.

Meantime, other writers were preparing records of the life of Jesus. The first Christian preaching apparently confined itself largely to retelling the story of the death and resurrection of Jesus, and to arguing that he was the Messiah. Before long, however, prospective converts wished to know more about him. When it became customary to give converts instruction on this subject before baptism, a standard form of teaching was found to be desirable, and written records added to the authority of missionaries who had never seen Jesus. Toward the middle of the first century, therefore, men began preparing records, though not always as formal biography. A Christian writer of the second century recorded that Matthew (one of the Twelve Apostles) "composed 'the Logia' [the Sayings, or the Oracles] in the Hebrew [Aramaic?] language, and each interpreted them as he could." Exactly what these Logia were we cannot say. If they were sayings of Jesus along general ethical lines, such as are now found in the Gospels, they should not have been difficult to interpret. It seems more probable that they were Old Testament prophecies in Hebrew about Jesus, many of which are mentioned in our Gospel according to Matthew. In any case, however, there certainly was a collection of the sayings of Jesus, and probably more than one. Typical of such sayings are those that make up the Sermon on the Mount. While no copies of these early collections of sayings survive, such sources were used freely by later Evangelists. Scholars often call them "Q"—from the German word Quelle, "source."

It is very doubtful whether any one of our four Gospels was written by an eyewitness to the events it records. The earliest of them is that according to Mark, which possibly was the work of the John Mark mentioned three or four times in the Acts of the Apostles. Its author probably received from eyewitnesses much of the material which makes his narrative the most lifelike of the four. Apparently he used written sources as well. It seems likely that he wrote at Rome

during the late fifties or early sixties. Several years later the Gospel
according to Matthew appeared. Its author used Mark as a principal
source, rewriting the earlier record and adding much material from
the collections that we call "Q." There is no good evidence concerning this author's identity.

The third Gospel and the Acts of the Apostles are the work of
the same man, and together they form a history of the period from
the birth of Jesus to the arrival of Paul at Rome in 60. Many passages
in the second half of Acts are told in the first person, indicating that
they were written by a companion of Paul on his travels. This author
is generally identified with the person whom Paul once referred to
as "Luke, the beloved physician." This man probably was a Hellenized Jew who wrote up his travels in 62 while Paul was awaiting trial
in Rome, for his narrative comes to a sudden ending and gives no
indication of what happened to Paul at the trial or afterward. According to one theory, Luke resumed his literary labors several years
later, writing the Gospel and combining his personal narrative with
other materials to form our Acts. Other authorities hold that both
Gospel and Acts were given approximately their present form in 62.
The author tells us explicitly that he knew "many" accounts of the
teaching of Jesus, and he obviously used Mark and "Q" when composing his Gospel. He also used other material (presumably collected while he was at Caesarea with Paul) dealing with the life of
Jesus and the early days of the church. He was more highly educated
than the other Evangelists, and he wrote in the manner of a Greek
historian. Conspicuous in his Gospel are many parables, such as
those of the Prodigal Son and the Good Samaritan, which are not
found elsewhere. Wherever he may have got these stories, his artistic
talent is responsible for their present form; and, as befitted a good
physician, he always showed compassion for the sick and the needy.
Renan once declared the third Gospel to be "the most beautiful
book in the world."

The fourth Gospel differs widely from the first three. A few episodes are repeated, but the greater part of the Gospel deals with
other matters. Occasionally the author used good sources, yet his
account is generally considered less authentic than that of his

predecessors. He was not a historian but a theologian and a mystic. While the earlier Evangelists make Jesus talk mostly about ethical principles and the Messianic kingdom, the fourth Gospel pictures him as speaking especially of immortality, of sin and forgiveness, of his own relation to God, and of the symbolism of the Eucharist. This mystical Gospel has always been the most popular of the four with Christians. It is difficult to accept the tradition which identifies the author of the fourth Gospel with the Galilean fisherman named John who became one of the Twelve Disciples, but there is no good evidence as to what other John he may have been. The Gospel emanated from the church at Ephesus several years after the others were written. There are also three brief Epistles attributed to John in the New Testament. Perhaps they are the work of this same unknown author.

The last book of the New Testament, the Revelation of John, also came from Ephesus, but its author was not the man who wrote the Gospel. The book tells of visions seen by its author while on the island of Patmos in the Aegean, and it resembles the other great apocalypses that had been current among the Jews ever since Maccabaean times. This work, like those of contemporary Jewish writers, is bitterly hostile to Rome—which it calls "the Mother of Harlots and of the Abominations of the Earth"—whereas such men as Paul and Luke appreciated the true greatness of the Roman Empire. Critics believe that it was composed at a rather late date, perhaps in the days of Domitian, when persecution had turned the Christians against Rome. The author's powerful imagination and literary ability, the poetic beauty of many passages, and the promise of a good time to come shortly, have conspired to make the book a favorite with many readers.

In addition to these works the New Testament contains five other Epistles—Hebrews, James, I and II Peter, and Jude. While all have been attributed to persons with celebrated names, in no case can we be sure of their authorship. Though cast in the form of Epistles, they are really brief sermons, and none of them has been considered very important. Some may have been written late in the first century, but others (*e.g.*, II Peter) probably did not appear before the middle of the second century.

Not all the writings of Christians in the first century are preserved in the New Testament. For example, we still have copies of a long letter written by a certain Clement of Rome to the Corinthian church about 96. Several other Christian works from the first half of the second century have likewise been preserved. Some are epistles, others are apologetic works defending Christianity before the pagans, still others are apocalypses such as the "Shepherd" by Hermas and the "Revelation of Peter." The *Didache*, or "Teaching of the Twelve Apostles," is a brief tract giving instructions for leading a Christian life. There are also ancient references to other gospels written in the second century, among them a Gospel according to the Hebrews, a Gospel according to the Egyptians, a Gospel of Peter, and others. Only a few brief fragments of these "apocryphal gospels" now remain, and they are of very doubtful authority. Even if historically accurate they would add nothing important to our knowledge of Jesus. Their value to us lies rather in showing what Christians liked to imagine about him. There are also a few second-century lives of apostles and martyrs, and an interesting romance entitled "The Acts of Paul and Thekla."

The appearance of so many Christian books forced church officials to decide on a "canon," or list of books officially accepted for public reading and teaching. In general, these officials followed the principle that only those books might be used which they believed (sometimes mistakenly) to be of apostolic origin. There was no dispute about the Pauline Epistles, and before the end of the second century our four Gospels were accepted as the only authentic ones. It was also agreed that Acts and the Revelation of John should be included in the canon. The dispute regarding the lesser Epistles, however, was long and bitter. Many authorities wished to exclude one or more of them, or to include various other works not found in our Bibles. Not until the fourth century did the canon assume final form. Moreover, the exact text of the various books was not certain. Verses here and there, and a few whole episodes, were added while others were dropped out. At last, during the fourth century, church authorities established a standard text to which manuscripts were thereafter made to conform. From this text most modern Bibles are translated. Only during the last century has the discovery of a few very ancient manuscripts and papyri enabled scholars to go behind this standard text of the fourth century and attempt a reconstruction of earlier forms. In modern translations, notably the so-called Revised Version, doubts regarding the authenticity of several passages are expressed by putting them in square brackets or lowering them to footnotes. The most famous of these stories, found only in a few of the ancient manuscripts of John, is that of the Woman Taken in Adultery. The story may well be authentic, however, for apparently it came from the apocryphal Gospel of Peter and was inserted here when that Gospel went out of circulation.

Gentile Christianity

The recruits attracted by Christianity during the second century differed greatly from the first-century Christians. Nearly all the early converts had been Jews, or else Gentiles already interested in Judaism. After the first generation, however, recruits came directly from paganism. Christians continued to read the Old Testament in the Septuagint Greek translation, they retained many forms and ceremonies inherited from the synagogues, and they spoke of themselves as the "true Israel," but much that they had inherited from Judaism now seemed unimportant. Their efforts to adapt themselves to a Jewish heritage which they did not understand brought new developments in theology, ritual, and church organization whose general direction was determined during the century here under discussion.

Theological speculation gave rise to divergent theories and much controversy. As the church leaders desired uniformity in doctrine, they began calling unacceptable teachings "heresies" (from the Greek word for a school of philosophy) and expelled those who held them from membership in the church. Converts from paganism often retained so many of their old philosophical and religious ideas that for a while Christianity seemed in danger of becoming just another form of Hellenistic Gnosticism. Another agitation which threatened Christian unity was that known as Montanism. Toward the middle of the second century, Montanus—who was a Phrygian priest of Cybele before his conversion to Christianity—began preaching an austere and ascetic morality and insisting that the days of prophecy were not yet over. He and his two daughters claimed the gift of prophecy and took great liberties in editing the New Testament to make it conform to their views. For a while they enjoyed considerable success but their teachings were eventually rejected by the church.

The most important of all the theological questions which disturbed the early church concerned the person of Jesus. The early Jewish Christians had accepted him as the Messiah foretold in the Old Testament and had anticipated that he would soon return to establish a period of general felicity. Gentile Christians laid little emphasis upon this aspect of the Gospel and came more and more to follow John in his mysticism or Paul in regarding Jesus as a Savior-God who assured his followers of a blessed immortality by himself dying and rising from the dead. The theological reorientation entailed by this changed point of view was long and difficult, and many attempts were made to define Jesus' relation to God. Some theologians considered him a mere man and others insisted that he was a god who had merely seemed to take on human attributes. Neither of these views proved acceptable, but a formula which most Christians could accept was not found until one hundred and fifty years later. Jesus was then declared by the church authorities to be both perfect God and perfect man.

Early Church Government

The second century was also the time when foundations were being laid for a world-wide organization of Christianity. At first the local churches—or groups of Christian converts—had been under the immediate care of the missionary who established them. It had been Paul's practice, when he left a community, to appoint "elders" (*presbyteroi*) who continued this care, and to give his churches a permanent organization resembling that of the synagogues from which they had broken away. Each synagogue was presided over by a group of men who owed their position to their age, dignity, piety, or learning, although anyone might be invited to participate in the Sabbath services by speaking or reading the Scriptures. Likewise, many sorts of persons took part in the services of the early churches. New Testament writers mention apostles (missionaries), prophets, evangelists, pastors, teachers, and those speaking with tongues, as well as workers of miracles, healers, and administrators. Persons in the earlier categories, along with still others perhaps, were sometimes spoken of collectively as "those speaking the word of God." These persons were highly respected, but apparently they were not identical with the "elders" even though some individuals may have been members of both groups. When the churches became better organized, these freer activities were discouraged. Prophesying, for example, was not absolutely forbidden but churches were strongly cautioned to beware of false prophets, and tests were set up for recognizing true prophets which it was difficult to meet.

We also hear of persons called "bishops" and "deacons"—in Greek the former means "overseer" and the latter "servant"—who became the rulers of the community. The "bishops," of whom each church had several at one time, were for a while the same as the "elders." One bishop often stood out among the others, however, perhaps because of personal prestige or administrative ability, or perhaps because efficient management required centralized responsibility. Before the end of the second century it was customary to have only one bishop in a city, with the remaining "presbyters" ("elders" or "priests") holding an intermediate position below the bishop and above the deacons. The bishop, chosen by the presbyters with the approval of the Christian community, held office for life. The various bishops in a province sometimes assembled in synods, but not until the fourth century was there a church council attended by bishops from all parts of the Christian world.

Christians as the "Third Race"

These early Christians also developed new ideas regarding the nature of the Church and its relation to society. Much of this thinking, being of a mystical and theological nature, need not detain us here, but a few points may be mentioned. From the earliest times Christians called their community the *Ecclesia*. This Greek word had once been used to designate the political assembly of a Greek city, but the Christians took it from the Greek Old Testament where it was applied only to the Jewish people assembled for religious purposes. The word therefore had a technical meaning long before Christians began using it. An *Ecclesia* was the religious assembly of a nation or people. By adopting this word the early Christians showed that they considered themselves a "nation" or "people." This idea was expressed by Paul when he spoke of the Christians as the "true Israel" or as "Israel after the spirit" in contrast to "Israel after the flesh." I Peter, going further, spoke of them as "an elect race, a holy nation, a people." In the next century Christians sometimes referred to themselves as a "third race"—third, that is, in addition to Greeks and Jews—while pagans reviled them with the same epithet. And it must be admitted that the Christians were in a sense a "race" or "nation." They constituted a considerable body of people united, not by a real or fictitious common ancestry, but by an ardent consciousness of their unity, by a strong mutual loyalty, by a distinctive way of life, by a common intellectual background, and by a common hope. United by bonds such as these and governed by an organized clergy, the Christians had come to form an ecclesiastical empire within the Roman Empire. Eventually they absorbed and took over that Empire.

Notes

Edward Gibbon

Edward Gibbon (1737–94) is one of the world's most famous historians. He was the only surviving child of a well-to-do country gentleman and member of Parliament. After a lonely, sickly, and bookish childhood he entered Oxford, at the age of 15, "with a stock of erudition that might have puzzled a doctor and a degree of ignorance of which a schoolboy would have been ashamed." There he passed several unhappy months until a momentary conversion to Roman Catholicism forced his withdrawal. His father hustled him off for reconversion to the family of a Protestant clergyman at Lausanne, Switzerland, where he lived happily for five years. While in Switzerland he fell in love with Suzanne Curchod, later the wife of J. Necker, the famous minister of France; but when his father forbade the match, Gibbon "sighed as a lover and obeyed as a son." During the Seven Years War Gibbon was a captain in his father's regiment of the Hampshire militia, but he saw no service abroad.

Upon the restoration of peace in 1763, Gibbon again traveled through France, Switzerland, and Italy; and in 1768 he established himself in London as a literary man. He joined Dr. Johnson's famous literary club and associated freely with the leading men of that brilliant day. In 1774 he entered Parliament to represent one of the seven "rotten boroughs" controlled by his cousin's husband, Edward Eliot, later Lord Eliot, the father-in-law of the younger William Pitt. For eight years Gibbon sat in Parliament, voting but never speaking. At first he (and Eliot) voted with Fox against the North ministry, but presently Gibbon accepted a lucrative sinecure on the Board of Trade, and thereafter he voted with North: he thus lost Eliot's favor and with it his seat in Parliament. North presently procured for him another seat, but when North's ministry fell (1782) Gibbon lost both seat and sinecure. As his income was insufficient to support him in style at London, he returned to Switzerland, which he had always regarded as a second fatherland. There he passed the remainder of his life, except for two brief visits to England, during the second of which he died (1794).

In an oft-cited passage of his *Memoirs* Gibbon tells how, on October 15, 1764, as he sat musing in the Church of the Ara Coeli at Rome, the idea of writing the decline of Rome first started to his mind. Not until several years later did he seriously set to work, and the first volume of *The History of the Decline and Fall of the Roman Empire* appeared in 1776. Two further volumes appeared in 1781, and three more completed the work in 1788. The first volume covered the period from the Antonines to the retirement of Diocletian (305); the second and third carried the story to 476; the fourth dealt with the age of Justinian; and the last two were devoted to a cursory survey of the Byzantine Empire and the East down to the fall of Constantinople in 1453. Among the many famous passages in the history are Gibbon's brilliant survey of the Roman Empire in the second century (chaps. 1–3), his account of the rise of Christianity (chaps. 15–16) which caused great scandal in its day because he approached the question from a rationalistic point of view, the stories of Julian the Apostate (chaps. 22–24) and Justinian (chaps. 40–43), the chapter on Roman law (chap. 44), and those on Mohammed and Mohammedanism (chaps. 50–51).

After completing his history Gibbon wrote his *Memoirs of My Life and Writings,* one of the great autobiographies in English literature. A much edited text was published after his death by his friend Lord Sheffield, and Gibbon's own texts were first published by John Murray in 1897. There is an important annotated edition by G. B. Hill (1900). The story of Gibbon's life has often been retold, less well, by lesser men, but new material about Gibbon is added by D. M. Low, *Edward Gibbon, 1737–1794* (1937). The *Decline and Fall* has remained a "best seller" for more than a hundred and fifty years. In the present century it has appeared in several inexpensive editions (Modern Library, Everyman's Library, Oxford Classics). For scholarly purposes the best edition is that of J. B. Bury (7 vols., 1896–1900; revised and expanded, 1909–14; 2nd ed., 1926–9), whose excellent notes indicate the advance of scholarship since Gibbon's day. The most recent edition (3 vols., The Heritage Press, 1946) omits the footnotes containing only scholarly apparatus but adds about fifty splendid etchings, made in Gibbon's day by G. Piranesi, which show what the Roman ruins were like before the archeologists started clearing them up. The etchings give us a new conception of what Gibbon understood by "decline" as he sat musing among the ruins in 1764.

Michael Rostovtzeff

Michael Ivanovitch Rostovtzeff was born at Kiev, Russia, in 1870. After studies in Russian and German universities and in the classic lands, he became a professor at St. Petersburg, where he remained until after the Bolshevik revolution. In 1920 he came to the United States, became Professor of Ancient History at the University of Wisconsin, and held a similar post at Yale from 1926 until his retirement in 1944. A thoughtful Russian living at the turn of the twentieth century could hardly avoid taking an interest in agrarian problems, and Rostovtzeff studied the land question in antiquity. He made his reputation with an important work, published in German under the title *Studien zur Geschichte des römischen Kolonates* (1910); a special study of *A Large Estate in Egypt in the Third Century B.C.* appeared in this country in 1922; and many articles discuss other aspects of the economic and general history of Hellenistic and Roman times. His two most important works, summing up the studies of a lifetime, are the *Social and Economic History of the Roman Empire* (1926) and the magisterial *Social and Economic History of the Hellenistic World* (3 vols., 1941).

The changes that have come over the study of ancient history in the course of one hundred and fifty years cannot be studied better than by comparing Rostovtzeff's *Roman Empire* with the first volume of Gibbon's *Decline and Fall.* Each author was a thorough scholar, at home with both the literary sources and the scholarship of his day. Gibbon found this scholarship in a few dozen bulky tomes, written in Latin or French; but the absence of large public libraries forced him to buy his own copies of the books he used. Rostovtzeff's reading, done largely in university libraries, covered hundreds of books and articles written in half a dozen modern languages. Gibbon had to rely almost entirely upon the ancient literary sources for his knowledge of Roman history; Rostovtzeff made extensive use of archeology (an archeologist in his own right, he had a large share in the important dig at Doura on the Euphrates) as well as of thousands of inscriptions, the papyri, and the coins. These new sources gave him an enormous amount of information not available to Gibbon. This new information appears on every page of the *Roman Empire*. Gibbon's first three chapters are a brilliant and famous survey of the Roman Empire in the second century; Rostovtzeff makes a similar survey in his chapters IV–VIII. So great are the differences between the two accounts that the reader is sometimes tempted to rub his eyes and wonder whether the two writers are really describing the same empire.

The differences between Gibbon and Rostovtzeff rest upon more than the information made available since Gibbon's day. If Gibbon had had all Rostovtzeff's facts before him, his book would have been very different, but it would not have been like Rostovtzeff's. Each author included in his text only those facts which he considered important. Gibbon therefore dealt largely with politics, war, and religion; Rostovtzeff deals primarily with economic life. Gibbon was a friend of the famous economist Adam Smith (whose *Wealth of Nations* was issued by the same publisher in the same year as the first volume of the *Decline and Fall*), but he almost never touched upon economic matters in his history. Rostovtzeff knows how interesting religious history is (he wrote a little book entitled *Mystic Italy* [1927] describing the cults of Pompeii), but his great works pass lightly over that aspect of things. And finally, while Gibbon was a literary artist of the first magnitude, he had little knowledge or understanding of the other arts: editions of his great history appearing during his lifetime contained only one illustration—a portrait of the author! Rostovtzeff does not attempt a formal history of art, but his books are lavishly illustrated, and his comments on the illustrations bring out vividly the connections between art and social history. Gibbon and Rostovtzeff each reflect the interests and intellectual atmosphere of their times—Gibbon of the eighteenth century, Rostovtzeff of the twentieth.

The differences between the two men and their times stand out especially when we compare their attitudes toward the "Fall of Rome." Gibbon was a good eighteenth-century philosopher who attributed that catastrophe to the moral decay of the ruling classes at Rome; Rostovtzeff seeks economic causes. In particular, he develops a theory that Rome's ruin came as a result of the civil wars of the third century: the armies that waged these wars, he believes, were composed of peasants who took fearful vengeance on the city dwellers who exploited them and in so doing they destroyed ancient civilization. Perhaps there is a little truth in the charge of certain critics that, in writing thus, Rostovtzeff was thinking of the fate of Tsarist Russia as he described that of ancient Rome. Or perhaps it might better be said that the misfortunes of his own class and country opened Rostovtzeff's eyes to what had happened in Rome. Even the critics would doubtless agree with Rostovtzeff, however, that the causes of Rome's decline were primarily economic rather than moral. Eighteenth-century historians were primarily moralists, but most writers today seem to hold that economic and social forces are more important than morals in determining the rise and fall of empires. Our two authors therefore reflect the spirit of their times as well as relating the bald facts of history. In fact, they could not do otherwise.

XIV A Century of Turmoil

MARCUS AURELIUS DIED ON THE 17TH OF MARCH, 180, AND was succeeded by his son Lucius Aurelius Commodus. Each of Marcus's four predecessors had been childless and had therefore been uninfluenced by parental partiality when selecting a successor. Marcus, on the other hand, had a son whom he had trained from infancy to rule the world, and he would consider no one else. Born on August 31, 161, shortly after his father took over the Empire, Commodus became Caesar at the age of six, consul and co-ruler with his father at sixteen, and he succeeded as emperor when only eighteen years old. He was murdered on December 31, 192, at the age of thirty-one. The twelve years of his reign were a turning point in the history of the Roman Empire.

Commodus

Commodus's enemies attacked him bitterly during his lifetime, contrasting the degenerate son with his noble father. Later moralists, ancient and modern, pagan and Christian, were led into the same temptation, and Commodus has usually been pictured by historians as a debauched and drunken tyrant, proud of his physical strength but devoid of ideas and policies in government. Only in recent years have scholars made more serious attempts to understand Commodus and his difficulties. Their researches show him to have been a rather pathetic young man, born to a position much too big for him. He was thoroughly frightened by repeated attempts upon his life, and his pathological mental state revealed itself in periods of great exaltation which were followed by extreme depression when he sought relief in drunkenness, in the society of gladiators, or in his harem of three hundred concubines.

Marcus Aurelius had died in the midst of a military campaign against German tribes on the Danube frontier. Commodus made peace on terms of a return to prewar conditions, and at once proceeded to Rome where he proclaimed himself the harbinger of peace and prosperity. Critics accused him of throwing away in cowardly fashion the fruits of thirteen years of warfare at the moment when final victory was in sight. More likely peace was dictated by the debility of the Empire after long years of plague, famine, and war. At any rate, the populace was delighted with the peace. Commodus had ended the wars, but he could not end the economic depression. He pared down expenditures and made strenuous efforts to collect more revenue, thus causing the rich to call him a tyrant, but the treasury remained empty. Another disastrous plague swept over the Roman world in 187; crop failures and famines afflicted numerous provinces; and a large part of Rome was burned in 189. Italy and the provinces were overrun with unemployed persons who turned to brigandage to fend off starvation. Revolts flared up in Gaul, Spain, and Africa. The eastern provinces had continued restless ever since the revolt of Avidius Cassius (177), and Alexandria was more disaffected than ever. Cynic philosophers preached openly in that city against the vicious emperor, and they circulated seditious tracts luridly depicting the sufferings of "martyrs" to his tyranny.

As if all this were not enough, Commodus was systematically sabotaged by the senate. The conduct of affairs therefore fell to court officials, mainly equestrians or provincials, whom senatorial critics saw fit to accuse of pandering to the emperor's lusts. Commodus took great care to retain the loyalty of the army, especially that of the praetorian guard (as was indeed necessary in such troubled times), and he always favored the lower classes against the rich. Gifts of money were distributed among the Roman populace seven times during his reign, and official propaganda promised the return of former felicity under a new social order.

Unfortunately, Commodus's promises were just political propaganda and were not followed by substantial economic and political reform. Nevertheless, the propaganda itself continued throughout his reign. No effort was spared to impress men with the emperor's great and beneficent qualities. He celebrated triumphs for minor frontier engagements, the months were called by his various titles, and Rome itself was renamed Colonia Commodiana. Even his 735 public appearances as a gladiator or wild-beast hunter were presumably for political effect. Though these appearances shocked and disgusted the educated upper classes at Rome and elsewhere, they may well have convinced the populace that this intrepid warrior was just the man they wanted to protect them from all threatening dangers. Commodus's choice of Hercules as his personal god, with whom he eventually identified himself, may have been less the result of that hero's physical prowess than of the teaching of Cynic philosophers that he had fought and suffered for the welfare of mankind. Still opposition was not silenced. Several senators were executed for resisting Commodus's innovations, and their places were given to his friends among whom, the historians plaintively report, were freedmen and other persons of low origin. At last intriguers at court hired the emperor's wrestling partner to strangle him. We are told that he had intended to assume the consulship on the next day, clad in the costume of a gladiator (December 31, 192).

The plot that ended Commodus's life had been so hurriedly concocted that the conspirators had no candidate ready for the succession. Faced with this emergency, the praetorian prefect nominated for the office an able official named Pertinax, who had served under both Marcus Aurelius and Commodus. The choice was ratified by the praetorian guard and later by the senate. Pertinax announced a return to the good old ways and permitted the senate to repeal several of Commodus's measures. His insistence upon discipline so angered the praetorians, however, that they murdered him eighty-seven days after they had made him emperor. The guard next chose a rich senator, Didius Julianus. Gossip reported that his socially ambitious wife and daughter goaded the old man into offering the guard larger bribes than any other candidate. In any case, the choice was made by the praetorians and their proclamation suggested to other troops that they too might select emperors. Three men were so chosen. Niger was proclaimed emperor by the legions in Syria and Egypt, Septimius Severus by the troops in Illyria and the Danube provinces, and Albinus somewhat later by those in Gaul and Britain. Julianus and his family were murdered after a reign of only sixty-five days, but it took almost four years of civil war to rid Severus of all rival claimants. Niger was defeated and executed in 194, but not until 197 was Albinus destroyed. Two years were then spent by Severus in a war against the Parthians and two more in settling the eastern provinces. The victor did not return to Rome until 202, after which he and his family ruled the empire for more than thirty years.

The Severi

Septimius Severus was born at Leptis Magna in North Africa in 146. His native community was Punic, and though Severus was largely of Roman blood, he spoke Latin with a slight accent. As emperor he favored the African provinces, relied upon African assistants, established the worship of Carthaginian gods at Rome, and even went out of his way to repair the tomb of Hannibal in Bithynia. His wife, Julia Domna, was a Syrian woman of high intelligence and great force of character whose father had been hereditary high priest of a sun god worshiped at Emesa near Damascus. She played a great part in the political, intellectual, and religious history of the Empire in her day. After Septimius's death the Empire was ruled by three successive members of his family, all of whom were dominated by Julia Domna, her sister, or her niece. The accession of the Severi thus marks another step in the conquest of the Roman Empire by its provinces.

Severus's political policies were determined principally by two facts: he was a usurper who owed his position to the army; and his early wars had aggravated the economic depression which had prevailed since the last days of Marcus Aurelius. Like Vespasian, who had come to power under rather similar circumstances, Severus planned to found a dynasty since only an assured succession could prevent a renewal of civil war at his death. Though Severus announced himself the champion of the senate and avenger of Pertinax, he was soon forced by circumstances to reverse himself and to continue the policies of Commodus. He announced that he had been secretly adopted by Marcus Aurelius and spoke of Commodus as his "brother."

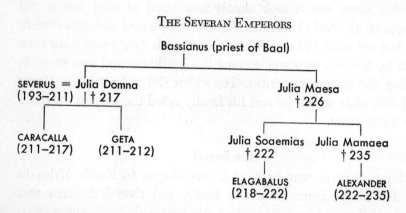

THE SEVERAN EMPERORS

Bassianus (priest of Baal)

SEVERUS = Julia Domna
(193–211) | † 217

Julia Maesa
† 226

CARACALLA   GETA
(211–217)   (211–212)

Julia Soaemias   Julia Mamaea
† 222   † 235

ELAGABALUS   ALEXANDER
(218–222)   (222–235)

Necessity also forced Severus to rely upon military power, and, like Vespasian again, he relied upon the legions rather than upon the praetorian guard. In fact, he disbanded the old guard, made up of Italians, and recruited a new one composed of provincials from the legions. He also stationed a legion of provincials in Italy, which was the first time since Augustus that Italy had seen troops. He pacified and won the favor of the Roman populace by the traditional method of lavish gifts, and he spent huge sums for building, perhaps as a form of unemployment relief. He devoted especial care to the provinces, largely because he recruited his legions there. He usually disregarded the senate, except when packing it with his friends. Heretofore Italians had retained a slight majority in that body, but now they made up barely a third of its members. While most provincial senators had formerly come from the Latin provinces of the West, they now came from Africa, Asia Minor, and Syria, and almost no western provincials were left in that body. The Roman Empire was rapidly being orientalized.

Severus's efforts met with a certain success, and conditions gradually improved throughout the Empire, especially in Africa and

Caracalla *(Berlin Museum)*

Elagabalus *(Louvre Museum)*

Julia Mamaea *(Louvre Museum)*

Plate 24

Plate 25.   Mithra Slaying a Bull

Syria. When he died, the treasury had a working balance for the first time in almost half a century. A large part of this money had been acquired by the confiscation of the estates of hostile senators and other wealthy men, however, and this precedent was destined to have the most disastrous consequences. Historians sometimes depict Severus as a great democratic reformer, seeking only to help the people, but others picture him as a military despot reducing all his subjects to the same abject level before him. In the long run the latter tendency prevailed, though Severus and his close advisers were by no means devoid of humanitarian idealism.

Severus died in 211 and was succeeded, as he had planned, by his two sons. The elder, officially named Marcus Aurelius Antoninus Severus after his supposed adoptive grandfather, is now commonly called Caracalla; the younger was Publius Septimius Geta. Severus intended that the two boys should rule jointly, each administering a half of the Empire, but Caracalla would brook no rival, and in less than a year he had Geta murdered (212). Caracalla liked to think of himself as a new Alexander the Great, yet throughout his life his policies were directed by his mother along lines laid down by his father. His only act of importance was the edict, known as the *Con-*

• Note for Plate 25. This relief, showing Mithra slaying a bull, is now in Paris but it was found at Rome during the Renaissance, in the ruins of a Mithreum (temple to Mithra) on the Capitoline Hill under the foundations of the present church of the Ara Coeli. Though several important parts of the relief (including the head and arm of Mithra, parts of the neck and foreleg of the bull, most of the dog) are modern restorations, the general outline is certain for several other reliefs have been found which closely resemble the one shown here. There are also many ancient statues and carvings, in other forms, showing Mithra killing the bull, which was the central event in Mithraic mythology. Note the typical Persian caps worn by Mithra and the two torch bearers. The dog, the serpent, and the scorpion also played an important part in the myth of Mithra. The charioteers above are the sun (left) and moon (right), each preceded by a boy (Phosphorus and Hesperus, respectively). On the side of the bull is carved an inscription *Deo soli invicto Mitrhe*, "To the god, the unconquered sun, Mithra," followed by a date (badly damaged) which may be 229 A.D. See F. Cumont, *Textes et Monuments figurés relatifs aux mystères de Mithra*, II (1896), pp. 193 ff.

stitutio Antoniniana (212), by which he extended Roman citizenship to every freeman in the Empire except those of the lowest class. While this decree has been much discussed in recent years as an illustration of the democratic, or leveling, policy of the Severi, it attracted little attention at the time. Our knowledge of it today is so scanty that we cannot say what class or classes of society actually profited by it: perhaps it was designed to favor the proletariat of the provincial cities. Wars then called Caracalla to the East, where he was murdered in the spring of 217. For about a year the Empire was nominally governed by an African soldier named Macrinus, until he was defeated by troops whom Caracalla's aunt, Julia Maesa, persuaded to defend the claims of her grandson, Elagabalus.

This amazing young man, three of whose four grandparents were full-blooded Syrians, was only fourteen years old when he became emperor. Already he was priest of the mountain god after whom he is usually called (*El,* god; *gabal,* mountain) and throughout life he was chiefly interested in his priestly functions. Conservative Romans were shocked, but Elagabalus's activities were highly characteristic of the new order then arising in the Roman world. Matters of state were left to Julia Maesa and her Syrian advisors. After a reign of less than four years, Elagabalus was murdered in 222, and was succeeded by his thirteen-year-old cousin Severus Alexander. Julia Maesa continued to dominate the government until her death in 226, when her place was taken by her daughter Julia Mamaea, who ruled until she and her son were murdered in 235. Ancient writers contrast Alexander with the other Severi, picturing him as an excellent ruler. He avoided the debaucheries and religious eccentricities of Elagabalus, yet it is hard to see any fundamental change in political policy. As a matter of fact, the boyish emperors had little influence upon public policy, and the court continued as before. Economic conditions were perhaps not quite so bad as before, but if there was less friction between the emperor's officials and the senate, it was because the senate had ceased to exist as an independent institution. The Roman Empire had by this time become an oriental military monarchy with no place for senators.

Anarchy in the Empire

Severus Alexander was succeeded by Maximinus, a Thracian peasant who had begun his career as a soldier in the ranks. His early advancement came about especially through his great physical strength, which aroused the admiration of his fellows. He was proclaimed emperor by his soldiers in 235 and murdered by them in 238. As these few words adequately summarize the lives of most of his successors during the next fifty years, no attempt need be made to chronicle the fate of each emperor separately. Historians often name twenty persons as ruling between 235 and 285,[1] but such lists are quite misleading. They include only those emperors whom the senate recognized (usually under duress) and do not indicate whether or not these men actually ruled, or what they ruled. Each of the twenty had rivals, backed by powerful armies, who sometimes held large parts of the Empire. It is impossible to draw up a complete list of those whom somebody recognized as emperor during these anarchic years, but their number would rise well above one hundred. At last Diocletian made himself sole ruler of the Empire in 285, and for twenty years he held this position with the aid of various associates. His resignation in 305 was followed by new civil wars, and not until 324 did Constantine restore order and unity to the Roman world.

Each of these "barrack-room emperors" was dependent upon the army that put him into office, and if once he ceased pampering his troops it was more than likely that they would murder him and replace him by a more compliant rival. As such emperors could not

---

[1] The usual list of these emperors is as follows:

Maximinus	235–238	Aemilianus	253	Carinus	283–285
Gordianus I	238	Valerian	253–260	Numerian	283–284
Gordianus II	238	Gallienus	253–268	Diocletian	284–305
Balbinus	238	Claudius II	268–270	Maximian	286–305
Pupienus	238	Aurelian	270–275	Constantius	305–306
Gordianus III	238–244	Tacitus	275–276	Galerius	305–311
Philip	244–249	Florian	276	Licinius	311–324
Decius	249–251	Probus	276–282	Constantine	306–337
Gallus	251–253	Carus	282–283		

give careful attention to the defense of the frontiers, and as such troops would not and could not fight vigorously, the barbarians quickly learned that they could raid Roman territory with impunity. Commodus had been much criticized for coming to terms with the Germans, though the long peace which followed showed the folly of the critics. These particular tribes are not heard of again for almost seventy-five years, and at no point did Germans seriously threaten the frontiers until the last years of Severus Alexander. In the days of Maximinus the Goths of southwestern Russia began to invade Moesia (modern Bulgaria). Year by year they extended their incursions until they invaded Greece and sacked Ephesus in Asia Minor (267–8). Already the Marcomanni and the Alemanni (a tribe living east of the middle and upper Rhine) had crossed the Alps to invade the Empire, the former advancing into Italy as far as Ravenna in 254, the latter reaching the vicinity of Milan five years later. The Franks then crossed the lower Rhine to invade Gaul, and for several years the whole northern frontier, from the Black Sea to the Atlantic, was seriously endangered.

The Third Persian (Sassanian) Empire

Conditions were even more precarious in the East. The old Parthian kingdom had continued its struggles against Rome down to the days of Caracalla, but then it was overthrown by rebels at home. The leader of the rebels was Ardashir, whose ancestors had been minor nobles in the province of Persis along the northern shore of the Persian Gulf. Ardashir's father overthrew the feudal king of the province and was succeeded by his son in 208. After fifteen years spent in acquiring neighboring provinces, the young king was so powerful that his Parthian overlord, Artabanus, decided to destroy him. The unruly subject defeated and killed Artabanus about 227, and established his capital at Ctesiphon, where he had himself crowned King of Kings. Ardashir thus founded the Third Persian Empire (the first being the Achaemenid, founded by Cyrus; the second the Arsacid, or Parthian Empire) which is usually called Sassanian after his grandfather, Sassan. Ardashir died in 241 and was succeeded by his son Shapur, who ruled until his death in 272.

These two great kings established their monarchy upon a firm foundation. Zoroastrianism became the state religion, and its clergy were among the chief props of the throne. The economic and cultural life of Persia in Sassanian times was probably almost on a level with that of the decadent West. Persia remained a powerful state, chronically at war with her western neighbor, until overthrown by the Mohammedans in 642.

Had the Persian kings been more tactful, and had they refrained from extensive looting during their first invasions of Roman territory, they might have occupied all the lands east of the Mediterranean from the Taurus Mountains to the Red Sea. As it was, they occupied Armenia (252), captured and looted Antioch (253), and even overran Cappadocia in Asia Minor. The Roman fortress at Doura had to be abandoned in 257. Three years later, in 260, came the greatest military disgrace that had yet befallen the Roman Empire, when the Emperor Valerian was taken prisoner by the Persians and presently died in captivity. Antioch was looted again, and Persian raiders crossed Asia Minor almost to the Aegean.

The prestige of Rome throughout the East was thus destroyed, and an Arab sheik named Odenathus, ruler of Palmyra in the desert east of Damascus, managed to create what was virtually an independent state. After being rebuffed by the Persian king Shapur, to whom he had once made advances, this Odenathus set himself up as the champion of the East against Persian pillaging. Twice during the 260's his armies reached the gates of Ctesiphon. After his death, about 267, his work was continued by his widow, the famous Zenobia. She added Syria, Palestine, and Egypt to her domains, established a brilliant court at Palmyra, and was compared to Cleopatra. Finally, in 273, Roman armies took her prisoner and destroyed her capital city.

Postumus in Gaul

Within a year of Valerian's death at least five generals tried to wrest the Empire from his son Gallienus, who had been joint ruler with him, administering the West while Valerian was in the East. Each of these rivals acted separately, with armies supposedly raised to defend the frontiers though actually they contained many barbarians recruited outside the Empire. The most redoubtable of the rebels was Postumus, who had been stationed at Cologne. In 260 he was proclaimed emperor by his troops and soon controlled all Gaul. Later he was recognized in Britain and Spain and, for a short time, in northern Italy. As Gallienus could not drive him out, Postumus governed what amounted to an independent empire in the West until his death in 268. His successor was defeated in 274. While Postumus had his own senate, consuls, and army, his policy was not that of nationalistic separatism: he did not wish to found an independent Gallic state but to rule the whole Roman Empire. Actually he and his like were tearing that empire to pieces.

The New Monarchy

Domestic strife and foreign attack thus brought the Roman Empire to the verge of ruin. Then, just as utter collapse seemed inevitable, a new line of emperors defeated the barbarians and pulled the Empire together once more. These men are usually called the Illyrian emperors since they all were born in that province and were raised to power by legions stationed there. Illyria was a Latinized province whose population at that time was closely related to the Veneti and other north Italian peoples: the South Slavs who dominate the region today did not arrive until several centuries later. The Illyrian emperors therefore marked a revival of western influence in the Empire after the oriental domination that began with the Severi. Nevertheless, these western emperors were quite unable to hold back the rising tide of orientalism.

The first Illyrian emperor was Decius (249–251), but the line is more commonly said to begin with Claudius II (268–270), and it was continued, with interruptions, by a series of able Illyrians, notably Aurelian (270–275) and Probus (276–282). These men reunited the Empire, re-established discipline in the army, and resumed the wars with Persia. They even found time for various reforms at home. Probus's successor, Carus, another Illyrian soldier, intensified the war against Persia, captured the capital at Ctesiphon, and was planning to press eastward when he was murdered by his

soldiers (283). His two sons, Carinus and Numerian, had already
been declared Caesars and were ruling the West and East respectively. Numerian was recognized as Augustus by the army in Persia,
with which he was serving, but within a few weeks he too was
murdered (284), probably by his father-in-law, Aper, who hoped
thus to obtain the throne for himself. The soldiers preferred Diocletian, whom they proclaimed emperor after he had murdered Aper
(284), and he then ruled for twenty years.

Diocletian

The new emperor, who had once been named simply Diocles but
who now took the full name Gaius Aurelius Valerius Diocletianus,
was a Dalmatian peasant born about 245. He entered the army as a
youth, held various administrative posts, became governor of Moesia
under Probus, and commanded the emperor's bodyguard under
Carus. Like most of his predecessors for fifty years, he owed his
position to his soldiers, and it was largely luck that, unlike these
predecessors, he was not speedily murdered by them. Various rivals
arose, and there were frequent wars with Persians or Germans, but
Diocletian always managed to defeat his enemies and to hold the
Empire intact. His successes were less the result of his military
ability than of his skill in selecting able and trustworthy assistants.
Diocletian was fundamentally a conservative man, anxious to preserve as much as possible of the old Roman system, and his reforms
were usually along lines laid down by his predecessors. These conservative reforms were what saved the Roman Empire.

When Diocletian became emperor he knew that he would not
long survive unless he quickly devised a system of succession that
would deprive imperial aspirants of all desire to have him murdered.
He also knew that it would be quite impossible for him to give personal attention to every part of his vast and troubled empire. He
therefore selected a reliable Illyrian soldier, named Maximian,
whom he made a second Augustus (286). With this colleague he
shared the tasks of government, following a precedent tried repeatedly since the days of Marcus Aurelius and Verus. A few years later,
in 293, he selected two Caesars to succeed the two Augusti, again

following second-century precedent. His own Caesar was a man named Galerius; Maximian's was Constantius Chlorus, father of the famous Constantine. Each Caesar married the daughter of the Augustus whom he would succeed. Diocletian looked after affairs in the East and Maximian those in the West, with the Caesar in each case helping his father-in-law, but there was no fundamental division of the Empire. As each ruler's primary task was the military defense of the Empire, the division represented the assignment of frontiers to be defended. Maximian protected the upper Rhine and Danube frontiers from headquarters conveniently stationed at Milan; Constantius defended the lower Rhine from Trier; Galerius was stationed on the lower Danube at Sirmium in modern Yugoslavia; and Diocletian defended the eastern frontier with Nicomedia (in northwestern Asia Minor) as his principal place of residence. Diocletian attended to domestic revolts in Asia and Egypt, Maximian took care of those in southern Gaul and Britain. Meantime the civil administration of the Empire was conducted by the praetorian prefects in the names of the four emperors jointly.

Administrative Changes

Diocletian also recognized the danger of allowing provincial governors to command large bodies of troops with which they might launch rebellions. He therefore accelerated the subdivision of provinces which had been begun by Septimius Severus. When Diocletian died, the Empire contained about one hundred provinces, though the same area (plus Dacia) had been divided into only forty-two provinces under Antoninus. Italy no longer enjoyed a privileged status, and the whole peninsula, except the district within one hundred miles of Rome, was placed under provincial governors. This multiplication of provinces made necessary their arrangement in twelve groups, called dioceses, each under an official called a vicar. The vicars, in their turn, were responsible to the praetorian prefects who, since the second century, had directed the civil administration of the Empire with a status approaching that of a prime minister or vizier. Though the city of Rome was now rarely honored by the presence of an emperor, it retained its old prestige as capital of the

Empire. Diocletian embellished it with many new buildings, the most famous of which were his enormous baths.

The power and prestige of the senate had declined steadily throughout the third century, and by 285 they had reached so low an ebb that Diocletian did not bother to seek senatorial recognition as emperor. He usually ignored the senate, not deigning to abolish it or even to quarrel with it. On occasion he even made use of it and its members. Aurelian had forbidden senators to enter the army, thus greatly restricting the number of important offices they might hold. Diocletian further limited the field of their activities, though for a while he allowed them to govern a few senatorial provinces and hold other lucrative and honorific positions. At the same time he had equestrians of his own choice watch and supervise them. The troops in each province were commanded by an equestrian official called a *dux,* and the vicars and praetorian prefects were always equestrians. Diocletian's officials gradually took over all power, leaving the senators with nothing to do either individually or as a body.

The third century also saw great changes in the recruiting and organization of the army. In the second century the army had been made up almost entirely of infantry stationed in camps along the strongly fortified frontiers. Military service was looked upon as a burden by the civilian population, and the army became a professional and largely hereditary military caste. Soldiers married wives in the communities where they were stationed and resented being moved elsewhere. Sometimes commanders, unable to find other recruits, enlisted barbarians who had only recently entered the Empire. At first these barbarians were used only as auxiliaries, but later they were admitted even to the legions. Before the middle of the third century the army had lost its patriotism to such a degree that soldiers followed any leader who paid them regularly, and they did not hesitate to attack and loot the cities of the Empire itself.

Repeated disasters also showed that a new strategy of defense had become necessary. The barbarians had discovered that there were no mobile reserves behind the strong thin line of fortifications, so if this line were once broken there was no one to prevent them from looting whole provinces at will. It was at this time, too, that the Persians showed the power of their "cataphracts"—heavily armed cavalry resembling medieval knights in armor. Gallienus and Aurelian had tried to remedy these defects in Rome's system of defenses, but it was Diocletian who created a new army. Cavalry and archers were taught to fight as the Persians did. Large mobile reserves were stationed behind the frontiers. The legion was reduced in size for the sake of greater mobility while the standing army was increased from about 300,000 to about 400,000 men. It was not easy to find recruits, however, and Diocletian was forced to revive the old obligation of every citizen to serve in the army. He ordered each community to supply a certain number of soldiers, and when they were slow in fulfilling their duties, and the conscripts proved to be of low caliber, he enlisted barbarians in the legions on an unprecedented scale. As the high commands were filled from the ranks, Italians having long since lost their exclusive right to such posts, the army became more barbarized than ever. Nevertheless, Diocletian managed to maintain discipline in the army, and other conditions improved.

Court Ceremonial

Diocletian was also responsible for the rapid growth of a court ceremonial designed to set the emperor apart from his subjects. Emperors had been accustomed to associate freely with citizens and soldiers until the increasing frequency of assassinations or attempted assassinations showed the need of greater precautions. In the third century emperors rarely appeared in public, and only members of their families or of the court might approach them except on formal occasions. Maximinus had required those approaching him to kneel and kiss his hand or even his foot, thus reviving the oriental practice of *proskynesis* which had once caused so much trouble for Alexander the Great. Gallienus required this ceremony even from persons meeting him in the street, and Diocletian made them kiss the hem of his garment. Commodus had begun the practice of wearing, on formal occasions, a purple robe heavy with gold-threaded embroidery and precious stones. Aurelain wore the diadem—a gold band worn around the head by Persians as a symbol of royalty and later elaborated into the medieval crown or tiara. The emperor's seat became a formal throne, he held a scepter in his hand, and he was addressed as *dominus noster*—"our lord." All these trappings of royalty had been used in some degree by Diocletian's predecessors but he carried court ceremonial to greater extremes than ever before, reducing it to a formal system, and thereby disgusting the few remaining Romans of the old school. All this pomp was, however, symbolic and typical of the new day.

Economic and Social Changes

Italy's economic prosperity of the first century continued well into the middle of the second. It was in large part a consequence of the peace and world unity brought by the establishment of the Empire, and it was encouraged by the imperial policy of economic laissez faire. Nevertheless, this prosperity carried within it the seeds of its own destruction. The great conquests had opened up new territories, especially in the West, whose economic life was on a much simpler plane than that of the Hellenistic world. These regions had been opened to development by Italians during the century before Augustus. Before long, however, they reached as high a stage of economic development as Italy herself. She could no longer maintain her leadership, for the difficulty of communication prevented the growth of a highly centralized economic organization. In the second century several provinces were economically better off than Italy herself. When the limits of political expansion had been reached, the prosperity of Italy began to fail. The industrial system of Augustan Italy had been based upon the labor of slaves, most of them prisoners of war, and the long peace dried up this source of cheap labor. Italy's economic position was severely shaken before the middle of the second century; plagues and Germanic wars aggravated the weakness of the system; and economic depression began under Marcus Aurelius.

The economic decline of Italy in the second century was followed by the ruin of much of the Empire in the third. As Italy gradually lost its central position in the economic organization of the Roman world, provinces or groups of provinces tended to become self-sufficing economic units. This economic independence made possible the political independence of men like Postumus in Gaul. The activities of such leaders led to civil war, and eventually to terrific destruction throughout their provinces. Barbarian invasions had even more disastrous effects in the frontier provinces. The provinces which suffered most in the third century were among the richest in the Empire, notably Gaul, Asia Minor, and Syria, and even northern Italy, which was now the richest part of the peninsula. At the same time the economic machine began to wear out. Ephemeral emperors had neither the time nor the resources to keep roads and irrigation systems in repair, or to defend trade routes from brigands and pirates. Trade became difficult or impossible, and economic stagnation set in.

As economic disintegration progressed, the countryside was broken up into great estates, called villas, each of which provided most of its own necessities and was capable of defending itself against invaders. Such independent villas were especially numerous in the western provinces, where they became the predecessors of medieval manors. Production on these estates did not reach the high level maintained a century or two before, and famines frequently resulted from local crop failures. As the plight of independent farmers became intolerable, such men were glad to surrender their farms for the sake of security, and to become *coloni* on the great estates. Otherwise they lost everything they had, and turned brigand or migrated to the cities where they were supported by the emperors.

The cities were, if possible, even less happy than the country. The decline of trade robbed them of their markets, and lack of incentive caused workers and industrialists to lose their old skills. Manufactured goods became scarce and of low quality. The wealth of the cities made them attractive to barbarian and native looters, and they suffered terribly in the third century. Even Rome itself was not immune. The city had long been virtually undefended, but the Emperor Aurelian decided that it must be surrounded with walls. The walls he built still stand, twelve miles in length. The fact that this great expense was deemed necessary shows how low the power of the Empire had fallen. The wars were accompanied by plagues and famines which took a fearful toll of human lives, especially in the cities. It is estimated that during the third century the population of the Empire declined by at least one third, with the proportionate loss much higher in Italy and the West.

The economic depression and the wars played havoc with imperial finance. The emperors had never worked out a satisfactory system of taxation. In their best days they lived from hand to mouth, and in the third century they were always bankrupt. Only rarely did an emperor inherit anything from his predecessor; he had to give huge donatives to his troops at once; and usually he was unable to collect any taxes at all from more than a fraction of the Empire. In order to meet immediate requirements he was forced to confiscate the personal property of rich men—usually justifying himself by charging them with treason—and to debase the coinage. Both Trajan and Marcus Aurelius had reduced the silver content of coins slightly; under Commodus coins were cast with 30 per cent alloy, under Severus Alexander with 50 per cent, and under Philip with 60 per cent, and in 256 the amount of alloy reached 75 per cent. Eventually it reached 98 per cent, which meant that the imperial coinage was virtually worthless. Of course prices rose to correspond with this debasement of the coinage. Statistics are lacking, however, except for Egypt, where in 280 prices ranged from fourteen to twenty times what they had been a hundred years before. Diocletian began casting good coins once more, thus bringing about a great deflation to undo the earlier inflation, but he could not stabilize either the currency or prices. Money tended to disappear, and people reverted to the primitive system of barter, which encouraged the further growth of villa economy.

Regimentation

When the emperors found that taxation could no longer provide sufficient funds for the government, they resorted to other methods to obtain necessary services. The old system of "liturgies," which had proved so disastrous in ancient Greece but which had survived in Egypt, was revived and extended. Rich men were forced to provide public services at their own expense. The government simply seized food for the army, and ships to transport it. Peasants were forced to maintain roads, irrigation ditches, and other public works, as a form of taxation. The workers' *collegia* were ordered to supply articles of their own manufacture, and when members began withdrawing from these organizations to escape such impositions, the government forbade them to leave. A little later, sons were forced to follow their fathers' trades, in the vain hope of thus assuring an adequate supply of all sorts of labor. When landlords and manufacturers went bankrupt (as they often did in these difficult times), the government took over their estates or businesses and operated them with results that were disastrous for all concerned. Peasants and workers fled to the hills and forests to become brigands, land went out of cultivation, and industry vanished.

When Diocletian's reforms failed to stabilize business conditions, he issued a famous Edict of Prices (301) by which he attempted to set "ceiling prices" for every commodity and maximum wages for every type of labor. Inscriptions have preserved large sections of this edict, which has been much commented upon in recent years and which provides valuable information upon economic conditions at this time. This edict makes it quite clear that there were great extremes of wealth and poverty side by side and that the laboring classes had been reduced to coolie standards of living. We are surprised that they survived at all. Diocletian was quite unable to enforce his decree, and it is doubtful whether he even tried to do so in the West. Distances and communications being what they were, the rulers of the ancient world simply did not have the power to enforce the regimentation to which they were being driven by their declining economy.

The third century thus witnessed a fundamental social and economic revolution in the Roman Empire. The former upper classes were being wiped out; their accumulated capital was being dissipated; and in consequence men suffered terribly, especially in the cities of the West. The civilization of the ancient world was a city civilization and its doom was sealed by this decline of city life. The former upper classes were replaced by a new aristocracy of soldiers and freebooters who had seized and now defended their villas and estates. The significant life of the coming age was to be rural rather than urban; the foundations of feudalism were already being laid; and the ancient world was giving way before the onrushing Middle Ages.

The Classic Age of Roman Law

In matters of law, as in everything else, Augustus had made as few changes as possible, but it was inevitable that new sources of law should develop under the imperial regime and that the emperor should eventually become the sole fount of law. After Tiberius had deprived the popular assemblies of the right to enact legislation, the *senatus consultum* was for a time the principal source of law, but the emperors controlled the senate and its laws were really their work. So notorious was this fact in the second century that writers wishing to cite a law usually quoted the *oratio principis* in which the emperor proposed it rather than the *senatus consultum* by which it was enacted. Even this pretense of senatorial action was dispensed with after the second century, and the emperors simply proclaimed their laws. From early times, moreover, the emperors had issued orders (*constitutiones*) with the force of law. At first they did so rather sparingly, but Hadrian and his successors used them freely. These imperial constitutions were of four sorts: edicts (*edicta*), or laws proclaimed by the emperor; decrees (*decreta*), or decisions of the emperor based on existing law; rescripts (*rescripta*), or answers to inquiries about the law; and mandates (*mandata*), or instructions to subordinate officials. Orders of the last three types were usually of a temporary nature, though sometimes they were important as establishing rules of law. The edicts, on the other hand, became the principal source of Roman law.

Augustus also refrained carefully from interfering with the old courts presided over by praetors, where the formulary system of procedure still prevailed. Praetors continued to post their edicts, and thus to declare law, as their predecessors had done under the Republic (see p. 221). The emperors controlled elections, however, and made sure that the praetors were men sympathetic with the new regime. Hadrian then put an end to all pretense of praetorian legislation. He ordered a famous jurist named Julianus (grandfather of the ephemeral emperor of 193) to prepare a model *Edictum perpetuum* which all praetors were to follow thereafter. Slightly more than half a century later Septimius Severus abolished the praetorian courts, substituting others using a different procedure. The perpetual edict and jury trial were replaced by a judge who heard evidence, cross-examined the witnesses, and rendered judgment. These judges were imperial officials, drawn from the equestrian class, and they interpreted the old praetorian law in a new spirit.

The Classic Jurisconsults

The importance of jurisconsults in the growth of Roman law has already been emphasized. Augustus and his successors allowed these scholarly experts to continue expressing opinions regarding the law, but they selected a certain number to whom they gave an official status with the right of publicly answering questions about the law—the *ius publice respondendi*. Presumably, the men thus signalized shared the emperor's views on such matters. Their opinions were not law, but they carried great weight in court. Unofficial jurists continued to publish *responsa* on their own authority, however, and wrote treatises on law. We know the names of many jurisconsults and of schools of legal thought during the first two centuries of our era, but only one lawbook of the time has been preserved: it is a textbook, entitled *Institutes*. Written by a jurist named Gaius who lived under Antoninus Pius, its merits were so high that it was accepted as a classic for several centuries. A few years later the celebrated Scaevola, a legal advisor to Marcus Aurelius, wrote a large *Digesta* (a systematic treatise on law) as well as other books and *responsa*. Valuable as these works are, it must be admitted that in law, as in other fields of learning, the writers of the second century were compilers rather than original thinkers.

The period of the Severi was illuminated by a succession of brilliant jurists who made this the Classic Age of Roman Law. Aemilius Papinianus was born in Syria and possibly was related to the Empress Julia Domna, to whose circle at Rome he belonged. He studied law under Scaevola at Rome, having Septimius Severus as a classmate, and later he became this emperor's trusted confidant. After

serving as praetorian prefect for several years, he was murdered at
Caracalla's order in 212. In spite of his active bureaucratic and political career, Papinian found time to publish several works on jurisprudence. Julius Paulus was likewise a jurist who became praetorian
prefect, perhaps under Severus Alexander, but we know almost
nothing of his career. Another praetorian prefect under Alexander
was Domitius Ulpianus, a Tyrian by birth, who was murdered in
228. The last of the famous Severan jurists was Modestinus, a pupil
of Ulpian, who died about 240. These great lawyers held the highest
posts in the imperial bureaucracy, and their views were those of the
emperors themselves. The growing absolutism of the time is reflected in Papinian's famous dictum, "The will of the prince has the
force of law," but its humanitarianism appears in countless passages
of the jurisconsults and in the constitutions which they drew up for
the emperors. While the law taught in the third century was still the
old Roman law, the compilers of the second century had been succeeded by creative lawyers who knew how to preserve the spirit of
traditional law in the process of adapting it to the conditions and
ideals of a new age.

The line of the great jurisconsults ends abruptly with the Severi.
The violence of the next few decades was little conducive to legal
scholarship, yet the real causes for the decline of jurisprudence lay
deeper. The absolutism of the new day left no place for independent
lawyers. Even the great Severan jurists had been public functionaries, and thereafter only the emperor's council was permitted to
issue interpretations of the law. As young lawyers had formerly been
trained by the jurisconsults, it now became necessary to establish
imperial law schools for that purpose. The most famous law school
was at Beirut in Syria, whither students were attracted from all parts
of the Roman world. Like so many other things, Roman law had become the concern of a professional bureaucracy.

The Great Codes

Legislation was so active during the third century that a codification of the new laws presently became necessary. About 294 a certain Gregorius, perhaps a professor at Beirut, made a collection of
the imperial constitutions, a few of which dated from Hadrian while

others were the work of the Severi and Diocletian. Thirty years later Hermogenianus published a supplement bringing this collection up to date. The Emperor Theodosius II (408–450) issued an important Law of Citations (426) ordering that thereafter legal interpretations should be drawn from the writings of Gaius, Papinian, Paul, Ulpian, and Modestinus, greatest weight being given to the opinions of Papinian. Twelve years later, in 438, came the Theodosian Code, which assembled all the constitutions since Constantine.

The last step in the codification of the Roman Law came under the Emperor Justinian (527–565). Finding the law in a state of great confusion, he appointed committees of jurists to prepare a new edition of the whole law which would thereafter be the sole authoritative guide for the Empire. Within a remarkably short time these committees, under the chairmanship of Trebonian, produced the *Corpus Iuris Civilis* (529–534), which has ever since remained the classic statement of Roman law. The work fell into four parts: the *Institutes* was a textbook on general legal principles, resting heavily upon Gaius; the *Digest*, or *Pandects*, was an enormous collection of the opinions of jurists; the *Code* included the constitutions from Hadrian to Justinian that were still in force; and the *Novels* contained new edicts as they were issued. The most important of the four is the *Digest*. Its fifty volumes contain thousands of excerpts from the writings of the great jurists, systematically arranged to cover the whole field of law. Each excerpt is marked with the name of its author and the book from which it was taken. The Preface declares that its authors excerpted 2000 books (volumes), about 1625 of which are mentioned by name. The books thus cited were the work of thirty-nine jurists, but only a dozen writers living in the late second and third centuries were used extensively. About half of the excerpts came from Ulpian or Paul. The law of the *Digest* reflects the spirit of the Roman Empire at its best: it is intelligent, enlightened, sober, objective, humane.

The New Spirit in Philosophy

At no period in antiquity did so wide a section of the population enjoy an opportunity for schooling as under the Severi. Primary schools

were to be found even in the villages, and schoolmasters were protected by imperial legislation. Papyrus textbooks found in Egypt
show that schoolboys were taught the Greek classics, while adults
sought a painless education—or at least the semblance of one—by
studying the great works of the past in excerpts and epitomes. Antiquity too had its "hundred best books," with which it was good to
have at least a bowing acquaintance. The papyri have also restored
to us fragments from the works of countless minor authors whose
banal verse and melodious but empty prose had long been forgotten.
There was much reading and writing in the world, but none of it attained the intellectual level of former times.

The truth is that the men of this age were filled with vague fears
and forebodings. They sought comfort in degrading religions and
superstitions, and we can observe the steady progress of what has
been aptly characterized as a "failure of nerve." The troubled conditions of the day help to explain these forebodings and failures, but
we must remember that the enlightened rationalism of earlier times
was the creation and possession of a rather small intellectual aristocracy that had long since been liquidated. The intellectual leaders of
the new day were not the descendants of Cicero and Tacitus but
orientalized Greeks and Hellenized Orientals whose great-grand-
fathers had doubtless been even more superstitious than they.
From their point of view, the third century was a progressive period
giving expression to the ideas of a new world.

The new spirit of the third century is best illustrated by the
literary men, scholars, and philosophers whom the Empress Julia
Domna assembled in the *salon* over which she presided at Rome.
Some of these men were pedants capable of nothing more than making huge collections of excerpts from earlier writers; but others
(such as Papinian) were important leaders in the political and intellectual life of the time. Diogenes Laertius wrote the *Lives of the
Philosophers*, a gossipy volume to which we owe much of what we
know about the personal histories of the thinkers of classic Greece.
More important than he was Philostratus, whom the empress ordered to write a life of Apollonius of Tyana. Apollonius was a Neo-
Pythagorean philosopher and teacher, a native of Cappadocia, who

flourished under Nero and the Flavians. Philostratus's book is as much a wonder book and travelogue as it is an account of the life and opinions of the philosopher, who is made to appear as the perfect sage. Philostratus raised his hero's reputation for sanctity so high that presently pagan controversialists began to praise Apollonius as superior to Jesus. Their propaganda had such telling effect that a hundred years later the Christian Eusebius published a long attack upon the book and its hero. A modern reader can find very little that Jesus and Apollonius had in common, and we are amazed that the two teachers were ever mentioned in the same breath.

Mystery Religions and Neoplatonism

The third century was the golden age of the oriental mystery-religions. The cults of Cybele, Isis, Mithra, and the others, did not differ fundamentally amongst themselves, and each borrowed ideas and practices from the others. Thus arose a syncretism, or general commingling of religions, in which even Christianity had its share, both as contributor and as recipient. We have already seen how the mysteries taught that the world is transitory and evil, and that men are by nature sinful; they urged their followers to disregard the things of this world in order to cultivate those of the spiritual world, which are eternal and good; and they promised a blessed immortality to those who accepted their teachings. Their distrust of human powers caused them to base their claims on ancient revelations from on high, and their otherworldliness led them to impose ascetic practices upon all who sought salvation. The prestige of Julia Domna may have helped them a little in certain quarters, and the army certainly helped Mithra even more. Nevertheless, the popularity of these religions came ultimately from the fact that they provided positive answers to problems then tormenting many men and women. For a time in the third century it seemed that Mithra might perhaps win the world, and it is interesting to speculate upon what fundamental differences if any, would prevail in the world today had Mithra triumphed in the third century instead of Christ in the fourth.

Between the heyday of Mithra and the victory of Christianity came a brief interlude, in the second half of the third century, when the new syncretistic religion of Sol Invictus enjoyed high favor. This "Unconquered Sun," whose beneficence to mankind was of incalculable value, rose anew every morning after his decline of the day before, and though the days might grow short toward the end of the year, the Unconquered Sun was always victorious, and summer returned. His "birthday" was celebrated on December 25, when the days began to lengthen; and the week, which pagans first began to observe at this time, began with the *Dies solis*, or Sunday. Various emperors prized the inspiring mythology and symbolism of Sol Invictus; Aurelian sought to establish his worship as a state cult; and both Diocletian and Constantine paid him honor.

While religion was thus leading many persons to a life of asceticism and contempt of the world, others were being directed to the same goal by philosophy. The principal school of philosophy at this time was Neoplatonism, founded by Ammonius Saccas, an Alexandrian Christian who returned to paganism. As Ammonius wrote nothing, we know his teaching only through the writings of his pupils, chief of whom was Plotinus, the last of the great pagan philosophers. Plotinus was born in Egypt in 204 and for several years he studied under Ammonius at Alexandria. He accompanied the Emperor Gordian on his expedition against Persia in 244, hoping to reach India and there learn the wisdom of the East, but he got no farther than Mesopotamia. After a short stay in Antioch, he settled in Rome, where he passed the remainder of his life as a teacher. Plotinus was a man of great personal charm and of unforgettable personality, a saint, and a mystic who believed that he had achieved perfect union with God. Though he based his philosophy upon the writings of Plato, he explained them in a way that their author would scarcely have understood. He even asked Gallienus for land in Campania where he might establish a state governed like the one described in Plato's *Laws*. Had the request been granted, we can be sure that Plotinus's foundation would have resembled a monastery rather than the Platonic city-state. His highly abstruse writings can be understood today only by trained metaphysicians, yet for several centuries they dominated the highest philosophical thought of

Europe. His most famous pupil, Porphyry, collected the master's writings, wrote his life, and published a learned attack upon Christianity.

Neoplatonism was paganism's final answer to the riddle of the universe, and at the schools of Athens it was taught in more and more attentuated forms until Justinian ordered the schools closed (529). The resulting loss was not so great as has sometimes been alleged. Though the Neoplatonists were hostile to Christianity, their views on many matters were accepted by the Christians, and at the end of the fourth century St. Augustine, intellectually the greatest of the Church fathers, introduced much of their philosophy into Christian theology.

The Progress of Christianity[2]

The church historian Eusebius, writing in the first decade of the fourth century, declared that in all parts of the world conversions to Christianity multiplied under Commodus and that at Rome many persons distinguished for family or wealth then began turning to the new religion. These spectacular successes continued throughout the third century, and the resulting flood of converts gave the church a new character. The development of its intellectual life was especially noteworthy. Christianity had attracted men of superior intellect in the first century, but for a hundred years thereafter Christian thinkers and writers were unworthy of comparison with contemporary pagan intellectuals. Now Christianity began to attract men whose intellects equaled the best that the pagan world could show. Though Christians of the old sort accused these educated converts of corrupting the pure and simple faith of earlier times, the new leaders provided broader and stronger intellectual foundations for Christian theology. As might be expected of such pioneers, none of them attained complete orthodoxy according to the standards of later theologians, yet they gave the church an intellectual respectability that it had not hitherto enjoyed.

This intellectual progress of Christianity was in part the work of a famous school at Alexandria, founded by Pantaenus in the days of

---

[2] See notes on Adolf Harnack and Louis Duchesne, pp. 580 f.

Commodus. Pantaenus had once been a Stoic philosopher, and after his conversion to Christianity he continued in his profession as teacher. He now taught Christianity instead of Stoicism, but he taught other things too, and he gave his pupils a liberal education according to the best standards of his day. Pantaenus became important especially through his pupil and successor, Clement of Alexandria.

Clement was born about 150, probably at Athens, but he lived and taught for many years at Alexandria. In early life he was a pagan deeply read in the writings of the philosophers, and apparently he had been initiated into one of the mysteries. He thus acquired a broader and more sympathetic understanding of Greek culture than was common among earlier Christians. After his conversion he attempted to harmonize the best of this antique culture with Christianity. In one oft-quoted passage he remarked that God had prepared the Greeks for Christianity by means of their philosophy just as he had prepared the Jews for it by their law. Clement then strove to make Christianity palatable to educated Greeks. The rising status of Christians at this time is also shown by Clement's tract entitled *What Rich Man Is Saved?* Here he argued that wealth, rightly used, need not be unchristian—a view seldom expressed by earlier Christian writers. More famous than Clement, however, was his pupil Origen.

Origen

Origen was born in Egypt, probably at Alexandria, in 185. His father Leonidas was then a pagan—the name he gave his son means "Begotten of Horus"—but he was later converted to Christianity. He reared his son in that faith and he met a martyr's death in 202. During this persecution, which was aimed especially at converts to Christianity, Clement withdrew from Alexandria, never to return, but Origen was made of sterner stuff. He even courted death by publicly befriending martyrs until his mother kept him at home by hiding all his clothes. Origen had made such progress in his studies, both Christian and pagan, that he was given Clement's post as head of the Christian school, though only seventeen years old. During the next several years he devoted his time to teaching and study. He attended lectures by Ammonius Saccas, acquired a knowledge of Plato and other Greek philosophers, including contemporary Stoics and Neo-Pythagoreans, learned what Alexandria had to teach about literary criticism and kindred subjects, and in 218 he began publishing the books that were to make him famous. Fourteen years later, in 232, he left the city after quarreling with his bishop Demetrius, whose protégé he had once been. He then established his residence at Caesarea in Palestine. Here he was arrested and tortured during Decius's persecution, and though presently released from prison, he died shortly afterward, perhaps in 253.

Origen's writings cover a vast field. All his life he worked at an edition of the Greek Old Testament, even learning Hebrew—then a rare accomplishment for a Christian—and using the methods of Alexandrian textual criticism. The resulting edition was called the *Hexapla* because various versions appeared in six parallel columns, with Origen's corrections and preferences indicated by symbols. Origen also wrote *Commentaries* on many books of the Old and New Testaments, developing the methods of allegorical interpretation which he took from Clement and the Stoics. Origen was very quick—rather too quick, in fact—to declare that the Scriptures recounted many foolish and impossible things, and he taught that hidden ethical or philosophical meanings should be sought in these passages, and even in those presenting no such difficulties. Only this hidden meaning was of importance to him, and he devoted great ingenuity to formulating rules by which allegories might be interpreted. The church eventually condemned Origen's extreme views, but it never abandoned his methods. Another of his books, called *De Principiis* in the free Latin translation that is all we now have, was an elaborate philosophical explanation of the universe, with Neoplatonic ideas overshadowing those of a strictly Christian source.

The most interesting of Origen's books is the *Contra Celsum*, written to defend Christianity against the attacks of a pagan writer named Celsus, who had published his *True Word* about 180. As Origen copied out Celsus's book a paragraph at a time, following each quotation with his reply, it is possible to reconstruct the greater part of this pagan attack upon Christianity. Celsus sometimes brought scurrilous charges against the Christians, but usually he conducted the discussion on a high plane with philosophical and political arguments. His philosophical criticisms were those of a Platonist, and it is interesting to observe how little Origen's larger views differ from those of his pagan opponent.

For more than a century Origen's writings were highly regarded by the church. Most Greek theologians of the period, and many Latins, were influenced by his ideas, but many of his views were later rejected and Origen was denounced as heretical. Intellectually, he was the greatest of the Greek fathers.

The First Latin Fathers

Meantime, the Latin church too was developing the intellectual aspects of its faith. The earliest Christians at Rome had been Greek-speaking Orientals, but toward the end of the second century Latin Christians began to win the upper hand there. As was to be expected, the intellectual life of the Latin churches diverged markedly from that of contemporary Greeks. They showed much less concern with abstruse philosophy and more with the practical problems of daily life. While Clement and Origen were embellishing Christianity with the ideas of Greek philosophy, Latin writers were enriching it with Roman ideas of law and justice, government and world unity. And just as the city of Rome had produced few of the great authors of Latin literature, so the church at Rome produced few of the Latin Fathers. Most of the early intellectual leaders of Latin Christianity belonged to the African church.

Septimius Tertullianus was born at Carthage between 150 and 160, the son of a minor official. He received an excellent education in Greek and Latin, and for several years he practiced law. Many scholars believe that he was the author of two legal treatises cited in the *Digest*. When over thirty years of age Tertullian became a Christian, and having once embraced that faith he devoted himself wholeheartedly to its cause. His writings include moral essays preaching puritanical austerity and asceticism, attacks upon Gnosticism, and a defense of Christianity called the *Apologeticum*. This famous tract differs widely from Origen's *Contra Celsum*. Ignoring philosophical argument, Tertullian adopted the style of a lawyer pleading in court and invoked legality, natural justice, and the virtues of the Christians in behalf of the new religion. He had none of Clement's sympathy with Greek thought, exclaiming on one occasion, "What has Jerusalem in common with Athens, or the Church with the Academy?" The puritanical zeal and the new prophecy of the Montanists (see p. 529) attracted him greatly, and for several years he tried in vain to persuade the church to accept Montanism. He then withdrew from the church, and spent his last days as a heretic. Nevertheless, his writings were widely used by his successors, who repeated his ideas, often in his own words, even when they did not care to cite the heretic by name.

Another notable African, Caecilius Cyprianus, was born to a wealthy family of the Roman aristocracy at Carthage about 200. At first he was a professor of rhetoric, and not until about 247 did he become a Christian. Soon thereafter Cyprian was elected bishop of the church in his native city. During the persecution of 250 he went into hiding, but eight years later, during the persecution of Valerian, he was beheaded. While a careful student of Tertullian (whom he called *magister,* "master"), Cyprian managed to avoid Montanism, and his great concern was with matters of church policy and government. His most important book is a treatise *On the Unity of the Catholic Church.*

Church Government

Meantime other Christians were perfecting the organization of their church, whose rapid growth raised new problems and opened new opportunities. The three orders of clergy—bishops, priests, and deacons—had by this time been established. In the third century the duties and functions of these orders differed much from those of officials bearing the same titles today. In each city or town the bishop was head of the church organization, and now there was only one bishop in each town. As there usually was only one church in the community, the bishop presided there in person at public worship, he regulated matters concerning the church, and he virtually ruled the Christians in his city. In the larger places the bishop was assisted by priests who preached, instructed converts, did pastoral work, and held services in neighboring villages, but who differed from modern parish priests in that they had no specific churches of their own. As every town had its bishop, there were more bishops and fewer priests than would be required for an equal number of Christians today. About 250 the clergy of Rome consisted of one bishop, forty-six priests, and seven deacons. In Alexandria, there were seventeen priests in the city and nineteen others in nearby Mareotis, all under one bishop. In lesser places the bishop might have only one or two priests, or none at all.

In the third century the deacons took charge of church property, and the archdeacon, or principal deacon, was the most important man in the church after the bishop. Christians owned their cemeteries, which sometimes developed into underground caverns where the dead were buried and religious services held. These were the celebrated catacombs, where Christians could hide in times of persecution (Plate 27). Services had ordinarily been held in private houses until the third century, but then the more important Christian communities began to erect church buildings somewhat resembling those of today. The church owned other lands and houses given by pious persons, and there was a treasury for the alms of the people. About 250 the Roman church supported fifteen hundred widows and other unfortunates with its funds. Ordinarily the clergy were not paid. The bishops were elected by the people from the clergy. The usual practice was to elect a deacon, who would be better informed than the priests regarding the business affairs of the church.

As great power fell to the bishops, the office attracted many able men in the third century. Among them were some who, like Cyprian, sprang from classes of society that would formerly have taken an active part in ruling the Empire, but whose services were not desired by the military autocrats then controlling the government. The statesmanship of these early bishops was an asset of incalculable value to the growing church. Sometimes it showed itself in their government of churches, sometimes in their dealings with other bishops, sometimes in their policies toward the state. The treatment of penitents, and especially of those who had denied the faith in time of persecution, gave ample scope for such statesmanship. Energetic bishops also found many occasions to exercise legislative powers, as when Calixtus I of Rome issued rules for Christian marriage that differed widely from those fundamental to Roman law.

The more difficult problems of church government were discussed in church councils attended by all the bishops of a Roman province. Such councils issued "canons" (laws) governing the Christians of the province, clergy and laity alike. One step more would have led to a world council of bishops, or selected bishops, which might have governed the whole church much as the senate had once governed Rome's empire. Such an "ecumenical" or world council was actually held at Nicaea in 325, but only three others followed during the next century and a quarter. Church government developed along other lines.

The power and prestige of the bishop of Rome advanced greatly during the third century, and the bishops often claimed that they were entitled to rule the whole Christian church. Pope Victor (189–198) was an aggressive champion of such Roman supremacy, and his successors included other able men with the same ambition. The Roman church gained an increasing influence in the affairs of the church as a whole, though other bishops and theologians found it difficult to concede more than prestige to their colleagues at Rome. Eastern bishops spoke bitterly of Roman pretentions, Origen denied the papal theory categorically, and Cyprian resisted Roman claims so vigorously that Pope Stephen, at the time of his martyrdom (257), was about to sever relations with the African bishop. Stephen's successor continued the quarrel, but within a short time Cyprian too met a martyr's death. About 270 Paul of Samosata. bishop of Antioch, was declared a heretic by his fellow bishops and expelled from the church. When he refused to surrender the church property at Antioch to his rival, his opponents took the matter to Aurelian. The emperor's decision favored the rival bishop, who was recognized by the bishops of Italy and Rome. Controversialists sometimes cite this case as evidence that Aurelian himself recognized Roman supremacy over the whole Christian church. It is more probable that the decision was determined by the fact that Paul had been closely associated with the rebel Queen Zenobia at Palmyra. The incident is significant, however, as showing how impossible it had become for Church and State to ignore each other.

Christianity and the Roman State

Modern ideas as to the desirability of a complete separation of church and state were unknown in antiquity. From the earliest times Rome's state cult had been an important part of her public life, and even so enlightened a man as Cicero contended that religion should be fostered by the state. The colleges of priests, and especially the *pontifex maximus,* wielded powers sufficient to arouse the ambitions of politicians as realistic as Caesar. After 12 B.C. the emperor himself was always *pontifex maximus.* Emperor worship tightened the connection of the government with religion, and beginning with Commodus the emperors made great efforts to promote this worship. Aurelian frankly called himself *deus et dominus* ("god and lord") and Diocletian advertised his "divine majesty." The desire to obtain religious sanctions for their government also led the emperors to apply the word *sacer* ("sacred") to everything that touched them. Their persons were declared "sacred," their palace was the *sacrum palatium,* their capital city (Rome) was the *urbs sacra,* their rescripts were *sacrae litterae* or *sacrae constitutiones,* their coins were *sacra moneta.* The word "sacred" came to mean nothing more than "imperial." The Empire was becoming an oriental theocracy, a state supposedly governed by the divine powers through their chosen agents. Such a state dared not ignore any rival religious organization.

Roman authorities had from early times attempted to determine what religious practices were permissible, either to Roman citizens, or to foreigners resident in Rome, or to provincials in their provinces. Usually these officials were very tolerant. Greek cults, notably those of Apollo, were brought from southern Italy, and Cybele was introduced from Asia Minor. When Aurelian established the cult of Sol Invictus, therefore, and when Constantine later did the same for

Christianity, they were merely following ancient precedent. Provincials were allowed to continue their ancestral worships unless they entailed barbarous practices such as human sacrifice—or others, such as circumcision, which Romans considered barbarous. These provincial cults were rigorously suppressed, however, if they took on political importance. The famous law of 186 B.C. forbade Bacchic societies but permitted individuals to worship the god in private. The worship of Isis at Rome was prohibited during the wars against Egypt, but later it was encouraged. The Druids were suppressed in Gaul because of their share in fomenting political separatism, and the Jews were punished severely for political rebellion. As soon as the government was sure of Jewish loyalty, on the other hand, it restored complete freedom of worship. Jews were excused from sacrifices to the emperors; the laws against circumcision were suspended for their benefit; and we read of Christians whom Marcus Aurelius condemned to labor in the Sardinian mines because of their anti-Semitic violence: one of the men thus punished later became Pope Calixtus I.

The First Persecutions

The first official opposition to Christianity is to be explained primarily by Roman suspicions that the new religion was of a seditious nature. Pontius Pilate permitted the crucifixion of Jesus when the Jews accused him of aspiring to kingship, and Pilate presumably reported the affair to Rome. A few years later Herod Agrippa, while pacifying the disturbances that followed Caligula's attempt to set up his statue in the Temple at Jerusalem, saw fit to execute the apostle James and to arrest Simon Peter; he too undoubtedly made a report to Rome. Shortly thereafter, Herod's friend Claudius, still nervous because of the confusion attendant upon Caligula's death, expelled Christians from Rome for rioting (41). Within a dozen years of the crucifixion, therefore, officials at Rome were convinced that Christianity might become a dangerous source of sedition. Several years later, in 64, when Nero was looking for someone to blame for the great fire at Rome, it seemed plausible to accuse the Christians, several of whom were executed. Such at least is Tacitus's account of the affair. Other ancient authors, including Suetonius and various Christian writers, tell of the Neronian persecution without mentioning the fire, and imply that the Christians were executed simply for being Christians. At any rate, Peter and Paul were executed in 67 for other reasons than the fire. Coming in the last days of Nero's reign, when opposition was rising on every hand, these executions again suggest that the authorities suspected the loyalty of Christians. The persecutions in Domitian's last years, about which very little is known, support this suggestion.

Pliny's famous letter to Trajan, written about 112, shows that in his day Christianity was considered illegal, though there is no mention here or elsewhere of laws specifically forbidding the religion. The prohibition to which Pliny refers was probably stated in a decree interpreting the laws against secret societies. Perhaps it dated from Nero's first persecution. Tertullian speaks of an *institutum neronianum* according to which Christians were not permitted to be—*non licet esse christianos*. Yet proceedings against the Christians must have been rather uncommon, for Pliny, who had been a practicing lawyer all his adult life and a high official of the Empire for many years, declared that he had never witnessed such a case in court. Nevertheless, he was familiar with the forms of court procedure to be used against them. Christians were ordered to sacrifice to the emperor. If they consented, they were set free; if they refused, they were punished. The Christians, of course, considered such sacrifice to be gross idolatry and a denial of Christ, whereas the pagans took it as a mere gesture (comparable perhaps to saluting the flag with us) and regarded refusal as clear evidence of disloyalty. Punishment for Roman citizens who refused to sacrifice was exile or beheading. Non-citizens were subjected to more ignominious punishments such as forced labor in the mines or fighting wild beasts in the arena.

Pliny's letter also shows that the proceedings against the Christians in Bithynia were instigated, not by the government, but by private individuals who anonymously denounced them. On many other occasions persecution was the work of mobs hostile to Christians. It is not easy to give a full account of the reasons for this popular hostility, but a major cause lay in the fact that in those early days conversion compelled a Christian to sever most of his connections with the pagan world. Idolatry and worship of the gods entered into every phase of pagan life, and there were many institutions, such as the gladiatorial shows, of which a Christian could not approve. Criticism of such things in the name of a higher morality angered many persons and inspired others (such as Lucian) to ridicule the critics. Enlightened pagans might preach a high morality and denounce the shows with impunity, for they continued to live in the world they denounced and they had no reputation for disloyalty to live down. Christians, on the other hand, conscientiously withdrew into their own small groups. Cases are on record where a wife's Christianity seriously compromised her husband's standing in society because she refused to continue her former associations with his pagan friends, and perhaps even left him. Deserted husbands

---

• Note for Plate 26. The first picture shows a *graffito,* or scratching, on a plaster wall, which dates from the second or third century after Christ and was found in the ruins of a building on the Palatine Hill. It depicts a man with an ass's head being crucified, before whom stands a worshiper. The Greek letters spell three words meaning, "Alexamenos worships God." Presumably this caricature was drawn by someone who wished to ridicule a Christian fellow servant. The sketch at the right is added to bring out the essential lines in the *graffito.*

The second picture shows a papyrus from Theadelphia in Egypt. It is a certificate declaring that its possessor had publicly sacrificed to the pagan gods during the persecution of Christianity by Decius. Note the three separate handwritings: that of the scribe who made out the certificate, at the top and bottom; that of the witnesses, two lines near the center; and the signature of Hermas himself, the man who had sacrificed and who wrote in large letters, apparently not being much accustomed to writing. The certificate reads, in translation: "To those in charge of the sacrifices under Aurelia Charis of the village of Theadelphia. I have always sacrificed and lived piously before the gods, and now I have sacrificed and tasted the victim in your presence in obedience to the edict. I request you to certify this for me. May you fare well. [Second hand] We, the Aurelii, Serenus and Hermas, have seen you sacrifice. [Third hand] I, Herm[as], have signed. [First hand] In the first year of the Emperor Caesar Gaius Messius Quintus Traianus Decius Pius Felix Augustus, Payni 22 [June 16, 250]."

Caricature of the Crucifixion

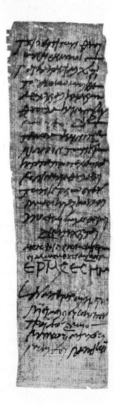

Certificate of Sacrifice

Plate 26.   Christianity and Rome

Catacomb

Christian Agapé

Plate 27.   Early Christianity

naturally became bitter against Christianity. It was also charged that Christian slaves or servants secretly converted the master's children, thus ruining their chances for distinguished marriages or careers.

When Christians had made themselves thoroughly unpopular, it was inevitable that ill-founded accounts of their activities should circulate in pagan society. Ignorant persons justified their brutalities by telling of Christian orgies culminating in incest and cannibalism. The former charge was made perhaps because Christians addressed one another as brother and sister, and saluted each other with a kiss of brotherhood, while the latter accusation may have come from reports of the Eucharist at which Christians said they partook of the body and blood of Christ. Others loudly accused the Christians of "atheism," and still others held them up to ridicule, saying, among other things, that they worshipped an ass's head (see Plate 26). Educated persons and government officials gave little heed to such absurd stories, but they could not ignore charges of sacrilege and lèse majesté, and they never ceased suspecting Christians of disloyalty.

Official Reluctance to Persecution

The conditions described by Pliny continued unchanged for many years. Disturbances arose from time to time, Christians were accused before the magistrates, and a few were executed for refusing to sacrifice. In the difficult times under Marcus Aurelius, disturbances became more common, Christians were accused more frequently, and there were terrible examples of mob fury, notably at

---

• Note for Plate 27. These two pictures come from the catacomb of Calixtus in Rome, which dates from the early third century. The upper picture shows a *cubiculum*, or family burial vault. The rooms were also used as chapels, where religious services might be held. Sometimes these chapels were elaborately decorated, and the origins of much Christian art may be traced back to them. The lower picture reproduces a wall painting of a Christian Agapé, or Love Feast. Here the assembled Christians ate ordinary food—in this case, bread and fish. The Agapé was not a solemn sacrament, but a "church supper," and it must not be confused with the Eucharist or Communion Service.

Lyons in 177. It must be added that the imperial authorities often showed a great distaste for persecution, but the Christians, goaded to fanaticism by the mob, made the judges' tasks more difficult. Thus, when a few Christians in Africa refused to sacrifice, the judge ordered them to think it over for thirty days, apparently hoping that the mob would by then have forgotten its fury, which would enable him safely to forget the whole matter. Instead, the Christians replied that there was nothing to think over and forced him to proceed to judgment. On another occasion a crowd voluntarily appeared before a judge and declared themselves Christians: after ordering a few ringleaders punished, the judge said to the others, "Fools, if you wish to die, you have ropes and precipices!" and had them thrown out of court. Sometimes judges eloquently urged the condemned to sacrifice, even suggesting subterfuges by which they might do so without violating their consciences. If this failed, the judge might apply torture to compel a sacrifice in the hope of thus sparing himself the necessity of ordering an execution.

Septimius Severus met strong opposition in the East and apparently he believed that Christians and Jews were in part responsible for his difficulties there. Jews had taken up arms against him, and his son celebrated a triumph over them. Christianity had made great progress at Edessa, in the buffer state of Osrhoëne, north of Syria, where a strong Syriac church and extensive Syriac Christian literature had sprung up in the second century. Apparently the client-king of Osrhoëne, Abgar IX (179–216), was a Christian—the first Christian king in history—and several of his close advisors had accepted the new religion. Osrhoëne revolted against Severus in 195 and thus presumably added to Roman fear of Christian disloyalty. Severus was greeted in Egypt with riotous disturbances while other mobs attacked the Christians. The emperor issued edicts in 202 forbidding the conversion of pagans to Judaism or Christianity. During the next few years many Christians were executed, especially in Egypt and North Africa.

Except for these edicts of Septimius, Christianity enjoyed peace and even imperial favor under Commodus and the Severi. In the days of Commodus the Christians had received spectacular aid from the beautiful Marcia who had been raised a Christian but had become one of Commodus's concubines. It was with her aid, for example, that Pope Victor obtained the release of Christian prisoners in the Sardinian mines. Septimius had a Christian nurse for his son and allowed Christians to hold high positions at court. Caracalla and Elagabalus gave little thought to the Christians, but Severus Alexander and his mother showed a sympathetic interest in them. Alexander erected statues of Abraham and Christ beside those of Orpheus and Apollonius of Tyana in his private chapel. He ordered the Golden Rule inscribed on public buildings, and his mother Julia Mamaea summoned Origen to Antioch to teach her the doctrines of Christianity. The next emperor, Maximinus (235–238), executed a few Christians in Rome and Syria: Pope Pontianus and his rival Hippolytus were exiled to Sardinia, where both soon died, and Origen barely escaped arrest. The peace of the church then continued unbroken for fifteen years and the Emperor Philip the Arabian was so favorable to the Christians that a false report credited him with secret conversion.

Christian Intransigeance

We naturally wonder why Christians did not take advantage of these conditions to establish a *modus vivendi* with the government. A series of able popes, including Victor (189–198), Calixtus (217–222), and Fabian (236–250), had influential friends at court who might have helped them gain legal recognition. Jews were disliked by the populace as much as the Christians were, and they had repeatedly risen in armed revolt against the government, which the Christians never did. Nevertheless, the emperors excused all Jews from sacrifices and other obligations incompatible with their religion. They never granted similar privileges to the Christians, and their greatest concession was to look the other way for forty years. Had Christians seriously tried to reach an understanding with the imperial authorities, they might have been accorded a status comparable to that enjoyed by the Jews, but we hear of no efforts on their part to regularize their position.

This intransigeance had developed under persecution. Nothing in

the Gospels suggests that Jesus opposed the Roman government
(he is even reported by the Gospels to have said, "Render unto
Caesar the things that are Caesar's"), and Paul, proud of his Roman
citizenship, ordered Christians to give the authorities due reverence
and obedience, saying "The powers that be are ordained of God."
It is true that several years later, after the Neronian persecutions,
the Apocalypse spoke bitterly of Rome as "drunk with the blood
of the saints," but many early Christians questioned the divine inspiration of this book. Christians often expressed the view that in
this world they were strangers and sojourners, and many of them
still expected an early return of Jesus to establish his Messianic kingdom. Even in the second century Christians rarely showed hostility
to the Roman state as such.

Nevertheless, open hatred flared up in the East under Septimius
Severus. The eighth book of a strange work called the Sibylline
Oracles is largely a Christian prophecy. Much of it is devoted to a
long recital of Rome's crimes, and it culminates in a prediction of
her fall in the year 195. A few years later a Christian named Judas
published an exposition of Daniel in which he tried to show that the
anti-Christ should be expected in 202—actually the year in which
Severus began his persecution. This persecution, not caused by mob
violence but officially ordered by the emperor, did much to embitter
the Christians against the state. Clement of Alexandria, who had
hitherto shown a sympathetic and receptive attitude toward the
better pagans, now wrote in praise of martyrdom, saying that the
Christian must forsake his country and disregard its laws. In Africa,
Tertullian began to preach that it was impossible for a true Christian
to share at all in the public life of the pagan world.

Several years later Origen was equally hostile to the Roman state.
Replying to Celsus's charge that the Christians formed a secret society in violation of the law, Origen declared that it was right to
form such associations against a tyrannical government. In other
passages he contrasted the law of God with the law of man. When
Celsus complained that Christians would not serve in the army or
defend the Empire, Origen justified their conduct, remarking that if

everyone were a Christian there would be no more wars! When Celsus eloquently urged Christians to support the state, Origen replied with a categorical "No!" The gulf separating the Christian church from the Roman state could not be bridged. As Origen published his apology in 248, just when the government was endeavoring to stimulate imperial patriotism by elaborate ceremonies in honor of the one thousandth anniversary of the founding of Rome, such remarks may well have aroused indignation in official quarters.

Decius and Diocletian

·In that very year (248) the Goths again invaded the Empire. Philip lost his life in battle, and after a period of confusion Decius became emperor. Rioting against the Christians broke out in 249, and in the next year Decius launched an energetic campaign against them. He was the first Illyrian emperor, and he may deliberately have reversed the tolerant policies of his oriental predecessors, the Severi and Philip. His native province was scarcely touched by Christianity, and as a soldier he may have resented Christian attacks upon his profession. Moreover, it is possible that Decius sincerely believed that the unprecedented afflictions under which the Empire then groaned were a punishment for neglect of the Roman gods and that a universal supplication might bring back their favor. At any rate, he ordered that every person in the Empire sacrifice publicly, that after doing so he be given a written certificate (several such certificates have been recovered in Egypt: see Plate 26), and that those who refused to sacrifice be punished with death.

The ensuing persecution was the bloodiest that Christianity had yet suffered, making thousands of martyrs in all parts of the Empire. Countless Christians weakened and sacrificed. Others hired pagans to sacrifice for them or bought forged certificates, even though the church declared that those who cheated were little better than those who sacrificed. Yet the relatively small number of victims—certainly not 1 per cent of the Christians in the Empire—shows that Decius's order was not well enforced. As it is difficult to believe that all except a few thousand Christians either sacrificed or cheated, we must as-

sume that most of them managed to avoid the officials. The persecution came to a sudden end with Decius's death in 251, but after a
respite of a few years it was resumed by Valerian. Soon thereafter,
Valerian was captured by the Persians, and his son Gallienus made
peace with the church (260). Christians were granted toleration and
permitted to own churches and cemeteries, and for the first time
they were recognized as a body with legal rights.

The death of Gallienus was followed by a slight reaction, but the
church was not subjected to serious persecution again for more than
forty years. Diocletian officially ignored the Christians during the
early years of his reign, allowing them to hold high commands and
to govern provinces. His wife and daughter were Christians, and a
large Christian church faced his palace at Nicomedia. But his son-
in-law and Caesar, Galerius, hated the Christians, against whom he
became aggressive after his victory over the Armenians in 297. As
Armenia was largely Christianized, even its king having been converted, Galerius may have feared or suspected Christian aid to his
enemies. His first step was to purge his army of Christians—very
few Christians voluntarily entered the army, but soldiers or officers
often remained in military service after conversion—and in 303 he
persuaded Diocletian to inaugurate a general persecution.

At first Diocletian insisted that there be no bloodshed, and the first
decree merely confiscated church property, destroyed Christian
books, removed Christians from public office, and deprived them of
all legal rights. Two fires in the palace, which Galerius attributed to
the Christians but which they attributed to him, were followed by
more stringent measures. Bishops and priests were arrested, and a
few were executed when they refused to sacrifice. Finally, in 304,
the government revived Decius's plan and ordered all Christians to
sacrifice. Thousands of martyrs died, and still the persecution was
no more successful than Decius's had been. The persecution continued for several years after Diocletian's retirement, but at last
Galerius, old, sick, and discouraged, admitted that he could not
abolish Christianity. Shortly before his death in April, 311, he signed
an edict granting equal toleration to all religions.

Christian Victory

The Christians had won in their great struggle with the Roman state. We have no means of knowing the number of those who suffered during the various persecutions of three hundred years. Fantastic figures were formerly suggested, and it is still possible to find sober writers who say that more than a million Christians became martyrs: 1 per cent of that figure would certainly be too low, but 10 per cent would probably be too high. Regardless of their numbers, the importance of these martyrs cannot be overestimated. Their steadfastness under persecution impressed the pagans, and in the long run it earned a high reward. As Tertullian exclaimed, "The blood of the martyrs was the seed of the church." Christians came to be respected by the pagans. The old slanders about incest and cannibalism were rarely repeated now—if we may judge from the silence of the later apologists—and the populace behaved quite differently at the executions. Polycarp and others in the second century had died amidst the howls of the mob. When Cyprian was executed in 258, pagans stood by in grim silence while the Christians, present in large numbers without being molested, were allowed to carry his body away in a triumphal procession. Under Diocletian pagan mobs sometimes reviled the executioners and occasionally snatched Christians from their hands. Local officials enabled prisoners to escape, and we are told that sometimes they would simply carry a Christian before the altar, falsely report that they had seen him sacrifice, and let him go. Maximian and Constantius, the Augustus and the Caesar in the West, ceased enforcing the edicts after a few weeks. Public opinion had definitely turned against persecution.

Christianity was still primarily a religion of the cities, though under Diocletian it was beginning to penetrate the villages and countryside, and it was much stronger in the eastern provinces than in the West. A leading authority on the subject (Harnack) believes that in the days of Diocletian a majority of the population of Asia Minor was Christian, as were strong minorities in Syria and Egypt,

Greece, central and southern Italy, north Africa, Spain, and southern Gaul. At the same time Christianity had won only a small minority in Palestine and the rest of Asia, northern Italy and Illyria; and its progress was negligible in northern Gaul, Britain, and along the Rhine-Danube frontier. Other writers have estimated that there were in all six or eight million Christians in the Empire, or about 10 per cent of the total population.

More important than their numbers, however, was the quality of the new converts. They included persons from every class of society and of every stage of culture. Many among them were thoroughly discouraged by the changes that had swept over the Empire since Marcus Aurelius. Some sought refuge from the turbulence of the new day. Others were attracted to the church because it offered a new hope while retaining much of the old spirit of Greece and Rome. Clement and Origen stood far from Plato and the Stoics, it is true, but not so far as did Plotinus and Porphyry. Tertullian differed much from Cato the Censor, but not so much as Septimius Severus did. Cyprian possessed a larger share of the old Roman virtues than Decius or Valerian. Christianity was almost ready to absorb the Roman world, whose better qualities it perpetuated along with its own distinctive Gospel.

Notes

Adolf Harnack

At the beginning of the twentieth century the best-known historian of early Christianity was Adolf Harnack (1851–1930). Born at Dorpat in Estonia, Harnack was the son of a Lutheran professor of theology whose family were Baltic Germans long resident in Russia. After taking his degree at Leipzig, he taught in various German universities until 1888 when he became Professor of Church History at Berlin. Here he played a leading part in the intellectual life of Germany. A member of the Prussian Academy of Sciences, he participated actively in many of that body's scholarly undertakings and wrote its history (1899); he was made librarian of the Royal Library (1905), which under his direction became one of the best in the world; and he maintained a close personal friendship with the Kaiser and other important political personages. He made himself a leader of the liberal religious forces in Germany, especially by his demand that candidates for ordination to the Lutheran ministry should not be required to subscribe to the Apostles' Creed. Harnack's liberal views regarding the divinity of Christ greatly distressed the Kaiser who, it is said, refused to discuss theology with him after the professor had publicly criticized a statement made by the Emperor in the heat of a controversy over Babylonian influences in the Old Testament—the so-called Babel-Bibel controversy that raged in Germany about 1903. Harnack visited the United States in 1904, where he had many friends and admirers among American scholars, several of whom were his former pupils. He was also well-known in England. Before and during World War I Harnack strongly disapproved of the propaganda of the Pan-German League, but his family connection with the Baltic lands caused him to favor the establishment there of an independent state under German protection. In politics, as in theology, Harnack was a distinguished example of the liberal element in Imperial Germany, but he had no sympathy with the Weimar Republic, and in his declining years he felt lonely and forsaken.

Harnack made his reputation with a large *History of Dogma* (3 vols., 1885-9; Eng. tr. in 9 vols., 1896-9) which nominally covered the whole history of Christianity down to the end of the Reformation period but which dealt largely with the first five or six centuries. In this work of his youth Harnack stressed the influence of Greek philosophy in shaping Christian theology and strongly implied that these Greek accretions were not essential to Christianity. When the Prussian Academy decided to publish a new edition of the Greek Fathers, Harnack prepared the way with what is perhaps his most important work, the *Geschichte der altchristlichen Litteratur bis Eusebius* (2 vols. in 4, 1893-1904). Here he assembled information about every piece of Christian writing, except the New Testament, that has been preserved or is mentioned from that early time. In *Die Mission und Ausbreitung des Christentums in den ersten drei Jahrhunderten* ("Missions and the Expansion of Christianity in the First Three Centuries," 1902, Eng. tr.) he traced the establishment of the new religion throughout the Roman Empire. In addition to writing these large books, Harnack found time to edit an impressive series of *Texte und Untersuchungen*, monographs dealing with different phases of the early church. Some he wrote himself but the great majority were the work of his pupils. In his later years Harnack had the pleasure of seeing many of his pupils hold important positions in the churches and universities of Germany and other Protestant countries.

Harnack's most popular work was *Das Wesen des Christentums* (1900; Eng. tr., *What Is Christianity?* 1901). Originally delivered as a course at the University of Berlin, these lectures were taken down in shorthand by an admiring student and later published in book form. About 70,000 copies of the German edition of this book were sold, and it was translated into fourteen languages. Harnack here made Christianity something agreeable to liberal Germans at the turn of the century. These men were little given to asceticism and other religious excesses but, while hostile to socialism, they were aware of the unfortunate state of the poor and altruistically willing to do something to relieve it; they were very respectful toward the constituted authorities; they vaguely felt that material progress by itself was not enough; and they were impatient with ancient creeds and dogmas. Harnack discovered that these very things were the essence of the original Gospel of Jesus. He then declared that this primitive Gospel was soon perverted by the Greek and Roman churches but rediscovered by Luther after many centuries. The book is really a liberal Protestant sermon rather than a history, but its fundamental ideas permeate Harnack's more esoteric works of high scholarship. For further details of Harnack's life, see the biography by his daughter, Dr. Agnes Zahn-Harnack, *Adolf von Harnack* (1936).

Louis Duchesne

The leading French student of early ecclesiastical history in the opening years of the twentieth century was Mgr. Louis Duchesne (1843–1922). The son of a Breton fisherman and educated in Brittany and at Rome, Duchesne was ordained to the Catholic priesthood in 1867. After taking his doctor's degree at the University of Paris (1877), he became Professor of Church History at the Institut Catholique in Paris. Ten years later he began teaching at the École des Hautes Études—a state institution, part of the University of Paris—and in 1895 the government appointed him director of the French School at Rome. This post he held the rest of his life. Under his administration the school became one of the best in the world for training archeologists, classicists, and students of Roman history. At Rome Duchesne was on excellent terms with Pope Leo XIII, who had a high regard for scholars. He was given many important tasks in the church, and it was even rumored that he might become a cardinal.

Duchesne owed his first reputation as a scholar to his edition (1884) of the "Liber Pontificalis," an ancient set of lives of the popes which is of prime importance to students of the early history of the church at Rome. Other works by Duchesne dealt with various phases of the early ecclesiastical history of France and with the history of Christian worship. His great work, however, is the *Histoire ancienne de l'Église* (3 vols., 1906–9, Eng. tr). Though the author limits his subject rather narrowly, largely ignoring the social background and pagan rivals of early Christianity, this book remains our best general survey of church history from post-apostolic times to the end of the fifth century.

Duchesne's skepticism regarding ancient legends and traditions won him many enemies in the church, and all his life he was in trouble with ecclesiastical authorities. Even his doctor's thesis was denounced at Rome when it first appeared. As long as Leo XIII was alive, Duchesne's enemies got nowhere, but under the next pope they redoubled their attacks. At last they were successful and in 1912 the *Histoire ancienne de l'Église* was placed on the Index—the official list of books which Catholics are forbidden to read. As a loyal son of the church, Duchesne bowed to this decision. Not until after his death did the long-awaited fourth volume of the great history appear, under the title *L'Église au VIième siècle* (1924). See J. Guiraud, "Monseigneur Duchesne: sa vie et son œuvre," in *Revue des questions historiques,* 97–98 (1922–23); and *Dictionnaire d'archéologie chrétienne et de liturgie,* art. "Historiens du Christianisme, XXXVII, Monsignor Duchesne," VI (1925), cols. 2680–2735.

XV   The End of the Ancient World

DIOCLETIAN AND MAXIMIAN RETIRED FROM OFFICE ON May 1, 305, and within a short time the Roman Empire was again being torn asunder by rival claimants. Galerius and Constantius became Augusti in the East and the West respectively, just as Diocletian had planned, but thereafter everything went wrong. First Galerius chose two friends named Maximin Daïa and Severus as Caesars, thereby mortally offending Maxentius and Constantine, sons respectively of Maximian and Constantius. When Constantius died a year later (July 306), his troops hailed his son Constantine as emperor. Galerius was furious, but he could do nothing except promote Severus to the rank of Augustus and recognize Constantine as Caesar. Maxentius was then proclaimed Caesar at Rome by troops that had once served under Maximian. Severus marched against him, was captured, and was killed. The aged Maximian thereupon resumed his position as Augustus (307), formed a fragile alliance with Constantine, to whom he gave his sister Fausta in marriage, and proclaimed his son and his son-in-law Augusti. Meantime Galerius had found a successor for Severus in the person of a competent soldier named Licinius, and Maximin Daïa, angry at being passed over, had assumed the rank of Augustus.

Six Augusti thus claimed the Roman world, but when friends urged Diocletian to resume power as a seventh Augustus, that retired statesman wisely refused. He ended his days peacefully and forgotten a few years later. After quarreling with his son Maxentius,

Maximian tried to seduce Constantine's army, and when he failed, he committed suicide at his son-in-law's suggestion (310). Galerius died a year later, and the world fell to the four remaining Augusti: Maximin Daïa held Asia and Egypt; Licinius held Illyria and the Balkans; Maxentius held Italy and Africa; and to Constantine went Britain, Gaul, and Spain.

There had been little actual fighting during these six years, but civil war broke out as soon as Galerius's restraining hand was removed in 311. Licinius and Constantine entered into an alliance which was sealed by the betrothal of Constantine's sister to Licinius, and Maxentius allied himself with Maximin Daïa, who had antagonized Licinius by seizing Asia Minor after Galerius's death. Constantine invaded Italy a few months later and defeated his rival decisively in a famous battle at the Milvian bridge just outside Rome (Oct. 28, 312). Early in the next year Constantine and Licinius held a conference at Milan and Licinius married Constantia. In the spring Licinius marched against Daïa, who had invaded Europe, and on May 1 he won an important victory near Adrianople. Daïa fled to Asia, where he committed suicide at Tarsus. For the next several years Constantine ruled the West and Licinius the East, but their truce ended in 324 and Constantine defeated his rival at Chrysopolis —near Scutari on the Asiatic shore of the Bosporus, opposite Byzantium. The victor, listening to the pleas of his sister, spared Licinius's life for the moment, but executed him a little later on charges of treason. Constantine ruled the whole Roman world thereafter, until his death in 337.

Constantine a Revolutionary Usurper

Constantine was one of the world's great revolutionists and, like Alexander, he may be taken as introducing a new period in history. Though he might have posed as another of the Illyrian emperors, he had many reasons to hate the system established by Diocletian. When he was born during the 270's at Nish (in the modern Yugoslavia), his father Constantius was a soldier as yet unaware of the greatness that awaited him. His mother was a Bithynian woman named Helena, a servant in a tavern, who had run off with the young soldier. When Constantius began to prosper politically, he discarded his concubine and married Theodora, the stepdaughter of Maximian, but the young Constantine remained loyal to his mother. Brought up at Diocletian's court, Constantine was held there more or less as a prisoner, and was snubbed and set aside in favor of his father's legitimate children. He therefore developed strong feelings against the tetrarchy and rebelled openly when Galerius failed to make him a Caesar. Though his position in the Empire was eventually recognized as legal, he was in reality a usurper. He was a man of great energy and will power, but of so limited an education that he spoke Greek with difficulty. His insatiable ambition rose above all moral scruples. He forced his father-in-law Maximian to commit suicide, he ordered the death of his brother-in-law Licinius after promising to spare him, and he was responsible for the murder of his son Crispus and of his wife Fausta. Whatever the cost, Constantine was determined to rule the world.

As soon as Constantine was firmly established as ruler of the West, he began issuing radical decrees, nearly three hundred of which have been preserved. He may have disliked Diocletian and his system, but circumstances and ambition forced him to follow the lines laid down by his predecessors of the third century. His reforms often seem exaggerations or intensifications of processes already noted under Commodus or the Severi, and especially under Diocletian. But while Diocletian was fundamentally conservative, preserving as much as possible of the old spirit, Constantine was a radical who cared little for the past. In his later years he ruled as an absolute monarch, surrounded by oriental pomp, flattery, and intrigue. He was served by an enormously expanded bureaucracy, proud in the multiplicity of its new titles. The people were regimented in a manner never before known. A veritable army of spies was employed to report the slightest signs of disaffection. All these measures were then sanctified with the aid of religion. Like so many of his predecessors, Constantine proclaimed himself the harbinger of a new day, and in his case, more than any other, the claim was justified. He was the principal creator of the Byzantine political and social system.

Constantine's new city on the Bosporus, which has ever since been called Constantinople (at least among Europeans, though now its official name is Istanbul), may well be taken as a symbol of the new day. Rome had ceased to be the capital of the Empire in more than name, and it was visited but rarely by the emperors, for the center of things had shifted to the East. Diocletian had resided at Nicomedia in Asia Minor, but Constantine selected the ancient Greek city of Byzantium, about fifty miles away on the European side of the Bosporus, as the capital of the world. Located at the crossing between Europe and Asia, the city stands at the southern end of the Bosporus on a rather narrow peninsula between the Golden Horn and the Propontis. The Golden Horn is an arm of the Bosporus reaching about four miles to the northeast and forms an excellent harbor. The site is healthful and beautiful, and it is so easily defended that hostile armies have rarely entered the city. Constantine began the expansion and rebuilding of Byzantium soon after the defeat of Licinius, and the new capital, called Constantinople, was formally dedicated in 330. He himself called the city "New Rome," and in countless ways he tried to make it resemble the old Rome. It was built on seven hills and divided into fourteen regions; it had its forum, its hippodrome, its porticoes, its aqueducts, its baths; and it even had a senate which was a feeble replica of Rome's. The city was decorated with works of art collected from all parts of the Empire, as well as with much that was new. In their architecture, paintings, and mosaics, the churches and public buildings showed the influence of the new Byzantine art which combined oriental and Christian styles. For a thousand years this proud city was the center of European culture and after Jerusalem, Athens, and Rome, it must be ranked fourth among the cities of antiquity that have deeply influenced the history of Europe.

Constantine and Christianity

The most radical of Constantine's departures from the old system was his acceptance of Christianity. Rationalistic historians in the nineteenth century often explained away his "conversion" as the trick of a coolheaded politician seeking Christian support. Such an interpretation of his actions is difficult to defend, and today it is rejected by nearly all scholars. Neither Constantine nor anyone else in his day was a nineteenth-century rationalist in matters of religion. On the contrary, all were guilty of what we—or even such enlightened pagans as Cicero and Horace—would consider the grossest superstition. Though Constantine unquestionably exploited the Christians for political ends, such action does not prove that he put no faith in the power of their God. We cannot even dismiss the famous story of his vision of the cross so disdainfully as was done a generation or two ago. This story is given by two almost contemporaneous authorities—Lactantius, a Christian who wrote in 317 or 318, five or six years after the events in question, and Eusebius, who wrote shortly after Constantine's death. Various bits of pagan evidence, dating from the period shortly before or after the events, add to our knowledge of what happened. We now have a much more plausible account of Constantine's conversion than that given by the rationalistic historians of the last century.

It had long been the custom for emperors to claim a close connection with the divine powers, and there is no reason to suspect that they were any less sincere than are modern politicians in their talk about democracy and other lofty ideals. Most emperors since Aurelian had favored Sol Invictus, to whom Constantius and Constantine were likewise attached. Diocletian too paid high regard to the Unconquered Sun, but he preferred the ancient gods of Rome, and took the surname Jovius while Maximian called himself Herculius. When Constantius married Theodora he transferred his allegiance from the Sun to Hercules, with Constantine apparently following in his father's footsteps. Constantine's marriage to Maximian's daughter Fausta in 308 strengthened this alliance with Hercules. The quarrel with his father-in-law in 310 broke the alliance, however, and Constantine returned to his and his father's former god, Sol Invictus. He identified this deity with Apollo, and in the summer of 310, only a few weeks after Maximian's death, he permitted an official panegyrist to announce that Apollo had appeared to him in a vision and promised him victory. Maxentius, on the other hand, remained loyal to Hercules and the old Roman gods, and in the summer of 312, as his struggle with Constantine approached its climax, he loudly proclaimed that these deities supported him. He busied himself with supplications, auguries, and sacrifices; and he was much encouraged by a cryptic oracle which prophesied that "the enemy of the Romans would perish."

It was at this moment that Constantine placed himself and his armies under the protection of the Christian God. According to Eusebius, he took this step in consequence of a vision of the cross seen in full daylight and followed by a dream at the beginning of the campaign; according to Lactantius it was in consequence of a dream the night before the battle. The two writers obviously refer to two separate visions. The contenders at the battle of the Milvian Bridge being thus ranged under rival gods, Constantine later showed appropriate gratitude to the deity to whom he attributed his victory. Even the pagans shared this view of Constantine's success. A panegyrist in 313 recognized divine intervention in the emperor's behalf, and the inscription on the famous arch in Rome, set up by the subservient senate in 315, declares that "by the inspiration of the deity and the power of his own mind" (*instinctu divinitatis, mentis magnitudine*) Constantine "avenged the Republic on the tyrant [Maxentius] and his faction in a just war." It must be noted, however, that both senate and panegyrist left it quite vague as to which divinity had aided the new emperor.

Constantine's Christianity

Why did Constantine thus turn to the Christian God? Many things may have predisposed him in this direction. His father had been friendly to the Christians, virtually ignoring orders to persecute them. The court officials at Nicomedia, whom Constantine detested, had been persecutors. The Christians were already pointing out that the great persecutors, such as Galerius, had come to wretched deaths while such rivals as Constantius had passed away in peace. Above all, the Christian God had obviously endowed his worshipers with the strength to conquer ferocious persecution. Considerations such as these may have preyed upon Constantine's mind, but it is doubtful whether he reached his conclusion by cold calculation. He was an impulsive and superstitious man, in a state of high excitement, and his dreams of Apollo and Christ may well have determined his conduct. Nor is it incredible that such a man, in such a state of mind, should see visions. But though Constantine ordered his soldiers to mark a cross upon their shields, he was not prepared in 312 to burn his bridges behind him by renouncing all other gods. Many of his own statements are as vague as the senate's inscription as to which deity had helped him. He recognized the power of other gods (or other manifestations of the one true God) and he retained the position of pagan *pontifex maximus*—as did all his Christian successors until 382. As late as 330 he still issued coins bearing the image of Sol Invictus. Not until he reached his death bed in 337 did he formally become a Christian by baptism, and only rarely did he make an effort to direct his life in accordance with the precepts of the Gospels.

The battle at the Milvian Bridge was scarcely won when Constantine found occasion to repay the favors he had received from his new God. Maximin Daïa had resumed the persecution of Christianity in the Orient soon after Galerius's death, and several Christians had met martyrdom. Constantine now expostulated with him strongly, and the persecutions came to an end, or at least they were reduced to minor proportions. Early in the next year (313), Constantine and Licinius agreed at Milan upon a policy of complete toleration for pagans and Christians alike, and even decided to restore the church property seized under Galerius. The edict by which Licinius ordered these policies carried out in his provinces has been preserved and is sometimes erroneously called the Edict of Milan. Constantine had no need to issue similar orders for he had already established such policies in his half of the world. In spite of his formal toleration of Christianity, Licinius remained a worshiper of Sol Invictus. We are told that shortly before his victory over Maximin Daïa this god appeared to him in a vision and dictated a hymn. Licinius taught the hymn to his soldiers, who sang it while marching against Daïa. Not since Homeric times had the divine powers intervened so openly in human affairs. Licinius presently became more hostile to the Christians, pestering them in minor ways, and the final

war between the two rivals assumed the aspect of a struggle between Christianity and paganism, with Licinius's numerous Christian subjects openly favoring Constantine.

Constantine's Aid to the Church

Meantime, Constantine was favoring Christianity in other ways.
His legislation at times had a humanitarian spirit that may have
been partly of Christian inspiration. So many privileges were extended to the Christian clergy that the rush of applicants for ordination had to be checked by new laws. Sunday was declared a legal
holiday, but, presumably out of regard for Licinius, the law ordered
rest on the *dies solis* (the Day of the Sun) rather than on the *dies
dominica* (the Lord's Day) which was the Christian name for the
first day of the week.

Constantine was lavish in his gifts to the church, and his generosity was supplemented by that of his mother. At Rome he gave the
palace of the Lateran to the popes, who used it for many centuries
as their official residence. Other palaces and basilicas were given to
the church, new churches were built, and old ones were repaired
and restored. Two of these churches were dedicated to St. Peter
and St. Paul, the former at the site of the present Renaissance structure and the latter outside the walls. The huge basilica beside the
forum, begun by Maxentius for other purposes, was completed as a
Christian church by Constantine. The church, not far from the Lateran, that is now called Santa Croce in Gerusalemme was the gift of
his mother Helena, who had followed him into Christianity. She was
much interested in the sacred sites of Palestine, which she visited
as a pilgrim. There she found many relics, among them what she
believed to be the true cross. The church at Rome was built in
honor of this discovery, and in it is preserved a part of what she
found. Constantine and Helena also built large churches at Jerusalem, Bethlehem, and other places. While Constantine did not exclude paganism from his new capital, he intended that the city
should be Christian. In it he built several famous churches, among
them the Church of the Twelve Apostles, in which he was buried,

and the Church of the Holy Wisdom (Hagia Sophia), at the site now occupied by the magnificent Byzantine church of the same name that was built two centuries later by Justinian.

Constantine had scarcely announced his conversion when Christians began calling upon him to settle quarrels within their church. They had always been anxious to preserve their corporate unity, yet from the earliest times they had quarreled among themselves. Diocletian's persecution precipitated especially troublesome controversies regarding the proper treatment for Christians who had weakened under stress and later wished to be readmitted to the church. Parties favoring severity and others favoring leniency arose everywhere, but especially at Rome, in Egypt, and above all in Africa. In the latter province two leaders, named Caecilian and Donatus, who favored leniency and severity respectively, were contenders for the office of bishop, and they managed to drag theological considerations as well as questions of policy into the controversy. As early as April, 313, friends of the austere Donatus had requested Constantine to set up a committee of bishops to settle the difficulty, and the matter assumed practical importance for the emperor when he decided at Milan to restore confiscated church property. Which faction was to get this property? At Constantine's order nineteen bishops assembled at Rome and there decided in favor of Caecilian. Once more the Donatists appealed to Constantine and a second, much larger, council convened at Arles: again the decision favored Caecilian, and again the Donatists refused to accept the decision. Constantine first tried persuasion and later sent recalcitrant Donatists into exile. As persecution only stimulated fanaticism, Constantine then proclaimed toleration in 321. In fact, a Donatist church continued in Africa for more than a hundred years.

A second and much more serious controversy arose in the East concerning the theology of an Alexandrian priest named Arius. Again Constantine intervened, apparently at the request of bishops meeting at Antioch. He summoned and presided over the first ecumenical (world-wide) church council, which was held at Nicaea in 325 and attended by about three hundred bishops from various parts of the Empire. In this case, too, Constantine attempted to enforce the decision of the council, and again neither persuasion nor exile convinced the defeated faction.

These various activities do not prove that Constantine desired to dominate the church. Christians had asked him to intervene, and it occurred to no one to deny his right to do so; and while the losers resisted what they deemed a wrong decision, the winners loudly called upon him to enforce what they considered a correct decision. Constantine's principal wish was for unity within the church. He pleaded with the Donatists to accept the decision of the councils, and at Nicaea he long and patiently sought a formula that all would accept, but when persuasion failed he was prepared to try force. We cannot say whether this desire for unity came from political or from religious considerations—from his desire for the united political support of the whole church or from his belief that all worshipers of the one true God should be united in one church. Probably he felt the force of both arguments. But even if Constantine did not deliberately plan to dominate the church, conditions drove him and his successors in that direction, and by the time of Justinian the system known as "Caesaropapism" was firmly established in the East. Under this system the emperor was head of both church and state. Such ideas have dominated the Eastern Church until our own day, but they have been less successful in the West. The Eastern Church today regards Constantine as *Isapostolos*—equal to the Twelve Apostles and above all other saints—but the Roman Church is not even sure that he got to heaven. At least, it has never accorded him the honor of canonization.

After Constantine

Constantine died in 337, after which a general massacre of his relatives and friends secured the government to his three sons. The three young men ruled jointly—Constantine II, who was twenty-one years old, took Britain, Gaul, and Spain; Constantius II, aged twenty, took Asia and Egypt; and Constans, who was only eighteen, took Italy, Africa, and the Balkans including Constantinople. Less than three years later, Constantine lost his life while attempting to seize his youngest brother's inheritance, and Constans ruled all the

West, until he was killed when a usurper arose in 350. Thereafter Constantius II ruled the whole empire until his death in 361. Two of Constantine's nephews had been spared during the massacres of 337 because of their tender years. The elder of these boys, Gallus, was made Caesar in 351 and executed in 354; the younger was the famous Julian who became Caesar in 355 at the age of twenty-three, drove German invaders from the Rhine provinces, was proclaimed sole emperor in 360. Three years later he lost his life in a campaign against the Persians. The dynasty of Constantine then came to an end twenty-six years after his death.

THE FAMILY OF CONSTANTINE

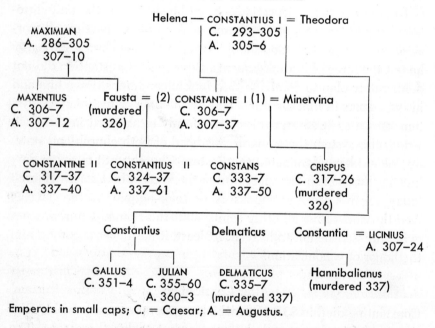

Helena — CONSTANTIUS I = Theodora

MAXIMIAN
A. 286–305
307–10

C. 293–305
A. 305–6

MAXENTIUS
C. 306–7
A. 307–12

Fausta = (2) CONSTANTINE I (1) = Minervina
(murdered   C. 306–7
326)   A. 307–37

CONSTANTINE II   CONSTANTIUS II   CONSTANS   CRISPUS
C. 317–37   C. 324–37   C. 333–7   C. 317–26
A. 337–40   A. 337–61   A. 337–50   (murdered
                                                    326)

Constantius   Delmaticus   Constantia = LICINIUS
                                                 A. 307–24

GALLUS   JULIAN   DELMATICUS   Hannibalianus
C. 351–4   C. 355–60   C. 335–7   (murdered 337)
            A. 360–3   (murdered 337)

Emperors in small caps; C. = Caesar; A. = Augustus.

The army chose an emperor (Jovian) who made peace with the Persians, surrendering the territory won by Diocletian, and died early in the next year (364). The Empire then fell to Valentinian (364–375) who, at the insistence of the army, shared rule with his younger brother Valens. He took the West while Valens ruled the East. Gratian (375–383) succeeded his father Valentinian in the

West, and ruled the whole empire for a short time after the death of
Valens in 378. Theodosius I took over the East in 379; and after the
deaths of Gratian and his younger brother Valentinian II (383–392)
and after the defeat of two usurpers, Theodosius ruled the West as
well until his death in 395. He was the last man to rule the whole
Roman Empire.

This political history is reminiscent of the chaotic third century,
but perhaps things were not quite so bad as before. The army continued to make emperors, but not so frequently. Usurpers arose, but
they were not so successful. Murder remained an instrument of
political policy, but while the Christian emperors used it widely
against their rivals, they suffered from it less frequently themselves.
There were twenty emperors between 235 and 285, but there were
only ten between 337 and 395, and only three usurpers managed to
hold large areas for more than a few weeks. Economic conditions
may have improved a little, though they still were appallingly bad.
Constantine had settled barbarians inside the empire, hoping to
bring abandoned farms back to cultivation, and his successors often
repeated the experiment. Emperors sometimes sought popularity by
remitting taxes that they could not collect. Julian found it necessary
to repeat Diocletian's attempt at price-fixing, and he too failed. Economic distress brought riots and civil disturbances. As the government's only answer to these troubles was increased regimentation
and the multiplication of rapacious officials, a sullen opposition arose
which prepared the way for the disasters of the fifth century.

Paganism was not yet dead, and various persons attempted to give
it a new lease on life. Maximin Daïa, the persecutor of Christianity,
had dreamed of renewing paganism by extensive reforms. Constantine showed little inclination to persecute the pagans, but he suppressed abuses and in the long run this purification helped paganism. Constantine's sons took more aggressive measures against the
old religions, ordering the closing of temples and the suspension of
certain sacrifices. Temples were torn down or converted into
churches; temple property was confiscated and sold; idols were
melted down when Christians shouted, "Send the gods to the mint!";
and the zeal of individual Christians often expressed itself in deeds

of violence against pagans. Because of all this, discontent rose among the pagans. They complained that the troubles of the time were a punishment for neglect of the old gods, and they only awaited a leader to demand revision of Constantine's laws. Such a leader appeared in the person of the Emperor Julian.

Julian the Apostate

Julian was born and raised a Christian, but the murder of his parents and cousins in 337, when he was five years old, prejudiced him against the new religion. This bad impression was made worse by the rigorous Christian education that was forced upon him during the next few years, when he was a prisoner with his brother Gallus in a remote part of Asia Minor. Secret reading of the Greek classics presently gave him a romantic enthusiasm for pagan culture. At the age of twenty he was allowed to visit Athens, where he was initiated into the mysteries at Eleusis and became acquainted with Neoplatonists and other pagans who remained his friends thereafter.

Julian threw aside the mask and openly proclaimed himself a pagan shortly before the death of Constantius II (361), whom he feared and detested. As soon as he became emperor he ordered the pagan temples reopened and the sacrifices resumed; he dismissed Christians from court and from the army; he forbade them to teach in schools, on the ground that they could not satisfactorily teach a literature permeated with gods in whom they did not believe; he even wrote a book against Christianity, parts of which we still possess. But there was no active persecution of Christians. Julian's interest lay rather in rehabilitating paganism, even by reforms learned from the new religion. He set up pagan priests whose close organization resembled that of the Christian clergy. He insisted that these priests be men of outstanding piety and virtue and that they look after the poor and unfortunates in their communities. However, his plans were foredoomed to failure. Christians were no longer content with the toleration for which they had recently prayed. They insisted that theirs should be the only religion tolerated by the state. They smashed idols when they were set up, they rioted, and there were lynchings by both sides. Persons who had acquired the property of pagan temples refused to give it up. On the other hand, Julian's revived paganism appealed only to a few romantics like himself. His dream ended with his death, and long afterward a legend arose that as he lay dying in his tent in Mesopotamia he exclaimed, "Galilean, thou hast conquered!"

The state of the pagans grew steadily worse thereafter. Sometimes pagans suffered violence, as when the bishop of Alexandria led a mob which destroyed the Serapeum in 391, or when Egyptian monks lynched the beautiful and talented Hypatia in 415. At other times the measures against paganism were of a more orderly nature, as when Theodosius ordered all pagans to become Christians (380) or when he crowned a long series of antipagan laws by forbidding anyone to offer sacrifices or otherwise honor the old gods (392). Especially significant was the case of the Altar of Victory which the Emperor Augustus had erected in the Senate House and on which sacrifices were regularly offered. Constantius II removed the altar in 357, Julian restored it four years later, and Gratian again ordered it removed in 382, in spite of strong protest by the pagans. It was set up again in 393 by a usurper named Eugenius, who had occupied the city, but in 394 it was finally removed by Theodosius. As Gratian had refused the pagan title *pontifex maximus* (382), the government no longer maintained official relations with the pagan gods.

There was little pagan literature in Greek after the age of the Severi, but the fourth century saw a revival of letters in the West, where paganism was still strong. Here a Latin literature arose that surpassed anything produced since Juvenal, and two authors of this period deserve especial mention. Claudian is sometimes called "the last Latin poet." Though he was a native of Egypt and received his first education in Greek, Claudian's poems, written in the 390's, are filled with praise of Rome and her eternal empire. Endowed with true poetic gifts and filled with reminiscences of Vergil, he expressed the idealism of the old Roman Empire which had brought law and peace to the world and made its subjects into citizens; but he added so much to the old story that one keen critic (Boissier) has seen papal Rome as well as Augustan Rome in this pagan poet's ideal. The other important Latin author is the historian Ammianus Marcellinus. A Syrian born at Antioch, Ammianus served for several years in the army, accompanied Julian on his ill-starred expedition to Persia, and eventually settled in Rome as a literary man. Enlightened and urbane, an admirer of Julian, remarkably free from the superstition which then enthralled nearly everyone from Constantine and Julian down to the most ignorant peasant, Ammianus wrote a history of the Roman Empire from Trajan to his own day as a sequel to the work of Tacitus. We still have the books covering the years 353 to 378, and as history they compare favorably with the best in the Latin language. Ammianus studied and loved the Roman writers of the great days, but he referred to them as having lived "in antiquity."

The Church in the Fourth Century

The Christian emperors of the fourth century devoted great attention to the church and the heresies by which it was distressed. Constantine had hoped in vain that the Nicene formula, supplemented by the exile of a few recalcitrants, would end the Arian troubles. Nevertheless, Arianism presently became so powerful, even at court or especially at court, that the emperor recalled the exiles and granted them his favor. He ordered the church at Alexandria to receive Arius back, but the heretic died suddenly on the eve of his triumph (336). A few months later Constantine received baptism from Eusebius of Nicomedia, an Arian bishop whom he had once exiled. Constantius continued to support Arianism, but the heresy declined after his time, and Theodosius was a great champion of orthodoxy.

Heresies usually began with doctrinal disputes, but they were much aggravated by nationalistic and class feeling, for heresy served as a means of protest against the political and theological absolutism that emanated from Constantinople. Church and state therefore united in the support of orthodoxy. Theodosius was even more severe against heretics than he was against pagans, and during his reign a number of unfortunates at Bordeaux were executed for their heretical beliefs. They were the first Christians to be executed—not merely lynched—by their fellow Christians for heterodoxy. A practice was thus inaugurated which continued to disgrace Christianity for many centuries to come.

The churches were so delighted with the emperor's gifts and with the aid of his police against heretics that they rarely resented his interference in religious affairs. The emperors therefore came to exercise great influence over the churches, even over the church at Rome. Constantine had paid little attention to Pope Sylvester (314–335), who did not attend the council at Nicaea, and whose two representatives took little part in the proceedings. Constantius exiled Liberius (352–366) because he refused to follow the new policy toward Arianism. The emperor replaced him with a man named Felix (355–365), but when Liberius, after reconsideration, accepted Constantius's demands he was allowed to return to Rome. The two rival popes spent the rest of their lives quarreling with each other. After their deaths a certain Damasus was elected pope, but the more rigorous Christians, unwilling to accept him because he had served Felix as deacon, set up Ursinus as antipope. Riots ensued, during one of which the partisans of Damasus killed 137 persons and wrecked a large Roman church (now S. Maria Maggiore: see Plate 28). Valentinian thereupon exiled Ursinus. Damasus lived in such extravagance that the pagan prefect of Rome once remarked, laughing, that he would become a Christian at once if they would make him bishop. Damasus (366–384) was much interested in having the rest of the Christian world accept the primacy of the Roman church —he was the first to refer to the papacy as the "apostolic see"—but he never forgot that he owed his position to the emperor. His successor, Siricius (384–398), was a peaceful man who, so far as our evidence goes, was the first to issue decretals (interpretations of church law) which were supposedly binding on the whole church and which were actually accepted widely in the West. But he was not the man to defy an emperor.

Nevertheless, the emperors did not have everything their own way. Athanasius, bishop of Alexandria from 328 to 373, was expelled from his city five times by various emperors because of his opposition to Arianism, yet he refused to accept the emperor's orders and championed orthodoxy even though it might bring him into conflict with the whole world: in later years men spoke admiringly of *Athanasius contra mundum.* At the end of the century Ambrose, bishop of Milan (374–397), went even further. This ambitious man had been attached to the imperial service before he became bishop, and after his ordination he continued to strive for worldly power. He made his bishopric the most powerful in the West, claiming equality with Rome and imposing his rule upon the bishops of all northern Italy, Illyria, and even Macedonia. As Milan was the seat of Imperial headquarters for Italy and the West, Ambrose had many contacts with the emperors. He twice humiliated Theodosius publicly. The first occasion came when a synagogue was destroyed by a Christian mob and Theodosius ordered the bishop of the town to have it rebuilt. Ambrose denounced the emperor to his face from the pulpit, reminded him that he owed his empire to God, and compelled him to rescind the order. A few years later, in 391, Ambrose found a much better complaint against Theodosius. The emperor had ordered his soldiers to massacre a large number of persons at Thessalonica because of a riot there. Ambrose excluded him from the church and forced him to do penance before readmitting him. Theodosius learned his lesson well, and was careful not to offend the formidable bishop again. Ambrose thus became the first Christian to assert the right of the church to dominate the state.

• Note for Plate 28. The Church of Santa Maria Maggiore in Rome is one of the older Christian basilica churches, though churches of this type had been in use for a hundred years before this one was built. It was begun in 432, on the site of an earlier basilica church, which may have been a pagan basilica remodeled. The church was considerably altered in the detail of decoration during the Middle Ages, and it now has a Renaissance appearance, but it still retains the fundamental features of the old Roman basilicas that were used as law courts. Note the two rows of pillars supporting the central part of the roof, and the windows in the clerestory above them. In Roman times the judge sat where the altar now stands, and the central part of the building was reserved for persons having business with the court. The space between the pillars and the main wall, in the old basilicas, was often given over to booths and shops.

Constantine *(Conservatori, Rome)*   Julian *(Louvre Museum)*

Basilica of Santa Maria Maggiore, Fifth Century

Plate 28

Hermits and Monks

When Constantine made it easy and even fashionable to profess Christianity, the flood of converts quickly lowered the level of enthusiasm and austerity within the church. Christians of the old school, who had suffered and risked their lives for the faith, were much concerned over this decline. Disgusted by the worldly interests often shown by new converts, enthusiasts exaggerated the aloofness and asceticism that had characterized Christianity from the first, and they began saying that, in spite of Constantine, it was still impossible to lead a Christian life in the midst of worldly society. Even during the peace of the third century, lasting from Gallienus to Galerius, ardent Christians of this sort in Egypt had withdrawn into the desert to lead more perfect lives. During the fourth century such men became hermits or anchorites in many parts of the East. Flight from the world was encouraged by the economic and political distress of the times, when all worldly things seemed to be going badly. Long before the advent of Christianity, Egyptian peasants had reacted to similar conditions in the same way, and in the fourth century many reverted to this ancient form of asceticism.

The first Christian anchorites went out as individuals, living alone or in small groups in caves or ruins, praying, fasting, mortifying the flesh, and struggling against the demons that beset them from every side. Antony and Paul, semi-legendary hermits of the days before Constantine, made enormous reputations by living thus, and their deeds were imitated by lesser men. Somewhat later a Syrian anchorite carried world flight to its ultimate form by passing thirty years on top of a pillar, his admirers bringing him food and water which he pulled up in a basket. This man, now known as St. Simeon Stylites, was beyond doubt in a pathological mental state, and if it were possible to imagine that the poor fellow had ever heard of Aristophanes, we would be tempted to accuse him of too literal an application of a joke in the *Clouds* (see Vol. I, p. 456). Nevertheless, his contemporaries admired him greatly, huge crowds flocked to see him, and after his death the pillar was visited by countless pilgrims. Around it they built a famous church whose ruins are now studied by archeologists because of its importance in the development of Byzantine architecture.

The hermit fleeing to the wilderness illustrates an important aspect of the social and religious history of the fourth century, but it was not long before monasteries provided better refuges for Christians who wished to lead holy lives apart from the everyday world. Such monasteries were nothing new. In the second century before Christ the Serapeum near Memphis sheltered recluses dedicated to the god. Shortly after the time of Christ, the Jewish writer Philo described a similar community of Jews near Alexandria who were called Therapeutae. The contemporary Essenes had monasteries near the Dead Sea and elsewhere in Palestine, and Neo-Pythagoreans had similar houses in the West. The first organizer of Christian monasticism was an Egyptian named Pachomius. He was converted about 314, lived for several years as an anchorite, drew up a rule for the guidance of monks, and organized his first community near Thebes in Upper Egypt in 323. Similar communities sprang up in many parts of the East, and a few were to be found in the West. Sometimes these monasteries became huge establishments housing a hundred or more monks, who lived frugal and sober lives by dividing their time between work and prayer, owning their scanty property in common, and usually avoiding the extreme mortifications and other excesses of the anchorites. In the second half of the fourth century, Basil, bishop of Caesarea in Asia Minor, drew up a rule still followed by monks in the Eastern Church. Western monasticism more generally followed the rule of Benedict, who about 520 established a famous monastery at Monte Cassino—a site in central Italy made famous in World War II. During the next several centuries the Benedictine order exercised a most beneficent influence upon the cultural life of western Europe.

The Great Fathers

The fourth century was also the great age of the Greek Fathers. At its beginning stood Eusebius (264–340), whose *Ecclesiastical History* is our principal guide to the history of the church from the

Apostles to Constantine. He wrote theological and apologetic works, but he became entangled in the snares of Arianism. Another prolific theological writer was Athanasius (c. 296–373), a pillar of orthodoxy, enemy of Arius and Constantius, and friend of the monks. At the middle of the century came three eminent Cappadocian theologians: Basil (329–379) and his brother Gregory of Nyssa (331–394), who had known Julian at Athens, and Gregory of Nazianzus (329–389). At the close of the fourth century there was John Chrysostom (347–407), whose sermons are among the most famous in Christendom. Unfortunately, the good man fell into disfavor with the emperor, and was exiled from Constantinople: he had had the effrontery to preach a sermon in which he cited the fact that Helena had become a saint as conclusive proof of the omnipotence of God.

Contemporary with these Greeks was the Latin Jerome (340–420), the greatest scholar of his day and translator of the "Vulgate" version of the Bible. This version is sometimes said to share with the King James Version in English and with Luther's German version the honor of being, from the purely literary point of view, an improvement upon the original Greek and Hebrew. Jerome was also a historian, a biographer, and an active writer of tracts. Other Christian writers were developing other types of literature. A Spaniard named Juvencus, who lived in the days of Constantine, put the Gospels into monotonous hexameters imitating Vergil; and somewhat later Prudentius, likewise a Spaniard but of greater ability as a poet, wrote numerous poems, long and short, on theological and moral topics.

Augustine and the "Christian Epic"

Above all these Fathers stands the massive figure of St. Augustine. Aurelius Augustinus was born in Numidia, west of Carthage, in 354. His father was a pagan but his mother, Monica, was an exceptionally devout Christian. After receiving a superior education, Augustine established himself as a professor of literature at Rome and later at Milan. His restless interest in religious and philosophical problems led him for a time to Manichaeism (a mixture of Zoroastrianism,

Gnosticism, and Christianity, founded by a Persian named Manes about 250 A.D.) and later to Neoplatonism. At Milan he came to admire Ambrose, under whose influence he was converted to Christianity (387). A year or two later Augustine returned to Africa, where he became a priest in 391, and bishop of Hippo in 395. This post he held until his death in 430.

Augustine has ever since been regarded as the greatest of Christian theologians. Not all his followers could wield so mighty a sword, however, and on occasion those who tried cut themselves badly. Countless heretics in the Middle Ages drew their errors from his writings, and Luther and Calvin were deeply influenced by him. Many of his books were of a controversial nature, directed against Manichaeans or Neoplatonists, against Donatists (who were still numerous in Africa), or against other contemporary heretics, but he wrote large treatises on such subjects as the Trinity and grace and free will.

The two of Augustine's books whose appeal has reached beyond professional theologians are his *Confessions* and the *City of God*. The latter is an enormous work to which Augustine devoted more than fifteen years. Alaric the Visigoth had sacked Rome in 410—under circumstances to be described below—and pagans at once revived their complaint that Rome's misfortunes were the result of her neglect of the old gods. Augustine set out to refute this charge by showing that Rome had also suffered when these gods were worshiped. The subject grew on him as he wrote and eventually he introduced most of his philosophy of life into the great book. He came to look upon the Christian church as a new empire rising out of the ruins of old Rome, but one that had existed from the beginning of time. He supported his theory with arguments drawn from history, political science, philosophy, and theology, and he set forth views somewhat resembling those of Ambrose on the proper relations of church and state. Few books in all history have been more influential than this *City of God*.

The Spanish priest Orosius shared Augustine's philosophy of history and expressed his views in a history of the world under the strange title, *Seven Books of Histories against the Pagans*. Orosius's ideas about the world and its history were the creation of a long line of Christian thinkers—theologians, poets, historians—from St. Paul to Augustine. For his facts Orosius relied especially upon Eusebius and Jerome, but he also drew from such pagan authors as Sallust, Livy, Trogus, and Tacitus. Augustine felt a true sympathy with such pagans as Cicero and Vergil, but his pupil did not, and he painted the pagan world in very dark colors. The whole long story is cast in the frame of the Four Monarchies mentioned in the Book of Daniel and elsewhere, with Assyria, Macedonia, Carthage, and Rome preparing the way for the Fifth Monarchy (the Christian Church), which had now superseded them and would last forever. Orosius took this idea from Jerome—whose translation of Eusebius's *Chronicle* made all history revolve around Assyria, Persia, Macedonia, and Rome, with the church again appearing as the eternal Fifth Monarchy. It is interesting to note, however, that a pagan contemporary, the poet Claudian, had recently used that very same ancient prophecy to prove the eternity of Rome, after the fall of Assyria, Media, Persia, and Macedonia. Orosius's history tells the long story of humanity from Adam and the Garden of Eden to the fifth century after Christ, with the central thread following the Old Testament narrative and with the great events of pagan history—Egypt and Assyria, the Trojan War, Romulus and his successors—thrown in as minor diversions. After long struggles and many horrors, pagan history reached its climax in the days of Augustus and Christ, after which the victory of Christianity restored the ancient unity of Eden to mankind. This Christian philosophy of history dominated the historical thought of western Europe until the eighteenth century. A few years ago the American philosopher George Santayana, with his usual felicity of expression, called the whole splendid story "the Christian epic."

Collapse

When Theodosius died in 395 he left the Empire to his two sons, Arcadius and Honorius, who had been declared Augusti in 383 and 393 respectively. Theodosius had intended that the two should rule jointly, as other emperors had so often done, with Arcadius administering the East and Honorius the West. But the youth of the boys made regencies necessary, and the regents virtually tore the Empire in two. An Aquitanian Gaul named Rufinus became regent in the East while a Vandal named Stilicho was regent in the West. These two men were thoroughly Romanized, in spite of their barbarian origin, and while each realized that he could scarcely become emperor himself, each hoped to found a dynasty by marrying into the imperial family.

The intrigues and quarrels of these regents came at a moment when the barbarians were pushing more vigorously than ever against the Rhine-Danube frontier. Tens of thousands of Germans already had peacefully entered the Empire, where they were allowed to occupy waste lands, but such individual immigration was no longer enough, for whole peoples in Germany were being driven to seek new homes. Fighting along the frontier increased in intensity, with many minor raids into Roman territory, until the Visigoths, or West Goths, crossed the Danube into Moesia (Bulgaria) in 376. Two years later they defeated and killed the Emperor Valens at Adrianople. Theodosius later made peace with the invaders, gave them land, called them allies, and received their aid in his wars. As soon as he was dead, however, trouble recommenced.

Alaric, king of the Visigoths, now demanded a high command in the Roman army. Barbarians had held such commands before, but these earlier commanders were men who had entered the Empire as individuals, not the rulers of an invading people; and while their soldiers were mostly Germans, they enlisted as individuals, not as tribes. Alaric's request was so different, and obviously so dangerous to the Empire, that it was refused. Angered at this refusal, the Visigoths started to march against Constantinople, then suddenly veered off to Greece, where they exacted tribute from Athens, sacked Corinth, and laid waste the Peloponnesus. Stilicho seized this occasion to intervene and marched against them in 397, hoping to drive them from Greece and add that province to his western half of the empire. Revolts in Africa forced him to abandon the project, but before leaving Greece he made an alliance with Alaric against the Eastern emperor. The regent Rufinus had by this time been murdered, and his place was taken by a eunuch, Eutropius, who made peace with Alaric, giving him the coveted military title and lands in Epirus. A few years later, in 401, Alaric invaded Italy, where he was defeated by Stilicho and consented to become his ally in Illyria.

When various German tribes invaded Italy from the north in 406, Stilicho drove them out, but the imperial authorities were helpless before the armies of Vandals who crossed the Rhine on the last day of that year and looted Gaul to their hearts' content. Eventually these Vandals settled down in new homes within the empire. Court intriguers took this occasion to plant doubts as to Stilicho's loyalty in the emperor's mind, and in 408 Honorius deprived himself of his only capable defender by having Stilicho murdered.

Alaric was not slow to profit by the new situation, and once more he marched into Italy. Here his forces were joined by large numbers of slaves and peasants who had run away from their lords. At first Alaric merely demanded lands for his men, but soon he made it clear that he hoped to succeed Stilicho as imperial minister and the power behind the throne. When his demands were refused, he set up a puppet emperor who promised him what he wanted and whom he deposed when the promises were not fulfilled. Alaric then marched on Rome and in August, 410, he entered and sacked the city. The capture of the Eternal City by barbarians caused the civilized world to shudder, but it also ruined Alaric's dream of a career within the empire. After three days he left Rome, laden with her spoils, and proceeded to southern Italy in the hope of crossing to Africa. His ships were destroyed by a storm, and he died soon thereafter (410).

Alaric was succeeded by his brother-in-law Ataulf, who led the Visigoths back through Italy into Gaul. At Narbonne he married Honorius's sister, Galla Placidia. This lady had indignantly refused to marry Stilicho, whose death she helped to compass, but now being in a chastened mood, she was willing to accept a barbarian husband. She presently bore him a son, named Theodosius after her father. The baby was intended to be emperor, but he died within a few months, and his father was murdered shortly thereafter (415).

Orosius reports a remark of Ataulf which probably gives an accurate statement of his views and Alaric's: "I once ardently desired to wipe out the very name of Rome and to change the Roman into a Gothic Empire, but when long experience taught me that the wild barbarism of the Goths was incompatible with laws, and that without laws there is no state, I decided instead to seek the glory of restoring and augmenting the Roman name with Gothic strength. I hope to be remembered as the restorer of Rome since I cannot replace her." The pagan poet Claudian had recently expressed similar sentiments in a panegyric on Stilicho.

Barbarian Rulers in the West

While Alaric was supporting his puppet emperor in Rome, at least three other usurpers were claiming power in the West, and still others arose during the next few years. Each of these men was a Roman supported by an army of barbarians, but often the claimant to empire was merely a straw man set up by some barbarian chieftain. These pretenders could be defeated by the imperial authorities only with armies composed of barbarian allies, who were quick to profit by the situation. After Ataulf had defeated a pretender in Spain, his people were allowed to settle in Aquitania as independent allies, and later they added most of Spain to their kingdom. Meantime the Franks had established themselves in northern France and Belgium, the Alemanni had crossed the Rhine into Alsace, and the Burgundians had occupied the Rhone valley. Their kingdoms were now recognized as independent by the imperial government, which thus abandoned all claim to Gaul and Spain. Early in the fifth century a usurper in Britain had withdrawn the Roman troops there to Gaul; the Britons were left to shift for themselves, and presently Angles, Saxons, and Jutes began invading the island from north Germany and Denmark, disregarding Rome. The Roman Empire of the West fell to pieces.

At the same time western Europe and even Italy itself were suffering invasion by more transitory marauders. Perhaps the worst was Attila the Hun, sometimes called "the scourge of God." The Huns had entered central Europe from Asia in the fourth century, and at times they had served as mercenaries in the Roman army. Attila in-

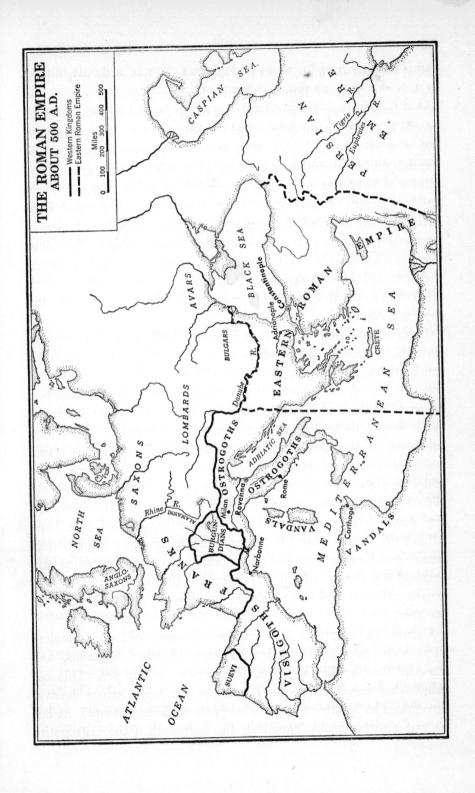

THE ROMAN EMPIRE
ABOUT 500 A.D.

Western Kingdoms
Eastern Roman Empire

Miles
0 100 200 300 400 500

CASPIAN SEA

PERSIAN EMPIRE

Tigris R.
Euphrates R.

BLACK SEA

AVARS

BULGARS

Danube R.

Constantinople
Adrianople

EASTERN ROMAN EMPIRE

CRETE

LOMBARDS

SAXONS

ADRIATIC SEA

OSTROGOTHS

OSTROGOTHS

Milan
Ravenna
Rome

Rhine R.
ALAMANNI

BURGUN-DIANS

FRANKS

VANDALS

Carthage

VANDALS

MEDITERRANEAN SEA

NORTH SEA

ANGLO-SAXONS

ATLANTIC OCEAN

Narbonne

VISIGOTHS

SUEVI

vaded Gaul in 451 and almost reached Orleans before he was turned back by an army of Romans and barbarians. The next year he invaded Italy and again withdrew. His death followed in 453, and his people then disappeared from history. Within three years, however, Italy was invaded again, this time by Vandals from the south. These Vandals had advanced from Gaul to Spain, whence they crossed the Straits of Gibraltar (429) and occupied all north Africa without much difficulty. A generation later, Vandal raiders crossed from Africa to Italy and sacked Rome in 455. In each case these bodies of invaders were rather small—the most numerous were the Vandals, who numbered only 80,000, including women and children, when they entered Africa—and usually they were more hostile to each other than to the Romans, yet they spread fearful devastation during their wanderings.

During the twenty years that followed Attila's invasion, one incompetent emperor followed another in the West. The emperor's residence had by this time been moved from Milan to Ravenna, and this city, now famous for its Byzantine churches and their mosaics, became the scene of the death agonies of the Roman Empire in the West. Here Stilicho was murdered in 408, and here his only worthy successor—Aetius, sometimes called "the last of the Romans"—met a similar fate in 454. Here a German general named Ricimer made and unmade five emperors and actually governed Italy from 455 to 472, though without aspiring to the purple himself. After his death real power fell to a barbarian named Orestes. He had once been Attila's private secretary, but later he married into a high Roman family and now he expelled an emperor named Nepos, whose 12-year-old son Romulus he placed upon the throne (475). This boy, usually called Romulus Augustulus, was the last of the emperors in the West.

German mercenaries had demanded allotments of land, and when these were refused, they slew Orestes, banished Romulus, and crowned their leader Odoacer (476). For seventeen years Odoacer ruled what remained of the Empire in the West, where he was recognized as "patrician" by the emperor at Constantinople. At last he was overthrown by Theodoric the Ostrogoth. (The Ostrogoths, or East Goths, had separated from their Visigothic cousins in the fourth century, and in the 470's they invaded the Balkan Peninsula where they became allies of the emperor at Constantinople.) When Germans in the service of Odoacer felt themselves aggrieved, Theodoric was sent by the emperor to invade Italy and aid them. After a long siege he captured Ravenna and treacherously murdered Odoacer (493). The Ostrogoth was then recognized by the emperor as ruler of a kingdom that included Italy, the Danube provinces, and Dalmatia—all that remained of the Empire in the West. Theodoric ruled well until his death in 526, and various successors continued his work until the last Ostrogothic king was killed by a general of Justinian in 553. Italy then became a part of the Empire once more, and was ruled from Ravenna by an "exarch" appointed by the emperor at Constantinople.

In spite of the disasters which overwhelmed the western world, and in part because of them, Christianity and the Roman Church advanced rapidly in the fifth century. The conversion of the upper classes was completed and progress was made with the peasants, who remained the last adherents of paganism. (Our word "pagan" is derived from the Latin *paganus*, "peasant," from *pagus*, "country," and "heathen" comes from a Germanic word of the same meaning.) Various new practices in Christian worship, notably the cult of the saints, made conversion of the peasants easier. The popular mind readily substituted saints for the old gods of paganism, and the old festivals, so dear to the hearts of the people, were continued as before except for slight changes in proper names.

At the same time the prestige of the Roman Church was enhanced by able popes who assumed popular leadership at times when the incompetent and helpless civil authorities had failed. It was Leo I who protected Rome against the Huns and the Vandals. The popes also were able to boast the name Roman against Ravenna. Also the Arian faith of most German invaders was an asset to the papacy. The Goths had been converted to Christianity in the days of Constantius II by a missionary from Constantinople named Ulfilas—his translation of the Gospels into Gothic is our earliest writing in a Germanic tongue—and he taught them Arian Christianity. It thus came about that, while Arianism was the religion of high social and political circles at Constantinople in the fourth century, it was regarded in the West one hundred years later as the religion of barbarian invaders. Orthodoxy and the papacy became symbols of civilization against Arian barbarism. But while the Germans who had invaded the more civilized parts of the West were Arians, and gave their religion a bad name, the pagan Franks were converted by orthodox missionaries from Rome. They looked up to the pope, and he was friendly to them. These Franks presently conquered their Arian rivals, and forcibly converted them to orthodoxy. At the same time Benedictine monks were teaching the people what they knew of ancient civilization. The Roman Church thus became the principal agency by which classical culture and learning were transmitted to the Middle Ages. It has been well said that this Roman Church was, in a way, the continuation of the Roman Empire in the West.[1]

The Empire in the East

The eastern half of the Empire suffered less catastrophically than the West in the fifth century. Invaders entered from the north and the east, but the emperors were able to buy them off or drive them out, and little territory was permanently lost. Asia Minor and Egypt were not invaded at all, and while Egypt was often convulsed by rebellion, Asia Minor remained relatively peaceful and prosperous. Thereafter it was the heart of the Empire. The emperors of the fifth century were persons of little consequence, yet they laid foundations for the great Justinian (527–565).

Justinian's first ambition was to restore political unity to the Mediterranean world, and with the aid of two brilliant generals, Belisarius and Narses, he almost attained this goal. The Vandals in Africa were conquered rather easily in 534, but the reconquest of Italy required twenty years of war against the Ostrogoths (535–554), and only a part of Spain was regained from the Visigoths

---

[1] "And if a man consider the originall of this great Ecclesiasticall Dominion, he will easily perceive that the *Papacy* is no other than the *Ghost* of the deceased *Romane Empire*, sitting crowned upon the grave thereof: For so did the Papacy start up on a Sudden out of the Ruines of that Heathen Power." This famous judgment is from the pen of one of England's deepest thinkers, Thomas Hobbes, *Leviathan* (1651), p. 386.

(555). No attempt was made to re-establish the imperial power in Gaul, but at last Justinian was able to call the Mediterranean "our sea." His long and bloody wars with the Persians were less successful. In domestic matters Justinian exalted his own person and that of his wife, the beautiful and notorious Theodora; he strengthened the bureaucracy and established a rigid absolutism; and he published the Justinian Code. The Christian church played a major role in his scheme of things and he dominated it completely, even the popes being subservient to him in his last years. Justinian had a keen eye for heresy and was ruthless in its extirpation. His policies were summed up in the phrase, "One empire, one church, one law." It was he who perfected the system of bureaucratic Caesaropapism ordinarily associated with the Byzantine Empire. His efforts left the Empire exhausted, however, and new misfortunes soon befell it.

A few years after Justinian's death, Mohammed was born in Arabia, and when he died in 632 his new religion was accepted in many parts of that country. Within ten years Moslem armies had conquered Syria, Palestine, Persia, and Egypt, and while their advances were less rapid thereafter, they did not stop until they reached the frontiers of India and China in the East and the Atlantic in the West. They entered Europe at Gibraltar in 711, and overthrew the Visigothic kingdom. Though the Moors were turned back by the Franks at the Battle of Tours in 732, and soon left Gaul, they retained large parts of Spain for several centuries. Throughout this vast territory Christians and pagans accepted Mohammedanism readily.

Such military and religious successes are amazing, even though many factors aided the Moslems. Exhausted Constantinople could not raise the armies needed to hold its provinces. The peoples of Asia and Africa often looked upon the Arabs as liberators freeing them from the bureaucrats and bishops of the hated Byzantine autocracy. But in the long run Moslem successes may best be regarded as the triumph of the Orient over European invaders. Almost a thousand years had passed since Alexander overthrew the first Persian Empire. During all that time a small aristocracy of Europeans and Europeanized Orientals had dominated a vast oriental population. Orientals now became masters in their own house once more. Except during the Crusades, they remained so until the nineteenth century. Nevertheless, the Moslem conquests did not cause a total eclipse of European culture in the Near East. The conquerors accepted much Greek science and learning, and for several centuries the Near East was again the most highly civilized part of the world. When the West at last was ready to absorb more of ancient culture than the monks had preserved, Moslems in Spain, Sicily, and elsewhere provided a second channel through which the legacy of antiquity passed to the modern world.

While the Arabs were seizing large sections of Justinian's restored empire in Asia and Africa, other invaders occupied European provinces. Lombards and other Germanic conquerors seized all Italy except a few Byzantine outposts in the southern part, and Slavic peoples invaded the Balkans. Constantinople ruled only Asia Minor, Thrace, part of Greece, and the Italian outposts. The Byzantine Empire, stripped of its outlying possessions, showed surprising vitality, however, and was a bulwark of civilization throughout the Middle Ages. Justinian was the last of the emperors who spoke Latin as his mother tongue. Thereafter the ruling classes came mostly from Asia Minor, but tradition was so powerful that the Byzantines called their empire Roman and though they spoke Greek they called their language "Roman." They preserved much old Greek culture, which they eventually passed on to Europe. Their greatest achievement, however, was the conversion and civilizing of the Slavs. Down to the present day the South Slavs and Russians show by their alphabet, their favorite personal names, their political ideas and practices, their art, and their religion that they are the true heirs of Byzantium.

Epilogue

The Fall of Rome

THE FIRST VOLUME OF EDWARD GIBBON'S SIX-VOLUME *History of the Decline and Fall of the Roman Empire* appeared in 1776, and only after five years was it followed by two more volumes. The author had then filled thirty-eight chapters, or about 1700 pages, with the history of the Empire from the middle of the second century down to the events of 476. At this point Gibbon decided to insert a ten-page essay entitled "General Considerations on the Fall of the Roman Empire in the West." His example is not a bad one. In the course of our present study we have repeatedly seen empires decline and fall, yet the "fall of Rome," which Gibbon once called "the greatest, perhaps, and the most awful scene in the history of mankind," remains the classic example of political and cultural decline. The problems it raises are both important and fascinating, and from Gibbon's day to our own, historians of Rome have usually permitted themselves a few General Considerations on this vast topic as a fitting conclusion to their studies.

The reader who reaches Gibbon's essay after reading through the first three volumes of the History may perhaps be disturbed by the fact that the picture here presented of the fall of Rome does not tally with what has gone before. The General Considerations are not a summary of the three volumes, and it would almost seem that they were written by another author who had not read the preceding chapters. As a matter of fact, Gibbon tells us himself that the essay was written before the first volume of the History appeared. Perhaps it was written as early as 1767, when Gibbon was only thirty years of age and much under the influence of the Scottish philosopher

David Hume. The essay expresses views similar to Hume's, and it even contains a sentence or two paraphrased from a letter written by the philosopher to the historian in that year. Gibbon started with a philosophical concept about the fall of Rome and set about writing his big history to illustrate it. As he progressed in his study, however, he broke away from Hume and developed quite different views about what had happened and why. Then in 1781 he dug up his youthful essay and inserted it at the end of his third volume without bothering to bring it up to date. His negligence on this matter shows us how his big book was written. Many others have followed Gibbon's example in starting with a ready-made philosophical theory, but, unlike him, they have not allowed their subsequent studies to change their preconceptions.

The study of the decline of Rome is also made difficult by the fact that the very word "decline" oozes morality. Students therefore end by writing what amounts to a sermon on an edifying theme. Even Gibbon did not escape this pitfall, and it was this moralizing aspect of Gibbon that Charles Dickens saw fit to ridicule in *Our Mutual Friend.* There were plenty of people in nineteenth-century England, many of them with intellectual endowments ampler than those of Mr. and Mrs. Boffin in the novel, who felt their morale fortified by the contemplation of Gibbon's vivid picture of Roman decline. This moralizing made an edifying sermon, but it was quite subjective and it was not scientific history.

If a student wishes to be scientifically objective in his study of Rome's decline he must first of all define exactly what he means by the word "decline." This is no easy task. In the final analysis, the difference between "progress" and "decline" lies wholly in each individual's conception of what things are worth while. A change that we like is progress, one that we dislike, decline; and one and the same change may be progress to the man who holds one philosophical point of view and decline to the man who holds another.[1] The

---

[1] The importance of such presuppositions will be strikingly apparent if we examine Bossuet's *Discours sur l'histoire universelle*—an excellent statement of the "Christian epic" which the good bishop prepared in 1681 for the instruction of the Dauphin of France. The author seems to make the decline begin with Romulus himself. Though Bossuet found much to admire in the ancient Romans, whom he regarded as the best

simple historian has no authority to choose between these points of view, but he may record a few of the views from which the fall of Rome has been considered. In attempting such a record we may start by asking, when did Rome fall?

Gibbon dated the "fall of Rome" in 476. In that year soldiers put a German named Odoacer on the throne in place of Romulus Augustulus, who was a Roman. Little can be said in favor of this date. Odoacer was scarcely more foreign than some of the emperors of the third century, whose rule likewise rested upon armies of foreign mercenaries. Once in power, Odoacer changed things very little, and before long he was succeeded by Theodoric who, though an Arian Goth, was anxious to preserve the old Roman system. The events of the year 476 are therefore quite insignificant in Roman history. It is equally difficult to defend the traditional thesis that Rome fell at a somewhat vaguer period in the fifth century because of the barbarian invasions. Barbarians had been invading the empire ever since the second century, usually peacefully but sometimes under arms. Those who came in the fifth century were few in number and they entered an exhausted empire, incapable of defending itself. Rome was already far gone in decline, and the barbarians only gave a final blow to the tottering edifice.

Some authorities like to date the decline from the time when the imperial authorities ceased to preserve law and order at home. No ancient government maintained modern standards in such matters, but the highest level of good government in antiquity unquestionably came in the period of about two and a half centuries between the Battle of Actium (31 B.C.) and the death of Severus Alexander (235 A.D.). Persons who prefer to judge a period by its literary and artistic achievements are apt to start the great decline in the second

---

of the pre-Christian peoples, his story of their first eight centuries is fundamentally a tale of horror, with things reaching their worst in the days of Julius Caesar. Improvement began under Augustus, but was checked by frequent relapses until the time of Constantine. Thereafter progress was rapid until at last the Christian Empire was founded by Charlemagne in 800. This view of Roman history must not be dismissed lightly. Bossuet was a very learned man, and those who agree with him as to what is the most important thing in history (namely, the conversion of the world to Christianity) will not find it easy to escape his conclusion that the centuries from 300 to 800, usually regarded as the period of the great decline, were in reality a time of rapid "progress."

century after Christ, with the passing of Tacitus and Lucian, though they add at once that this Silver Age was vastly inferior to the Golden Ages of Augustus and Pericles. There was, however, a slight literary revival in the Latin West at the end of the fourth century, and the fifth and sixth centuries saw the creation of the splendid new art preserved in the Byzantine monuments of Constantinople and Ravenna. Others judge a period by its economic prosperity as shown either by the accumulation of large fortunes or by the economic well-being of the masses, or by a rather even but liberal distribution of wealth. The first century before Christ was the period of great fortunes, while the middle and lower classes probably did best in the second century after Christ. A new wealthy class arose in the fourth century, after the horrors of the third, but not many fortunes in the West survived the holocaust of the fifth century when everybody suffered. Still others, following Sallust and pointing to the moral or economic consequences of the great wars, date the decline from the second century before Christ. If we turn to philosophy and religion, we can trace the progressive "failure of nerve" which began in the second, or perhaps even first, century after Christ and became catastrophic in the third. Many present-day writers prefer to date the end of Rome and the beginning of the Middle Ages from the conversion of Constantine—a view for which much may be said. Our decision as to when ancient civilization went into decline is therefore as subjective as are the criteria by which we judge civilization in general.

If we seek the causes of Rome's decline we find that most modern historians explain it by social, economic, or political forces. They sometimes point to the loss of man power in the late second and third centuries because of plagues, famine, and war; but they fail to explain why these losses were not presently repaired, as after similar disasters at other times. As a matter of fact, the permanent loss of population was a result rather than a cause of the decline. Other writers declare that the economic decline of the third century was caused by the civil wars, while in the next breath they attribute the wars to the economic decline. The constant financial difficulties of the imperial government have attracted the attention of some writers and it has been said, only half jestingly, that Rome fell because no one in that day happened to think of a funded debt or an income tax. The numbing influence of the late imperial bureaucracy has been blamed by others for the collapse. It should be pointed out, however, that this bureaucracy did not take over until the old system had failed, and that in the East it managed to keep the old machine lumbering along for several centuries. Other writers attribute the decline to the new governing classes under the Empire. Government fell more and more to men who had learned the techniques required to keep the machine going but who could not understand the spirit that had created it.

Education too has come in for its share of blame. Ancient education always was a very aristocratic affair, with its liberal aspects confined to the happy few. When these upper classes were liquidated, as took place in Greece in the fourth and third centuries before Christ, and in Rome in the first century before Christ, and again in the third century after Christ, no one remained who was capable of understanding or even of continuing the higher cultural traditions of earlier times. Rome could not educate her new rulers and she could no longer make Romans of the barbarians who flocked into the Empire. Similarly, Christianity has been accused of causing the decline of ancient civilization. "I have described the triumph of barbarism and religion," wrote Gibbon near the end of his book. It is true that many Christians showed the same subserviency and otherworldliness that characterized the pagans of the decaying empire, but it is likewise true that these humble, sober, and hard-working Christians were an asset rather than a liability, and that they were responsible for saving most of what was saved from the wreckage of ancient civilization.

None of these social explanations of the decline of Rome is very satisfactory, and some have sought to avoid the subjectivity inherent in them all by invoking purely physical causes. It has been suggested that the climate of the Mediterranean basin was somewhat cooler in early times than under the late Empire, and it has been pointed out that a slight rise in the annual temperature would make a climate debilitating rather than stimulating. Unfortunately, the evidence for such a change in climate is not very strong. Soil exhaustion and deforestation can be observed in Italy in the first century after Christ and still earlier in Greece, but land elsewhere apparently remained as fertile as ever. When climate and soil exhaustion fail, some writers turn to biology, saying that the quality of the racial stock declined. They maintain that Asiatic slaves replaced their former Nordic masters, and talk about hybridization and the "extermination of the best." They have little biological evidence to support their theories, in whose favor little can be said.

The forces here enumerated may have disturbed the serenity of life in the late Roman Empire, but it is hard to believe that any of them, or all of them taken together, produced the great changes that are summed up in the fall of Rome. Nor does it seem likely that other forces of the same sort, as yet unnoticed by scholars, will provide more satisfactory explanations. Perhaps, therefore, it would be better to approach the problem from a different angle. The demand for an explanation of the "decline" follows from the belief, so widely held in the eighteenth and nineteenth centuries, that "progress" is the law of life and that seeming departures from this general rule need an elaborate explanation. Today people are not so sure about this automatic and inevitable progress. The forces of nature are, if anything, on the side against progress. We may prefer our present state to that of our early ancestors, but our superior happiness is the result of our own efforts, of the things that we have created—the material ones such as houses and tools and more especially the immaterial ones such as liberty and scientific knowledge. They can be preserved only by constant care and vigilance. The real problem is to explain how men came to create all these things, not why some of their creations failed to last forever.

Viewed in this light, the history of mankind is the story of how men have learned to make things that are useful. Sometimes these things are purely material and serve primitive needs—houses and clothes, weapons and tools—but more important are the immaterial and intangible things that men have created. The latter include social institutions such as the family and law, forms and ideals of government, skills and techniques in agriculture and industry, languages and writing, methods and content of education, scientific knowledge, works of literature and art, beliefs about God. They constitute civilization, and they are passed on from generation to generation as a priceless heritage. The first beginnings of human activity along each of these lines are hopelessly lost in the darkness that enshrouds the history of early man, but it is possible for the historian to show how later men took over and adapted this heritage to meet their own needs. He can describe this heritage and the state of the men who inherited it; he can indicate what they tried to do with it; he can suggest reasons why their alterations and additions to it took one form rather than another; and sometimes he can show why certain traditional ways of doing things were abandoned while others were retained.

Moreover, the historian can show that there were certain periods in the past when men were quick and eager to accept new ideas, either from other peoples with a different inheritance or from members of their own group who had stumbled upon something new and useful. These were periods of high enthusiasm and feverish activity, when men expressed their ideas in brilliant form. The historian can picture the background of such a period, the need for change, and the origin of the new ideas, but who can tell why men suddenly become enthusiastic and do great things?

Such glorious periods rarely last more than a generation or so, for within that short space of time the new ideas reach their logical development and receive their classic expression. The children of the innovators then spend their lives perfecting a social organization based upon the new knowledge and the new ideas. The more intricate this social organization becomes, the greater is the likelihood of its collapse or of its domination by routine bureaucrats. But we may perhaps derive some consolation from observing that cultural collapse is never complete, even though it be as great and as long-continued as the death agonies of the Roman Empire. Later generations have never escaped from the powerful legacy of the ancient world, and they never will. No great civilization ever passes completely away.

One of the intangibles which men have created, and which they pass on from generation to generation, is a knowledge of their own past. As civilizations become more elaborate, men devote greater care and skill to perpetuating this knowledge. The fact that men everywhere and always have wished to know their history, even if they know it only in the false and primitive form that we call mythology, is sufficient proof that such knowledge has been found to serve some useful purpose. It is not always easy, however, to show wherein the practical value of historical knowledge lies. Historians have sometimes fondly believed that by collecting and arranging the "facts of history" they could create a "science of society" that would be of immense value to the human race. We may doubt the possibility of creating so vast a science from our scrappy and often

---

• Note for Plate 29.   This view of the Roman forum shows the present state of what once was the center of the world. To the left, slightly outside the picture, rises the Palatine Hill; in the background and to the right stands the Capitoline; between them, in the center of the picture, lies the forum itself. In late Republican times the Palatine was the fashionable quarter of Rome, and here Augustus erected an enormous residence, to which his successors added other buildings. Our word "palace" is derived from these buildings on the Palatine. In early times the *arx*, or citadel, stood on the Capitoline, and beside it was the great temple to Jupiter. The forum was a swamp until drained by the Etruscans, after which it became the center of Rome's business and political life. Eventually it was so filled with public buildings that new forums, located to the right of the area shown in the photograph, were built by the emperors to serve as business centers.

The three columns standing near the center of this picture were once part of a temple to the twin gods, Castor and Pollux. The first temple on this site was said to date from the fifth century before Christ, but it was rebuilt often, and these pillars come from a reconstruction by Augustus. Next to these pillars, toward the camera, may be seen the ruins of the temple to Vesta, a round building on whose altar a perpetual fire was tended by the Vestal Virgins. The open space nearby is the Atrium of Vesta, on each side of which are ruins of the residence of the Vestals. The ruins further to the right, near the center of the picture, are those of the Regia, once the dwelling place of the kings and later the official residence of the pontifex maximus. To the left of the temple of Castor was a large temple and library, erected by Tiberius and dedicated to the Divus Augustus; the part still standing is now a church. Beyond the temple to Castor may be seen two double rows of broken pedestals with three arches at the end. They are the ruins of the Basilica Julia, erected by Caesar in 46 B.C. on the site of the earlier basilica built by Tiberius Gracchus the Elder in

Plate 29. Roman Forum Today

unreliable bits of information, and certainly it was for no such purpose as this—smacking as it does of the scientific optimism of recent times—that for hundreds and even thousands of years men have preserved records of their deeds.

Historical study is not a form of scientific research but a form of art, comparable to poetry or philosophy, to theology, or to the dreaming up of brave new worlds. As such it has given pleasure to millions of persons. Yet men usually expect that historical studies, like other works of art, will have a practical as well as an aesthetic value. Historians such as Polybius and Plutarch used to justify themselves by saying that they pictured the great men of the past as models for others to follow. The Old Testament writers and Christian historians such as Eusebius and Orosius—and, as we have seen,

---

169. The six columns beyond the basilica were the front of the temple of Saturn, once used as the treasury. The two columns slightly to the right formed the corner of a temple built by Vespasian, beside which stood a temple to Concord. The triumphal arch was erected in honor of Septimius Severus in 203 A.D. Beside it stands the Curia, once the meeting place of the senate. This building was put up by Casear to replace the one burned in 52 B.C., but it was remodeled by Diocletian; eventually it became a church. In front of the Curia was the the Comitium, the open space where the assemblies met in Republican times; part of the Rostrum, from which the speakers addressed the citizens, may still be seen. Beside the Curia was the Basilica Aemilia, built by Aemilius Lepidus in 179 B.C.; its ruins do not appear in this photograph. Next came the temple of Faustina, dedicated by Antoninus Pius to his wife; a few of its columns show in the picture. The octagonal roof with a cupola belongs to a church, part of which was a pagan temple in the days of Maxentius, and in the foreground at the right are ruins of the Basilica of Constantine, a huge church built by the first Christian emperor. The large building with a tower at the far end of the forum was erected in the Middle Ages, but it rests upon the foundations of the ancient Tabularium, where official records were kept.

In the upper right of the picture may be seen the Church of the Ara Coeli. It is built upon the site of the ancient temple to Juno Moneta ("Juno the Reminder"), which was one wing of the Capitol. In this building the Romans established their first mint in 269 B.C. (Our words "mint" and "money" are derived from "Moneta.") In the third century a Mithreum stood on this spot (see Plate 25). The present church was built during the Middle Ages, and it was here that the young Edward Gibbon sat musing on the evening of October 15, 1764, when the idea of writing the decline of Rome first started to his mind. In the far distance, against the horizon, may be seen the dome of St. Peter's.

Gibbon himself— made the course of human events a lesson in theology or ethics. Various modern writers have rearranged the story of the past in different ways in order to laud and magnify one country or another. These historians are trying to generate enthusiasm for something or other. No less a thinker than Goethe once remarked that the chief value of history lies in the enthusiasm it stimulates. The importance of enthusiasm cannot be denied, and therefore that of inspirational history should not be minimized. Of course such a historian is merely playing the fifes and drums while someone else determines the goal and the line of march, but the historian helps arouse the enthusiasm without which co-operative effort is difficult or impossible. Such history is an asset to any society. Unfortunately, however, the historians who write it are apt to seek emotional stimulation at the expense of the truth, and their constructions are very apt to collapse—to the great dismay of those who hastily accepted them as true.

Nevertheless, it is possible to learn much about the world from a study of its past. We do not claim that learned historians are the men who best understand the present. Heaven forbid! But those who understand the present usually have a fair knowledge of history too. There are countless parallels in the past to events in our own day. These parallels are never perfect, for history does not repeat itself exactly, but the student who examines them carefully, noting the resemblances and especially the differences between two periods, will acquire a deeper view of his own time. Parallels with our own day may be found everywhere in history, but the history of antiquity is of special value to persons interested in such studies. Modern studies in this field are written with rather less nationalistic bias than those in other fields, perhaps, and ancient history is a rich field because of its vast expanse, covering every stage of culture, from the simplest to the highly complex. During the past thousand years countless persons have learned to understand their own world better and have thereby become more useful citizens by studying the history of antiquity. If the present volume should stimulate even a few to think more deeply about the problems facing the world today, the labor it has cost will not have been spent in vain.

Bibliography

Works of Reference

The Cambridge Ancient History, ed. J. B. Bury and others, 12 vols., 1923–39, and 5 vols. of plates, prepared by C. T. Seltman, 1927–39. A full history of the ancient world, each chapter written by a specialist. Full bibliographies and many maps. Vols. 7–12 cover the period from Alexander to Constantine.

Dictionary of Greek and Roman Antiquities, ed. William Smith (1847; 3rd ed. in 2 vols., 1890) is now quite out of date, but the *Smaller Classical Dictionary*, reprinted in Everyman's Library (1910; new ed., 1937) is a handy little volume.

Dictionnaire des antiquités grecques et romains, ed. C. V. Daremberg and E. Saglio, 5 vols., 1877–1919. Earlier volumes somewhat out of date, but many excellent articles.

Encyclopædia Britannica, 11th ed., 28 vols., 1910–11. The articles in this edition are good, and usually to be preferred to the watered-down versions in later editions.

Encyclopædia of Religion and Ethics, ed. James Hastings, 13 vols., 1908–27.

Oxford Classical Dictionary, ed. M. Cary [and others], 1949.

Paulys Real-Encyclopädie der classischen Altertumswissenschaft, ed. G. Wissowa and W. Kroll, 1894 — —. To be completed in about 60 volumes of which five or six were yet to appear in 1940. Exhaustive and fundamental articles on all subjects connected with classical antiquity.

Historical Atlas, W. E. Shepherd (1911).

Atlas of Ancient and Classical Geography, Everyman's Library (1907; new ed., 1933).

A. THE HELLENISTIC WORLD

Alexander

The principal sources are Arrian, *The Anabasis of Alexander* and Plutarch, *Life of Alexander* and *The Fortune of Alexander*.

Berve, H., *Das Alexanderreich auf prosopographischer Grundlage* (2 vols., 1926), a fundamental work containing biographies of all known persons of the period.

Bevan, E. R., "Alexander III. the Great," in *Encyclopædia Britannica* (11th ed., 1910, and subsequent eds.).

Droysen, J. G., *Geschichte Alexanders des Grossen* (1833; new ed., 1917).

Ehrenberg, V., *Alexander and the Greeks* (1938).

Hogarth, D. G., *Philip and Alexander of Macedon* (1897).

Jouguet, P., *Macedonian Imperialism and the Hellenization of the East* (1926; Eng. tr., 1928).

Meyer, Ed., "Alexander der Grosse und die absolute Monarchie" (1905), in *Kleine Schriften* (1924), I, 265–314.

Radet, G., *Alexandre le grand* (1931), an unusual book.

Robinson, C. A., *Alexander the Great* (1947).

Tarn, W. W., *Alexander the Great* (2 vols., 1948).

Wheeler, B. I., *Alexander the Great* (1900).

Wilcken, U., *Alexander the Great* (1931; Eng. tr., 1932).

Hellenistic Political History

The principal sources are Polybius and Plutarch, *Lives* (Agis and Cleomenes, Aratus, Demetrius, Eumenes, Philopoemen).

Beloch, K. J., *Griechische Geschichte* (vol. 4, 2nd ed., 1925).

Bell, H. I., *Egypt from Alexander the Great to the Arab Conquest* (1948).

Bevan, E. R. *Egypt under the Ptolemaic Dynasty* (1927). *The House of Seleucus* (2 vols., 1902).

Bouché-Leclercq, A., *Histoire des Lagides* (4 vols., 1903–07). *Histoire des Séleucides* (2 vols., 1913–14).

Bury, J. B., and others, *The Hellenistic Age* (1923).

Cary, M., *The Legacy of Alexander* (1932).

Debevoise, N. C., *A Political History of Parthia* (1938).

Ferguson, W. S., *Greek Imperialism* (1913). *Hellenistic Athens* (1911).

Jones, A. H. M., *The Cities of the Eastern Roman Provinces* (1937).

Jouguet, P., *Macedonian Imperialism and the Hellenization of the East* (1926; Eng. tr., 1928).

Kaerst, J., *Geschichte des Hellenismus* (2 vols., 1901–09; 2nd ed., 1917–26).

Kahrstedt, U., *Syrische Territorien in hellenistischer Zeit* (1926).

Macurdy, Grace H., *Hellenistic Queens* (1932).

Meyer, Ed., *Die Blüte und Niedergang des Hellenismus in Asien* (1925).

Niese, B., *Geschichte der griechischen und makedonischen Staaten seit der Schlacht bei Chaeronea* (3 vols., 1893–1903).

Rostovtzeff, M., *Social and Economic History of the Hellenistic World* (3 vols., 1941), the outstanding book in the field, see note, p. 533.

Tarn, W. W., *Antigonos Gonatas* (1913).

Tscherikower, V., *Die hellenistischen Städtegründungen von Alexander dem Grossen bis auf die Römerzeit* (1927).

Hellenistic Culture

Bailey, C., *Epicurus* (1926). *The Greek Atomists and Epicurus* (1928).

Bevan, E. R., *Later Greek Religion* (1927). *Stoics and Sceptics* (1913).

Dickins, G., *Hellenistic Sculpture* (1920).

Fyfe, T., *Hellenistic Architecture* (1936).

Goodenough, E. R., *The Political Philosophy of Hellenistic Kingship* (1928).

Heath, T. L., *Archimedes* (1920). *Aristarchus of Samos, the Ancient Copernicus* (1913).

Hicks, R. D., *Stoic and Epicurean* (1910).

More, P. E., *Hellenistic Philosophies* (1923).

Rostovtzeff, M., *A Large Estate in Egypt in the Third Century B.C.* (1922). "The Foreign Commerce of Ptolemaic Egypt," in *Journal of Economic and Business History,* IV (1931), 728–69.

Tarn, W. W., *Hellenistic Civilization* (1927; 2nd ed., 1930).

Wendland, P., *Die hellenistisch-römische Kultur* (3rd ed., 1912).

Westermann, W. E., "The Greek Exploitation of Egypt," in *Political Science Quarterly,* XL (1925), 517–39.

Wenley, R. M., *Stoicism and Its Influence* (1923).

Zeller, E., *Stoics, Epicureans, and Sceptics* (Eng. tr., 1880).

The Near East in the Second and First Centuries B.C.

The principal sources include Polybius and Livy, XXXVIII–XLV, *passim;* Diodorus, fragments of Bks. XXVII–XXXII; Josephus, *Antiquities,* XII–XVII; Justin, XXX–XLII; the Book of Daniel and the books of the Apocrypha, especially I and II Maccabees.

Bevan, E. R., *Jerusalem Under the High Priests* (1904).

Bickermann, E., *Der Gott der Makkabäer* (1937), important. *Maccabees: An Account of Their History from the Beginnings to the Fall of the Hasmoneans* (1947).

Jones, A. H. M., *The Herods of Judaea* (1938).

Jouguet, P., "Les Lagides et les indigènes égyptiens," *Revue belge*, II (1923), 419–45.

Kolbe, W., *Beiträge zur syrischen und jüdischen Geschichte* (1926).

Meyer, Ed., *Ursprung und Anfänge des Christentums* (vol. 2, 1921).

Oesterley, W. O. E., and Robinson, T. H., *A History of Israel* (vol. 2, 1932).

Otto, W., "Herodes," in Pauly-Wissowa *Real-Encyclopädie*, Supp. vol. 2.

Préaux, C., "Esquisse d'une histoire des révolutions égyptiennes sous les Lagides," *Chronique d'Egypte*, XI (1936), 522–52.

Reinach, Th., *Mithridate Eupator, roi de Pont* (1890).

Schlatter, A., *Geschichte Israels von Alexander dem Grossen bis Hadrian* (1901; 3rd ed., 1925).

Schürer, E., *A History of the Jewish People in the Time of Jesus Christ* (3 vols., 1886–90; 4th ed., 1901–07; Eng. tr. 1890).

Swain, J. W., "The Theory of the Four Monarchies: Opposition History Under the Roman Empire," *Classical Philology*, XXXV (1940), 1–21. "Antiochus Epiphanes in Egypt," *ibid.*, XXXIX (1944), 73–94.

Tarn, W. W., *The Greeks in Bactria and India* (1938).

Willrich, H., *Das Haus des Herodes zwischen Jerusalem und Rom* (1929).

B. THE ROMAN REPUBLIC

General Histories

Boak, A. E. R., *A History of Rome to 565 A.D.* (1921; 3rd ed., 1942).

Cary, M., *A History of Rome down to the Reign of Constantine* (1935).

De Sanctis, G., *Storia dei Romani* (4 vols., 1907–23).

Ferrero, G., and Barbagallo, C., *A Short History of Rome* (2 vols., Eng. tr., 1918–19).

Frank, T., *A History of Rome* (1923). *Roman Imperialism* (1914).

Geer, R. M., *Classical Civilization: Rome* (1940).

Glotz, G., ed., *Histoire romaine* (4 vols., 1926–47), separate volumes by E. Pais and J. Bayet, G. Bloch and J. Carcopino, L. Homo, M. Besnier and A. Piganiol.

Heitland, W. E., *The Roman Republic* (3 vols., 1909).

Kornemann, E., *Römische Geschichte* (2 vols., 1938–39).

Jones, H. S., *A Companion to Roman History* (1912).

Mommsen, Th., *A History of Rome* (3 vols., 1853–56; Eng. tr. in 5 vols., 1862–4), a classic, see note, p. 368.

Piganiol, A., *Histoire de Rome* (1939).

Sandys, J. E., *A Companion to Latin Studies* (1910).

Appreciations of the Roman Genius

Bailey, C., *The Legacy of Rome* (1923).

Greene, W. C., *The Achievement of Rome* (1933).

Grenier, A., *The Roman Spirit in Religion, Thought, and Art* (1925; Eng. tr., 1926).

Heitland, W. E., *The Roman Fate* (1922).

Showerman, G., *Eternal Rome* (2 vols., 1924). *Rome and the Romans* (1931).

Stobart, J. C., *The Grandeur That Was Rome* (1912).

Republican Constitution and Law

Abbott, F. F., *A History and Description of Roman Political Institutions* (1901; 3rd ed., 1911).

Botsford, G. W., *The Roman Assemblies* (1909).

Buckland, W. W., *A Manual of Roman Private Law* (1925).

Declareuil, J., *Rome the Law Giver* (1924; Eng. tr., 1926).

Fowler, W. W., *The City State of the Greeks and Romans* (1893).

Gelzer, M., *Die Nobilität der römischen Republik* (1912).

Girard, P. F., *Manuel élémentaire de droit romain* (1895; 8th ed., 1929).

Greenidge, A. H. J., *Roman Public Life* (1901). *The Legal Procedure of Cicero's Time* (1901).

Homo, L., *Roman Political Institutions* (1927; Eng. tr., 1929).

Jolowicz, H. F., *A Historical Introduction to the Study of Roman Law* (1932).

Mommsen, Th., *Römisches Staatsrecht* (3 vols., 1871–75; 3rd ed., 1887), the great historian's *magnum opus*. *Römisches Strafrecht* (1899). *Juristische Schriften* (3 vols., 1905–07) contains many articles of high value.

Münzer, F., *Römische Adelsparteien und Adelsfamilien* (1920), see note, p. 122.

Sohm, R., *The Institutes*: *a Text-book of the History and System of Roman Private Law* (1883; 17th ed., 1923; Eng. tr., 3rd ed., 1907).

Täubler, E., *Imperium Romanum* (1913).

Willems, P., *Le Sénat de la république romaine* (3 vols., 1878–85).

Economic Life

Brehaut, E., *Cato the Censor on Farming* (1933).

Frank, T., *An Economic History of Rome* (1920; 2nd ed., 1927). *An Economic Survey of Ancient Rome* (vol. 1, 1933), deals with Italy, presenting the principal sources with translations and commentary.

Hatzfeld, J., *Les trafiquants italiens dans l'Orient hellénique* (1919).

Heitland, W. E., *Agricola* (1921).

Louis, P., *Ancient Rome at Work* (1912; Eng. tr., 1927).

Rostowzew [Rostovtzeff], M., *Studien zur Geschichte des römischen Kolonates* (1910).

Scalais, R., a series of articles on Italian agriculture in the *Musée belge*, 1923–28.

Toutain, A., *The Economic Life of the Ancient World* (1927; Eng. tr., 1930).

Weber, Max, *Die römische Agrargeschichte in ihrer Bedeutung für die Staats- und Privatrecht* (1891).

Religion and Philosophy

Altheim, F., *A History of Roman Religion* (Eng. tr., 1938).

Arnold, E. V., *Roman Stoicism* (1911).

Bailey, C., *Phases in the Religion of Ancient Rome* (1932).

Carter, J. B., *The Religious Life of Ancient Rome* (1911).

Farrington, B., *Science and Politics in the Ancient World* (1932).

Fowler, W. W., *The Religious Experience of the Roman People* (1911). *Roman Festivals* (1899). *Roman Ideas of Deity* (1914).

Frazer, J. G., *The Fasti of Ovid* (5 vols., 1929), edited with translation and elaborate commentary.

Halliday, W. R., *Lectures on the History of Roman Religion* (1923).

Hicks, R. D., *Stoic and Epicurean* (1910).

Rostovtzeff, M., *Mystic Italy* (1927).

Sikes, E. E., *Lucretius, Poet and Philosopher* (1936).

Wissowa, G., *Religion und Kultus der Römer* (1902; 2nd ed., 1912).

Literature

Most of the Latin classics are available in English translation in the Loeb Library, with Latin and English texts on opposite pages. George Howe and G. A. Harrer, *Roman Literature in Translation* (1924), and C. Bailey, *The Mind of Rome* (1926), present long passages translated by masters. The series known as *Our Debt to Greece and Rome* contains a small volume on each important Roman writer.

Duff, J. W., *A Literary History of Rome from the Origins to the Close of the Golden Age* (1909).

Frank, T., *Life and Literature in the Roman Republic* (1930).

Mackail, J. W., *Latin Literature* (1897).

Schanz, M., *Geschichte der römischen Literatur* (vol. 1, 4th ed., by
C. Hosius, 1927), very full.
Teuffel, W. S., *Geschichte der römischen Literatur* (vol. 1, 6th ed., by
W. Kroll and F. Skutsch, 1913).

Roman Art

Anderson, W. J., Spiers, R. P., and Ashby, T., *The Architecture of Ancient
Rome* (1927).
Cagnat, R., and Chapot, V., *Manuel d'archéologie romaine* (2 vols.,
1916–20).
Cambridge Ancient History, Vol. 4 of Plates (1934).
Platner, S. B., and Ashby, T., *A Topographical Dictionary of Ancient
Rome* (1929).
Rodenwaldt, G., *Die Kunst der Antike (Hellas und Rom)* (1927), vol. 3
of the Propyläen Kunstgeschichte, lavishly illustrated.
Strong, E. S., *Art in Ancient Rome* (2 vols., 1928).

Military Science

Clark, F. W., *The Influence of Sea Power on the History of the Roman
Republic* (1915).
Coussin, P., *Les armes romaines* (1926).
Delbrück, H., *Geschichte der Kriegskunst* (vol. 1, 1900; 3rd ed., 1920).
Griffith, G. T., *The Mercenaries of the Hellenistic World* (1935).
Kromeyer, J., and Veith, G., *Heerwesen und Kriegführung der Griechen
und Römer* (1928).
Parker, H. M. D., *The Roman Legions* (1923).
Starr, C. G., *The Roman Imperial Navy* (1941).
Tarn, W. W., *Hellenistic Military and Naval Developments* (1930).
Thiel, J. H., *Studies on the History of Roman Sea-Power in Republican
Times* (1946).

Social and Private Life

Blümner, H., *Die römischen Privataltertümer* (3rd ed., 1911).
Dobson, J. F., *Ancient Education* (1932).
Förtsch, B., *Die politische Rolle der Frau in der römischen Republik*
(1935).
Fowler, W. W., *Social Life at Rome in the Age of Cicero* (1908).
Frank, T., *Aspects of Social Behaviour in Ancient Rome* (1932).

Grose-Hodge, H., *Roman Panorama* (1946).
Gwynn, A., *Roman Education from Cicero to Quintilian* (1926).
Johnston, H. W., *The Private Life of the Romans* (1903; 2nd ed., 1932).
Marrou, H. I., *Histoire de l'éducation dans l'antiquité* (1948).
Moore, F., *The Roman's World* (1937).
Moore, R. W., *The Roman Commonwealth* (1942).
Treble, H., and King, K. M., *Everyday Life in Rome* (1930).

Rome's Western Neighbors

Frank, T., *An Economic Survey of Ancient Rome* (vols. 3–4, 1937–38), sources collected, translated, and commented by various scholars.
Whatmough, J., *The Foundations of Roman Italy* (1937).
Dennis, G., *The Cities and Cemeteries of Etruria* (1848; 3rd ed., 1883), a classic.
Fell, R. A. L., *Etruria and Rome* (1924).
Randall-MacIver, D., *The Etruscans* (1927). *Italy Before the Romans* (1928).
Schachermeyer, F., *Etruskische Frühgeschichte* (1929).
Freeman, E. A., *History of Sicily* (3 vols., 1891–92).
Randall-MacIver, D., *Greek Cities in Italy and Sicily* (1931).
Ehrenberg, V., *Karthago* (1927).
Gsell, S., *Histoire ancienne de l'Afrique du nord* (vols. 1–6, 1913–27).
Meltzer, O., and Kahrstedt, U., *Geschichte der Karthager* (3 vols., 1879–1913).
Bouchier, E. S., *Spain under the Roman Empire* (1914).
Sutherland, C. H. V., *The Romans in Spain* (1939).
Clerc, M., *Massalia* (1927).
Jullian, C., *Histoire de la Gaule* (vols. 1–2, 1908; 3rd ed., 1914).

Studies of Special Periods

The Early Republic

The principal sources include Livy, I–X; Dionysius of Halicarnassus; Plutarch, *Lives* (Timoleon, Pyrrhus); much source material in T. Frank, ed., *Economic Survey*, (vol. 1, 1933).

Beloch, K. J., *Römische Geschichte bis zum Beginn der punischen Kriege* (1926).
Homo, L., *Primitive Italy and the Beginnings of Roman Imperialism* (1925; Eng. tr., 1926).

Nap, J. M., *Die römische Republik um das Jahr 225 v. Chr.* (1935).

Piganiol, A., *La conquête romaine* (1927).

Scullard, H. H., *A History of the Roman World from 753 to 146 B.C.* (1935).

Spaeth, J. W., *A Study of the Causes of Rome's Wars from 343 to 265 B.C.* (1926).

The Scipionic Age

The principal sources include Livy, XXI–XLV; Polybius; Plutarch, *Lives* (Fabius, Marcellus, Flamininus, Cato Major, Aemilius Paullus); Nepos, *Lives* (Hannibal); Appian, VI–VIII; Diodorus, XXV–XXIX.

Baker, G. P., *Hannibal* (1930).

Colin, G., *Rome et la Grèce de 200 à 146 avant J.-C.* (1908).

Groag, E., *Hannibal als Politiker* (1929).

Haywood, R. M., *Studies in Scipio Africanus* (1933).

Holleaux, M., *Rome, la Grèce et les monarchies hellénistiques au IIIe siècle avant J.-C.* (1921).

Liddell-Hart, B. H., *A Greater than Napoleon: Scipio Africanus* (1926).

Meyer, Ed., "Hannibal und Scipio," in *Meister der Politik* (vol. 1, 1923).

Schur, W., *Scipio Africanus und die Begründung der römischen Weltherrschaft* (1927).

Scullard, H. H., *Scipio Africanus in the Second Punic War* (1930).

Walbank, F. W., *Philip V of Macedon* (1940).

The Decline of the Roman Republic

The principal sources include Appian, *Civil Wars*, I; Cicero, *Letters and Orations;* Dio, *Roman History*, XXXVI–XL; Plutarch, *Lives* (Caesar, Cato Minor, Cicero, Crassus, Tiberius and Gaius Gracchus, Lucullus, Marius, Pompey, Sertorius, Sulla); Velleius Paterculus. Greenidge, A. H. J., and Clay, A. M., *Sources for Roman History, 133–70 B.C.* (1903) present many sources in Greek or Latin; see also Hardy, E. G., *Roman Laws and Charters* (1912) for the texts of several important laws in translation.

Bennett, H., *Cinna and His Times* (1923).

Bloch, G., "M. Aemilius Scaurus," *Mélanges d'histoire ancienne* (1909).

Boak, A. E. R., "The Extraordinary Commands from 80 to 48 B.C." *American Historical Review*, XXIV (1918), 1–25.

Boissier, G., *Cicero and His Friends* (1865, Eng. tr.), a delightful book. *La conjuration de Catilina* (1905).

Carcopino, J., *Autour des Gracques* (1928). *Sylla, ou la monarchie manquée* (1931).

Cobban, J. M., *Senate and Provinces, 78–44 B.C.* (1935).

Drumann, W., *Geschichte Roms in seinem Übergange von der republikanischen zur monarchischen Verfassung* (2nd ed., by Groebe, 6 vols., 1899–1929).

Ferrero, G., *The Greatness and Decline of Rome* (5 vols., 1901–07; Eng. tr., 1907–09).

Fuchs, H., *Der geistige Widerstand gegen Rom in der antiken Welt* (1939).

Greenidge, A. H. J., *A History of Rome, 133–104 B.C.* (1904).

Hardy, E. G., *The Catilinarian Conspiracy* (1924).

Haskell, H. J., *The New Deal in Old Rome* (1939). *This Was Cicero* (1942).

Holmes, T. R., *The Roman Republic and the Founder of the Empire* (3 vols., 1923).

Kroll, W., *Die Kultur der Ciceronischen Zeit* (2 vols., 1933).

Marsh, F. B., *A History of the Roman World from 146 to 30 B.C.* (1935). *The Founding of the Roman Empire* (1927).

Meyer, Ed., *Cäsars Monarchie und das Principat des Pompejus* (1918).

Oman, C. W. C., *Seven Roman Statesmen* (1902), interesting biographies.

Parks, M. E., *The Plebs in Cicero's Day* (1918).

Petersson, T., *Cicero, a Biography* (1920).

Robinson, F. W., *Marius, Sulla, und Glaucia* (1912).

Sihler, E. G., *Cicero of Arpinum* (1914).

Strachan-Davidson, J. L., *Cicero and the Fall of the Roman Republic* (1903).

Taylor, Lily Ross, *Party Politics in the Age of Caesar* (1949).

The Civil Wars

The principal sources include Appian, *Civil Wars*, II–V; Caesar, *Civil War;* Cicero, *Letters* and *Philippics;* Dio, *Roman History*, XLI–LI; Plutarch, *Lives* (Antony, Brutus, Caesar, Cato Minor, Cicero, Pompey); Nicolaus of Damascus, *Life of Augustus* (tr. C. M. Hall, 1923); Lucan, *Civil War;* Suetonius, *Lives of the Twelve Caesars* (Caesar, Augustus); Velleius Paterculus, II.

Buchan, J., *Augustus* (1937). *Julius Caesar* (1932).

Deutsch, M. E., *Caesar's Son and Heir* (1928).

Fowler, W. W., *Julius Caesar* (1904).

Gundolf, F., *The Mantle of Caesar* (1924; Eng. tr., 1929).

Hadas, M., *Sextus Pompey* (1930).

Holmes, T. R., *The Architect of the Roman Empire* (vol. 1, 1928).

Lindsay, J., *Marc Antony* (1936).

Macurdy, Grace, *Hellenistic Queens* (1932), Cleopatra.

Radin, M., *Marcus Brutus* (1939).

Syme, R., *The Roman Revolution* (1939).

Tarn, W. W., "The Battle of Actium," *Journal of Roman Studies*, XXI (1931), 173–99.

Walter, G., *Brutus et la fin de la république* (1938).

C. THE IMPERIAL PERIOD

General Histories

Many of the histories of the Republican period, listed above, continue into the Imperial period.

Albertini, E., *L'empire romaine* (1929).

Bloch, E., *L'empire romaine—évolution et décadence* (1922).

Cavaignac, E., *La paix romaine* (1928).

Gibbon, E., *The History of the Decline and Fall of the Roman Empire* (6 vols., 1776–88; ed. J. B. Bury in 7 vols., 1909–14), a classic, see note, p. 531.

Homo, L., *L'empire romaine* (1925).

Jones, H. S., *The Roman Empire, B.C. 29-A.D. 476* (1908).

Nilsson, M. R., *Imperial Rome* (Eng. tr., 1926).

Rostovtzeff, M., *A Social and Economic History of the Roman Empire* (1926), see note, p. 533.

Stevenson, G. H., *The Roman Empire* (1930).

Wells, J., and Barrow, R. H., *A Short History of the Roman Empire to the Death of Marcus Aurelius* (1931).

Augustus and the Julio-Claudian Emperors

The principal sources include the *Monumentum Ancyranum;* Tacitus, *Annals* and *Histories;* Suetonius, *Lives of the Twelve Caesars;* Dio, LI–LX; Josephus, *Jewish War* and *Antiquities,* XVIII–XX; Velleius Paterculus. T. Frank, *Economic Survey* (vol. 5, 1940).

Dessau, H., *Geschichte der römischen Kaiserzeit* (2 vols., 1924–30).

Salmon, E. T., *A History of the Roman World from 30 B.C. to A.D. 138* (1944).

Buchan, J., *Augustus* (1937).

Firth, J. B., *Augustus Caesar* (1903).

Holmes, T. R., *The Architect of the Roman Empire* (2 vols., 1928–31).

Schuckburgh, E. S., *Augustus, the Life and Times of the Founder of the Roman Empire* (1903).

Winspear, A. D., and Geweke, L. K., *Augustus and the Reconstruction of Roman Government and Society* (1935).

Reinhold, M., *Marcus Agrippa, a Biography* (1933).

Marsh, F. M., *The Reign of Tiberius* (1931).

Rogers, R. S., *Studies in the Reign of Tiberius* (1943).

Balsdon, J. P. V. D., *The Emperor Gaius* (1934).

Momigliano, A., *Claudius the Emperor and His Achievements* (1934).

Scramuzza, V. M., *The Emperor Claudius* (1940).

Henderson, B. W., *The Life and Principate of the Emperor Nero* (1903). *Civil War and Rebellion in the Roman Empire* (1908).

Vespasian to Diocletian (70–305)

Parker, H. M., *The Roman World from A.D. 138 to 337* (1935).

Gsell, S., *Essai sur le règne de l'Empereur Domitien* (1894).

Henderson, B. W., *Five Roman Emperors, A.D. 69–117* (1927). *The Life and Principate of the Emperor Hadrian* (1925).

Hüttl, W., *Antoninus Pius* (2 vols., 1933–37).

Sedgwick, H. D., *Marcus Aurelius, a Biography* (1921).

Platnauer, M., *The Life and Reign of the Emperor Severus* (1918).

Hopkins, R. V. N., *The Life of Alexander Severus* (1907).

Homo, L., *Essai sur le règne de l'Empereur Aurélien* (1904).

Seston, W., *Dioclétien et la Tétrarchie* (1946).

Constitution and Law

Abbott, F. F., and Johnson, A. C., *Municipal Administration in the Roman Empire* (1926).

Boissier, G., *L'opposition sous les Césars* (1875)

Brinton, Crane, *From Many One* (1948).

Hammond, M., *The Augustan Principate* (1937).

Hirschfeld, O., *Die kaiserliche Verwaltungsbeamten bis auf Diokletian* (2nd ed., 1905).

Howe, L. L., *The Pretorian Prefect from Commodus to Diocletian* (1942).

Keyes, C. W., *The Rise of the Equites in the Third Century* (1915).

Lambrechts, P., *La composition du sénat romain de Septime Sévères à Dioclétien* (1937).

Mattingly, H., *The Imperial Civil Service of Rome* (1910).

Mommsen, Th., *Römisches Staatsrecht* (3rd ed., 1887).

Reid, J. S., *The Municipalities of the Roman Empire* (1913).
Stein, A., *Der Römische Ritterstand* (1927).

The Provinces

Frank, T., ed., *An Economic Survey of Ancient Rome* (vols. 2–4, 1936–8).
Mommsen, Th., *The Provinces of the Roman Empire from Caesar to Diocletian* (1885; Eng. tr., 2 vols., 1886).
Chapot, V., *The Roman World* (1927; Eng. tr., 1928).
Fuchs, H., *Der geistige Widerstand gegen Rom in der antiken Welt* (1938).
Bouchier, E. S., *Spain Under the Roman Empire* (1914). *Syria as a Roman Province* (1916).
Broughton, T. R. S., *The Romanization of Africa Proconsularis* (1929).
Chapot, V., *La province romaine d'Asie* (1904).
Collingwood, R. G. *The Archaeology of Roman Britain* (1930). *Roman Britain* (1923; 3rd ed., 1934).
Haverfield, F., and Macdonald, G., *The Roman Occupation of Britain* (1924).
Jones, A. H. M., *The Cities of the Eastern Roman Provinces* (1937).
Jouguet, P., *La vie municipale dans l'Egypte romaine* (1911).
Jullian, C., *Histoire de la Gaule* (vols. 4–8, 1913–26).

Social and Intellectual Life

Abbott, F. F., *Society and Politics in Ancient Rome* (1914).
Barrow, R., *Slavery in the Roman Empire* (1928).
Carcopino, J., *Daily Life in Ancient Rome* (1939; Eng. tr., 1940).
Carrington, R., *Pompeii* (1936).
Charlesworth, M. P., *Five Men: Character Studies from the Roman Empire* (1936). *Trade Routes and Commerce of the Roman Empire* (1926).
Davis, W. S., *The Influence of Wealth on Imperial Rome* (1910).
Dill, S., *Roman Society from Nero to Marcus Aurelius* (1905).
Duff, A. M., *Freedmen in the Early Roman Empire* (1928).
Friedländer, L., *Roman Life and Manners Under the Early Empire* (1862–71; Eng. tr., in 3 vols., 1908–13).
La Piana, G., "Foreign Groups in Rome During the First Centuries of the Empire," *Harvard Theological Review*, XX (1927), 183–403.
Mau, A., *Pompeii, its Life and Art* (Eng. tr., 1899).

Rostovtzeff, M., *Caravan Cities* (1932).
Tucker, T. G., *Life in the Roman World of Nero and St. Paul* (1910).

Literature

Duff, J. W., *A Literary History of Rome in the Silver Age* (1927).
Boissier, G., *Tacitus* (1903; Eng. tr., 1906).
Conway, R. S., *Harvard Lectures on the Vergilian Age* (1928).
Frank, T., *Catullus and Horace* (1928). *Vergil, a Biography* (1922).
Glover, T. R., *Studies in Virgil* (1904; 6th ed., 1930).
Laistner, M. L. W., *The Greater Roman Historians* (1947).
Rand, E. K., *The Magical Art of Virgil* (1931).
Schanz, M., *Geschichte der römischen Literatur* (vol. 2, 4th ed., by C. Hosius, 1935; vol. 3, 3rd ed., by C. Hosius and G. Krüger, 1922).
Teuffel, W. S., *Geschichte der römischen Literatur* (3 vols., 6th ed., by W. Kroll and F. Skutsch, 1913–20).
Thackeray, H. St. J., *Josephus, the Man and the Historian* (1929).

Paganism

Angus, S., *The Mystery Religions and Christianity* (1925). *The Religious Quests of the Graeco-Roman World* (1929).
Beurlier, E., *Le culte impériale* (1897).
Bidez, J., *La vie de Porphyre* (1918).
Boissier, G., *La fin du paganisme* (2 vols., 1891). *La religion romaine d'Auguste aux Antonins* (2 vols., 1874).
Cumont, F., *Oriental Religions in Roman Paganism* (1906; 4th ed., 1929; Eng. tr., 1911). *After Life in Roman Paganism* (1922). *Astrology and Religion Among the Greeks and Romans* (Eng. tr., 1912). *The Mysteries of Mithra* (Eng. tr., 1911).
Deissmann, A., *Light from the Ancient East* (1908; 4th ed., 1923; Eng. tr., 1927).
Geffcken, J., *Der Ausgang des griechisch-römischen Heidentums* (1920; 2nd ed., 1929).
Glover, T. R., *The Conflict of Religions in the Early Roman Empire* (1909).
Graillot, H., *Le culte de Cybèle, mère des dieux* (1912).
Halliday, W. R., *The Pagan Background of Christianity* (1925).
Hyde, W. W., *Paganism to Christianity in the Roman Empire* (1946).
Labriolle, P. de, *La réaction païenne: étude sur la polémique anti-chrétienne du Ier au VIe siècle* (1934).

Nock, A. D., *Conversion: the Old and the New in Religion from Alexander the Great to Augustine of Hippo* (1933).

Norden, E., *Agnostos Theos* (1923).

Reitzenstein, R., *Hellenistische Mysterienreligionen* (1911; 3rd ed., 1927).

Réville, J., *La religion à Rome sous les Sévères* (1886).

Scott, K., *The Imperial Cult Under the Flavians* (1936).

Sihler, E. G., *From Augustus to Augustine* (1923).

Taylor, L. R., *The Divinity of the Roman Emperor* (1931).

Wendland, P., *Die hellenistisch-römische Kultur in ihren Beziehungen zu Judentum und Christentum* (3rd ed., 1912).

Willoughby, H. R., *Pagan Regeneration* (1929).

Christianity

Jewish Background

The principal source for the history of the Jews in the first century is Josephus, *Jewish War* and *Antiquities*, XVIII–XX. See also, R. H. Charles, ed., *Apocrypha and Pseudepigraphia of the Old Testament* (2 vols., 1913) which contains Jewish apocalypses and other literature of the period in Eng. tr., with commentary.

Bertholet, A., *Die jüdische Religion von der Zeit Esras zum Zeitalter Christi* (1911).

Bousset, W., *Die Religion des Judentums im späthellenistischen Zeitalter* (1902; 3rd ed., 1926).

Charles, R. H., *Religious Development Between the Old and New Testaments* (1914).

Goodenough, E. R., *An Introduction to Philo Judaeus* (1940).

Grant, F. C., *The Economic Background of the Gospels* (1925).

Guignebert, C., *The Jewish World in the Time of Jesus* (1935; Eng. tr., 1939).

Herford, R. T., *Judaism in the New Testament Period* (1928). *The Pharisees* (1924).

Juster, J., *Les juifs dans l'empire romain* (2 vols., 1914).

Meyer, Ed., *Ursprung und Anfänge des Christentums* (3 vols., 1921–23).

Moore, G. F., *Judaism in the First Three Centuries of the Christian Era* (3 vols., 1927).

Oesterley, W. O. E., and Box, G. H., *The Religion and Worship of the Synagogue* (1907).

Pfeiffer, Robert H., *History of New Testament Times* (1949).

Jesus of Nazareth

Cadbury, H. J., *The Peril of Modernizing Jesus* (1937).
Case, S. J., *Jesus, a New Biography* (1929).
Goguel, M., *Life of Jesus* (1932; Eng. tr., 1933).
Guignebert, C., *Jesus* (1933; Eng. tr., 1935).
Klausner, J., *Jesus of Nazareth* (tr. from Hebrew, 1925).
Knox, J., *The Man Christ Jesus* (1941).
Olmstead, A. T., *Jesus in the Light of History* (1942).
Otto, R., *The Kingdom of God and the Son of Man* (1934; Eng. tr., 1938).
Renan, E., *Life of Jesus* (1863, Eng. tr.), see note, p. 491.
Schweitzer, A., *The Quest of the Historical Jesus* (1906; Eng. tr., 1910), see note, p. 492.

Paul of Tarsus

Deissmann, A., *Paul, a Study in Social and Religious History* (1911; Eng. tr., 1926).
Glover, T. R., *Paul of Tarsus* (1925).
Kennedy, H. A. A., *St. Paul and the Mystery Religions* (1913).
Klausner, J., *From Jesus to Paul* (Eng. tr. from Hebrew, 1943).
Knox, W. L., *St. Paul and the Church of Jerusalem* (1925). *St. Paul and the Church of the Gentiles* (1939).
Lietzmann, H., *Petrus und Paulus in Rom* (1915).
Nock, A. D., *St. Paul* (1938).
Ramsay, W. M., *The Cities of St. Paul* (1907). *Pauline and Other Studies* (1906). *St. Paul the Traveller and the Roman Citizen* (1896).
Schweitzer, A., *The Mysticism of Paul the Apostle* (1930; Eng. tr., 1931). *Paul and his Interpreters* (1911; Eng. tr., 1912).

The Church in the First Century

Case, S. J., *The Evolution of Christianity* (1914).
Craig, C. T., *The Beginnings of Christianity* (1945).
Enslin, M. S., *Christian Beginnings* (1938).
Foakes-Jackson, F. J., and Lake, K., *The Beginnings of Christianity* (5 vols., 1920–33), a very comprehensive and scholarly work.
Goguel, M., *La naissance du christianisme* (1946). *L'Église primitive* (1948).
Lietzmann, H., *The Beginnings of the Christian Church* (1932; Eng. tr., 1937).
McGiffert, A. C., *A History of Christianity in the Apostolic Age* (1897).

Ramsay, W. M., *The Church in the Roman Empire before 170 A.D.* (1893).

Riddle, D. W., and Hutson, H. H., *New Testament Life and Literature* (1946).

Scott, E. F., *The Nature of the Early Church* (1941).

Streeter, B. H., *The Primitive Church* (1930).

Weiss, J., *The History of Primitive Christianity* (2 vols., 1914–17; Eng. tr., 1937).

New Testament Criticism

Schweitzer, A., *The Quest of the Historical Jesus* (1906; Eng. tr., 1910).

McCown, C. C., *The Search for the Real Jesus* (1940).

Cadbury, H. J., *The Making of Luke-Acts* (1927).

Dibelius, M., *From Tradition to Gospel* (1919; 2nd ed., 1933; Eng. tr., 1935).

Dodd, C. H., *The Apostolic Teaching and its Development* (1937).

Goodspeed, E. J., *The Formation of the New Testament* (1926).

Grant, F. C., *The Earliest Gospel* (1943). *Form Criticism* (1934), translations of two essays by R. Bultmann and K. Kundsin.

James, M. R., *The Apocryphal New Testament* (1924), translations of all the apocrypha with notes.

Kenyon, F. G., *Our Bible and the Ancient Manuscripts* (1895; 4th ed., 1940). *The Bible and Archaeology* (1940). *The Text of the Greek Bible* (1937).

Knox, J., *Marcion and the New Testament* (1942).

Lake, Kirsopp, *The Text of the New Testament* (6th ed., 1928).

Lake, Kirsopp, and Lake, Sylvia, *An Introduction to the New Testament* (1937).

Moffatt, J., *An Introduction to the Literature of the New Testament* (1911; 3rd ed., 1918).

Montefiore, C. G., *The Synoptic Gospels* (2 vols., 1909; 2nd ed., 1927), by an eminent Jewish scholar.

Scott, E. F., *The Literature of the New Testament* (1932).

Strack, H. L., and Billerbeck, Paul, *Kommentar zum Neuen Testament aus Talmud und Midrash* (4 vols., 1922–28).

Streeter, B. H., *The Four Gospels* (1924; 4th ed., 1930).

Torrey, C. C., *Documents of the Primitive Church* (1941). *Our Translated Gospels* (1936).

Full commentaries on most of the books of the New Testament may be found in the *International Critical Commentary* and *The Moffatt New Testament Commentary,* of which the latter is the more recent.

The Church in the Second and Third Centuries

The principal narrative source for the history of the Church before Constantine is Eusebius, *Church History*, but all the early Fathers supply material. Most of the Fathers of this period are available in English in the *Ante-Nicene Fathers* (10 vols., 1885–87); those of the next two centuries in the *Nicene and Post-Nicene Fathers* (28 vols., 1886–1900). See also the *Apostolic Fathers* (2 vols.) and Eusebius, *Church History* (2 vols.), in the Loeb Library. A group of Roman Catholic scholars has recently announced a new translation of the principal Fathers, to be published in 72 volumes under the title *Ancient Christian Writers*: two volumes appeared in 1947 and it is hoped that the series will be complete within six years.

Ayer, J. C., *A Source Book of Ancient Church History* (1913).

Cadoux, C. J., *The Early Church and the World* (1925).

Duchesne, L., *Early History of the Christian Church* (3 vols., 1906–10; Eng. tr., 1909 ff.). *Christian Worship, Its Origin and Evolution* (Eng. tr., 1912), see note, p. 582.

Faye, E. de, *Gnostiques et gnosticisme* (1913). *Origène, sa vie, son oeuvre, sa pensée* (3 vols., 1923–28). *Origen and his Work* (1926).

Fliche, A., and Martin, V., eds., *Histoire de l'église* (vols. 1–3, 1938–39; Eng. tr., 1942–45).

Hardy, E. G., *Christianity and the Roman Government* (1894).

Harnack, A., *Constitution and Law of the Church in the First Two Centuries* (Eng. tr., 1910). *The Expansion of Christianity in the First Three Centuries* (2 vols., Eng. tr., 1904–05). *Geschichte der altchristlichen Litteratur bis Eusebius* (2 vols., 1893–1904), see note, p. 580.

Kidd, B. J., *A History of the Church to A.D. 461* (3 vols., 1922). *The Roman Primacy to A.D. 461* (1936).

Labriolle, P. de, *A History of Christian Latin Literature* (Eng. tr., 1925).

Lietzmann, H., *The Founding of the Church Universal* (1936; Eng. tr., 1938). *Messe und Herrenmahl* (1924).

Mommsen, Th., "Religionsfrevel nach römischen Recht" (1890), in *Gesammelte Schriften* (1907), III, 389–422.

Monceaux, P., *Histoire littéraire de l'Afrique chrétienne* (7 vols., 1901–23).

Neumann, K. J., *Die römische Staat und die allgemeine Kirche* (1890).

Troeltsch, E., *The Social Teaching of the Christian Churches* (Eng. tr., 1931).

Workman, H. B., *Persecution in the Early Church* (1906).

Constantine and His Successors

The sources include Ammianus Marcellinus; Julian, *Against the Galileans* (Loeb Library); Eusebius, Lactantius, Athanasius, Ambrose, Jerome, Augustine (Nicene Fathers); Orosius (tr. Raymond, 1936).

Alföldi, A., *The Conversion of Constantine and Pagan Rome* (1948).

Baynes, N. H., *Constantine the Great and the Christian Church* (1929).

Baynes, N. H., and Moss, H. B., *Byzantium* (1948).

Bidez, J., *Vie de l'Empereur Julien* (1930).

Boissier, G., *La fin du paganisme* (2 vols., 1891).

Bury, J. B., *History of the Later Roman Empire* (vol. 1, 1923).

Dill, S., *Roman Society in the Last Century of the Empire* (1898).

Firth, J. B., *Constantine the Great* (1923).

Glover, T. R., *Life and Letters in the Fourth Century* (1901).

Lot, F., *Les invasions germaniques: la pénétration mutuelle du monde barbare et du monde romain* (1935). *The End of the Ancient World* (1927; Eng. tr., 1931).

Piganiol, A., *L'Empereur Constantin* (1932).

Schwartz, E., *Kaiser Constantin und die christliche Kirche* (1913; 2nd ed., 1936).

Seeck, O., *Geschichte des Untergangs der antiken Welt* (6 vols., 1897–1920).

Stein, E., *Geschichte des spätrömischen Reiches* (vol. 1, 1928).

Index

It often happens that two or more Romans appear whose names are identical. Wherever possible these men are distinguished by giving the year in which they held high office: *c.*, consul; *cen.*, censor; *t.p.*, tribune.

272 167